ARIS & PHILLIPS HISPANIC CLASSICS

Rainy Days

Días de lluvia

Short Stories by Contemporary Spanish Women Writers

Edited, with an Introduction and Notes by

Montserrat Lunati

Short Stories translated into English by

Marilyn Myerscough and Charles Kelley
(1st edn)   *(2nd edn)*

LIVERPOOL UNIVERSITY PRESS

First published 2018 by
Liverpool University Press
4 Cambridge Street
Liverpool
L69 7ZU

www.liverpooluniversitypress.co.uk

British Library Cataloguing-in-Publication data
A British Library CIP record is available

ISBN 978-1-910572-29-0 hardback
ISBN 978-1-910572-30-6 paperback

Typeset by Tara Evans

Printed in Poland by BooksFactory.co.uk

Cover image: *A Girl in Her Room* by Mercè Lluís

To Jordi

To Roger, Anna and Isaac

CONTENTS

ACKNOWLEDGEMENTS
(SECOND EDITION)

I must first express my gratitude to all the women writers who have made this collection of short stories possible with their kindness and generosity in allowing me to use their texts, some of them for the second time, as most of the cuentos included in this second edition of *Rainy Days* were also part of the first. Equally, I want to say a big thank you to the hugely talented artist Mercè Lluís for allowing me to use one of her beautiful paintings for the cover. I am very grateful to Professor Jonathan Thacker, Director of the Aris Phillips Hispanic Classics Series from Liverpool University Press. He has been very patient and kind throughout the long process of putting together this extended anthology, and his comments and suggestions have been extremely helpful (any errors, of course, are my sole responsibility). Professor Will Fowler kindly facilitated my access to the Library of the University of St Andrews and I am extremely grateful to him for that, and to him and his wife Caroline for their friendship. Chloe Johnson, from Liverpool University Press, has always been kind and efficient: a wonderful point of contact. Tara Evans has been a superb typesetter: I am very grateful to her for her patience and careful attention to detail. Colleagues and friends have helped at particular times by providing me with support and useful contacts and references: many thanks to Professor Abigail Lee Six, Dr Carlos Sanz Mingo, Professor Nuria Capdevila-Argüelles, Professor Christine Henseler, Professor Ángeles Encinar, Dr Catherine Barbour and Dr María-José Blanco. Thank you also to Dr Charles Kelley, my former colleague at Cardiff University, who translated the new stories included in this edition of *Rainy Days* with great care. Above all, I want to express my gratitude to my son Roger and his wife Anna for their perceptive observations, and to Jordi, for his insightful comments, they have been a huge help throughout the compilation of this second edition of *Rainy Days*.

Montserrat Lunati
Crail, May 2018

ACKNOWLEDGEMENTS
(FIRST EDITION)

The first word of acknowledgement should go to all the authors of each of the texts collected in this anthology, both for their talent in writing the stories and for their generosity in allowing me to include them in this book. I owe a most particular debt of gratitude to Professor Catherine Davies whose comments, suggestions and recommendations I found extremely helpful and illuminating. I would also like to thank Lucinda Phillips for commissioning me to prepare this book and for being always such a supportive and enthusiastic publisher, and to all the staff in Aris & Phillips, especially Janet Davis, who have been so patient and courteous. Thanks are also due to my former colleagues Dr Catrin Redknap and Dr Jean Andrews, and most especially to my colleague Dr Charles Kelley who is always willing to offer me his good humoured support. My appreciation is also due to Marilyn Myerscough who translated the stories with her usual care. And last but not least, I want to express my deepest gratitude to Jordi who has helped me in many ways through the lengthy process and to Roger, for coping so well with a working mother.

Montserrat Lunati
Cardiff, June 1997

'FUGITIVE ALCHEMY': SOME NOTES ON THE SECOND EDITION OF *RAINY DAYS*

Twenty years have passed since the first edition of *Rainy Days / Días de lluvia: Short Stories by Contemporary Spanish Women Writers*. Before I introduce this second edition of a collection of *cuentos* of female authorship, perhaps it will not be out of place to consider how women's lives in Spain, which changed significantly with the restoration of democracy in the latter quarter of the twentieth century, have continued to evolve. It is undeniable that their social visibility has increased thanks to a new sensitivity that equality-inspired policies, mostly promulgated under the pressure exerted by feminist thought, have made possible. And yet, it would be too optimistic to say that Spanish society is free from prejudices against women, prejudices that sometimes come hand in hand with other discriminations, such as racism, especially against female immigrants. In these twenty years the world has experienced major transformations, the forced displacement of millions of people from areas of war and persecution, and the difficulties that refugees face to be accepted in the countries where they try to establish themselves, being two of them. Another change that has had an enormous impact on everyday life is the access to information and interaction through internet technology. Websites of all kinds, social media, and electronic communication have changed radically the way people keep themselves informed and relate to each other. Things that happen in one part of the world have an instant reverberation everywhere, from calls to protest against social injustices that go viral in minutes, to all sorts of news that find an immediate response worldwide. For instance, after Donald Trump's inauguration as president of the United States on 18 February 2017, big demonstrations of (mostly) discontented women followed, not only in different American cities but in many European ones too, including Barcelona and Madrid (Noain, 2017). Another example would be the #MeToo campaign after Harvey Weinstein's sexual harassment and violence against many women was made public, which revealed the ubiquity of sexual assault, how systemic the problem is, how 'it is ongoing […], the backdrop to many women's lives' (Moore, 2017).

The campaign, which proved to be a watershed moment in the fight against sexual harassment of all sorts, prompted some to ask not just that the victims come forward, but also that the perpetrators be named and shamed (Valenti, 2017). Calls for the #MeToo movement to become a truly global phenomenon have also been made (Pankhurst, 2018), especially when those who speak out about sexual abuse are being bullied on social media (Argento, 2018). The endless possibilities that new technology offers, although extremely positive in many respects, have not always meant progress in every sense. Old hideous misogyny has simply found a quicker and more effective way of spreading its poisonous message. Without proper internet regulations to allow legal sanctions in order to protect women (or any other vulnerable group or individual), they often get abuse targeting their physical appearance (how they look, what they wear, etc.). No matter how important women's achievements have been, they are reduced once again to their physicality, an old strategy to undermine their status as social and historical subjects. Social media have also been misused to publicize irrational and random violence against women. Recently, for example, a young man was charged with GBH and sexual discrimination against women: he stamped on an unsuspected female victim with two feet on a street in Barcelona while a friend of his recorded it to post the video on social media in order to show how the woman in question was left wounded and dazed on the floor (*El Periódico*, 11 February 2017). It was later revealed that the aggressors had done it in Benidorm, Madrid and twice in Barcelona, and they explained their actions on the grounds that they wanted to humiliate and ridicule women only because of their sex. Despite significant advances made by women in Spain both in their private and public lives, and with more women than ever of all political persuasions occupying prominent positions, being a woman in the public eye, rather than commanding respect, often makes her the target of sexist remarks: Manuela Carmena, Madrid's Mayoress, and Ada Colau, Barcelona's Mayoress, have often been on the receiving end of this type of gender prejudice.[1] In the workplace, women report that, regarding promotion, it is not uncommon for them to be treated differently because of their gender. This is definitely the case vis-à-vis the gender pay gap, although the phenomenon is not just observable in Spain (Kean, 2017). A

---

1   Félix de Azúa, the lastest writer to be elected a member of the Real Academia de la Lengua, declared that Ada Colau should be 'sirviendo en un puesto de pescado' [serving at a fishmonger's stall] (Remacha, 2016), which is not only sexist but also offensive against people in that profession by dint of 'feminising' it, an antiquated and despicable form of misogyny, and the kind of insult that would have not been inflicted on a male Mayor.

recent article in *The Guardian* claimed that 'Gender pay figures reveal eight in ten UK firms pay men more' (Topping, Barr and Duncan, 2018). The NHS is one of the institutions where the gender pay gap has been more strongly contested: after Professor Jane Dacre, President of the Royal College of Physicians, declared that she would lead an independent review into gender pay inequality, the Secretary of State for Health and Social Care, promised to eliminate doctors' gender pay gap (BBC, 28 May 2018). According to a report published by Eurostat on the 2016 Women's Day, progress in the gender pay gap in Europe had stalled, with the financial crisis affecting women more than men. Spain had the sixth biggest gender pay in Europe (Bolaños, 2016). The situation was not much better a year later, and the data provided by the European Commission on the 2017 Women's Day specifically highlights the precarious position of single mothers (Martínez, 2017). Significantly, a survey has revealed that 82% of Spaniards across the political spectrum believe that the gender pay gap is a reality society must face (Alvárez, 2018).

Admittedly, judges are now far less reluctant to condone male violence against women – there are more women judges than in the past, although they do not always act in a different way to that of their male colleagues. However, despite restriction orders being issued more frequently (statistically, according to the database *Mujeres en cifras*, on the *Instituto de la Mujer* website, husbands are the most frequent killers), gender and domestic violence is still endemic and the figures published in 2017 do not a show any substantial improvement in relation to 2016. *Mujeres en cifras* (consulted on 24 August 2017), gives as 36 the number of victims since the beginning of the year, a first semester that has registered a 47.6% increase in relation to 2016 (RTVE, 30 June 2017). The number of children who have been victims of violent fathers is six times worse than in the previous year (RTVE, 30 June 2017). In 2016, there were 44 women killed, and 60 in 2015. According to *Mujeres en cifras*, numbers oscillated in the previous decades (73 in 2010; 76 in 2008; 71 in 2003; 50 in 2001; 63 in 2000; 54 in 1999), but statistics remain grim.

When writer Clara Janés was elected a member of the Real Academia de la Lengua in 2015, thus becoming the tenth woman to be chosen in three hundred years (and currently one of eight women out of a total of forty-six members), she avoided questions about the dearth of female presence at the RAE. Instead, she said that she was concerned about gender violence: 'A mí lo que me preocupa es la violencia de género. Ahí es donde me duele el

asunto y sobre lo que habría que actuar con fuerza. Es terrible lo que está pasando' [What worries me is gender violence. This is what I find painful and what requires strong action. What is happening is terrible] (Remacha, 2016). She considered this to be women's worst predicament in Spain, and a more pressing issue than the symbolical value of allowing women access to places of privilege, like the RAE, a historically male-dominated institution. As statistics show, her concern was well-founded. However, the lack of women in the RAE cannot be ignored, as it constitutes an indictment of how gender discrimination has been deeply ingrained in Spanish culture, and still is.

In July 2017, a new and widely discussed Pacto de Estado contra la Violencia de Género [State Pact against Gender Violence] was announced as a landmark to combat gender violence and its implementation was funded to the tune of 1,000 million euros, thus recognising that violence against women (and children who are often victims of the same violence) is one of the 'mayores lacras del país' [one of the worst scourges in the country] (Rodríguez-Pina, 2017a). All political or interested parties had been involved in the discussion, but finally the Comisión de Igualdad [Equality Commission] approved the Pact with twenty-nine votes in favour and seven abstentions from Unidos Podemos [Together We Can], which thought the Pact to be insufficient (Rodríguez-Pina, 2017b). The Partido Feminista [Feminist Party], part of Unidos Podemos, was instrumental in that abstention as their Comisión Política e Ideológica [Political and Ideological Commission] rejected the Pact as just a mirroring of the 28 December 2004 Law whose implementation after twelve years they considered ineffective. They highlighted some weaknesses that had been left unresolved in the new Pact, especially regarding the impunity granted to perpetrators (custody, parental visitation, prison sentences not completed) while women were still represented as not capable or ill. They also noted that the PP (the then ruling Partido Popular, the Conservative Party) had rushed into finalizing the Pact in order to take political advantage from it (*Público*, 27 July 2017). In an article published shortly before the Pact was announced, Isabel Muntané (2017), co-director of the MA in Gender and Communication at the UAB (Universitat Autònoma de Barcelona), expressed her concern that the Pact might fall short of the expectations that had initially been raised in the wake of more than 600 proposals from city councils, autonomous communities and feminist and women's associations. She stressed that the final report had been postponed three times, many of the 80 testimonies had been contested, and the Spanish

government had consistently failed to meet the CEDAW's [Convention for the Elimination of All Forms of Discrimination against Women], established by the UN in 1979, and the Istanbul Convention's recommendations which extended the concept of gender violence well beyond the domestic sphere to include genital mutilation, forced marriages, obstetric violence, violence against migrant women in domestic service, and elderly or disabled women.

The Pact has also been criticized for 'forgetting' to enter women in school and text books. Luz Martínez Ten, responsible for *Mujer y Políticas de Igualdad de la Federación de Empleados Públicos de UGT* [Woman and Equality Policies of the General Workers Union, Public Servants Federation] declared that 'esta invisibilización tiene consecuencias terribles, porque a largo plazo influye en la creación de la brecha salarial, en la perpetuación de la violencia de género y en la pérdida ingente del potencial intelectual' [this lack of visibility has terrible repercussions, as in the long term it influences the gender pay gap, the perpetuation of gender violence and the loss of intellectual potential] (Kohan, 2017). Her words say it all: it is a vicious circle.

Ana Morgade, stand-up comic and 'monologuista' [author of monologues], as she defines herself, when presenting the XX Max Theatre Prizes on 25 June 2017 seized the opportunity to denounce the discrimination against women in her profession. In a humorous tone, she declared that she was hoping that her speech would become obsolete soon, as this would mean that things were finally changing. But this is a general phenomenon: only a quarter of the films shown at the 61st BFI London Film Festival were directed by women (Brown, 2017,), and music critics are aware that contemporary movements with working class roots, like 'heavy' or 'punk', have always been distinctively male, with very few women as leaders of bands, and that is very difficult for all-female groups with an uncompromising feminist stand to make a name for themselves in the music industry (Vicenç and Vinardell, 2017).

Fortunately, a new attitude vis-à-vis all these issues can be detected amongst young people, as epitomised by the website borradasdelmapa.hol.es, which was created in 2016 by seven students from the Universidad Juan Carlos I, in Madrid, while working on a project for a course on Interactive Publicity. They stated that:

Cegados por las cifras de las muertes causadas por la violencia de género, a menudo nos olvidamos de que existe una realidad detrás de cada una de ellas. Borradas del mapa es un proyecto que nace con la intención de mostrar que la violencia de género está más cerca de lo que creemos.

[Blinded by the number of deaths due to gender violence, we often forget that there is a reality behind each of them. 'Wiped out off the map' is a project that begins with the purpose of showing that gender violence is nearer than we think.]

With a view to making gender violence more visible, they used an interactive map of Spain (with names and places) exposing the brutal reality of gender-related murders in different parts of the country. Even though lack of funds has prevented the website from being interactive or developing further, it is still available on a free server. What is encouraging is that this group of students thought their project was politically and socially relevant and went ahead with it. Will the next generation make a difference? If the graphic book *Lola Vendetta. Más vale Lola que mal acompañada* (2017) is anything to go by, we can be optimistic. Raquel Riba Rossy's *Lola Vendetta* was a success on social media and gained followers almost immediately. Lola is an irreverent, impulsive, uncompromising feminist character who debunks taboos about maternity and menstruation (her black and white drawings are occasionally tinted with red), she is ironic to the point of sarcasm and has little time for any form of *machismo*, and she always advocates female empowerment. A Pussy Riot type of character, her focus on issues of identity, body and gender politics in a country where cultural and social habits take time to evolve, is a positive and refreshing development. And so is the huge response to the call for a women's general strike across Spain on 2018 Women's Day. Although the Partido Popular and Ciudadanos, the two most right-wing political parties in the Spanish Parliament, did not support the strike, its success was phenomenal, and it was seen as 'una explosión empujada por las más jóvenes' [an explosion prompted by the youngest girls] (Alvárez and Rodríguez-Pina, 2018), that is, by those who will build Spain's immediate future. Some of the placards that women carried with them at the demonstrations say it all. Just two examples: ''Quiero dejar de tener miedo!!! Basta Ya' [I don't want to live in fear!!! Enough is enough][2]

---

2   It is difficult not to read this claim in the light of the verdict returned by three Spanish judges against a group of five men, including a member of the Spanish Armed Forces and a Civil Guard, who called themselves 'La Manada', a nickname which has been translated as 'the wolf pack' (Rosell, 2018), and were accused of gang raping an 18-year-old woman during the 2016 *Sanfermines*, the popular Pamplona *fiesta.* The lenient sentence for 'sexual abuse' (nine years in prison, instead of the thirteen asked for by the prosecution) led to a social outcry (Albalat, 2018). To add insult to injury, one of the judges was in favour of their acquittal and neo-Nazi groups encouraged the lynching of the victim on social media (Pardo, 2018).

(Alvárez and Rodríguez-Pina, 2018), and 'Lo contrario al feminismo es la ignorancia' [The opposite to feminism is ignorance] (Ibarz, 2018).

The *cuentos* in the second edition of *Rainy Days*

There were twelve stories in the 1997 edition of *Rainy Days*. This second edition has been extended to include sixteen short stories. Four new stories by Berta Marsé, Luisa Castro, Juana Salabert and Nuria Amat have been added to it. Of the twelve stories of the first edition, Paloma Díaz-Mas's 'La obra maestra' has been replaced by 'Los mayorales exhaustos', which is more in tune with what the author is writing these days and provides a good example of the narrative trend that has been termed 'self-fiction', also observable in Luisa Castro's story 'Mi madre en la ventana'. In the last few decades, self-fiction has been followed by many contemporary writers, some of them included in the first edition of *Rainy Days*. Whether they take the form of novels, short stories, or are openly declared biographical texts such as memoirs or diaries, these are all works which offer a fascinating insight into the life of the writer while socially and politically contextualising it. This is the case, for example, of Cristina Fernández *Cubas's Cosas que ya no existen* (2001); Soledad Puértolas's *Con mi madre* (2001); Luisa Castro's *Viajes con mi padre* (2003) and *La segunda mujer* (2006); Paloma Díaz-Mas's *Como un libro cerrado* (2005); Laura Freixas's *Adolescencia en Barcelona hacia 1970* (2007), *Una vida subterránea: Diario 1991–1994* (2013), and *Todos llevan máscara. Diario 1995–1996* (2018), amongst others, such as Carme Riera's *Temps d'una espera* (1998) and *Temps d'innocència* (2013), both in Catalan. This narrative trend is not just a Spanish phenomenon, but a general one in Western literature. Anna Caballé (2017) discusses the genre's characteristics and, taking Marta Sanz's *La lección de anatomía* (2008, revised in 2014) as an example, analizes how women writers use it. Sanz's is, she says,

> …un texto que nos hace pensar en cómo las escritoras abordan la autoficción, su utillaje es muy distinto: pueden entrar a saco en los conflictos cuerpo e identidad [sic] –como hace Sanz o también Cristina Grande en *Naturaleza infiel*–, pero se desinteresan por la reflexión metaliteraria tan característica de la obra de Enrique Vila-Matas, Javier Marías o Javier Cercas, por poner algunos ejemplos. Es decir que no problematizan la cuestión del narrador, no al menos de la misma manera. (Caballé, 2017)

[...a text which reminds us of how women writers tackle self-fiction, their way of using it is very different: they can be uncompromising about conflicts regarding body and identity – as Sanz does, and also Cristina Grande in *Naturaleza infiel* – but they are not interested in the metafictional reflection so characteristic of the work of Enrique Vila-Matas, Javier Marías or Javier Cercas, to give some examples. That is to say, they do not problematize the issue of the narrator, at least not in the same way.]

Paloma Díaz-Mas's 'Los mayorales exhaustos' is a fine and multi-layered example of self-fiction. With its ironic and enigmatic title, it gives voice to a narrator who retraces her childhood memories in order to understand better the adult she has become, and it rescues from sweeping generalisations a female character who represents a rather conventional teacher during Francoism. Doña Rosita is devoted to the Catholic Church as well as the dictator, and yet she is an inspiring teacher who instils in her young pupils a thirst for knowledge that will have a remarkably beneficial effect on the narrator later on in life. Although it would be wrong to read this text, or any other for that matter, as a thinly disguised autobiographical account of Paloma Díaz-Mas's childhood, it reminds us of her book *Como un libro cerrado* (2005).

It may seem a straightforward discourse, but self-fiction always goes through a complex process of elaboration: it involves not only a subjective approach, but a distance mediated by the (selective) memory of the experiences that make us who we are and its rendition into text. In this rendition, memory and imagination go hand in hand. In other words, once 'life' is textualized, put into words (or converted into images), it becomes, inevitably, fiction, whether its origin be a pure invention, the memory of something that never happened (Suárez 1994, 7), or a lived occurrence. Gonzalo Suárez (1994, 7) once wrote: 'La vida sobre el papel, deja de ser vida. La letra impresa siempre es recuerdo' [Life on paper ceases to be life. The printed word is always memory]. The past can never be re-enacted in its entirety, but this impossibility, this unsurmountable gap is what prompts the writer (or the filmmaker, or the artist), to use their imagination to transform personal memories into a creative narrative that can be shared. In the article mentioned above, Anna Caballé regards self-fiction as a less complex narrative:

Con la irrupción de la autoficción la novela española dejó de novelar para enredarse en el sempiterno problema del escritor que se ve escribir. Al novelista ya no le fue necesario inventarse un mundo imaginario, unos personajes, un paisaje. Con la autoficción no requiere un andamiaje. (Caballé, 2017)

[With the eruption of self-fiction, the Spanish novel ceased to imagine in order to get entangled with the everlasting problem of the writer who watches himself write. The novelist didn't need to invent an imaginary world, some characters, a landscape. With self-fiction, no scaffolding is needed].

I do not entirely agree with this statement, for self-fiction may have no plot but it requires a degree of literary elaboration. At the time of writing these notes, I happened to attend Maggie O'Farrell's presentation[3] of her memoir *I am, I am, I am* (the title is a quotation from Sylvia Plath's *The Bell Jar*), which is subtitled *Seventeen Encounters with Death* (2017). As is often the case in O'Farrell's fiction, it does not follow the 'tyranny' (her word) of conventional chronology, the narrator is an 'I', or a 'she', depending on the need the said narrator has to distance herself from the diegesis, and the names of people have been changed: by reading her memoir it is obvious that in the process she describes as being more 'excavation than creation', 'excavation' itself is a complicated and fascinating task. In self-fiction, even though memories provide the raw material for the narrative, re-creation is always at work. The story 'El reloj de Bagdad', by Cristina Fernández Cubas, is also a deep 'excavation' into her childhood, as can be inferred by reading her autobiographical texts, such as 'Elba, el origen de un cuento' (1996), but its origin does not make it less literary and it certainly does not mean that it has to be read as a biographical account. Quite the contrary. And memories come from everywhere. Talking about her novel *El sueño de Venecia* (1992), in particular its chapter three, set in the nineteenth century and entitled 'El Indio' (the name of a chocolate shop in Madrid), Paloma Díaz-Mas comments that, with its intricate plot and its urban setting, it was read as an elaborate homage to Galdós, while, in a stimulating fusion, it was also full of hidden biographical detail: 'en un escritor, lo autobiográfico no es solo lo que se ha vivido, sino también lo que se ha leído' (Díaz-Mas, 2006, 48) [for a writer, what is autobiographical is not just what they have lived, but what they have read]. Interestingly, this comment leads us to another of the stories included in the first edition of *Rainy Days*: 'Memoria en venta', by Laura Feixas. Its protagonist is Ernestina, a forty-year old woman who, overwhelmed by the burden of her memories, decides to get rid of them. When she tries to sell or give them all away, we discover that most are literary memories, snippets from the books she has read: indeed, what we read is also part of the experience that constitutes us. Having disposed of

---

3 The presentation took place at the Topping bookshop in St Andrews (Scotland) on 20th September 2017.

her past, Ernestina tries to retrieve one specific memory, that of a first love (which ironically evokes Alexandre Dumas's fils's *La Dame aux camélias* and Verdi's *La Traviata*), and she is totally lost: in a world reminiscent of science-fiction, to have no memories means to have no sign of identity left. This turns the story into a political allegory of the controversial 'pact of silence' regarding the Civil War and Franco's dictatorship which prevailed in Spain from the Transition to practically the beginning of the twenty-first century: if you 'lose' your past, you are in danger of 'forgetting' who you are.

When preparing this anthology, whose title, *Días de lluvia / Rainy Days*, comes from the wonderfully evocative story by Pilar Cibreiro, a tale that reminds us of the power of literature, of storytelling, to create worlds with words, I looked for stories that were a good read and celebrated the uniqueness of the *cuento* form in different ways. The genre has historically struggled to be commercially attractive, hence to appeal to the publishers' interest, but I would say that it has gained prominence and, in an era where genre demarcations are less prescriptive, very few see it as a minor literary product, inferior to the novel.[4] There are as many short-story writers as poetics of the genre, and very often editors of anthologies invite the authors to produce a brief text specifying their approach to the genre. There is even one anthology that collects only poetics of the *cuento* (Becerra, 2006). Among the many incisive attempts to describe it, I have selected a few which highlight the immense possibilities afforded by the literary tension, the 'fugitive alchemy', as James Lasdun subtly defines it (2009), of the brief narrative form. By connecting with the enigmatic and extremely seductive nature of her stories which are fantastic (in a Todorovian sense), Cristina Fernández Cubas says that 'el cuento es un género escurridizo que se nos escapa de las manos a la menor ocasión; un género en el que vale tanto lo que se dice como lo que se oculta; un género

---

4   See 'A Selection of Anthologies of Spanish *cuentos* and Studies on the Short-story Genre in Spain since 1997' at the end of this volume. The number of collective anthologies published in the last twenty years is quite impressive. Some have been put together with a theme in mind, others have the more ambitious objective of being representative of the last century, or of the newest generations of writers, such as those edited by José María Merino, Ángeles Encinar, Andrés Neuman or Fernando Valls. An interesting case is that of *Última temporada. Nuevos narradores españoles 1980–1989*, edited by Alberto Olmos (2013), which includes the same number of women and men writers, an unusual decision for which he was criticized by a literary establishment still anchored in the past (Yuste, 2013). From the list, it is obvious some publishers are to be commended for their dedication to the genre: Páginas de Espuma, Salto de Página, Lengua de Trapo, or Menoscuarto. It is to be noted that more conventional publishers such as Cátedra, Anagrama, Alfaguara or Destino, among others, have also published short stories too, which is an indicator of the growing respect for the genre.

en el que muy a menudo, se cuenta sobre todo lo que se oculta' (Fernández Cubas, 2006, 22–23) [the short story is a slippery genre that gets easily out of our control; a genre in which what is told is as important as what is untold; a genre in which often what is being told is what is hidden]. Succinctly echoing the closeness of the short-story to the poem, Ana María Matute (2001) puts it thus: 'El cuento es la poesía de la prosa' [The short story is the poetry of prose]. Mercedes Cebrián conveys the same idea in a different register but with similar conviction:

> …no debería haber frases saltables en un relato, ni espacios desaprovechados; el relato no es un país con grandes extensiones de terreno poco pobladas, es más bien un recinto tokiota donde se hacinan palabras e ideas, pero a la vez hay que permitirle que actúe como un flâneur, que recale en lo quizá obvio para muchos, que elija las mil palabras frente a la tan ponderada imagen. (Cebrián, 2006, 156)

> […there should be no sentences to spare in the short story, no wasted spaces; the short story is not a country with large extensions of scarcely populated land, it is rather a Tokio-like space where words and ideas are stacked together, but at the same time it should be allowed to be a flâneur, to pay attention to what is perhaps obvious to many, to choose the thousand words instead of the celebrated image.]

Although many scholars insist that one of the features that defines most of the contemporary Spanish practitioners of the genre is 'el apego a lo cotidiano' [a fondness for every day's life] (M. A. V., 1998), or realism broadly understood, that is, in its many forms and shapes (Encinar and Valcárcel, 2012),[5] diversity prevails. As Mercedes Abad says, the short story, being less commercial, 'es un género mucho más libre, donde uno puede permitirse el lujo de jugar, buscar y experimentar para quizá encontrar formas nuevas de contar las mismas historias de siempre' (Abad, 2006, 88) [it is a genre that offers more freedom, within which you can play, experiment and look for new forms to tell the same stories all over again]. This freedom has been instrumental in the way the genre has developed since Edgar Allan Poe's 'tale of effect'. Indeed, the short story no longer seems to need an unexpected ending, although some stories in *Rainy Days* come close to that

---

5　A specialist in the Spanish short story in Spain, Ángeles Encinar has published extensively on the genre (see her publications in the 'Selected Bibliography of Anthologies of Spanish *cuentos* and Studies of the Short-Story Genre in Spain since 1997'; see also those of Fernando Valls and Andrés Neuman, editors of well-known anthologies of *cuentos*).

model. María Eugenia Salaverri's 'Cirugía plástica', with its magnificent closing scene, offers a (relative) surprise. However, it is also an open ending which leaves Irma with choices: what will she do now that all veils have been removed and she has been confronted with the painful revelation that her husband is cheating on her?

Mercedes Abad's 'Pasión defenestrante', with its comical approach to excessive love, is arguably the story that uses the most unexpected final effect. Most of the rest of the stories avoid a shocking revelation: they leave the characters in medias res, as it were, their existences suspended in the middle of something they were doing, as in the case of Soledad Puértolas's 'Viejas historias', with the two protagonists walking side by side on the street, without saying to each other everything that they have to say. Characters are occasionally pushed to the side of their lives: as in Maruja Torres's 'Desaparecida', one of the most dramatic stories in the volume, in which the loneliness that defines the woman protagonist in a TV studio is as compelling as that felt by the protagonists of Rosa Montero's 'El abuelo' and Adelaida García Morales's 'El encuentro', all of them offering a devastating criticism of conventional family structures.

When collecting the short stories, I was also interested in those which say something about writing from the margins, from a location that implicitly acknowledges or exposes otherness. The stories by Rosa Montero and Adelaida García Morales have male characters as protagonists but, either because of age or social discrimination, they are also decentered individuals, examples of society's unconventional 'other', a presence that, in García Morales's story, suggests the Romantic theme of the feared double. For different reasons, the protagonists of 'Nueve meses y un día', by Marina Mayoral, 'Penélope', by Lourdes Ortiz, 'Cirugía plástica', by María Eugenia Salaverri, and 'Desaparecida', by Maruja Torres, are female characters who find themselves displaced in a world where men continue to have privileges that deeply affect them. However, by refusing to appear happier than they are, or by literally disappearing when they have become already invisible to those around them, they all reject being contented with the subordinate role that history, legend, culture or sheer lack of consideration have given them.

'Viejas historias', by Soledad Puértolas, and 'Pasión defenestrante', by Mercedes Abad, are about couples, or, rather, about (im)possible partners. Either by ironically mocking the trap of romantic love in Abad's case, or by desiring some sense of fulfilment in human relationships, which is the characters' driving force in Puértolas's case, these are stories which

make a female protagonist the center of consciousness and offer a nuanced perspective that inevitably shows men around them under a critical, and often amusing, light.

Most of the new stories added to this new edition of *Rainy Days* deal with young girls. They join 'El reloj de Bagdad', by Cristina Fernández Cubas, with a narrator who goes back to her childhood as a young teenager rapidly growing up and discovering in her own body the effects of time. Time is a multi-layered concept in the story and is superbly symbolized by the foreign clock of the title which provides the basis for a fantastic story which leaves readers guessing about the effects the clock has had in the narrator's family.

The girls in the new stories of this second edition are extremely relevant to historical and gender issues in contemporary Spain: the stories in which they appear have a political dimension that shows how social and cultural environments shape people's lives. Berta Marsé's 'Cocinitas' is an ironic and funny, if rather bitter-sweet tale about how young girls are the product of the society they live in, how values can be internalised, how their socialisation reflects what they see at home, on television or in the world around them, and, as in many traditional children's tales, how they are as cruel to each other as adults can be. Marsé's story also highlights how vulnerable they are, how the world constructed for them to mimic puts them at risk of suffering without according them any protection.

Marina Mayoral's 'Nueve meses y un día', already collected in the first edition, does something quite unusual: in a touching but radical move, it gives voice to a mother, it offers the perspective of a figure so often silenced, and it does so in a story that ends with a mourning scene of intimate but epic proportions. In Luisa Castro's 'Mi madre en la ventana', another example of the relatively new trend of the mother-daughter theme, now told through the voice of a daughter, we find a different strategy to make the mother figure relevant. The vigilant *madre* at the window who at first seems harsh and uncaring, will provide her daughter with the resources and the resilience that in the long term will allow her to fend for herself. In this story there is no trace of what Adrienne Rich (1986, 235) has termed 'matrophobia' (the daughter's fear of becoming like her own mother that pushes girls away from their mothers); on the contrary, the mother figure is rescued from misogyny and prejudice. Intertextual echoes of Luisa Castro's *Viajes con mi padre* (2003) can easily be identified here.

The protagonist of the story by Nuria Amat, 'Hipatia', is that formidable historical figure from the once culturally flourishing Alexandria of the

Ptolemies which, in her time, was in the hands of the Romans. She lived between the 3rd and the 4th centuries and was a respected philosopher, a brilliant mathematician and a distinguished astronomer. Hypatia is a great example of how, over the centuries, great women have risen above the prejudice imposed on their gender and, against all the odds, achieved something extraordinary. Whether they have been conveniently forgotten is another matter. That Hypatia should occupy centre stage from the very title of the story is an act of justice. If we bear in mind the way Hypatia met her death at the hands of misogynistic religious fundamentalists, the story is also a cry against intolerance. Not history as such, but the history of Western literature and its legendary male myths is what Lourdes Ortiz questions in 'Penélope': by giving the female character the centre of consciousness (cleverly indicated by the title), the story of Odysseus is revised from an alternative perspective, that of the woman who has waited twenty years for the return of her husband and, when it happens, discovers how time has ravaged their bodies, laments the wasted opportunities for pleasure and prefers to be alone rather than join in the celebrations.

Juana Salabert's delicate and extremely moving story, 'Serás aire volador', deals with the devastation caused by drug addiction to a generation of young adults in the 1980s, and uses the music and lyrics of the electronic band Mecano as the cultural clues to define their social identity. Not quite the fighters against dictatorship their older brothers might have been, it was the generation that attempted to live a free life in a new, fragile democracy, and became some of its most vulnerable victims. The narrator, who sees his twin brother succumb to heroine and tells the story with great tenderness, paints a picture that is almost a sociological portrait of Spain at the time: there is a Francoist father, a (French) free-spirited mother, a socially aspirational older brother and his wife. It has all the elements of a first-period Almodóvar film that have turned tragically sad.

Whether the enjoyment derived from a good short story comes from aesthetic, gender or social concerns, or, as Frank O'Connor said, from the attention given to 'submerged populations' (cited in Lasdun, 2009), that is, of finding in the characters something of the 'marginal, isolated figures such as Chekhov's clerks, Maupassant's prostitutes or Sherwood Anderson's provincial school teachers, eking out thin existences at the edges of society' (Lasdun, 2009), that deeply touches us, we hope that this new version of *Rainy Days*, with sixteen diverse and powerful stories, provides exciting and pleasurable food for thought.

Works cited

Mercedes Abad, 'Grandeza y locura del cuento', in E. Becerra (ed.), *El arquero inmóvil. Nuevas poéticas sobre el cuento* (Madrid: Páginas de Espuma, 2006), 83–88.

J. G. Albalat, 'Els jutges exculpen "La manada" de violació i desencadenen la indignació social', *El Periòdic*, 26 April 3028.

Pilar Alvárez and Gloria Rodríguez-Pina, 'Una explosión empujada por las más jóvenes', *El País*, 7 March 2018. https://politica.elpais.com/politica/2018/03/07/actualidad/1520447384_040798.html

Rafael J. Alvárez, 'El 82% de los españoles de todas las ideologías cree que hay brecha salarial', *El Mundo*, 6 October 2018. http://www.elmundo.es/espana/2018/03/06/5a9e8e3c22601d7a088b4649.html

Asia Argento, 'I've ben called a whore for my part in the #MeToo campaign. It won't stop me', *The Guardian*, 20 April 2018. www.theguardian.com/commentisfree/2018/apr/20/asia-argento-metoo-harvey-weinstein-italy

BBC, 'Hunt "determined" to eliminate doctors' gender pay gap', 28 May 2018. www.bbc.co.uk/news/health-44251506

Eduardo Becerra (ed.), *El arquero inmóvil. Nuevas poéticas sobre el cuento* (Madrid: Páginas de Espuma, 2006).

Alejandro Bolaños, 'La brecha salarial de género en España, la sexta más alta de Europa', *El País*, 8 March 2017. https://economia.elpais.com/economia/2016/03/07/actualidad/1457378340_855685.html

Mark Brown, 'Only a quarter of movies at 20017 film festival are directed by women', *The Guardian*, 31 August 2017. https://www.theguardian.com/film/2017/aug/31/only-a-quarter-of-movies-at-2017-london-film-festival-are-directed-by-women

Anna Caballé, '¿Cansados del yo?', *El País* (Babelia), 6 January 2017. http://elpais.com/cultura/2017/01//06/babelia/1483708694_145058.html

Luisa Castro, *Viajes con mi padre* (Barcelona: Planeta, 2003).

Luisa Castro, *La segunda mujer* (Barcelona: Seix Barral, 2006).

Mercedes Cebrián, 'Cualquier parecido con la realidad es pura poética', in E. Becerra (ed.), *El arquero inmóvil. Nuevas poéticas sobre el cuento* (Madrid: Páginas de Espuma, 2006), 153–57.

Paloma Díaz-Mas, *El sueño de Venecia* (Barcelona: Anagrama, 1992).

Paloma Díaz-Mas, *Como un libro cerrado* (Barcelona: Anagrama, 2005).

Paloma Díaz-Mas, 'Cómo se escribe una novela histórica (o dos)', in J. Jurado Morales (ed.), *Reflexiones sobre la novela histórica* (Cádiz: Servicio de Publicaciones de la Universidad de Cádiz, 2006), 37–49.

Ángeles Encinar and Carmen Valcárcel (eds), *En breve. Cuentos de escritoras españolas (1975–2010). Estudios y antología* (Madrid: Biblioteca Nueva, 2012).

Cristina Fernández Cubas, 'Elba, el origen de un cuento', *Lucanor* 6 (1991), 114–16.

Cristina Fernández Cubas, 'En China donde viven los chinos', in E. Becerra (ed.), *El arquero inmóvil. Nuevas poéticas sobre el cuento* (Madrid: Páginas de Espuma, 2006), 21–26.

Cristina Fernández Cubas, *Cosas que ya no existen* (Barcelona: Tusquets, 2011).

Laura Freixas, *Adolescencia en Barcelona hacia 1970* (Barcelona: Destino, 2007).

Laura Freixas, *Una vida subterránea: Diario 1991–1994* (Madrid: Errata Naturae, 2013).

Laura Freixas, *Todos llevan máscara: Diario 1995–1996* (Madrid: Errata Naturae, 2018).

Cristina Grande, *Naturaleza infiel* (Barcelona: RBA, 2008).

Mercè Ibarz, 'Vaga', *Vilaweb*, 8 March 2018.

Istanbul Coventions, http://ec.europa.eu/justice/gender-equality/files/gender_based_violence/160316_factsheet_istanbul_convention_en.pdf

Danuta Kean, '"Why'd he get promoted? Because he has a dick": Sexism in publishing survey reveals widespread frustration. Majority of women report being treated differently at work due to gender', *The Guardian*, 1 July 2017. https://www.theguardian.com/books/2017/jun/29/sex-in-publishing-survey-reveals-man-who-won-promotion-because-he-had-a-dick

Marisa Kohan, 'El Pacto de Estado contra la Violencia de Género "olvida" meter a las mujeres en los libros de texto', *Público*, 27 July 2017. http://www.publico.es/sociedad/violencia-machista-pacto-violencia-genero-olvida-meter-mujeres-libros-texto.html

EFE, 'La brecha salarial se sitúa en España en el 23,25%, según un informe de la UGT', *Expansión*, 20 February 2017. http://www.expansion.com/economia/2017/02/20/58aafb61e2704e33078b464d.html

James Lasdun, 'The view from somewhere else', *The Guardian* (Review), 4 April 2009. https://www.theguardian.com/books/2009/apr/04/short-story-debuts

M. A. V., 'Merino destaca el apego a lo cotidiano como rasgo del cuento español', *El País* (*Cultura*), 21 October 1998.

Silvia Martínez, 'La reducció de la bretxa salarial entre homes i dones s'estanca a Europa', *El Periòdic*, 7 March 2017.

Ana María Matute, 'El hechizo del relato', *El País* (Babelia), 18 August 2001.

Suzanne Moore, 'It's not just one monster. "Me too" reveals the ubiquity of sexual assault', *The Guardian*, 16 October 2017. https://www.theguardian.com/commentisfree/2017/oct/16/harvey-weinstein-women-sexual-assault-me-too

Ana Morgade, https://www.youtube.com/watch?v=sXP5ILYXQjM

Mujeres en cifras. http://www.inmujer.gob.es/MujerCifras/Violencia/Victimas MortalesVG.htm (consulted 24th August 2017).

Isabel Muntané, 'Últim avís per a un pacte d'estat contra la violència de gènere', *Ara*, 19 July 2017.

Idoya Noain, 'La resistencia a Trump se organiza', *El Periódico*, 19 February 2017.

http://www.elperiodico.com/es/internacional/20170219/la-resistencia-a-trump-se-organiza-5845410

Maggie O'Farrell, *I am, I am, I am. Seventeen Encounters with Death* (London: Tinder Press, 2017).

Alberto Olmos, *Última temporada. Nuevos narradores españoles 1980–1989* (Madrid: Lengua de Trapo, 2013).

Helen Pankhurst, 'The #MeToo movement needs to be a truly global phenomenon' (*The Guardian*, 10 May 2018). https://www.theguardian.com/commentisfree/2018/may/10/metoo-me-too-movement-global-phenomenon-women-girls-workplace-abuse

Cristina Pardo, 'La Manada', *El Periòdic*, 1 May 2018.

El Periódico, 'El fiscal pide tres años de cárcel por una brutal patada a una joven, grabada y difundida en internet', 11 February 2017. http://www.elperiodico.com/es/sociedad/20170211/el-fiscal-pide-tres-anos-carcel-brutal-patada-joven-grabada-difundida-internet-5801363

Público, 'Absoluto rechazo del Partido Feminista ante el Pacto de Estado contra la violencia machista', 27 July 2017. http://www.publico.es/sociedad/absoluto-rechazo-del-partido-feminista-pacto-violencia-genero.html

Soledad Puértolas, *Con mi madre* (Barcelona: Anagrama, 2001).

RTVE, 'Un total de 31 víctimas de violencia de género en el primer semestre, la cifra más alta desde 2010', 30 June 2017. http://www.rtve.es/noticias/20170630/total-31-mujeres-asesinadas-primer-semestre-del-ano-cifra-mas-alta-desde-2010/1574040.shtml

Luis Rendueles and Vanessa Lozano, 'Grups neo-Nazis i ultres promouen el linxament de la víctima de "La manada"', *El Periòdic*, 17 May 2018. https://www.elperiodico.cat/ca/successos-i-tribunals/20180517/grups-neonazis-ultres-promouen-linxament-victima-la-manada-6820547

Belén Remacha, 'La curiosa miosoginia de la RAE', *eldiario.es*, 5 April 2016. http://www.eldiario.es/cultura/RAE-institucion-tradicionalmente-misogina_0_502200361.html

Raquel Riba Rossy, *Lola Vendetta. Más vale Lola que mal acompañada* (Barcelona: Lumen, 2017). http://www.lolavendetta.net/ https://www.instagram.com/lola.vendetta/?hl=en

Gloria Rodríguez-Pina, 'Pacto histórico para atajar la violencia contra la mujer', *El País*, 25 July 2017a. https://politica.elpais.com/politica/2017/07/24/actualidad/1500883885_958602.html

Gloria Rodríguez-Pina, 'Unidos Podemos se abstiene en el Pacto de Estado contra la violencia machista', 28 July 2017b. https://politica.elpais.com/politica/2017/07/28/actualidad/1501230577_729033.html

Adrienne Rich, *Of Woman Born: Motherhood as Experience and Institution* (London: Virago, 1986).

Carme Riera, *Temps d'una espera* (Barcelona: Columna, 1998).

Carme Riera, *Temps d'innocència* (Barcelona: Edicions 62, 2013).

Victoria Rosell, 'The "wolf pack" case showed the world how Spanish law is mired in misogyny', *The Guardian*, 26 June 2018.

Marta Sanz, *La lección de anatomía* (Barcelona: Anagrama, 2014).

Gonzalo Suárez, *El asesino triste* (Madrid: Alfaguara, 1994).

Alexandra Topping, Caelainn Barr and Pamela Duncan, 'Gender pay gap figures reveal that eight in 10 UK firms pay men more', *The Guardian*, 4 April 2018. https://www.theguardian.com/money/2018/apr/04/gender-pay-gap-figures-reveal-eight-in-10-uk-firms-pay-men-more

Jessica Valenti, '#MeToo named the victims. Now, let's list the perpetrators', *The Guardian*, 17 October 2017.

Clara Vicenç and Marina Vinardell, 'I en la música, on són les dones?', *Vilaweb*, 15 June 2017. http://.www.vilaweb.cat/notícies/i-en-la-musica/on-son/les-dones

Javier Yuste, 'Alberto Olmos', *El Cultural*, 7 December 2013. http://www.elcultural.com/noticias/buenos-dias/Alberto-Olmos/5681

INTRODUCTION TO THE FIRST EDITION

WOMEN WRITERS IN POST-FRANCO SPAIN: WRITING AS TRANSGRESSION?

To illustrate an article by Rosa Pereda, 'El pensamiento posfeminista' (1993, 6), the Spanish newspaper *El País* used a photograph from 1914 in which the suffragette Emmeline Pankhurst is being arrested by a uniformed policeman who carries her in his arms, presumably, away to the police station, as though she were a naughty child caught in a mischievous act. It could be argued that the picture was an appropriate choice to accompany Pereda's reflection that, after the 1980s, new strategies had to be found to keep alive the fight for women's rights because of the new, trendy conservatism threatening to undermine women's achievements. This conservatism was manifested in campaigns against abortion, increasing and much publicized mistrust of day-nurseries, claims that women were fed up with trying to be Superwoman and were missing out on life's natural pleasures, like motherhood and so on. It was as though the snapshot was used as a reminder of how difficult the struggle had been. But we could also read this picture of Emmeline Pankhurst (who looks admirably full of dignity in such uncomfortable circumstances) as being in keeping with the general, popular perception of the self-confessed feminist as someone who is eccentric almost to the point of ridicule. What I am referring to here is the kind of patriarchal attitude which, however great the success of women in public and private spheres, still dominates the lives and ways of thinking of a majority of people, whatever their race, gender or class. 'El masclisme és interclassista' [Macho culture cuts across social class],[1] said the last Director of the Instituto de la Mujer, the Catalan Marina Subirats, in an interview (Alberola, 1994, 38) before the March 1996 election in Spain gave power to the conservative *Partido Popular.*

Despite the many social and political gains made by women over the last century, which have been sanctioned by law in most democratic countries, the resilience of these all-pervasive patriarchal values, often presented as 'natural', justifies a gathering of texts written by women. Since language was dressed in men's clothes for so long, a collection of women's texts is,

---

1   Translated from Catalan.

to some extent, a small step towards a more equal society, a type of positive discrimination, no less political for being literary. Spanish critics and authors have often displayed a tendency to scorn collections of women's writings, dismissing them as either a hysterical response to perceived victimization on the part of feminist writers and academics, who are accused of sexism (although the same people never question anthologies featuring a majority of, or exclusively, men writers), or the product of marketing surveys carried out by commercially-minded publishers, since women writers nowadays sell very well and most of their readers are women.[2] Ignacio Soldevila-Durante states:

> ¿se hace realmente el mayor favor posible a las escritoras publicando monografías sobre su obra, o incrementando en los estudios globales el porcentaje respectivo de la atención a ellas dedicada? Es ésta cuestión de estricta justicia compensatoria, ya que debido a las condiciones reales en que la mujer ha vivido hasta el fin del franquismo, y con la honrosa excepción de los breves años de gobierno de izquierda entre 1936 y 1939 [*sic*], hacer un recuento de los catálogos de la Biblioteca Nacional en dos apartados – hombres y mujeres – dará como resultado un porcentaje más o menos equivalente al 10% de mujeres escritoras. (1990, 609)

This is a very low percentage indeed, and evidence of just how marginalized women have been in terms of cultural production in Spain up to the present day.

Joan L. Brown surveys the presence of women writers in what has been traditionally considered the canon in Spanish literary history, dividing it

---

2   This current situation is mainly due to two factors: first, women in Spain, as in many other countries, have been more actively involved in literary production than in any other area of cultural production (see Weedon, 1987, 144; Graham and Labanyi, 1995, 383–84), and secondly, reading is Spanish women's main cultural activity, in which they are far ahead of men, according to an invaluable survey carried out by the sociologist Enrique Gil Calvo (1992a), *La era de las lectoras: El cambio cultural de las mujeres españolas*. This is an important study whose conclusions coincide with several opinion polls on the subject published by the Spanish press, and also with a survey carried out by the magazine *Lire* on the femininization of the reading habits in France (quoted in Serra, 1995, 75). Gil Calvo highlights some relevant findings, like the fact that even at the 'turning point' (58) of women's lives, when they become mothers, and most of their other cultural activity is affected, their book-reading rates do not seem to decrease at all, along with evidence about 'la evidente superioridad del menú cultural de las activas respecto a los activos' (92), or figures which show the undeniable reality of the 'inequívoco avance que supone el desarrollo modernizador del comportamiento cultural femenino' (49).

into three – somewhat debatable – periods: 'before Franco (1100–1936), during the Franco era (1936–1975), and after Franco (1975 to the present)' (1990, 553–60).[3] Although the number of writers increases considerably from one period to the next, she finds that only six women from the first period, spanning eight centuries, have been consistently included in most literary histories and anthologies: Teresa de Jesús (sixteenth century), María de Zayas y Sotomayor (seventeenth century), Cecilia Böhl de Faber, who used a male penname: 'Fernán Caballero', Gertrudis Gómez de Avellaneda, Rosalía de Castro, and Emilia Pardo Bazán (nineteenth century). By stressing that only six were officially maintained at the centre of the literary establishment, Brown is signalling that equally, if not more, important is the number of women writers who have been forgotten. The pernicious effect of such an approach was pointed out by Elaine Showalter in 1977 when dealing with English writers:

> Criticism of women novelists, while focussing on these happy few [Austen, George Eliot, the Brontës, Woolf], has ignored those who are not 'great', and left them out of anthologies, histories, textbooks, and theories. Having lost sight of the minor novelists, who were the links in the chain that bound one generation to the next, we have not had a very clear understanding of the continuities in women's writing, nor any reliable information about the relationships between the writers' lives and the changes in the legal, economic, and social status of women. (1991, 7)

The general position of traditional Hispanism, that of taking seriously only one small group of women writers accorded the same, or nearly the same, critical consideration as their male counterparts, is the result of what Chris Weedon accurately deconstructs as

> the liberal-humanist criticism which claims to address both the unique individual and the universally human, but its gender blindness has created the conditions for a discourse which is profoundly conservative and patriarchal in its implications, The individual and the human nature for which it speaks are both normatively male, and the meaning and values which it privileges naturalize the social power relations of patriarchy. (1987, 139)

A rough calculation of the number of women poets, novelists and playwrights

---

3 This issue is also addressed by Brown in 'Women Writers of Spain: An Historical Perspective', in *Women Writers of Contemporary Spain: Exiles in the Homeland* (1991, 13–25).

of the first period – the eight-century time-span as established by Brown – gathered in a sample of female-only bio-bibliographic source books (Pérez 1988 and 1996; Gould Levine, Engelson Marson and Feiman Waldman 1993; the anthologies edited by Susan Kirkpatrick 1992 and Ángela Elena Bordonada 1989; and those *Mujeres del 27* included in an Ínsula's monographic issue of 1993, though some of their publications spill over into the second period) amounts to approximately one hundred women writers. The disparity between these figures – six as opposed to one hundred – needs no comment. Besides, this figure of one hundred could very easily double if we were to take into account earlier collections.[4] Indeed, however long the list turns out to be, we shall be always consigning to oblivion those whose literary output never reached publication, or those whose social status as women prevented them from 'attempting the pen'.[5]

Nowadays the situation has changed enormously. Unlike other occupations where women find it difficult in practice to combine successfully the role of professional and mother, in spite of a certain amount of social improvement,[6] female literary production is beginning to be highly coveted. Women writers sell well and that makes then attractive to publishers.[7] This is a relatively recent and extremely relevant factor which has no doubt helped the female author to become less invisible. The process started in the thirties and, after a relapse in the immediate aftermath of the Civil War, gathered momentum – thanks mainly to writers like Carmen Laforet, Ana María Matute, Carmen Martín Gaite, Elena Quiroga or Dolores Medio[8] and, later on, to those

---

4   See Janet Pérez (1988, 1–7) for bibliography on earlier accounts of Spanish women writers.
5   See the poem by Anne Finch, Countess of Winchelsea, quoted in Sandra Gilbert and Susan Gubar's *The Madwoman in the Attic* (1979, 3).
6   Enrique Gil Calvo (1992b) analizes the social and economic reasons which directly reinforce discrimination at home and in the workplace (different salaries according to the worker's sex: an average of 25% less for women, as recent figures published by the ILO – International Labour Organization – show; unequal opportunities for promotion; unequal allocation of job perks, and so on), preventing a more egalitarian distribution of tasks and keeping women and men trapped in the vicious circle of patriarchy.
7   Those publishers whose criteria have not been purely commercial, but literary or political (Anthropos, LaSal, Lumen, Tusquets) have also played an important role in the diffusion of women's writing.
8   The first women who started publishing after the Civil War had been born in the 1920s and early 1930s. They were brought up in a country which, with all its failures and political turmoil, was not the one that emerged after 1939 where the main role assigned to women was to stay at home and look after the family. This may account for women's early presence in the literary scene in spite of the hostile environment. This suggestion already made by

respected older figures who, after spending years in exile since the end of the Civil War, were re-entering the Spanish scene such as Rosa Chacel or the Catalan Mercè Rodoreda, as well as other important names who started publishing in the late sixties, such as Ana María Moix, or Esther Tusquets, whose first novel dates from 1978 – and took off with the splendid mushrooming of new names in the 1980s and 1990s, of whom, unfortunately, only twelve are represented in this anthology. However, for all the talent and the powerful presence of many of the women writers, the panorama is far from ideal. The number of pages devoted to them in influential reference books has increased steadily but very slowly.[9] At the same time, as Brown points out:

> Consonant with such low representation is the condescending manner in which [...] literary histories describe and categorize literature by women [...], [they] take pains to emphasize (though rarely to define) the 'feminine' nature of all literature by women. By inference, this label is understood to signify sentimentality. (1990, 555)

Here she is referring to criticism prior to 1975, and we might be tempted to believe that things are now so much better that there is hardly any need to complain; that well-informed critics, familiar with new theoretical trends, have put an end to all these discriminative and patronizing readings, and that Spanish literature written by women has received the attention it deserves.[10] However, some interesting points could be raised if we were

---

María del Carmen Riddel (1995, 7), coincides with José-Carlos Mainer's clever redistribution of the periodization of post-Civil War Spanish literature in *De postguerra (1951–1900)*:

En algún lugar he negado que la contienda de 1936 sea mojón de un nuevo período cultural:

Tras el final de las batallas y hasta 1950, más o menos, he creído ver que se extiende un período soterradamente epigonal cuyas claves se asientan en los años republicanos. (1994, 9).

9   Joan L. Brown (1990, 554) gives useful percentages of the number of female authors and pages dedicated to them in the most consulted histories of twentieth-century Spanish literature published between 1956 (29 pp. out of 815) and 1985 (120 pp. out of 440).

10   Apart from those journals which are dedicated to women's literature, like *Letras Femeninas*, or the recent *Lectora. Revista de Dones i Textualitat* (Universitat Autònoma de Barcelona), several others have published monographic issues on Spanish women writers:

Litoral 1986 (169–70)
Anales de la Literatura Española Contemporánea 1987, 12 (1–2)
Ventanal 1988 (14)
Revista de Estudios Hispánicos 1988 (22)
Revista Canadiense de Estudios Hispánicos 1990, 14 (3)

Monographic Review 1992 (8)
Ínsula 1993 (557)
Quimera 1994 (123)
Bulletin of Hispanic Studies 1995 (72)

A considerable number of multi- or single-authored books dealing with different women writers or with the representation of women in literature has also been published in recent years, the most significant being:

Concha Alborg, *Cinco figuras en torno a la novela de posguerra: Galvarriato, Soriano, Formica, Boixadós y Aldecoa* (Madrid: Ediciones Libertarias, 1993).

Isolina Ballesteros, *Escritura femenina y discurso autobiográfico en la nueva novela española* (New York: Peter Lang, 1994).

Joan L. Brown, ed., *Women Writers in Contemporary Spain. Exiles in the Homeland* (Newark: University of Delaware Press; Cranbury, NY: Associated University Presses, 1991).

Lou Charnon-Deutsch, *Gender and Representation: Women in Spanish Realist Fiction* (Amsterdam and Philadelphia: John Benjamins, 1990).

Lou Charnon-Deutsch, *Narratives of Desire: Nineteenth-Century Spanish Fiction by Women* (Pennsylvania: Pennsylvania State University Press, 1994).

Lou Charnon-Deutsch and Jo Labanyi, eds, *Culture and Gender in Nineteenth-Century Spain* (Oxford: Oxford University Press, 1995).

Lisa Condé and Stephen M. Hart, eds, *Feminists Readings on Spanish and Latin-American Literature* (Lewiston, NY: Edwin Mellen Press, 1991).

Catherine Davies, *Contemporary Feminist Fiction in Spain. The Work of Montserrat Roig and Rosa Montero* (Oxford and Providence, USA: Berg, 1994).

Myriam Díaz-Diocaretz and Iris M. Zavala, eds, *Breve historia feminista de la literatura española (en lengua castellana).* [Two volumes published to date: *Teoría feminista* (1993), and *La mujer en la literatura española. Modos de representación desde la Edad Media hasta el siglo XVII* (1995)] (Barcelona: Anthropos; Madrid: Dirección General de la Mujer).

María Ángeles Durán and M. D. Temprano, 'Mujeres, misóginos y feministas en la literatura española', in *Actas de las IV Jornadas de Investigación Interdisciplinaria,* 412–84 (Madrid and Zaragoza, 1986), 412–84.

Elena Gascón Vera, *Un mito nuevo: La mujer como sujeto/ objeto literario* (Madrid: Pliegos, 1992).

Francisca López, *Mito y discurso en la novela femenina de posguerra en España* (Madrid: Pliegos, 1995).

Roberto C. Manteiga, Carolyn Galerstein and Kathleen McNerney, eds, *Feminine Concerns in Contemporary Spanish Fiction by Women* (Potomac, MD: Scripta Humanistica, 1987).

María Jesús Mayans, *Narrativa feminista española de posguerra* (Madrid: Pliegos, 1991).

Beth Miller, ed., *Women in Hispanic Literature. Icons and Fallen Idols* (Berkeley: University of California Press, 1983).

Geraldine C. Nichols, *Escribir, espacio propio: Laforet, Matute, Moix, Tusquets, Riera y Roig por sí mismas* Minneapolis, MN: Institute for the Study of Ideologies and Literature, 1989).

Geraldine C. Nichols, *Des/cifrar la diferencia: Narrativa femenina de la España contemporánea* (Madrid: Siglo Veintiuno de España Editores, 1992).

to look at one of the most prestigious collections of essays on Spanish literary history published in the 1990s, the ninth volume of the *Historia y Crítica de la Literatura Española* (whose general editor is Francisco Rico): *Los nuevos nombres: 1975–1990* (edited by Darío Villanueva, 1992). This encyclopaedic volume covers the exact period of time during which the number of women writers in Spain has flourished. We should welcome the fact that the 'condescending manner' in which previous criticism used to deal with women's literature has entirely disappeared from this volume, and yet the inequality persists. Only 88 women writers are included as opposed to 560 male authors. The gender balance of scholars and academics contributing to this major collective work is also lop-sided: 17 are female while 63 are male. But the fact that of the 88 women writers 17 (19.2%) are studied in some depth, and only 64 (11.4%) of the 560 male writers are considered interesting enough to be discussed at some length, provides us with a rather ambivalent information: either the criteria for including men have been wider (writers at the beginning of their careers or those with only one book), or women writers, in spite of being a lesser presence, have been given more individual attention. Both explanations, somewhat contradictory, seem valid. Moreover, if we take into account the number

---

Elizabeth Ordóñez, *Voices of Their Own. Contemporary Spanish Narrative by Women* (Lewisburg: Bucknell University Press, 1991).

María del Carmen Riddel, *La escritura femenina en la posguerra española* (New York: Peter Lang, 1995).

Elizabeth A. Scarlett, *Under Construction. The Body in Spanish Novels* (Charlottesville: University Press of Virginia, 1994).

Noël Valis and Carol Maier, eds, *In the Feminine Mode. Essays on Hispanic Women Writers* (Lewisburg: Bucknell University Press, 1990).

[The list does not include the numerous articles on the subject in journals specializing in Hispanic Studies.]

There have also been contributions on Spanish women writing in books or journals with a European or transnational dimension:

Biruté Ciplijauskaité, 'Lyric Memory, Oral History, and the Shaping of the Shelf in Spanish Narrative'. *Forum for Modern Language Studies* 24.4 (1992). [This is a monographic issue: entitled *The Language of a Thousand Tongues: Contemporary European Fiction by Women*, ed. with a 'Foreword' by Catherine Davies].

Catherine Davies, 'Feminists Writers in Spain since 1990: From Political Surgery to Personal Enquiry', in Helena Forsås-Scott, ed., *Textual Liberation. European Feminist Writing in the Twentieth Century* (London: Routledge, 1991) 192–226.

Biruté Ciplijauskaité, *La novela femenina contemporánea (1970–1985). Hacia una tipología de la narración en primera persona* (Barcelona: Anthropos, 1988).

(See also selected bibliography on every autor included in this anthology.)

of women writers active[11] during the years covered by the volume who might have been included in it, we have to accept that not many names are missing.[12] This leads us to a grim conclusion: although the population is surprisingly gender-balanced – 51% is female in Spain, and 52% in the world (Navarro 1993, 14) – there are still fewer women than men writers, as there are fewer Members of Parliament than male ones.[13] Circumstances which enable women to develop to their full potential may have improved significantly, and the willingness to neutralize patronising attitudes towards literature written by women might be less hard to find than in previous decades, but the process towards parity is far from over.

Also enlightening in this respect is what Laura Freixas (a writer who knows the Spanish publishing milieu well) states in the introduction to *Madres e hijas*, a ground breaking anthology of short stories written by women:

11   The volume also refers to books published between 1975 and 1990 by writers who were known before 1975 and who, strictly speaking, were not 'new names'.

12   Bearing in mind that the volume was published in 1992, before new writers such as Enriqueta Antolín, Gabriela Bustelo, María Ángeles Caso, Maite Dono, Susana Fortes, Belén Gopegui, María Eugenia Salaverri, Ana Santos, Maite Dono, and others were known, the most striking absences are those of Maruja Torres, who had already published her first satirical novel in the 1980s and was a leading figure in Spanish journalism, and Carme Riera, who is mentioned four times always in relation to her scholarly work while nothing is said about her creative writing (other Catalan writers translated into Spanish are mentioned: Mercè Rodoreda, Montserrat Roig). Other possible names which could have been included are Aurora de Albornoz, Gloria Fuertes, Carmen Gómez Ojea, Julia Ibarra, Elena Martín Vivaldi, María Luz Melcón, Concha Lagos, Elena Santiago, Elena Soriano, Acacia Uceta, Arantxa Urretavizcaya and Concha Zardoya, all of them with books published between 1975 and 1990 which are neither more nor less important than those by some of their male counterparts which merited inclusion.

13   According to J. M. Calvo (1995, 18), the world's number of women MPs reached in 1988 its highest point since the struggle for female suffrage began: 14.8%. In 1995 it was reduced to 11.3%, in spite of the encouraging fact that female presence in parliaments is four times what it was in 1945 (figures, though, must have improved with the spectacular increase in the number of women MPs in the British Parliament after the May 1997 general election). The situation in Spain as far as the number of women in key positions of power is concerned has never been exemplary, but now, after the conservative *Partido Popular* won the general election in March 1996, it has definitely worsened:

> José María Aznar ha presumido de que en su Consejo de Ministros hay cuatro mujeres [pero] el PP no ha nombrado a ninguna secretaria de Estado [all 21 are men] y sólo a dos directoras generales [27 are men] y 12 secretarias generales. El último Gobierno de Felipe González tenía tres ministras, cinco subsecretarias de Estado, tres subsecretarias y 18 directoras generales. (Casqueiro, 1996, 22)

en el mundo editorial de aquí y ahora las mujeres *funcionan*: hay que añadir que ese reconocimiento suele ir acompañado de cierta condescendencia (se las llama *las chicas*), y que si están presentes (aunque, insistimos, de forma muy minoritaria) en la publicación y en los premios comerciales, su reconocimiento académico es harina de otro costal. De la Real Academia están prácticamente ausentes[14] así como de la nómina de los grandes premios institucionales; y como ha mostrado Geraldine Nichols,[15] las historias de la literatura española las ignoran o rebajan sistemáticamente. (1996, 18, her italics)

To this we could add that all too often academic papers still show unnecessary prejudice: in *Ínsula*'s recent issue dedicated to contemporary narrative, two different contributors use in their respective articles these somewhat derisory subheadings: 'Mujeres y autonómicos' (Gracia 1996, 30), and 'Mujeres: una lista' (Chicharro Chamorro 1996, 15). Literary debates organized by otherwise serious academic journals or cultural magazines reveal the same degree of unevenness. Looking at a few examples in recent years, we come across the same old tokenism: in 1986 *El Urogallo* brought together six writers for a discussion on 'Narradores de hoy', and only one of them was a woman; in 1988 *Ínsula* published a debate on 'El cuento' held in the Casona de Verines (Pendueles, Asturias) the previous year and, among twenty-eight writers and academics, only five were women; in 1994, five writers and one academic who acted as coordinator were invited by *Ínsula* to debate 'De últimos cuentos y cuentistas', but only one was a woman; six men – authors and critics – were asked to participate in the debates on *¿Qué va a ser de la literatura?* organized in 1996 by the cultural magazine *Lateral* both in Madrid and Barcelona, and only one woman writer was invited. We could go on.

Thus, for all the positive signs in publishing circles (for example, more series dedicated to female writers), the real issue at stake is the development of a new consciousness about women and gender, and the recognition by the

---

14   Carmen Conde, a poet of the so-called *Generación de 1936*, was appointed to replace the playwright Miguel Mihura in 1978, and she became the first woman ever to be a member of the Real Academia de la Lengua, to be followed by Elena Quiroga in 1984. After Conde's death in January 1996, she was replaced by the novelist Ana María Matute, but female presence in the institution is still intolerably scarce.

15   She refers to Geraldine C. Nichols's *Escribir, espacio propio: Laforet, Matute, Moix, Tusquets, Riera y Roig por sí mismas* (1989). Nichols's comments are not dissimilar to Brown's in this respect. Elizabeth J, Ordóñez also addresses the issue and draws the conclusion that 'a number of well-known and respected studies of contemporary Spanish fiction during the last two decades seemed uneasy about where or how to include works by women' (Ordóñez, 1991, 15).

literary establishment of women writers' success, not only as a sociological phenomenon, but also as a literary one. This recognition should lead to something more than just the mere addition of a few names to the canon. It should challenge the whole concept of the canon itself, a canon that, if it is to remain at all, should be an inclusive, non-hegemonic one.[16]

Some women writers seem to believe that the situation is slowly improving though it still leaves a lot to be desired. Others, on the contrary, deny that there is any discrimination against female authors, for example Cristina Fernández Cubas, who, at the same time, acknowledges the significance of their presence in post-Civil War narrative:

> Tenemos los mismos problemas que los hombres. Además en España siempre ha habido mujeres escritoras. Cuando yo era pequeña estaban Carmen Laforet, Ana María Matute, [un] poco más tarde Carmen Martín Gaite. Mujeres de éxito, que ganaban premios muy prestigiosos en la misma competencia con los hombres, en iguales condiciones. A nadie se le ocurría, en ningún momento, hacer una antología de esas tres mujeres. A nadie se le ocurrió decir 'son femeninas', en absoluto. Esta es una cosa posterior. Hemos nacido en un país en el cual ser escritora era una cosa normal. (Carmona *et al.*, 1991, 158)

Or Soledad Puértolas: 'Nunca he creído […] que las mujeres tengan mayores problemas para escribir que los hombres. Nunca se me ha ocurrido que las cosas deban plantearse de ese modo. Tampoco parece que tengan especiales dificultades para publicar sus textos. ¿Dónde reside la discriminación, si es que la hay?' (1993, 60).

The debate, tough, if such a debate exists, should be set within a larger framework: that of the women writers' approach to literature and the politicization of their writing.[17] The fight against gender inequalities has been tackled in different ways and with many strategies. In a collective interview Mercedes Abad made this highly significant point: 'Durante cuarenta años la literatura se dedicó casi exclusivamente a la lamentación organizada. Y no sólo la literatura, sino otros modos y otros movimientos, pongo por ejemplo a las mujeres. Yo, desde luego, no me dedico a lamentarme ('Narradores de hoy', 1986, 20).

---

16   See Lou Charnon-Deutsch (1994, 1–12) for a highly interesting discussion on the canon, this 'unstable concept determined by political and social contingencies, religious and moral beliefs, literary and aesthetic tastes, and, especially, the dynamics of a literary economic system' (3).

17   Both Monica Threlfall (1985) and Catherine Davies (1994) have competently addressed the issue.

A few years later, at the University of California, Abad, Fernández Cubas and Puértolas agreed on one thing: 'literatura y feminismo no tienen nada que ver' (Carmona *et al.*, 1991, 158). There is a widespread reluctance to accept any form of what Rosa Montero calls 'literatura utilitaria' (Davies, 1993, 383). A reluctance that reveals the profound mistrust for politics and the power of art to transform reality embedded in a society which had to cope with a dictatorial regime for so long. Adelaida García Morales, a committed socialist[18] and a writer whose fiction is dominated by complex female figures and gender relations, is also adamant that 'La lucha política y la literatura son cosas completamente distintas. [...] La literatura es un territorio imaginario' (Cano, 1996, 100).

Although I am aware of the risks of drawing general conclusions, I would suggest that recent Spanish history, and the way pre-1975 currents in Spanish cultural production were influenced by it, still cast a shadow over contemporary writers' views on literature. In 1939 the outcome of a bloody Civil War which lasted three years brought to power a military régime lead by General Franco. The dictatorship lasted until his death in 1975. The adversity and political isolation which Spaniards endured for four decades affected every single aspect of their lives. They were denied basic democratic rights and the former pluralistic society of pre-War Spain became, in the 1940s, one in which diversity was perceived as a threat to an illusory fascist sense of unity.[19] After the brutal repression which followed the Civil War, a short period of the so-called *realismo existencial* gave way to in the 1950s to political commitment as the predominant feature in literature –and in art in general. Many *engagé* writers, male and female, viewed literature

---

18   See her article 'La primavera socialista, a pesar de todo' in *El País,* 24 February 1996, published during the 1996 Spanish general election campaign.

19   For further reading on the situation of women before, under and after Franco, see: Concha Borreguero, *et al.*, *La mujer española: De la tradición a la modernidad (1960–1980)* (Madrid: Tecnos, 1986); Anny Brooksbank-Jones, 'Women, Politics and Social Change in Contemporary Spain', *Tesserae, Journal of Iberian and Latin American Studies* 1.2 (1995), 277–94; María Rosa Capel, *El trabajo y la educación de la mujer en España (1900–1931)* (Madrid: Ministerio de Cultura, 1982); Pilar Folguera, ed., *El feminismo en España: Dos siglos de historia* (Madrid: Ed. Pablo Iglesias, 1988), Helen Graham and Jo Labanyi, eds, *Spanish Cultural Studies: An Introduction. The Struggle for Modernity* (Oxford and New York: Oxford University Press, 1995); Olga Kenyon, 'Women under Franco and PSOE: The Discrepancy between Discourse and Reality', in Bernard McGuirk and Mark I. Millington, eds, *Inequality and Difference in Hispanic and Latin American Cultures* (Lewiston, NY: Edwin Mellen Press, 1995); Carmen Martín Gaite, *Usos amorosos de la postguerra Española* (Barcelona: Anagrama, 1987); Monica Threlfall, 'The Women's Movement in Spain'. *New Left Review* 151 (1985), 44–73.

as an instrument for political and social change – their inspiration, in some cases, was just not Sartre or Italian neo-realism, but also Spanish writers and artists living in exile. The literature – narrative, theatre, poetry – produced as a result of this closeness between the world and the text, responded to the creed of what has been labelled *realismo social* or *realismo crítico* or *dialéctico*: a testimonial writing strongly influenced by leftist thought.[20] A willingness to expose the hardship suffered by the people under Franco's authoritarian regime shaped most of the literary output of those years despite the strict censorship in force at the time. Writers tried to be 'objective' in their attempts to depict social injustice and political repression, and avoid the red pen of the censors. As the public and the writers themselves grew tired of *realismo social*, some of them, such as Luis Martín Santos, Juan Goytisolo or Juan Benet, questioned and escaped from its limitations without being any less critical of contemporary Spain. From the 1960s until the mid 1970s experimental literature flourished, both as a reaction to a frequently short-sighted belief in *objetivismo* and as a result of the influence of French structuralism and its insistence on the non-referentiality of literature. Many so-called 'anti-novels' were written. Formal experimentation was cleverly exploited, and together with a questioning of the very nature of language and its conventional use in fiction, this allowed writers to distance themselves from the naïve attempts at 'objectivism' of the previous decade. Writers still set out to destroy 'the images of security and wholeness sustained by the [Franco] Regime' (Herzberger, 1991, 253), but now language itself, and hence narration, became the locus for this new avant-garde, elitist struggle against totalitarianism. As Jo Labany says: 'Novelists and critics' increasing insistence that the writers' duty was to revolutionize language implied that no other revolution was possible; indeed it became fashionable to praise writers for the suicidal act of "destroying language"' (Graham and Labanyi, 1995, 296).

Since the mid 1970s, diversity and a postmodern license to break free from any remaining dominant trends have been the most obvious features of Spanish narrative, along with a renewed fondness for storytelling. The

---

20   By no means homogeneous (some literary historians even prefer to distinguish between *neorrealismo* and *social realism*), *realismo* encompassed young writers of the generation of 1950, for whom the Civil War had been a childhood experience and were generally committed to social and political change, and those of the generation of 1936, who experienced the Civil War as young adults, some of them on Franco's side, such as Camilo José Cela – a novelist with aesthetical rather than social concerns – or writers of a Christian persuasion, such as Miguel Delibes.

democratic press took over the former testimonial role of literature, and writers today reject 'literatura militante', to use Montero's words again (Davies 1993, 383), because amongst other possible reasons, it reminds them of what was fashionable and yet so restrictive only a few decades ago.

Some writers have no qualms about admitting being feminists, others are more reluctant to be labelled as such, as indeed they are about any labelling exercise. Among the first group we find Lourdes Ortiz (Porter 1990, 144), Maruja Torres (1996, 10), or Laura Freixas (Fidalgo 1996, 60), whose introductory words in *Madres e hijas* (1996, 9–20) offer a convincing comment on the issue of *literatura femenina*. Freixas emphasizes that *literatura femenina* is different from that produced by male writers and takes into account the French feminist notion of *écriture féminine*, which does not automatically exclude men's writing for biological reasons and, we may add, does not guarantee any writing with a female signature immediate inclusion in the alternative space of femininity. Ideally, her words should put an end to all those hopeless, and frequently biased, discussions in the Spanish press about 'the sex of literature' (for example, quizzes in which the readers are supposed to guess the 'sex' of the writers of anonymous pieces). The Catalan writer Marta Pessarrodona, in a Beauvoirian-inspired thought, once said: 'La literatura més que sexe, te gènere (masculí, femení), fonamentalment per raons socials' [Literature had gender (masculine, feminine), rather than sex, basically for social reasons] (Serra, 1995, 76).

Some authors feel definitely uneasy about the appropriation of their condition as women writers by certain critics, and demand to be free from political burdens. Rejection of what is seen as narrow-minded feminism, an imposition rather than personal choice, is clear in the following words by Paloma Díaz-Mas:

> Me resulta especialmente molesto que por el hecho de ser mujer te exijan que escribas en reivindicación [*sic*] [...]. Me parece perfectamente lícito que algunas escritoras elijan como tema la condición de la mujer, pero que no sea obligatorio porque eso me parece paternalismo por parte de las mujeres hacia las mujeres. Ya hemos estado bastante tuteladas durante siglos para que ahora nos vengan a tutelar los movimientos de liberación de la mujer. (Diéguez, 1988, 88)

These words are not far from what Suzanne Moore wrote à propos of the issue of women and their access to political power: 'Women want nothing more and nothing less than the privilege that men take for granted – that

their gender is not constantly noted' (1996, 6). This is a claim that in literary terms, is similar to that made by Puértolas, a writer who, on the other hand, has always insisted on favouring the androgynous approach (see Puértolas, 1993, 155):

> Lo perturbador es que de la mujer se espere, sobre todo, eso, el peculiar punto de vista femenino. ¿No resulta raro que pensemos que no puede ser tan amplio y diverso como el punto de vista masculino? Porque hombres hay de todas clases. Escritores, de todas clases. ¿Acaso las mujeres y dentro de esta categoría, las escritoras, están condenadas a ser extremadamente parecidas? (1993, 60–61)

Puértolas touches on an important issue, that of an alleged single female experience, both in writing and history, which feminist criticism is increasingly challenging. Julia Kristeva had already stressed in 'Women's Time' (first published in 1979) the plurality of female expressions and preoccupations. As Helen Graham writes: 'Gender cannot denote a single experience because it is always bisected by socio-economic class and other competing cultural and political identities' (Graham and Labanyi, 1995, 183).

Chris Weedon has also acknowledged such a risk in women's literature: 'The danger of formulating general laws about women's writing is that they render differences and contradictions invisible, differences which are at least as important as similarities and which tell us more about the precise discursive structuring of gender at any particular historical movement' (1987, 157). Weedon also insists that to study women's writing in isolation from male-authored books is beneficial for our understanding of patriarchy since '[t]he socially and historically produced concerns of women writers as depicted in fiction help to form a map of the possible subject positions open to women, what they could say or not from within the discursive field of femininity in which they are located' (1987, 157).

As Maggie Humm (1991, 2) points out, the way something is spoken about reveals how power relations operate. Socially – and historically – constructed gendered roles for men and women reveal themselves through language. Critics such as Gonzalo Navajas also advocate that women's literature needs to be treated separately because of gender-biased literary dissimilarities:

> Lo que justifica la autonomía del estudio de la literatura femenina es la especificidad de una estética dentro de la cual quedan interpeladas epistemológica y metodológicamente la literatura y la novela femeninas. Hay una distintividad del discurso femenino en general que afecta la naturaleza

del texto escrito por mujeres y que hace, además, que la textualidad femenina ocupe un emplazamiento especial dentro del paradigma de la literatura en general. (1996, 38)

However, it is not at all textual indications of women's, or men's, alleged essential natures that we should be searching for, but the exposure of the social construction of gender. Furthermore, it is not the author, nor a possible identification between the author and the text, nor the author and the characters, that should be addressed, but the text itself. And texts escape authorial control when they enter the reader's domain. Since Roland Barthes certified the 'death of the author' in his influential essay of the late sixties, and questioned once and for all unitary intentional subjectivity and the notion of an author pre-ordaining possible interpretations of the text, we understand that reading is a constantly deferred process of creating meaning, an open, historically placed dialogue between the reader and the text. Readers activate dormant intertextual presences, not always the result of the author's intention, identify different discourses, and explore possible interpretations from textual evidence. The post-structuralist approach, with its stress on the interactive role of the reader and on intertextuality, challenges and diffuses the notion of 'authority'. Texts should be read as proposals rather than as authorial statements, and the limits of interpretation are imposed only by the reader or by the text itself.

Rosa Montero's writing is exemplary in this. She refuses to call her own work 'feminist literature' (Davies, 1993, 383), possibly to avoid pigeon-holing it[21] and although her novels, short stories and journalistic work are too complex, ironic and multi-layered to be interpreted simply as feminist tracts, they show particular sensitivity to all kinds of discrimination, especially discrimination suffered by women. Therefore, we can read her from this perspective, as Catherine Davies does:

Fiction by women in Spain which articulates female experience is necessarily non-hegemonic. And if the writer supports the general objectives of the Women's Movement, that is, she critiques patriarchy and sexism, and questions ideological underpinnings of femininity, if she is engaged in the transformation of dominant power relations in society and considers the practice of writing a means of doing this, then she is perforce a feminist writer. (Davies, 1994, 5)

Whether we agree or not with Navajas when he says that '[es] la perspectiva genérico-sexual la que produce la especificidad estética, el elemento

---

21 An understandable reluctance since certain Spanish critics tend to be overzealous when it comes to labelling and packaging authors.

diferenciador [en] relación a formas convencionales vinculadas con una perspectiva humanista de raigambre masculina' (Navajas, 1996, 38), women writers enrich the plurality of alternative discourses because they carry with them a gender-branded History.

Postmodernism, with its decentering of hegemonic values, has allowed marginal voices to speak their differences. The activity of female writers is of crucial importance, not only 'when they perform the reflexive act of looking at themselves, an act of representation which legitimately collapses the distance between subject and object' (Pietropaolo and Testaferri, 1995, xi), but also because their increasing self-assurance and their access to certain mechanisms of cultural production are transforming the literary status quo, and this, in itself, is a development of historical relevance that needs to be acknowledged.

Cristina Peri Rossi, Uruguayan born but who has lived in Barcelona since 1972, thinks that the time has come 'para empezar a vender las transgresiones femeninas que, además, son transgresiones a normas que no han sido fijadas por ellas' (Peri Rossi, 1995, 5). Women's writing has the potential for transgression just by being there, by trying to share an equal space with the writings of a competitor whose only advantage is that he got there first.

The contemporary 'prose tale': a story of plurality and fragmentation

The number of collections of Spanish short stories[22] published in the last decade reflects the amount of attention which the genre has received. This

---

22   Some anthologies are notable for the comprehensive list of contemporary authors included:

Ángeles Encinar and Anthony Percival, eds, *Cuento español contemporáneo* (Madrid: Cátedra, 1993).

Joséluis González and Pedro de Miguel, eds, *Últimos narradores: Antología de la reciente narrativa breve española* (Pamplona: Hierbaola, 1993).

Juan Ramón Masoliver, ed., *The Origins of Desire: Modern Spanish Short Stories* (London: Serpent's Tail, 1993).

Fernando Valls, ed., *Son cuentos* (Madrid: Austral, 1993).

Among the anthologies of stories written by women, and after the pioneering example in 1982 of *Doce relatos de mujeres*, edited by Ymelda Navajo, Madrid: Alianza, the most significant are:

Ángeles Encinar, ed., *Cuentos de este siglo: 30 narradoras españolas* (Barcelona: Lumen, 1995).

Laura Freixas, ed., *Madres e hijas* (Barcelona: Anagrama, 1996).

interest is to be attributed not to a comeback as such of this narrative form, but rather to a new critical awareness of it and the challenging way in which a significant number of Spanish authors are employing it.

Nowadays, when genres cross boundaries, blurring the differences that have traditionally existed amongst them, it might seem inappropriate to identify generic peculiarities for the short story; yet, since the underlining of its importance in relation to the novel is still felt to be necessary to do it justice,[23] perhaps it is useful to deal with the issue again, however briefly.

A distinction has been established between the popular, usually fantastic tale, firmly rooted in the oral tradition – tales of anonymous origin included in medieval collections, or tales whose fame has outlived that of the writers who created or collected them (Perrault, Andersen, Hoffman, the Grimm Brothers) – and the modern short story that is clearly identified with an author. This distinction, though, between *cuento popular* and *cuento culto* may be seen as rather reductive. Fantasy, for example, once the domain of folk tales, has become a multifunctional strategy: 'esa inquietud que surge de lo cotidiano' (Fernández Cubas quoted in Moret, 1994, 32), especially after the beneficial influence of Latin-American writers such as Jorge Luis Borges and Julio Cortázar. It is the textual space where natural and supernatural meet in Cristina Fernández Cubas, José María Merino or Juan José Millás, or the instrument for parody in Laura Freixas, to mention only some of the writers keen to explore the fantastic in unusual ways. A practice potentially subversive since, as Mary Eagleton points out, '[t]o query the truth, coherence and resolution of realism is to undermine the symbolic order' (quoted in Hanson, 1989, 58), a statement which could be related to the connection established by Claire Hanson between the short story as the most appropriate genre to offer the other side of the 'official story', and fantasy as 'another mode of expression for repressed desire of knowledge' (Hanson, 1989, 6).

The literary history of the *cuento*, on the other hand, reflects the significance of the oral tradition and the close relationship between popular and authored short narrative. The first well-known collections of *cuentos* in fourteenth-century European literature kept the oral component as a narrative device to string the stories together, and provide evidence of how traditional tales, *fabliaux* (short narrative poems popular in France from the twelfth to the fourteenth century), fables and popular legends entered the world of the

---

23 See Fieta Jarque, 'Varios autores celebran en El Escorial el auge del cuento' in *El País*, 7 August 1996.

written world. In Boccaccio's *Decameron* ten Florentines, after taking refuge from the plague in a villa outside the city, relate one tale each for ten days; in Chaucer's *Canterbury Tales* pilgrims on the road to Canterbury tell stories to entertain each other, and in Don Juan Manuel's *El Conde Lucanor* (or *Libro de los enxiemplos del Conde Lucanor et de Patronio*), the young nobleman Lucanor seeks the advice of his steward Patronio, and is answered with enxiemplos (exemplary stories). These three major collections were all written in the fourteenth century and present influences from different earlier cultures such as the Greek, the Arabic or the Jewish. The catharsis experienced by the listeners to the tales – which the reader shares too – in all the earlier collections is also present in some contemporary works such as *El cinturón traído de Cuba*, by Pilar Cibreiro (1985). Soledad Puértolas finds a fascinating explanation for the origin of the *cuento* in its power to transform events rather than to chronicle them, and relates it to the oral tradition, to 'la necesidad fabuladora del hombre, acaso más fuerte que su necesidad de ser testigo de la realidad' (1991, 72). In a debate on 'De cuentos y cuentistas', five well-known short-story writers (Ignacio Martínez de Pisón, Pedro Zarraluqui, Juan Miñana, Cristina Fernández Cubas and Enrique Vila-Matas) agreed on the importance of orality in storytelling: 'Lo primero que yo recuerdo no es un libro, sino la narración de historias' (Fernández Cubas quoted in Valls, 1994, 5). As Walter Benjamin put it in 'The Storyteller': 'Experience which is passed on from mouth to mouth is the source from which all storytellers have drawn' (1992, 94).

After those first medieval examples many Spanish authors – Cervantes and María de Zayas among them – turned to short narrative in the centuries which followed. It was in the nineteenth century, however, and thanks to the key role played by the press (with regular sections in newspapers and magazines) that the genre blossomed. Gustavo Adolfo Bécquer, Emilia Pardo Bazán, Cecilia Böhl de Faber 'Fernán Caballero', Leopoldo Alas 'Clarín', Rosalía de Castro, Juan Valera, Armando Palacio Valdés and Pedro Antonio de Alarcón are amongst those writers whose short stories went a long way to gain literary respect for the *cuento literario*.[24]

---

24   Literary criticism on the nineteenth-century Spanish short story is abundant, but I would especially recommend the following titles: Mariano Baquero Goyanes, *El cuento español en el siglo XIX,* from 1949, and it is available from Biblioteca Virtual Cervantes: www.cervantes. virtual). [There is a 1992 revised edition by Ana Baquero Escudero: *El cuento español: Del Romanticismo al Realismo* (Madrid: Consejo Superior de Investigaciones Científicas.]; Lou Charnon-Deutsch, *The Nineteenth-Century Spanish Short Story. Textual Strategies of a Genre in Transition* (London:Tamesis, 1985).

At the turn of the century and until the 1930s, the short story – together with the novella – was very much in fashion. The first book ever published by Pío Baroja, *Vidas sombrías* (1900), was a collection of *cuentos*, and Valle-Inclán won several prizes, not always without controversy, in the many *certámenes de cuentos* organised in those days. Some of them were sponsored by periodicals such as *El Cuento Semanal* (1907–1912), which awarded the prize to Gabriel Miró in 1907. The role of this successful publication in popularizing the genre and in providing a model for others of a similar kind – *Los Contemporáneos* (1909–1926), *La Novela Corta* (1916), *La Novela Semanal* (1921–1925), *La Novela Mundial* (1926–1928), to name just a few – has been widely recognized.

At the same time, and along with older writers, some avant-garde figures such as Ramón Gómez de la Serna, Benjamín Jarnés or Samuel Ros were also devoted to the short story as were many women writers of different political persuasions who showed, possibly for the first time in Spanish literary history, a new professional, rather than just personal, approach to writing.[25]

But it was in the 1950s, when testimonial writing was the dominant trend and after a period of virtual stagnation, that the genre made a spectacular comeback. Realist novelists seemed to realise the potential of short narrative prose as a suitable form to 'portray' a *tranche de vie*, and some writers, such as Ignacio Aldecoa, Medardo Fraile or Daniel Suerio made their names through their quasi-exclusive dedication to the *cuento*. Other significant novelists who started writing stories in those years are Juan Benet, Rafael Sánchez Ferlosio, Alfonso Grosso, Juan García Hortelano, Juan Marsé, Jesús López Pacheco, Jesús Fernández Santos,[26] not forgetting an important group of women writers to whom I will refer later, and those living in exile since 1939 such as Max Aub, Francisco Ayala, Arturo Barea, Rosa Chacel, María Teresa León, Ramón J. Sender, and the Catalans Mercè Rodoreda and Pere Calders, whose works produced abroad were not to be fully distributed in Spain until the arrival of democracy.

It could be argued that from the 1950s onwards the short story has

---

25 For further reading on the Spanish short story in the decades prior to the Civil War, see: Ángela Ena Bordonada, ed., *Novelas breves de escritoras españolas 1900–1936* (Madrid: Castalia, 1989); Lily Litvak, *El cuento anarquista* (Madrid: Taurus, 1982); José María Martínez Cachero, ed., *Antología del cuento español 1900–1939* (Madrid: Castalia, 1982).
26 See the following anthologies for good collections of mid-twentieth century short stories: Medardo Fraile, ed. *Cuento español de posguerra* (Madrid: Cátedra, 1992).; Alicia Redondo Goicoechea, ed., *Relatos de novelistas españolas (1939–1969)* (Madrid: Castalia, 1993).

not experienced any serious relapse, although it has proved difficult for the genre to achieve the same critical recognition as the novel. However, since the early 1980s the appeal of the short story for many authors of the so-called *nueva narrativa* has led to its renovation and made critics and public more aware of it, and their favourable reception should be taken into account when considering the present popularity of the *cuento* in Spain.[27] Nevertheless, it is still commonplace to complain about the short story being the Cinderella of narrative prose, and to bemoan the dearth of scholarly work it has inspired – although some exceptions are readily acknowledged, such as Baquero Goyanes's seminal study *El cuento español en el siglo XIX* (first published in 1949), Anderson Imbert's *Teoría y técnica del cuento español contemporáneo* (1970), Erna Branderberger's *Estudios sobre el cuento español contemporáneo* (1973), Catharina V. de Vallejo's *Teoría cuentística del siglo XX (Aproximaciones hispánicas)* (1989), or Ana Rueda's *Relatos desde el vacío* (1992).[28] Such observations are somewhat surprising since there are now clear signs of critical attention: journals publish monographic issues on the *cuento* (*Ínsula*, for instance in 1988 and 1994, and *Las Nuevas Letras*, *República de las Letras* and *Monographic Review* also in 1988);[29]

---

27   Unusual for collections of short stories, the ones published in 1996 by Javier Marías, *Cuando fui mortal*, Madrid: Alfaguara, and by Almudena Grandes, *Modelos de mujer*, Barcelona: Tusquets, as well as the one mentioned above edited by Laura Freixas, *Madres e hijas*, have been in the best-seller lists for weeks.

28   The following titles may provide useful further reading for those interested in the *genre*:

Rosa M. Grillo de Filippo, *Racconto espagnolo. Appunti per una teoría del racconto e le sue forme* (Salerno: Palladio Editrice, 1985).

Clare Hanson, ed., *Re-reading the Short Story* (Basingstoke: Macmillan, 1989).

Peter Fröhlicher and Georges Günter, eds, *Teoría e interpretación del cuento* (New York: Peter Lang, 1995).

Susan Lohafer, *Coming to Terms with the Shor Story* (Baton Rouge and London: Louisiana State University Press, 1989).

Susan Lohafer and Ellyn Clarey, eds, *Short Story at a Crossroads* (Baton Rouge and London: Louisiana State University Press, 1989).

Charles E. May, ed., *Short Story Theories* (Athens, Ohio: Ohio University Press, 1976).

Charles E. May, *The New Shot Story Theories* (Athens, Ohio: Ohio University Press, 1994).

Vladimir Propp, *Morphology of the Folktale*, trans. L. Scott (Bloomington, Ind.: Research Center, Indiana University, 1958).

Ian Reid, *The Short Story* (London and New York: Methuen, 1977).

Valerie Shaw, *The Short Story: A Critical Introduction* (London and New York: Routledge, 1992).

29   *Ínsula*, issues 495 and 568; *Las Nuevas Letras*, 8; *República de las Letras*, 22. *Monographic Review*, vol. IV.

Lucanor, Revista del Cuento literario, a journal devoted entirely to the short story, was launched in 1988 and is now well established; publishers (Aguaclara, Alfaguara, Anagrama, Cátedra, Hierbaola, Libertarias, Lumen, Sirmio/Quaderns Crema, Tusquets and so on) are increasingly less reluctant to endorse collections of short stories, especially by successful writers, who pave the way for others; newspapers and magazines also publish short stories thereby continuing a nineteenth-century practice which helped popularize the genre; and, most importantly, writers are turning to it with conviction.[30] Santos Alonso has noted that a writer's dedication to the *cuento* is not an obstacle to achieving literary recognition (Alonso 1991, 44), as proved amongst others by Mercedes Abad, Agustín Cerezales, Pilar Cibreiro, Cristina Fernández Cubas, Ignacio Martínez de Pisón, Antonio Pereira, María Eugenia Salaverri, Juan Eduardo Zúñiga or the Catalans Quim Monzó and Sergi Pàmies. Occasionally writers talk and write about the genre as if they felt the need to persuade the reader of its value and to legitimize it once and for all. They do so by engaging in a combination of creative writing and aesthetic reflection pioneered by Edgar Allan Poe and used by other *cuentistas* in the Hispanic tradition, such as Emilia Pardo Bazán, 'Clarín', Julio Cortázar or Horacio Quiroga, a tradition which finds in Carmen Martín *Gaite's El cuento de nunca acabar* (1983) one of its finest contemporary examples.

In 1842, when reviewing Nathaniel Hawthorne's *Twice-Told Tales*, Poe listed some of the features he thought essential for the 'prose tale'. It required 'to be read at one sitting, [...] from a half-hour to one or two hours in its perusal, [because] of the immense force derivable from *totality*' (Poe, 1965, 107, his italics). With no interruptions in the act of reading, he thought, 'the author is enabled to carry out the fullness of his intention [and] the soul of the reader is at the writer's control' (198). Even if nowadays we are rather sceptical about the validity of such statements, brevity – intrinsically related to the possibility of reading without interruptions – is the chief characteristic of this form of narrative. Brevity also suggests that the tautness of the language brings the short story closer to the poem, its selection of words being more demanding than in the novel. Poe's comments on Hawthorne's stories could be applied to the genre in general: 'Every word *tells*, and there is not a word which does not tell' (112, his italics).

---

30 Fernando Valls and Nuria Carrillo (1991) carried out a survey on the number of collections of short stories published in Spanish in Spain between 1975 and 1990, and came up with figures which clearly indicate a progression: 12 in 1975, 33 in 1989, and 32 in 1990.

This idiosyncratic trait of the short story is still the one that best defines it according to contemporary writers such as José María Merino, who believes the *cuento* to be 'narración pura, en que lo sintético predomina sobre lo analítico, que tiende a la máxima expresividad en el menor espacio dramático possible' (Merino, 1988, 21), or Antonio Muñoz Molina, who compares the short story to the sonnet, because of 'la concentración absoluta y casi químicamente pura de sus normas, sus tareas y sus artificios' (Muñoz Molina, 1991, 152). The philosopher and writer Fernando Savater also claims that the *cuento* is '*domus aurea* de la creación verbal, menos sujeto a la retórica que la poesía, más concentradamente intenso que la novela, sin los requisitos espectaculares del drama teatral, capaz de una complejidad de contenido que no alcanza ni el chiste ni el aforismo' (1984, 6).

'Short', though, could also imply different things to today's reader. It could imply 'fragmented', that is, the awareness of the impossibility of an undisputed, totalizing discourse. In 1906 Chesterton had already pointed out similarities between the brevity of the form and the modern experience of being alive:

> Our modern attraction to the short story is not an accident of form; it is a sign of a real sense of fleetingness and fragility; it means that existence is only an impression, and, perhaps, only an illusion. We have no instinct of anything ultimate and enduring beyond the episode. (Chesterton quoted in Shaw, 1992, 17)

Contemporary writers and critics have broadened this early perception of the short story and see it as the ideal literary form to translate the broken and multifaceted nature of experience: 'Su fragmentariedad casa bien con la sensibilidad contemporánea, formada en la percepción de elementos aislados' (Jose Antonio Millán quoted in Alonso, 1991, 44).

Jose Luis Martín Nogales, editor of *Lucanor*, focuses his analysis of the contemporary short story entirely on what he calls the 'teoría de la fragmentariedad'. As opposed to the multifaceted linguistic nature of the novel and the complexity of its diachronic progress, the short story offers just a glimpse, an enlightening but self-consciously limited perspective: 'Si la novela es la reconstrucción de una globalidad, el cuento supone la captación de algo fragmentario' (Martín Nogales 1996, 34). In the twilight of ideologies 'el cuento se ha mostrado como el cauce literario adecuado para recoger los fragmentos dispersos de un mundo escindido' (34). Asked about the appropriateness of the genre to translate thematically and structurally

today's world, the five writers mentioned above who commented on *cuentos* and *cuentistas* were of the same opinion. 'El cuento responde a esa versión fragmentaria de la realidad', said Martínez de Pisón, and Zarraluqui added: 'El ser fragmentario no le impide ser también muy global. [...] es un territorio realmente poderoso y lleno de misterio. Quizá por ello tiene esa extraña y leve relación con la poesía' (Valls, 1994, 4).

As mentioned previously, storytelling has been, along with plurality, one of the most distinctive features of the *nueva narrativa española* since the mid 1970s. One of the literary critics of *El País* stated, perhaps too categorically, that 'Los experimentalismos se baten en retirada, la metaficción ha dejado de tener el papel que tenía y, aun cuando el espectro temático sea variado, la narratividad impone sus líneas con firmeza' (García-Posada, 1995, 32).[31]

Amongst narrative genres, the short story is precisely the most ambitious in terms of its technical and thematic diversity as, given its high degree of self-consciousness, it easily accommodates all types of formal experimentalism whilst sharing with the novel the ability to generate the enjoyment associated with the telling and reading of stories.

In 1990 Agustín Cerezales, one of the most innovative of short-story writers, describe the situation thus:

> En España se escribe con más libertad que nunca [...]. No me refiero sólo a la libertad ideológica, sino a la estética. [...] No hay escuela que valga. El resultado es variedad, profusión, riesgo, respuesta acorde a la urgencia de la demanda. [...] Estamos inmersos en una espléndida aventura. (Cerezales quoted in Alonso, 1991, 45)

This adventure is made even more exciting by the influence of Latin-American writers, with their undisputed talent for storytelling. If novelists, with remarkable exceptions such as Eduardo Mendoza,[32] have been reluctant to accept that there has been a beneficial dialogue between Spanish and Latin-American narratives, most short-story writers (and novelists who are also short-story writers) pay constant tribute to Jorge Luis Borges, Alejo Carpentier, Adolfo Bioy Casares, Julio Cortázar, Carlos Fuentes, Mario Vargas Llosa, Gabriel García Márquez, Juan Carlos Onetti, Juan Rulfo and

---

31 Although the tendency highlighted by García-Posada seems to be the dominant one, it would be wrong to conclude that the explicitly metafictional novel has gone out of fashion: the influential Nadal Prize for 1997 has been awarded to Carlos Cañeque for the novel *Quién*, which has been described as 'un juego metaliterario a la sombra de Borges [que] reflexiona sobre la literatura y la autoría de libros' (Moret, 1997, 30).

32 See Miguel Riera, 'El caso Mendoza. Entrevista', *Quimera* 66–67 (n.d.), 42–47.

other authors of the so-called 'boom' whose works have been published in Spain with enormous success since the 1960s, thanks to publishers such as Alianza, Salvat or Seix Barral. Fernando Valls acknowledges that '[p]arece que nos reconciliamos con el género gracias a los hispanoamericanos [...]. Ellos nos mostraron un modelo mucho más rico y brillante [...], que el cuento podía ser un género apropiado para hablar del mundo contemporáneo' (Valls, 1994, 4).

The diversity afforded by the *cuento* and its current 'expansión plural' (Carrillo 1994, 9) have been made possible by the porous quality of the genre, its readiness to absorb new techniques and structural innovations. From stories which follow Poe's preference for 'tales of effect' to those which incorporate elliptic cinematic strategies, with surprising or unremarkable endings, either conforming to or transgressing traditional models, contemporary short stories display a wide range of executions.

Collecting this anthology

The stories gathered for this anthology follow a rich and diverse tradition of female-authored short story-writing which goes back to the seventeenth century and to the short novels by María de Zayas, and almost two centuries later, to Rosario de Acuña, Emilia Pardo Bazán (the most prolific of nineteenth-century writers, with more than five hundred stories attributed to her credit), the Galician Rosalía de Castro, Cecilia Böhl de Faber 'Fernán Caballero' or María del Pilar Sinués. Stressing the suitability of the genre as the channel for an alternative discourse, Clare Hanson suggests that 'the short story has been from its inception a particular appropriate vehicle for the expression of the ex-centric, alienated vision of women' (Hanson, 1989, 3).[33] This notion can be confirmed by looking into the work of women writers of the first decades of the twentieth century who turned to the short story. Amongst them we find Caterina Albert, who used the penname 'Víctor Català', the name of one of his early male characters, and wrote in Catalan; Carmen de Burgos (whose favourite nom de plume was significantly a female one: 'Colombine'), Eva Carmen Nelken (hers was 'Magda Donato'), Concha Espina, Sofía Casanova, Blanca de los Ríos, Margarita Nelken, Pilar Millán Astray, Federica Montseny, María Teresa León, as well as Rosa Chacel's

---

33   See Mary Eagleton's discussion of 'Gender and Genre', in *Modern Genre Theory*, ed. David Duff (Harlow: Longman, 2000), 250–62. [The text was first published in Clare Hanson's *Re-reading the Short Story*, in 1989.]

cuentos in *Revista de Occidente*, and those of María de la O Lejárraga (who signed most of her works with her husband's name, 'Gregorio Martínez de la Sierra') for the popular periodical *El Cuento Semanal*.

After the Spanish Civil War, writers such as Carmen Martín Gaite or Ana María Matute, who at the beginning of their careers were associated with *realismo social*, successfully cultivated the genre, as did many others such as Josefina (Rodríguez) Aldecoa, Concha Alós, Eulalia Galvarriato, Carmen Kurtz, Carmen Laforet, Dolores Medio, Elizabeth Mulder, Marta Portal, Elena Quiroga and Elena Soriano, not to forget Mercè Rodoreda writing in Catalan from exile in France first, and later in Switzerland. Over the last twenty years the short story has appealed to almost every woman writer, and female author and generic form have become allied in the struggle to achieve unreserved literary acclaim.

Diversity and eclecticism are indeed the main features of Spanish women's short-story writing and they should be enough to counter any essentialist or prescriptive views on it. However, it is worth noting that a greater number of female central characters, female narratorial voices and female internal focalizations are found in woman-authored texts, a fact which has a clear impact on the way many issues are dealt with. Although by no means a female prerogative, further common ground is to be observed in the preference of some authors to write short stories for children, an activity in which Gloria Fuertes, Carmen Martín Gaite, Ana María Matute, Rosa Montero, Lourdes Ortiz and Soledad Puértolas have excelled.

Contemporary women writers have made the most of the *cuento*'s generic technical flexibility, as evidenced by those selected for this collection. They display a wide range of narrative strategies which include: first person narrators (Abad, Fernández Cubas, Díaz-Mas, García Morales, Puértolas, Salaverri); narratorial voices with internal focalization but not using a first person (Freixas, Ortiz, Torres); stream of consciousness techniques, underlining the absence of any intervening narratorial voice (Mayoral); ironically detached narrators (Abad, Montero, Freixas); stories with linear structures (Díaz-Mas, García Morales, Montero) or circular structures (Torres); stories with unexpected endings (Abad, Díaz-Mas), closed endings (Fernández Cubas) or open endings (Cibreiro, Freixas, Puértolas, García Morales, Mayoral, Montero, Ortiz, Salaverri, Torres); metafictional narratives which defamiliarize cultural conventions (Ortiz) or use parody to subvert generic ones (Freixas); evocative stories with no plot (Cibreiro) or with a clear dramatic unit (Fernández Cubas); stories where anecdote is central to

the diegetic progress towards 'effect' (Abad, Fernández Cubas, Díaz-Mas) or those whose anecdote is at the service of a character's paradigmatic situation (Freixas, García Morales, Mayoral, Montero, Ortiz, Puértolas); stories in which the order of the events narrated enhances the suspense of a magical atmosphere (Fernández Cubas) and those in which the immediacy of linearity is used for testimonial purposes (Montero), or in combination with the Romantic theme of the double (García Morales).

Plurality is equally obvious when literary tradition and familiar themes and motifs are intertextually explored in order to convey new concerns: realist and testimonial tales coexist with fantastic ones, meditations on the nature of fiction and textuality cohabit with psychological introspections or decentred discourses on women and tradition.

This anthology offers representative examples of the thematic diversity of the contemporary *cuento*. It includes stories which use fantasy as an instrument to gain access to a child's perspective and to the enigmatic side of experience (Fernández Cubas), and those in which fantasy becomes a feminist strategy (Freixas); testimonial stories exploring the margins of a ruthless society where no compassion is shown towards poverty and homelessness (García Morales) or old age (Montero); self-referential narratives in which intertextual presences are both highlighted and questioned in order to make new polemical or subversive statements, either by revising literary myths from a feminist perspective (Ortiz), by humorously incorporating literary references as part of a character's memory (Freixas), or by using artistic ones – a painting – to draw attention to the impossible quest for any lasting fulfilment, and to the importance of the way something – or somebody – is looked at in a story which could be read as metaphor for the reader's interactive role (Díaz-Mas).

There are stories with middle-aged, alienated female characters who, after a lifetime of serving everyone except themselves and having outgrown their role as wife and mother, overcome the demonizing labels of 'frustrated housewife' and 'social outcast' in different ways: by angrily refusing sexual conformity and passive domesticity (Ortiz); by leaving home – the space of inner exile – and seeking a new centre, a new life away from an oppressive existence which has gradually become empty (Torres), or by voicing their unhappiness almost tenderly, by writing her 'body' (Mayoral), although, ultimately, the private rebellions of these three female characters are hindered by the same cultural structures that they refuse to conform to.

There are stories about couples, all of them told by a female narrator who

is an ironic, but not altogether detached observer (Abad), an observer who is much more involved that at first appears (Puértolas), or the wife who endures the contradictions and infidelities of the husband (Salaverri); uncompromising yet unromanticised love stories where women find themselves swept away by prevailing male fantasies (Abad), powerless because traditional rules of sexual behaviour give men the privilege of initiative (Puértolas), or trapped in a routine that nevertheless leads to epiphany moments of self-discovery (Salaverri); stories of lost and unrequited love, sometimes collectively fantasized (Cibreiro), or with irretrievable moments of fulfilment experienced by a male narrator (Díaz-Mas); stories where issues of troubled identities and the search for the self are paramount, either embodying the equation of memory and identity in one individual character (Freixas), in a collective one (Cibreiro), with characters who struggle to identify an imaginary self beyond experiences inflicted upon them (Salaverri), or with characters trying to resist imposed values (García Morales, Mayoral, Ortiz, Torres).

Finally, the emphasis on multiple and dynamic perspectivism confirms the postmodern conviction that events and characters are constructed through language, in plural and unfixed discourses.

Juan José Millás once said that every tale leads to another through a secret door (quoted by Fernández Cubas in Moret, 1994, 32). This is especially evident in an anthology, where stories gathered together establish unprecedented links with one another: similarities are underlined, alternative strategies confront each other, a multi-layered perspective on comparable issues emerges, differences are celebrated and ultimately the reader has the power to explore any possible passage from one text to another, interconnecting threads, themes and preoccupations.

The twelve authors included in this anthology, all of them associated with the post-*Transición* years, provide a sample of young, or relatively young, contemporary Spanish women writers. Nevertheless, the collection is inevitably selective. Excellent writers had to be excluded – not only the great names already known before 1980, but also interesting new ones such as Luisa Castro, Belén Gopegui, Almudena Grandes, Ana María Novales, Beatriz Pottecher, Clara Sánchez or Mercedes Soriano, to name but a few. It is difficult to find a reason other than limited space.

Attempts to apply objective criteria were made when preparing the book: a) diversity of the authors (with different professional backgrounds: journalism, teaching, and so on; writers from different parts of Spain, some also publishing in Catalan or Galician; writers with an already established

reputation selected alongside others with only one promising book); b) formal and thematic variety of the stories; c) period in which the stories were first published (the 1980s and early 1990s); d) language in which the stories were originally written (in spite of the variety of regions represented by the authors, all the stories selected were first written in Spanish: this a bilingual collection and it seemed fitting to reproduce the original in *lenguaje creado*, rather than in a Spanish translation).

In addition to these objective criteria, personal preference and enjoyment also played a key role in the selection process, an enjoyment it is hoped will be shared with the readers of this book.

Comprehensive introductory notes and selected bibliographies are provided for every author. However, the number of items in these vary considerably according to the author's age, the number of books published and the amount of academic attention she has attracted. A few titles dealing with more than one author are included in every relevant 'further reading' list to make it easy for further research.

The stories are presented in chronological order. There is only one exception: 'Días de lluvia', by Pilar Cibreiro. This story, which gives the collection its title, is the one that is situated at the beginning because it so fittingly evokes both the power of literature to create worlds with words and the oral tradition of storytelling, a tradition in which women have been so instrumental.

References

Miquel Alberola, 'El masclisme és interclassista' [Interview with Marina Subirats], *El Temps*, 27 June 1994, 38–41.

Santos Alonso, 'Poética del cuento: Los escritores actuales meditan sobre el género', *Lucanor* 6 (1991), 43–54.

Enrique Anderson Imbert, *Teoría y técnica del cuento* (Buenos Aires: Ariel, 1970).

Roland Barthes, 'The Death of the Author', in *Image–Music–Text*, trans. S. Heath (London: Fontana, 1977), 142–48.

Walter Benjamin, 'The Storyteller', in *Illuminations*, trans. by H. Zohn (London: Fontana, 1992), 83–117.

Erna Brandenberger, *Estudios sobre el cuento español contemporáneo* (Madrid: Nacional, 1973).

Joan L. Brown, 'Women Writers in Spanish Literary History: Past, Present and Future', *Revista Canadiense de Estudios Hispánicos* 14.3 (1990), 553–60.

Joan L. Brown (ed.), *Women Writers of Contemporary Spain: Exiles in the Homeland*

(Newark: University of Delaware Press; Cranberry, NY: Associated University Presses, 1991).

Soledad Cano, '"El giro a la derecha supone un retroceso": Adelaida García Morales', *Cambio 16*, 25 March 1996, 100–101.

José María Calvo, 'El número de mujeres parlamentarias en el mundo es menor que hace siete años', *El País*, 28 August 1995, 18.

Vicente Carmona, Jeffrey Lamb, Sherry Velasco and Barbara Zecchi, 'Conversando con Mercedes Abad, Cristina Fernández Cubas y Soledad Puértolas: Feminismo y literatura no tienen nada que ver', *Mester* 20.2 (1991), 157–65.

Nuria Carrillo, 'La expansión plural de un género: el cuento 1975–1993', *Ínsula* 568 (1994), 9–11.

Javier Casqueiro, 'Escaparate de mujeres', *El País*, 26 May 1996, 22.

Lou Charnon-Deutsch, *Narratives of Desire: Nineteenth-Century Spanish Fiction by Women* (Pennsylvania: Penn State University Press, 1994).

Antonio Chicharro Chamorro, 'Del periodismo a la novela', *Ínsula* 589–90 (1996), 14–17.

Catherine Davies, 'Entrevista a Rosa Montero (Madrid, 22 de enero de 1993)', *Journal of Hispanic Research* 1.3 (1993), 383–88.

Catherine Davies, *Contemporary Feminist Fiction in Spain: The Work of Montserrat Roig and Rosa Montero,* (Oxford and Providence, USA: Berg, 1994).

María Luisa Diéguez, 'Entrevista con Paloma Díaz-Mas', *Revista de Estudios Hispánicos* 22.1 (1988), 77–91.

Ángela Ena Bordonada, *Novelas breves de escritoras españolas (1900–1936)* (Madrid: Castalia, 1989).

Feliciano Fidalgo, 'Laura Freixas, Soledad, Almudena, Clara… escritoras', *El País* 25 February 1996, 60.

Laura Freixas, 'Prólogo', in *Madres e hijas* (Barcelona: Anagrama, 1996), 11–20.

Miguel García-Posada, 'Nuevos paradigmas'. *El País*, 6 January 1995, 32.

Enrique Gil Calvo, *La era de las lectoras: El cambio cultural de las españolas* (Madrid: Ministerio de Asuntos Sociales, Instituto de la Mujer, 1992a).

Enrique Gil Calvo, 'A cargo del hogar', *El País*, 24 December 1992b, 8.

Sandra M. Gilbert and Susan Gubar, *The Madwoman in the Attic: The Woman Writer and the Nineteenth-Century Literary Imagination* (New Haven: Yale University Press, 1979).

Linda Gould Levine, Ellen Eagleton Marson and Gloria Feiman Waldman (eds), *Women Spanish Writers: A Bio-Bibliographical Source Book* (Westport, CT: Greenwood Press, 1993).

Jordi Gracia, 'Novela y cultura en el fin de siglo', *Ínsula* 589–90 (1996), 27–30.

Helen Graham and Jo Labanyi (eds), *Spanish Cultural Studies: An Introduction. The Struggle for Modernity* (Oxford and New York: Oxford University Press, 1995).

Clare Hanson (ed.), *Re-reading the Short Story* (Basingstoke: Macmillan, 1989).

David K. Herzberger, 'History, Apocalypse, and the Triumph of Fiction in the Post-War Spanish Novel', *Revista Hispánica Moderna* 44 (1991), 247–58.

Maggie Humm, *Border Traffic: Strategies of Contemporary Women Writers,* (Manchester: Manchester University Press, 1991).

Ínsula 1993. Monographic issue no. 557 dedicated to *Mujeres del 27.*

Susan Kirkpatrick (ed.), *Antología poética de escritoras del siglo XX* (Madrid: Castalia, 1992).

Julia Kristeva, 'Women's Time', in *The Kristeva Reader*, edited by Toril Moi (Oxford: Basil Blackwell, 1987), 187–213.

José Carlos Mainer, *De postguerra (1951–1990)* (Barcelona: Crítica, 1994).

Carmen Martín Gaite, *El cuento de nunca acabar (Apuntes sobre la narración, el amor y la mentira)* (Barcelona: Anagrama, 1983).

José Luis Martín Nogales, 'De la novela al cuento: el reflejo de una quiebra', *Ínsula* 589–90 (1996), 33–35.

José María Merino, 'El cuento: narración pura', *Ínsula* 495 (1988), 21.

Suzanne Moore, 'If I whirled the rules…' *The Guardian,* 19 July 1996, 6.

Xavier Moret, 'Cristina Fernández Cubas relata "la inquietud que surge de lo cotidiano"', *El País,* 14 May 1994, 22.

Xavier Moret, 'Carlos Cañeque gana el Premio Nadal con un juego metaliterario a la sombra de Borges', *El País,* 7 January 1997, p. 30.

Antonio Muñoz Molina, 'Contar cuentos', *Lucanor* 6 (1991), 152.

'Narradores de hoy' [unassigned], *El Urogallo* 2 (1986), 18–25.

Gonzalo Navajas, 'Narrativa y género. La ficción actual desde la mujer', *Ínsula* 589–90 (1996), 37–39.

Ana Navarro, 'La mujer y el nuevo paradigma', *El País,* 12 August 1993, 14.

Elizabeth Ordóñez, *Voices of Their Own: Contemporary Spanish Narrative by Women* (Lewisburg: Bucknell University Press, 1991).

Rosa Pereda, 'El pensamiento posfeminista', *El País* (Babelia), 23 October 1993, 6.

Janet Pérez, *Contemporary Women Writers of Spain* (Boston, MA: Twayne Publishers, 1988).

Janet Pérez, *Modern and Contemporary Spanish Women Poets* (New York: Twayne Publishers/ Prentice Hall, 1996).

Cristina Peri Rossi, 'Escribir como transgresión', *Lectora, Revista de Dones i Textualitat* 1 (1995), 3–5.

Laura Pietropaolo and Ada Testaferri, eds, *Feminisms in the Cinema* (Bloomington: Indiana University Press, 1995).

Edgar Allan Poe, *The Complete Works of Edgar Allan Poe*, edited by J. A. Harrison, Vol. IX (New York: AMS Press, 1965).

Phoebe Porter, 'Conversación con Lourdes Ortiz', *Letras Femeninas* 15.1/2 (1990), 139–44.

Soledad Puértolas, 'La gracia de la vida, la inmortalidad', *Lucanor* 6 (1991), 172.

Soledad Puértolas, *La vida oculta* (Barcelona: Anagrama, 1993).

María Rosa Riddel, *La escritura femenina en la postguerra española* (New York: Peter Lang, 1995).

Ana Rueda, *Relatos desde el vacío: Un nuevo espacio crítico para el cuento español* (Madrid: Orígenes, 1992).

Fernando Savater, 'Cuentos', *El País,* 13 August 1984, 6.

Montserrat Serra, 'Llegir, verb de dona', *El Temps,* 20 November 1995, 74–77.

Valerie Shaw, *The Short Story: A Critical Introduction* (London and New York: Routledge, 1992).

Elaine Showalter, *A Literature of Their Own: From Charlotte Brontë to Doris Lessing* (London: Virago, 1991 [1977]).

Ignacio Soldevila-Durante, 'Sobre la escritura femenina y su reivindicación en el conjunto de la literatura contemporánea en España. (A propósito de un reciente libro de Janet Pérez)', *Revista Canadiense de Estudios Hispánicos* 14.3 (1990), 606–22.

Monica Threlfall, 'The Women's Movement in Spain', *New Left Review* 151 (1985), 44–73.

Maruja Torres, 'Luchas de mujer', *El País Semanal,* 9 June 1996, 10.

Catharina V. de Vallejo, *Teoría cuentística del siglo XX (Aproximaciones hispánicas)* (Miami: Eds. Universal, 1989).

Fernando Valls and Nuria Carrillo, 'El cuento español actual. Cronología', *Lucanor* 6 (1991), 83–92.

Fernando Valls, 'De últimos cuentos y cuentistas', *Ínsula* 568 (1994), 3–6.

Darío Villanueva (ed.), *Los nuevos nombres: 1975–1990, vol IX) Historia y Crítica de la Literatura Española*, edited by F. Rico (Barcelona: Crítica, 1992).

Chris Weedon, *Feminist Practice and Poststructuralist Theory* (Oxford: Blackwell, 1987).

DÍAS DE LLUVIA

RAINY DAYS

Original Spanish text from
El cinturón traído de Cuba (Madrid: Alfaguara, 1985, 56–59)
© Pilar Cibreiro, 1985

PILAR CIBREIRO was born in 1952 in the Galician town of Vilaboa. She has lived in El Ferrol (Galicia), London and Madrid, and has now settled back in Galicia. She writes both in Galician and in Spanish, but her poetry is in Galician. She has published two books of poems: *O vasalo da armadura da prata* [*El vasallo de la armadura de plata*] in 1987, and *Feitura do lume* [*Hechura del fuego*] in 1994. Some of her early poems were included by Ramón Buenaventura in *Las diosas blancas: Antología de la joven poesía española escrita por mujeres*, published in 1985 and later translated into French. Her first book, *El cinturón traído de Cuba* (1985), is a very successful collection of short stories that can also be read as an episodic novel. It is the voice of collective memory, the memory of a pre-modern Galicia, with characters that live in a small village: from the emigrant who comes back from Cuba with no money, having lost his mind to an unrequited love, to people who disappear or commit suicide for enigmatic reasons. These stories are passed down from one generation to the next and remind us of the oral tradition of storytelling, the verbal strategy of keeping memories alive whilst they are slowly woven into the fabric of fiction. This is the reason why this anthology borrows the title from one of the stories in *El cinturón*: 'Rainy Days/Días de lluvia'. For years, *El cinturón traído de Cuba* has been a set text in Galician schools. The book in its entirety has been translated into French and Italian, and some of its stories into German and English. They also figure prominently in anthologies of Spanish *cuentos*. In 1990, Pilar Cibreiro published the novel *Arte de acecho*, a *Bildungsroman* set in 1970s London in which a female narrator embarks on a journey of self-discovery. In 2005, she published another collection of narrative proses, *El dueño del trigo*, which includes two novellas and two short stories, receiving excellent reviews.

Bibliography of Pilar Cibreiro
Novel
Arte de acecho (Madrid: Alfaguara: 1990).

Short story and novella collections
El cinturón traído de Cuba (Madrid: Alfaguara, 1985).
El dueño del trigo (Madrid: Caballo de Troya/Random House-Mondadori, 2005).

Poetry
O vasalo da armadura da prata (Barcelona: Sotelo Blanco Edicións, 1987; 2001).
Feitura do lume (Barcelona: Sotelo Blanco Edicións, 1995; 2001).
'O miña lengua' http://www.blogoteca.com/madeingaliza/index.php?cod=42247

Short stories published in anthologies and journals (a selection)
'Pilar de Campos', *Ínsula* 469 (1986).
'Un emigrante más'; 'Santalla el escapado'; 'Los novios', in B. Fernández Casasnovas and M. Iglesias Vicente (eds), *Relatos de mujeres. 2* (Madrid: Popular, 1988; 2011).
'Días de lluvia', in Á. Encinar (ed.), *Cuentos de este siglo: 30 narradoras españolas contemporáneas* (Barcelona: Lumen, 1995).

Further reading on Pilar Cibreiro
Irene Andres-Suárez 'La inmigración en la cuentística española contemporánea', in I. Andres-Suárez, M. Kunz and I. d'Ors, *La inmigración en la literatura española contemporánea* (Madrid: Verbum, 2002), 301–40.
Leopoldo Azancot, 'El cinturón traído de Cuba', *ABC*, 22 June 1985.
Nuria Carrillo, 'La expansión plural de un género: el cuento 1975–1993', *Ínsula* 568, (1994), 9–11.
Mario Couceiro, 'Pilar Cibreiro y su cinturón traído de Cuba', *La Voz de Galicia*, 9 May 1985.
Eva Díaz, 'El triunfo madrileño de una gallega ignorada en su tierra', *La Voz de Galicia*, 9 May 2005.
Luis Mateo Díez, 'Biografía de una aldea', *Guía del Ocio*, 5 August 1985, 38.
Ángeles Encinar, 'Tendencias en el cuento español reciente', *Lucanor* 13 (1995), 103–108.
José Manuel Fajardo, 'Narradores para el fin de siglo', *Cambio 16*, 21 October 1985, 139–36.
J. G., 'Deixalo chover: El cinturón traído de Cuba', *Cambio 16*, 10 June 1985, 183.
Juan Manuel González, 'La narrativa española, o el auge deseado de lo nuevo', *El Urogallo* 60 (1991), 24–31.
Xesus González Gómez, 'Las razones de un descubrimiento', *Quimera* 46–47 (1985), 108.

N. M., 'Tierras de la memoria: El cinturón traído de Cuba', *El País* (*Libros*), 16 June 1985.

Coro Malaxechevarría, 'Pilar Cibreiro', in *An Encyclopaedia of Continental Women Writers*, K. Wilson (ed.) (1991), 254. https://books.google.co.uk/books?id=2Wf1SV bGFg8C&pg=PA254&lpg=PA254&dq=Pilar+Cibreiro&source=bl&ots=QWoBv XHAtx&sig=Tkli0uM62UsAQgWWz-krDb4b87k&hl=en&sa=X&ved=0ahUK EwiKpdO1xPHRAhWKAsAKHfDRBs0Q6AEIYTAO#v=onepage&q=Pilar%20 Cibreiro&f=false

Ramón Mayrata, 'Más allá de la bruma', *La Gaceta del Libro*, 15 May 1985, 5.

Gregorio Moralesa Villena, 'Tres nuevos autores: Infancia y primera novela', *Ínsula*, 473 (1986), 5.

María José Obiol, 'El juego de las similitudes y las diferencias. Madurez en el oficio de contar', *El País* (*Libros*), 28 July 1985.

María José Obiol, 'Pilar Cibreiro, ecos de La Habana en Vilaboa', *La Gaceta del Libro*, 15 May 1985, 4–5.

Ángel L. Prieto de Paula, 'Idas y revueltas', *El País*, 19 March 2005. http://elpais. com/diario/2005/03/19/babelia/1111193416_850215.html

María Victoria Reyzábal, 'El cinturón traído de Cuba. Primera andadura narrativa', *Reseña* 159 (1985), 10.

Milagros Sánchez Arnosi, 'El cinturón traído de Cuba', *Ínsula* 468 (1985), 19.

Lynn K. Talbot, 'Entrevista con Pilar Cibreiro', *Letras Peninsulares* 2.3 (1989), 435–40.

Fernando Valls, 'El renacimiento del cuento en España (1975–1990)', *Lucanor* 6 (1991), 27–42.

Further online information Pilar Cibreiro (a selection)
http://centros.edu.xunta.es/cpideatios/datos/revista/html/ver. php?menu1=Sab%as%20que&menu2=Pedagox%a&id=245
http://opinoma.es/?tag=pilar-cibreiro
http://vianaemais.blogspot.co.uk/2016/05/pilar-cibreiro.html
https://bit.ly/2t218YE
http://www.edu.xunta.gal/centros/iesallerulloa/system/files/5_PILAR-CIBREIRO-Fatima_Fernandez.pdf
http://www.poesiagalega.org/uploads/media/cibreiro_1987_autopoetica.pdf
https://www.facebook.com/DaritaQ/posts/538742172810255

DÍAS DE LLUVIA

¡Cuánto se aprendía de la lluvia y del paso de sus días, de la calma que imponía y de su silencio, sólo interrumpido por el goteo del agua sobre los tejados, los charcos y los árboles!

Llovía durante días, mansamente y sin cesar. La humedad formaba una cortina de vapor que se espesaba a lo lejos hasta nublar el horizonte de los campos y las colinas, oscureciéndolo y envolviéndolo todo en su neblinoso velo gris.

Dentro de la casa, al abrigo del fuego, alguien desgranaba las doradas espigas del maíz y con los granos iban cayendo las palabras hasta formar historias que yo recogía con ávida fruición y también, alguna vez, con espanto.

Historias de mujeres que lucharon con hombres y vencieron, de amantes sorprendidos en la pasión culminante, de huidas y saltos por la ventana con la ropa en la mano, de burlas en los Antroidos, esfollas y fías; relatos de escarceos juveniles en los pajares y en los caminos, de agravios, de plantadas, de galanes valientes y de bonita voz; historias de emigrantes, de su fortuna y de su fracaso, relatos de visiones, difuntos y aparecidos, de jóvenes suicidas y mujeres poseídas por un espíritu extraño; relatos que hablaban de la vida y de la muerte, entremezcladas.

Cuando me cansaba de palabras subía al fayado a explorar lo ignoto: muebles y ropas caídas en desuso, arcas repletas de trigo que escondían en su morena superficie la invitación de las nueces y manzanas allí guardadas, la persecución de los ratones, las casas y caminos vecinos vistos desde lo alto y tamizados por la llovizna y los libros, sobre todo los libros.

Había varios de Historia y de Gramática, unos con ilustraciones en blanco y negro y otros en color, pero el más dotado de magia era un libro de viajes redactado en forma epistolar. Cada carta ofrecía un modelo distinto de letra –gótica, inglesa– y otras que no sabía diferenciar, ni siquiera descifrar. Se hablaba allí de los diferentes países y razas, en los dibujos aparecían las calles de Singapur o los minaretes de Tánger, a cada lugar le correspondía

RAINY DAYS

How much we learned from the rain and the passing of rainy days, from the sense of calm it instilled and from its silence, broken only by the steady drip of water onto the rooftops, into puddles, onto trees!

It would go on raining for days at a time, gently and on and on. The dampness would form a curtain of vapour which grew thicker in the distance, shutting out the light of the sun from the horizon of fields and hills and casting everything into darkness, enveloping all around in a grey misty veil.

Inside the house, warm near the fireside, someone was stripping the grains from golden ears of maize, and as the grains fell so did words, tumbling on until they became stories which I would glean with avid enjoyment and, occasionally, fear.

Stories about women who fought with men and won, of lovers surprised at the height of their passion, escaping and leaping through windows, clothes in hand, the jokes in the *Antroidos*, *esfollas* and *fías*;[1] tales of young lovers' fumblings in hay lofts and in country lanes; tales of people wronged, of revenge, about falling in and out of love, of courtships, and haughty fine-looking girls, of brave and handsome young men with silken voices; stories about emigrants, their good fortunes and their failures; tales of visions, the dead and apparitions, of young suicides and women possessed by spirits; stories that spoke of life and death, all jumbled together.

When I grew tired of words I'd climb to the lumber room at the top of the house to explore the unknown – pieces of furniture and old clothes fallen into disuse, wooden chests full of wheat, their dark surfaces hiding the appetizing walnuts and apples carved there, hunting for mice, the houses and neighbouring roads viewed from on high and filtered through a haze of rain. And the books, above all the books.

There were a number of History and Grammar books, some of them with illustrations in black and white, others in colour, but the one most endowed with magic was a travel book written as a series of letters, each presented in a different typeface – gothic script, roman type – and others I couldn't identify or even decipher. The letters told me about different countries, different races. The illustrations depicted the streets of Singapore or the minarets of

---

1   ***Antroidos, esfollas** and **fías***: Three Galician words which mean Carnival (*Antroidos*), the rituals and parties which accompany the stripping of maize leaves (*esfollas*), and the celebrations which take place at the time of the flax harvest (*fías*).

su estampa. Libros todos que me descubrían otros mundos lejanos y deconocidos, otras tierras, otras gentes, otras palabras.

Había también revistas de la época traídas por no sé quién. Allí, abandonadas entre viejos colchones de pluma de maíz, entre los bolillos para el encaje y los chalecos raídos, estaban las imágenes de Gary Cooper y su esposa en su viaje a España; el Che fumando un puro descomunal cuando era ministro en Cuba y todavía no había sido ensalzado y devorado por el mito, años más tarde; Brigitte Bardot –la melena espesa y rubia, los pantalones blancos y ajustados–, y Mao rodeado de un montón de chinos idénticos e indiferenciables.

El desván estaba lleno de cosas misteriosas y tentadoras. Afuera la lluvia y la niebla eran también un misterio indescifrable.

Llovía morosamente y la humedad lo impregnaba todo: el cuerpo, las paredes, los objetos. Si salíamos las zuecas chapoteaban y se hundían en el suelo mojado, en los caminos embarrados.

Dentro, en los hogares, se desgranaban las espigas y, a su ritmo, seguían cayendo las palabras, pacientes, lentas, repetidas. Eran las mismas historias una y otra vez, como un cuento siempre nuevo e interminable.

No se salía al campo en esos días. Sólo Antonio da Farruca, encapuchado en un saco de esparto, recorría febrilmente su regadío con la azada en la mano y desatascaba regatos o abría nuevos senderos de agua, indiferente a la lluvia, a la semioscuridad del día, al letargo.

Tangiers, each place having its own illustration. All these books opened up distant, unknown worlds to me, other lands, other peoples, other words.

There were also some magazines of the period, but I never knew who'd left them there. Lying where they'd fallen among old mattresses stuffed with corn silks, among the lace-making bobbins and threadbare waistcoats, were pictures of Gary Cooper[2] and his wife on a visit to Spain; Che[3] smoking an enormous cigar in the days when he was still a minister in Cuba, before he'd been elevated and devoured by the myth years later; Brigitte Bardot[4] – the thick cloud of blonde hair, her trousers white and close fitting – and Mao,[5] surrounded by a crowd of Chinese, all dressed the same and wearing identical expressions.

The attic was full of tempting, mysterious objects. And outside, the rain and the mist were another unfathomable mystery.

It rained gently but steadily, and the dampness permeated everything: your body, the walls, the things around you. If we went out our wooden clogs would squelch and sink into the wet earth and the muddy paths.

Inside the houses, ears of corn were stripped, and words – patient, slow, repetitive – would come tumbling out to the same rhythm. They were the same stories over and over again, like a tale that was forever new and unending.

Nobody would go out into the fields on rainy days. Only Antonio da Farruca went out, covering himself with a sack made of esparto grass, feverishly plying his way back and forth his plot of land, hoe in hand, unblocking the channels for the water to flow, or making new ones, indifferent to the rain, the half darkness of the day, and the lethargy.

---

2   **Gary Cooper**: US born film actor (1901–1961). A star for thirty years and winner of two Oscars for Best Actor, he received a Special Academy Award in 1960 for his many celebrated performances, most of them as the archetypal hero of Westerns.

3   **Che**: Ernesto 'Che' Guevara (1928–1967). Born in Argentina, he fought in the Cuban Revolution (1956–1959), and then held government posts under Fidel Castro until 1965, when he left Cuba to become a guerrilla leader in South America. He was killed in Bolivia.

4   **Brigitte Bardot**: French film actress born in 1934. She was an international sex-symbol for fifteen years after her success in *Et Dieu créa la femme* (1956), directed by her husband at the time, Roger Vadim. She is now known for her commitment to the cause of endangered animal species.

5   **Mao**: Mao Zedong or Mao Tse-tung (1893–1976). Leader and main theorist of the Chinese Communist Revolution which won national power in China in 1949. He held the posts of Chairman of the Chinese Communist Party and President of the People's Republic of China until his death. He is associated with policies to develop rural industry and provide infrastructure for agriculture, and with the Cultural Revolution, which he launched in 1966 as a radical mass movement to prevent the Chinese revolution from stagnating.

De él se decía que emigrando a Cuba muy mozo se enamoró allá de una mulata habanera y que ella no lo quiso. Y Antonio regresó, loco de amor, trastornado para siempre por el desdén de la cubana.

Desde hacía años pasaba por los caminos inaccessible y vestido de remiendos –no lo trataba bien la Farruca, su madre– o recogía colillas a la puerta de 'La Maravilla' desconociendo a todos sus vecinos, portando en su caminar de mendigo atolondrado un enigma imposible.

Alto y pacífico, Antonio, el del triste Viaje Sin Suerte y el del Amor Sin Fortuna, el que todo lo hacía con prisa, ensimismado y movido por un secreto furor, mientras hablaba a Mercedes, la perdida al otro lado del mar y recobrada luego en la locura, su mulata hermosa y fatal, nuestra mulata de figura ignorada y por algunos maldecida.

People said that he'd emigrated to Cuba as a very young boy and fallen in love with a *mulata* from Havana, who didn't requite his love. Antonio had returned home, crazy with love, his life forever turned upside down by the Cuban girl's disdain.

For years he'd just drifted around in a world of his own, dressed in rags – la Farruca, his mother, didn't look after him – picking up cigarette stubs in the doorway of 'La Maravilla' and ignoring his neighbours, carrying around with him an impossible enigma, in his confused beggar's wanderings.

Tall and unaggressive, Antonio, the man of the Great Misadventure, the man who was Unlucky in Love, the one who did everything in a rush, lost in a dreamworld and driven by a secret fever while he talked to Mercedes, the girl he lost on the other side of the ocean and then, in his madness, won back again, his beautiful and deadly *mulata*, our *mulata*, of the unknown countenance, cursed by some.

EL RELOJ DE BAGDAD

THE CLOCK FROM BAGHDAD

Original Spanish text from
Mi hermana Elba y Los altillos de Brumal
(Barcelona: Tusquets, 1988, 115–30)
© Cristina Fernández Cubas, 1980

CRISTINA FERNÁNDEZ CUBAS was born in 1945 in Arenys de Mar, a seaside town near Barcelona. After studying Law at the Universitat de Barcelona and Journalism at the Universidad Complutense, in Madrid, she spent several years travelling and living abroad. Her first two books were collections of short stories: *Mi hermana Elba* (1980), very well received by both public and critics, and *Los altillos de Brumal* (1983), which confirmed her preference for setting events in an ambivalent space where the natural seems to meet with the supernatural, and the fantastic requires the involvement of the reader's hesitation, as theorised by Tzvetan Todorov. Her first novel, *El año de Gracia* (1985), plays intertextually with Defoe's *Robinson Crusoe*, and her second, *El columpio* (1995), goes back to the recurrent themes of many of her *cuentos*: the lasting power of dreams and childhood memories. As other practitioners of the genre have noted on many occasions, she went on to consolidate her position as one of the most important and influential short story writers in the Spanish language by publishing two other collections: *El ángulo del horror* (1990) and *Con Agatha en Estambul* (1994). In these, the fantastic as a particular kind of anxiety emerging, in a very Freudian, 'uncanny' way, from ordinary objects, people and everyday events is a theme which can be seen in other titles, such as *Parientes pobres del diablo* (2006), or her latest collection, *La habitación de Nona* (2015), for which she was awarded the prestigious Premio de la Crítica in 2015, the Premio Dulce Chacón, and the Premio Nacional de Narrativa in 2016 (for other prizes to individual books, see bibliography below). As *Nona's Room*, it has been recently translated into English by Kathryn Phillips-Miles and Simon Deefholts. Cristina Fernández Cubas has also written books for children and theatre plays, as well as publishing a very celebrated autobiographical account, *Cosas que ya no existen* (2001), where the personal and the social inevitably meet.

Bibliography of Cristina Fernández Cubas

Novels
El año de Gracia (Barcelona: Tusquets, 1985).
El columpio (Barcelona: Tusquets, 1995).
La puerta entreabierta [under the pseudonym Fernanda Kubbs] (Barcelona: Tusquets, 2013) / Audiobook narrated by Lola Acevedo (Libribox, 2015).

Short story collections
Mi hermana Elba (Barcelona: Tusquets, 1980).
El vendedor de sombras (Barcelona: Argos-Vergara, 1982).
Los altillos de Brumal (Barcelona: Tusquets, 1983).
El ángulo del horror (Barcelona: Tusquets, 1990).
Con Agatha en Estambul (Barcelona: Tusquets, 1994).
Los atillos de Brumal. En el hemisferio sur (Barcelona: Plaza y Janés, 1998).
Parientes pobres del diablo (Barcelona: Tusquets, 2006) – *III Premio Setenil al Mejor Libro de Relatos publicado en España en 2006; Finalista Premio Salambó; 2007 Premio Xatafi-Cyberdark de Literatura Fantástica.*
Todos los cuentos [collection of the titles above] (Barcelona: Tusquets, 2008) – *Premi Ciutat de Barcelona; Premio Salambó de Narrativa; IV Premio Cálamo 'Libro del Año 2008'; Premio Qwerty; Premio Tormenta 2008.*
El vendedor de sueños. El viaje (Barcelona: Alfabia, 2009).
La habitación de Nona (Barcelona: Tusquets, 2015) – *Premio de la Crítica 2015; Prenio Dulce Chacón 2016; Premio Nacional de Narrativa 2016 – Nona's Room*, translated by Kathryn Phillips-Miles and Simon Deefholts (London: Peter Owen Publishers, 2017).

Short stories included in anthologies and journals (a selection)
'Omar, amor', in Y. Navajo (ed.) *Doce relatos de mujeres* (Madrid: Alianza, 1982).
'Algunas de las muertes de Eva Andrade', *Gimlet*, 3 May 1981.
'La ventana del jardín', in F. Valls (ed.) *Son cuentos. Antología del relato breve español, 1975–1993* (Madrid: Espasa Calpe, 1993).
'Omar, My Love' (trans. by Miriam Frank), in J. A. Masoliver Ródenas (ed.), *The Origins of Desire* (London: Serpent's Tail, 1993).
'Ausencia', in Á. Encinar (ed.), *Cuentos de este siglo: 30 narradoras españolas contemporáneas* (Barcelona: Lumen, 1995).
'Ausencia', in J. Andrews and M. Lunati (eds) *Contemporary Spanish Short Stories: Viajeros perdidos* (London: Bristol Classical Press, 1998).
'La mujer de verde', in M. Monmany (ed.), *Vidas de mujer* (Madrid: Alianza, 1998).
'El viaje', in J. L.González (ed.), *Dos veces cuento. Antología de microrrelatos* (Madrid: Ediciones Internacionales Universitarias, 1998; 2007).
'El reloj de Bagdad', in J. M. Merino (ed.) *Cien años de cuentos (1898–1998). Antología del cuento español en castellano* (Madrid: Alfaguara, 1999).

'El ángulo del horror', in R. Hernández Viveros (ed.), *Relato español actual* (México, DF: Universidad Nacional Autónoma de México; Fondo de Cultura Económica, 2002).

'En el hemisferio sur', in D. Roas and A. Casas (eds), *La realidad oculta. Cuentos fantásticos españoles del siglo XX* (Palencia: Menoscuarto, 2008).

'La mujerde verde', in J. J. Muñoz Rengel (ed.), *Perturbaciones. Antología del relato fantástico español actual* (Madrid: Salto de Página, 2009).

'Lúnula y Violeta', in L. Freixas (ed.), *Cuentos de amigas* (Barcelona: Anagrama, 2009).

'La ventana en el jardín', in Á. Encinar and C. Valcárcel (eds), *En breve. Cuentos de escritoras españolas (1975–2010)* (Madrid: Biblioteca Nueva, 2012).

Autobiographical
'Elba, el origen de un cuento', *Lucanor* 6 (1991), 114–16.

Cosas que ya no existen (Barcelona: Lumen, 2001; Barcelona: Tusquets, 2001) *VI Premio NH de Relatos*.

Play
Hermanas de sangre (Barcelona: Tusquets, 1998).

Children's literature
Cris y Cros. El vendedor de sombras (Madrid: Alfaguara, 1988).

De mayor quiero ser bruja [with illustrrations by Luisa Vera] (Barcelona: Malpaso, 2014).

Essays on literature and reflections on her own writing
'El amor y el tiempo', *El País* (Babelia), 2 March 1996.

Drácula de Bram Stoker, un centenario – Vampiros – banpiroak (San Sebastián: Diputación Floral de Guipúzcoa, 1997) [bilingual Spanish and Basque].

Emilia Pardo Bazán (Barcelona: Omega, 2001).

'En China donde viven los chinos', in E. Becerra (ed.), *El arquero inmóvil: nuevas poéticas sobre el cuento* (Madrid: Páginas de Espuma, 2006), 21–26.

'De donde vienen los cuentos', in I. Andres-Suárez and A. Casas (eds), *Cristina Fernández Cubas* (Madrid: Arco Libros, 2007), 11–17.

Further reading on Cristina Fernández Cubas
Concha Alborg, 'Cuatro narradoras de la Transición', in R. Landeira and L.T. González (eds), *Nuevos y novísimos. Algunas perspectivas críticas sobre la narrativa española desde la década de los 60* (Boulder, CO: Society of Spanish and Spanish-American Studies, 1987), 11–28.

Mercedes Alcalá Galán, 'Mujeres en el espejo. Cuentos de escritoras españolas sobre madres e hijas', in J. Romera Castillo and F. Gutiérrez Carbajo (eds), *El cuento*

en la década de los noventa: actas del X Seminario Internacional del Instituto de Semiótica Literaria, Teatral y Nuevas Tecnologías de la UNED (Madrid, 31 de mayo–2 de junio de 2000) (Madrid: Visor Libros; UNED, 2001), 177–86.

José Andrés Rojo, 'La invasion de la realidad', *El País* (Babelia), 17 March 2001.

Irene Andres-Suárez and Ana Casas (eds), *Cristina Fernández Cubas: Grand Séminaire de Neuchâtel. Coloquio Internacional Cristina Fernández Cubas, 17–19 mayo de 2005* (Madrid: Arco Libros; Neuchâtel, Suiza: Universidad de Neuchâtel, 2005).

J. Ernesto Ayala-Dip, 'El deseo de seducir: cinco relatos cortos de Cristina Fernández Cubas', *El País* (Babelia), 21 May 1994.

Ernesto Ayala-Dip, 'Cristina Fernández Cubas, *Todos los cuentos*', *El País* (Babelia), 20 December 2008.

Katarzyna Olga Beilin, 'Cristina Fernández Cubas: "Me gusta que me inquieten", *Conversaciones literarias con novelistas contemporáneos* (Woodbridge, Suffolk; Rochester, NY: Tamesis, 2004), 127–47.

Catherine G. Bellver, 'Two New Women Writers from Spain', *Letras Femeninas* 8.2 (1982), 3–7.

Catherine G. Bellver, '*El año de Gracia* and the Displacement of the World', *Studies in Twentieth-Century Literature* 16.2 (1992), 221–32.

Catherine G. Bellver, '*El año de Gracia*: El viaje como rito de iniciación', *Explicación de Textos Literarios* 22.1 (1993–1994), 3–10.

Catherine G. Bellver, 'Spectators and Spectacle: The Teathrical Dimension in the Works of Cristina Fernández Cubas', *Hispania* 90.1 (2007), 52–61.

Astrid A. Billat, *La imposibilidad de 'la mujer' presentada en cinco novelas postfranquistas* (New York: Peter Lang, 2004).

Mary-Lee Bretz, 'Cristina Fernández Cubas and the Recuperation of the Semiotic in *Los altillos de Brumal*', *Anales de la Literatura Española* 13.3 (1988), 177–88.

Pilar Cabañas, 'Los mecanismos de la perplejidad: la categoría de lo fantástico en las narraciones de Cristina Fernández Cubas', *Quaderns de Filologia. Estudis Lingüístics* 5 (2000), 187–203.

Vicente Carmona, Jeffrey Lamb and Sherry Velasco, 'Conversando con Mercedes Abad, Cristina Fernández Cubas y Soledad Puértolas: "Feminismo y literatura no tienen nada que ver"', *Mester* 20.2 (1991), 157–65. http://escholarship.org/uc/item/9wx441f1#page-4

Elena Carrera, 'La hermenéutica de la paranoia en *El columpio*', *Tesserae, Journal of Iberian and Latin American Studies* 13.1 (2007), 1–10.

Nuria Carrillo, 'La expansión plural de un género: el cuento 1975–1993', *Ínsula* 568 1994), 9–11.

Ana Casas, 'La epifanía del monstruo. Identidad y perversión en los cuentos de Cristina Fernández Cubas', in Á. Encinar and C. Valcárcel (eds), *En breve. Cuentos de escritoras españolas (1975–2010). Estudios y antología* (Madrid: Biblioteca Nueva, 2012), 105–22.

Asunción Castro, 'El cuento fantástico de Cristina Fernández Cubas', in M. Villaba Alvárez (ed.), *Mujeres novelistas en el panorama literario del siglo XX: I Congreso de narrativa española (en lengua castellana)* (Cuenca: Ediciones de la Universidad Castilla-La Mancha, 2000), 237–46.

Jennifer A. Colón, 'From Womb to Tomb: The Allegory of Motherhood in "Omar, amor" by Cristina Fernández Cubas', *Letras Peninsulares* 21.2–3 (2008–2009), 295–314.

María Dolores de Asís Garrote, *Última hora de la novela en España* (Madrid: Pirámide, 1996).

Maria DiFrancesco, *Feminine Agency and Transgression in Post-Franco Spain: Generational Becoming in the Narratives of Carme Riera, Cristina Fernández Cubas and Mercedes Abad* (Newark, DEL: Juan de la Cuesta, 2008).

Ángeles Encinar, 'Escritoras españolas actuales: una perspectiva a través del cuento', *Hispanic Journal* 13.1 (1992), 181–91.

Ángeles Encinar, 'Tendencias en el cuento español reciente', *Lucanor* 13 (1994), 103–108.

Ofelia Ferrán and Kathleen M. Glenn, '"El florecimiento caprichoso de un jacaranda": Writing and Reading the Palimsest in Cristina Fernández Cubas's "Lúnula y Violeta"', *Hispanic Studies* 27 (2002), 202–22.

Jessica A. Folkart, 'Desire, Doubling and Difference in Cristina Fernández Cubas's *El ángulo del horror*', *Revista Canadiense de Estudios Hispánicos* 24.2 (2000), 343–62.

Jessica A. Folkart, 'Interpretations of Gender: Performing Subjectivity in Cristina Fernández Cubas's *Los altillos de Brumal*', *Anales de la Literatura Española Contemporánea* 25.2 (2000), 389–416.

Jessica A. Folkart, 'Almost the Same, but not Quite: Re-orienting the Story of the Subject in Cristina Fernández Cubas's *El año de Gracia*', *Studies in the 20th Century Literature* 26.2 (2002), 285–309.

Jessica A. Folkart, *Angels on Otherness in Post-Franco Spain: The Fiction of Cristina Fernández Cubas* (Lewisburgh, PA: Bucknell University Press, 2002).

Luis García, 'Cristina Fernández Cubas', *Péndulo del Milenio* 14 (2001), 18–21.

Adolfo García Ortega, 'Españoles traducidos. Hacia la normalización', *El Urogallo* 23 (1988), 10–13.

M Geoffrion-Vinci and A. Guarino, 'Of Cookpots, Kettles and Codes: Language and Libido in Cristina Fernández Cubas as read through Hélène Cixous', *Anales de la Literatura Española Contemporánea* 29.1 (2004), 83–106.

Kathleen M. Glenn, 'Authority and Marginality in Three Contemporary Spanish Narratives', *Romance Languages Annual* 2 (1990), 426–30.

Kathleen M. Glenn, 'Gothic Indecipherability and Doubling in the Fiction of Cristina Fernández Cubas', *Monographic Review/Revista Monográfica* 8 (1992), 125–41.

Kathleen M. Glenn, 'Back to Brumal: Fiction and Film', *Romance Languages Annual* 4 (1992), 460–65.

Kathleen M. Glenn, 'Conversación con Cristina Fernández Cubas', *Anales de la Literatura Española Contemporánea* 18.2 (1993), 355–63.

Kathleen M. Glenn, 'Reading Postmodernism in the Fiction of Cristina Fernández Cubas, Paloma Díaz-Mas and Marina Mayoral', *South Central Review, The Journal of the South Central Modern Language Association* 18.1–2 (2001), 78–93.

Kathleen M. Glenn and Janet Pérez (eds), *Maping the Fiction of Cristina Fernández Cubas* (Newark, NJ: University of Delaware Press, 2005).

Kathleen M. Glenn, 'Transgresiones genéricas en unas narraciones de Carme Riera, Inma Monsó, Marina Mayoral y Cristina Fernández Cubas', in Pilar Nieva-de la Paz (ed.), *Roles de género y cambio social en la literatura española del siglo XX* (Amsterdam: Rodopi, 2009), 299–315.

Julie Gleue, 'The Epistemological and Ontological Implications in Cristina Fernández Cubas' *El año de Gracia*', *Monographic Review / Revista Monográfica* 8 (1992), 142–56.

Berna González Harbour, 'Cristina Fernández Cubas: "Importa lo que se dice y lo que se oculta"', *El País* (Cultura), 2 April 2015. http://cultura.elpais.com/cultura/2016/11/16/actualidad/1479296215_002315.html

Javier Goñi, 'Propuestas (en español) para una primavera', *El Urogallo* 48 (1990), 43–45.

Friederike Hassauer, 'Cristina Fernández Cubas: las agotadas tareas de interpetación', in Dieter Ingenschay and Hans-Jörg Neuschafer (eds), *Abriendo caminos: la literatura desde 1975* (Barcelona: Lumen, 1994), 111–22.

Beatriz Hernán-Gómez Prieto, 'La sombra en el espejo (el doble en los cuentos de Cristina Fernández Cubas)', in E. Perassi (ed.), *Tradizione, innovazione, modelli. Scrittura femminile del mondo iberico e americano* (Roma: Bulzoni, 1996), 431–65.

Shoshannah Rebecca Holdom, *Gothic Teatrality and Performance in the Works of Adelaida García Morales, Cristina Fernández Cubas and Pilar Pedraza* (PhD, University of Manchester, 2003).

Maryanne Leone, 'Going Global: Spain's Entrance into the European Union and National Identity in Cristina Fernández Cubas's *El año de Gracia*', *Anales de la Literatura Española Contemporánea* 31.1 (2006), 199–224.

María del Mar López Cabrales, 'Cristina Fernández Cubas. Los horrores de la memoria', in *Palabras de mujeres. Escritoras españolas contemporáneas* (Madrid: Narcea, 2000), 167–76.

John B. Margenot, 'Parody and Self-Consciousness in Cristina Fernández Cubas' *El año de Gracia*', *Siglo XX/20th Century* 11.1–2 (1993), 71–87.

Juan A. Masoliver Ródenas, 'La magia de la vida cotidiana', *La Vanguardia* (Libros), 4 May 2001.

M. R. Massei, 'La literatura fantástica y la voz femenina en el motivo del golem en

'Omar, amor' de Cristina Fernández Cubas', *Hispanic Journal* 25.1–2 (2004), 197–208.

Xavier Moret, 'Cristina Fernández Cubas relata "la inquietud que surge de lo cotidiano"', *El País* (La Cultura), 14 May 1994.

Miguel Ángel Muñoz, 'Entrevista a Cristina Fernández Cubas', in M. Á. Muñoz (ed.), *La familia del aire: entrevistas con cuentistas españoles* (Madrid: Páginas de Espuma, 2011), 33–40.

Enrique Murillo, 'Introducción', in Cristina Fernández Cubas, *El año de Gracia. Mi hermana Elba* (Barcelona: Tusquets, 1992), 7–13.

Geraldine C. Nichols, 'Entrevista a Cristina Fernández Cubas', *España Contemporánea* 6.2 (1993), 55–71.

Pilar Nieva de la Paz, 'Hacia la negación de lo real. Espacios irreales y espacios siniestros en las novelas y cuentos de Cristina Fernández Cubas, Carmen Gómez Ojea y Cristina Peri Rossi', in *Narradoras españolas en la transición política (Textos y contextos)* (Madrid Editorial Fundamentos, 2004), 313–31.

Carmen Esteban Núñez and Neus Samblancat Miranda, 'Los espejos del yo en la narrativa de Cristina Fernández Cubas', *Lectora* 1 (1995), 89–93.

María José Obiol, 'El sueño de la mujer despierta: Cristina Fernández Cubas reaparace con cuatro cuentos cinco años después', *El País* (Babelia), 10 June 1990.

María José Obiol, 'La escritora y el secreto: Cristina Fernández Cubas vuelve a la novela con *El columpio*', *El País* (Babelia), 25 March 1995.

María José Obiol, 'El rostro opaco de la infancia. Cristina Fernández Cubas presenta una obra de teatro sobre la maldad infantil', *El País* (Babelia), 23 May 1998.

José Ortega, 'La dimension fantástica en los cuentos de Fernández Cubas', *Monographic Review / Revista Monográfica* 8 (1992), 157–63.

Carlos Pardo, 'El corazón de Las ficciones. Cristina Fernández Cubas sigue fiel a su mundo narrativo en *La habitación de Nona*', *El País*, 1 April 2015.

Peregrina Pereiro, 'La presencia de la ausencia: la mediación de lo fantástico en *Con Agatha en Estambul* de Cristina Fernández Cubas', in *La novela española de los noventa: alternativas éticas a la postmodernidad* (Madrid: Pliegos, 2002), 81–109.

Janet Pérez, *Contemporary Women Writers of Spain* (Boston, MA: Twayne Publishers, 1988).

Janet Pérez, 'Fernández Cubas, Abjection, and the "retórica del horror"', in *Explicación de Textos Literarios* 24 (1996–1996), 159–71.

Janet Pérez, 'Narrative Unreliability and the Flight from Clarity, or the Quest for Knowledge in the Fog', *Hispanófila* 122 (1998), 29–39. http://www.jstor.org/stable/43807048

Alison Ribeiro de Menezes, 'On Civil-War Memory in Spanish Women's Writing: The Example of Cristina Fernández Cubas's *Cosas que ya no existen*', in M.

Bragança and P. Tame (eds), *The Long Aftermath: Cultural Legacies of Europe at War, 1936–2016*. (New York: Berghahn Books, 2015), 60–72.

Ana Rueda, 'Cristina Fernández Cubas: una narrativa de voces extinguidas', *Monographic Review / Revista Monográfica* 4 (1988), 257–67.

Robert C. Spires, *Post-Totalitarian Spanish Fiction* (Columbia, MO: University of Missouri Press, 1996). https://bit.ly/2JBR8MF

Luis Suñén, 'La realidad y sus sombras: Rosa Montero y Cristina Fernández Cubas', *Ínsula*, 446 (1986), 5.

Lynn K. Talbot, 'Journey into the Fantastic: Cristina Fernández Cubas's *Los altillos de Brumal*', *Letras Femeninas* 151.1–2 (1989), 37–47. https://www.jstor.org/stable/23022294?seq=1#page_scan_tab_contents

Maruja Torres, 'Cosas de Fernández Cubas', *El País Semanal,* 13 May 2001.

Fernando Valls, 'El renacimiento del cuento en España (1975–1990)', *Lucanor* 6 (1991), 27–42.

Fernando Valls, 'De últimos cuentos y cuentistas', *Ínsula* 568 (1994), 3–6.

Fernando Valls, 'Prólogo', in *Todos los cuentos. Cristina Fernández Cubas* (Barcelona: Tusquets, 2009), 9–20. https://tinyurl.com/y99rz2zx

Fernando Valls, 'De las certezas del amigo a las dudas del héroe. Sobre "La ventana en el jardín" de Cristina Fernández Cubas', *Ínsula* 568 (1994), 18–19.

Fernando Valls, 'CFC: la reina del relato', *El País* (Cultura), 17 November 2016. http://cultura.elpais.com/cultura/2016/11/16/actualidad/1479324628_085990.html

Phyllis Zatlin, 'Tales from Cristina Fernández Cubas. Adventures in the Fantastic', *Monographic Review / Revista Monográfica* 3 (1987): 107–18.

Phyllis Zatlin, 'Amnesia, Strangulation, Hallucination and Other Mishaps: The Perils of Being a Female in the Tales of Cristina Fernández Cubas', *Hispania* 79.1 (1995), 36–44.

Further online information on Cristina Fernández Cubas (a selection)

http://cultura.elpais.com/cultura/2016/11/16/actualidad/1479296215_002315.html

http://www.planetadelibros.com/autor/cristina-fernandez-cubas/000013202

http://escritoras.com/escritoras/Cristina-Fernandez-Cubas

http://www.elconfidencial.com/cultura/2016-11-16/cristina-fernandez-cubas-nacional-narrativa_1290447/

http://www.enriquevilamatas.com/escritores/escrfernadezcubasc1.html

ttps://lanaveinvisible.wordpress.com/2016/10/31/cristina-fernandez-cubas/

http://www.elcultural.com/noticias/letras/Cristina-Fernandez-Cubas-Con-el-cuento-aun-no-ha-podido-nadie/7695

http://www.elcultural.com/noticias/letras/Cristina-Fernandez-Cubas-Premio-Nacional-de-Narrativa-2016/10083

http://www.elperiodico.com/es/noticias/ocio-y-cultura/cristina-fernandez-cubas-nacional-de-narrativa-la-habitacion-de-nona-5632412

http://www.abc.es/cultura/libros/abci-cristina-fernandez-cubas-logra-premio-nacional-narrativa-habitacion-nona-201611161236_noticia.html

https://www.youtube.com/watch?v=QYs3f4mIBxM

http://www.revistavisperas.com/la-habitacion-nona-cristina-fernandez-cubas/

https://www.questia.com/library/literature/fiction/short-story-writers/cristina-fernandez-cubas

https://bit.ly/2LLHdF3

http://bayal.blogspot.co.uk/2016/11/cristina-fernandez-cubas.html

http://www.revistadelibros.com/articulos/hermanas-de-sangre-obra-teatral-de-cristina-fernandez-cubas

http://www.elsindromechejov.com/la-habitacion-de-nona-cristina-fernandez-cubas/

http://www.march.es/conferencias/anteriores/voz.aspx?p1=22888

http://zafra.hoy.es/noticias/201611/26/cristina-fernandez-cubas-logra-20161126150509.html

http://lamentable.org/vivimos-un-momento-de-profunda-irritacion/

https://pendientedemigracion.ucm.es/info/especulo/numero37/cfcubas.html

https://buleria.unileon.es/bitstream/handle/10612/4373/CRISTINA%20FERN%C3%81NDEZ%20CUBAS%20Y%20ANA%20CASAS.%20VIAJANDO%20A%20LO%20OTRO%20DESDE%20CUALQUIER%20LUGAR.pdf?sequence=1

http://www.ub.edu/cdona/lletradedona/parientes-pobres-del-diablo

https://www.sinjania.com/una-poetica-del-cuento/

http://www.bne.es/es/Actividades/Ciclos/Temporales/2015/Conversaciones ficticiasenlabne/Sesion1.html

http://msur.es/2016/01/29/cristina-fernandez-cubas/

http://www.rci.rutgers.edu/~zatlin/AboutCubas.htm

http://ilium.qdony.net/?p=3768

http://desequilibros.blogspot.co.uk/2008/07/el-viaje-cristina-fernndez-cubas.html#.WJNx239qEfI

http://www.slideshare.net/Mitxi/dossier-cristina-fernandez-cubas1

http://www.academia.edu/10315932/Entrevista_con_Cristina_Fernandez_Cubas

http://dspace.unive.it/bitstream/handle/10579/1764/825242-136572.pdf?sequence=2

http://www.letraslibres.com/mexico-espana/libros/parientes-pobres-del-diablo-cristina-fernandez-cubas

http://latormentaenunvaso.blogspot.co.uk/2006/06/parientes-pobres-del-diablo-cristina.html

http://antoncastro.blogia.com/2009/073001-cristina-fernandez-cubas-un-cuento.php

http://unlibroaldia.blogspot.co.uk/2013/10/fernanda-kubbs-cristina-fernandez-cubas.html

http://cultura.elpais.com/cultura/2013/02/13/actualidad/1360758812_120184.html

EL RELOJ DE BAGDAD

Nunca las temí ni nada hicieron ellas por amedrentrarme. Estaban ahí, junto a los fogones, confundidas con el crujir de la leña, el sabor de los bollos recién horneados, el vaivén de los faldones de las viejas. Nunca las temí, tal vez porque las soñaba pálidas y hermosas, pendientes como nosotros de historias sucedidas en aldeas sin nombre, aguardando el instante oportuno para dejarse oír, para susurrarnos sin palabras. 'Estamos aquí, como cada noche'. O bien, refugiarse en el silencio denso que anunciaba: 'Todo lo que estáis escuchando es cierto. Trágica, dolorosa, dulcemente cierto'. Podía ocurrir en cualquier momento. El rumor de las olas tras el temporal, el paso del último mercancías, el trepidar de la loza en la alacena, o la inconfundible voz de Olvido, encerrada en su alquimia de cacerolas y pucheros.

–Son las ánimas, niña, son las ánimas.

Más de una vez, con los ojos entornados, creí en ellas.

¿Cuántos años tendría Olvido en aquel tiempo? Siempre que le preguntaba por su edad la anciana se encogía de hombros, miraba por el rabillo del ojo a Matilde y seguía impasible, desgranando guisantes, zurciendo calcetines, disponiendo las lentejas en pequeños montones, o recordaba, de pronto, la inaplazable necesidad de bajar al sótano a por leña y alimentar la salamandra del último piso. Un día intenté sonsacar a Matilde. 'Todos los del mundo', me dijo riendo.

La edad de Matilde, en cambio, jamás despertó mi curiosidad. Era vieja también, andaba encorvada, y los cabellos canos, amarilleados por el agua de colonia, se divertían ribeteando un pequeño moño, apretado como una bola, por el que asomaban horquillas y pasadores. Tenía una pierna renqueante que sabía predecir el tiempo y unas cuantas habilidades más que, con el paso de los años, no logro recordar tan bien como quisiera. Pero, al lado de Olvido, Matilde me parecía muy joven, algo menos sabia y mucho más inexperta, a pesar de que su voz sonara dulce cuando nos mostraba los cristales empañados y nos hacía creer que afuera no estaba el mar ni la playa, ni la vía del tren, ni tan siquiera el Paseo, sino montes inaccesibles y escarpados por los que correteaban hordas de lobos enfurecidos y hambientos. Sabíamos –Matilde nos lo había contado muchas veces– que ningún hombre temeroso de Dios

THE CLOCK FROM BAGDAD

I was never afraid of them, nor did they ever do anything to frighten me. They were just there, next to the kitchen range, mingling with the crackle of the firewood, the taste of bread fresh from the oven, the swish of the old women's skirts. I was never afraid of them, perhaps because in my deams I pictured them as pale and lovely, hanging like us on the thread of tales set in nameless villages, waiting until the time was right to make themselves heard, to wisper wordlessly to us: 'Here we are, just like every night.' Or else take refuge in the heavy silence that would presage: 'Everything you're listening is true. Tragically, painfully, sweetly true.' It could happen at any minute. The low murmur of the waves after the storm, the passing of the last goods train, the rattle of the crockery in the larder, or the unmistakable voice of Olvido, locked away in her alchemy of pots and pans:

'They're the souls of the dead, child, the souls of the dead.'
More than once, my eyes half closed, I believed in them.

How old would Olvido have been at the time? Whenever I asked her about her age the old lady would shrug her shoulders, cast a sideways glance at Matilde, and carry on impassively shelling peas, darning socks, arranging lentils in little heaps, or would suddenly remember some all-pressing need to go down to the cellar for firewood and stoke up the central-heating stove on the top floor. One day, I tried pumping Matilde for some information. 'All the years in the world', she told me laughing.

Matilde's age, on the other hand, never aroused my curiosity. She too was old, she walked with a stoop, and her white hair, stained with yellow by eau de cologne, joyously peeped from the edges of a little bun, tight as a ball, through which bobby pins and hairgrips poked out. She had a gammy leg which knew how to forecast the weather and a number of other skills as well, which, as the years have gone by, I can no longer remember as clearly as I'd like. But compared with Olvido, Matilde seemed much younger to me, not quite as wise and much more inexperienced, in spite of the fact that her voice sounded soft whenever she pointed out the steamed-up windows to us and made us believe there was no sea outside, nor any beach, nor any train track, not even the Paseo, but only craggy and inaccessible mountains over which packs of rabid and hungry wolves roamed. We knew – Matilde had told us so time and again – that no God-fearing man should abandon the warmth of his

debía, en noches como aquéllas, abandonar el calor de su casa. Porque ¿quién, sino un alma pecadora, condenada a vagar entre nosotros, podía atreverse a desafiar tal oscuridad, semejante frío, tan espantosos gemidos procedentes de las entrañas de la tierra? Y entonces Olvido tomaba la palabra. Pausada, segura, sabedora de que a partir de aquel momento nos hacía suyos, que muy pronto la luz del quinqué se concentraría en su rostro y sus arrugas de anciana dejarían paso a la tez sonrosada de una niña, a la temible faz de un sepulturero atormentado por sus recuerdos, a un fraile visionario, o tal vez una monja milagrera… Hasta que unos pasos decididos, o un fino taconeo, anunciaran la llegada de incómodos intrusos. O que ellas, nuestras amigas, indicaran por boca de Olvido que había llegado la hora de descansar, de comernos la sopa de sémola o de apagar la luz.

Sí, Matilde, además de su pierna adivina, poseía el don de la dulzura. Pero en aquellos tiempos de entregas sin fisuras yo había tomado el partido de Olvido, u Olvido, quizá, no me había dejado otra opción. 'Cuando seas mayor y te cases, me iré a vivir contigo'. Y yo, cobijada en el regazo de mi protectora, no conseguía imaginar cómo sería esa tercera persona dispuesta a compartir nuestras vidas, ni veía motivo suficiente para separarme de mi familia o abandonar, algún día, la casa junto a la playa. Pero Olvido decidía siempre por mí. 'El piso será soleado y pequeño, sin escaleras, sótano ni azotea'. Y no me quedaba otro remedio que ensoñarlo así, con una amplia cocina en la que Olvido trajinara a gusto y una gran mesa de madera con tres sillas, tres vasos y tres platos de porcelana… O, mejor, dos. La compañía del extraño que las previsions de Olvido me adjudicaban no acababa de encajar en mi nueva cocina. 'Él cenará más tarde', pensé. Y le saqué la silla a un hipotético comedor que mi fantasía no tenía interés alguno en representarse.

Pero en aquel caluroso domingo de diciembre en que los niños danzaban en torno al bulto recién llegado, me fijé con detenimiento en el rostro de Olvido y me pareció que no quedaba espacio para una nueva arruga. Se hallaba extrañamente rígida, desatenta a las peticiones de tijeras y cuchillos, ajena al jolgorio que el inesperado regalo había levantado en la antesala. 'Todos los años del mundo', recordé, y, por un momento, me invadió la certeza de que la silla que tan ligeramente había desplazado al comedor no era la del supuesto, futuro y desdibujado marido.

Lo habían traído aquella misma mañana, envuelto en un recio papel de embalaje, amarrado con cordeles y sogas como un prisionero. Parecía un gigante humillado, tendido como estaba sobre la alfombra, soportando las

hearth on nights like that. For who but a sinful soul, condemned to wander amongst us, would dare defy such darkness, such cold, such terrifying groans from the bowels of the earth? And then Olvido would take up the tale. Slowly, deliberately, confident and aware that from that moment on she would hold us in the palm of her hand, that very soon the light of the oil lamp would focus on her face and the wrinkles of the old woman would turn into the apple blossom skin of a child, the terrible face of a grave digger tormented by his memories, a visionary friar, perhaps some miracle-working nun… Until firm footsteps or clincking heels would announce the arrival of some tiresome intruder. Or that they, our friends, using Olvido as a mouthpiece, would suggest it was time for us to rest, to eat our bland soup made with semolina or time to put out the light.

Yes, Matilde, in addition to her prophesying leg, possessed the gift of gentleness. But in those days of wholehearted commitment, I had taken Olvido's side, or perhaps Olvido had left me with no other option. 'When you're older and get married, I'm going to live with you.' And, sheltered in the lap of my protectress, I couldn't imagine what that would be like, a third person wanting to share our lives, or see a good enough reason to move away from my family or some day to abandon the house next to the beach. But Olvido always decided for me. 'The flat will be sunny and small, with no stairs, no basement and no roof terrace.' And there was nothing else for it but to dream of it like that, with a spacious kitchen where Olvido would bustle about to her heart's content, and a big wooden table with three chairs, three glasses and three china plates… Or better still, two. The company of the outsider assigned to me in Olvido's prophesies didn't quite fit into my new kitchen. 'He'll have his dinner later', I thought. And I removed his chair to a hypothetical dining room my imagination had no interest whatsoever in conjuring up.

But on that warm Sunday in December, as the children danced around the recently arrived package, I kept my eyes firmly fixed on Olvido's face and it seemed to me there was no room left for even one new wrinkle. She was strangely stiff, taking no notice of the calls for scissors or knives, not joining in the fun the unexpected gift had unleashed in the hallway. The words 'All the years in the world' came to mind, and for a moment I was possessed by the certainty that the chair so hastily removed to the dining room was not that of the hypothetical, future and still indistinct husband.

They had delivered it that very morning, all done up in thick wrapping paper, tied round with string and ropes lik a prisoner. Stretched out like that on the rug it looked like a giant brought low and having to tolerate the dancing

danzas y los chillidos de los niños, excitados, inquietos, seguros hasta el último instante que sólo ellos iban a ser los destinatarios del descomunal juguete. Mi madre, con mañas de gata adulada, seguía de cerca los intentos por el misterio. ¿Un nuevo armario? ¿Una escultura, una lámpara? Pero no, mujer, claro que no. Se trataba de una obra de arte, de una curiosidad, de una ganga. El anticuario debía de haber perdido el juicio. O, quizá, la vejez, un error, otras preocupaciones. Porque el precio resultaba irrisorio para tamaña maravilla. No teníamos más que arrancar los últimos adhesivos, el celofán que protegía las partes más frágiles, abrir la puertecilla de cristal y sujetar el péndulo. Un reloj de pie de casi tres metros de alzada, números y manecillas recubiertos de oro, un mecanismo rudimentario pero perfecto. Deberíamos limpiarlo, apuntalarlo, disimular con barniz los inevitables destrozos del tiempo. Porque era un reloj muy antiguo, fechado en 1700, en Bagdad, probable obra de artesanos iraquíes para algún cliente europeo. Sólo así podía interpretarse el hecho de que la numeración fuera arábiga y que la parte inferior de la caja reprodujera en relieve los cuerpos festivos de un grupo de seres humanos. ¿Danzarines? ¿Invitados a un banquete? Los años habían desdibujado sus facciones, los pliegues de sus vestidos, los manjares que se adivinaban aún sobre la superficie carcomida de una mesa. Pero ¿por qué no nos decidíamos de una vez a alzar la vista, a detenernos en la esfera, a contemplar el juego de balanzas que, alternándose el peso de unos granos de arena, ponía en marcha el carillón? Y ya los niños, equipados con cubos y palas, salían al Paseo, miraban a derecha e izquierda, cruzaban la vía y se revolcaban en la playa que ahora no era una playa sino un remoto y peligroso desierto. Pero no hacía falta tanta arena. Un puñado, nada más, y, sobre todo, un momento de silencio. Coronando la esfera, recubierta de polvo, se hallaba la última sorpresa de aquel día, el más delicado conjunto de autómatas que hubiéramos podido imaginar. Astros, planetas, estrellas de tamaño diminuto aguardando las primeras notas de una melodía para ponerse en movimiento. En menos de una semana conoceríamos todos los secretos de su mecanismo.

Lo instalaron en el descansillo de la escalera, al término del primer tramo, un lugar que parecía construido a posta. Se le podía admirar desde la antesala, desde el rellano del primer piso, desde los mullidos sillones del salón, desde la trampilla que conducía a la azotea. Cuando, al cabo de unos días, dimos con la proporción exacta de arena y el carillón emitió, por primera vez, las notas de una desconocida melodía, a todos nos pareció muchísimo más alto y hermoso. El reloj de Bagdad estaba ahí. Arrogante, majestuoso, midiendo

and screeching of excited, restless children, convinced right up to the very last minute that the colossal plaything was intended for them. My mother, showing all the guile of a pampered she-cat, stood close by and watched the efforts at unveiling the mystery. A new cupboard? A sculpture? A lamp? But no, of course not. This was a work of art, a curio, a bargain. The antique dealer must have been out of his mind. Or perhaps it was old age, a mistake, other things to worry about. Because the price had turned out to be absurdly low for such a wonderful thing. We just had to rip off the last bits of sticky tape, the cellophane protecting the most fragile parts, open the little glass door and hook in the pendulum. A free-standing clock almost ten feet tall, with gold-plated numbers and hands and a simple yet perfect mechanism. We would have to clean it up, make sure it stood level, varnish over the inevitable wear and tear that comes with age. Because it was a very old clock, bearing the date 1700, and it had been made in Baghdad, probably by Iraqui craftsmen for some European customer. This was the only interpretation that could be put out on the fact that the numerals were in Arabic and the lower part of the casing was embossed with a group of human figures in festive mood. Dancers? Guests at a banquet? The years had worn their features smooth, the folds of their clothing, the delicacies that could still be made out on the worm-eaten surface of a table. How was it that not one of us made the decision to raise our eyes, to let them dwell on the clock-face, to gaze at the set of balances that set the chimes in motion when they were altered by the weight of a few grains of sand? And now the children, armed with buckets and spades, were going out to the promenade, looking to right and left, crossing the railroad track and turning somersaults on the beach that was no longer a beach but a remote and dangerous desert. But there was no need for so much sand. One handful, no more and, above all, a moment of silence. Crowning the face of the clock, covered in dust, appeared the final surprise of the day, the most delicate set of automata that we could ever imagine. Heavenly bodies, planets, tiny little stars waiting for the opening notes of a tune to set them going. In less than a week we would know all the secrets of its mechanism.

It was installed on the stair landing, at the top of the first flight, a place that looked as if had been specially built for it. It could be admired from the hallway, from the first floor landing, from the big comfortable chairs in the living room, from the trap-door that led out onto the roof terrace. When, after a few days, we had worked out the exact amount of sand and the chimes had for the first time sounded the notes of some unfamiliar tune, we all thought it looked even taller and more beautiful. The Baghdad Clock had arrived.

con su sordo tictac cualquiera de nuestros movimientos, nuestra respiración, nuestros juegos infantiles. Parecía como si se hallara en el mismo lugar desde tiempos inmemoriales, como si sólo él estuviera en su puesto, tal era la altivez de su porte, su seguridad, el respeto que nos infundía cuando, al caer la noche, abandonábamos la plácida cocina para alcanzar los dormitorios del ultimo piso. Ya nadie recordaba la antigua desnudez de la escalera. Las visitas se mostraban arrobadas, y mi padre no dejaba de felicitarse por la astucia y la oportunidad de su adquisición. Una ocasión única, una belleza, una obra de arte.

Olvido se negó a limpiarlo. Pretextó vértigos, jaquecas, vejez y reumatismo. Aludió a problemas de la vista, ella que podía distinguir un grano de cebada en un costal de trigo, la cabeza de un alfiler en un montón de arena, la china más minúscula en un puñado de lentejas. Encaramarse a una escalerilla no era labor para una anciana. Matilde era mucho más joven, y llevaba, además, mucho menos tiempo en la casa. Porque ella, Olvido, poseía el privilegio de la antigüedad. Había criado a las hermanas de mi padre, asistido a mi nacimiento, al de mis hermanos, ese par de mocosos que no se apartaban de las faldas de Matilde. Pero no era necesario que sacase a relucir sus derechos, ni que se asiera con tanta fuerza de mis trenzas. 'Usted, Olvido, es como de la familia'. Y, horas más tarde, en la soledad de la alcoba de mis padres: 'Pobre Olvido. Los años no perdonan'.

No sé si la extraña desazón que iba a adueñarse de la casa irrumpió de súbito, como me lo presenta ahora la memoria, o si se trata, quizá, de la deformación que entraña el recuerdo. Pero lo cierto es que Olvido, tiempo antes de que la sombra de la fatalidad se cirniera sobre nosotros, empezó a adquirir actitudes de felina recelosa, siempre con los oídos alerta, las manos crispadas, atenta a cualquier soplo de viento, al menor murmullo, al chirriar de las puertas, al paso del mercancías, del rápido, del expreso, o al cotidiano trepidar de las cacerolas sobre las repisas. Pero ahora no eran las ánimas que pedían oraciones ni frailes pecadores condenados a penar largos años en la tierra. La vida en la cocina se había poblado de un silencio tenso y agobiante. De nada servía insistir. Las aldeas, perdidas entre montes, se habían tornado lejanas e inaccesibles, y nuestros intentos, a la vuelta del colegio, por arrancar nuevas historias se quedaban en preguntas sin respuestas, flotando en el aire, bailoteando entre ellas, diluyéndose junto a humos y suspiros. Olvido parecía encerrada en sí misma y, aunque fingía entregarse con ahínco a fregar los fondos de las ollas, a barnizar armarios

Arrogant and majestic, its muffled tick measuring every one of our movements, the breaths we took, our childish games. It felt as if it had been in that same place from time immemorial, as if it were the only thing that had ever stood in its place, such was the haughtiness of its bearing, its confidence, the respect it commanded in us when, as night fell, we gave up the peaceful kitchen to climb the stairs to our bedrooms on the top floor. Nobody remembered how bare the old stairway used to be. Visitors declared themselves enchanted by it and my father never stopped congratulating himself on his good luck and astuteness in acquiring it. A unique find, a thing of beauty, a work of art.

Olvido refused to clean it. She claimed to be afraid of heights, she pleaded migraines, old age and rheumatism. She hinted at problems with her sight, she who could distinguish a grain of barley in a sack of wheat, the head of a pin in a heap of sand, the tiniest pebble in a handful of lentils. Scaling a step ladder was no job for an old lady. Matilde was much younger, and anyway she had been in the house for a shorter length of time. For she, Olvido, enjoyed the privilege of seniority. She had brought up my father's sisters, had been there at my birth, at the births of my brothers, that pair of freckled faces who never left Matilde's side. But she didn't have to harp on about her rights so much, or hold on so tight to my plaits. 'You, Olvido, are like one of the family.' And hours later, in the solitude of my parents' bedroom: 'Poor Olvido. The years are taking their toll.'

I don't know if the strange sense of unease that was soon to take over the house erupted suddenly, which is how my memory makes it feel now, or if it's to do, perhaps, with the distortion that lies at the heart of memory. But one thing was certain, which was that Olvido, some time before the shadow of fate started to hang over us, began to take on the appearance of a suspicious cat. Her ears always pricked, her hands would twitch, alert to every breath of wind, the least noise, doors creaking, the passing of the goods train, the fast-through train, the express, or the everyday rattle of saucepans on shelves. Only now it wasn't the souls who were calling for prayers, or sinful friars condemned to wander the earth for years on end. Life in the kitchen was invaded by a tense and oppressive silence. It was no use going on about it. The remote villages in the mountains had turned into far off and inaccessible places, and when we came home from school our efforts to tease out new tales were left as questions to which no replies were given, floating in the air, hovering amongst them, vanishing into nothing, along with the smoke and the whispers. Olvido seemed a prisoner inside herself, and although she pretended to be absorbed in scrubbing the

y alacenas, o a blanquear las junturas de los mosaicos, yo la sabía cruzando el comedor, subiendo con cautela los primeros escalones, deteniéndose en el descansillo y observando. La adivinaba observando, con la valentía que le otorgaba el no hallarse realmente allí, frente al péndulo de bronce, sino a salvo, en un mundo de pucheros y sartenes, un lugar hasta el que no llegaban los latidos del reloj y en el que podía ahogar, con facilidad, el sonido de la inevitable melodía.

Pero apenas hablaba. Tan sólo en aquella mañana ya lejana en que mi padre, cruzando mares y atravesando desiertos, explicaba a los pequeños la situación de Bagdad, Olvido se atrevió a murmurar: 'Demasiado lejos'. Y luego, dando la espalda al objeto de nuestra admiración, se había internado por el pasillo cabeceando enfurruñada, sosteniendo una conversación consigo misma.

—Ni siquiera deben ser cristianos—dijo entonces.

En un principio, y aunque lamentara el súbito cambio que se había operado en nuestra vida, no concedí excesiva importancia a los desvaríos de Olvido. Los años parecían haberse desplomado de golpe sobre el frágil cuerpo de la anciana, sobre aquellas espaldas empeñadas en curvarse más y más a medida que pasaban los días. Pero un hecho fortuito terminó de sobrecargar la enrarecida atmósfera de los últimos tiempos. Para mi mente de niña, se trató de una casualidad; para mis padres, de una desgracia; para la vieja Olvido, de la confirmación de sus oscuras intuiciones. Porque había sucedido junto al bullicioso grupo sin rostro, ante el péndulo de bronce, frente a las manecillas recubiertas de oro. Matilde sacaba brillo a la cajita de astros, al Sol y la Luna, a las estrellas sin nombre que componían el diminuto desfile, cuando la mente se le nubló de pronto, quiso aferrarse a las balanzas de arena, apuntalar sus pies sobre un peldaño inexistente, impedir una caída que se presentaba inevitablemente. Pero la liviana escalerilla se negó a sostener por más tiempo aquel cuerpo oscilante. Fue un accidente, un desmayo, una momentánea pérdida de conciencia. Matilde no se encontraba bien. Lo había dicho por la mañana mientras vestía a los pequeños. Sentía náuseas, el estómago revuelto, posiblemente la cena de la noche anterior, quién sabe si una secreta copa traidora al calor de la lumbre. Pero no había forma humana de hacerse oír en aquella cocina dominada por sombríos presagios. Y ahora no era sólo Olvido. A los innombrables temores de la anciana se había unido el espectacular terror de Matilde. Rezaba, conjuraba, gemía. Se las veía más unidas que nunca, murmurando sin descanso, farfullando frases inconexas,

bottoms of kitchen pans, in varnishing cupboards and larders, or whitening the grouting between the mosaic tiles, I knew she would be moving through the dining room, cautiously mounting the bottom treads, standing still on the little landing and just looking. I would imagine her just standing there looking at it with the courage that came from not really being there in front of the bronze pendulum, but instead safe in her world of cooking pots and frying pans, a place where the ticking of the clock didn't reach and where the sound of the inevitable chimes could easily be drowned out.

But she scarcely spoke. Only on that now distant morning when my father, crossing seas and traversing deserts, explained to the children where Baghdad was, Olvido had dared to mutter: 'Too far away.' And then, turning her back on the object of our admiration she made her way along the corridor, shaking her head grumpily, talking to herself as she went.

'They can't even be Christians', she then added.

In the beginning, and even though I regretted the sudden change that had taken place in our lives, I attached no great importance to Olvido's ramblings. The years seemed to have suddenly come crashing down on the old woman's fragile body, on those shoulders which were determined to grow more and more hunched as the days went by. But a chance event proved the final straw for the rarified atmosphere of those days. To me, with my child's mind, it was an accident; to my parents, it was a piece of bad luck; to Olvido, it was the confirmation of her suspicions. Because it had taken place alongside the noisy faceless group in front of the bronze pendulum, facing the little gold-plated hands. Matilde was bringing up the shine on the little box of heavenly bodies, the Sun and the Moon, the nameless stars which made up the tiny procession, when her mind suddenly went blank, she made a grab for the sand balances, tried to position her feet on some non-existent step, to prevent a fall which looked inevitable. But the fickle step ladder refused to support that wobbling body any longer. It was an accident, a fainting fit, a momentary blackout. Matilde didn't feel well. She had been saying so just that morning as she was getting the little ones dressed. She felt sick, her stomach was upset, it could have been last night's dinner, who was to say it wasn't a secret and treacherous drink taken by the warmth of the fire. Yet it was impossible to make yourself heard in that kitchen dominated by omens. And now it wasn't just Olvido. To the old lady's unnameable fears had been added Matilde's spectacular terror. She would pray, she would ward off spirits and she would wail. They were more united than ever, muttering

intercambiándose consejos y plegarias. La antigua rivalidad, a la hora de competir con su arsenal de prodigios y espantos, quedaba ya lejos. Se diría que aquellas historias, con las que nos hacían vibrar de emoción, no eran más que juegos. Ahora, por primera vez, las sentía asustadas.

Durante aquel invierno fui demorando, poco a poco, el regreso del colegio. Me detenía en las plazas vacías, frente a los carteles del cine, ante los escaparates iluminados de la calle principal. Retrasaba en lo posible el inevitable contacto con las noches de la casa, súbitamente tristes, inesperadamente heladas, a pesar de que la leña siguiera crujiendo en el fuego y de que de la cocina surgieran aromas a bollo recién hecho y a palomitas de maíz. Mis padres, inmersos desde hacía tiempo en los preparativos de un viaje, no parecían darse cuenta de la nube siniestra que se había introducido en nuestro territorio. Y nos dejaron solos. Un mundo de viejas y niños solos. Subiendo la escalera en fila, cogidos de la mano, sin atrevernos a hablar, a mirarnos a los ojos, a sorprender en el otro un destello de espanto que, por compartido, nos obligara a nombrar lo que no tenía nombre. Y ascendíamos escalón tras escalón con el alma encogida, conteniendo la respiración en el primer descansillo, tomando carrerilla hasta el rellano, deteniéndonos unos segundos para recuperar el aliento, continuando silenciosos los últimos tramos del camino, los latidos del corazón azotando nuestro pecho, unos latidos precisos, rítmicos, perfectamente sincronizados. Y, ya en el dormitorio, las viejas acostaban a los pequeños en sus camas, niños olvidados de su capacidad de llanto, de su derecho a inquirir, de la necesidad de conjurar con palabras sus inconfesados terrores. Luego nos daban las buenas noches, nos besaban en la frente y, mientras yo prendía una débil lucecita junto al cabezal de mi cama, las oía dirigirse con pasos arrastrados hacia su dormitorio, abrir la puerta, cuchichear entre ellas, lamentarse, suspirar. Y después dormir, sin molestarse en apagar el tenue resplandor de la desnuda bombilla, sueños agitados que pregonaban a gritos el silenciado motivo de sus inquietudes diurnas, el Señor Innombrado, el Amo y Propietario de nuestras viejas e infantiles vidas.

La ausencia de mis padres no duró más que unas semanas, tiempo suficiente para que, a su regreso, encontraran la casa molestamente alterada. Matilde se había marchado. Un mensaje, una carta del pueblo, una hermana doliente que reclamaba angustiada su presencia. Pero ¿cómo podia ser? ¿Desde cuándo Matilde tenía hermanas? Nunca hablaba de ella pero conservaba una hermana en la aldea. Aquí estaba la carta: sobre la cuadrícula del papel una mano temblorosa explicaba los pormenores del imprevisto. No tenían más que

ceaselessly, jabbering unconnected phrases, exchanging advice and prayers between themselves. The rivalry of yesterday, the pitting of their arsenal of marvels and terrors against each other, was now a thing of the distant past. You might say those stories which used to make us quake with excitement were no more than games. Now, for the first time, I felt that they were afraid.

During the winter I gradually took longer and longer to get home from school. I would linger in the empty squares, in front of cinema posters, in front of the bright shop windows in the high street. I would put off for as long as possible the inevitable contact with nights at home, suddenly sad, unexpectedly icy, in spite of the fact that the firewood still crackled in the hearth and the aroma of freshly baked rolls and popcorn still floated out of the kitchen. My parents, long immersed in getting ready for a trip, appeared to be unaware of the sinister cloud that had gathered over us. And they left us alone. A world of old ladies and children left alone. Climbing the stairs Indian file, holding hands, not daring to speak, to catch each other's eye, to catch the other in a burst of terror that, by being shared, might compel us to name that which had no name. And we would go on up, step after step, our hearts in our mouths, holding our breath on the first landing, running as fast as we could to the next, pausing for a few seconds to catch our wind, continuing on the last few treads of the stairway in silence, the beating of our hearts pounding in our chests – precise, rhythmic, perfectly sunchronized beats. And, once in the bedroom, the old ladies would put the children to bed, children who had forgotten their capacity for tears, their right to ask questions, their need to stave off their unconfessed terrors with words. Then they would bid us goodnight, kiss us on the forehead and, as I was lighting the little night light by the side of my bed, I would hear them shuffling along to their bedroom, opening the door, whispering to one another, complaining and sighing. And then to sleep, without bothering to turn off the weak light cast by the bare light bulb, restless dreams that louldly announced the hushed-up reason for their daytime worries, the Unnamed Lord, the Master and Owner of our lives in old age and in childhood.

My parents' absence lasted no more than a few weeks, time enough though for them to find the house annoyingly altered when they returned. Matilde had left. Some message, a letter from the village, a sister in trouble anxiously demanding her presence. But how could that be? Since when did Matilde have sisters? She never talked about one, yet she still had a sister in the village. Here was the letter: on the scrap of squared paper a trembling hand explained the details of the unforeseen occurrence. They only had to

leerla. Matilde la había dejado con este propósito: para que comprendieran que hizo lo que hizo porque no tenía otro remedio. Pero era una carta sin franqueo. ¿Cómo podía haber llegado hasta la casa? La trajo un pariente. Un hombre apareció una mañana por la puerta con una carta en la mano. ¿Y esa curiosa y remilgada redacción? Mi madre buscaba entre sus libros un viejo manual de cortesía y sociedad. Aquellos billetes de pésame, de felicitación de cambio de domicilio, de comunicación de desgracias. Esa carta la había leído ya alguna vez. Si Matilde quería abandonarnos no tenía necesidad de recurrir a ridículas excusas. Pero ella, Olvido, no podía contestar. Estaba cansada, se sentía mal, había aguardado a que regresaran para declararse enferma. Y ahora, prostrada en el lecho de su dormitorio, no deseaba otra cosa que reposar, que la dejaran en paz, que desistieran de sus intentos para que se decidiera a probar bocado. Su garganta se negaba a engullir alimento alguno, a beber siquiera un sorbo de agua. Cuando se acordó la conveniencia de que los pequeños y yo misma pasáramos unos días en casa de lejanos familiares y subí a despedirme de Olvido, creí encontrarme ante una mujer desconocida. Había adelgazado de manera alarmante, sus ojos parecían enormes, sus brazos, un manojo de huesos y venas. Me acarició la cabeza casi sin rozarme, esbozando una mueca que ella debió suponer sonrisa, supliendo con el brillo de su mirada las escasas palabras que lograban aflorar a sus labios. 'Primero pensé que algún día tenía que ocurrir', masculló, 'que unas cosas empiezan y otras acaban…' Y luego, como presa de un pavor invencible, asiéndose de mis trenzas, intentando escupir algo que desde hacía tiempo ardía en su boca y ya empezaba a quemar mis oídos: 'Guárdate. Protégete… ¡No te descuides ni un instante!'

Siete días después, de regreso a casa, me encontré con una habitación sórdidamente vacía, olor a desinfectante y colonia de botica, el suelo lustroso, las paredes encaladas, ni un solo objeto ni una prenda personal en el armario. Y, al fondo, bajo la ventana que daba al mar, todo lo que quedaba de mi adorada Olvido: un colchón desnudo, enrollado sobre los muelles oxidados de la cama.

Pero apenas tuve tiempo de sufrir su ausencia. La calamidad había decidido ensañarse con nosotros, sin darnos respiro, negándonos un reposo que iba revelándose urgente. Los objetos se nos caían de las manos, las sillas se quebraban, los alimentos se descomponían. Nos sabíamos nerviosos, agitados, inquietos. Debíamos esforzarnos, prestar mayor atención a todo cuanto hiciéramos, poner el máximo cuidado en cualquier actividad por

read it. Matilde had left it with this aim in mind: that they might understand that what she'd done, she had done because there was no alternative. But it was a letter without a postage mark. How could it have got as far as the house? A relative had delivered it. A man appeared at the door one morning with a letter in his hand. And that curious and affected wording? My mother looked amongst her books for an old guide to good manners and social etiquette. Those little notes of condolences, of congratulations for some change of address, the communication of an unhappy event. She had read that letter before. If Matilde wanted to leave us, she had no need to resort to ridiculous excuses. But she, Olvido, could not answer. She was tired, she felt poorly, she had waited until they came home before saying she was ill. And now, stretched out on the bed in her room she wanted nothing more than to rest, to be left in peace, for them to stop trying to get her to eat a little something. Her throat refused to swallow any food or to take even a sip of water. When it was agreed it would be a good idea if the little ones and I should spend a few days with some distant relatives, I went up to say goodbye to Olvido, and I thought I was standing before a woman I didn't know. She had lost an alarming amount of weight, her eyes looked enormous, her arms were all bones and veins. She stroked my head almost without touching me, twisting her face into what she must have thought was a smile, making up for the few words that managed to fall from her lips with the glitter of her eyes. 'At first I thought it had to happen one day', she mouthed, 'that certain things would begin, and others come to an end...' And then, as if in the grip of some invincible dread, she grasped at my plaits, trying to spit out something that had been burning in her mouth for a long time and now began to burn in my ears: 'Be on your guard. Look after yourself... Don't be careless for even a second!'

Seven days later, when I got home, I found a room that was meanly empty, smelling of disinfectant and chemist's cologne, the floor shining, the walls whitewashed, not one single object or item of personal clothing in the wardrobe. And at the far end, under the window that looked out over the sea, all that was left of my beloved Olvido: a bare mattress, rolled up on top of the rusty bed-springs.

But I scarcely had time to feel her absence. Disaster had decided to vent its spleen on us without allowing us pause for breath, denying us the rest that was proving so imperative. Objects fell from our hands, chairs broke, food went off. We felt nervous, agitated, worried. We had to make an effort to pay greater attention to everything we did, to afford maximum care to

nimia y cotidiana que pudiera parecernos. Pero, aún así, a pesar de que lucháramos por combatir aquel creciente desasosiego, yo intuía que el proceso de deterioro al que se había entregado la casa no podía detenerse con simples propósitos y buenas voluntades. Eran tantos los olvidos, tan numerosos los descuidos, tan increíbles las torpezas que cometíamos de continuo, que ahora, con la distancia de los años, contemplo la tragedia que marcó nuestras vidas como un hecho lógico e inevitable. Nunca supe si aquella noche olvidamos retirar los braseros, o si lo hicimos de forma apresurada, como todo lo que emprendíamos en aquellos días, desatentos a la minúscula ascua escondida entre los faldones de la mesa camilla, entre los flecos de cualquier mantel abandonado a su desidia... Pero nos arrancaron del lecho a gritos, nos envolvieron en mantas, bajamos como enfebrecidos las temibles escaleras, pobladas, de pronto, de un humo denso, negro, asfixiante. Y luego, ya a salvo, a pocos metros del jardín, un espectáculo gigantesco e imborrable. Llamas violáceas, rojas, amarillas, apagando con su fulgor las primeras luces del alba, compitiendo entre ellas por alcanzar las cimas más altas, surgiendo por ventanas, hendiduras, claraboyas. No había nada que hacer, dijeron, todo estaba perdido. Y así, mientras, inmovilizados por el pánico, contemplábamos la lucha sin esperanzas contra el fuego, me pareció como si mi vida fuera a extinguirse en aquel preciso instante, a mis escasos doce años, envuelta en un murmullo de lamentaciones y condolencias, junto a una casa que hacía tiempo había dejado de ser mi casa. El frío del asfalto me hizo arrugar los pies. Los noté desmesurados, ridículos, casi tanto como las pantorrillas que asomaban por las perneras de un pijama demasiado corto y estrecho. Me cubrí con la manta y, entonces, asestándome el tiro de gracia, se oyó la voz. Surgió a mis espaldas, entre baúles y archivadores, objetos rescatados al azar, cuadros sin valor, jarrones de loza, a lo sumo un par de candelabras de plata.

Sé que, para los vecinos congregados en el Paseo, no fue más que la oportuna melodía de un hermoso reloj. Pero, a mis oídos, había sonado como unas agudas, insidiosas, perversas carcajadas.

Aquella misma madrugada se urdió la ingenua conspiración de la desmemoria. De la vida en el pueblo recordaríamos sólo el mar, los paseos por la playa, las casetas listadas del verano. Fingí adaptarme a los nuevos tiempos, pero no me perdí detalle, en los días inmediatos, de todo cuanto se habló en

whatever activity, however trifling and routine it might appear to us. But even so, in spite of the fact that we fought to combat that growing disquiet, I sensed that the process of deterioration to which the house had succumbed could not be stopped by resolution and good will alone. There were so many things we forgot to do, so numerous the oversights, so incredible the mistakes we made time and again that now, with hindsight, I look back on the tragedy that blighted our lives as a logical and inevitable event. I never knew whether we forgot to take out the braziers that night, or whether we did so in a hurry, like everything else we did in those days, neglectful of some tiny ember hidden amongst the flaps of the table that had the heater under it, between the fringes of some tablecloth carelessly flung down… But, with shouts and screams, they plucked us from our beds, wrapped us in blankets, and we rushed down the terrifying staircase, suddenly filled with dense, black, choking smoke, as if we were suffering from some fever. And then, safe now, a few yards away, in the garden, there was a huge and unforgettable sight. Violet, red, yellow flames, eclipsing the early dawn light with their glow, competing with one another to see which could reach the greatest height, bursting through windows, cracks in the brickwork, skylights. There was nothing that could be done, they said, all was lost. And thus it was that, immobilized by panic, as we stood there watching the hopeless battle against the fire, it seemed as if my life was about to be extinguished at that very instant, at just twelve years old, enveloped in a murmur of lamentations and expressions of sympathy, beside a house that had ceased to be my home some time ago. The cold of the asphalt made me scrunch my feet. They looked enormous, ridiculous, to me – almost like the calves of my legs that were sticking out from my too short and too tight pyjama bottoms. I covered myself up with the blanket and then, dealing me the *coup de grâce*, I heard the voice. It came from behind me, from between trunks and filing cabinets, things rescued at random, worthless pictures, earthware jugs, the best things a pair of silver candlesticks.

I know that for the neighbours gathered on the promenade it was only the untimely chime of a beautiful clock. But to my ears it had sounded like a sharp, treacherous, perverse shout of laughter.

That same early morning the ingenuous conspiracy of poor memory started its plotting. Of life in the village we were to recall only the sea, the walks along the beach, the striped summer bathing tents. I pretended to adapt myself to the new times, but in the days that followed I never missed a word of

mi menospreciada presencia. El anticuario se obstinaba en rechazar el reloj aduciendo razones de dudosa credibilidad. El mecanismo se hallaba deteriorado, las maderas carcomidas, las fechas falsificadas... Negó haber poseído, alguna vez, un objeto de tan desmesurado tamaño y redomado mal gusto, y aconsejó a mi padre que lo vendiera a un trapero o se deshaciera de él en el vertedero más próximo. No obedeció mi familia al olvidadizo comerciante, pero sí, en cambio, adquirió su pasmosa tranquilidad para negar evidencias. Nunca más pude yo pronunciar el nombre prohibido sin que se culpase a mi fantasía, a mi imaginación, o a las inocentes supersticiones de ancianas ignorantes. Por la noche de San Juan, cuando abandonábamos para siempre el pueblo de mi infancia, mi padre mandó detener el coche de alquiler en las inmediaciones de la calle principal. Y entonces lo vi. A través del humo, los vecinos, los niños reunidos en torno a las hogueras. Parecía más pequeño, desamparado, lloroso. Las llamas ocultaban las figuras de los danzarines, el juego de autómatas se había desprendido de la caja, y la esfera colgaba, inerte, sobre la puerta de cristal que, en otros tiempos, encerrara un péndulo. Pensé en un gigante degollado y me estremecí. Pero no quise dejarme vencer por la emoción. Recordando antiguas aficiones, entorné los ojos.

Ella estaba allí. Riendo, danzando, revoloteando en torno a las llamas junto a sus viejas amigas. Jugueteaba con las cadenas como si estuvieran hechas de aire y, con sólo proponérselo, podía volar, saltar, unirse sin ser vista al júbilo de los niños, al estrépito de petardos y cohetes. 'Olvido', dije, y mi propia voz me volvió a la realidad.

Vi como mi padre reforzaba la pira, atizaba el fuego y regresaba jadeante al automóvil. Al abrir la puertecilla, se encontró con mis ojos expectantes. Fiel a la ley del silencio, nada dijo. Pero me sonrió, me besó en las mejillas y, aunque jamás tendré ocasión de recordárselo, sé que su mano me oprimió la nuca para que mirara hacia el frente y no se me ocurriera sentir un asomo de piedad o tristeza.

Aquélla fue la última vez que, entornando los ojos, supe verlas.

what was said in my unheeded presence. The antiques dealer dug his heels in about taking the clock back, advancing reasons of dubious credibility. The mechanism had deteriorated, the woodwork was worm-eaten, the dates had been fiddled with… He denied ever having at any time owned such an unduly large object in such out-and-out bad taste and advised my father that he should sell it to a rag-and-bone man or get rid of it on the nearest rubbish tip. My family ignored the words of the absent-minded dealer, and instead acquired an ashtonishing calmness in order to deny the obvious. I could never again speak the proscribed name out loud without my fantasy, my imagination or the innocent superstitious of ignorant old women getting the blame. But on St John's Eve,[1] when we turned out our backs forever on the village where I'd spent my childhood, my father ordered the hired car to stop near the main street. And then I saw it. Through the smoke, the neighbours, the children gathered round the blazing bonfire. It looked smaller, forsaken, sad. The flames hid the figures of the dancers, the set of automata had sprung from the casing and the dial was hanging down, motionless, on top of the glass door which had at one time enclosed the pendulum. It reminded me of a decapited giant and I shivered. Yet I didn't want to allow my emotions to get the better of me. Remembering former fondness, I screwed up my eyes.

She was there. Laughing, dancing, fluttering round the flames with her old friends. She was playing with the chains as if they were made of air and by just thinking of it she could fly, leap, merge without being seen with the whoopings of the children, with the tremendous noise of firecrackers and rockets. 'Olvido', I said, and my own voice brought me back to reality.

I watched how my father was banking up the pyre, stoking the fire and returning to the car, out of breath. On opening the car door he found himself looking into my expectant eyes. True to the law of silence, he said nothing. But he smiled at me, kissed me on both cheeks and, though I shall never have occasion to remind him of it, I know his hand pressed the back of my neck to make me look straight ahead and it didn't cross my mind to feel the slightest trace of pity or sadness.

Through half-closed eyes, that was the last time I succeeded in seeing them.

---

1   **St John's Eve**: on the night of 23rd of June, the eve of St John's Day, the beginning of summer is celebrated with bonfires in some areas of Spain, such as Catalonia.

EL ENCUENTRO

A CHANCE ENCOUNTER

Original Spanish text
first published in *Sur Express* 3 (1987),
later collected in *Relatos de mujeres. 2*
(Madrid: Popular, 1988, 51–66)
© Adelaida García Morales, 1987

ADELAIDA GARCÍA MORALES was born in Badajoz in 1945, and at the age of eleven moved to Seville, the city where her family came from. She graduated in Philosophy from the Universidad Complutense, Madrid, and went on to study script writing at the Escuela Oficial de Cinematografía. She worked as a secondary school teacher, a translator and a model. She was also part of Esperpento, an independent theatre group based in Seville. Her first book, published in 1985, consisted of two novellas, *El sur* and *Bene. El sur*, an intense exploration of the relationship between a Republican father struggling to cope with interior exile in Franco's Spain and his devoted daughter, won Adelaida García Morales acclaim before it was even published. Written in 1981, it provided the basis for the film of the same title which Víctor Erice, her husband at the time, directed with great success in 1983. Even though producer Elías Querejeta withdrew his economic support before it was finished, *El sur* remains one of the best films ever made in Spain. The characters created by Adelaida García Morales are key to examine the devastating effects of the dictatorship on those who lost the Civil War but continued to live in Spain. In 1985, she published one of her most successful novels, *El silencio de las sirenas*, for which she was awarded the Premio Herralde. It is a tale of romantic love in which an Adèle Hugo-like character is observed by a bemused female friend, the narrator of the story. In 1985, Adelaida García Morales also won the Premio Ícaro, an accolade bestowed to the best literary newcomer of the year by the newspaper *Diario 16*. She went on to publish nine more novels and a collection of short stories, all of them with solitary, enigmatic and complex female characters that often have to deal with mystery, suspense and horror: 'lo innombrable', as Ignacio Echevarría described it in 1990 (see bibliography below). A committed left-

wing thinker, in the 1990s she occasionaly published articles (such as 'La primavera socialista, a pesar de todo', *El País*, 24 February 1996) in which she talked openly about her politics. However, she gradually withdrew from public life, which helped to create an image of her as a forgotten figure by the time she died of heart failure on 22 September 2014, in the Sevillian town of Dos Hermanas. Then controversy began when, in 2016, the novelist Elvira Navarro published a book with the misleading title of *Los últimos días de Adelaida García Morales*, which gives the impression that it is a biographical account of the writer at the end of her life. However, Elvira Navarro, as she herself admitted, never researched Adelaida's biography: 'yo no me he sumergido en su biografía sino [...] en su leyenda. Adelaida García Morales es en mi libro una excusa para abordar algunos temas que me inquietan, como la desaparición, la relación entre el arte y las instituciones o el desamor de este país hacia su patrimonio' [I have not immersed myself in her biography, but in her legend. In my book AGM is an excuse to deal with issues that concern me, such as how someone can disappear, the relationship between art and institutions, and the lack of care in this country regarding its patrimony] (http://www.abc.es/cultura/cultural/abci-adelaida-garcia-morales-estaba-fuera-canon-201609191312_noticia.html). The book is based entirely on a story told to Navarro by a friend: Adelaida went to the Delegación de Igualdad of the Dos Hermanas City Council and asked for 50 euros to go to Madrid to see her younger son, a petition that was denied as nobody in the City Council knew who she was. Taking this as a starting point, the book fantasizes about Adelaida García Morales's life as a recluse and creates characters and situations with the apparent intention of exposing the invisibility of women writers in Spain. Although Navarro's *Los últimos días de Adelaida García Morales* received mixed reviews, and some critics welcomed its quality as a 'falso documental' [false documentary], as it is described on the book's blurb, the result is far from convincing. Indeed, it encourages the 'legend' of the writer as a hermit and as a pauper, someone with an excentric personality who is too fragile to face the world. But even if that were the case, the uninformed appropriation and problematic representation of Adelaida García Morales as the main character discussed by others in Navarro's book, show very little genuine respect for one of the most interesting contemporary Spanish writers. Rather, it is a way of using Adelaida García Morales's persona for Navarro's literary benefit, and elaborates on her 'legend' to a perilous point of explotation: *ABC* run an article entitled 'Adelaida García Morales, el ángel negro de la literatura

española' [AGM, the black angel of Spanish literature] (http://www.abc.
es/cultura/cultural/abci-adelaida-garcia-morales-angel-negro-literatura-
espanola-201609190411_noticia.html). Víctor Erice, the father of Adelaida's
younger son, published an article entitled 'Una vida robada' in *El País* (http://
cultura.elpais.com/cultura/2016/09/29/babelia/1475153443_790435.html)
complaining against Navarro's book: 'Adelaida no fue una persona común;
tampoco una fantasmagoría. Nunca logró integrarse en la sociedad, y eso
la honra' [Adelaida was neither an ordinary person nor a ghost. She never
managed to fit into society, and she deserves credit for that]. Erice regrets
that the book does not consider the harm that it may inflict on others like
Pablo, their seventeen-year old son. He adds: 'El libro entraña una falsa
reividicación de Adelaida; banaliza su memoria como escritora y su identidad
como ser humano' [The book is a false vindication of Adelaida: it trivialises
her memory as a writer and her identity as a human being]. When Adelaida
García Morales died, most obituaries in Spanish newspapers claimed that
she had been forgotten and that, if she was remembered at all, it was in
relation to Erice's film. It is not unusual for a woman writer to see her work
reduced to one of her titles, especially if that association involves a male
figure, but this claim was not entirely correct: she might have been forgotten
in Spain, but she certainly was not among Anglosaxon academics with an
interest in female authors from Spain: in 2006 Abigail Lee Six published a
monograph exploring the Gothic elements of her fiction, *The Gothic Fiction
of Adelaida García Morales: Haunting Words* (see bibliography below), that
placed her novels within a European tradition in which Mary Shelley, the
author of *Frankenstein* (1816–1817), is a prominent figure. There were also
scholarly articles on her fiction as late as 2013. Besides, Abigail Lee Six is
currently writing a monograph on Spanish vampire fiction to be published
by Routledge, in which a discussion of Adelaida García Morales's last
novel, *La lógica del vampiro*, will be a significant inclusion. Even if she was
forgotten in Spain because she had chosen to live her life in a different and
more personal way, the use of her persona as a metaphor is a questionable
strategy to restore the reputation she deserves. The fact that it may have
been done as a defence of female authorship should be no excuse.

Bibliography of Adelaida García Morales

Novels

El sur seguido de *Bene* (Barcelona: Anagrama, 1985).

El silencio de las sirenas (Barcelona: Anagrama, 1985) – *Premio Herralde 1985; Premio Ícaro 1985.*

La lógica del vampiro (Barcelona: Anagrama, 1990).

Las mujeres de Héctor (Barcelona: Anagrama, 1994).

La tía Águeda (Barcelona: Anagrama, 1995).

Nasmiya (Barcelona: Plaza & Janés, 1996).

La señorita Medina (Barcelona: Plaza y Janés, 1997).

El accidente (Madrid: Anaya, 1997).

El secreto de Elisa (Madrid: Debate, 1999).

Una historia perversa (Barcelona: Planeta, 2001).

El testamento de Regina (Madrid: Debate, 2001).

Short story collection

Mujeres solas (Barcelona: Plaza & Janés, 1996).

Short stories in anthologies (a selection)

'El encuentro', *Sur Express*, 3 (1987).

'El encuentro', in *Relatos de mujeres (2)* (Madrid: Popular, 1987).

'La carta', in M. Monmany (ed.), *Vidas de mujer* (Madrid: Alianza, 1998).

'El legado de Amparo', in *Mujeres al alba* (Madrid: Alfaguara, 1999).

'La mirada', F. Marías (ed.), *Don Juan* (Zaragoza: 451 Editores, 2008).

Further reading on Adelaida García Morales

Lourdes Albuixech, 'Recurring Themes and Techniques in Adelaida García Morales 's Narrative', *Hispanófila* 151 (2008), 93–103. http://www.jstor.org/stable/43808498

Ernesto Ayala-Dip, 'Fallece la escritora Adelaida García Morales', *El País*, 24 September 2014. http://cultura.elpais.com/cultura/2014/09/24/actualidad/1411565352_547495.html

Miguel Bayón, 'Mujeres escritoras: la mirada que ve desde el rincón', *Cambio 16*, 24 November 1986, 149–52.

Katarzina Olga Beilin, 'Por qué no somos transparentes? *El silencio de las sirenas* de Adelaida García Morales como un viaje filosófico de Hegel a Lacan', *Anales de la Literatura Española Contemporánea* 28.3 (2003), 39–60.

Ana Bundgård, 'Adelaida García Morales: *El silencio de las sirenas* (1985)', in *La dulce mentira de la ficción: ensayos sobre narrativa española actual* (Bonn: Romanistischer Verlag, 1995), 15–30.

Soledad Cano, 'Adelaida García Morales: "El giro a la derecha supone retroceso"', *Cambio 16*, 25 March 1995, 100–101.

Lucille C. Charlebois, 'Adelaida García Morales. *El testamento de Regina*', *España Contemporánea* 15.2 (2002), 115–17.

Lucille C. Charlebois, 'Adelaida García Morales. *Una historia perversa'*, *España Contemporánea* 16.1 (2003), 123–26.

Aristófanes Cedeño, '*El silencio de las sirenas* o la ambivalencia mítica de la destrucción del monstruo', *Letras Peninsulares* 15.3 (2002), 645–66.

Biruté Ciplijauskaite, 'Una historia de amor desde la perspectiva kafkiana', *Ínsula,* 488–89 (1987), 24.

Biruté Ciplijauskaite, 'Intertextualidad y subversión en *El silencio de las sirenas*, de Adelaida García Morales', *Revista Hispánica Moderna* 49 (1988), 167–73.

Birute Ciplijauskaité, *La novela femenina contemporánea (1970–1985). Hacia una tipología de la narración en primera persona* (Barcelona: Anthropos, 1994).

Biruté Ciplijauskaite, 'Intertextualidad y subversión en *El silencio de las sirenas* de Adelaida García Morales', in *La construcción del yo femenino en la literatura* (Cádiz: Servicio de Publicaciones de la Universidad de Cádiz, 2004), 157–67.

Malcom Allan Compitello, 'Making *El sur*', *Revista Hispánica Moderna* 46.1 (1993), 73–86.

María Dolores de Asís Garrote, *Última hora de la novela en España* (Madrid: Pirámide, 1996).

Itziar de Francisco, 'Adelaida García Morales: "La mujer es la reserva de la vida. El hombre ha jugado su partida con la existencia y la ha perdido"', *El Cultural*, 17 January 2001. http://www.elcultural.com/revista/letras/Adelaida-Garcia-Morales/13341

Mercedes de Grado, *La rebelión de las sirenas: identidad y debate feminista en la narrativa de Adelaida García Morales* (PhD, University of Durham, 2002).

Luis de la Peña, 'Sobre la fragilidad del amor', *El País* (Babelia), 2 March 1996.

Luis de la Peña, 'La melancolía de García Morales', *El País* (Babelia), 29 November 1997.

Thomas G. Deveny, *Contemporary Spanish Film from Fiction* (Lanham, MD: Scarecrow Press, 2003).

Ignacio Echevarría, 'Lo innombrable: Adelaida García Morales aborda con delicadeza la fantasía y el terror', *El País* (Libros), 3 June 1990.

Peter Evans and Robin Fiddian,'Víctor Erice's *El sur*: A Narrative of Star-Cross'd Lovers', *Bulletin of Hispanic Studies* 54.2 (1987), 127–35.

Andrés Fernández Rubio, 'Adelaida García Morales plantea en su nueva obra la complejidad de un triángulo amoroso. *Nasmiya* indaga en las posibilidades del amor "fuera de los esquemas culturales"', *El País*, 23 January 1996. http://elpais. com/diario/1996/01/23/cultura/822351603_850215.html

Carmela Ferradans, 'Identidad y transcendencia. La respuesta sublime de Adelaida

García Morales', *Letras Peninsulares* 7.2–3 (1994–1995), 473–84. https://works.bepress.com/carmela_ferradans/17/

Adolfo García Ortega, 'Españoles traducidos. Hacia la normalización', *El Urogallo* 23 (1988), 10–13.

Anna M. Gil, 'La lògica del vampir', *Avui* (Cultura), 27 September 2001.

Kathleen M. Glenn, 'Gothic Vision in García Morales and Erice's *El sur*', *Letras Peninsulares* 7.1 (1994), 239–50.

Shoshannah Rebecca Holdom, *Gothic Teatrality and Performance in the Works of Adelaida García Morales, Cristina Fernández Cubas and Pilar Pedraza* (PhD, University of Manchester, 2003).

Francisco Javier Higuero, 'Segmentariedades desterritorializadas en *Mujeres solas* de Adelaida García Morales', in J. Romera Castillo and F. Gutiérrez Carbajo (eds), *El cuento en la década de los noventa: actas del X Seminario Internacional del Instituto de Semiótica Literaria, Teatral y Nuevas Tecnologías de la UNED (Madrid, 31 de mayo-2 de junio de 2000)* (Madrid: Visor Libros; UNED, 2001), 197–206.

Francisco Javier Higuero, 'Prevalencia diegética de segmentariedades en *Mujeres solas* de Adelaida García Morales', *Hispanófila* 137 (2003), 69–82.

Yvonne Jehenson, 'Adelaida García Morales', in L. Gould Levine, E. Engleson Marson and G. Feiman Waldson (eds), *Spanish Women Writers: A Bio-Bibliographical Source Book* (Westport, CT and London: Greenwood Press, 1993), 211–18.

Abigail Lee Six, 'Mens's Problems: Feelings and Fatherhood in *El sur* by Adelaida García Morales and *París* by Marcos Giralt Torrente, *Bulletin of Spanish Studies* 79 (2002), 753–70.

Abigail Lee Six, *The Gothic Fiction of Adelaida García Morales: Haunting Words* (Woodbridge: Tamesis, 2006).

Abigail Lee Six, 'Regina in *El testamento de Regina*', in *Gothic Terrors, Incarceration, Duplication, and Bloodlust in Spanish Narrative* (Lewisberg: Bucknell University Press, 2010), 47–60.

Abigail Lee Six, '"Confusa la historia y clara la pena". The Child's Perspective in *El sur* and *Bene*, by Adelaida García Morales', *Forum for Modern Languages Studies* 49.2 (2013), 184–91.

Montserrat Lunati, 'Breaking Silences, Dealing with the Past: *El sur*, by Adelaida García Morales (1985) and Víctor Erice (1983)', in J. London and D. George (eds), *Spanish Film, Theatre and Literature in the Twentieth Century,* (Cardiff: University of Wales Press, 2007), 146–59.

Coro Malaxechevarría, 'Mito y realidad en la narrativa de Adelaida García Morales', *Letras Femeninas* 17.1–2 (1991), 43–49.

Roberto Manteiga, 'From Empathy to Detachment: The Author-Narrator Relationship in Several Spanish Novels by Women', *Monographic Review / Revista Monográfica*, 8 (1992), 19–35.

Mercedes Mazquiarán de Rodríguez, 'The Metafictional Quest for Self-Realization and Authorial Voice in *El silencio de las sirenas*', *Romance Languages Annual* 2 (1990), 477–81.

Mercedes Mazquiarán de Rodríguez, 'Gothic Imagery, Dreams and Vampirism: The Haunting Narrative of Adelaida García Morales', *Monographic Review / Revista Monográfica* 8 (1992), 164–82.

Isaac Montero, ''¿Nuestra realidad ausente?', *República de las Letras* 8 (1987), 64–68.

Barbara Morris, 'Father, Death and the Feminine: The Writer's "Subject" in Adelaida García Morales's *El sur*', *Romance Languages Annual* 1 (1989), 559–64.

Gonzalo Navajas, 'Narrativa y género. La ficción actual desde la mujer', *Ínsula* 589–590 (1996), 37–39.

Gonzalo Navajas, *Más allá de la posmodernidad. Estética de la nueva novela y cine españoles* (Barcelona: Ediciones Universitarias de Barcelona, 1996).

Clare Nimmo, 'García Morales's and Erice's *El sur*: Viewpoint and Closure', *Romace Studies* 26 (1995), 41–49.

María José Obiol, 'El juego de las similitudes y las diferencias. Madurez en el oficio de contar', *El País* (Libros), 28 July 1985.

Joan Oleza, 'Un realismo posmoderno', *Ínsula* 589–90 (1996), 39–42.

Elizabeth J. Ordóñez, 'Writing Ambiguity and Desire: The Works of Adelaida García Morales', in J. L. Brown (ed.), *Women Writers of Contemporary Spain. Exiles in the Homeland* (Newark: University of Delaware Press, 1991), 258–77.

Elizabeth J. Ordóñez, 'Beyond the Father: Desire, Ambiguity, and Transgression in the Narrative of Adelaida García Morales', in *Voices of Their Own. Contemporary Spanish Narrative by Women* (Lewisburgh: Bucknell University Press, 1991), 174–92.

Janet Pérez, *Contemporary Women Writers of Spain* (Boston, MA: Twayne Publishers, 1988), 173–74.

Milagros Sánchez Arnosi, 'Adelaida García Morales: La soledad gozosa', *Ínsula* 472 (1986), 4.

Lluís Satorras, 'Mujeres atormentadas': Adelaida García Morales publica dos novelas en las que predominan los mundos privados femeninos', *El País*, 17 March 2001.

Elizabeth A. Scarlett, 'Nomads and Schizos: Postmodern Trends in Body Writing', in *Under Construction. The Body in Spanish Novels* (Charlottesville and London: 1994), 166–85.

Currie K. Thompson, 'Adelaida García Morales' *Bene* and That Not-So-Obscure Object of Desire', *Revista de Estudios Hispánicos* 22.1–2 (1988), 99–106.

Currie K. Thompson, '*El silencio de las sirenas:* Adelaida García Morales' Revision of the Feminine "Seescape"', *Revista Hispánica Moderna* 45.2 (1992), 298–309.

Antonio Ubach Medina, 'La infancia malvada. Rosa Chacel, Adelaida García

Morales y Almudena Grandes', in M. Arizmendi and G. Arbona Abascal (eds), *Letra de mujer. La escritura femenina y sus protagonistas analizados desde otra perspectiva* (Madrid: Ediciones del Laberinto, 2008), 301–11.

Further information online on Adelaida García Morales (a selection)

http://www.elmundo.es/cultura/2016/09/17/57dc245a46163f6c0d8b4626.html

http://cultura.elpais.com/cultura/2016/10/01/actualidad/1475344637_671002.html

http://cultura.elpais.com/cultura/2016/09/23/babelia/1474645760_427680.html

http://escritoras.com/escritoras/Adelaida-Garcia-Morales

http://www.revistavisperas.com/el-sur-de-adelaida-garcia-morales/

https://www.youtube.com/watch?v=I7utc7lHMwY

http://fama2.us.es/fco/frame/frame2/estudios/1.6.pdf

http://www.academia.edu/5539571/Imagenes_de_la_soledad_en_El_sur_y_Bene_de_Adelaida_Garcia_Morales

http://www.elperiodico.com/es/noticias/ocio-y-cultura/muere-adelaida-garcia-morales-autora-sur-3546263

http://www.biografiasyvidas.com/biografia/g/garcia_morales.htm

http://www.diariodesevilla.es/ocio/Sur-llora-Adelaida-Garcia-Morales_0_846815821.html

http://blogs.elconfidencial.com/cultura/mala-fama/2016-09-21/adelaida-garcia-morales-elvira-navarro-el-sur_1262765/

https://www.ahorasemanal.es/adelaida-garcia-morales-coleccionista-de-nostalgias

http://www.lavanguardia.com/obituarios/20140925/54416318483/adelaida-garcia-morales-origenes-el-sur.html

http://www.elespanol.com/cultura/libros/20160916/155984744_0.html

http://www.laopiniondezamora.es/blogs/hablamos-de-mujeres/adelaida-garcia-morales.html

http://www.zgrados.com/adelaida-garcia-morales/

http://desdelaciudadsincines.blogspot.co.uk/2016/11/los-ultimos-dias-de-adelaida-garcia.html

http://www.revistadelibros.com/articulos/la-senorita-medina-de-adelaida-garcia-morales

http://lamedicinadetongoy.blogspot.co.uk/2016/10/los-ultimos-dias-de-adelaida-garcia.html

http://www.andalan.es/?p=12791

http://unlibroaldia.blogspot.co.uk/2016/11/adelaida-garcia-morales-el-sur-seguido.html

https://fernandezpaton.net/2016/10/02/la-ficcion-a-partir-de-adelaida-garcia-morales-que-ha-escrito-elvira-navarro/

http://www.swarthmore.edu/Humanities/mguardi1/espanol_11/garciamorales.htm

http://www.ieturolenses.org/revista_turia/index.php/actualidad_turia/la-soledad-y-los-silencios-de-adelaida-garcia-morales

https://periodicoirreverentes.org/2016/10/13/adelaida-garcia-morales-mercant ilizacion-del-%C2%A8malditismo%C2%A8/

http://cultura.elpais.com/cultura/2014/09/24/actualidad/1411565352_547495.html

http://www.abc.es/cultura/libros/20140924/abci-adelaida-garcia-morales-201409241121.html

EL ENCUENTRO

De vez en cuando, forzado por el paso descontrolado del tiempo por mi vida, trato de detenerme con el fin de evaluar, clasificar, o simplemente recordar, mis actividades de la última semana. Pero un turbulento marasmo, constituido por retazos de lo vivido, entremezclados y confusos, aislados unos de otros, se adueña de mi memoria. Siempre recuerdo, más o menos, lo mismo: voy de aquí para allá, me dejo caer por el bar de la esquina, por el café de Milagros o por la cervecería de la plaza. A veces busco encuentros fortuitos por el barrio, forzando tontamente el azar, o bien me otorgo el derecho de introducirme en conversaciones ajenas. Si algo no puedo soportar es el silencio. No estoy capacitado para resistir un día entero sin hablar, sin decir cualquier cosa, lo que sea. Aunque no me importa reconocer que carezco de empatía y que tampoco soy de esos hombres que poseen una vocación definida. A pesar de las apariencias, detesto a los charlatanes y, de ningún modo, he decidido esta dispersión callejera a la que ya me he resignado. Lo que sucede es que para la otra alternativa, la de permancer en mi estrecha vivienda así, sin más, sin un televisor siquiera, sin ocupaciones y obligado a un mutismo absoluto, no me veo con aptitudes. Y menos aún ahora que acabo de renunciar a la comida diaria que me ofrecía mi hermana entre consejos y reprobaciones. Me había convertido en el blanco de todas las iras familiares. Incluso mis sobrinos más pequeños habían aprendido, imitando a sus padres, a juzgarme con parcialidad por cualquioer menudencia. No pienso volver a visitarles. Que se peguen entre ellos. He cumplido los treinta años y, dados los tiempos en que vivimos, se me puede considerar todavía un joven parado. Aunque mi cuñado, azuzado por la hostilidad que me profesa, asegura que mi desocupación nada tiene que ver con el paro actual. Afirma que lo mío es de otra índole, que son motivos muy diferentes a los comunes los que me mantienen alejado del trabajo. Yo diría que, por la animadversión con que me habla y por la delectación con que me insulta, cree haber descubierto móviles delictivos en mi infortunio. Hace apenas dos días nos enzarzamos en una enconada discusión, a raíz de mi inasistencia a una cita que él mismo había concertado. Me negué a acudir sólo por dignidad. Estaba convencido de que aquel supuesto conocido suyo, del que lo único que sabía era que se apellidaba Núñez, tampoco dispondría

A CHANCE ENCOUNTER

From time to time, forced by the hurtling passage of time in my life, I endeavour to slow down a bit so as to evaluate, classify, or simply recall what I did the week before. But a turbulent paralysis comprising snippets of personal experience all jumbled together and in no particular order, one isolated from the other, takes hold of my memory. I always remember more or less the same thing: I'm on my way from here to there, I drop in at the bar on the corner, the Milagros café or the pub in the square. Sometimes I'm on the lookout for chance encounters around the neighbourhood, stupidly pushing my luck, or else awarding myself the right to barge my way into somebody else's conversation. If there's one thing I can't stand is silence. I'm just not capable of going a whole day without speaking, without saying something, anything. I don't mind admitting, though, I have no empathy, neither am I one of those men who have some definite vocation. In spite of appearances, I detest smooth-talking tricksters and there's no way this wandering the streets I've resigned myself to now was my decision. The thing is, the other alternative – the one of staying put like this in my cramped room, with nothing else, not even a television, nothing to do and forced into total silence – I'm not capable of that. And even less so now that I've just given up the meal my sister used to provide me every day along with advice and reprimands. I'd become the target for all the family's wrath. Even the youngest of my nephews, copying their parents, had learned to sit in prejudiced judgement on me for every little thing. I don't think I'll go and see them again. Let them fight among themselves. I've reached the age of thirty and, given the times we live in, I might still be regarded as a young man who's out of work. Though my brother-in-law, egged on by the hostility he bears towards me, claims my not having a job's got nothing to do with the current unemployment statistics. He says that in my case it's something else, that the reasons that keep me out of a job are very different to the usual ones. I'd say that from the animosity he shows when he talks to me and the delight he takes in insulting me, he thinks he's uncovered criminal motives behind my misfortune. Scarcely two days ago we got involved in a heated row because I'd failed to turn up to some appointment he himself had set up. I refused to turn up solely out of self-respect. I was convinced that that so-called acquaintance of his, about whom the only thing I knew was that his name was Núñez, didn't have a job for me in his

de un empleo para mí en su Agencia. Ya a las últimas entrevistas que me había impuesto, me presenté desesperanzado, sin cambiar mi atuendo de costumbre, verstido al desgaire, sin preocuparme por lucir la indumentaria correcta. Finalmente, aunque guardé la tarjeta de visita, por si acaso, tuve el coraje de responderle verbalmente a sus ofensas y de despedirme jurando que, en lo sucesivo, sería para ellos sólo un muerto.

Aquella misma noche, gracias a las vicisitudes de la suerte, conecté con un viejo enjuto y barbicano, merodeador de papeleras públicas, basuras y otros deshechos. Casi tropiezo con él. Su deslucida figura se irguió de pronto ante mí, como surgiendo de entre grandes cubos repletos de desperdicios. El movimiento de sus dedos, casi vertiginoso, me retuvo a su lado, admirándole durante varios minutos. Estoy seguro de que en aquellos momentos no le incomodó mi curiosidad. Incluso me atrevería a afirmar que le complacía el disponer de un espectador ante el que exhibir la destreza de malabarista con que hizo volar el contenido íntegro de un cajón de madera. Pensé que el virtuosismo de aquellos dedos, tan extraño a la torpeza general del resto de su cuerpo, no podía ser sino el resultado de un prolongado y pertinaz entrenamiento. 'Nada, no hay nada!' protestó mientras, con un ademán rutinario de mendicidad, me tendía la mano hasta casi rozarme. Le di las buenas noches con agrado y permanecí inmóvil junto a él, como si acabara de llegar a una cita. El viejo murmuró algo a guisa de saludo y se arregló el nudo de la corbata que, a falta de cinturón, le sujetaba los pantalones. Debido a que no era un trasnochador y al quebrantamiento de mi ánimo por la ruptura familiar, pese a la independencia que ésta suponía, volví a desearle buenas noches, ahora con el fin de despedirme y continuar el camino hacia mi casa. '¡Espera, no te vayas! ¡Quédate conmigo hasta que se apaguen las luces de las calles, hasta que se haga de día!' Al escuchar su voz suplicante pensé que era un loco y aún así, me detuve. No me sentía capaz de salir corriendo sin responderle, sin mirarle siquiera, y menos aún de pasar la noche vagando a su lado por el asfalto. Enseguida intuí que no me resultaría fácil torcer su voluntad. Así que, abocado sin remedio a postergar la despedida, le invité a que me acompañara en mi recorrido. Su abrumador agradecimiento me forzó a precisar con descortesía que sólo andaríamos juntos hasta mi puerta. ¿Qué necesidad tenía yo de agobiarme creando compromisos en un encuentro tan insignificante? Pero, observando su lánguida figura, frente a mí, encogiéndose resignada en el interior de su

agency anyway. At the last interviews he'd forced down my throat I turned up without any real expectations, without altering the way I usually looked, without bothering to change the slovenly way I usually dressed, without bothering to wear the 'right' sort of clothes. Finally, and even though I kept the visiting card just in case, I found the courage to tackle him to his face about his offensive remarks, and then I left swearing that the next time they saw me I'd be in my coffin.

That same night, thanks to the vicissitudes of fortune, I bumped into a gaunt old man with a grey beard, a forager of public litter bins, rubbish tips and other sources of garbage. I nearly collided with him. His shabby figure suddenly reared up before my very eyes as if surging up from the midst of great bucketfuls of refuse. The giddy movement of his fingers held me at his side marvelling at him for several minutes. I'm convinced that during that time my curiosity didn't bother him. I'd even go as far as to say he was pleased to have an audience before which to exhibit how he could make the full contents of a wooden box vanish with all the dexterity of a juggler. I thought the great virtuosity of those fingers, so strangely at odds with the general clumsiness of the rest of his body, could only be the result of some extended and dedicated training. 'Nothing, there's nothing!' he complained, meanwhile stretching out his hand in a routine begging gesture until he was almost grazing me. I wished him a cheery good evening and stood still beside him, not moving a muscle, as if just turning up for an appointment. The old man muttered something by way of a greeting and arranged the knot of the tie that in the absence of a belt was holding up his trousers. Since I was not a night owl, and as my spirits were pretty low after the family bustup, despite the independence that implied, I again wished him good night, planning now to take my leave of him and continue on my way home. 'Wait, don't go! Stay with me 'till they turn out the street lights, 'till the morning comes!' Hearing his pleading voice I thought he was crazy, but even so I stopped. I felt I couldn't just run off without giving him an answer, without even looking at him, and even less spend the night wandering the streets with him. I guessed straightaway that it wouldn't be easy for me to change his mind. So, forced into agreeing to delay the leave-taking, I invited him to accompany me as I walked. His overwhelming gratitude drove me to make it rudely clear that we would only be walking together as far as my door. What need did I have to overburden myself by creating awkward situations in such a meaningless encounter? Yet watching his languid figure in front of me, resignedly cringing inside his coat, I was tempted to prolong the

chaqueta, estuve tentado a prolongar el paseo, pues nos hallábamos a pocos pasos de mi domicilio. No obstante, supe contenerme.

Emprendimos así una silenciosa marcha que a él debió parecerle un perfecto fraude, ya que, al detenerme para introducir la llave en la cerradura, sin esperar mi consentimiento, a modo de represalia, me comunicó que subiría conmigo.

'Nada de eso!' le dije con visible fastidio. Y, enseguida, mecánicamente, para suavizar mi negativa, añadí que no había ascensor y que, además, vivía en el ático. '¡Mejor!' exclamó el viejo, aclarando sin tardanza que despreciaba todos los aparatos eléctricos en general, pero que a los ascensores precisamente no los soportaba. Jamás se había dejado elevar por ninguno de ellos. No me importaba demasiado mostrarme grosero con él, o mezquino, o incluso duro, pero tampoco su presencia me repelía hasta el punto de dejarme enredar en un forcejeo que, tal vez, se prolongara durante toda la madrugada. Por otra parte, no encontré, en aquellos momentos, ninguna razón contundente que me impulsara a emplear la violencia con un pobre estólido. Y, ante todo, no se puede olvidar que era la primera vez en mi vida que alguien se empeñaba con testarudez en conseguir mi compañía. Claro que tal extravagancia más que complacido, me dejó desconcertado e indefenso ante aquel vagabundo que me observaba ansioso, casi con temor, como si esperase de mí algo parecido a una sentencia.

Emprendimos el ascenso a un ritmo normal hasta que, a mitad de la escalera, se detuvo jadeante. Ya en el último tramo tuve que transportarle, colgado por completo de mi cuello. Por fortuna, su cuerpo parecía consistir sólo en un esqueleto o armazón de alambre, cubierto directamente por la ropa. Atravesamos la azotea, sin prisa, hasta alcanzar mi propiedad: un estrecho rectángulo situado en una de las esquinas. Al entrar en la salita, el viejo se reanimó de golpe. Y como si hubiera sido impulsado por un resorte oculto, se entregó sin perder un instante a lo que, sin lugar a dudas, parecía ser la razón misma de su existencia. Todas sus facultades se pusieron, de inmediato, al servicio de sus dedos. Escrutó, palpó y tiró cuanto alcanzaron sus ojos. Nada podía satisfacerle. Y, como en cumplimiento de una mission fatídica, hizo volar un cenicero vacío, una bufanda, un peine mellado, unos calcetines, un frasquito de colirio, una caja de zapatos, recibos, periódicos y otros objetos abandonados sobre la gran mesa que ocupa, con exactitud geométrica, la mitad de la habitación. Después, pasó al otro lado, encaramándose con un pie en la butaca y el otro en el velador del rincón. En esta postura tenía acceso

walk since we were by this time just a few steps away from where I lived. Nevertheless, I managed to contain myself.

Thus we set off on a silent walk that to him must have seemed a complete fraud, because when I stopped to put the key in the lock, without waiting for my consent, by way of a reprisal, he said he'd come up with me. 'Oh no you won't!' I told him with visible annoyance. And then, almost immediately, mechanically, so as to smooth over my having said no, I added there was no lift and what was more I lived in the attic. 'All the better!' cried the old man, clarifying this without further ado by explaining that he had no time for electrical apparatus in general but it was lifts in particular he really couldn't abide. He'd never allowed himself to be carried up in one. I didn't care very much about how rude or mean or even callous I appeared to him, yet neither did his presence repel me to the point where I would allow myself to get embroiled in some struggle that might well go on into the early hours of the morning. On the other hand just then I found no convincing reason to drive me to use violence against a poor blockhead. Above all you mustn't forget this was the first time in my life that anybody had been so pig-headedly determined to seek out my company. Of course, such extravagance, rather than making me feel pleased, left me bewildered and defenceless in the presence of this tramp who was watching me anxiously, almost fearfully, as if were expecting something approaching a verdict from me.

We started our climb at a normal pace until halfway up the stairs he paused for breath. By the time we got to the first flight I was already having to carry him, his whole weight hanging from my neck. Fortunately his body seemed to be nothing more than a skeleton or wire framework covered only by his clothes. We made our unhurried way across the flat roof until we reached my place: a narrow rectangle situated at one of the corners. As we entered the tiny room the old man suddenly recovered his wind. And as if driven by some hidden force, without another second's ado, he set about what appeared to be the undoubted reason for his very being. All his talents were immediately at the service of his fingers. He examined, he felt and threw aside everything his eyes lit upon. There was no satisfying him. And as if in fulfilment of some fateful mission he sent an empty ashtray flying, a scarf, a comb with some of its teeth missing, some socks, a little bottle of eyedrops, a shoe box, receipts, newspapers and other things scattered about the big table that with geometric precision takes up half of the room. Then he crossed to the other side of the room, perching with one foot on the armchair and the other on the small table in the corner. In this position he

a una estantería, cuyo contenido: unos pocos libros y un plato de cerámica rudimentaria, tampoco logró interesarle. Bajó contrariado, murmurando algo y cayendo directamente en el cuarto contiguo: mi dormitorio. Su afán desenfrenado de búsqueda, su vertiginoso registro, no se detuvo ante mis pertenencias más íntimas. No respetaba nada, incluso llegó a levantar el colchón de la cama. Una vez hubo convertido mi hogar en una gigantesca papelera, se echó al suelo con el propósito de levantar las baldosas más inestables. Entonces creí adivinar sus verdaderos móviles en medio de tanto teatro. No es ningún inocente, me dije, busca dinero. Y, saliendo al fin de mi estupor, le increpé: '¡Menudo sinvergüenza está usted hecho, amigo!' 'Nada, no hay nada!' protestaba él por su cuenta, invulnerable a mis insultos. Le llamé ratero varias veces y, abriendo la puerta con autoridad, le ordené salir inmediatamente, mientras le señalaba la oscura intemperie de la azotea. Incluso le amenacé con denunciarle a la policía si no abandonaba mi vivienda. Me aclaró entonces, con una vehemencia desproporcionada, que ante todo deseaba evitar que le confundieran con un ladrón. Por eso, rara vez buscaba entre los objetos en venta de las tiendas o de los puestos de mercadillos. Temía, por encima de cualquier otra desventura, que le recluyeran de nuevo en lo que llamó un presidio infantil. Sus palabras me confundieron, me desconcertaron, incluso lograron que me avergonzara de mi crueldad. 'Entonces ¿qué anda usted buscando?' le pregunté. Pero ya no me respondió. Sentándose en la butaca de la salita, me miró con fijeza, igual que si tuviera ante sí un ilimitado vacío. Por primera vez tuve ocasión de observarle con detenimiento. La huella de una antigua ferocidad permanecía en sus facciones. Bajo sus pobladas cejas, una mirada rota, desvanecida tras una película blanquecina, prestaba a su rostro el gesto perdido de un ciego. Ni siquiera me veía. Cerró los ojos e, inmediatamente, sin ningún proceso previo, sin que pasara el tiempo, comencé a escuchar los estertores de su respiración. Y digo 'estertores' porque más que a un sosegado reposo, su sueño se asemejaba a una agitada agonía. Pensé que estaría enfermo, muy enfermo.

A la mañana siguiente, al despertarme, ya tenía el firme propósito de arrojar de mi vida a aquel individuo sin sentido, imagen viva de la mala fortuna que me acechaba. Era la encarnación misma de un mal presentimiento. Le zarandée sin cuidado y le fui despabilando por el camino, mientras cruzaba la azotea, cargando a medias con él sobre mis hombros. En cuanto pisamos la acera, le tendí la mano en señal de despedida. Pero él me negó la suya. Se había agarrado al borde de mi chaqueta para formular lo que

could reach a shelf, the contents of which – a few books and a crude ceramic dish – also failed to catch his interest. Annoyed, he got back down, muttering something, and immediately fell on the adjoining room: my bedroom. His uncontrolled urge to search, his mind-boggling rummaging, didn't stop even when he got to my most intimate belongings. He respected nothing, even going so far as to lift up the mattress on my bed. Once he'd turned my home into a huge waste bin, he threw himself onto the floor so that he could start lifting up some of the looser tiles. At this point I thought I guessed the real motives behind this pantomime of his. This is no simpleton, I told myself, he's looking for money. And coming out of my stupor at last I upbraided him: 'You cheeky devil, you!' 'Nothing, there's nothing', he complained, ignoring me, unmoved by my insults. I called him a sneak thief several times, and holding open the door with authority I ordered him to get out there and then, all the time showing him the inclement darkness outside on the flat roof. I even threatened to report him to the police if he didn't leave my home. He then pointed out to me with a vehemence out of all proportion that what he wanted above anything else was to avoid being taken for a thief. That was why he rarely rummaged through things on sale in shops or on stalls. More than any other misfortune, he feared that they would lock him away again in what he called a young offenders institution. His words confused me, bewildered me, even managed to make me feel ashamed at how cruel I'd been. 'So what are you looking for?' I asked him. But this time he didn't answer. Sitting in the armchair in my tiny room he stared at me, as if he were peering into some boundless void. For the first time I had a chance to examine him carefully. The mark of some former ferocity was still etched on his features. Under his heavy brows the broken look in his eyes, masked over with a whitish film, gave his face the lost expression of a blind man. He didn't even see me. He closed his eyes and immediately, without further ado, without any time elapsing, I began to hear the death rattle in his throat. And I say 'death rattle' because instead of peaceful repose his sleep resembled agitated death throes. I thought he must be ill, very ill.

The next morning when I woke up I'd already made up my mind to throw this absurd old man out of my life, this vivid image of the bad luck that was lying in wait for me. He was the very incarnation of a bad premonition. I shook him roughly and roused him out of his sleep all the while walking crossing the roof terrace with him half-slung over my shoulders. As soon as we stepped onto the pavement I stretched out my hand towards him in a gesture of farewell. But he refused to give me his. He'd grabbed the edge

muy bien podría ser una invitación. Al punto supe que comía casi a diario en una institución de Caridad. Pretendía que yo le acompañara con el fin de que aprendiera el camino y así poder beneficiarme, en el futuro, de su misma fuente de alimentación. Ni me sorprendió, ni me molestó que me hubiera tomado por un igual. Nada tenía de extraño. Con el tiempo y las contrariedades, me he vuelto perezoso, abúlico, descuidando hasta límites inadmisibles mi aspecto externo. Quién sabe la apariencia que puedo yo ofrecer ahora a alguien que carezca de la mirada indulgente con que, en virtud de tantos años de convivencia, me aceptan los vecinos de mi barrio. Pese a la insistencia del viejo infortunado, rechacé su propuesta con desdén, desabrido, tal vez por temor a ir cayendo, poco a poco, solapadamente, en su misma forma de desamparo si frecuentaba lugares de mendicidad. Así pues, me despedí de él alegando que tenía un compromiso. Debía acudir a una entrevista importante, una cuestion de trabajo. Saqué de mi bolsillo la tarjeta de visita que había recibido de mi cuñado y se la enseñé. No pretendía que la leyera, ni tampoco que la mirase. Me bastaba con nombrarla, con exhibirla como prueba incuestionable de nuestras diferencias, como señal inequívoca de que yo no era de los suyos. Y, para convencerme de que aquella desvalida criatura no era precisamente mi espejo, me alejé con la intención de ignorarle en lo sucesivo.

Nos hallábamos en una de esas calles céntricas y angostas, en las que la irrupción del tiempo moderno se manifiesta reduciendo a mero estorbo todo cuanto albergan. Allí mismo, en una esquina cualquiera, en medio de un agitado trasiego, se detuvo el viejo, aceptando mi desprecio con naturalidad. Adosado a la fachada porosa, adherido a ella como si la sucia superficie penetrara su cuerpo traslúcido, extendió su mano mendicante, armonizando con cuanto le rodeaba, igual que una mancha de humedad o un desconchado en un edificio en ruina.

Minutos más tarde, entré en la Agencia que dirigía el señor Núñez, siguiendo las indicaciones que colgaban en la puerta: 'Entre sin llamar'. Asimismo logré introducirme, con la tarjeta de visita en la mano, en su propio despacho sin que nadie tratara de impedírmelo. El director, a pesar de su atuendo juvenil, era un hombre maduro y castigado. Primero me miró con sobresalto. Después, al escuchar mis lacónicas palabras de identificación, dijo impertinente: '¡Ah, eres tú!' Contuve a tiempo la tentación de excusarme. Pues ¿qué le iba a decir, lo siento pero soy yo? ¡De ningún modo! Arrostrando

of my coat to formulate what might well have been an invitation. I instantly learned that he ate virtually every day at some charitable institution. He tried to get me to go with him so that I would know the way and thus in future be able to take advantage of this same source of food. It neither surprised nor bothered me that he'd taken me as an equal. There was nothing odd about that. Over the years, with all the setbacks I've suffered, I've grown lazy, apathetic, intolerably careless about my appearance. Who knows how I might look now to anybody who might lack the indulgent eye with which my neighbours in the district, by dint of the many years we lived so close to each other, accept me. Despite the hapless old man's persistence, I turned down his offer scornfully, a little sharply, possibly out of fear I would fall, gradually and insidiously, into the same helpless state were I to frequent those places where the beggars roamed. And so I took my leave of him claiming I had an appointment. I had to attend some important interview, it was to do with work. I took the visiting card I'd got from my brother-in-law out of my pocket and showed it to him. I didn't want him to read it or even look at it. It was enough for me to mention it, to hold it up as unquestionable proof of the difference between us, as an unmistakable sign that I was not the same as him. And in order to convince myself that that destitute creature was not my mirror image, I walked away with the intention of ignoring him from then on.

We found ourselves in one of those downtown narrow streets where the inrush of modern times manifests itself by reducing everything that such areas cherish to just a nuisance. At that very spot, on some corner or other, in the midst of frenetic to-ings and fro-ings the old man stopped still, accepting my contempt as if it were the most natural thing in the world. With his back against the porous façade, stuck to it as if the dirty surface were biting into his translucent body, he stretched out his begging hand, blending in with his entire surroundings like a damp stain or a place where the plaster has come away from a dilapidated building.

Minutes later I entered the agency run by Señor Núñez, following the instructions hanging on the door: 'Enter without knocking.' With the visiting card in my hand I likewise managed to get into his own office without anybody trying to stop me. In spite of the youthful way he was dressed, the manager was a mature and careworn man. Initially he looked taken aback. Then on hearing my terse words of identification he said peevishly: 'Oh, it's you!' I managed to curb the temptation to apologize in time. After all, what was I going to say to him, 'Sorry, but yes, it's me?' Not likely! Braving

su injusta incomodidad ante mi presencia, le informé sobre el motivo de mi visita. '¿Qué sabes hacer?' me preguntó expeditivo. 'Si se trata de menudencias... tareas simples... no sé... cualquier cosa'. Percibí al punto que mi respuesta no satisfizo y, además, que conmigo sólo deseaba ahorrar: tiempo, palabras, saludos, sonrisas, amabilidad e incluso ademanes, pues me observaba mirándome de lado, a hurtadillas, en una postura rígida y manifiestamente incómoda, negándome la mínima deferencia de girar para hablarme abiertamente de frente.

'¿Sabes taquigrafía?' Por el tono de su voz, más que una pregunta, sus palabras me parecieron una adivinanza. 'Pues... no la considero demasiado difícil', respondí yo, dispuesto a no dejarme humillar. 'Pero ¿sabes o no sabes?' Ante su insistencia articulé un movimiento de hombros y cabeza, un gesto incalificable que logró acrecentar su desprecio. '¿Hablas inglés?' 'Si me empeño...' '¿Qué quieres decir?' 'Pues que si me lo propusiera...' 'En fin –protestó– ahora no hay nada, pero se te hará una ficha." Llamó entonces a uno de sus empleados y, sin la menor dilación, se abrió la puerta para dejar paso, no a la persona solicitada, sino a la desvencijada figura del viejo callejero. Había entrado inocentemente, avanzando hasta el centro de la habitación. Allí se detuvo y me dedicó una inoportuna risita de júbilo, como si pretendiera congratularse con mi fracaso. Ante un individuo así, impertinente, osado, fuera de cualquier regla de juego, nada más lógico que una reacción brusca y despectiva. Mientras el director, indignado, trataba de expulsarle, yo me mantenía a distancia, indiferente, disimulando nuestro reciente trato. Ni siquiera intervine cuando le agarró con violencia por un brazo, lastimándole, para conducirle hasta la salida. Tampoco me sumé, como hubiera sido lo natural, a los comentarios del oficinista en cuyas manos me dejó el señor Núñez. Sin llegar a darme más pistas sobre el posible trabajo, sin dejarme entrever ni la menor esperanza de conseguirlo, sin despedirse siquiera, me abandonó precipitadamente, dispuesto a recuperar el tiempo perdido entre mi visita y la del intruso. No es difícil comprender que, viéndome en el trance de rellenar una ficha en esas condiciones y convencido de su ineficacia para justipreciar mis capacidades, cayera en un hondo abatimiento.

De nuevo en la calle, no me extrañó descubrir al viejo esperándome con una inexplicable sonrisa de satisfacción, casi de regocijo. No le reprendí, ni le exigí que justificara su comportamiento. No le dije nada. Me abandoné a la

his unjust irritation at my being there, I told him of the reason for my visit. 'What can you do?' he promptly asked me. 'If you're talking about bits and bobs ... simple jobs... I don't know ... anything.' I immediately realized my reply was unsatisfactory and that anyway he only wanted to save things – time, words, greetings, smiles, being friendly, gestures even – for he was looking at me out of the corner of his eye, pretending not to, in a stiff and obviously uncomfortable posture, denying me even the basic courtesy of turning round to speak to me face to face.

'Can you do shorthand?' From the tone of his voice, his words sounded like a guessing game to me rather than a question. 'Well ... I don't consider it too difficult', I replied, unwilling to allow myself to be humiliated. 'Well, do you know how to or don't you?' In view of his insistence I sketched a movement with my shoulders and head, a gesture into which nothing could be read, and which managed to deepen his scorn. 'Do you speak English?' 'If I try hard enough...' 'What do you mean?' 'Well, if I were to really put my mind to it...' 'Well', he stated, 'at that moment there's nothing, but we'll fill out a form for you.' Then he called one of his employees and, without delay the door opened to let somebody into the room, not the person he'd asked to come in but the broken-down figure of the old man who lived on the streets. He'd entered innocently enough, advancing to the middle of the room. There he stopped and let out an untimely snigger of jubilation in my direction as if to congratulate himself on my failure. Faced with someone like that – impertinent, daring, beyond any set of rules – the only logical thing was a rude and contemptuous reaction. While the manager, who was angry by now, tried to throw him out I kept my distance, indifferent, concealing the fact of our recent dealings. I didn't even intervene when the director seized him roughly by the arm, hurting him, so as to lead him to the way out. Nor, as would have been the natural thing to do, did I add my voice to the comments made by the clerk in whose hands Señor Núñez left me. Without giving me any clues about the potential job, without allowing me the last glimmer of hope of landing it, without even say goodbye, he rushed off and left me, seeking to make up for the time that had been wasted on my visit and that of the intruder. Finding myself at the critical point of effectively appraise my capabilities, it's not hard to understand why I should fall into a deep depression.

Back on the street again it didn't surprise me to find the old man waiting for me with an inexplicable smile of satisfaction, and almost of delight, on his face. I didn't reprimand him, neither did I demand an explanation for his

deriva, conducido por él, ignorando que ahora había tomado un rumbo fijo. Supe que nos hallábamos en su territorio cuando, al entrar en un bar, siguiendo siempre su iniciativa, un camarero le saludó, llamándole por su nombre: Simón. Y, no obstante haberle advertido sobre mi imposibilidad de pagar, pidió con entusiasmo una botella de buen vino y dos vasos. Inmediatamente, antes incluso de empezar a beber, quiso abonar el importe. De un bolsillo de su chaqueta extrajo una cartera de piel desgastada y, ante mi estupor, la hizo bailar entre sus dedos hasta dejarla abierta en mis manos. Contenía una considerable cantidad de dinero. Se la devolví enseguida, desconcertado, incapaz de admitir que mi compañero, por llamarle de alguna manera, había sido el artífice, él solo, de tan importante hurto. Y, mientras barajaba con su habilidad de malabar el resto del botín: unos pocos papeles y algunos documentos, se me apareció fugazmente el rostro severo del señor Núñez, enmarcado en una pequeña fotografía. De golpe, aunque por breves instantes, me alarmé. Si éste no disponía de otras referencias sobre mi persona que las que hubiera podido recibir de mi cuñado, estaba perdido. Por fuerza haría recaer sobre mí toda la culpabilidad. Claro que este mal presagio se desvaneció muy pronto. Pues ¿acaso no resultaba a todas luces evidente que el sospechoso era el otro, el viejo pordiosero que había logrado colarse en su oficina con tanta desfachatez? Una vez tranquilizado, le di unas palamadas en la espalda a guisa de reconocimiento y ¿por qué no decirlo? también de admiración. No se puede negar que, dadas las circunstancias en que se produjo y conociendo, por otra parte, sus temores, semejante intrepidez exigía un talante heroico. Y así, aquella vida en ruina que, hasta entonces, me había sugerido su miserable figura, de súbito se me apareció transfigurada, como un paisaje desconocido, inquietante, incluso amenazador. Sin embargo, cuando, algo más tarde, le oí murmurar de nuevo: '¡Nada, no hay nada!' mientras hurgaba en la cesta de una vendedora de tabaco, le zarandée impaciente y le hablé como a un loco: '¡Dígame qué está buscando, hombre, yo puedo ayudarle!' Nos hallábamos en un pasadizo subterráneo, un paso de peatones que conducía, además, a las taquillas del metro. Le había seguido hasta allí sólo por inercia, porque no pensaba asistir más a la comida en casa de mi hermana, porque no tenía, en aquellos instantes, un punto más atractivo al que dirigirme. No sé por qué, me sentía con derecho a sonsacarle. Pero en aquel trance no se mostraba receptivo a ninguna pregunta. Tal vez ni siquiera me había escuchado. Y tampoco parecía dispuesto a desvelar a nadie el secreto de su extravagancia.

behaviour. I didn't say a word. I allowed myself to be drawn along, following where he led, unaware that he had now taken a fixed course. I knew we were in his territory when, on entering a bar always following his lead, a waiter greeted him, addressing him by his name: Simón. And notwithstanding the fact that I had warned him I couldn't possibly pay, he enthusiastically called for a bottle of good wine and two glasses. Immediately, before we even began to drink, he wanted to settle the bill. He took a battered leather wallet out of a pocket in his jacket and, as I watched in astonishment, made it twirl a couple of times between his fingers before laying it open in my hands. It contained a good deal of money. I immediately gave it back to him, disconcerted, unable to admit that my companion, for lack of a better word, had been the sole architect of such a sizeable theft. And as he, with his juggler's skill, was shuffling the remains of the haul: a few papers and some documents, the severe features of Señor Núñez appeared fleetingly before my eyes, framed in a little photograph. Suddenly, albeit for only a few brief seconds, I was alarmed. If the manager had no other references about what sort of person I was other than those he'd been able to get from my brother-in-law, I was sunk. The full blame would necessarily fall on me. However, this strong sense of foreboding soon evaporated. Wasn't it blatantly obvious that the suspect should be the other man, the old beggar who had managed to gatecrash his office so brazenly? Once I'd calmed down, I patted him once or twice on the back in acknowledgment and – why not admit it? – admiration too. You can't deny that given the circumstances it took place under and, on the other hand, knowing about his fears, such an intrepid action called for an heroic disposition. And now, the ruined life that up until that moment had been suggested by his miserable figure, suddenly appeared to have been transfigured, like an unknown landscape, disturbing, menacing even. Nonetheless, when a little while later I heard him again mumble: 'Nothing, there's nothing!' as he was rummaging through a tobacco vendor's basket, I shook him impatiently and spoke to him as if to a mad person: 'Tell me what you're looking for – I can help you!' We were in an underground passage, a pedestrian subway that also led to the ticket office for the Metro. I had followed him thus far out of sheer inertia, since I wasn't planning to go to eat at my sister's house any more, and because just then I had nowhere better to go. I don't know why but I felt I had the right to wheedle it out of him. But at that juncture he didn't look as if he'd be receptive to any questions. Perhaps he hadn't even been listening to me. And neither did he seem ready to reveal the secret of his extravagance to anybody.

Finalmente, la vendedora, que por su tolerancia podría ser una antigua conocida, perdió la paciencia: '¡Bueno, ya está bien!' '¡Mira cómo me está poniendo todo!' Simón soltó malhumorado una caja de cerillas y nos dio la espalda. Ignorándonos a ambos, cruzó la multitud de peatones con dificultades, abriéndose paso en dirección perpendicular a la de ellos. Le observé mientras se alejaba, flotando entre los transeúntes, como una forma sólo ligeramente humana, como un simulacro de hombre, como si su búsqueda imposible, entre deshechos y objetos insignificantes, no fuera más que un puro desmoronamiento convertido en acción, una manera activa de disparatar. '¡Otro!' exclamó la vendedora de tabaco mirándome a mí, no con desprecio sino con un deje de lástima y conmiseración tal que me hizo sentir frío. Su 'otro' me reflejaba, como un espejo resquebrajado, una imagen mía descompuesta e irreconocible, pero tremendamente familiar a un tiempo. 'Una cosa que le dé suerte. Eso es lo que busca', me aclaró la vendedora arrugando la nariz en una mueca de desprecio, molesta conmigo, como si pensara que yo le había obligado a decir una tontería. Tenía el pelo canoso y rizado en una permanente pasada de moda. Mientras se arreglaba el peinado, ajustándose bien las horquillas, me dijo en son de burla que también yo podría encontrar la cosa, sí, la cosa que me daría suerte y cambiaría mi vida. Sólo tenía que estar atento, hurgar en todas partes, incluso en los lugares más insólitos, incluso en los más repugnantes. Hablaba con tal desprecio que, de haberla escuchado en otras circunstancias, me habría pronunciado en defensa del viejo, habría improvisado algún gesto de solidaridad con él. Pero en aquel preciso instante sus palabras sólo me inspiraron un pesado aburrimiento. Alcé mi voz bruscamente, por encima de la suya, decidido a hacerla callar. No me faltaba más que enredarme en una conversación tan insensata. En aquel momento pude haberme marchado, salir al exterior y reintegrarme al ritmo natural de mis días. Pero no lo hice. Me dispuse a buscar a Simón con el propósito de despedirme una vez más. No tardé mucho en encontrarle. Se había acomodado en el suelo, junto a un hombre pulcro y maduro que informaba de su miseria por escrito, con letras mayúsculas, en un cartón que le colgaba del cuello. Me detuve a su lado, mirándole desde arriba y separado de él por una línea imaginaria pero perfectamente definida. Allí estaba el viejo, entonando una canción inclasificable, una suerte de

Finally, the tobacco vendor, who from the way she put up with him could have been a very old acquaintance, lost patience: 'OK, that's enough now! Look what a mess you're making of everything!' With a show of bad temper, Simón let go of a box of matches and turned his back on us. Ignoring both of us he made his way with difficulty through the crowd of pedestrians, cutting a vertical line through their mass. I watched him as he moved farther and farther away, floating amongst the passers-by like a shape that was only vaguely human, a semblance of a man, as his impossible search amongst the rubbish and worthless things were no more than straightforward breakdown converted into action, an active way of behaving absurdly. 'Another one!' exclaimed the tobacco vendor looking at me, not scornfully but with such a hint of sadness and commiseration that it made my blood run cold. Her 'another one' reflected back to me, as if from some cracked mirror, an image familiar that was distorted and unrecognizable, yet at the same time very familiar. 'Something that will bring luck. That's what he's looking for', explained the woman selling the tobacco, wrinkling her nose in a grimace of scorn, offended with me as if she thought I'd forced her into saying something silly. She had greying hair that was curled into an outdated perm. Whilst she sorted out her hair-do, carefully adjusting the kirby-grips, she told me in a taunting voice that I too would be able to find the thing, yes, the very thing that would bring me luck and change my life. I only had to be observant, to rummage everywhere, even in the most unwanted, the most repugnant, places. She was saying this with such derision that, had I been listening under any other circumstances, I would have spoken up in defence of the old man, would have improvised some gesture of solidarity with him. But at that precise instant her words inspired in me nothing more than a heavy sense of boredom. I raised my voice rudely above hers, resolved to make her shut up. That was all I needed, to get myself involved in such a stupid conversation. I could have stalked off right then, gone outside and reintegrated myself into the natural rhythm of my days. But I didn't do it. I got ready to go in search of Simón so I could say my farewells one more time. I didn't have to wait long before I found him. He was settled on the ground, next to a tidily dressed middle-aged man who was advising the world of his poverty in writing, in capital letters, on a piece of cardboard that was hanging round his neck. I stopped next to him, looking down at him from above, separated from him by an imaginary but perfectly defined line. Here was the old man, intoning some song you couldn't quite identify, in

quejido, tal vez un torpe simulacro de saeta. Había extendido ante sí una cartulina con varias estampas pegadas. Todas eran de la virgen de Triana. Rocé con mi pie, suavemente, el bolsillo de su chaqueta, abultado por la cartera recién adquirida. '¿No te basta con esa suerte?' le pregunté tuteándole, sin pensarlo, por primera vez. 'Eso es otra cosa', me respondió distraído, con indiferencia. Entonces me dejé deslizar por la pared, poco a poco, hacia abajo, doblando las rodillas hasta caer a su lado, en aquel suelo de asfalto, inaccessible para mí sólo unos segundos antes. Fue como si hubiera resbalado en el límite mismo de lo que siempre había considerado la normalidad. Y sentí que el mundo entero se desplomaba allá arriba, desvaneciéndose en mi cabeza, dentro de ella. Durante breves minutos, fugaces e irrepetibles, me entregué a un descanso impensable. Una moneda vino rodando hasta mis rodillas. Nadie la reclamó.

a kind of wailing, perhaps some ungainly sham of a *saeta.*[1] He had a piece of thin cardboard laid out in front of him on which various holy pictures had been stuck. All showed the Virgin of Triana. I used my foot to brush gently against the pocket of his jacket, which was bulging with the recently acquired wallet. 'Isn't that luck enough for you?' I asked, using the familiar form of address for the first time without thinking. 'That's another matter', he replied distractedly, indifferently. Then I let myself gradually slide down the wall, bending my knees until I was down at his side on that concrete ground, a place that had been inaccessible to me just a few seconds earlier. It was as if I had slipped on the very edge of what I had always regarded as normality. And I felt that the whole world was coming crashing down from above, dispersing itself onto my head, inside it. For a few short fleeting and unrepeatable minutes I consigned myself to an unthinkable rest. A coin came rolling towards my knees. Nobody picked it up again.

---

1 **saeta**: a short flamenco verse sung at the passing of a procession during Holy Week in Southern Spain.

PENÉLOPE

PENELOPE

Original Spanish text from
Los motivos de Circe.Yudita
(Madrid: Castalia/Instituto de la Mujer, 1991, 75–85)
© Lourdes Ortiz, 1988

LOURDES ORTIZ was born in Madrid in 1943. She is an academic who has published extensively on the cultural history of art and literature. For many years, she was a Professor of Art History at the Madrid's Real Escuela de Arte Dramático and, in the 1990s, she became the Director of the institution. Lourdes Ortiz is a respected and much studied novelist, short-story writer and playwright. During Spain's transition years from dictatorship to democracy, she was a true trailblazer, creating a number of female characters that offered inspirational new models at a period of crucial social change for women: amongst them, the first female detective in Spanish literature, Bárbara Árenas, in the thriller *Picadura mortal* (1979), and the fictionalization of the twelfth-century Castilian queen Urraca in the eponymus 1982 novel, a fine example of historiographic metafiction. *Urraca* gives the queen Urraca a voice and tells of the conflict with her son, the future king Alfonso VII, who ended up imprisoning her. The novel offers an alternative discourse on a real-life figure of Spanish history, who, although unforgiving and scheming, has, in Ortiz's version, a credible human dimension that is often ignored by official history. Both in her narrative and in her plays, Lourdes Ortiz takes historical, biblical, literary or mythical figures and re-imagines them from a contemporary perspective: Penélope, Circe, Salomé, and even García Lorca's Bernarda Alba, among others, become characters with new nuances which enrich our modern perception of them. One of the most moving female characters Lourdes Ortiz has created is Fátima, in the collection of *cuentos, Fátima de los naufragios* (1998). Fátima is a North-African woman who has lost her son and her husband to the sea when they were trying to emigrate and longs for them on the beach, waiting for their return. As a writer who was for a while involved in left wing Spanish politics, social and collective preoccupations

often constitute the background of Ortiz's novels, stories and plays: from the scathing representation of Spanish socialism of the post-Franco period in *Antes de la batalla* (1992) to the illegal trafficking of children from countries such as Peru and Rumania to the opulent West in *La fuente de la vida* (1995). In her last two novels, she has come back to the detective genre with a political dimension in *Cara de niño* (2002), and has drawn on her vast knowledge of art history in *Las manos de Velázquez* (2006). Over the years, Lourdes Ortiz has been a regular contributor to Spanish newspapers, radio and television, and is the translator into Spanish of canonical French authors, Gustave Flaubert and the Marquis of Sade, amongst them, as well as relevant contemporary figures such as Alain Bourdin, Jean Jolivet, Jacques Le Goff, Georges Bataille, Pierre Vilar, and Michel Tournier.

Bibliography of Lourdes Ortiz

Novels

Luz de la memoria (Madrid: Alkal, 1976; 1986).
Picadura mortal (Madrid: Sedmay, 1979).
En días como estos (Madrid: Alkal, 1981).
Urraca (Barcelona: Puntual Ediciones, 1982, Madrid: Debate, 1998).
Arcángeles (Barcelona: Plaza y Janés, 1986).
Antes de la batalla (Barcelona: Planeta 1992).
La fuente de la vida (Barcelona: Planeta, 1995) – Finalista Premio Planeta 1995.
La liberta. Una mirada insólita sobre Pablo y Nerón (Barcelona: Planeta, 1999).
Cara de niño (Barcelona: Planeta, 2002; 2015).
Las manos de Velázquez (Barcelona: Planeta, 2006).

Plays

Las murallas de Jericó (Madrid: Hiperión, 1980; Pamplona: Ediciones Peralta, 1980) –Finalista Premio Premio Aguilar de Teatro.
Penteo (1982).
Fedra (1983).
Yudita (1986).
Electra-Babel (1991).
El local de Bernardeta A (1994; also in Raquel García-Pascual (ed.), *Dramaturgas españolas en la escena actual* [Madrid: Castalia Ediciones, 2011], 5–77).
El cascabel al gato (Ciudad Real: Ñaque Editora, 1996).
Dido en los infiernos (1996).
La guarida (1999; Madrid: Ediciones Irreverentes, 2007) – Premio 'El Espectáculo Teatral'.
Rey loco (1999).
Carmen (2002).
Aquiles y Pentesilea (Madrid: Instituto Nacional de Artes Escénicas y de Teatro, 2016).

Short story collections

Los motivos de Circe (Madrid: Ediciones del Dragón, 1988); re-edited as *Los motivos de Circe. Yudita*, F. González Santamera (ed.), (Madrid: Castalia, 1991); re-edited as *Voces de mujer*, N. Morgado (ed.), (Madrid: Iberoamericana; Frankfurt am Main: Vervuert, 2007).
Fátima de los naufragios. Relatos de tierra y mar (Barcelona: Planeta, 1998).
Cenicienta y otros relatos (Madrid: Compañía Europea de Comunicaciones e Información, 1991).

Children's literature
La caja de lo que pudo ser (Madrid: Altea/ Santillana, 1981).
Los viajeros del futuro (Madrid: Santillana, 1982).
El jardín de Aixa, with illustrations by Antonio Acebal (ONGD del Principado de Asturias, 2007).

Short stories included in anthologies (a selection)
'Paisajes y figuras', in Y. Navajo (ed.), *Doce relatos de mujeres* (Madrid: Alianza, 1982).
'Salomé', in B. Fernández Casasnovas and M. Iglesias Vicente (eds), *Relatos de mujeres. 1* (Madrid: Popular, 1988).
'Alicia', in L. Freixas (ed.), *Cuentos eróticos* (Barcelona: Grijalbo, 1988).
'...Y te lo hace en 3D', in L. Freixas (ed.), *Los pecados capitales (Catorce cuentos inéditos)* (Barcelona: Grijalbo, 1990).
'El espejo de las sombras', in Á. Encinar and A. Percival (eds), *Cuento español contemporáneo* (Madrid: Cátedra, 1993; 2001).
'Eva', in *Historias con nombre de mujer* (Madrid: Popular, 1994).
'El inmortal', in Á. Encinar (ed.), *Cuentos de este siglo: 30 narradoras españolas contemporáneas* (Barcelona: Lumen, 1995).
'El puente', in *Érase una vez la paz* (Barcelona: Planeta, 1996).
'Salomé', in J. Andrews and M. Lunati (eds), *Contemporary Spanish Short Stories: Viajeros perdidos* (London: Bristol Classical Press, 1998).
'El sabueso', in Á. Encinar (ed.), *Historias de detectives* (Barcelona: Lumen, 1998).
'Danae 2000', in M. Monmany (ed.), *Vidas de mujer* (Madrid: Alianza, 1998).
'Alicia', in L. Freixas (ed.), *Cuentos eróticos* (Barcelona: Grijalbo, 1988). Later included in C. Estévez (ed.), *Relatos eróticos escritos por mujeres* (Madrid: Castalia/Instituto de la Mujer, 1990).
'Adagio', in *Cuentos solidarios* (Madrid: ONCE, 1999).
'CruciGama', in *De Madrid ... al cielo* (Barcelona: Muchnik Editores, 2000).
'Impacto y favor', in M. F. Reina (ed.), *La paz y la palabra. Letras contra la Guerra* (Madrid: Odisea Editorial, 2003).

Essays on literature, theatre, women, and on her own writing
Larra: escritos políticos (ed.) (Madrid: Ciencia Nueva, 1967).
Comunicación crítica (Madrid: Pablo del Río, 1977).
Conocer Rimbaud y su obra (Barcelona: Dopesa, 1979).
'El cuerpo de la mujer como expresión simbólica', in P. Folguera (ed.), *Nuevas perspectivas sobre la mujer: actas de las Primeras Jornadas de Investigación Interdisciplinaria* (Vol. 1) (Madrid: Universidad Autónoma de Madrid, Seminario de Estudios de la Mujer, 1982), 223–31.
La sombra del actor (Técnica actoral) (Madrid: RESAD – Real Academia Superior de Arte Dramático, 1984; 1999).

El Cairo (Barcelona: Grijalbo, 1985).

Camas. Un ensayo irreverente (Madrid: Temas de Hoy, 1989).

El sueño de la pasión (Los cambios en la concepción y la expresión de la pasión amorosa a través de los grandes textos literarios de la tradición occidental. Desde la Antigüedad hast el siglo XIX) (Barcelona: Planeta, 1997).

'Una carta sobre la creación', in A. Percival (ed.), *Escritores ante el espejo: estudio de la atividad literaria* (Barcelona: Lumen, 1997), 225–36.

'Prólogo', in E. Liébana (ed.), *Hijas del frío: relatos de escritoras nórdicas* (Madrid: De la Torre, 1997), 7–15.

Las mujeres en Honduras, with photographs by Belén Aznar de Miguel (Colectivu de Moces y Muyeres, 2005).

'La pereza del crítico; historia-ficción', in J. Jurado Morales (ed.), *Reflexiones sobre la novela histórica* (Cádiz: Servicio de Publicaciones de la Universidad de Cádiz, 2006), 17–29.

Don Juan, el deseo y las mujeres (Sevilla: Fundación Jose Manuel Lara, 2007).

Further reading on Lourdes Ortiz

John C. Ackers, 'The Generation of Spanish Novelists after Franco', *The Review of Contemporary Fiction* 8.2 (1988), 292–99.

Concha Alborg, 'Cuatro narradoras de la transicion', in R. Landeira and L.T. González del Valle (eds), *Nuevos y novísimos. Algunas perspectivas críticas sobre la narrativa española desde la década de los 60* (Boulder, CO: Society of Spanish and Spanish-American Studies, 1987), 11–28.

Santos Alonso, 'La transición: hacia una nueva novela', *Ínsula* 512–13 (1989), 11–12.

Mara Aparicio, '*Urraca*', *Nueva Estafeta* 48–49 (1982), n.p.

Leopoldo Azancot, '*Arcángeles*', in *ABC*, 17 May 1986.

Isolina Ballesteros, *Escritura femenina y discurso autobiográfico en la nueva novela española* (New York: Peter Lang, 1994).

Luis Blanco Villa, 'Un personaje perdido en la ciudad', *Ya*, 21 May 1986.

María del Carmen Bobes Naves, 'Novela histórica femenina', in J. Romero Castillo, F. Gutiérrez Carbajo and M. García-Page (eds), *La novela histórica a finales del siglo XX* (Madrid: Visor Libros, 1996), 39–54.

Sharon Elaine Bolton, *Dialogue in the Work of Carmen Martín Gaite, Rosa Montero y Lourdes Ortiz* (PhD, University of Manchester, 2002).

Argelia F. Carracedo, 'Síntesis del tiempo en *Urraca* de Lourdes Ortiz', *Journal of Interdisciplinary Literary Studies / Cuadernos Interdisciplinarios de Estudios Literarios* 2 (1990), 97–108.

Daniela Cavallaro, 'Playing with Tradition and Transgression: Lourdes Ortiz's *Fedra*', *Estreno* 26 (2000), 21–25.

Birute Ciplijauskaité, 'Historical Novel from a Feminine Perspective: *Urraca*', in R. C. Manteiga, C. Galersntein and K. McNerney (eds), *Feminine Concerns in*

Contemporary Spanish Fictions by Women (Potomac, MD: Scripta Humanistica, 1987), 29–42.

Birute Ciplijauskaité, 'Lyric Memory, Oral History, and the Shaping of Self in Spanish Narrative', *Forum for Modern Language Studies* 28.4 (1992), 390–400.

Birute Ciplijauskaité, *La novela femenina* contemporánea (1970–1985). *Hacia una tipología de la narración en primera persona* (Barcelona: Anthropos, 1994).

Biruté Ciplijauskaité, 'La novela histórica desde la perspectiva famenina: *Urraca*', in *La construcción de yo femenino en la literatura* (Cádiz: Servicio de Publicaciones de la Universidad de Cádiz, 2004), 311–20.

Rafael Conte, 'En busca de la novela perdida', *Ínsula* 464–65 (1985), 1, 24.

Josefina de Andrés Argente, *Lourdes Ortiz* (Madrid: Ediciones del Orto, 2003).

María Dolores de Asís Garrote, *Última hora de la novela en España* (Madrid: Pirámide, 1996).

Luís de la Peña, 'Sobre las almas heridas', *El País* (Babelia), 4 July 1998.

María José Díaz de Tuesta, 'Lourdes Ortiz revisa la figura de Nerón', *El País* (La Cultura), 26 September 1999.

Dru Dogherty. 'Lourdes ante Lorca', in Wilfred Floech and María Francisca Vilches de Frutos (eds), *Teatro y sociedad en la España actual* (Madrid: Iberoamericana; Frankfurt am Main: Vervuert, 2004), 139–50.

Ángeles Encinar, 'La sexualidad y su significación en la novelística española actual', *Asclepio* 42.2 (1990), 63–74.

Ángeles Encinar, '*Luz de la memoria* de Lourdes Ortiz', in *Novela española actual: la desaparición del héroe* (Madrid: Pliegos, 1990), 112–27.

Ángeles Encinar, 'Escritoras españolas actuales: una perspectiva a través del cuento', *Hispanic Journal* 13.1 (1992), 181–91.

Ángeles Encinar,'*Urraca*: una recreación actual de la historia', *Letras Femeninas* 20.1–2 (1994), 87–99.

Carmen Estévez, 'Introducción', in C. Estévez (ed.), *Relatos eróticos escritos por mujeres* (Madrid: Castalia, 1990), 7–26.

D. Flesler, 'De Cluny a Schegen: Europa y la heterogeneidad étnica de España en *Urraca* de Lourdes Ortiz', *Buletin of Spanish Studies* 85.5 (2008), 603–20.

Jessica A. Folkart, 'Of Prostitutes and Parchments: Sex, Immigration and a Poetics of Skin in Lourdes Ortiz's *Fátima de los naufragios*, *Revista Canadiense de Estudios Hispánicos* 40.2 (2016), 333–56.

José Luis García Barrientos, 'Dramatología del tiempo y dramaturgias femeninas (Diosdado, Ortiz, Pedrero, Reina, Resino)', in José Romera Castillo and Francisco Gutiérrez Carbajo (eds), *Dramaturgias femeninas en la segunda mitad del siglo XX:espacio y tiempo* (Madid: Visor/UNED, 2005), 43–66.

Raquel García-Pascual, 'Epílogo para curios@s', in *Dramaturgas españolas en la escena actual* (Madrid: Castalia Ediciones, 2011), 315–62 [329–34 on *El local de Bernadeta A.*].

Pablo Gil Casado, *La novela deshumanizada española (1958–1998)* (Barcelona: Anthropos, 1990).

Alicia Giralt, *Innovaciones y tradiciones en la narrativa de Lourdes Ortiz* (Madrid: Pliegos, 2001).

María Gómez Martín, *No son batallas lo que quiero contar: la mujer medieval en la novela histórica de autora* (Oviedo: KRK, 2012).

Felicidad González Santamera, 'Introdución', in Lourdes Ortiz, *Los motivos de Circe. Yudita* (Madrid: Castalia, 1991), 7–42.

Edward T. Gurski, '*Urraca*: Metahistory and Self-Discovery', *Revista Hispánica Moderna* 52.1 (1999), 171–79. https://www.jstor.org/stable/30203558?seq=1#page_scan_tab_contents

Patricia Hart, 'The Picadura and the Picardía of Lourdes Ortiz', in *The Spanish Sleuth. The Detective in Spanish Fiction* (London and Toronto: Fairleigh University Press, 1987), 172–81.

Christine Henseler, 'The Art of Seduction: *Urraca*, by Lourdes Ortiz', in *Contemporary Spanish Women's Narrative and the Publishing Industry* (Urbana and Chicago: University of Illinois Press, 2003), 42–57.

Nuria Ibáñez Quintana, *Visiones convergentes: mito, historia y arquetipo en la dramaturgia de Lourdes Ortiz, Sabina Berman y Diana Raznovich* (PhD, Western Michigan University, 2008). https://books.google.co.uk/books?id=NbbxP-Ge Tu8C&pg=PA14&lpg=PA14&dq=lourdes+ortiz&source=bl&ots=HjL_cTD_ rz&sig=_-plghFFy7hL4QBrDLiONJuWLOc&hl=en&sa=X&ved=0ahUKEw jYq5S7t4PSAhWKCsAKHZgQApQ4ChDoAQhKMAc#v=onepage&q=lourd es%20ortiz&f=false

Nuria Ibáez Quintana, 'Eros y tradición en *Fedra,* de Lourdes Ortiz', in in Á. Encinar y C. Valcárcel (eds), *Escritoras y compromiso. Literatura española e hispanoamericana de los siglos XX y XXI* (Madrid: Visor, 2009), 869–80.

Anjouli Janzon, '*Urraca*: un ejemplo de metaficción historiográfica', in J. Romera Castillo, F. Gutiérrez Carbajo and M. García-Page (eds), *La novela histórica a finales del siglo XX* (Madrid, Visor, 1996), 265–73.

Fietta Jarque, 'Lourdes Ortiz enfrenta a dos generaciones en su novela *Arcángeles*', *El País*, 15 March 1986. http://elpais.com/diario/1986/05/15/ cultura/516492014_850215.html

Mercedes Julià, 'Feminismo, historia y postmodernidad en la novela *Urraca* de Lourdes Ortiz', *Revista Hispánica Moderna* 51.2 (1998), 376–90.

José Jurado Morales (ed.), *Reflexiones sobre la novela histórica* (Cádiz: Servicio de Publicaciones de la Universidad de Cádiz; Fundación Fernando Quiñones, 2006).

Maryanne L. Leone, 'Colonizing Voices and Visions: Lourdes Ortiz's *Fátima de los naufragios* and *La piel de Marcelinda*', *Revista Canadiense de Estudios Hispánicos* 30.3 (2006), 449–69. http://www.jstor.org/stable/27764080

Aurora López, 'Tejer con urdimbres nuevas. Penélope en Lourdes Ortiz e Itziar Pascual', *Elvira* 2.5 (2002), 31–44.

Martín López-Vega, 'Lourdes Ortiz: "La desorientación es el signo de nuestra época"', *El Cultural*, 6 May 2015. http://www.elcultural.com/revista/letras/Lourdes-Ortiz/4952

Roberto Manteiga, 'From Empathy to Detachment: The Author-Narrator Relationship in Several Spanish Novels by Women', *Monographic Review / Revista Monográfica* 8 (1992), 19–35.

A. Marco 'La cara oculta de los mitos: *Los motivos de Circe* de Lourdes Ortiz', in E. Méndez and A. Delgado (eds), *Lengua y cultura. Enfoques didácticos* (Las Palmas de Gran Canaria: Servicio de Publicaciones de la Universidad de Las Palmas, 2001), 407–16.

Lynn A. McGovern, 'History and Metafiction in Lourdes Ortiz's *Urraca*', *Cincinnati Romance Review* 13 (1994), 197–205.

Lynn McGovern-Waite, 'Entrevista a Lourdes Ortiz', *Letras Peninsulares* 10.2–3 (1997-1998), 321–32.

Lynn A. McGovern, *Contando historias. Las primeras novelas de Lourdes Ortiz* (Madrid: Pliegos, 2004).

Lynn A. McGovern, '*La fuente de la vida*: Lourdes Ortiz denuncia la fuente de las crecientes desigualdades entre el norte y el sur', in F. Sevilla and C. Alvar (eds), *Actas del XIII Congreso de la Asociación Internacional de Hispanistas, Madrid 6–11 julio de 1998*, Vol. 2 (Madrid: Castalia, 2000), 712–18.

Alison Maginn, 'Breaking the Contract in the Female Detective Novel: Lourdes Ortiz's *Picadura mortal*', *Letras Femeninas* 28.1 (2002), 45–56.

James Mandrell, '"Experiencing Technical Difficulties": Genre, Gender, Translation and Difference: Lourdes Ortiz, Maria Antònia Oliver and Blanca Álvarez', *Journal of Narrative Technique* 27.1 (1997), 55–83.

Safiya Maouelainin, 'El poder del discurso y los discursos del poder en *Urraca* de Lourdes Ortiz', *Hispania* 99.3 (2016), 483–91.

Nina L. Molinaro, 'Resistance, Gender, and the Mediation of History in Pizarnik's *La condesa sangrienta* and Ortiz's *Urraca*', *Letras Femeninas* 19.1–2 (1993), 45–54.

Gregorio Morales Villena, 'Entrevista con Lourdes Ortiz', *Ínsula* 479 (1986), 1, 10.

Gregorio Morales Villena, 'Lourdes Ortiz y Álvaro Pombo, ópera quinta', *Ínsula* 480 (1986), 13.

Carmen Morán Rodríguez, ''Una escritura libremente pensada' [Prologue], in L. Ortiz, *Pensar la escritura* (Valladolid: Secretariado de Publicaciones e Intercambio Editorial, 2010), 9–21.

Nuria Morgado (ed.), *Voces de mujer/ Lourdes Ortiz* (Valladolid: Cátedra Miguel Delibes; Madrid: Iberoamericana Vervuert, 2007).

Nuria Morgado, 'Rewriting Classical Myths: Women's Voices in "Los motivos

de Circe" and "Penélope"', *Culture and History Digital Journal*, 2.1 (2013). http://cultureandhistory.revistas.csic.es/index.php/cultureandhistory/article/viewArticle/23/99

Gonzalo Navajas, 'Narrativa y género. La ficción actual desde la mujer', *Ínsula* 589–90 (1996), 37–30.

Pilar Nieva de la Paz, 'La intencionalidad política global. El "mosaico colectivo" en *Luz de la memoria* y *En días como éstos*, de Lourdes Ortiz, y *Lloran las cosas sobre nosotros*, de Rosa Romá', in *Narradoras españolas en la transición política (Textos y contextos)* (Madrid: Editorial Fundamentos, 2004), 256—60.

Pilar Nieva de la Paz, 'La reinterpretación transgresora de la Historia: *Urraca, de Lourdes Ortiz'*, in *Narradoras españolas en la transición política (Textos y contextos)* (Madrid: Editorial Fundamentos, 2004), 398–409.

Elizabeth J. Ordóñez, 'Reading Contemporary Spanish Narrative by Women', *Anales de la Literatura Española Contemporánea* 7 (1982), 237–51.

Elizabeth J. Ordóñez, 'Inscribing Difference: *L'écriture féminine* and New Narrative by Women', *Anales de la Literatura Española Contemporánea* 12.1–2 (1987), 45–58.

Elizabeth J. Ordóñez, 'Writing "Her/story": Reinscriptions of Tradition in Texts by Riera, Gómez Ojea, and Ortiz,' in *Voices of Their Own: Contemporary Spanish Narrative by Women* (Lewisburg: Bucknell University Press, 1991), 127–48.

Anthony Percival, '*La casa de Bernarda Alba* en el teatro actual: *El local de Bernadeta A*, de Lourdes Ortiz', in P. Guerrero Ruiz (ed.), *Federico Garcia Lorca en el espejo del tiempo* (Alicante: Aguaclara, 1998), 167–76.

Anthony Percival, 'Arte y diseño en 'Venus dormida' de Lourdes Ortiz', *Romance Quarterly* 5.1 (2004), 60–66.

Janet Pérez, 'Lourdes Ortiz', in *Contemporary Women Writers of Spain* (Boston, MA: Twayne Publishers, 1988), 165–67.

Janet Pérez, 'Characteristics of Erotic Brief Fiction by Women in Spain', *Monographic Review/Revista Monográfica* 7 (1991), 173–95.

Phoebe Porter, 'Conversaciones con Lourdes Ortiz', *Letras Femeninas* 15.1–2 (1990), 139–44.

Amalia Pulgarín, 'La necesidad de contar por sí misma: *Urraca* de Lourdes Ortiz', in *Metaficción historiográfica: la novela histórica en la narrativa hispánica posmodernista* (Madrid: Fundamentos, 1995), 153–201.

María José Ragué, 'Penélope, Agave y Fedra, personajes femeninos griegos en el teatro de Carmen Resino y Lourdes Ortiz', *Estreno, Cuadernos del Teatro Español Contemporáneo* 15.1 (1989), 23–34.

Carmen Rivera Villegas, 'Cuerpo, palabra y autodescubrimiento en *Urraca*, de Lourdes Ortiz', *Bulletin of Hispanic Studies* 74.3 (1997), 307–14.

Mercedes Rodríguez Pequeño, '*En el umbral de la hoguera* de Josefina Molina y *Urraca* de Lourdes Ortiz', in E. Moral Padrones and A. de la Villa Lallana

(eds), *La mujer, alma de la literatura* (Valladolid: Secretariado de Publicaciones e Intercambio Editorial de la Universidad de Valladolid, 2000), 73–92.

A. Sánchez, 'Discovering History in Lourdes Ortiz's *Urraca*', *Bulletin of Hispanic Studies* 84.2 (2007), 179–96.

Nuria Sánchez Villadangos, *Mujer y memoria en las novelas de Lourdes Ortiz* (Vigo: Editorial Academia del Hispanismo, 2013).

Santos Sanz Villanueva, 'Generación del 68', *El Urogallo* 26 (1988), 28–60.

William M. Sherzer, *The Spanish Literary Generation of 1968: José María Guelbenzu, Lourdes Ortiz and Ana María Moix* (Lanham, MD: University Press of America, 2012).

Gonzalo Sobejano, ''Ante la novela de los años setenta', *Ínsula* 396–97 (1979), 1, 22.

Gonzalo Sobejano, 'La novela poemática y sus alrededores', *Ínsula* 464–65 (1985), 1, 26.

Robert C. Spires, 'A Play of Difference: Fiction after Franco', *Letras Peninsulares*, 1. 3 (1988), 285–98.

Robert C. Spires, 'Lourdes Ortiz: Mapping the Course of Postfrancoist Fiction', in J. L. Brown (ed.), *Women Writers of Contemporary Spain. Exiles in the Homeland* (Newark: University of Delaware Press, 1991), 198–216.

Luis Suñén, 'Escritura y realidad', *Ínsula* 464–65 (1985), 5.

Luis Suñén, 'Bajar a los infiernos', *El País*, 23 October 1986.

Lynn K. Talbott, 'Lourdes Ortiz's *Urraca*: A Re-vison/ Revision of History', *Romance Quarterly* 38.4 (1991), 437–48.

Lynn K. Talbott, 'The Politics of a Female Detective Novel: Lourdes Ortiz's *Picadura mortal*', *Romance Notes* 35.2 (1994), 163–69.

Juan Tébar, 'Novela criminal española de la transición', *Ínsula* 464–65 (1985), 4.

Antonio Sánchez Uribe, 'Una crónica medieval moderna: *Urraca* de Lourdes Ortiz', *Analecta Malacitana* 18.2 (1995), 319–44.

Juan Villarín, 'Viaje por nuestra ignorada novela policíaca', *Alfoz* 86 (1992), 123–26.

Further online information on Loudes Ortiz (a selection)

http://lourdesortiz.blogspot.co.uk/
http://escritoras.com/escritoras/Lourdes-Ortiz
http://www.biografiasyvidas.com/biografia/o/ortiz_lourdes.htm
http://elpais.com/autor/lourdes_ortiz/a
http://www.edicionesirreverentes.com/narrativa/OjosdeGato.html
http://www.edicionesirreverentes.com/teatro/FEDRA_LourdesOrtiz.html
http://www.mareditor.com/narrativa/endiascomoestos.html
https://fernando2009.wordpress.com/2011/08/28/lourdes-ortiz-urraca/
http://www.noticiasirreverentes.com/entrevistas/lourdes_ortiz.htm
http://www.laopiniondemurcia.es/opinion/2016/11/06/mujer-mito-lourdes-ortiz/780417.html

http://www.compartelibros.com/autor/lourdes-ortiz/1

https://www.youtube.com/watch?v=i01jYRhYKZE

http://www.resad.es/acotaciones/acotaciones12/12casado.pdf

http://www.revistadelibros.com/articulos/fatima-de-los-naufragios-de-lourdes-ortiz

https://www.ruor.uottawa.ca/handle/10393/29415

http://www.ugr.es/~arenal/articulo.php?id=41

http://leyendoconmar.blogspot.co.uk/2014/11/picadura-mortal-de-lourdes-ortiz.html

http://viajealdesbordantebarroco.blogspot.co.uk/2014/10/urraca-de-lourdes-ortiz.html

http://viparnaso.blogspot.co.uk/2010/11/la-fuente-de-la-vida-lourdes-ortiz.html

http://www.abc.es/cultura/cultural/abci-lourdes-ortiz-resultaria-frustrante-tras-tanto-luchar-vuelva-imponerse-guerra-201604011501_noticia.html

http://delamanchaliteraria.blogspot.co.uk/2009/12/el-mito-y-la-figura-femenina-en-la-obra.html

http://cultura.elpais.com/cultura/2016/04/06/actualidad/1459971780_822269.html

http://www.revistadelibros.com/articulos/cara-de-nino-de-lourdes-ortiz

PENÉLOPE

'Vuélvete a tu habitación. Ocúpate de las labores que te son propias, el telar y la rueca, y ordena a las esclavas que se apliquen al trabajo … y del arco nos ocuparemos los hombres y principalmente yo, cuyo es el mando de esta casa'.

Son palabras de Telémaco. Ella, Penélope, acata y se repliega: veinte años permitiendo que Atenea, la de los ojos de lechuza, ponga a sus ojos un plácido sueño. Duerme sin cesar… duerme y teje una tela inacabable de deseos insatisfechos. Allá, en lo alto de la magnífica casa, contempla cómo se vence su carne mientras se indigna ante la desvergüenza joven de las esclavas que aprovechan la fiesta y los hombres que acuden al panal siempre oferente de un lecho que se hurta y se brinda.

'Pretendíamos a la esposa de Odiseo –cuenta Anfimedonte, al llegar al lugar donde reposan los muertos– y ella ni rechazaba las odiosas nupcias, ni quería celebrarlas'.

Ni rechazaba, ni aceptaba: sólo el sueño sobre ese lecho de olivo labrado por el marido, lecho inamovible, cinturón de castidad adornado con oro y con marfil, como promesa de un regreso que condena a una espera cubierta de fantasmas. Recluida en la noble casa, en aquella hacienda confortable

PENELOPE

'Go back to your room. Attend to your own work – the loom and the distaff – and order the slaves to get on with theirs ... and men will look after the bow, and especially I who am master of this house.'[1]

These words are spoken by Telemachus.[2] She, Penelope,[3] obeys and withdraws; twenty years of permitting Athene,[4] she of the owl-like gaze, to bathe her eyes in a peaceful sleep. She sleeps without end ... she sleeps and weaves an endless fabric of unsatisfied desires. There, high up in that magnificent house, she ponders on how her flesh is getting older while she gets angry at the youthful brazenness of the female slaves who are taking advantage of the holiday and the men who are flocking round the ever-tempting honeycomb of a bed that is both snatched away and offered.

'We were suitors for the hand of Odysseus's wife',[5] says Amphimedon[6] when he arrives at the place where the dead repose, 'and she didn't reject the odious nuptials, nor want to celebrate them.'

She neither rejected nor accepted: only the dream on that olive-wood bed carved by her husband, the unmoveable bed, chastity belt decorated with gold and ivory, like the promise of a return that condemns her to a period of waiting, full of ghosts. Shut away in that noble house, on that comfortable

---

1 See *Odyssey*, XXI, 350–54.
2 **Telemachus**: the son of Odysseus, King of Ithaca, and Penelope.
3 **Penelope**: the wife of Odysseus. She waited for her husband for ten years, while he fought in the Trojan War, and ten more while he travelled back home. For three years she avoided the pleas of over a hundred suitors by pretending to weave a shroud for her father-in-law, Laertes, while unravelling it secretly by night. Odysseus returned secretly and slaughtered all the suitors. Penelope has come to symbolize faithfulness and loyalty beyond endurance.
4 **Athene**: also known as Pallas Athena and identified by the Romans with Minerva, is the virgin goddess of arts, crafts and war. Patroness of Athens, she is believed to have created the olive-tree and her symbol is the owl.
5 **Odysseus**: the king of Ithaca and hero of Homer's *Odyssey*, the account of his journey back to Ithaca after being in the Trojan War. Also known as Ulysses or Ulixes, his Latin name. He left his homeland to help the Greek Prince Menelaus when his wife Helen was abducted by the Trojan Prince Paris. Helen was considered the most beautiful woman in the world and her many suitors – Odysseus had been one of them before he married Penelope – agreed among themselves that whoever she eventually married would be defended by all the others. When Paris carried Helen off to Troy, the Greek leaders organized the expedition against Troy which lasted ten years. During the Trojan War Odysseus was respected for his intelligence and wiliness.
6 **Amphimedon**: one of Penelope's suitors; see *Odyssey* XXIV, 125–27.

que labrara el esposo antes de la partida. Esposa fiel, que se deja tentar, mientras tasa con los ojos semi-abiertos y una sonrisa apenas perceptible de Core, eternamente joven, a los hombres que acuden y compiten por ella. Recatada y triste, tejiendo y recordando las palabras, los cuentos del incansable narrador, aquel diestro en embustes que rompió su doncellez y le hizo un hijo, ese hijo que ahora crece, como imagen del padre, frente a ella y que vuelve a recordarle una y otra vez quién es el amo:

'Vuélvete a tu habitación...'

Habitación poblada por los hilos tenues de un sudario que es sudario de la propia carne; paños mojados de una túnica precursora que deja huellas como de bronce, cinceladas sobre una piel que ya ha olvidado las delicias del abrazo, piel guardada en alcanfor, bañada en la nostalgia ... anhelante, como una flor de cardo que apenas desprende aroma y recogida, resguardada en un rechazo pertinaz, cabezón e inútil que la va convirtiendo en estatua que conserva la calidez sedosa del mármol más pulido.

Ellos, los pretendientes, llenan la casa con sus gritos, sus borracheras y sus modos de hombre. Ella desde su alcoba huele el deseo de los varones, se estremece con sus risotadas, presiente el recorrido ávido de sus manos sobre el cuerpo limpio y fragante de las esclavas jóvenes. Al anochecer, a la luz de las antorchas, ascienden las voces y la música de agua que no deja de manar de la cítara, sube el olor caliente del sebo quemado, de la grasa chisporreante de la carne recién asada... hay un olor untuoso y turbio de sudor y cuerpos entremezclados, como en un friso de bruscos ademanes, donde centauros lúbricos atenazan a las doncellas no espantadas, sino complacientes y, mientras se vacían las cubas y se llenan las cráteras, ella puede escuchar aún la melopea lánguida de las canciones.

Ha aprendido a distinguir las voces ... la voz segura y firme de Antínoo... Conoce bien sus chanzas y sus valentonadas ... el más diestro y agudo, el más hermoso de los pretendientes; la voz delicada, casi femenina de Eurímaco que regala sus oídos con tiernos elogios que a veces le hacen olvidar que el tiempo pasa...; la voz sensata, madura de Anfínomo... Oye desde lejos sus charlas y siente un temblor que la hace refugiarse y encogerse entre las pieles de cabra cuando oye el relato desvergonzado de las hazañas amorosas.

estate worked by her husband before his departure. The faithful wife, who allows herself to be tempted, while with half-open eyes and a scarcely perceptible Core-like[7] eternally-young smile she weighs up the men who come and compete for her hand. Modest and sad, weaving and recalling the words, the tales of the indefatigable narrator, that expert in telling lies who ruptured her maidenhead and created a child in her who is today growing up, in the image of his father, in front of her and who reminds her again and again who is the master: 'Go back to your room...'

A room full of the slender threads of a shroud which is a shroud for her own flesh; damp pieces of cloth of a robe foretelling death, which leaves marks as if of bronze, engraved on a skin which has now forgotten the delights of an embrace, skin preserved in camphor, bathed in nostalgia ... eager, like the flower of the thistle that hardly gives off any aroma, and secluded, shielded in prolonged, obstinate and useless rejection that is turning her into a statue that retains the silky quality of the most highly polished marble.

They, the suitors, fill the house with their shouts, their drunkenness, and their men's ways. She, from her room, smells the desire of the males, she trembles at their guffaws, can imagine them avidly running their hands over the clean, sweet-smelling bodies of the young slave girls. When night falls, in the light of the torches, their voices rise as does the watery music which never stops flowing from the zither. The warm smell of burnt grease and the crackling fat of recently roasted meat rises ... there's an unctuous and murky smell of sweat and bodies intermingled, like a frieze depicting rough movements, where lewd centaurs grip young virgins who are not afraid but obliging and, while the barrels are emptied out and the drinking vessels are filled up, she can still hear the languid *melopoeia* of songs.

She has learned to distinguish the voices ... the firm, assured voice of Antinous ... she knows all about his jokes and bluster ... the most shrewd and witty, the most handsome of the suitors; the delicate, almost feminine, voice of Eurymachus who regales her ears with tender eulogies that at times make her forget that time is passing...; the sensible, mature voice of Amphinomus...[8] She listens from afar to their talk and feels a shiver that makes her seek refuge and shrink between the goatskins when she hears the shameless story of amorous exploits.

---

7 **Core**: or Kore, means Maid; the enigmatic smile refers to the Archaic Greek statues of young girls also known as Cores.

8 **Antinous, Eurymachus** and **Amphinomous**: three of Penelope's suitors.

Les ve jugar al atardecer en el patio, ante el umbral de la casa. Y conoce y distingue cada músculo de sus cuerpos, tensos al tirar la jabalina o el disco: la precisión de Antinoo, la dulzura, que es casi debilidad, de Eurímaco, la seguridad protectora de Anfínomo... Todos allí, día tras día, sólo por ella ... acechando, esperando el momento en que se presente una vez más en el umbral, enmarcada por sus doncellas, como en una comitiva sacra para la entrega de un peplo, y se coloque ante ellos en silencio, siempre altiva, con el velo cubriéndole el rostro, disimulando y ocultando las arrugas... allí, entre las columnas, mientras siente el látigo acuciante de las miradas y se sabe señora de voluntades, insinuando y desmintiendo.

'A todos les da esperanzas –cuenta Antínoo– y a cada uno en particular le hace promesas y le envía mensajes'.

De tarde en tarde se cruza con cualquiera de ellos y baja los ojos como si se sonrojara ... tal vez tú ... y luego se retira llevándose a la alcoba el roce de esos dedos que por un instante ... el calor de aquel aliento que ... la procacidad descarada, provocativa de la risa de Antínoo, la broma burda del que intenta retenerla contra el muro, aquellos labios que durante un segundo...

Al anochecer desciende al calor del hogar y aguarda en silencio, sintiéndose observada, admirada, presintiendo ... mientras los hombres escuchan la voz templada del aedo que canta las hazañas de aquéllos que debieron partir, esa historia oída ya mil veces, donde se narran las aventuras de los héroes, de aquel Odiseo, su esposo, que marchó un día camino del Ilión... y entonces esas dos lágrimas como de ámbar, la representación de una tristeza coribante, expresada con la serenidad del rito, que no puede ocultar la rebelión y un cierto aburrimiento:

'¡Femio! Pues que sabes otras muchas hazañas de hombres y de dioses que recrean a los mortales y son celebradas por los aedos, canta algunas de éstas, sentado ahí en el centro y óiganlas todos silenciosamente y bebiendo

She sees them as night falls gambolling in the garden, in front of the house. And she knows and can distinguish every muscle of their bodies, taut as they throw the javelin or the discus: the accuracy of Antinous, the gentleness, which is almost weakness, of Eurymachus, the protective security of Amphinomus... All of them there, day after day, just for her ... watching, waiting for the moment when she shows herself once more at the front of the house, framed by her ladies in waiting, as if in a sacred procession to hand over a *peplos*[9] and she stations herself before them in silence, ever haughty, with a veil covering her face, disguising and hiding the wrinkles ... there, between the pillars, while she feels the piercing whiplash of their eyes and knows herself to be mistress of their wishes, teasing and rejecting.

'She gives hope to everybody', says Antinous, 'and she makes promises and sends messages to each one individually.'

Now and then she comes face to face with one or other of them and lowers her eyes as if she was blushing ... perhaps you ... and then she moves away taking back to her room with her the brush of those figures that for just an instant ... the warmth of that breath that ... the brazen cheek of Antinous's provocative laugh, the coarse joke of the man who tried to pin her against the wall, those lips that for a second...

When night comes she goes to the warmth of the hearth and waits there in silence, feeling herself observed, admired, full of foreboding ... while the men listen to the tuneful voice of the *aedos*[10] who sings of the feats of those who had to depart, that story heard a thousand times already, in which they tell of the adventures of the heroes, of that Odysseus, her husband, who set off one day for Ilium ...[11] and then those two amber-like tears, the representation of a corybantic[12] sadness expressed with ritual serenity, that cannot hide the rebellion and a certain boredom:

'Phemius![13] Since you know about many other feats of men and the gods who recreate mortals and who are celebrated by the *aedos*, sing about some of them, sitting there in the middle, and let everybody listen to them in

---

9   **Peplos**: an outer robe or shawl worn by women in Ancient Greece.

10   **aedos**: minstrel.

11   **Ilium**: another name for the city of Troy.

12   **corybantic**: refers to the male attendants of Cybele, the fertility goddess. The Corybantes celebrated the goddess's rites with armed dances during which they clashed spears and shields and beat cymbals. When the infant god Zeus was being hunted by his father, the Corybantes saved him by drowning out his crying with their frenzied din.

13   **Phemius**: a minstrel or *aedos* in Odysseus's household. He was forced to serve Penelope's suitors during his master's absence, but Odysseus spared his life on his return.

vino; pero deja ese canto triste que constantemente me angustia el corazón en el pecho…'

Y envuelta en su dolor como en un manto sepulcral vuelve a su alcoba y teje.

Veinte años que ella cuenta en los metros de hilo, tela de araña que se anuda y se hace densa y en la que puede leerse el tejido rechinante del tiempo; la lanzadera en su ir y venir, ágil entre sus dedos, crea un ritmo de olas, de tempestades y de ausencias mientras ella sueña con barcos que se enfrentan a mares embravecidos, y con prudentes y benévolos mensajeros de los dioses que recorren las nubes y se aproximan a su lecho… Intenta recordarle. A veces, cuando mira a Telémaco cree reconocer los rasgos ya desdibujados del padre bajo aquellas facciones firmes, en los pómulos, bajo aquellos miembros del varón-niño que se arquean en el aire y trazan perspectivas y escorzos entre las recias columnas de piedra blanca. Y cuando él, su hijo, se calza las sandalias y se dobla percibe las piernas duras de Ulises y vuelve a sentir la presión de aquellos muslos firmes contra los suyos, el calor de los tendones prietos, la fortaleza de aquellas piernas preparadas para la carrera y curtidas por todos los vientos. Y entonces repara en los otros: ve la gallardía de Antínoo, la complacencia de Eurímaco, la nobleza de Anfínomo y en el sueño protector que le depara la diosa macho, la diosa guerrera –lo mismo que el escultor va haciendo brotar de la dura piedra los rasgos seguros, sonrientes y serenos del adolescente que descolla en el pugilato–, ella acaricia con la mente la materia suave del recuerdo con la que va modelando, perfilando y corrigiendo los rasgos del esposo perdido y él aparece allí de nuevo, como un fantasma que regresa del Hades para hablarle y dormir a su lado sobre aquellas pieles sedosas del carnero que ella mantiene limpias y oreadas desde que él marchó:

'Pero a mí me envía algún dios pesadillas funestas. Esta misma noche acostóse a mi lado un fantasma, muy semejante a él, como era Odiseo cuando partió con el ejército; y mi corazón se alegraba, figurándose que no era sueño sino veras'.

Y en ese momento los brazos duros de Antínoo, la sonrisa de Eurímaco, la fortaleza de Anfínomo se convierten en bosquejos inacabados, torpes de aquél que se mantiene intacto con el paso del tiempo, divinal y joven para ella a través de sus ruegos y ensoñaciones de malcasada. Y luego,

silence and drink their wine; but no more of that sad song that never fails to wring my heart.'

And, enveloped in her grief as if in a winding-sheet, she returns to her room and weaves.

Twenty years that she measures out in the metres of thread, a spider's web that gets into knots and gets thicker and in which she can read for herself the creaking weave of time; the shuttle in its plying back and forth, agile between her fingers, creates the rhythm of waves, of storms and of absences while she dreams of boats that confront roaring seas, and of judicious and kindly messengers from the gods who fly through the clouds and come close to her bed... She tries to remember him. Sometimes, when she looks at Telemachus, she thinks she recognizes the lines, now blurred, of the father beneath those firm features, in the cheek-bones, under those manly boy limbs that arch in the air and trace perspectives and foreshortenings between the solid pillars of white stone. And when he, her son, puts on his sandals and bends down she can see the strong legs of Ulysses[14] and once again she feels the pressure of those firm thighs against her own, the warmth of the taut tendons, the power of those legs ready for the race and weathered by the wind. And then she notices the others: she sees the gallantry of Antinous, the kindness of Eurymachus, the nobility of Anphinomus and in the protective dream provided for her by the virile goddess, the warrior goddess – in the same way as the sculptor continuously brings forth from the hard stone the sure, smiling and serene features of the adolescent who excels at boxing – in her mind she caresses the smooth material of the memory with which she goes on modelling, profiling and correcting the features of her lost husband and he appears again, like a ghost who has returned from Hades[15] to talk to her and sleep at her side on those silky sheepskins that she has kept clean and aired ever since he went away:

'But some god sends me funereal nightmares. This very night there lay beside me a ghost, who looked a lot like him, like Odysseus used to be when he left with the army; and my heart became happy, imagining that it wasn't a dream but was real.'

And at that moment the firm arms of Antinous, Eurymachus's smile, Amphinomus's strength, become unfinished, rough sketches of the man who remains intact with the passage of time, god-like and young for her through her entreaties and fantasies of an unhappily married woman. And

---

14 **Ulysses**: see note 5.
15 **Hades**: the abode of the dead.

como si un mal espíritu burlón se introdujera en la alcoba, llega hasta ella nítida, como un crótalo repiqueante, la risa de Mantinao que se revuelca en el atrio con cualquiera de los pretendientes y siente unos celos que muerden sus entrañas desgarrándola y la hace presentir a todas las Circes, las Calipsos, las posibles mujeres de rasgos exóticos y técnicas maduras, infinitamente sabias en el arte del amor, mujeres de cabelleras desatadas de Gorgona insaciable y cree escuchar de pronto los gemidos entrecortados de Ulises que se mezclan, se superponen a la risa desatada de la doncella y se levanta del lecho y querría azotar el cuerpo blanco de la niña para castigar en aquella piel el deseo enloquecido del esposo; huele la semilla del varón sobre la carne apenas cubierta por la túnica de algodón blanca y gime y acude de nuevo al telar, deshace la labor y recomienza, se pierde en los hilos cruzados, en el ir y venir de la lanzadera … y puede verle, escucha el bramido ronco de su garganta y las olas se mezclan con el batir de los remos y se arremolinan las estrellas haciendo perder el Norte, mientras él cabalga como Tritón sobre las olas y la risa argentina de Circe traspasa los muros de piedra y se clava, como la aguja del más fino metal, en su vientre, y maldice a las brujas incontinentes que retozan en lechos cubiertos con pieles de animales nunca antes contemplados y beben de un vino obscuro y fuerte que se agarra a los labios y deja manchas rojas sobre el torso del hombre, y siente la sequedad de su carne que se va arrugando como se secan los higos dulces en los almacenes, amarilleándose, retorciéndose y perdiendo la suavidad de pulpa de la blanca savia perfumada y fresca.

Y entonces convoca a las doncellas y hace que cubran su rostro de arena

then, as if an evil, mocking spirit had come into the bedroom, the laugh of Mantinaos[16] who indulges in amorous pursuits with one or other of the suitors in the inner courtyard, reaches her clearly, like a merrily pealing rattlesnake, and she feels jealous pangs gnawing at her entrails, tearing her apart and causes her to sense the presence of all Circes[17], the Calypsos[18], the potential women with exotic features and mature techniques, infinitely wise in the art of love, women with heads of loose flowing hair like the insatiable Gorgon,[19] and suddenly she thinks she hears the laboured groans of Ulysses that mingle with, superimpose themselves on, the loose laugh of the young virgin and she gets up from her bed and wants to whip the white body of the young girl, to punish in that skin the maddened desire of her husband; she smells the seed of the man on flesh scarcely covered by the white cotton tunic and she moans and goes back to her weaving, unpicking what she's done and starting again, losing herself in the crossed threads, in the coming and going of the shuttle ... and she can see him, hear the rough roar in his throat and the waves mingle with the stroking of the oars and the stars begin to whirl and eddy until the North is lost, while he rides the weaves like Triton[20] and the silvery laugh of Circe passes through the stone walls and, like a needle made of the finest metal, penetrates her belly, and she curses the lascivious witches that frolic in beds covered with the skins of animals that have never been seen before and drink of a dark strong wine that clings to the lips and leaves red stains on the torso of the man, and she feels the dryness of her flesh that is becoming wrinkled as sweet figs dry out in store-houses, turning yellow, shrivelling and losing the succulent softness of the perfumed and fresh white sap.

And then she summons the maids and tells them to cover her face with

---

16 **Mantinaos**: although her name is not mentioned in the *Odyssey*, she is supposed to be one of the twelve girls who, having engaged in erotic liaisons with the suitors, are eventually killed by Telemachus.

17 **Circe**: a sorceress who lived in the island of Aeaea. When returning to Ithaca after the Trojan War, Odysseus stopped at Aeaea. Circe transformed half of his men to stone, but after falling in love with Odysseus she changed his men back to their original form. Odysseus lived with her for a year before resuming his homeward journey.

18 **Calypso**: a goddess or nymph who lived alone on the island of Ogygia, where Odysseus was washed ashore after being shipwrecked. She fell in love with him and kept him with her for seven years, after which, Odysseus, missing his wife and son, resumed his journey to Ithaca.

19 **Gorgons**: three ugly sea-monsters, the sisters Stheno, Euyale and Medusa, who had their hair laced with snakes.

20 **Triton**: son of Poseidon and Amphitrite, Triton is a minor sea-god; a merman, he is fish below the waist and a man above it.

ocre y perfilen sus ojos, que perfumen de resina su cuerpo y desciende al zaguán y se muestra con un brillo en la retina que incita y reclama, como la hembra del cabrito atrae al macho.

Pero allí observándola, censurándola, alerta siempre cual el cazador que otea la pieza, está Telémaco, ese hijo que habla discretas palabras:

'Vuelve a tu habitación ... ocúpate de las labores que te son propias'.

Sabe del reproche; conoce la mirada del hijo, pidiendo cuentas: los cuerpos destripados de los cerdos en la continua matanza, como en unas bacanales perpetuas; las vísceras sangrantes de los bueyes devorados, las ancas del animal troceadas y girando noche tras noche en el asador; la hacienda de mi padre ... mi herencia; los puercos que se alimentan con bellotas son cuidados con esmero para mi mayoría de edad, mientras tú...

¡Esa puerca de Helena...! Hay orgullo y desprecio cuando piensa en aquélla a la que debe su desgracia. Ella no resistió: se dejó llevar, como cualquier criada por el primero que alabó sus rubios cabellos y puso calambres en sus dedos. Helena. Pero ella, Penélope, juró entonces y ha vuelto a jurar día tras día durante veinte años que habría de lavar la mancha que sobre su pueblo y sobre los suyos cayó desde que el adulterio trajera desdicha a las tierras de Itaca. Ella no cederá. Aguarda como un perro fiel para desmentir a los viejos cantores que manchan sus bocas maldiciendo a la mujer que, como Pandora, abrió la cajita de todos los males... ¡Qué tonto fuiste, Menelao! Porque Helena, la argiva, fue débil y se dejó seducir por el primer forastero, Ulises tuvo que partir. Por eso Penélope desprecia a Helena y se ha encerrado en un largo mutismo que la condena a una soledad atormentada por los develos y las lágrimas.

A veces sube al desván donde guarda las arcas que contienen los ricos peplos y los delicados mantos y acaricia el arco de Ulises. Nadie tras él, ninguna mano se ha atrevido a tocarlo. Era ágil y diestro, y certero con la aguda flecha. Y ella, como el arco, era también flexible y tersa, dócil y manejable, entre las manos suaves y precisas, las manos poderosas del varón. ¡Aquella extraña mezcla de fortaleza y ternura, de agilidad y brío

ochre sand and outline her eyes, perfumed her body with resin, and she goes down to the vestibule and shows herself with a sparkle in her eye that incites and demands attention, as the female goat attracts the male.

But there looking at her, censuring her, ever alert as the hunter stalking his prey, is Telemachus, that son who utters the judicious words:

'Go back to your room … attend to your own work.'

She knows it is a reproach; she knows that look of her son, calling her to account: the butchered bodies of the pigs in the continual slaughter, as if in some eternal bacchanalia; the bloody entrails of the devoured oxen, the animal haunches cut up and turning night after night on the spit; my father's estate – my inheritance; the pigs that are fed with acorns and looked after with care for my coming of age, while you…

'That swine Helen…!'[21] There's arrogance and scorn when she thinks about that woman to whom she owes her misfortune. She didn't resist: she allowed herself to be carried away like any little maid by the first man to praise her blonde hair and make her fingers tingle. Helen. But she, Penelope, swore then and has gone on swearing day after day for twenty years that she would have to wash away the stain that fell on her people and on her loved ones after that adulterous act brought shame to the lands of Ithaca. She will not give in. She stands guard like a faithful dog to contradict the old singers who stain their mouths cursing the woman who, like Pandora,[22] opened the little box containing all the ills of the world… What a fool you were, Menelaus![23] It was because Helen of Argos was weak and allowed herself to be seduced by the first stranger, that Ulysses had to go away. That is why Penelope scorns Helen and has locked herself away in a long silence which condemns her to a solitary existence, tortured by troubles and tears.

Sometimes she goes up into the attic where she keeps the chests that store the rich *peplos* and finely-woven cloaks and she strokes the bow that belongs to Ulysses. Nobody after him, no hand has dared to touch it. He was agile and skilful, and sure with the sharp arrow. And she, like the bow, was flexible and smooth too, docile and yielding, in the soft and experienced hands, the strong hands of the man. That strange mix of strength and tenderness, of

---

21   **Helen**: see note 5.
22   **Pandora**: according to Hesiod, the first woman made out of clay by Hephaestus and adorned by the gods with special qualities (her name means 'all gifts'). Married to Epimetheus, she brought with her a jar or a box with all sorts of evils, which she released on earth, keeping only hope inside.
23   **Menelaus**: see note 5.

que condensa la serenidad imperecedera y grácil del templo … la ligereza de las columnas, la solidez del mármol!...

Y ahora ha llegado. Dicen que es él, ese hombre anciano y sin fuerza en los músculos que viste como mendigo y trae el polvo de los caminos en las sandalias mal curtidas. Y hay un momento de espanto, una vacilación que la hace renegar de aquel tiempo pasado, un miedo … y permanence muda, sin despegar los labios porque tiene el corazón estupefacto. Y entonces, una vez más, Telémaco percibe la vacilación y la reprime con dureza:

'Madre mía … descastada madre, ya que tienes el ánimo cruel, ¿por qué te pones tan lejos de mi padre, en vez de sentarte a su lado y hacerle preguntas y enterarte de todo? Ninguna mujer se quedaría así, con ánimo tenaz, apartada de su esposo, cuando él después de tantos males, vuelve en el vigésimo año a la patria tierra. Pero tu corazón ha sido siempre más duro que una piedra.'

Veinte años esperando y ahora aquel anciano…

'Ni me encono, ni me tengo en poco, ni me admiro en demasía, pues sé muy bien *cómo eras* cuando partiste de Itaca en la nave de largos remos'.

Y Ulises habla y describe morosamente el lecho que tan sólo él podía conocer y Penélope siente un desfallecimiento, un vértigo y, tras recuperarse, balbucea:

'No te enojes conmigo … ya que eres en todo el más circunspecto de los hombres y las deidades nos enviaron la desgracia y no quisieron que gozáramos juntos de la mocedad, ni que juntos llegáramos al umbral de la vejez'. Porque los años del esposo le han devuelto sus propios años, esas canas que pintaba y repintaba, esa delgadez de la piel que comienza a separarse de la carne, como sudario prematuro.

Ya no habrá pretendientes que devoren la cosecha y la carne de los animales bien cebados, ya no habrá salmodias, ni canciones al anochecer, ni el juego del eterno ofrecimiento y el rechazo, ni lides en el patio, ni el sudor agrio de los cuerpos desnudos, ni el delirio de la orgía.

Los pretendientes han muerto por la mano de Ulises… Sierva del hijo fue como sierva del padre… Objeto del deseo que puede ser disputado, poseído y conquistado y es anhelado en la medida en que con su fidelidad establecía la mediación. Hay un Otro que no estaba y que en su ausencia

agility and verve that is captured in the imperishable and graceful serenity of the temple ... the lightness of the pillars, the solidity of marble...!

And now he has arrived. They say it's him, that old man with no power in his muscles, dressed like a beggar, and carrying the dust of the highways on his rough leather sandals. And there is a moment of terror, a hesitation that makes her vigorously deny that time has gone by, a fear ... and she remains silent, not opening her lips because her heart remains speechless. And then, once more, Telemachus notices her hesitation and harshly upbraids her:

'Oh mother mine – my cold, indifferent mother, you have a cruel heart now, why do you stand so far apart from my father instead of taking your place at his side and asking him questions and finding out all he has done: no wife would be like that, with such tenacious nerve, separated from her husband when he, after so many bad things, returns to his homeland after twenty years away. But your heart has always been harder than a stone'.[24]

Twenty years waiting and now that old man...

'I'm not angry, nor do I think of myself as someone unimportant, but neither do I think too much of myself, because I know full well *how you used to be* when you set off for Ithaca in the ship with the long oars'.[25]

And Ulysses talks and slowly describes the bed that he alone was able to know and Penelope feels a faintness coming on, an attack of dizziness, and after recovering herself, she stammers:

'Don't get angry with me ... for you are in all things the most circumspect of men and the gods sent us misfortune and didn't want us to enjoy our youth together, or for us to arrive at the threshold of old age together.'[26] Because the age of her husband has returned her to her own age, those grey hairs that she would dye and re-dye, that thinness of the skin that is beginning to come away from the flesh, like a premature shroud.

No longer will there be suitors to eat up the harvest and the flesh of well-fattened animals, no longer will there be psalmodies or singing as night falls, nor the game of the eternal offering and refusing, nor fights in the garden, nor the bittersweat of naked bodies, nor the delirium of the orgy.

The suitors have died at the hand of Ulysses... As she was the slave of the son so she is the slave of the father... Object of desire that can be wrangled over, possessed and conquered and is longed for insofar as her fidelity acted as arbiter. There is Another who was not there and who in

---

24   See *Odyssey*, XXIII, 97–104.
25   *Ibid.* 174–47.
26   *Ibid.* 209–12.

seguía poseyendo… Todos, incluso el hijo, que compite por ella en el torneo, querían ocupar el lugar de ese otro… Y cuando el otro, Ulises, vuelve y se asienta en el hogar, Penélope deja de existir y pasa a ser la sombra que trasiega en el cuarto de las mujeres.

Todos los jóvenes de Itaca, los más hermosos han muerto ya. Ahora, por las noches, cuando Atenea, la de los ojos de lechuza, cierra sus ojos y la incita al sueño, recuerda el murmullo de las voces, los encuentros furtivos en las esquinas del patio tras las columnas y acaricia con melancolía la piel reseca y fría del esposo que a su vez sueña con los brazos siempre frescos de Circe, con la juventud de Nausica o el encanto hechicero de Calipso.

La divinal Penélope en aquella cama de olivo, que fue su lazo, contempla a Ulises que ha regresado y llora: él tiene tras sí una historia para narrar y ante él una hacienda que reconstruir y un reino que legará a su hijo. Ella, la esposa, que ya no está en edad de volver a ser madre, y renunció, cuando era tiempo, al tacto de los cuerpos jóvenes, se refugia en el sueño y deja que los fantasmas de los pretendientes le devuelvan el eco de un goce que ya no puede ser: la risa de Eurímaco … la belleza de Antínoo … la fortaleza de Anfínomo. Y como en un lamento percibe desde el fango caliente de la tierra el rugido denso y quejumbroso de las bacantes y la risa dominadora, seca de Atenea que pone lanzas y esculpe sobre los páramos.

his absence continued to possess... Everybody, including her son, who competes for her in the tournament, wanted to take the place of that other... And when that other, Ulysses, comes back and takes his seat at the hearth, Penelope ceases to exist and turns into the shadow that moves about the women's room.

All the young men of Ithaca, the most beautiful ones, have died now. Now, when Athene of the owl-like eyes, closes hers at night and spurs her on to sleep, she recalls the murmur of the voices, the furtive encounters in the corners of the courtyard behind the pillars and sadly she strokes the dry, cold skin of her husband who in turn dreams of the ever young arms of Circe, of the youthfulness of Nausicaa[27] or the bewitching charms of Calypso.

The divine Penelope on that bed of olive-wood that was her snare looks at Ulysses who has come back and she weeps: he has behind him a story to tell and ahead of him an estate to rebuild and a kingdom to leave to his son. She, the wife, who is no longer of an age when she can be a mother again and who, while there was still time, renounced the touch of young bodies, takes refuge in dreams and allows the ghosts of the suitors to give her back the echo of a pleasure that can no longer be: the laughter of Eurymachus ... Antinous's beauty ... Amphinomus's great strength. And as in a lament, she perceives from the hot mire of the earth the heavy, querulous roar of the Bacchantes[28] and the domineering, dry laughter of Athene that throws down spears and sculpts the waste land.

---

27 **Nausicaa**: daughter of Alcinous, king of the Phaeacians, and Arete. The shipwrecked Odysseus begged assistance of Nausicaa when she was washing clothes at the seashore. She greeted him and told him how to win the help of her parents. Alcinous offered her in marriage to Odysseus, but he refused out of loyalty to his wife.

28 **Bacchantes**: also known as Maenads, they are female followers of Bacchus or Dionysos, god of wine and of vegetation in general. As priestesses they also took part in the wild celebrations and orgiastic rites of the festival of Bacchus.

MEMORIA EN VENTA

MEMORIES FOR SALE

Original Spanish text from
El asesino en la muñeca
(Barcelona: Anagrama, 1988, 15–26)
© Laura Freixas

LAURA FREIXAS was born in Barcelona in 1958. A former student of the French Lycée, she was awarded a degree in Law from the University of Barcelona. She then went to Paris for a year, where she attended the École des Hautes Études en Sciences Sociales and studied the Russian feminist Alexandra Kollontai. Returning to Barcelona, she worked for a literary agency before spending two academic years teaching Spanish at the English Universities of Bradford and Southampton. She was then offered a post at the Barcelona publishing house Grijalbo where she became the director of the series *El espejo de tinta* (1987–1994), which gave her the opportunity to introduce authors and genres still relatively new to the Spanish public: Amos Oz, Elfriede Jelinek, Clarice Lispector, Paul Bowles, the correspondence between Pasternak, Rilke and Tsvetaeva, the letters of Sylvia Plath to her mother, the diaries of Joe Orton and Virginia Woolf, etc. In 1988, she published her first collection of short stories, *El asesino en la muñeca,* a book influenced by Cortázar and where the passing of time and its complexities, as its title indicates, is a prominent theme. Since then, she has published four novels and another collection of short stories, *Cuentos a los cuarenta* (2001), and contributed to several anthologies of brief narrative. However, her interest for the genre goes beyond this: she has been the inspired editor of very successful anthologies of *cuentos* whose central themes had been neglected in Spanish literature: relationships between mothers and daughters, and between female friends. These subjects clearly connect with her preoccupations as a feminist literary critic and, as her essays indicate, one who is particularly interested in the cultural and social aspects of women's literary production in Spain. She has contributed regularly to several newspapers and cultural magazines such as *El País*, *Claves*, *El Europeo*, *El Urogallo* or *Letras Libres* and, since 2001, she has been a regular critic and columnist for

La Vanguardia. Laura Freixas has translated from French and English, focusing particularly on the genre of the private diary (Andre Gide; Virginia Woolf), since this is one of her main interests not just as a translator but as a writer and editor: in 2013, she published *Una vida subterránea: Diario 1991–1994*, the first instalment of her own diary, and a second volume has been published in 2018: *Todos llevan máscara: Diario 1995–1996*. As a mover and a shaker in the field of cultural feminism in Spain, she lectures and gives workshops on women's literature, women's social issues, and creative writing at, among other venues, the Biblioteca Nacional, the Círculo de Bellas Artes, Casa Encendida, Fundación March, Instituto Cervantes, and the Librería de Mujeres in Madrid, the city where she lives since 1991. She has been a visiting lecturer at the Universities of Virginia, Darmouth, Illinois, Syracuse (New York) and St Andrews (Scotland). From 2009 to 2017, she was the President of the association Clásicas y Modernas para la Igualdad de Género en la Cultura and is currently its Honorary President (www.clasicaymodernas.org). Laura Freixas is a member of the European Cultural Parliament.

Bibliography of Laura Freixas
Novels
Último domingo en Londres (Barcelona: Plaza y Janés, 1997).
Entre amigas (Barcelona: Destino, 1998).
Amor o lo que sea (Barcelona: Destino, 2005).
Los otros son más felices (Barcelona: Destino, 2011; 2018).

Autobiographical
Adolescencia en Barcelona hacia 1970 (Barcelona: Destino, 2007).
Una vida subterránea: Diario 1991–1994 (Madrid: Errata Naturae, 2013).
Todos llevan máscara: Diario 1995–1996 (Madrid: Errata Naturae, 2018).

Short story collections
El asesino en la muñeca (Barcelona: Anagrama, 1988).
Cuentos a los cuarenta (Barcelona: Destino, 2001).

Short stories in anthologies and journals (a selection)
'La eternal juventud', *Lucanor* 3 (1989), 34–37.
'Final absurdo', in F. Valls (ed.), *Son cuentos. Antología del relato breve español, 1975–1993* (Madrid: Espasa Calpe, 1993).
'The Clyptoderm' (trans. by Helen Lane), in J. A. Masoliver Ródenas (ed.), *The Origins of Desire* (London: Serpent's Tail, 1993).
'La intérprete', *Lucanor* 12 (1994), 24–32.
'El asesino en la muñeca', in Á. Encinar (ed.), *Cuentos de este siglo: 30 narradoras españolas contemporáneas* (Barcelona: Lumen, 1995).
'Miss Hyde y el dragón', in M. Monmany (ed.), *Vidas de mujer* (Madrid: Alianza, 1998).
'Don Mariano y la tribu de los Freixolini', in A. Vallejo-Nájera (ed.), *Hijas y padres* (Barcelona: Martínez Roca, 1999).
'Final absurdo', in J. R. King (ed.), *Short Stories in Spanish: New Penguin Parallel Text* (London: Penguin, 1999).
'Joven promesa', in R. Hernández Viveros (ed.), *Relato español actual* (México, DF: Universidad Nacional Autónoma de México; Fondo de Cultura Económica, 2002).
'Daydream Island', in P. Bush and L. Dillman (eds.), *Spain's: A Traveller's Literary Companion* (Berkeley, CA: Whereabouts Press, 2003).
'Final absurdo', in J. J. Muñoz Rengel (ed.), *Perturbaciones. Antología del relato fantástico español actual* (Madrid: Salto de Página, 2009).

As editor of short story anthologies and essay collections
Cuentos eróticos (Barcelona: Grijalbo, 1988).
Los siete pecados capitales (Catorce cuentos inéditos) (Barcelona: Grijalbo, 1990).
Special issue of *Revista de Occidente* on the genre of the private diary, 182–83 (1996)
Madres e hijas (Barcelona: Anagrama, 1996).
Retratos literarios: escritores españoles del siglo XX evocados por sus contemporáneos (Madrid: Espasa Calpe, 1997).
Ser mujer (Madrid: Temas de Hoy, 2000).
Cuentos de amigas (Barcelona: Anagrama, 2009).
Libro de las madres (Madrid: 451 Editores, 2009).

Essays on literature, women's literature, diaries, and creative writing
'Diarios íntimos españoles: un recuento', *Revista de Occidente* 160 (1994), 155–223.
'Auge del diario ¿íntimo? en España', *Revista de Occidente* 182–83 (1996), 5–15.
'Animales que se alimentan de sí mismos (Antología del diario íntimo)', *Revista de Occidente* 182–83 (1996), 147–59.
'Carmen Martin Gaite', in L. Freixas (ed.), *Retratos literarios: escritores españoles del siglo XX evocados por sus contemporáneos* (Madrid: Espasa Calpe, 1997), 303–305.
Taller de narrativa (Madrid: Anaya, 1999).
Literatura y mujeres: escritoras, público y crítica en la España actual (Barcelona: Destino, 2000).
Clarice Lispector (Barcelona: Omega, 2001).
'Prólogo', in Colette, *Amores contrariados* (Barcelona: Alba, 2002), 9–22.
'Qué significa "de mujeres/ para mujeres/ femenino" en la crítica literaria actual', in C. Henseler (ed.), *En sus propias palabras: escritoras españolas ante el mercado literario* (Madrid: Torremozas, 2003), 97–117.
'Madre hay más que una', in C. Ramblado-Minero (ed.), *Construcciones culturales de la maternidad en España: la madre y la relación madre-hija en la literatura y el cine contemporáneos* (Alacant: Centre d'Estudis sobre la Dona, Universitat d'Alacant, 2006), 9–18.
La novela femenil y sus lectrices: la desvalorización de las mujeres y lo femenino en la crítica literaria española actual (Córdoba: Servicio de Publicaciones de la Universidad de Córdoba, 2008). *XII Premio Leonor de Guzmán.*
Ladrona de rosas: Clarice Lispector, una genialidad insoportable (Madrid: La Esfera de los Libros, 2010).
'Postfacio', in Constance de Salm, *Veinticuatro horas en la vida de una mujer sensible* (Madrid: Funambulista, 2011), 141–63.
'Prólogo', in Virgina Woolf, *Paseos por Londres* (Madrid: La Línea del Horizonte, 2014), 9–13.

El silencio de la madres (y otras reflexiones sobre las mujeres en la cultura) (Barcelona: Aresta, 2015).
'Publicity and Secrets: Publishing a Private Diary', in M. J. Blanco and C. Williams (eds), *Feminine Singular: Women Growing Up through Life-Writing in the Luso-Hispanic World* (Oxford: Peter Lang, 2017), 75–85.

Children's literature
Melina y el pez rojo (Madrid: Hotel Papel Ediciones, 2008).

Further reading on Laura Freixas
A comprehensive list of Laura Freixas's bibliography, including novels, collections of short stories, articles, essays and contributions to courses on Creative Writing, as well as a selection of articles on her work and reviews of her books, can be found on her oficial website www.laurafreixas.com. What follows is a list of items that deal with her work and are not included (totally or partially) on her oficial website.

Alba Alsina, 'De amicitia', *Avui*, 14 January 1999.
M. Ángeles Cabré, 'Escribirás con dolor', *La Vanguardia* (Culturas), 7 July 2000.
M. Ángeles Cabré, 'Un verano en Cadaqués', *La Vanguardia* (Culturas), 30 November 2011.
Nuria Carrillo, 'La expansión plural de un género: el cuento 1975–1993', *Ínsula* 568 (1994), 9–11.
Amelia Castilla, '14 escritoras cuentan en una antología la relación entre madres e hijas', *El País,* 28 February 1996.
Pilar Damron, '*Cuentos de amigas*', *Hispania* 30.1 (2010), 160–61. http://www.jstor.org/stable/25703421
Feliciano Fidalgo, 'La mirada virgen no existe' [Interview with Laura Freixas], *El País*, 26 February 1996.
Javier Goñi, 'Novela epistolar a varias voces', *El País* (Babelia), 1 March 1997.
Teresa Hernández, 'Ventana al futuro: Laura Freixas reúne varios relatos de escritoras españolas', *Diario 16* (Libros), 9 March 1996.
Sonia Hernández, 'En la mitad del camino', *La Vanguardia* (Culturas), 31 October 2007.
Sonia Hernández, 'La mujer de los libros', *La Vanguardia* (Culturas), 9 September 2009.
Juan Losa, 'Laura Freixas: "El feminismo pasará de moda, será el momento de las verdaderas feministas"', *Público*, 7 March 2018. http://www.publico.es/culturas/laura-freixas-feminismo-pasara-moda-sera-momento-verdaderas-feministas.html
Montserrat Lunati, 'Memoria e intertextualidad en "Memoria en venta", de Laura

Freixas', *Moenia, Revista Lucense de Lingüística and Literatura* 8 (2002), 419–30.

Juan Marín, 'Porque el pasado envejece', *El País* (Babelia), 21 November 1998.

Juan A. Masoliver Ródenas, '*El asesino en la muñeca*', *La Vanguardia Española*, 7 July 1988.

Juan A. Masoliver Ródenas, 'La mujer en la creación', *La Vanguardia* (Cultura), 2 February 1996.

Juan A. Masoliver Ródenas, 'En favor de la ternura', *La Vanguardia* (Libros), 8 January 1999.

Mariela Michelena, 'Laura Freixas: "Tenía muchas ganas de ser impúdica"', *Mujerhoy*, 31 May 2018. http://www.mujerhoy.com/vivir/protagonistas/201805/31/laura-freixas-diario-todos-llevan-mascara-20180528085506.html

Lilian Neuman, 'El espejo de tinta', *La Vanguardia* (Culturas), 31 March 2018.

Nuria G. Noceda, 'Madres-hijas: Una relación de igual a igual tensa y ambivalente', *Diario 16*, 3 March 1996.

Isabel Núñez, 'Sueños de la vida madura', *La Vanguardia* (Libros), 11 May 2001.

María José Obiol, 'Una aportación propia', *El País* (Babelia), 2 March 1996.

María José Obiol, 'Despertar el debate', *El País* (Babelia), 1 July 2000.

Eva Piquer, 'L'escriptora acomplexada', *Avui* (Cultura), 15 June 2000.

Peio H. Riaño, 'Laura Freixas: "Los hombres no permiten la consolidación de las escritoras"', *El Español*, 7 May, 2018. https://www.elespanol.com/cultura/libros/20180507/laura-freixas-mujeres-editoras-no-apuestan-escritoras/305469808_0.html

Santos Sanz Villanueva, '*El asesino en la muñeca*', *Diario 16*, 29 October 1988.

Susan M. Squier, 'Fetal Voices: Speaking from the Margins Within', *Tulsa Studies in Women's Literature* 10.1 (1991), 17–30.

Angélica Tanarro, 'Luces y sombras de una joven escritora', *El Norte de Castilla*, 4 June 2018. Blogs.elnortedecastilla.es/angelicatanarro/

Fernando Valls, 'Mujeres que cuentan', *El Mundo*, 23 March 1996.

Isabel Verdú, 'La voluntad de la escritura', *Heraldo de Aragón,* 26 April 2018.

Marina Villalba Alvárez, 'Vida vs. Muerte en la narrativa de Laura Freixas: *El asesino en la muñeca* o la inútil medición del tiempo', in J. Romero (ed.), *Actas del IV Simposio Internacional de la Asociación Española de Semiótica: describir, inventar, transcribir el mundo* (Madrid: Fundamentos, 1992), 845–51.

Further online information on Laura Freixas (a selection)
www.laurafreixas.com

www.laurafreixasenglish.htm

http://escritoras.com/escritoras/laura-freixas

http://www.rtve.es/alacarta/videos/para-todos-la-2/para-todos-2-entrevista-laura-freixas/3087873/

http://elpais.com/autor/laura_freixas
http://www.lavanguardia.com/autores/laura-freixas.html
http://erratanaturae.com/autor/laura-freixas/
http://www.circulobellasartes.com/blog/laura-freixas-literatura/
http://dinora-lu.blogspot.co.uk/2015/05/laura-freixas-literatura-y-mujeres.html
http://cultura.elpais.com/cultura/2015/04/22/actualidad/1429708867_227600.html

Reviews of books by Laura Freixas and reviews of books by others written by Laura Freixas are listed on https://www.jstor.org/action/doBasic Search?Query=laura+freixas

MEMORIA EN VENTA

El día que cumplió cuarenta años, la señorita Ernestina decidió deshacerse de todos sus recuerdos.

Era ésta, desde luego, una decisión dolorosa, y tanto más incomprensible –a primera vista– cuanto que, hasta entonces, la señorita Ernestina había prodigado a sus recuerdos un cariño y atención sin igual: no sólo había ido acumulando, con los años, un número extraodinario de ellos, sino que los conservaba, además, en impecable estado; pero precisamente por eso, se le habían vuelto una carga demasiado pesada.

Sólo quien tiene una buena colección de recuerdos sabe el trabajo, el tiempo y los desvelos que su mantenimiento requiere. Para empezar, hay que vigilar constantemente su buen orden; pues uno evoca un recuerdo cualquiera y son, por lo menos cuatro o cinco que emergen, prendidos al primero por nexos insospechados; y si uno se descuida, dejándose llevar por los tentadores senderos del pasado, serán no cinco o seis, sino hasta veinte o treinta los que salgan de sus escondrijos por sorpresa, recuerdos olvidados uniéndose al cortejo. Es necesario devolverlos luego, con todo cuidado, a sus fechas respectivas, a fin de volver a encontrarlos fácilmente la próxima vez que uno quiera revivirlos. Eso por no hablar de los cuidados sin fin que su conservación exige: quitar cada día el polvo, hacer limpieza a fondo los sábados, y renovar regularmente las bolas de naftalina; de lo contrario, se corre el consabido riesgo –la señorita Ernestina, tan cuidadosa, se enfermaba sólo de pensarlo– de que al ir a buscar un recuerdo un poco antiguo, digamos de la primera infancia, lo encuentre uno mohoso, apolillado, todo descolorido o, lo que es peor, roído hasta la médula por los ratones del olvido.

Mencionemos por último la cuestión del espacio. La capacidad de la memoria es limitada, y la de la señorita Ernestina estaba rebosando. Además de los recuerdos propios –y no eran pocos–, tenía un sinfín de ajenos: recuerdos de familia que le legó su madre, por ejemplo, u otros que le prestaron y cuyo desmemoriado propietario había olvidado reclamarle. La cosa llegaba hasta tal punto, que en los últimos tiempos la señorita Ernestina los iba perdiendo por la calle.

–Perdone, señorita– la interpelaba al darle alcance un caballero galante y sudoroso. –¿No será suyo este Primer Beso a la Luz de la Luna que acabo de encontrarme por el suelo? Por poco lo piso, y la verdad, hubiera sido

MEMORIES FOR SALE

On the day of her fortieth birthday, Miss Ernestina decided to get rid of all her memories.

This was, of course, a painful decision and one, moreover, that at first sight was all the more difficult to understand, given that until that time Miss Ernestina had lavished an unrivalled amount of love and attention on her memories: not only had she been accumulating an extraordinary number of them over the years, she had also kept them in an impeccable condition; but this was precisely why they had now become a burden too heavy to bear.

Only someone who has a fine collection of memories knows the work, the time, and the care needed to maintain them. To start with, constant attention must be paid to keeping them in the right order; one evokes some memory or other, and at least four or five will pop up, each linked to the first by some unsuspected connection; and if you're not careful and allow yourself to be drawn down the tempting byways of the past, there won't only be five or six but as many as twenty or thirty forgotten memories flushed out of their hiding places and joining the procession. You need therefore to take the utmost care to return them to their respective dates so that you can easily find them again the next time you want to revive them. And that is to say nothing of the endless care demanded in their preservation: dusting them off each day, with a jolly good clean on Saturdays, and regularly renewing the mothballs; were it otherwise, you would run the timeworn risk – Miss Ernestina, so very careful in her ways, would feel ill just thinking about it – that when setting out in search of some rather ancient memory, let's say one from early childhood, you'd find one that was mildewed, moth-eaten, badly faded, or worse, gnawed to the marrow by the mice of oblivion.

Finally, let us mention the question of space. The capacity of the memory is limited, and Miss Ernestina's was full to overflowing. In addition to her own memories – and these were not few – she had an endless supply of other people's: family memories which had been bequeathed her by her mother, for example, or others which had been lent her and whose absent-minded owner had forgotten to reclaim. It reached such a stage that Miss Ernestina had of late started losing them in the street.

'Excuse me, Señorita', a polite gentleman bathed in sweat would ask as he caught up with her, 'would this be yours, this First Kiss in the Moonlight which I've just found on the ground? I very nearly trod on it, and to tell the

una lástima…– Se lo mostraba delicadamente en la palma de la mano, y la señorita Ernestina, reconociéndolo, daba las gracias confusa y se lo metía en el bolso.

Pero no eran, en definititiva, esos incidentes menores los que habían determinado la irrevocable decision de la señorita Ernestina; ni tampoco trataba, con ella, de ahorrarse trabajo; no la movían, en fin, consideraciones de orden práctico, sino algo más profundo: le dolían sus recuerdos. Saboreándolos, como caramelos, los gastaba; y a la vez, se hacían más bellos: pues es bien sabido que están hechos de una materia indefinible, frágil y brillante como alas de mariposa, que el tiempo y el uso van tornando irisada y sutil, casi translúcida, vaga y dramática al igual que los sueños; y con los años, comienzan traicioneramente a rezumar nostalgia, hasta volverse amargos. Los placeres de la memoria se envenenan: cuando pretendía, con ternura, acariciar sus recuerdos preferidos, la señorita Ernestina se encontraba con un dolor punzante como el mordisco de un gato.

La señorita Ernestina tenía un amigo novelista; su primera idea fue cederle en bloque todos sus recuerdos para que, aplicando las venerables recetas de la alquimia poética, los mezclase –invocando a las Musas– con claros de luna y amargos vocativos, sueños robados e ilusiones perdidas; y añadiendo luego un mechón de pelo blanco de Madame Arnoux, migajas de cierta famosa madalena y otras sagradas reliquias, los convirtiese en libros. Mas acabó por descartar tal solución, pues le repugnaba la idea de poner sus recuerdos, aun así transformados, en millares de manos anónimas y ajenas, y condenarlos a repetirse eternamente, sin final ni reposo, al capricho de lectores desatentos. Casi era preferible arrojarlos al mar, y dejar que una niña, un día, encontrase, acurrucados en una caracola, los recuerdos de otra niña, ya en la tumba. (La señorita Ernestina imaginó también, por un momento, el susto que se llevaría una pescadera cuando al abrir un besugo en el año dos mil hallase en su interior el recuerdo grandioso, deslumbrante y sonoro de una noche en la Ópera).

Repartir sus recuerdos entre los pobres, como sin duda le habría aconsejado

truth that would have been a shame…' He would hold it out to her delicately in the palm of his hand, and Miss Ernestina, recognizing it, would thank him, embarrassed, and would put it away in her handbag.

But when all was said and done, it wasn't these minor incidents that drove Miss Ernestina to take her irrevocable decision; neither was she trying to save herself work; at any rate it was not considerations of a practical nature that moved her to act, but something more profound: her memories were causing her pain. Like sweets, savouring them melted them down; and at the same time, they became sweeter: it is, after all, a well known fact that they are made of a substance that is beyond definition, fragile and shimmering like butterfly wings, that time and use make rainbow-hued and subtle, almost transparent, hazy and dramatic just like dreams; and that with the passing of the years, they treacherously start to ooze nostalgia until they turn bitter. The pleasures of the memory become tainted: when she tried tenderly to stroke her favourite memories, Miss Ernestina would experience a sharp pain like the bite of a cat.

Miss Ernestina had a friend who was a novelist: her first idea was to transfer all her memories to him lock, stock and barrel so that by applying ancient recipes from poetic alchemy, he could – by summoning up the Muses – mix them with shafts of moonlight and bitter laments, stolen dreams and illusions; and then by adding a tuft of Madame Arnoux's[1] white hair, crumbs from a certain madeleine cake[2] and other sacred relics, turn them into books. But she eventually ruled out any such solution because the idea of putting her memories, even transformed in that way, into thousands of anonymous and alien hands and condemning them to be repeated forever, without end, without rest, at the whim of some inattentive reader, repelled her. It would almost be better to cast them into the sea and let some little girl some day find, curled up in a shell, the memories of another little girl now in her grave. (Miss Ernestina also imagined for a second a fisherwoman's fright as she slit open a sea bream in the year two thousand and found nestling in its innards a splendid, brilliant and sound-filled memory of a night at the Opera.)

To share out her memories amongst the poor, which is undoubtedly

---

1   **Madame Arnoux**: a female character from the novel *L'Éducation sentimentale* by the French writer Gustave Flaubert (1821–1880). Her white hair shocks the male protagonist, who had been in love with her since his youth, when he sees her years later, and discovers that she has aged by seeing how her hair has become white.

2   **Madeleine cake**: in *Du Cote de Chez Swann*, the first novel of the series *À la Recherche du temps perdu* by French writer Marcel Proust (1871–1922), the taste of a *petite madeleine* (small French sponge cake) dipped in tea triggers the workings of memory for the narrator.

su pía bisabuela, le parecía tan ostentoso como donarlos a un archivo o a un museo; sin contar con que los pobres, ya se sabe, son en extremo susceptibles, y el regalo de recuerdos usados podría ofenderles. Así que finalmente, y a falta de mejor solución, la señorita Ernestina optó por poner a la venta sus recuerdos.

Redactó pues el siguiente anuncio, que hizo insertar en el periódico local: 'SE VENDEN DIEZ MIL RECUERDOS EN BUEN ESTADO. Al por menor o al detall. Precios razonables. Curiosos abstenerse.'

Y se sentó junto al teléfono en espera de eventuales compradores.

El primero en llamar fue un jeque árabe. Estaba muy interesado, según dijo, en adquirir recuerdos invernales, ya que sólo durante un reciente viaje a Suiza –a fin de concluir un importante negocio de trueque de camellos por relojes de cuco, precisó– había descubierto los encantos del invierno. La señorita Ernestina respondió que tendría algunos.

–¿Con nieve?– preguntó el jeque, esperanzado.

–Bueno– empezó la señorita Ernestina, que era muy servicial– nieve, lo que se dice nieve…, en mi ciudad no nieva, pero si se conforma con granizo…

–¡Ni hablar!– exclamó el jeque, con voz de hombre importante. –He dicho nieve, ¡nada de imitaciones! ¡Y además quiero auroras boreales, esquimales, ventiscas, iglúes, icebergs y trineos tirados por pingüinos!

–Será por renos– corrigió educadamente la señorita Ernestina; pero en ese preciso instante, novecientos treinta y cinco relojes de cuco comenzaron a dar las once (hora de Kuwait). Una terrible maldición islámica fue lo ultimo que oyó. El jeque había colgado.

Poco tiempo después telefoneó una dama muy afable, que comenzó preguntando si tendría recuerdos literarios. La señorita Ernestina, llena de buena voluntad, tomó carrerilla y se lanzó a declamar:

–¡Con diez cañones por Mancha, de cuyo nombre no quiero acordarme…! No, me parece que no era exactamente eso– añadió en voz más baja.

what her pious great grandmother would have advised her to do, seemed to her as ostentatious as donating them to an archive or a museum; this is to say nothing of the fact that the poor, as we already know, are extremely sensitive, and the gift of used memories might offend them. So finally, and in the absence of any better solution, Miss Ernestina opted to put her memories up for sale.

So she compiled the following advertisement and had it inserted in the local newspaper:

'FOR SALE: TEN THOUSAND MEMORIES IN GOOD CONDITION. To be sold as a job lot or piecemeal. Reasonable prices. No browsers please.'

The first person to call was an Arab sheikh. He was very interested, he said, in acquiring memories of winter since it had only been during a recent visit to Switzerland, undertaken to clinch an important deal concerning an exchange of camels for cuckoo clocks, he explained in some detail, that he had discovered the delights of that season. Miss Ernestina replied that she had a few.

'With snow?' asked the sheikh hopefully.

'Well', began Miss Ernestina, who was a very helpful sort of person, 'snow, what you call snow … it doesn't actually snow in my town, but if you don't mind hailstones…'

'Not another word', exclaimed the sheikh, sounding like a man of substance. 'I said snow. I don't want any imitations! And besides, I want aurora borealis, Eskimos, blizzards, igloos, icebergs and sledges drawn by penguins!'

'That would be reindeer,' corrected Miss Ernestina, politely; but just at that moment nine-hundred and thirty-five cuckoo clocks all began simultaneously to strike eleven o'clock (Kuwait time). A dreadful Islamic curse was the last thing she heard. The sheikh had hung up.

A little while later a very affable lady telephoned and began by asking if she had any literary memories. Miss Ernestina, willing as ever, took a deep breath and launched into a recital:

'*¡Con diez cañones por Mancha, de cuyo nombre no quiero acordarme…!*[3] No, I don't think it went quite like that', she added in a lower tone of voice.

---

3   *¡Con diez cañones … acordarme!*: ingenious intertextual combination of the openings of two canonical works of Spanish literature. They are a poem by José Espronceda (1808–1842), *Canción del pirata,* whose first lines are: 'Con diez cañones por banda / viento en popa a toda vela / no corta el mar, sino vuela / un velero bergantín', and *El ingenioso hidalgo Don Quijote de la Mancha*, by Miguel de Cervantes (1547–1616), whose famous beginning is as follows: 'En un lugar de la Mancha, de cuyo nombre no quiero acordarme…'.

La dama, con mucho tacto, aprovechó ese momento de vacilación para continuar:

–No, verá, señorita, lo que sucede es que estoy escribiendo la biografía novelada de una princesa rusa de principios de siglo y me hacen falta recuerdos, cómo le diría yo, pues eso, novelescos. Bueno, pues he visto su anuncio en el periódico y me he dicho, digo, Carmelina, a lo mejor este caballero, o esta señorita, te podrían ayudar. Yo no le podría pagar mucho, la verdad, y claro está que si por casualidad fuese usted una princesa rusa, no vendería sus recuerdos por cuatro pesetas. Pero mire, la cosa está en que yo me conformaría con recuerdos, digamos, de Hamburgo o de Estrasburgo, si no los tiene de San Petersburgo, porque, claro, usted en San Petersburgo no habrá estado nunca, pero mire si a eso vamos, yo tampoco, pero el lector medio mucho menos, no sé si me entiende, y mientras suene exótico… En fin, que usted me vende los recuerdos que tenga de duelos, collares de esmeraldas, lobos esteparios, amores imposibles, suicidios con daga, adulterios…, me haría un buen precio, ¿verdad?, siendo de segunda mano…, Bueno, a lo que iba: yo entonces cambio todos los nombres para que suenen a ruso, si es Martínez, Martinoff, si es García, Garciovsky, y así (licencia poética, le llamamos a eso en nuestra jerga); pongo aquí y allá un grupo de campesinos bailando la balalaika, una horda de bolcheviques feroces con la hoz y el martillo al cinto, y vamos, que me queda bordado. ¿Qué le parece?

La señrita Ernestina dudó un rato.

–¿Amores imposibles dice usted que le sirven?– preguntó por fin. –Porque de eso…– añadió en un murmullo –de eso, alguno tengo.

–Si es con duques o marquesas, desde luego– respondió la dama con firmeza.

–Ah, no– replicó la señorita Ernestina–. Sólo puedo ofrecerle, si usted no la ha leído, mi recuerdo de *El rojo y el negro*.

–Rojos, por supuesto– respondió su interlocutora, con evidente suspicacia–, pero ¿me quiere usted decir que pinta un negro en San Petersburgo en 1910?

–Dejémoslo– propuso la señorita Ernestina, algo desanimada.

The lady most tactfully took advantage of this moment of hesitation to continue:

'No, you see, Señorita, the thing is I'm writing a biography in the form of a novel about a Russian Princess who was living at the beginning of the century and I need some memories that are, how shall I put it, well yes, like something out of a novel. So, having seen your advertisement in the paper I said to myself, Carmelina, I said, this gentleman, or this lady, might be able to help you. In truth I wouldn't be able to pay very much, and of course if you happened by any chance to be a Russian Princes, you wouldn't just sell your memories for peanuts. But look, the thing is this, I would be happy with some memories of, let's say, Hamburg or Strasbourg, if you don't have any of St Petersburg, because obviously you could never have been to St Petersburg, but look, if it comes to that, I haven't either, much less the average reader, I don't know if you can follow me, and as long as it sounds exotic... Well, so you sell me any memories you might have of duels, emerald necklaces, wolves on the Steppes, impossible love affairs, people committing suicide with a dagger, adulterous affairs ... you'd give them to me for a good price, wouldn't you, their being second hand... Well, as I was saying: I then change all the names so they sound Russian –Martinoff for Martínez, Garciovsky for García and so on (we call that 'poetic licence' in our trade); I pop in a group of peasants here and there dancing to the balalaika, a horde of angry Bolsheviks with hammers and sickles at their belts, hey, I'm making a fantastic job of it. What do you think?'

Miss Ernestina hesitated a moment.

'Do you think impossible love affairs might do?' she asked at last. 'Because', she added in a whisper, 'I do have some of those.'

'Only if they involve dukes or marquises, of course', replied the other lady firmly.

'Ah, no', replied Miss Ernestina. 'But, if you haven't already read it, I can only offer you my memory of *Scarlet and Black*.'[4]

'The Reds, of course', replied the woman on the other side of the phone, clearly suspicious, 'but what on earth was a black man doing in St Petersburg in 1910?'

'Let's just leave it', suggested Miss Ernestina, somewhat discouraged.

---

4 ***Scarlet and Black***: *Le Rouge et le noir*, a novel by the French writer Stendhal, pseudonym of Henri Beyle (1783–1842). The colours of the title suggest some of the social interests of the protagonist Julian Sorel in the context of 19th-century France: black for the clergy, red for the army.

Telefonearon o escribieron aún varias personas más: el inevitable representante del *Guinnes Book of Records*; la directora de un orfelinato de provincias que deseaba adquirir varios lotes de recuerdos de infancias felices con vistas a obtener una subvención del Ministerio; un condenado a cadena perpetua que pedía recuerdos eróticos para entretener la vaciedad de sus noches –pero había que mandárselos disimulados en el relleno de un pastel de chocolate o en el doble fondo de una caja de galletas–; y un ciego de nacimiento, deseoso de comprar recuerdos de colores, especialmente el lila, del que le habían hablado tan bien. A éste, por lo menos, Ernestina pudo enviarle por correo el recuerdo de la espléndida buganvilla que ornaba la fachada de la casa de su bisabuela. Pero pasaban los días, y el grueso de su memoria seguía intacto y sin comprador.

'Qué lástima de recuerdos', meditaba una tarde la señorita Ernestina, tristemente. 'Yo me había encariñado con ellos y bien veo que no valen nada… Si antes pretendía venderlos, ahora estaría dispuesta a regalarlos; y si ni regalados los quiere nadie, los quemaré, o los enterraré bien hondo, y yo con ellos.'

En ese preciso instante llamaron a la puerta. Era el trapero del barrio. Olía a vinagre y a conejo.

–¿E' aquí 'onde venden recuerdo'?– preguntó sin más preámbulo.

–Sí, aquí es– respondió ella algo desconcertada.

El trapero que ya se había metido en la sala, les echó un vistazo y propuso rápidamente:

–Ze lo' compro a peso.

–No, no hace falta– respondió la señorita Ernestina con fatiga–. Ya no los quiero para nada y me hará un favor si se los lleva.

Sin perder el tiempo en comentarios, el ropavejero comenzó a recoger recuerdos a puñados, y algunos sueños e ilusiones que había también en el montón, y los fue metiendo hechos un revoltijo en el saco que llevaba.

–Pero, dígame– inquirió tímidamente la señorita Ernestina–, ¿qué hará con ellos?

–Pué verá– contestó el hombre, sin dejar la faena–, tengo un cliente amnézico que zeguramente me comprara tó' er lote, zi ze lo dejo baratito–. La señorita Ernestina guardaba silencio, admirada por tanto sentido práctico. –Y zi no– concluyo él–, pue pa' quemá' en la e'tufa o pa' relleno de colchone'.

Several other people phoned or wrote: the inevitable representative of the *Guinness Book of Records*; the female head of an orphanage somewhere in the provinces who wanted to acquire several batches of happy childhood memories with a view to obtain some sort of a grant from the Ministry; a man condemned to life imprisonment who was asking for erotic memories to help fill the emptiness of his nights –although she would have to send them smuggled inside the filling of a chocolate cake or in the false bottom of a box of biscuits; and a man blind from birth, hoping to purchase some memories of colours, particularly lilac, of which he had heard so many nice things. To the latter at least Ernestina had been able to send a letter containing the memory of the wonderful bougainvillaea which had adorned the front of her great grandmother's house. But the days passed, and the bulk of her memory remained intact and without a purchaser. 'What a pity about my memories', mussed Miss Ernestina sadly one evening. 'I used to be so extremely fond of them and now I can see they're not worth anything... Even though I was trying to sell them before, now I'd be ready to give them away; and if nobody even wants them as a gift, I'll burn them, or bury them good and deep, and me along with them.'

At that very moment there was a knock at the door. It was the local rag-and-bone man. He smelt of vinegar and rabbits.

'Is this where's 'ems selling mem'ries?' he asked without preamble.

'Yes, it's here...' she replied, slightly taken aback.

The rag-and-bone man, who had by now come into the living room, cast his eyes over them and soon made his decision:

'I'll buy 'em from ya by weight.'

'No, there is no need for that', replied Miss Ernestina wearily. 'I don't want them any more, and you'll be doing me a favour if you just take them away.'

Waiting no time on niceties, the rag-and-bone man began picking up memories by the fistful, along with a few dreams and illusions that were also included in the heap, and stuffed them higgledy-piggledy into the sack he was carrying.

'But tell me', ventured Miss Ernestina, 'what are you going to do with them?'

'Well, see', answered the man, without pausing in what he was doing, 'I've gotta client who's lost his mem'ry oo'll surely buy the lot off me if I let 'im 'ave 'em cheap.' Miss Ernestina said no word, marvelling at such common sense. 'An' if 'e don't', the man concluded, 'well per'aps I'll burn 'em in the stove or use 'em to stuff mattresses.'

Y tras recoger los últimos recuerdos desparramados por el suelo –entre los que la señorita Ernestina tuvo tiempo de reconocer el del entierro de su padre y el de un osito de peluche que tuvo de pequeña y al que quería con locura–, el atareado trapero se fue como había venido.

Los meses siguientes, la vida de la señorita Ernestina fue apacible, si no feliz. Dormía a pierna suelta y sin sueños; comía con apetito, y nunca se distraía de lo que estaba haciendo ni se equivocaba de parada de autobús, como antes le sucedía con frecuencia. Por los documentos que había conservado, sabía su nombre, domicilio, fecha de nacimiento y número de cartilla del seguro; nadie le pedía que supiera algo más. En sus ratos libres, miraba arrobada la televisión. Pagaba religiosamente sus impuestos, y creía a pies juntillas las noticias de los periódicos y los discursos de las autoridades. Era, en suma, la ciudadana modelo.

Pero un día sucedió algo extraño. Iba por la calle, atenta a los semáforos y dócil a las indicaciones de los guardias, cuando oyó a alguien gritar: '¡Armando!', y tuvo un terrible sobresalto. Como una iluminación, una voz interior le dijo que Armando era el nombre de su primer amor; pero no le dijo más. En vano buscó ella, detenida y como fulminada en medio de la acera, la historia de aquel amor perdido en su vacía memoria; no halló sino varios fragmentos: el eco de una ciudad –París, tal vez– y un ramo de gladiolos de color impreciso.

Desesperada, pues acababa de descubrir que la pérdida de un recuerdo querido duele más que todos los recuerdos juntos, la señorita Ernestina se precipitó a su casa y escribió un nuevo anuncio:

'EXTRAVIADO PRIMER AMOR. Muy cariñoso. Responde al nombre de Armando. Signos distintivos: París y gladiolos. Se gratificará espléndidamente a quien lo devuelva sano y salvo a su desconsolada propietaria'.

Esta vez, sin embargo, no tuvo la paciencia de aguardar junto al teléfono. Como también había olvidado la visita del ropavejero, no tenía idea de qué podía haberse hecho de aquel precioso recuerdo, y creyó haberlo perdido esa misma mañana. Volvió, pues, a la calle fatídica, y a gatas por el suelo, comenzó a recorrer los adoquines palmo a palmo.

And having scooped up the final memories scattered about the floor – amongst them one that Miss Ernestina just had time to recognize as her father's funeral, and another of a teddy bear she'd had when she was a little girl and that she'd loved to bits – the busy rag-and-bone man left as suddenly as he'd arrived.

During the months that followed Miss Ernestina's life was peaceful if not happy. She slept soundly and dreamlessly; she had a good appetite and never got distracted from what she was doing or got off at the wrong bus stop, which was something that had happened before on a number of occasions. From the documents she'd kept she knew her name, address, date of birth and National Insurance number; nobody expected her to know anything more. In her free moments she would watch television, entranced. She religiously paid her taxes, and believed absolutely what she read in the papers and the platform speeches of the authorities. She was, in short, the model citizen.

But then, one day something happened. She was walking along the street, watching the traffic lights and dutifully obeying the signals of the policemen, when she heard somebody shout: 'Armando!'[5] and her heart gave a great lurch. Like an illumination, a voice inside her told her that Armando was the name of her first love; but it didn't tell her anything else. Standing there stock still as if struck by lightning in the middle of the pavement, she cast around in vain in her empty memory for the story of that lost love; she could find nothing more than vague fragments: the echo of a city – Paris, perhaps – and a bunch of gladioli the colour of which she couldn't make out.

In despair, having just discovered that the loss of a cherished memory hurts more than all the other memories put together, Miss Ernestina rushed home and wrote out another advertisement:

'MISLAID – ONE FIRST LOVE. Very loving. Answers to the name of Armando. Distinguishing features: Paris and gladioli. Handsome reward to the person who returns it safe to its disconsolate lady owner.'

This time, however, she didn't have the patience to wait by the phone. Since she'd also forgotten about the visit of the rag-and-bone man, she had no idea what could have become of that precious memory, and believed she'd lost it just that morning. So she went back to the fateful street, and dropping down on all fours she began to go over the paving slabs inch by inch.

---

5   **Armando**: ironic use of a male name with Romantic undertones; Armand Duval and Marguerite Gautier are the main characters in the 19th-century French play, *La Dame aux camélias* (1848) by Alexander Dumas, *fils* (1824–1895), based on his own novel of the same title. The work was the source of Giuseppe Verdi's opera *La Traviata* (1853). Apart from the name of the male protagonist, 'Paris' and 'gladioli' reinforce this intertexual connection.

Al verla rebuscar con tanto ahínco, varios transeúntes se le acercaron solícitos. Los hombres creían que había perdido el reloj o un billete de mil; las mujeres, que se le había roto el collar de perlas buenas; y los niños tiraban del brazo de sus madres para que les dejasen ayudar a la señora a encontrar la canica o la lagartija que seguramente andaba buscando. A todos los apartaba con nerviosismo la señorita Ernestina.

–Hagan el favor de no pisar– les decía irritada–. ¿No ven que estoy buscando un recuerdo, y que podrían aplastarlo?

Entonces, los niños preguntaban: 'Mamá, ¿qué es un recuerdo?', y los adultos seguían su camino con ofendida dignidad, disgustados de haber perdido el tiempo.

Por fin, un viejecito que la había estado observando en silencio se le acercó para decirle:

–Debería usted alegrarse, señorita. Créame que la envidio. Usted podrá disfrutar del presente, construir un futuro; no como yo, que atrapado por innumerables recuerdos, vivo con la vista vuelta atrás e inmóvil.

La señorita Ernestina levantó la cabeza:

–¡Cómo que debería alegrarme!– replicó, dolida–. ¡Es el recuerdo de mi primer amor lo que he perdido! ¿Se da cuenta?

El anciano movió la cabeza compasivamente.

–¿Ha probado en el Ayuntamiento?– sugirió, tras un breve silencio.

–¿En el Ayuntamiento?– repitió la señorita Ernestina.

–Sí– dijo el anciano–. En la Oficina de Recuerdos Perdidos podría ser que lo tuvieran.

La señorita Ernestina dio las gracias y corrió al Ayuntamiento. Allí la atendió una señora muy amable.

–Verá– comenzó la señorita Ernestina, sofocada aún por la carrera–, no tiene pérdida: es el recuerdo de un primer amor llamado Armando, con gladiolos rojos, o tal vez blancos o amarillos, y atardeceres en París; por lo que más quiera, dígame: ¿lo han encontrado?

La funcionaria la contempló en silencio, con una mirada que a la señorita Ernestina, sin saber por qué, le pareció triste, y la invitó a seguirla.

Atravesaron varios corredores tenebrosos en cuyas paredes se alineaban, sobre estanterías, recuerdos polvorientos clasificados por orden alfabético. En la sección de la A, y a medida que avanzaban, la señorita Ernestina pudo distinguir recuerdos de abnegación y de abanicos, de acrobacias, achaques y achuchones, de adulterios y alpiste, de Antípodas y arañas, de arenques y arzobispos… Atravesaron varias secciones más, hasta llegar a la P.

Seeing her searching so intently, several passers-by approached and asked if there was anything they could do. The men thought she'd lost her watch or a thousand peseta note; the women, that her string of good pearls had broken; and the children tugged at their mothers' arms that they might be allowed to help the lady find the marble or the little gecko she was surely looking for. Miss Ernestina nervously shooed them all away:

'Please, don't step here', she told them irritably. 'Can't you see I'm looking for a memory and you might trample on it?'

Then the children asked: 'What's a memory, mama?' and the adults continued on their way with offended dignity, annoyed at having wasted their time.

Finally, a little old man who'd been watching her in silence went up to her and said:

'You should cheer up, Señorita. Believe me, I envy you. You can enjoy the present, build a future; not like me, trapped in endless memories, I live looking over my shoulder, unable to move.'

Miss Ernestina lifted her head.

'What do you mean, I should cheer up!' she answered, hurt. 'It's the memory of my first love I'd lost! Do you understand?'

The old man nodded his head compassionately.

'Have you tried at the Town Hall?' he suggested after a brief silence.

'At the Town Hall?' repeated Miss Ernestina.

'Yes', said the old man. 'The Lost Memories Office might have it.'

Miss Ernestina thanked him and hurried along to the Town Hall. There she was attended by a very kind lady.

'You see', began Miss Ernestina, still out of breath from rushing, 'You can't miss it: it's the memory of a first love, called Armando, with red gladioli, or perhaps they were white or yellow, and of sunsets in Paris; by all you hold most dear, please tell me: have you found it?'

The clerk gazed at her in silence, with a look that struck Miss Ernestina as sad, though she didn't know why, then invited her to follow her.

They went down a number of gloomy corridors with walls lined with shelves on which were stacked dusty memories filed in alphabetical order. As they made their way along, in the section marked A Miss Ernestina was able to make out memories of abnegation, fans, acrobatics, attacks of ill health and assaults, adulterous affairs and bird-seed, the Antipodes and arachnids, of herrings and archbishops.[6] They went through a number of further sections before they came to the letter F.

---

6 **Abnegation ... archbishops**: note that in Spanish all these words begin with A.

–Sección de Primeros Amores sin Dueño– anunció su guía, con amplio y fatigado gesto–. Usted misma.

Y, dando media vuelta, se marchó.

Hace de esto diez o doce años. La señorita Ernestina lleva examinando alrededor de siete mil recuerdos, lo que representa apenas una décima parte del total. A veces, en un arrebato de desesperanzada furia, lo tira todo por el suelo, y se pone a llamar a voces a su Armando, o a oler el aire, porque está segura de poder reconocer su olor entre millares; pero sólo huele a polvo, y sólo el silencio le contesta.

'First Loves – no Owners', announced her guide with a sweeping but weary gesture of her hand. 'Help yourself!'

And, turning on her heels, she left.

This happened ten or twelve years ago. Miss Ernestina has looked at around seven thousand memories, which scarcely represent a tenth of the total. Sometimes, in a fit of hopeless anger she hurls everything onto the floor, and calls out to her Armando, or sniffs at the air because she's certain she'd be able to recognize his smell amongst thousands; but she is only sniffing at dust, and only the silence answers her.

NUEVE MESES Y UN DÍA

NINE MONTHS AND A DAY

Original Spanish text from
Morir en tus brazos y otros cuentos
(Alicante: Aguaclara, 1989, 70–73)
© Marina Mayoral, 1989

MARINA MAYORAL was born in Mondoñedo, Galicia, in 1942. She studied in Santiago de Compostela, and in Madrid, where she obtained a doctorate with a PhD dissertation on the Galician post-Romantic poet Rosalía de Castro, the subject of several of her scholarly books. As well as being a prolific and successful novelist and short story writer, she is a Professor of Literature at the Universidad Complutense, in Madrid. Her published works combine literary creation and literary criticism in equal measure. She has edited several books by the nineteenth-century Galician novelist and short story writer Emilia Pardo Bazán and the poet Rosalía de Castro. Most recently, she has edited a modernized edition of *Cantar de Mio Cid*, the oldest documented Castilian epic poem. She has also reflected on her own writing and edited several books on narrative aspects of literary theory. Some of her novels use her scholarly knowledge to play in an engaging way with the metafictional mode, such as *Dar la vida y el alma* (1993). Marina Mayoral writes both in Spanish and in Galician and several of her novels have been translated from Galician into Spanish and vice versa (see bibliography below). She has attracted a well-deserved interest in Anglo-Saxon feminist academic circles, particularly with her texts on friendship between women, such as *Recóndita armonía* (1994), a reworking of 'De su mejor amiga, Celina' (a *cuento* included in *Morir en tus brazos,* 1989), and, to some extent, *Querida amiga* (1996), a collection of short stories in epistolary form. Whether in Spanish or in Galician, many of her fictional works are set in the imaginary town of Brétema, one of many significant literary locations in Spanish literature. In 1992, she was awarded the Premio Fernández Latorre for her contribution to journalism (for prizes to her individual books, see bibliography below). Marina Mayoral's fiction has been translated into German, Italian, Polish, Chinese, Portuguese and Catalan. *El amor, la vida*

y más allá (2017) is her latest collection of short stories. In 2017 she was elected a member of the Real Academia Galega and her inauguration speech in Galician was entitled *Por que Murguía destruíu as cartas de Rosalía?*

Marina Mayoral's official website [marinamayoral.es] is a useful tool where you can find information about her scholarly and creative publications, as well as visual and audio material related to the reception of her work and her cultural activities.

Bibliography of Marina Mayoral

Novels

Cándida, otra vez (Barcelona: Ámbito Literario, 1979; Madrid: Castalia, 1992; Madrid: Alfaguara, 2001). *Premio Ámbito Literario 1979.*

Al otro lado (Madrid: Magisterio Español, 1980; Madrid: Alfaguara, 2001) *Premio Novelas y Cuentos 1980.*

Unha árbore, un adeus (Vigo: Galaxia, 1988; 2004, 5th edn; La Coruña: La Voz de Galicia, 2002) – *Un árbol, un adiós* (Madrid: Acento Editorial, 1996; Madrid: Suma de Letras, 2004).

La única libertad (Madrid: Cátedra, 1982; Madrid: Alfaguara, 2002).

Contra muerte y amor (Madrid: Cátedra, 1985; Madrid: Punto de Lectura, 2008).

O reloxio da torre (Vigo: Galaxia, 1988). *El reloj de la torre* (Madrid: Mondadori, 1991).

Chamábase Luis (Vigo: Edicións Xerais, 1989; 2017, 19th edn) - *Premio Losada Diéguez 1989 – Se llamaba Luis* (Barcelona: Grijalbo, 1995; Barcelona: Círculo de Lectores, 1997; Madrid: Anaya, 2004).

Recóndita armonía (Madrid: Alfaguara, 1994; 2000, 6th edn; Madrid: Alfaguara, 1996).

Tristes armas (Vigo: Xerais, 1994; 2017, 29th edn; Madrid: Anaya, 2001; 2017, 19th edn).

Dar la vida y el alma (Madrid: Alfaguara, 1996; 1999, 5th edn)

La sombra del ángel (Madrid: Alfaguara, 2000).

Bajo el magnolio (Madrid: Alfaguara, 2004; Madrid: Suma de Letras, 2005) – *Ao pé do magnolio* (Vigo: Galaxia, 2004).

Casi perfecto (Madrid: Alfaguara, 2007) – *Case perfecto* (Vigo: Edicións Xerais, 2007).

¿Quién mató a Inmaculada de Silva? (Madrid: Alfaguara, 2009) – *Quen matou a Inmaculada de Silva?* (Vigo: Edicións Xerais, 2009).

Deseos (Madrid: Alfaguara, 2011).

O Anxo de Eva (Vigo: Edicións Xerais, 2013).

El abrazo (Barcelona: Stella Maris, 2015).

Short story collections

Morir en tus brazos y otros cuentos (Alicante: Aguaclara, 1989).

El tiburón, el ángel y otros relatos (Madrid: Hachette Pilipacchi/ Difusión Directa Édera, 1998).

Querida amiga (Vigo: Galaxia, 1995; 1999, 5th edn) *Premio Losada Diéguez 1996 – Querida amiga* (Madrid: Alfaguara, 2001).

Recuerda, cuerpo (Madrid: Alfaguara, 1998).

Solo pienso en ti (Madrid: H. Liczkowski, 2006).

El amor, la vida y más allá (Santiago de Compostela: Teófilo Edicións, 2017).

Short stories included in anthologies and journals (a selection)

'Ensayo de comedia' [Premio Hucha de Oro 1982], in *Ensayo de comedia y doce cuentos más* (Madrid: Confederación Española de Cajas de Ahorro, 1983).

'El único camino', in *El pájaro y nueve relatos más* (Madrid: Publicaciones del Gabinete de Información y Relaciones Externas de RENFE, 1983).

'Ensayo de comedia', in E. Olazagastegui (ed.), *Sorpresas* (Philadelphia: Harcourt College Publishers, 1993; 2002, 3rd edn).

'De su mejor amiga, Celina', in F. García Pavón (ed.), *Antología de cuentistas españoles contemporáneos (1966–1980)* (Madrid: Gredos, 1984).

'En los parques, al anochecer', *El País*, 6 May 1990.

'En los parques, al anochecer', in C. Estévez (ed.), *Relatos eróticos escritos por mujeres* (Madrid: Castalia/ Instituto de la Mujer, 1990).

'El fantasma de la niña negra', *Panorama*, 24 September 1990.

'Nueve meses y un día', in *Spanische Erzählungen* (München: Deutscher Taschenbuch Verlag, 1992).

'El final', in J. González and P. de Miguel (eds), *Últimos narradores. Antología de la reciente narrativa breve española* (Pamplona: Hierbaola, 1993).

'Entonces empezó a olvidar', in A. Encinar and A. Percival (eds), *Cuento español contemporáneo* (Madrid: Cátedra, 1993; 2001).

'El asesino y la víctima', in J. A. Hernández and E. Guillermo (eds), *Cuentos españoles contemporáneos / Modern Short Stories for Intermediate through Advanced Students* (Lincolwood, IL: National Textbook Company, 1993).

'Querida amiga', in Á. Encinar (ed.), *Cuentos de este siglo: 30 narradoras españolas contemporáneas* (Barcelona: Lumen, 1995; Barcelona: Círculo de Lectores, 1997).

'Los crímenes de Cecilia Böhl de Faber', in Á. Encinar (ed.), *Historias de detectives* (Barcelona: Lumen, 1998).

'Solo pienso en ti', *Interviu,* 9–15 October 1995.

'A través del tabique', in F. Valls (ed.), *Son cuentos. Antología del relato breve español, 1975–1993* (Madrid: Espasa Calpe, 1993; 1996, 5th edn).

'A través del tabique', in J. M. Merino (ed.), *Cien años de cuentos (1898–1998). Antología del cuento español en castellano* (Madrid: Alfaguara, 1999).

'Recuerdo imborrable', *El País Semanal,* 20 August 2000.

'Nunca más', *Mujer de Hoy*, 18–24 August 2001.

'A través del tabique', in *Historias médicas. ¿Qué me pasa, doctor?* (Madrid: Páginas de Espuma, 2001).

'Amores de mujer', in J. Fernández Vallejo (ed.), *Cuentos de cine* (Madrid: Castalia, 2002).

'El final', in R. Hernández Viveros (ed.), *Relato español actual* (México, DF: Universidad Nacional Autónoma de México; Fondo de Cultura Económica, 2002).

'Viaje al Polo Norte', *Mujer de Hoy*, 25 July 2003.

'Los coches de mi vida', in *Mujeres en ruta* (Madrid: Línea Recta, 2005).

'Antes que el tiempo muera', in I. Pertusa and N. Vosburg (eds), *Un deseo propio. Antología de escritoras españolas contemporáneas* (Barcelona: Bruguera, 2009).

'Querida amiga', in *Anthology of Contemporary Galician Short Stories* (Brighton: Foreign Demand, 2008).

'Imagen LIX', in Á. Olgoso and J. M. Merino (eds), *Nocturnario* (Granada: Nazarí, 2016).

Reflections on her own work

'La perspectiva múltiple', in M. Mayoral and G. Gullón (eds), *El oficio de narrar* (Madrid: Cátedra / Ministerio de Cultura, 1990), 159–70.

'La autonomía del personaje', in M. Mayoral (ed.) *El personaje novelesco* (Madrid: Cátedra / Ministerio de Cultura, 1990), 101–108.

'Reflexiones sobre mi propia narrativa', in J. Arancibia, A. Mandel and Y. Rosas (eds), *Literatura femenina contemporánea de España. VII Simposio Internacional de Literatura* (Northridge: California State University & Instituto Literario y Cultural Hispánico, 1991), 15–19.

'Nunca más un hombre. Reflexiones no muy optimistas sobre la vejez femenina', in *Como mujeres. Releyendo a escritoras del siglo XIX y XX* (Oviedo: Consejería de Educación y Cultura, Principado de Asturias, 1994), 209–10.

'Romper los esquemas de lo esperado', in M. Mayoral (ed.), *La risa y la sonrisa (El humor visto por sus autores)* (Madrid: Espasa Calpe, 2001), 45–53.

'Una mirada hacia adentro', in M. Mayoral (ed.), *La risa y la sonrisa (El humor visto por sus autores)* (Madrid: Espasa Calpe, 2001), 9–14.

'Nací mujer. Condicionamientos sociales sobre la mujer escritora', in *Palabra de mujer.* [CD produced by the Instituto Andaluz de la Mujer, Junta de Andalucía, 2004].

'¿Dónde viven mis personajes?', in J. H. Valdivieso and L. T. Valdivieso (eds), in *Madrid en la literatura y las artes* (Phoenix, Arizona: Orbis Press, 2006), 71–75.

Literary criticism

Poesía española contemporánea. Análisis de Textos (Madrid: Gredos, 1973).

La poesía de Rosalía de Castro (Madrid: Gredos, 1974).

Rosalía de Castro y sus sombras (Madrid: Fundación Universitaria Española, 1976).

Análisis de cinco comedias [with Andrés Amorós and Francisco Nieva] (Madrid: Castalia, 1977).

Análisis de Textos (Poesía y prosa españolas) (Madrid: Gredos, 1977).

Rosalía de Castro (Madrid: Cátedra, 1986).

Critical editions

Rosalía de Castro, *En las orillas del Sar* (Madrid: Castalia, 1978; 1990, 4th edn).
Emilia Pardo Bazán, *Cuentos y novelas de la tierra* (2 vols.) (Santiago de Compostela: Sálvora, 1984).
Emilia Pardo Bazán, *Los pazos de Ulloa* (Madrid: Castalia, 1986).
Emilia Pardo Bazán, *Insolación* (Madrid: Espasa Calpe, 1987).
Emilia Pardo Bazán, *Dulce dueño* (Madrid: Castalia, 1989).
Rosalía de Castro, *Follas novas* (Vigo: Xerais, 1990) [with Blanca Roig].
Emilia Pardo Bazán, *La quimera* (Madrid: Cátedra, 1991).
Rosalía de Castro, *Obras completas* (2 vols) (Madrid: Turner, 1993).
Emilia Pardo Bazán, *Los pazos de Ulloa* (Madrid: Ollero y Ramos Editores – Random House Mondadori, 2006).
Cantar de Mío Cid (Tenerife: La Página Ediciones, 2014).

As editor of collections of essays

Estudios sobre Los pazos de Ulloa (Madrid: Cátedra/ Ministerio de Cultura, 1989).
El oficio de narrar (Madrid: Cátedra Ministerio de Cultura, 1989; 1990).
Las escritoras románticas españolas (Madrid: Fundación Banco Exterior, 1990).
El personaje novelesco (Madrid: Cátedra/ Ministerio de Cultura, 1990).
La risa y la sonrisa (El humor visto por sus autores) (Madrid: Espasa Calpe, 2001).
Poemas de amor a través de los siglos (Madrid: Ediciones Sial, 2006).
Memoria de la guerra civil de las escritoras españolas (Madrid: Ediciones Sial, 2011).

For a complete list of Marina Mayoral's contributions to academic journals and collections of essays, please go to www.marinamayoral.es.

Further reading on Marina Mayoral

Concha Alborg, 'Marina Mayoral's Narrative: Old Families and New Faces from Galicia', in J. L. Brown (ed.), *Women Writers of Contemporary Spain. Exiles in the Homeland* (Newark: University of Delaware Press, 1991), 179–97.
Concha Alborg, 'Las artes plásticas en la narrativa de Marina Mayoral: De metaficción a metarte', *Revista Hispánica Moderna* 54.1 (1991), 144–49.
Concha Alborg, 'Marina Mayoral', in L. Gould Levine, E. Engleson Marson and G. Feiman Waldson (eds), *Spanish Women Writers: A Bio-Bibliographical Source Book* (Westport, CT and London: Greenwood Press, 1993), 330–36.
Mónica Álvarez Pérez, 'La narrativa de Marina Mayoral: algunas reflexiones sobre su obra', in M. Villalba Álvarez (ed.), *Mujeres novelistas en el panorama literario del siglo XX* (Cuenca: Ediciones de la Universidad de Castilla-La Mancha, 2000), 255–62.
J. Ernesto Ayala-Dip, 'La metáfora del deseo imposible', *El País*, 11 March 2000.

Ana L. Baquero Escudero, 'Marina Mayoral: *Querida amiga*', in *La voz femenina en la narrativa epistolar* (Cádiz: Publicaciones de la Universidad de Cádiz, 2003), 194–201.

Catherine C. Bellver, 'Entrevista con Marina Mayoral', *Letras Peninsulares* 6.2–3 (1993–1994), 383–90.

Catherine G. Bellver, 'Al compás del reloj: la dialéctica del tiempo en una novela de Marina Mayoral', in A. López de Martínez, (ed.), *Homenaje a Victoria Urbano* (Madrid: Editorial Fundamentos, 1994), 101–108.

Catherine G. Bellver, 'Gender Difference and Metafictional Gaze in Marina Mayoral's *Dar la vida y el alma*', in O. Ferrán and K. M. Glenn (eds), *Women's Narrative and Film in Twentieth-Century Spain: A World of Difference(s)* (New York and London: Routledge, 2002), 184–201.

Nagore Beltrán de Guevara, 'Marina Mayoral, *La sombra del ángel*', *Letras Femeninas* 26.1–2 (2007), 243–44.

Maryellen Bieder 'Ambigüedad narrativa y compromiso social en Marina Mayoral: ¿víctimas o asesinas?', in Á. Encinar y C. Valcárcel (eds), *Escritoras y compromiso. Literatura española e hispanoamericana de los siglos XX y XXI* (Madrid: Visor Libros, 2009), 351–68.

Carmen Blanco, 'A Galicia mindoniense de Marina Mayoral', in *Literatura Galega da muller* (Vigo: Xerais, 1991), 357–63.

María Luisa Brey, 'Marina Mayoral', in *O Intelectual Galego e Deus* (Vigo: Sociedade de Estudos, Publicacións e Traballos, 1998), 129–38

Nuria Carrillo, 'La expansión plural de un género: el cuento 1975–1993)', *Ínsula* 568 (1994), 91–11.

Anne Charlon, 'Brétema: la Galice remémorée ou inventée de Marina Mayoral', in E. Larraz (ed.), *Parcours et repères d'une identité regionale*, vol. 23 (Dijon: Hispanistica XX, 2006), 277–97.

Anne Charlon, 'Les auteurs et l'autorité: absence ou refus. Le cas de Marina Mayoral', *Collection l'Intime, 2/Représentations de l'écrivain dans la literature contemporaine*, 1 June 2012. http://revuesshs.u-bourgogne.fr/intime/document. php?id=241

Rosalía Cornejo-Parriego, 'Conversando con Marina Mayoral', *Letras Peninsulares,* 13.3 (2000-2001), 815–25.

Rosalía Cornejo-Parriego, 'Entre érôs y philía: amistades femeninas en la obra de Marina Mayoral', *Tesserae, Journal of Iberian and Latin American Studies* 8.1 (2002), 13–28. http://www.tandfonline.com/doi/ abs/10.1080/14701840220143968?journalCode=cjil20

Rosalía Cornejo-Parriego, '¿Feminismo posfeminista? Reflexiones culturales a propósito de *Recuerda, cuerpo* de Marina Mayoral', *Bulletin of Hispanic Studies* 80.5 (2003), 593–609.

Rosalía Cornejo-Parriego, *Entre mujeres. Política de la amistad y el deseo en la*

narrativa española contemporánea. [Chapter 5 is devoted to the works of Marina Mayoral] (Madrid: Biblioteca Nueva, 2007).

María Dolores de Asís Garrote, *Última hora de la novela en España* (Madrid: Pirámide, 1996).

Giovanni Battista de Cesare, 'Marina Mayoral, *Recóndita armonía*', in *Annali dell'Università di Napoli L'Orientale*, Sezione Romanza 49.2 (2007), 675–79.

Francesca de Cesare, 'Declinazioni del desiderio in *Recuerda, cuerpo* di Marina Mayoral', in G. Volpe (ed.) *Amistades que son ciertas. Estudi in onore di Giovanni Battista de Cesare* (Napoli: Think Thanks, 2015), 31–41.

Luis de la Peña, 'Cuentos sobre el deseo', *El País*, 7 November 1998.

Paloma Díaz-Mas, 'Un itinerario por los sentimientos', *Ínsula* 535 (1991), 24.

Santos Doval Vega, 'La obra narrativa de Marina Mayoral', *Cuadernos para la Investigación de la Literatura Hispánica* 37 (2012), 130–40.

Ángeles Encinar, 'Tendencias en el cuento español reciente', *Lucanor* 13 (1995), 103–108.

Carmen Estévez, 'Introducción', in C. Estévez (ed.), *Relatos eróticos escritos por mujeres* (Madrid: Castalia, 1990), 7–26.

José María García Rey, 'Marina Mayoral: la sociedad que se cuestiona en medio de una dudosa realidad', *Cuadernos Hispanoamericanos* 394 (1983), 214–21.

Kathleen M. Glenn, 'Marina Mayoral's *La única libertad*: A Postmodern Narrative', in in J. Fernández Giménez, J. J. Labrador Herraiz and L. T. Valdivieso (eds), *Estudios en homenaje a Enrique* Ruiz Fornells (Erie, PA: ALDEEU, 1990), 267–73.

Kathleen M. Glenn and M Carreno, 'Marina Mayoral's *La única libertad*: A Postmodern Narrative', *Actas do Congreso de Estudios Galegos* (Vigo: Galaxia, 1998), 405–12.

Kathleen M. Glenn, 'Reading Postmodernism in the Fiction of Cristina Fernández Cubas, Paloma Díaz-Mas and Marina Mayoral', *South Central Review, The Journal of the South Central Modern Language Association* 18.1/2 (2001), 78–93.

Kathleen M. Glenn, 'Transgresiones genéricas en unas narraciones de Carme Riera, Imma Monsó, Marina Mayoral y Cristina Fernández Cubas', in P. Nieva de la Paz (ed.), *Roles de género y cambio social en la literatura española del siglo XX* (Amsterdam: Rodopi, 2009), 301–15.

Cristina González Moral, 'Estereotipos del personaje femenino en Marina Mayoral', *Lectora, Revista de Dones i Textualitat* 9 (2003), 1–15.

Javier Goñi, 'Taller de pruebas', *El País*, 1 December 2001.

Germán Gullón, 'La perezosa modernidad de la novela española (y la ficción más reciente)', *Ínsula* 464–65 (1985), 8.

Germán Gullón, 'El novelista como fabulador de la realidad: Mayoral, Merino, Guelbenzu...', in R. Landeira and L.T. González del Valle (eds), *Nuevos y*

novísimos. Algunas perspectivas críticas sobre la narrativa española desde la década de los 60 (Boulder, CO: Society of Spanish and Spanish-American Studies, 1987), 59–70.

Germán Gullón, 'La cambiante representación de la mujer en la narrativa española contemporánea: *Chamábase Luis* de Marina Mayoral', in A. López de Martínez (ed.), *Discurso femenino actual* (San Juan de Puerto Rico: Editorial de la Universidad de Puerto Rico, 1995), 33–51.

Sonja Herpoel, 'Vivir es sufrir. *Dar la vida y el alma* de Marina Mayoral', in M. Villalba Álvarez (ed.), *Mujeres novelistas en el panorama literario del siglo XX* (Cuenca: Ediciones de la Universidad de Castilla-La Mancha, 2000), 247–53.

Vance R. Holloway, 'Inmutabilidad y emancipación en las novelas de M. Mayoral', in *El postmodernismo y otras tendencias de la novela española (1917–1995)* (Madrid: Editorial Fundamentos, 1999), 310–34.

Roberta Johnson, 'La narrativa revisionista de Marina Mayoral', *Alaluz, Revista de poesía, narración y ensayo* 22.2 (1990), 57–63.

Roberta Johnson, 'Marina Mayoral's *Cándida, otra vez*: Invitation to a Retrospective Reading of *Sonata de Otoño*', in C. Maier and R. L. Salper (eds). *Ramón María del Valle-Inclán: Questions of Gender* (Lewisburg: Bucknell University Press, 1994), 239–59.

Margaret E. W. Jones, 'Different Wor(l)ds: Modes of Women's Communication in Spain's *narrativa femenina*', *Monographic Review / Revista Monográfica* 8 (1992), 57–69.

Margaret E. W. Jones, 'El mundo literario de Marina Mayoral: visión posmoderna y técnica de palimsesto', *España Contemporánea* 5.1 (1992), 83–91.

Mayte Lama, 'Al otro lado de Marina Mayoral: entrevista', *Confluencia* 19.1 (2003), 19–27. http://www.jstor.org/stable/27922942

Adelaida López Martínez, 'La cambiante representación de la mujer en la narrativa española contemporánea : *Chamábase Luis* de Marina Mayoral', in A. López Martínez (ed.), *Discurso femenino actual* (San Juan de Puerto Rico:, Editorial de la Universidad de Puerto Rico, 1995), 33–51.

Abraham Martí-Maestro, 'La novela española en 1982 y 1983', *Anales de la Literatura Española Contemporánea* 9.1–3 (1984), 149–74.

Carmen Martín Gaite, 'Buen ejercicio literario. *Cándida, otra vez* de Marina Mayoral', in *Tirando del hilo* (Madrid: Editorial Siruela, 2006), 379–81.

Ellen C. Maycock, 'La sexualidad en la construcción de la protagonista en Tusquets y Mayoral', *Espéculo: Revista de Estudios Literarios* 22 (2002). https://pendientedemigracion.ucm.es/info/especulo/numero22/tusq_may.html

Eunice Doman Myers, 'El cuento erótico de Marina Mayoral: transgrediendo la Ley del Padre', in S. Cavalho (ed.), *Estudios en honor de Janet Pérez. El sujeto femenino en escritoras hispánicas (*Potomac, MA: Scripta Humanistica, 1998), 39–51.

Gonzalo Navajas, 'Narrativa y género. La ficción actual desde la mujer', *Ínsula* 589–90 (1996), 37–39.

Pilar Nieva de la Paz, 'Entre dos mundos; la vida del campo y la provincia en las novelas de Marina Mayoral y Elena Santiago', in *Narradoras españolas en la transición política (Textos y contextos)* (Madrid: Editorial Fundamentos, 2004), 135–46.

María Camino Noia Campos, 'Estructuras narrativas na obra de Marina Mayoral', *Boletín Galego de Literatura* 9 (1992), 57–91.

María Camino Noia, 'Claves de la narrativa de Marina Mayoral', *Letras Femeninas* 19.1–2 (1993), 33–44.

Elena Olazagasti-Segovia, '*Recóndita armonía*, de Marina Mayoral, y la amistad entre mujeres', *Bulletin of Hispanic Studies* 75.4 (1998), 435–41. http://online. liverpooluniversitypress.co.uk/doi/abs/10.3828/bhs.75.4.435?journalCode=bhs

Janet Pérez, 'Marina Mayoral', in *Contemporary Women Writers of Spain* (Boston, MA: Twayne Publishers, 1988), 157–57.

Janet Pérez, 'Characteristics of Erotic Brief Fiction by Women in Spain', *Monographic Review / Revista Monográfica* 7 (1991), 173–95.

Milagros Sánchez Arnosi, 'Entrevista a Marina Mayoral', *Ínsula* 431 (1982), 4–5.

Santos Sanz Villanueva, 'Generación del 68', *El Urogallo* 26 (1988), 28–60.

Carmen Servén, 'Variedades sobre identidades femeninas en la Historia de la Literatura: *Querida amiga* (1995) de Marina Mayoral', in B. Sánchez Dueñas and M. José Porro Herrera (eds), *Estudios de Literatura Española desde una perspectiva de género* (Córdoba: Grupo de Investigación Solarha, 2011), 265–74.

María Sergia Steen, 'Un magnolio para dos: la novela de Marina Mayoral', *Espéculo: Revista de Estudios Literarios*, 35 (2007). http://www.ucm.es/info/especulo/ numero35/magnolio.html

María Socorro Suárez Lafuente, 'El pentagrama de la historia y las notas de la identidad en *Recóndita armonía*', *Deva* 3 (1995), 3–8.

María Socorro Suárez Lafuente, 'Subversión e intertexto en la obra de Marina Mayoral', *Letras Hispanas* 1.1 (2004), 47–54. http://gato-docs.its.txstate.edu/ jcr:e98a221b-ecc2-4435-bd05-c048b3f2654f/suarez.pdf

Lynn K. Talbot, 'Self-Discovery and History in the Galician World of Marina Mayoral', *Letras Peninsulares* 5.3 (1992–1993), 451–64.

Anxo Tarrío Varela, 'Marina Mayoral, una voz para Galicia', *Ínsula* 514 (1989), 20.

Phyllis Zatlin, 'Detective Fiction and the Novels of Mayoral', *Monographic Review / Revista Monográfica* 3.1–2 (1987), 279–87.

Phyllis Zatlin, 'Women Novelists in Democratic Spain: Freedom to Express the Female Perspective', *Anales de la Literatura Española Contemporánea* 12 (1987), 29–44.

María Teresa Zubiaurre Wagner, 'Una primera aproximación a *Dar la vida y el alma*: identidad femenina, metaficción y polifonía en la narrativa de Marina Mayoral',

in S. Cavalho (ed.), *Estudios en honor de Janet Pérez. El sujeto femenino en escritoras hispánicas (*Potomac, MA: Scripta Humanistica, 1998), 187–200.

Further online information on Marina Mayoral (a selection)
http://www.marinamayoral.es/
http://www.marinamayoral.es/biografia/index.html
http://www.marinamayoral.es/libros/index.html
http://www.marinamayoral.es/prensa/index.html
http://www.marinamayoral.es/investigacion/index.html
http://www.marinamayoral.es/investigacion/bibliografia.html
http://www.marinamayoral.es/videos.html
http://www.marinamayoral.es/informacion/index.html
http://escritoras.com/escritoras/Marina-Mayoral
http://www.mcnbiografias.com/app-bio/do/show?key=mayoral-diaz-marina
http://www.lavozdegalicia.es/firmas/marina-mayoral
https://mmayoral.wordpress.com/
http://www.laopinioncoruna.es/contraportada/2008/09/10/marina-mayoral-hombres-
  tragaron-dona-emilia/219886.html
http://brazaldelasletras.blogspot.co.uk/2014/05/marina-mayoral-escritora-y-
  catedratica.html
https://www.youtube.com/watch?v=DRLv3DpioHs
http://www.march.es/conferencias/anteriores/voz.aspx?p1=21624
http://www.diariosur.es/v/20110608/cultura/marina-mayoral-deseo-
  impulsa-20110608.html
https://biblioteca.ucm.es/escritores/marina_mayoral/
http://www.cuv3.com/2011/02/17/la-escritora-gallega-que-se-llevo-la-nube-puesta/
www.blogs.elcorreogallego.es/tendencias/ecg/teofilo-edita-escritora-proxima-
  academica-rag-marina-mayoral/idEdicion-2017-11-28/idNoticia-1087107/
https://www.elprogreso.es/gl/articulo/a-marina-mayoral-34-hai-sucesos-fan-pensar-
  vida-despois-da-morte34/201712011934401283340.html

NUEVE MESES Y UN DÍA

Todo empezó aquella noche en que le dije a Juan: 'hoy no hace falta que te lo pongas'. O quizá, para ser más exactos, empezó antes, bastante antes, cuando el médico me dijo que el esterilet me estaba haciendo una úlcera, o antes aún, un día, inclinada sobre la taza del water, mientras me limpiaba las babas con papel higiénico entre arcada y arcada; entonces pensé que tendría que buscar otro procedimento porque aquellas náuseas me estaban haciendo cogerle asco hasta a los ratitos buenos. Así que la cosa viene de lejos, aunque en sentido estricto empezó aquella noche. A Juan le cayó mal, pero eso tampoco es una novedad, también los otros, Marieta y Juan Carlos, le cayeron como una patada. En cierto modo lo de éste fue más bien extrañeza, '¿estás segura?' dijo y 'ya hablaremos', porque ese día tenía reunión de filatélicos y yo creo que con la ilusión de una serie nueva por la que estaba muy interesado se le pasó un poco el susto y lo dejó estar. Peor fue con Marieta. Yo quería decírselo a ella la primera, al fin es mujer y tiene que comprenderlo, así que me armé de valor y se lo dije: 'Marieta, nena vas a tener…' Pero en el último momento me corté. Marieta siempre ha sido muy seca, muy despegada, y de pronto la vi allá tan lejana, comiéndose su filete con patatas fritas sin esperar siquiera que llegase su padre, pero se me cruzaron las palabras y le dije: 'Marieta, nena, vas a tener un hijo'. Y ella, sin levantar la vista del plato y de la revista que tenía al aldo, engullendo a toda velocidad, me dijo: 'no digas tonterías, mamá, es que no he desayunado'. Debía haberlo dejado, no era seguramente el momento adecuado, pero con ella nunca se sabe y además siempre viene a escape, de modo que insistí y se lo dije. Se lo tuve que decir dos veces, fue muy desagradable, me sentí tan avergonzada como si fuera un delito, sin ninguna razón. Marieta ha heredado esa forma de mirar de mi suegra, me acuerdo cuando la conocí, todavía no se me notaba nada, pero tuve la sensación de que la tripa me crecía de repente y me abultaba las faldas,

NINE MONTHS AND A DAY[1]

It all began that night when I said to Juan: 'You really don't need to wear one tonight.' Or perhaps, to be more precise, it started before that, quite a long time before that, when the doctor told me the coil was giving me an ulcer, or even before that, one day, crouched over the lavatory bowl as I cleaned up the spittle between one bout of vomiting and the next with toilet paper; and then I thought I'd have to find some other method because those nauseous spells were making me feel sick in the pit of my stomach and spoiling even the good times I enjoyed in bed with him. So it had been going on for some time, though strictly speaking it started that night. Juan didn't take it very well, though that isn't anything new either; the others, Marieta and Juan Carlos, had also come as a bolt out of the blue to him. In a way this third one came as rather a surprise to him, 'Are you sure?' he said, and 'We'll talk about it later', because he had a meeting of his stamp collectors club that day and I think that because he was looking forward so much to a new issue he was really interested in, the shock wore off a bit and he put it out of his mind. It was worse with Marieta. I wanted her to be the first one I told about it, after all she's a woman and she should understand, so I plucked my courage and I said to her: 'Marieta, my darling, you're going to have a…'. But at the last second I stopped short. Marieta's always been very self-contained, very detached, and all of a sudden I had this vision of her, so distant, eating her steak and chips without even waiting for her Dad to arrive, but the words just kept tumbling out and I said: 'Marieta, darling, you're going to have a baby.' And without raising her eyes from her plate or the magazine she had next to it, bolting down her food as fast as she could, she said: 'Don't talk rubbish, Mum, it's just that I haven't had any breakfast today.' I should have left it at that, it obviously wasn't the right time, but you never know with her and anyway she is always about to dash off, so I persisted and told her. I had to tell her twice, it was really unpleasant, I felt so ashamed, as if it were a crime, though there was no need to feel like that. Marieta has inherited that look of hers from my mother-in-law, I remember when I first met her, there was nothing showing yet, but I had the feeling my belly was suddenly swelling, my skirts were filling out, much worse than with

---

1   A connection between pregnancy and a prison sentence is established by the title, which incorporates '*and a day*', the Spanish formula that is added sometimes to the time that a condemned person has to spend in jail.

mucho peor que con mi padre, dónde va a dar, mi padre fue quien bajó la cabeza anonadado, yo lo comprendo, no teníamos un real y, además, yo era su niña, dieciocho años eran muy pocos para casarse así, de penalty, pero qué se le iba a hacer. Y Marieta me miró igual que mi suegra, sin ninguna piedad, yo diría que con el mismo odio, pero, ¿por qué, Señor?, ¿qué me reprocha?, ¿qué hay de malo en eso? Yo desde niños se lo expliqué a los dos, se lo conté todo, la verdad, nada de la cigüeña, de una forma bonita, 'a los niños los tienen las mamás en un nidito junto al corazón, un poco más abajo' y después, cuando fueron mayorcitos les di un libro muy bien hecho, que lo encargué a Francia a unos amigos porque aquí todavía no había, ni era frecuente hablar a los niños de esas cosas, pero yo quería que lo supieran desde el comienzo, que lo aprendieran bien, no como yo ni como su padre. Y cuando se fue en el verano a Inglaterra hace ya bastantes años, yo le hablé de la píldora, no era agradable para mí, me parecía tan niña, dicecisiete años, pero yo sabía por experiencia lo que puede pasar a esa edad y mejor prevenir que lamentar, a los padres siempre nos coge por sorpresa, pero ella me cortó muy seca: 'ya tomo mis precauciones, mamá, yo no me voy a casar de penalty'. Ni de penalty ni de nada, ya se ve. No sé qué me reprocha, ni cómo tiene el valor de hablarme así. Cuando dijo que se iba a vivir con Pablo ¿qué esperaba que hiciéramos? ¡cómo para alegrarse, vamos, vaya situación! Aún ahora cuando la gente me pregunta ¿qué les voy a decir?, 'pues no, no se ha casado', 'pues sí, vive con uno', hasta para presentarlo a los amigos es una complicación no poder decir 'mi yerno' o 'mi hijo político' o 'el marido de Marieta', lo normal; pues no: Pablo para aquí y Pablo para allá y todos disimulando y echando capotes. Y encima tan seca, tan dura, a mí me parece bien que venga a comer, que vengan los dos y que Juan les pase un dinero todos los meses, pero, por Dios, un poco de comprensión con las debilidades de los otros, que yo admito que son debilidades, pero tiene que darse cuenta de que no soy una vieja y que tengo las mismas necesidades que ella y que un error lo comete cualquiera.

Pero ella siempre ha sido así, ya me lo esperaba, en cierto modo me ha dolido más lo de Juan Carlos; si le digo que tengo lepra no me mira con más horror. Él fue desde pequeño mucho más cariñoso que la niña, sin

my Dad, well for goodness sake my dad was the one who drooped his head, dumbfounded. I can understand why, we didn't have a penny to our name, and anyway I was his little girl, eighteen is very young to get married like that, a shot-gun wedding, but what else could one do? And Marieta looked at me the same way as my mother-in-law, without the slightest understanding of what I was feeling, without the slightest sympathy, sympathy is not the right word, without mercy. I'd say with the same hatred, but why, Lord? What's she reproaching me for? What's so wrong about this? Even when they were children I explained things to them, told them everything, told them the truth in a nice way, none of that rubbish about storks: 'Mummies have babies in a little nest next to their hearts, but a little bit further down' and then, when they were a bit older I gave them a book, very well written, that I asked some friends to bring back from France because they still didn't have anything like that here, it wasn't the done thing to talk to children about those things, but I wanted them to know about it from the very beginning, so they'd learn properly, nor like me or their father. And when she went off to England that summer some years ago now, I talked to her about the pill, it wasn't very nice for me, she seemed so young, just seventeen, but I knew from experience what can happen at that age, and better safe than sorry, it always catches us parents by surprise, but she just snapped at me: 'I'm already taking my own precautions, Mum, because I don't want a shot-gun wedding.' No shot-gun wedding, no nothing, that's clear to everybody. I don't know why she's reproaching me, or how she has the nerve to talk to me like that. When she said she was going to live with Pablo, what did she expect us to do? Be over the moon about it, come on, what a situation! Even now when people ask, what am I going to say about it? 'Well no, they're not married', 'Well yes, she lives with somebody', even introducing him to our friends is complicated. I can't say 'my son-in-law' or 'my son by marriage' or 'Marieta's husband', the usual things; no: it's Pablo here and Pablo there and everybody putting on a show and a pretence. And she is so self-contained, so cold, but it's OK by me if she comes here to eat, if they both come, and if Juan slips them money every month, but, for God's sake, spare me a moment of human frailty, I admit it is human frailty, but what she has to realize is that I'm not an old woman and I've got the same urges as she has and that anybody can make a mistake.

But she's always been like that, I was expecting it, but in some ways Juan Carlos has hurt me even more than she has: if I had told him I had leprosy he couldn't have looked at me with more horror. Ever since he was

comparación, lo que pasa es que en estas cosas me preocupa, hay algo que no va bien, yo no sé si los frailes … no sé, pero no me parece a mí normal tanto desinterés. Yo no soy como mi suegra que quería a su hijo para ella sola, por muy viuda que fuera ya podía suponer que alguna se lo había de llevar un poco antes o un poco después, no era para tomárselo así. A mí me gustaría que Juanca saliese con chicas y, en fin, lo normal a su edad, lo que pide la naturaleza. Cuando se me empezó a notar volvía la vista hacia otro lado, como si fuera algo repugnante y eso que llevaba unos vestidos muy monos y muy disimulones, y ahora igual, le voy a dar un beso y tuerce la cara. Me preocupa este chico y me duele que reaccione así, en el fondo es egoísmo, no querer enterarse de los problemas de una. De modo que si la familia hace eso, ¿qué vas a esperar de los de fuera?, 'estás loca', 'qué insensatez', '¡a estas alturas!'. Hasta el médico, '¿ha calculado usted los riesgos?', calculado, qué barbaridad, como si fuese una máquina; ni una palabra de aliento, nadie. El único, Juan, 'a lo hecho, pecho', como siempre, no es un gran consuelo, pero tampoco lo de los otros. Más de dos me han recomendado un viaje a Londres, Marieta también. Pero yo eso no lo quiero, no es por ser católica, que sí lo soy, pero me parece horrible, como planear un crimen, a escondidas y en un país con esa lengua que no se entiende nada. Además, le decía yo a Gloria, que ella sí que fue hace años a Londres y es de las que me animaban al viaje, mi abuela tuvo dieciocho hijos, estuvo pariendo casi hasta los cincuenta y no le salió ninguno mal. Y ella me decía, 'pero tú qué sabes si de los seis que se le murieron de niños había alguno tonto', y en eso tiene razón, cuando son pequeños se les nota menos y sobre todo antes, que la medicina estaba más atrasada. Pero el mío no, el mío no era tonto. Era un niño hermoso y parecía fuerte. Nació justo a los nueve meses y un día. Nació muerto. Fue el momento del parto, el chico venía bien, pero tardé mucho en dilatar y después algo falló, no tenía ganas de empujar, no sé por qué sería. Me dio mucha pena. Entonces sí que me sentí vieja, que ya no servía, que ya no sirvo. Porque la verdad es que yo lo quería, quería a ese niño, desde aquella noche, desde antes. Yo me acuerdo de cuántas angustias con Marieta y con Juanca, llegaron y cargamos con ellos, pero lo que se dice quererlos, antes, antes de verlos ya aquí, pues no, no los quería, y después estábamos deseando dejárselos a mi

little he's been much more loving than the girl, there's no comparison, but the thing is he worries me in this respect, there's something that's not quite right, I don't know if the monks… I don't know, but such a lack of interest doesn't seem normal to me. I'm not like my mother-in-law who wanted to have her son all to herself, she might well have been a widow, but she must have known that some girl was going to take him away sooner or later, she didn't have to react like that. I'd be happy if Juanca went out with girls, after all it's normal at his age, it's what nature intended. When I began to show he averted his eyes from me, as it were something repulsive, and although I was wearing pretty dresses that hid everything, and even now if I go to give him a kiss he turns his face away. That boy worries me and it hurts me he reacts like that, it's all down to selfishness, not wanting to get involved in somebody else's problems. So if the family behave like that, what can you expect from other people: 'Are you mad?', 'How stupid!', 'At your time of life!.' Even the doctor, 'Have you calculated the risks?' Calculated, what a thing to say, as I were a machine; not a word of encouragement, not from anybody. Only Juan, 'Let's try and make the best of it', same as always, he's not a lot of comfort, but he's not as bad as the others. More than one person recommended the trip to London, including Marieta. But I don't want that, it's not because I'm a Catholic, of course I am, but it seems horrible to me, like plotting a murder in secret, and in a country where they speak a language you can't understand a word of. Besides, I said to Gloria, she's the one who went to London a few years back and who was among those pushing me to go, my grandmother had eighteen children, she went on giving birth until she was almost fifty and they were all OK. And she said to me: 'But you don't know if one of the six who died in childhood was backward', and she was right about that, when they are little it's less obvious and anyway, in those days medicine was much less advanced. But not mine, mine wasn't retarded. He was a beautiful boy and he looked strong. He was born at exactly nine months and a day. He was still born. It happened just as he was being born, the baby was coming out alright, but I was very late dilating and then something went wrong, I didn't want to push, I don't know why that should be. It caused me so much sorrow. After that of course I felt old, felt I was useless, that I am useless. Because the truth of it is that I wanted him, I wanted my baby, from that night, from before that. I remember how much distress there was with Marieta and Juanca, they arrived and we were saddled with them, but what you might call wanting them, before, before seeing them born, well no, I didn't want them, and afterwards we wanted

madre, nos apetecía salir, y con sólo una habitación y aquella cocinita tan pequeña y siempre llena de humos, nos arreglábamos muy mal, no nos iba a alquilar un palacio, decía mi suegra… Ahora tenemos una casa grande y un dinerillo ahorrado y una asistenta por horas y yo tengo tanto tiempo libre. Juan se pasa las horas en el estudio o en la obra y después muchos días con los filatélicos, y yo estoy aquí, esperando que aparezca Marieta y me cuente algo, o el chico. Juan se enfada conmigo, dice que no entiende por qué me siento vieja, que él se encuentra en plena forma, está pensando en apuntarse al maratón, siempre le ha gustado hacer deporte. Así que yo vengo aquí, a este cuarto donde pensaba poner la cuna, junto a la ventana, para que al crecer pudiera ver el árbol y los pájaros que vienen algunas mañanas, y me siento aquí, y lloro un rato.

to leave them with my mother, we longed to go out and, with just one room and that tiny little kitchen so small and always full of smoke, things were really difficult for us, she wasn't going to rent a palace for us, my mother-in-law used to say… Now we have a big house and a bit of money put by and a daily help and I have so much free time. Juan spends his time in the study or at work and a lot of time at the stamp club, and here I am, waiting for Marieta to show up and tell me something, or the boy. Juan gets cross with me, he says he doesn't understand why I feel old, that he feels on top of the world, he's thinking of putting his name down for the Marathon, he's always enjoyed being involved in sport. Anyway, I come in here, into this room where I was thinking of putting the cot next to the window, so that as he got older he'd be able to see the tree and the birds that come some mornings, and I sit here and I cry a while.

PASIÓN DEFENESTRANTE

UNCONTROLLED PASSION

Original Spanish text from
Felicidades conyugales (Barcelona:Tusquets, 1989, 13–21)
© Mercedes Abad, 1989

MERCEDES ABAD was born in Barcelona in 1961, where she studied at the French Lycée and graduated in Journalism from the Universitat Autònoma de Barcelona. Although the first of her novels, *Sangre* (2000), is a fascinating exploration of a mother-daughter relationship, and the second one, *El vecino de abajo* (2007), a complex and enjoyable reflection on how to relate with others, she is primarily known as a short-story writer, and few anthologies of contemporary Spanish *cuentos* fail to include one of her stories. With six collections of stories to her name, this is a literary genre that suits her ironic wit thanks to her excellent ear for dialogues and a fluent humorous discourse that, she says, has mellowed over the years. With *Ligeros libertinajes sabáticos* (1986), she was one of the first women writers in the post-Franco period to use erotic themes in literature from a female perspective, a perspective that had always been considered taboo in such a patriarchal society. A journalist by trade, she has contributed to the written press (*El País*; *El Periódico*) and has worked extensively for other media such as radio (Cadena Ser; Com Radio) and television (TV3; Canal Digital TVE). She currently writes for the German publication *Ecos* (Spotlight Verlag). Always very interested and involved in the theatre, she has written three plays in Catalan, which all premiered in the 1990s. In 2000 she adapted Christopher Hampton's *Dangerous Liaisons* for the theatre, and in 2002 the Marquis de Sade's *La Philosophie dans le boudoir* for the experimental Catalan theatre group *La fura dels baus*. Mercedes Abad has translated Georges Simenon, Vanessa Duriès and Diane Brasseur into Spanish, and teaches creative writing at the Escola d'Escriptura of the Barcelona's Ateneu. Her books have been translated into several languages such as Italian, German, Portuguese, Finnish and Dutch.

Bibliography of Mercedes Abad

Novels

Sangre (Barcelona: Tusquets, 2000).
Negra y criminal (Granada: Zoela, 2003) [detective novel written collectively with other eleven writers].
El vecino de abajo (Madrid: Alfaguara, 2007).

Short story collections

Ligeros libertinajes sabáticos (Barcelona: Tusquets, 1986) – *VIII Premio La Sonrisa Vertical.*
Felicidades conyugales (Barcelona: Tusquets, 1989).
Soplando al viento (Barcelona: Tusquets, 1995).
Amigos y fantasmas (Barcelona: Tusquets, 2004) – *Premio Mario Vargas Llosa NH de Relatos.*
Media docena de robos y un par de mentiras (Madrid: Alfaguara, 2009).
La niña gorda (Madid: Páginas de Espuma, 2014).

Short stories included in anthologies and journals (a selection)

'Ligeros libertinajes sabáticos' and 'Pascualino y los globos', in C. Estévez (ed.), *Relatos eróticos escritos por mujeres* (Madrid: Castalia/ Instituto de la Mujer, 1990).
'La joie de vivre', in L. Freixas (ed.), *Los siete pecados capitales (Catorce cuentos inéditos)* (Barcelona: Grijalbo, 1990).
'Una bonita combinación', in Á. Encinar (ed.), *Cuentos de este siglo: 30 narradoras españolas contemporáneas* (Barcelona: Lumen, 1995).
'Sueldo de marido', in J. A. Masoliver Ródenas and F. Valls (eds), *Los cuentos que cuentan* (Barcelona: Anagrama, 1998).
'Aquel verano del 1975', in P. J. Ramírez (ed.), *Aquel verano* (Madrid: Espasa Calpe, 1996).
'Servicio de caballeros', in J. de las Muelas (ed.), *29 Martinis (That's the Limit!)* Barcelona: Edhasa, 1999).
'Ideogramas húmedos', in A. Estevan (ed.), *Cuentos eróticos de Navidad* (Barcelona: Tusquets, 1999) [Translated into Chinese in 2004, Eurasian Press].
'As I fall', translated by Graham Thomson, *Barcelona Review, International Review of Contemporary Fiction* 25 (2001).
'El placer de callar', in A. Neuman and J. M. Merino (eds), *Pequeñas resistencias. Antología del nuevo cuento español* (Madrid: Páginas de Espuma, 2002).
'Un hombre de temple', in R. Hernández Viveros (ed.), *Relato español actual* (México, DF: Universidad Nacional Autónoma de México; Fondo de Cultura Económica, 2002).

'La corza blanca', in L. Silva (ed.), *Leyendas de Bécquer (*Zaragoza: 451 Editores, 2007).
'Cap d'en Font, 27 de septiembre de 2008', in E. Berbel (ed.), *27 de septiembre. Un día en la vida de las mujeres* (Málaga: Alfama, 2009).
'Una bonita combinación', in A. Billat (ed.), *Three Centuries of Spanish Short Stories (Literary Selections and Activities for the Student of Spanish)* (Newburyport, MA: Focus Publishing/ R Pulins Company, 2010).
'Cosas difíciles de explicar', in C. Velasco Rengel (ed.), *Watchwomen: narradoras del siglo 21* (Zaragoza: Institución Fernando el Católico, 2011).
'Retrato de Emma en el jardín. Técnica mixta', in Á. Encinar and C. Valcárcel (eds), *En breve. Cuentos de escritoras españolas (1975–2010)* (Madrid: Biblioteca Nueva, 2012).
'Amigas', in Á. Encinar (ed.), *Cuento español actual (1992–2012)* (Madrid: Cátedra, 2013).
'Viaje con turbulencias'. http://ebiblioteca.org/?/ver/28228

Plays
Pretèrit perfecte (premiered in 1992 and directed by Jordi Llop)
Si non è vero (premiered in 1995 and directed by Jordi Llop)
Bunyols de Quaresma (Hotel de mala mort) (premiered in 1997 and directed by Joan Anton Sánchez-Aznar)

Essays and reflections on her own writing
Sólo dime dónde lo hacemos (Madrid: Temas de Hoy, 1991).
'Simpatía por lo menor', in A. Neuman and J. M. Merino (eds), *Pequeñas resistencias. Antología del nuevo cuento español* (Madrid: Páginas de Espuma, 2002), 29–36.
'Grandeza y locura del cuento', in E. Becerra (ed.), *El arquero inmóvil: nuevas poéticas sobre el cuento* (Madrid: Páginas de Espuma, 2006), 83–88.
[On the contemporary Spanish short story and the influences on her own writing – no title], in Á. Encinar (ed.), *Cuento español actual (1992–2012)* (Madrid: Cátedra, 2013), 93–94.

Collection of press articles
Titúlate tú (Barcelona: DeBolsillo, 2000).

Further reading on Mercedes Abad
Concha Alborg, 'Desaveniencias matrimoniales en los cuentos de Mercedes Abad', in A. Redondo Goicoechea (ed.), *Mujeres novelistas: jóvenes narradoras de los noventa* (Madrid: Narcea, 2003), 31–43.
Concha Alborg, 'Amistades peligrosas en *Amigos y fantasmas* de Mercedes Abad',

in Á. Encinar and C. Valcárcel (eds), *En breve. Cuentos de escritoras españolas (1975–2010). Estudios y antología* (Madrid: Biblioteca Nueva, 2012), 21–33.

Ana Alcaina, 'Entrevista a Mercedes Abad', *Barcelona Review* 25 (2001).

María Luisa Blanco, 'Mercedes Abad: "Lo pornográfico y lo obsceno son conceptos distintos"', *Cambio 16*, 8 July 1996, 25.

Vicente Carmona, Jeffrey Lamb and Sherry Velasco, 'Conversando con Mercedes Abad, Cristina Fernández Cubas y Soledad Puértolas: "Feminismo y literatura no tienen nada que ver"', *Mester* 20.2 (1991), 157–65. http://escholarship.org/uc/item/9wx441f1#page-4

Maria DiFrancesco, *Feminine Agency and Transgression in Post-Franco Spain: Generational Becoming in the Narratives of Carme Riera, Cristina Fernández Cubas and Mercedes Abad* (Newark, DEL: Juan de la Cuesta, 2008).

Ángeles Encinar, 'Escritoras actuales frente al cuento: autoras y tendencias', in J. Romera Castillo and F. Gutiérrez Carbajo (eds), *El cuento en la década de los noventa* (Madrid: Visor, 2002), 129–49.

Carmen Estévez, 'Introducción', in C. Estévez (ed.), *Relatos eróticos escritos por mujeres* (Madrid: Castalia, 1990), 7–26.

María Isabel Jiménez Morales, 'Mercedes Abad, entre el erotismo, el humor y la crueldad', in A. A. Gómez Yebra (ed.), *Aula de Letras 1994–1995. Cien años de letras españolas* (Málaga: Universidad de Málaga, 1995), 3–13.

Elena Lorente, 'Generaciones cruzadas: Beatriz de Moura / Mercedes Abad', *El País*, 14 August 1996.

James Mandrell, 'Mercedes Abad and *La Sonrisa Vertical*: Erotica and Pornography in Post-Franco Spain', *Letras Peninsulares* 6.2–3 (1993), 277–99.

Jaume Martí-Olivella, '*Felicidades conyugales*', *Letras Peninsulares* 5.1 (1992), 181–83.

Jaume Martí-Olivella, 'The Hispanic Post-Colonial Tourist', *Arizona Journal of Cultural Studies* 1 (1997), 23–42.

Miguel Ángel Muñoz, 'Entrevista a Mercedes Abad', in M. Á. Muñoz (ed.), *La familia del aire: entrevistas con cuentistas españoles* (Madrid: Páginas de Espuma, 2011), 150–55.

'Narradores de hoy: cumplirán los 40 en el año 2000', *El Urogallo* 2 (1986), 18–25.

Janet Pérez, '*Soplando al viento*', *España Contemporánea* 10.1 (1997), 181–83.

Janet Pérez, 'Characteristics of Erotic Brief Fiction by Women in Spain', *Monographic Review / Revista Monográfica* 7 (1991), 173–95.

Janet Pérez, 'Mercedes Abad o el arte de contar', in Á. Encinar and K. M. Glenn (eds), *La pluralidad narrativa. Escritores españoles contemporáneos (1984-2004)* (Madrid: Biblioteca Nueva, 2005), 61–73.

Ana Rueda, 'Mercedes Abad: *Felicidades conyugales*', *España Contemporánea* 4.1 (1991), 150–54.

Fernando Valls, 'La literatura erótica en España entre 1975 y 1990', *Ínsula* 530 (1990), 29–30.

Nancy Vosburg, 'Entrevista con Mercedes Abad', *Letras Peninsulares* 6.2–3 (1993), 221–30.

Further online information on Mercedes Abad (a selection)

http://percebesabad.blogspot.com.es/
http://escritoras.com/escritoras/Mercedes-Abad
https://www.escritores.org/biografias/4569-abad-mercedes
http://www.elcultural.com/revista/letras/-Mercedes-Abad/2136
http://elpais.com/diario/2004/03/19/cultura/1079650803_850215.html
http://elpais.com/autor/mercedes_abad/a
http://www.elcultural.com/noticias/buenos-dias/Mercedes-Abad/6073
http://www.elmundo.es/encuentros/invitados/2000/10/231/
http://www.diariodenavarra.es/noticias/mas_actualidad/cultura/2014/03/30/
    mercedes_abad_quot_todos_llevamos_gordo_dentro_quot_153446_1034.html
http://www.poemas-del-alma.com/blog/especiales/la-nina-gorda-mercedes-abad
https://www.youtube.com/watch?v=wogQvNVwq8s
https://www.youtube.com/watch?v=wwJ0aBdfSH4
http://www.espacioluke.com/2005/Marzo2005/joseluis2.html

PASIÓN DEFENESTRANTE

A Darlos Icaria

Érase un día tórrido y húmedo, una carretera mal cosida, un coche que anhelaba la jubilación y, en el interior del vehículo, un hombre y una mujer. La mujer –yo– conducía con evidente torpeza a causa de los incesantes manotazos que daba al aire en un vano intento de ahuyentar un enjambre de moscas especialmente tenaces, que absolvían a su compañero de viaje y concentraban en ella toda su furia. La predilección de los insectos hacia mí era cuestión que no lograba explicarme y que había verificado a lo largo de penosos veranos durante los cuales picores y escozores me habían impedido entregarme a cualquier actividad que no fuera la de rascarme el pellejo mientras los bichos, semejantes a una aureola mística, seguían ejecutando su frenética danza en torno a mí.

Ríos de sudor y perversos afluentes estriaban mi rostro.No pude evitar maldecir en voz alta, con la consiguiente ofuscación del hombre que iba a mi lado, un simple desconocido, interesado en la compra de una mansión que ni siquiera me pertenecía. Maldije el momento en que, ignoro si llevada por un masoquismo profundamente arraigado o, simplemente, para demostrar que era capaz de hacerlo, acepté encargarme de todos los asuntos relacionados con la venta de la propiedad que Paula había abandonado meses atrás. Al morir Igor, ella había jurado no volver a poner los pies en aquel extraño lugar, morada fantasmagórica de la demencia del difunto.

Cuando, tras nuestra lenta y dificultosa ascensión, llegamos a lo alto de la colina donde se hallaba la casa, tanto mi posible cliente como yo ofrecíamos un aspecto lamentable: desgreñados, empapados en sudor y cubiertos de polvo. Antes de cruzar la verja que daba acceso a la mansión, y aun a sabiendas de que el impacto de lo real superaría con creces cuanto yo pudiera decir, me dispuse a poner en antecedentes al hipotético comprador –creo recordar que se llamaba Julius Capdefila– acerca de las innumerables virtudes del lugar: precio francamente irrisorio, amplitud del terreno circundante, paisaje idílico salpicado de árboles exóticos y sombras bienhechoras, piscina octagonal con un fauno en el centro haciendo las veces de surtidor y una náyade bañándose en sus aguas, jardín romántico donde se apretujaban más de un centenar de esculturas cuyos estilos eran absolutamente dispares, edificio construido bajo los preceptos de la arquitectura minimalista y una

UNCONTROLLED PASSION

To Darlos Icaria

Once upon a torridly hot and humid day, a road in a bad state of repair, a car hankering after retirement, and inside the vehicle a man and a woman. The woman – me – was driving all over the road as the result of taking incessant swipes at the air in a vain attempt to drive away a swarm of particularly tenacious flies that ignored her travelling companion and concentrated all their fury on her. The insects' preference for me was something I never managed to work out, but which had been confirmed during the course of painful summers when bites and stings had prevented me from concentrating on anything other than scratching at my skin while the horrid little creatures, like some mystic halo, continued to execute their frenetic dance around me.

Rivers of sweat and perverse tributaries streaked my face. I couldn't help cursing out loud to the resultant bewilderment of the man at my side, a mere stranger, who was interested in the purchase of a mansion that didn't even belong to me. I rued the day on which – I don't know whether I was driven by some deeply-ingrained masochism or simply to show I could do it – I agreed to take on the responsibility for anything related to the sale of the property that Paula had just up and left some months before. When Igor died she'd sworn she'd never again set foot in that strange place, that haunted abode of the dead man's insanity.

When, after our slow and hard climb, we reached the top of the hill on which the house stood, both my potential client and I looked a sorry sight: dishevelled, bathed in sweat and covered in dust. Before passing through the iron gates that gave access to the mansion, and even though I knew full well the impact of the house itself would far exceed any words I might utter, I wanted to give the would-be purchaser – I seem to recall his name was Julius Capdefila – some background to the innumerable virtues of the place: a price that was frankly laughable, the extensive grounds in which it was set, idyllic landscape dotted with exotic trees and providential areas of shade, an octagonal swimming pool with a faun in the middle that acted as a fountain and a naiad bathing in its waters, a romantic garden where room had been found for more than a hundred sculptures of utterly different styles, a building constructed under the precepts of minimalist architecture, and a tiny Baroque

capillita barroca que Igor había transformado en un taller de pintura y cuyos frescos sorprenderían a más de un avezado pornógrafo. El conjunto no podía ser más absurdo. Considerado por separado, cada elemento era bello en sí mismo, pero su arbitraria yuxtaposición hacía imposible cualquier armonía, por heterodoxa que fuera. A causa de ello, y aunque Paula, poco interesada en el dinero que la venta de semejante pastiche pudiera proporcionarle, había bajado el precio una y otra vez, nuestros propósitos de venta se estrellaban contra la previsible reticencia de los visitantes. Desmoralizada como estaba, y absorta en mil y una tretas, tardé en advertir el interés que manifestaba mi acompañante. Mientras inspeccionábamos el interior de la vivienda, Julius Capdefila observaba atentamente cada uno de los objetos que se apiñaban en mesas y estanterías. Me explicó que coleccionaba objetos antiguos o simplemente curiosos y que se hallaba sinceramente sorprendido ante el desapego de la propietaria hacia piezas tan valiosas. Percibí cierto recelo de hombre honesto en su mirada estrábica, como si sospechase que aquellos objetos podían ser producto del robo, y la casa, una hermana gemela de la guarida donde Alí Babá y sus cuarenta compinches ocultaban sus tesoros. Supuse que el precio de auténtico saldo que pedíamos a cambio no hacía sino acentuar semejante impresión y, al ver que el escrupuloso coleccionista permanecía mudo y expectante, a la espera de una explicación plausible que aniquilara de una vez por todas a cualquier gusanillo roedor de conciencias, decidí relatarle las razones que impulsaban a mi amiga Paula a deshacerse de aquella bicoca al precio que fuera.

Cuando Paula conoció a Igor —ya no me acuerdo en qué circunstancias, aunque juraría que debieron ser tan absurdas como todo lo que aconteció después— su primera sensación, según me contó días más tarde, fue que ninguna de las partes que componían la excéntrica personalidad del checo se avenía a integrarse en una totalidad ordenada y coherente. Más adelante yo misma tendría la ocasión de comprobarlo. Igor era caótico, pero también obsesivamente meticuloso en cuestiones de orden, capaz también de mentir con sinceridad, exhibicionista y exageradamente púdico a la vez, y hurón solitario y estrella indiscutible de todas las fiestas. Era precisamente esa cualidad bífida de su naturaleza la que mayor encanto y poder de seducción le confería.

Paula, a quien lo insólito atraía sistemáticamente, no tardó en sucumbir a los turbios encantos del checo y, en vista de que éste correspondía con notable ardor a los galanteos de mi amiga, todo permitía augurarles una inolvidable secuencia de pasión y felicidad. Las cosas, sin embargo, empezaron a torcerse mucho antes de lo previsto.

chapel that Igor had transformed into a painter's studio and whose frescoes would surprise more than one experienced pornographer. The whole thing couldn't have been more absurd. Each element taken separately was beautiful in itself, but its arbitrary juxtaposition made any sort of harmony, however heterodox it might be, impossible. As a result, and even though Paula, who was little interested in the money the sale of such a pastiche might yield her, had dropped the price more than once, our sales prospects were dashed on the rocks of the visitors' predictable reluctance. Demoralized as I was, and engrossed in a thousand and one stratagems, I was slow to notice the interest my companion was showing. As we inspected the inside of the house, Julius Capdefila paid careful attention to each and every one of the objects piled together on tables and shelves. He explained that he collected antiques or simply curios and was genuinely surprised at the owner's indifference to such valuable pieces. From his squinting look I noted a certain honest man's mistrust, as if he suspected those objects might have been the proceeds of some robbery and the house a twin sister to the lair where Ali Baba and his forty chums hid their treasure. I supposed that the knock-down price we were asking in exchange could only add to that impression and, noting that the scrupulous collector kept silent and expectant, waiting for some plausible explanation that would lay once and for all whatever prickings of conscience were gnawing at him, I decided to come clean as to the reasons that compelled my friend Paula to rid herself of that plum property at any price.

When Paula first met Igor – I don't now remember under what circumstances, though I'd be willing to swear they must have been as absurd as everything else that subsequently took place – her first reaction, according to what she told me a few days later, was that none of the parts that made up the Czech's eccentric personality had managed to blend into one ordered and cohesive whole. I would later have occasion to verify this for myself. Igor was chaotic, but he was also obsessively meticulous on matters of order, capable, too, of lying with sincerity, an exhibitionist yet at the same time exaggeratedly modest, a shy loner yet the indisputable star of any party. It was precisely this doubled-stranded quality of his nature that gave him even greater charm and powers of seduction.

Paula, who was systematically attracted by the unusual, lost no time in succumbing to the Czech's dark charms, and given the fact that the latter responded with notable ardour to my friend's flirting, the scene was fully set for an unforgettable sequence of passion and happiness. Things, nevertheless, began to go wrong long before they were expected to.

Muy poco tiempo después del inicio de su relación con Igor, Paula me llamó un día por teléfono y me rogó, sin más aclaraciones, que acudiera a su casa lo antes possible. De su tono de voz deduje que era presa de una viva agitación, de modo que me reuní con ella inmediatamente. Nada más llegar a su casa, me deslumbró la visión de un magnífico clavicordio. Alevosamente, Paula me dejó paladear durante unos instantes mi estupor sin decir palabra: luego señaló hacia un rincón de la sala donde mi atónita mirada tropezó con un inmenso colmillo de elefante. Habida cuenta de la precaria situación económica en que se hallaba mi amiga, la repentina aparición de objetos tan costosos no dejaba de ser sorprendente. Estaba a punto de preguntarle a Paula si le había tocado la lotería cuando ella, llorosos los ojos y temblorosos los labios, me anunció que era Igor quien le había regalado, no solo el clavicordio y el colmillo, sino un sinfín de otros objetos, aunque de tamaño indudablemente más modesto, que se alineaban en anaqueles antaño desnudos. Paula me contó que todo había empezado un día en que Igor y ella se hallaban en el casco antiguo de la ciudad y pasaron casualmente frente al escaparate del anticuario donde estaba expuesto aquel hermoso clavicordio. Paula se detuvo unos instantes a contemplar el instrumento; luego ambos prosiguieron su paseo. En este punto del relato, mi amiga se empeñó en jurarme que ella nunca había pedido nada a Igor; yo, que la conocía bien, sonreí ante sus intentos de justificación: Paula era la persona menos interesada de cuantas había conocido. Sea como fuere, el clavicordio apareció en casa de Paula al día siguiente, acompañado de una nota en la que Igor le rogaba aceptar aquel humilde presente. Ella, halagada, agradeció el gesto. Sin embargo ese gesto revistiría con el tiempo un significado absolutamente siniestro. Tras aquel primer regalo un auténtico diluvio de ellos invadió la vida de Paula. Todas las sinceras protestas de mi amiga resultaron vanas; no pasaba un solo día sin que, cuando salían juntos, Igor la arrastrara al interior de alguna tienda y la obligara a salir de ella con un montón de objetos que Paula ni siquiera había deseado. Él firmaba los cheques con auténtico deleite, como si ésa fuera su única misión en la vida y, si ella intentaba rehusar los regalos, él se sentía mortalmente ofendido.

El día que me lo confesó todo, una Paula visiblemente desconcertada me pedía un consejo que yo no fui capaz de ofrecer; balbuceé torpemente y sin convicción alguna que los regalos muy bien podían ser un reclamo afectivo, o tal vez una tradición checa poco conocida en nuestro país o un experimento psicológico revolucionario. Pasamos horas y horas cavilando sin que ninguna lucelilla se encendiera en nuestras mentes. Con todo, el

Shortly after her relationship with Igor had started, Paula called me on the phone one day and, without proffering any further explanation, begged me to go to her house as soon as possible. From her tone of voice I deduced that she was in a real state of turmoil, so I went over to see her immediately. I had scarcely got to her house when I was dazzled by the sight of a magnificent clavichord. Slyly, Paula allowed me to wallow in astonishment for a few seconds without saying a word; then she pointed to a corner of the room where my astounded gaze fell on a huge elephant tusk. Knowing the precarious financial situation my friend was in, the sudden appearance of such costly items couldn't help but come as a surprise. I was on the point of asking Paula if she'd won the lottery when, her eyes filled with tears and her lips trembling, she announced that Igor had given them to her as presents, not just the clavichord and the tusk but an endless list of other things too, though undoubtedly more modest in size, which were now ranged on the hitherto bare shelves. Paula told me it had all started one day when she and Igor had found themselves in the old quarter of the city and had passed by chance in front of an antique dealer's shop window where that beautiful clavichord had been on display. Paula stopped for a second to look at the instrument; then the pair had continued on their walk. At this point in the story my friend insisted in telling me that she had never asked Igor for anything; I, who knew her well, smiled at her attempts at justification: Paula was the least materialistic person I'd ever known. Be that as it may, the clavichord turned up at Paula's house the next day, accompanied by a note in which Igor begged her to accept that humble present. She, flattered, thanked him for the gesture. Nevertheless, that gesture was, with time, to take on a truly sinister significance. After that first present an absolute deluge of things invaded Paula's life. All my friend's genuine protests proved in vain; whenever they went out together Igor would without fail drag her inside some shop and force her to come out again with a pile of things Paula hadn't even wanted. He signed the cheques with true delight as if that were his only mission in life, and if she tried to refuse the presents he'd feel mortally offended.

On the day she confessed all this to me, a visibly disturbed Paula asked for advice that I was incapable of providing: I stammered awkwardly and without conviction something about how the gifts might very well be a call for her attention, or perhaps a Czech custom not widely known in our country, or a revolutionary psychological experiment. We spent hours and hours going back and forth over it all without any glimmer of light being

mero hecho de haberse confiado a mí alivió sensiblemente a mi amiga; al despedirnos, su estado de ánimo, sin ser precisamente el óptimo, había mejorado de forma ostensible.

Cuando volvimos a encontrarnos, Paula me contó, no sin un mohín irónico, que se había convertido en una adicta a los regalos; si bien era cierto que seguían provocándole cierta inquietud acerca de la salud mental de Igor, si transcurrían un día o dos sin que él le hubiera ofrecido algún presente, una horrible ansiedad se apoderaba de ella. Entre risas de abierta complicidad, Paula me dijo que había amenazado a Igor: si no le regalaba una casa donde cupieran ella y sus regalos, daba por terminada su relación. Reímos juntas y olvidamos el asunto durante unas horas en las que me alegré de encontrar de nuevo a la Paula de siempre, confiada, risueña y vital.

El tiempo transcurrió de regalo en regalo. Cuando Igor compró la casa de la colina para Paula, ella ya había logrado aceptarlo todo sin graves problemas de conciencia. Las compras compulsivas de Igor se habían convertido en placentera normalidad. Y por temor a resultar inconveniente, ella nunca se atrevió a indagar acerca de las fuentes de ingresos del checo; se contentaba con pensar que, si él despilfarraba el dinero de aquella manera, era porque sin duda podía permitirse ese lujo. Pero como las personas felices tienen la penosa costumbre de asumir, como algo evidente e incuestionable, la felicidad de sus seres más queridos, la tragedia pilló a Paula desprevenida. Cuando Igor, con todas sus cuentas bancarias agotadas y deudas espectaculares –lo atestiguan ciertos papeles que la policía encontró en los bolsillos de la chaqueta del cadáver–, saltó por la ventana del noveno piso de un edificio, el mundo se desmoronó sobre Paula y los regalos. Un psiquiatra se vio obligado a internarla temporalmente en una clínica para enfermos de los nervios. Ella no llevó ningún regalo consigo. Postrada en su cama del hospital, alarmó a todos los médicos y enfermeras de la clínica con sus delirios, infatigables repeticiones de misteriosos inventarios de objetos rarísimos entre los cuales destacaba un clavicordio.

Cuando Paula, una vez restablecida, salió del hospital, se negó a volver a la casa de la colina; cada uno de los regalos que ahí se amontonaban era un dardo clavado en su cerebro. Me dijo que me regalaba la mansión y, cuando logré hacerla entrar en razón y persuadirla de que lo mejor sería venderla, puso como condición que fuese yo quien se ocupara de todo.

kindled in our minds. Nevertheless, the mere fact of having confided in me brought my friend significant relief; when we said goodbye to each other her spirits, without exactly being good, had clearly improved.

The next time we met up, Paula, with a grimace, told me that she'd turned into a gift junkie: even though it was true they continued to cause her a certain amount of disquiet about the state of Igor's mental health, if one or two days went by without his proffering her some present or other she'd be seized by a dreadful anxiety. Amid openly complicit laughter, Paula told me that she'd threatened Igor: if he didn't give her a house where she and his presents would fit, their relationship would be over. We laughed together and put the matter to one side for a couple of hours, during which I was happy to rediscover the Paula of old – trusting, smiling and vital.

Time passed from gift to gift. By the time Igor bought the house on the hill for Paula she had already managed to accept the whole thing without any serious problems of conscience. Igor's compulsive purchases had turned into agreeable normality. And fearful of its proving an unwise thing to do she never dared inquire into the sources of the Czech's income: she contented herself with thinking that if he was squandering his money like that it was because he could undoubtedly allow himself that luxury. But since happy people have the dangerous habit of taking for granted the happiness of their loved ones as something obvious and unquestionable, the tragedy caught Paula off guard. When Igor, his bank accounts exhausted and with spectacular debts – these were attested to by certain documents the police found in the pockets of the jacket that the corpse was wearing – jumped through the window of a ninth floor of a building, the world crashed around Paula and the gifts. A psychiatrist was forced to admit her temporarily into a clinic for people undergoing nervous breakdowns. She didn't take a single gift with her. Stretched out on her hospital bed she alarmed all the doctors and nurses at the clinic with her delirious, tireless repetitions of mysterious inventories of extremely rare objects, among which the clavichord stood out.

When Paula, her health restored, left the hospital, she refused to go back to the house on the hill; every one of the gifts that were piled up there was a dart hammered into her brain. She told me that she was giving the mansion to me, and when I managed to get her to see sense and persuaded her that the best thing would be to sell it, she stipulated that it should be I who took care of everything.

Al concluir mi relato, el semblante de Julius Capdefila, coleccionista desconfiado y hombre intachable y ejemplar, expresaba el más profundo estupor. Todo cuanto había relatado, me dijo, añadía más valor a una casa que, desde el primer momento, lo había seducido. Capdefila quiso aclarar algunos detalles de nuestro trato y la venta quedó acordada. Anochecía ya cuando subimos al coche para iniciar el regreso y, como suele ocurrirme a esa hora del día a menos que interponga una tenaz resistencia, empezó a embargarme la melancolía. La alimenté recordando a Igor y la ansiedad que parecía gobernar todos sus actos, su avidez por la vida, su talante risueño, los accesos de hilaridad que tan frecuentemente lo estremecían y que siempre acababa contagiándonos a Paula y a mí, sus largos y repentinos silencios y su mirada llena de fuego. Y luego los regalos, todos los regalos, desfilaron por mi mente en siniestra comitiva. Había algo en aquella historia que no encajaba: faltaba una pieza en el rompecabezas. Tras la muerte de Igor, esa vaga sospecha me había inducido, sin que Paula lo supiera, a investigar la vida del checo. Hablé con personas que lo habían conocido, recorrí consulados y departamentos de inmigración y metí la nariz en todos sus papeles, sin encontrar jamás indicio alguno que me permitiera comprender lo que había sucedido. Desanimada, al cabo desistí de mi búsqueda. Pero la pieza seguía faltando y nada podía convencerme de lo contrario.

Tras la firma del contrato de venta de la casa de la colina, Paula tomó el dinero obtenido y, en un gesto tan absurdo como liberador, lo repartió entre todos aquéllos que habían querido a Igor y lamentaron sinceramente su muerte. A modo de desquite, Paula dio a la parte que le había tocado un destino muy peculiar: hizo construir un panteón para Igor en el cementerio más bonito de la ciudad. La pesadilla de Paula se convertía en chiste.

Yo había desistido ya de mi empeño en encontrar la pieza que faltaba en el rompecabezas cuando un día recibí una llamada telefónica de Julius Capdefila. Temerosa de que el coleccionista hubiera tenido algún problema relacionado con la casa, me estremecí al oír su voz, pero él se apresuró a tranquilizarme; había encontrado en la rendija de una puerta una carta de Igor dirigida a Paula. Capdefila me rogó que avisara a la destinataria de la misiva y fuéramos inmediatamente a la casa de la colina. Yo protesté aduciendo que Paula no querría volver a aquel lugar, y Capdefila, tan comprensivo como siempre, se avino a que nos encontrásemos en un bar. Paula ya estaba esperando cuando yo llegué; sostenía una copa de vino con mano trémula.

When I got to the end of my story the face of Julius Capdefila, a mistrustful collector and an irreproachable and exemplary man, registered the most profound astonishment. Everything he'd been told, he said, added more value to a house that had seduced him from the very first moment. Capdefila wanted to clarify a few details of our transaction and the sale was agreed. Night was already beginning to fall when we got into the car to start our return journey, and, as usually happens with me at that time of the day unless I put up a really strong resistance, I began to feel overwhelmed with sadness. I fuelled this by remembering Igor and the anxiety that appeared to govern everything he did, his lust for life, his cheerful personality, the fits of mirth that shook him so frequently and always ended up infecting Paula and me, his long and sudden silences and his eyes filled with fire. And then the gifts, all the gifts, filed through my brain in a sinister procession. There was something in that story that didn't fit: a piece of the jigsaw was missing. After Igor's death this vague suspicion, without Paula knowing anything about it, had prompted me to look into the Czech's life. I talked to people who had known him, I scoured Consulates and Immigration Departments, and poked my nose into all his papers without ever finding any clue that would allow me to understand what had happened. Discouraged, I eventually gave up my search. But the piece stayed missing, and nothing could convince me otherwise.

After the signing of the contract for the sale of the house on the hill, Paula took the money and in a gesture as absurd as it was liberating, shared it out between all those people who had loved Igor and who sincerely mourned his death. As a way of making amends, Paula used the share that had come to her for a truly singular purpose: she had a pantheon built for Igor in the most beautiful and expensive cemetery in the city. Paula's nightmare had turned into a joke.

I had already given up my quest for the missing piece in the jigsaw when one day I got a phone call from Julius Capdefila. Afraid that the collector may have run into some problem with the house I trembled when I heard his voice, but he quickly tried to reassure me; in the crack of some door he'd found a letter from Igor addressed to Paula. Capdefila begged me to let the addressee of the missive know of its existence and said we should go immediately to the house on the hill. I protested that Paula wouldn't want to go back to that place, and Capdefila, as understanding as ever, agreed we should meet in a bar. Paula was already waiting when I got there; she was holding a glass of wine in a trembling hand. She was extremely pale and

Estaba tan pálida y tensa y sus ojos miraban al vacío de una manera tan enajenada que, incluso en un lugar tan repleto de gente como aquel bar, llamaba poderosamente la atención. Julius Capdefila no tardó en aparecer y entregar la carta a Paula. En el interior de un sobre sucio y arrugado había una hoja pequeña de papel y un par de líneas que decían así:

'Querida Paula:

He pasado media vida buscando un pretexto para suicidarme. No sabes cuánto agradezco tu colaboración. Gracias mil,

Igor'

tense and her eyes looked into space in such a deranged way that, even in a place as crowded with people as that bar was, she caught their attention. Julius Capdefila was not long in showing up and handing over the letter to Paula. Inside a dirty envelope, all crumpled up, there was a little piece of paper with a couple of lines that read as follows:

'Dear Paula,
I've spent half my life looking for a pretext to commit suicide. You can't know how grateful I am for your collaboration. A thousand thanks,
Igor'

EL ABUELO

THE GRANDFATHER

Original Spanish text from
El País Semanal, 29th July 1990, 4
© Rosa Montero, 1990

ROSA MONTERO was born in Madrid in 1951. She began writing for the Madrid press while she was still at university, where she studied Psychology and Journalism. During those years, she was an active participant in independent theatre groups such as Tábano and Canon, and contributed to a number of newspapers and magazines until, in 1977, she started working for *El País,* the newspaper she has been associated with ever since. From 1980 to 1981, she was the director of its Sunday Supplement. Over the years, she has written for the press all over the world: *Clarín (*Argentina), *El Mercurio* (Chile), *Stern* (Germany), *Libération* and *La Montagne* (France), and *The Guardian* (UK). One of her favourite journalistic genres is the interview. She has excelled in developing a distinctive style that, as her official website notes, is now being studied at Journalism faculties both in Spain and in Latin America. Her chronicles and articles for *El País*, as well as her interviews to leading world figures have been collected in several books. Rosa Montero's socially-minded approach has led her to debate the most controversial issues: from racism to ageism, from mental health to the horrors of war to terrorism. She pays especial attention to women's rights: domestic violence, sexual harassment, as well as intolerant attitudes and habits that are difficult to eradicate even when they are banned by law, are often her topics for discussion. A particularly exemplary work is her series entitled *Historias de mujeres* (collected in a book in 1995): these are biographical accounts of fifteen 'formidable' (as she describes them) women across time and place. They feature, amongst others, María de la O Lejárraga (1874-1956), who wrote works that her husband, Gregorio Martínez de la Sierra, took the credit for, and who exemplifies the ultimate form of discrimination, that of being invisible, of being erased from historical memory. Rosa Montero is a prolific and widely studied novelist with fifteen novels to her name, all of which

have been translated into a number a different languages. A very versatile and prolific writer, she has successfully used different narrative genres: from realistic and testimonial accounts to futuristic science-fiction-*cum*-thriller novels, like *Lágrimas en la lluvia* (2011) or *El peso del corazón* (2015), both featuring the female sleuth Barbara Husky, a valiant android with all the qualities and weaknesses of a human being. Of a more intimate nature are the celebrated *La loca de la casa* (2003), a somewhat autobiographical account full of literary references, and *La ridícula idea de no volver a verte* (2016), a complex and fascinating mourning narrative written after the death of her partner of twenty years that cleverly weaves her reflections during her period of grief with Marie Curie's diary after the sudden death of her husband Pierre. In her latest novel, *La carne* (2016), the 'body' as the location of desire, solitude, and the passing of time as experienced by a mature woman takes centre stage. Rosa Montero has taught Spanish literature in many universities, given guest lectures at cultural events all over the world, and received the most distinguished awards both as a fiction writer and as a journalist. They are too many to list here: for more detailed information about all her activities and accolades, see her comprehensive official website www.rosamontero.es

Bibliography of Rosa Montero

Based on the extensive bibliographical research carried out by Alicia Ramos-Mesonero, Rosa Montero's official website, www.rosamontero.es, provides information about her novels, and about the numerous editions that each one of them has had, as well as the many translations of her books into English, Danish, Swedish, German, French, Korean, Greek, Italian, Norwegian, Portuguese, Turk, Romanian, Dutch, Croatian, Slovenian, Chinese, Bulgarian, Polish, Russian, Serb, Ukrainian and Estonian. The website also offers a complete list of her short stories published in collections and in the press, her prologues to a variety of books, her biographies, interviews, articles and pieces of travel writing. Rosa Montero's contributions to cinema, television, theatre and opera are also listed as are the papers presented at Conferences and all the Courses she has taught at Universities all over the world. It includes the Prizes awarded to her: literary, journalistic, and others related to issues she cares for, such as Human Rights or Mental Illness. The website also collects reviews appeared in newspapers, magazines and online. In order not to repeat what is so easily accessible from her official website, I have listed below only the first edition of her books and the individual prizes awarded to them.

Novels

Crónica del desamor (Barcelona: Debate, 1979).

La función Delta (Madrid: Debate, 1981).

Te trataré como a una reina (Barcelona: Seix Barral, 1983).

Amado amo (Madrid: Debate, 1988).

Temblor (Barcelona: Seix Barral, 1990).

Bella y oscura (Barcelona: Seix Barral, 1993).

La hija del caníbal (Madrid: Espasa Calpe, 1997; 2001; 2007) – *Premio Primavera de Narrativa 1997; Premio Círculo de Críticos de Chile 1999.*

El corazón del tártaro (Madrid: Espasa Calpe, 2001); in graphic novel format, with illustrations by Rafa Alvárez (Madrid: Editorial Funambulista, 2014).

La loca de la casa (Madrid: Alfaguara, 2003) – *Premio Qué Leer 2004; Premio Grinzane Cavour al Mejor Libro Extranjero publicado en Italia 2005; Premio Roman Premier, St. Emilion (France) 2005–2006.*

Historia del rey transparente (Madrid: Alfaguara, 2005) – *Premio Qué Leer 2005; Premio Mandarache 2007.*

Instrucciones para salvar el mundo (Madrid: Alfaguara, 2008) – *Festival of European Literatures Prize, Cognac (France).*

Lágrimas en la lluvia (Barcelona: Seix Barral, 2011); in graphic novel format,

with illustrations by Damián Campanario and Alessandro Voldrighi (Barcelona: Planeta Comic, 2011) – *Premio de los Lectores del Salón del Comic de Barcelona 2012.*

La ridícula idea de no volver a verte (Barcelona: Seix Barral, 2013) – *Premio de la Crítica de Madrid 2014; Prix du Livre Robinsonnais, Bibliothèque du Plessis Robinson.*

El peso del corazón. El regreso de Bruna Husky (Barcelona: Seix Barral, 2015).

La carne (Madrid: Alfaguara, 2016).

Short story collection
Amantes y enemigos. Cuentos para parejas (Madrid: Alfaguara, 1998) – *Premio Círculo de Críticos de Chile 1999.*

Biographies, collections of articles and interviews, and essays on literature
España para ti ... para siempre (Madrid: A. Q. Ediciones, 1976).
Cinco años de país (Madrid: Debate, 1982).
La vida desnuda (Madrid: El País/ Aguilar, 1994) – *Premio Mundo 1978; Premio Nacional de Periodismo 1994.*
Historias de mujeres (Madrid: Santillana/ Alfaguara, 1995).
Entrevistas (Madrid: Aguilar, 1996).
'Montserrat Roig', in L. Freixas (ed.), *Retratos literarios. Escritores españoles del siglo XX evocados por sus contemporáneos* (Madrid: Espasa Calpe, 1997), 347–48.
Pasiones: amores y desamores que han cambiado la historia (Madrid: El País/ Aguilar, 1999).
Lo mejor de Rosa Montero (Madrid: Espejo de Tinta, 2006).
Estampas bostonianas y otros viajes ((Madrid: Península, 2002; Madrid: Punto de Lectura, 2008).
El amor de mi vida (Madrid: Alfaguara, 2011).
Maneras de vivir (Miami: La Pereza, 2014).

Children's literature
El nido de los sueños (Madrid: Siruela, 1991).
Las barbaridades de Bárbara (Madrid: Alfaguara, 1996).
El viaje fantástico de Bárbara (Madrid: Alfaguara, 1997).
Bárbara contra el Doctor Colmillos (Madrid: Alfaguara, 1998).

Further reading on Rosa Montero
Also based on Alicia Ramos-Mesonero's research, a very thorough list of bibliography on Rosa Montero's works is provided on her website: http://www.rosamontero.es/pdf/Bibliografia_Completa_Rosa_Montero.pdf

Under the subtitle 'Estudios críticos', the scholarly work carried out on Rosa Montero's literary output is divided into: books entirely dedicated to her; collections of essays; PhD dissertations on many aspects of her production, and academic articles published in Journals and Conference Proceedings.

What follows is a number of items that have not been included:

Concha Alborg, 'Cuatro narradoras de la transicion', in R. Landeira and L.T. González del Valle (eds), *Nuevos y novísimos. Algunas perspectivas críticas sobre la narrativa española desde la década de los 60* (Boulder, CO: Society of Spanish and Spanish-American Studies, 1987), 11–28.

Samuel Amell, 'El motivo del viaje en tres novelas del posfranquismo', in J. Fernández Jiménez, J. J. Labrador Herraiz and T. L. Valdivieso (eds), *Estudios en homenaje a Enrique Ruiz Fornells* (Erie, PA: ALDEEU, 1990), 12–18.

Samuel Amell, 'Tradición y renovación: un difícil balance en la novela española actual', *Crítica Hispánica* 14.1–2 (1992), 5–11.

Inés Arribas, 'Poder y feminismo en *Amado amo* de Rosa Montero', *Romance Languages Annual* 3 (1991), 348–53.

Antonio Chicharro Chamorro, 'Del periodismo a la novela', *Ínsula* 589–90 (1996), 14–17.

Birute Ciplijauskaité, *La novela femenina contemporánea (1970–1985). Hacia una tipología de la narración en primera persona* (Barcelona: Anthropos, 1994).

Rafael Conte, 'En busca de la novela perdida', *Ínsula* 464–65 (1985), 1–24.

Judith Drinkwater, 'Postmodern Identities: Writing by Women and Rosa Montero's' *Amado amo'*, in R. Christie, J. Drinkwater and J. Macklin, *The Scripted Self: Textual Identities in Contemporary Spanish Narrative* (Warminster: Aris & Phillips Ltd, 1995), 153–66.

Carlos Galán Lorés, 'Los más jóvenes de los jóvenes', *Ínsula* 512–13 (1989), 14–15.

Claudia Gatzemeier, '"El corto invierno de la anarquía": *La hija del caníbal* de Rosa Montero', in Ulrich Winter (ed.), *Lugares de memoria de la Guerra Civil y el franquismo: representaciones literarias y visuales* (Madrid: Iberoamericana; Frankfurt am Main: Vervuert, 2006), 93–100.

Marie-Lise Gazarian Gautier, 'Rosa Montero', in *Interviews with Spanish Writers* (Elmwood Park, IL: Dalkey Archive Press, 1991), 208–15.

Viviana-Claudia Giménez, 'Subversión en *Te trataré como a una reina* de Rosa Montero', *Romance Languages Annual* 3 (1991), 454–59.

Kathleen M. Glenn, 'Fantasy, Myth and Subversion in Rosa Montero's *Temblor*', *Romance Languages Annual* 3 (1991), 460–64.

Kathleen M. Glenn, 'Escritura e identidad en *La hija del cannibal*, de Rosa Montero', in M. Villalba Álvarez (ed.), *Mujeres novelistas en el panorama literario del siglo XX* (Cuenca: Ediciones de la Universidad de Castilla-La Mancha, 2000), 273–80.

María Gómez Martín, *No son batallas lo que quiero contar: la mujer medieval en la novela histórica de autora* (Oviedo: KRK, 2012).

Marisa Herrera Postlewate, '*La hija del caníbal*: In Search of Self-realization', in *How and Why I write: Redefining Hispanic Women's Writing and Experience* (New York: Peter Lang, 2003), 57–93.

Dieter Ingenschay and Hans-Jörg Neuschafer (eds), *Abriendo caminos. La literatura española desde 1975* (Barcelona: Lumen, 1994).

Ángel Juristo, 'Señales de cambio', *El Urogallo* 85 (1993), 28–31.

Rubén Loza Aguerrebere, 'Rosa Montero, el amor y la pasión', in *Palabras abiertas (entrevistas)* (Montevideo: Ediciones B Uruguay, 2011), 52–56.

José Ramón Masoliver, '*Temblor* de Rosa Montero', *Ínsula* 525 (1990), 19–20.

Salvador Oropesa, 'El encuentro con la otredad: "Estampas bostonianas" de Rosa Montero', in J. Fernández Giménez, J. J. Labrador Herraiz and L. T. Valdivieso (eds), *Estudios en homenaje a Enrique Ruiz Fornells* (Erie, PA: ALDEEU, 1990), 472–78.

Peregrina Pereiro, 'El retorno del compromiso colectivo en *La hija del caníbal* de Rosa Montero', in *La novela española de los noventa: alternativas éticas a la postmodernidad* (Madrid: Pliegos, 2002), 111–32.

Jeremy Squires, 'Variations upon the fantastic in Rosa Montero's short stories', *Journal of Romance Studies* 15.2 (2015), 77–93.

Carol Stos, '*Bella y oscura* de Rosa Montero: un acercamiento ecofeminista', in R. Cornejo Parriego and A. Villamandos (eds), *Un hispanismo para el siglo XXI. Ensayos de crítica cultural* (Madrid: Biblioteca Nueva, 2011), 122–38.

Katica Urbanc, *Novela femenina, crítica feminista: cinco autoras españolas* (Toledo, Ohio: Textos Toledanos, 1996).

Fernando Valls, 'La literatura femenina en España: 1975–1989', *Ínsula* 512–13 (1989), 13.

Anne L. Walsh, *Chaos and Coincidence in Contemporary Spanish Fiction* (Bern: Peter Lang, 2011).

Phyllis Zatlin, 'The Contemporary Spanish Metanovel', *Denver Quarterly* 17.3 (1982), –62–73.

Phyllis Zatlin, 'La reaparición de nuevas corrientes femeninas en la novela española de posguerra', *Letras Femeninas* 9 (1983), 35–42.

Phyllis Zatlin, '*Crónica del desamor* y *La función Delta*', *Hispanófila* 84 (1985), 121–23.

Further online information online on Rosa Montero (a selection)
http://www.rosamontero.es/
http://escritoras.com/escritoras/Rosa-Montero
http://www.biografiasyvidas.com/biografia/m/montero_rosa.htm
http://www.rtve.es/alacarta/videos/pagina-dos/pagina-dos-rosa-montero/3719826/

http://www.elespanol.com/reportajes/20160506/122737963_0.html

http://www.diariodenavarra.es/noticias/cultura_ocio/cultura/2016/09/07/rosa_montero_novelistas_estamos_obsesionados_muerte_483580_1034.html

http://cultura.elpais.com/cultura/2010/11/29/actualidad/1290985206_850215.html

http://blog.entreescritores.com/rosa-montero-las-editoriales-quiebran-muchos-escritores-no-encuentran-editor-y-de-seguir

www.anikaentrelibros.com/autores/autores-destacados/7131-rosa-montero/

http://www.zendalibros.com/la-carne-arde-los-60-otras-cosas-rosa-montero-nunca-me-dijo/

http://www.planetadelibros.com/autor/rosa-montero/000012593

https://www.yenny-elateneo.com/entrevistas/rosa-montero-el-paso-del-tiempo-el-amor-y-otras-obsesiones/

EL ABUELO

Debería haber sospechado algo por la propina que le dieron: 200 pesetas que el hombre le metió en la mano, con torpe disimulo, mientras aparentaba estar absorto en la contemplación del letrero roto de la gasolinera. Debería haberlo sospechado, porque, además, no tenía la pinta de dar buenas propinas. Con ese aspecto de mirarlo todo por las comisuras de los ojos, y la camisa de manga corta abrochada hasta el gaznate. En cuanto que retiró la manguera, el hombre se metió en el coche como una bala y salió zumbando. Bueno, le costó un poco arrancar. Estaba nervioso: arrancaba y se le calaba, y entonces echaba el cuerpo hacia delante, como intentando impulsar el vehículo con los hombros. Por fin, el utilitario petardeó y allá fueron los tres en el coche encarnado: el tipo que nunca miraba a los ojos, la mujer gorda que se mordía los labios y el niño que, en el asiento de atrás, aplastaba la nariz contra el cristal y bizqueaba. Mariano no sabía por qué, pero se había fijado en ellos. Quizá por las 200 pesetas. Pero más bien porque tenían algo ligeramente raro y especial. Desagradable.

Como era el principio de las vacaciones había mucho movimiento en la gasolinera, de modo que Mariano tardó en darse cuenta. Luego le vio ahí, de pie junto a la puerta de los lavabos. Era un viejo alto y delgado, pulcramente vestido. Llenó Mariano los depósitos de unos cuantos coches y el viejo seguía ahí, tieso como una estaca, aunque le estaba cayendo encima un sol africano. Mariano se enjugó las manos con un trapo y se acercó a él:

—¿Desea usted algo?

El viejo le miró y pestañeó con aire confundido. Tenía la frente cubierta de gotitas de sudor y la calva congestionada y con manchones rojos. Sonrió.

—Quiero una coca-cola.

'Acabáramos', se dijo Mariano; 'si no le llegó a preguntar, se nos derrite', Abrió el arcón congelador, sacó un bote de cola y se lo dio.

—¿Y la pajita?—preguntó el anciano, frunciendo reprobadoramente el ceño.

—Aquí no tenemos pajitas—resopló Mariano mientras miraba las filas de acalorados automovilistas que esperaban para repostar—. Son 125 pesetas.

—Yo no tomo coca-cola sin pajita—explicó el viejo con educada firmeza.

—Mire, a mí me dan lo mismo sus costumbres—gruñó Mariano, que era un hombre más bien brusco—. Usted ha abierto el bote y me lo tiene que pagar: 125 pesetas.

THE GRANDFATHER

He should have suspected something from the tip he was given: 200 pesetas, which the man slipped into his hand with awkward dissimulation as he pretended to be absorbed in the broken sign over the petrol station. He should have suspected him anyway because he didn't look like the sort who'd give a good tip. With that way he had of looking at everything out of the corner of his eye and his short-sleeved shirt buttoned fast up to his gullet. As soon as he pulled out the nozzle the man had shot into the car like a bullet and roared off. OK, he had a bit of trouble getting started. He was nervous: he tried to start the car several times and flooded the engine, and then threw his body forward as if trying to propel the vehicle with his shoulders. Finally the engine of the little blood red car back-fired and there they went, the three of them, inside it: the chap who never looked anyone in the eye, the fat woman gnawing at her lip, and the kid in the back seat pressing his nose against the glass and making himself go cross-eyed. Mariano didn't know why, but he had noticed them. Perhaps it was because of the 200 pesetas. But more likely it was because there was something rather strange and special about them. Unpleasant.

Being the beginning of the holidays, there was a lot of coming and going at the petrol station, so it took Mariano a while to realise what was going on. Then he saw him, standing there, next to the door to the toilets. He was a tall, thin elderly man, tidily dressed. Mariano filled up the tanks of a few more cars and the old man went on standing there, stiff as a post, even though the heat of an African sun was beating down on him. Mariano wiped his hands on a rag and went over to him:

'Can I get you something?'

The old man looked at him and blinked as if confused. His brow was covered with droplets of sweat and his balding head was flushed with big red blotches. He smiled.

'I want a coca-cola.'

'I get it', said Mariano to himself; 'If I hadn't asked him, he'd have melted.' He opened the fridge, took out a can of cola and handed it to him.

'That's 125 pesetas.'

'What about the straw?' asked the old man, frowning with disapproval.

'We don't have straws here', sighed Mariano, keeping an eye on the rows of tired, hot drivers waiting to have their cars filled up. 'That's 125 pesetas.'

El anciano se irguió, digno como un duque. Le sacaba por lo menos media cabeza a Mariano, pero era todo puro pellejo y huesos, una menudencia casi transparente.

–No llevo dinero encima. Tendrá que esperar usted a que vuelva mi hijo.

–¿Su hijo? ¿Y adónde se ha marchado su hijo?

El viejo parpadeó; extendió el brazo y señaló alrededor, con un vago ademán en el que cabía con holgura la inmensidad del mundo. Mariano miró en torno suyo: el páramo en el que estaba instalada la gasolinera refulgía bajo un sol infernal. Tierras desérticas y sucias, sembradas de latas y papeles. Mariano resopló haciendo acopio de paciencia y regresó a los surtidores. Se pasó un buen rato llenando depósitos y el viejo seguía ahí, con toda la solanera en su cabeza, aferrado como un poseso a su lata de cola. Y entonces, de pronto, Mariano comprendió. No era un hombre inteligente; sobre todo no era un hombre de pensamiento rápido. Pero al fin comprendió. Se puso tan nervioso que derramó parte del combustible por el suelo y dejó un automóvil a medio servir. Corrió hacia el anciano:

–¿Cómo es su hijo?

El viejo dio un respingo y le miró con cara de susto.

–¿Y cómo es el coche? Porque venían ustedes en coche, ¿no?– insistió angustiado.

Y entonces, a trompicones, el anciano confirmó sus sospechas. Sí, el coche era rojo; sí, iba con el nieto y con la nuera. Sí, él había entrado en los retretes y…

Mariano se pasó la manaza por la cara. Que le tuviera que ocurrir esto a él. A finales de julio. Con el trabajo que había. Con el calor que hacía. Y tener que hacerse cargo de un viejo chocho. Le miró con inquina por el rabillo del ojo: ahí estaba, sudoroso y purpúreo, achicharrado. Ahora sólo faltaba que el anciano la *palmara* de una insolación. Mariano rugió bajito, limpió con un trapo la banqueta y la puso en la sombra, pegada a la pared de la oficina.

–Venga. Siéntese aquí– gruñó.

'I don't drink coca-cola without a straw', explained the old man in a firm well-mannered voice.

'Look, I don't give a damn what you do or what you don't', growled Mariano, who was a rather rude man. 'You've opened the can and now you've got to pay me: 125 pesetas.'

The old man straightened up, dignified as a duke. He was at least half a head taller than Mariano, but he was all skin and bones, a virtually transparent little man.

'I don't carry any money on me. You'll have to wait until my son comes back.'

'Your son? And where's your son gone?'

The old man blinked; he stretched out his arm and made a broad, vague signalling gesture that widely encompassed the immensity of the world. Mariano looked around him: the bleak plateau that formed the setting for the petrol station sparkled under the hellish sun. It was a dirty wasteland littered with cans and bits of paper. Mariano sighed. He was doing his best to be patient. He went back over to the petrol pumps. He spent quite a lot of time filling up tanks and the old man went on standing there, with the full force of the sun beating down on his head, clinging to his can of cola like a man possessed. And then suddenly Mariano understood. He wasn't an intelligent man; and he certainly wasn't a man who could think on his feet. But at last he understood. He got so nervous he spilled some petrol on the ground and left a car he was halfway through filling up. He ran over to the old man:

'What does your son look like?'

The old man gave a start and looked at him with a frightened face.

'And what does the car look like? Because you did come by car, didn't you?' he insisted anxiously.

And then, in fits and starts, the old man confirmed his worst suspicions. Yes, the car was red; yes, he'd been with his grandson and his daughter-in-law. Yes, he'd gone off to the toilet and...

Mariano wiped his broad hand across his face. How could something like this happen to him? At the end of July. With the work he had to do. In this heat. And to have to take charge of some old dodderer. He looked at him with resentment out of the corner of his eye: there he was, sweaty and red in the face, frying to a crisp. All it needed now was for the old man to peg out from sunstroke. Mariano growled, wiped the bench with a rag and moved it over into the shade, hard up against the wall of the office.

'Come on. Sit yourself down here', he grunted.

El viejo obedeció dócilmente y se dejó caer en la banqueta con un suspiro de alivio. Se mantenía muy serio y erguido, sujetando con toda majestad su coca-cola intacta. Mariano mandó al chico que telefoneara a la Guardia Civil para que vinieran a recogerle.

–Vamos a la playa–dijo de pronto el viejo con una sonrisa complacida–. Mi nieto sabe nadar. Mi nieto me quiere mucho. Es un buen chico.

–Ya.

Se había corrido la voz por la estación y los clientes miraban al anciano como quien mira la jaula de los monos. 'A ver si llegan los civiles de una vez', se dijo Mariano. *Pelona* se acercó al viejo renqueando y le olisqueó amistosamente con su hocico fino y tembloroso. También ella había aparecido por allí un buen día, con señales de haber llevado collar y evidentemente abandonada, medio muerta de hambre y arrastrando una pata aplastada que nunca llegó a recuperar. Mariano había dejado que la perra durmiera en la gasolinera, y además la alimentaba, pero, claro, un viejo era otra cosa.

El anciano parpadeó e inclinó la cabeza hacia él.

–Es que, ¿sabe usted?, tengo un poquito de incontinencia– explicó en un penetrante susurro–. Por eso tuve que ir al excusado mientras echaban gasolina… Claro, yo comprendo que para los demás debe ser muy cansado…

Por primera vez en muchos años, Mariano pensó: 'Menos mal que soy un solterón'. Luego se acercó al congelador, sacó un zumo y arrancó la pajita que venía adherida al cartón.

–Tenga, su maldita paja–dijo adustamente.

Y el viejo la cogió con avidez, la hundió en el bote y comenzó a chupar, con un ruidito de lactante y una expresión de dicha absoluta, el caldo recalentado y pegajoso.

The old man obeyed meekly and dropped down onto the bench with a sigh of relief. He remained unsmiling and ramrod straight, clinging with full majesty to his untasted coca-cola. Mariano sent the boy off to phone the Guardia Civil for them to come and pick him up.

'We're going to the beach', said the old man suddenly with a happy smile. 'My grandson knows how to swim. My grandson loves me very much. He's a good boy.'

'Sure he is.'

Word had spread around the petrol station and the customers were looking at the old man in the same way as they would a cage of monkeys. 'Let's see if the Guardia Civil turn up for once', muttered Mariano to himself. *Pelona* limped up to the old man and sniffed at him in a friendly way with her sensitive and trembling nose. She too had just turned up there one fine day, with signs of having once worn a collar but now obviously abandoned, half dead from hunger and dragging one crushed paw which had never recovered. Mariano had let the dog sleep in the petrol station and had fed her, but of course an old man was a different matter.

The old man blinked and leaned his head towards him.

'The thing is you know, I'm a bit incontinent', he explained in a piercing whisper. 'That's why I had to go to the toilet while they were filling the tank… Of course, I know it must be very tiresome for everybody else…'

For the first time in many years Mariano thought: 'It's not such a bad thing I never got married.' Then he went over to the fridge, took out a carton of juice and yanked off the little straw that was stuck to it.

'Here, take your bloody straw', he said gruffly.

And the old man took it eagerly, plunged it into the can and, and making little noises like a baby at the breast, he began to suck at the hot, sticky liquid, with an expression of absolute happiness on his face.

HIPATIA

HYPATIA

Original Spanish text from *Amor breve*
(Barcelona: Muchnik Editores, 1990, 22–33);
later collected in *El siglo de las mujeres*
(Barcelona: Ediciones del Bronce, 2000, 49–60)
© Nuria Amat, 1990

NURIA AMAT was born in Barcelona. She studied Information Science, Library Studies and Hispanic Philology at university. She did her PhD in Information Science and has taught Library Studies at the Escuela Universitaria de Biblioteconomía y Documentación in Barcelona. She is currently based in Barcelona, but has lived in Colombia, Mexico, Paris, Berlin and the United States. Some of these places provide the setting for her novels, such as the Colombian set *Reina de América* (2001), which won the Premi Ciutat de Barcelona. A versatile author, Nuria Amat has written novels, short stories, poetry, theatre and essays. In 2004, she translated the poetry of Emily Dickinson in a very personal and free manner: it was a poetic exercise which combined an homage and an 'appropriation' of the American poet that inspired her to write more personal poetry in *Poemas impuros* (2008). Her poetry has been translated into English by Carol Maier, translator of María Zambrano and Rosa Chacel, among others. Nuria Amat is better known for her novels, especially those that cross genres in a sophisticated fashion which includes psychoanalysis, social comment, feminist concerns, metafictional awareness and, lately, political engagement. Nuria Amat's fiction has been translated into English, Italian, Portuguese, German and Swedish. She writes mostly in Spanish but her novel *Amor i guerra* (2011) was first published in Catalan and awarded the prestigious Premi Ramon Llull de les LLetres Catalanes. In 2008 Nuria Amat was invited by Carlos Fuentes and Gabriel García Márquez to occupy the Cátedra Julio Cortázar at the Universidad de Guadalajara, in Mexico, and in 2013 she was distinguished with the Venezuelan Orden Alejo Zuloaga.

Bibliography of Nuria Amat
Novels
Pan de boda (Barcelona: La Sal, Edicions de les Dones, 1979).
Narciso y Armonía (Barcelona: Puntual, 1982).
Todos somos Kafka (Madrid: Anaya, 1993; 2004; Paris: Allia, 2008).
Viajar es muy difícil: manual de ruta para viajeros periféricos (Madrid: Anaya & Mario Muchnik, 1995).
La intimidad (Madrid: Alfaguara, 1997).
El país del alma (Barcelona: Seix Barral, 1999) – *Finalist Premio Rómulo Gallegos 2001.*
Reina de América (Barcelona: Seix Barral, 2001) – *Premi Ciutat de Barcelona 2002* –*Queen Cocaine* (San Francisco: City Lights, 2005) – *Shorlisted for the IMPAC Literary Prize 2007.*
Deja que la vida llueva sobre mí (Barcelona: Lumen, 2007).
Amor i guerra (Barcelona: Planeta, 2011) – *Premi de les Lletres Catalanes Ramon Llull* – *Amor y guerra* (Barcelona: Planeta, 2011) – *Feu d'été* (Paris: Robert Laffont, 2011).
El sanatorio (Barcelona: EDLibros, 2016).

Short story collections
El ladrón de libros y otras bibliomanías (Barcelona: Muchnik, 1988).
Amor breve (Barcelona: Muchnik, 1990).
Monstruos (Madrid: Anaya & Mario Muchnik, 1991).
El siglo de las mujeres (Barcelona: Ediciones del Bronce, 2000).

Short stories included in anthologies and journals (a selection)
'Amor breve', in M. Monmany (ed.), *Vidas de mujer* (Madrid: Alianza, 1998).
'Casa de verano', in *Mujeres al alba* (Madrid: Alfaguara, 1999).
'Summer House', translated by Graham Thomson, *Barcelona Review, International Review of Contemporary Fiction*, 12 (1999). http://www.barcelonareview.com/amat/e_na.htm
'Pim, pam y pum', in *Mudances / Mudanzas* (Barcelona: Columna, 1999).
'La loca que hay en mí', in *Las vidas de Eva* (Barcelona: Destino, 2007).
'Sin amante', in L. Freixas (ed.), *Cuentos de amigas* (Barcelona: Anagrama, 2009).
'The Weeding', in P. Bush and L. Dillman (eds), *Spain: A Traveler's Literary Companion* (Berkeley, CA: Whereabouts, 2003).
'Amor breve', in in Á. Encinar and C. Valcárcel (eds), *En breve. Cuentos de escritoras españolas (1975–2010)* (Madrid: Biblioteca Nueva, 2012).

Poetry
Amor infiel. Emily Dickinson por Nuria Amat (Madrid: Losada, 2004).
Poemas impuros (Barcelona: Bruguera, 2008).

Play
Pat's Room (premiered in 1997, Sala Becket, Barcelona).

Essays on literature
De la información al saber (Madrid: Fundesco, 1990).
El libro mudo: las aventuras del escritor entre la pluma y el ordenador (Madrid: Anaya Mario Muchnik, 1994).
Letra herida (Madrid: Alfaguara, 1998).
La nostalgia de los libros perdidos (La Laguna, Tenerife: Universidad de la Laguna, 1998).
Juan Rulfo, el arte del silencio (Barcelona: Omega, 2003).
Escribir y callar (Madrid: Siruela, 2010).

Further reading on Nuria Amat
César Aira, 'Voces entre la selva', *El País* (Babelia), 30 March 2002.
Ana Alcaina, 'Interview with Nuria Amat', trans. by S. Brownbridge, *Barcelona Review*, 1999. http://www.BarcelonaReview.com/12/e_na_int.htm
Aldo Albònico, 'Donne e uomini svelati: l'oracolo manual di Nuria Amat', in S. Regazzoni and L. Buonomo (eds), *Maschere. Le scritture delle donne nelle culture iberiche* (Roma: Bulzoni, 1994), 63–67.
Marta E. Altisent, '*El país del alma* en las geografías literarias de Nuria Amat', in E. L. Bergmann and R. Herr (eds), *Mirrors and Echoes: Women's Writing in Twentieth-Century Spain* (Berkeley: Global Area, and International Archive; University of California Press, 2007), 151–63.
Marta Altisent, 'Escritoras y escritura en la narrativa breve de Nuria Amat', in Á. Encinar and C. Valcárcel (eds), *En breve. Cuentos de escritoras españolas (1975–2010). Estudios y antología* (Madrid: Biblioteca Nueva, 2012), 35–54.
Samuel Amago, *True Lies: Narrative Self-Consciousness in the Contemporary Spanish Novel* (Lewisburgh, PA: Bucknell University Press, 2006).
J. Ernesto Ayala-Dip, 'Crónica de un amor burgués', *El País* (Babelia), 26 June 1999.
Isolina Ballesteros, 'Intimidad y mestizaje literario: una entrevista con Nuria Amat', *Letras Peninsulares* 11.2–3 (1998–1999), 679–92.
Carme Basté, 'Un divertimento sin puntos ni comas', *Mundo Diario*, 14 February 1979.
Anna Becciú, 'Raíces de Rulfo', *El País* (Babelia), 31 January 2004.
Ma. Ángeles Cabré, 'Autobiografía inventada', *La Vanguardia* (Culturas), 21 May 2008.
Mario Campaña, 'Entrevista a Nuria Amat', *Guaraguao* 14.35 (2010), 11–122. http://www.jstor.org/stable/23266252
Nuria Capdevila-Argüelles, 'Viaje hacia el estado de novela. Bildungsroman literario y transgenérico de la voz de Nuria Amat', *Quimera* 186 (1999), 55–64.
Nuria Capdevila-Argüelles, *Challenging Gender and Genre in the Literary Text: The*

Works of Nuria Amat' (New Orleans: The University Press of the South, 2002).

Nuria Capdevila-Argüelles, 'Textual Silence and (Male) Homosexual Panic in Nuria Amat's *La intimidad*, *Tesserae, Journal of Iberian and Latin American Studies* 8.1 (2002), 5–12.

Pilar Castro, '*Amor y guerra*', *El Mundo* (Cultural), 24 February 2012.

Carlos Fuentes, 'La sombra dilatada de Kafka', *El País* (Babelia), 25 September 2004.

Carlos Fuentes, 'Nous somme tous Kafka', *L'Herne. Cahier Fuentes* 87, 103–104. https://www.scribd.com/document/32323897/Cahier-N-87-Fuentes

Carlos Fuentes, 'Nuria Amat', *El País*, 6 September 2008.

Roberto García Bonilla, 'Nuria Amat: algunos retratos de Juan Pérez Vizcaíno', *Espéculo* 28 (2004–2005). http://www.nuriaamat.com/dossier/robertogarciabonilla.pdf

Juan Goytisolo, 'Escritora a secas', *El País* (Babelia), 29 March 2008.

Julià Guillamon, 'Maldito Franco, maldito Stalin', *La Vanguardia* (Culturas), 30 March 2011.

Eduardo Haro Tecglen, 'Una infancia literaria', *El País* (Babelia), 12 April 1997.

Carol Maier, 'Love Unfaithful but True: Reflections on *Amor infiel: Emily Dickinson por Nuria Amat'*, *The Emily Dickinson Journal* 18.2 (2009), 77–93.

Andreu Manresa, 'Núria Amat gana el Llull con una novela ambientada en 1936', *El País*, 4 February 2011.

Ana María Moix, 'Prólogo', in N. Amat, *Viajar es tan difícil. Manual de ruta para escritores periféricos* (Barcelona: Bruguera, 2008), 7–10.

Ana María Moix, 'Literatura hecha biografía', *El País* (Cataluña), 13 March 1997.

Zulema Moret, 'La loca, la lectora y contar la vida en *La intimidad* de Nuria Amat', in M. Villaba Álvarez (ed.), *Mujeres novelistas en el panorama literario del siglo XX* (Cuenca: Universidad de Castilla-La Mancha, 2000), 317–27.

Matías Néspolo, 'Carlos Fuentres y Gabo invitan a Nuria Amat a la Cátedra Julio Cortázar', *El Mundo* (Cultura), 7 June 2008.

Luis Nogales Pita, 'Amor infiel y fidelidad al amor', *El Semanal* 444 (2004). http://www.nuriaamat.com/dossier/amorinfiel.htm

Ana Nuño, 'Desnudar la voz. Entrevista a Nuria Amat', *Quimera* 182 (1999), 8–12.

Julio Ortega, 'Remedio para melancólicos', *El País*, 16 August 1997.

Jose Miguel Oviedo, '*Poemas impuros*, de Nuria Amat', *Letras Libres*, 115 (2008). http://www.letraslibres.com/mexico/libros/poemas-impuros-nuria-amat

Felip Palou, 'Núria Amat gana el Ramon Llull con su primera novela en catalán', *La Vanguardia* (Cultura), 4 February 2011.

Isabel Punzano, 'La poetisa Nuria Amat', *El País*, 12 April 2008.

Susanna Regazzoni, 'Escritoras españolas hoy. Rosa Montero y Nuria Amat', in A. del Toro and D. Ingenschay (eds), *La novela española actual. Autores y tendencias* (Kassel: Edition Reichenberger, 1995), 253–70.

José Ribas, 'Entrevista con Nuria Amat', *Ajoblanco* 120 (1999), 20–4.

Lluís Satorras, 'La hija de Kafka', *El País*, 28 November 1998.

Ricardo Senabre, '*Reina de América*', *El Mundo* (Cultural), 10 April 2002.

Ricardo Senabre, '*Deja que la vida llueva sobre mí*', *El Mundo* (El Cultural), 28 February 2008.

Juan Senís Fernández, 'Entre el ensayo, la novela y el libro de viajes. Un ejemplo de indefinición genérica: Viajar es muy difícil, de Nuria Amat', in *Novela y ensayo. VIII Simposio Internacional sobre Narrativa Hispánica Contemporánea* (El Puerto de Santa María: Fundación Luis Goytisolo, 2001), 165–74.

Virginia Trueba Mira, 'La escritura de *La intimidad* (una novela de Nuria Amat), *Notas y Estudios Filológicos* 14 (1999), 265–79.

Carlos Zanón, 'Una dona anomenada cavall: Parlem de literatura, de talent i ofici, parlem de *Reina de América*', *Avui*, 23 March 2003.

Further online information on Nuria Amat (a selection)

http://www.nuriaamat.com/

http://elpais.com/autor/nuria_amat/a

http://escritoras.com/escritoras/Nuria-Amat

https://www.escritores.org/biografias/133-nuria-amat

http://www.elcultural.com/revista/letras/NURIA-AMAT/4188

http://trabalibros.com/escritores/i/780/56/nuria-amat

http://www.20minutos.es/noticia/949221/0/

http://www.letraslibres.com/mexico-espana/libros/reina-america-nuria-amat

https://www.ecured.cu/Nuria_Amat

http://www.mcnbiografias.com/app-bio/do/show?key=amat-nuria

http://www.lavanguardia.com/libros/20110203/54109695129/nuria-amat-gana-el-llull-con-su-obra-amor-i-guerra.html

http://www.radio.cz/es/rubrica/notas/nuria-amat-praga-se-parece-mucho-a-cataluna

http://blogs.brown.edu/ciudad_literaria/2006/02/08/la-intimidad-de-nuria-amat/

http://salamancartvaldia.es/not/79831/nuria-amat-ldquo-en-el-mundo-hispano-la-literatura-peca-de-machismo-porque-los-propios-autores-varones-apartan-a-sus-posibles-competidoras-rdquo-

http://www.lainformacion.com/arte-cultura-y-espectaculos/literatura/nuria-amat-critica-la-marginacion-a-la-que-se-ven-sometidas-las-escritoras_cX6G72pUrDBHiEVzd5nPf5/

http://elpais.com/diario/2004/04/17/cultura/1082152801_850215.html

http://www.elcultural.com/revista/letras/Amor-infiel-Emily-Dickinson-por-Nuria-Amat/9675

For more information on her work, political views, and interviews for radio and television, see her comprehensive website http://www.nuriaamat.com

HIPATIA

Cuando el milenio contaba con 370 años, Hipatia nació en Alejandría. Fue bibliotecaria. Y fue también matemática, astrónoma, física y directora de la escuela neoplatónica. Y fue la última científica que trabajó en la Biblioteca. Y la última filósofa. Después de su muerte el saber humano entró en una barbarie que perduró mil años.

HYPATIA

When the millennium was 370 years old, Hypatia[1] was born in Alexandria.[2] She was a female librarian. And she was also a female mathematician, astronomer, physicist and head of the Neo-platonic School.[3] And she was the last female scientist to work in the Library. And the last female philosopher. After her death human knowledge entered into a barbaric period which lasted one thousand years.

---

1 **Hypatia of Alexandria**: born *c*. 355ce in Alexandria, she was a philosopher, a mathematician (the earliest female mathematician documented) and an astronomer who, in her time, was a leading world figure in all these disciplines and an immensely respected teacher, as substantiated by the 160 letters written to her by her pupil Synesius of Cyrene. She was the daughter of Theon of Alexandria, himself a mathematician and an astronomer and the last attested member of the Alexandrian Museum. Theon worked on the preservation of Euclid's Elements and on Ptolemy's Almagest and Handy tables. Hypatia followed her father's steps in preserving the Greek mathematical and astronomical heritage. She was a Neoplatonist and seen by Christians as a pagan. She lived in the Alexandrian Roman-Egyptian era, in the 3rd–4th centuries, an era of increasing turbulent religious tensions that would eventually destroy the multicultural, cosmopolitan and tolerant city that Alexandria once was. She was brutally murdered by Christian fanatics, allegedly encouraged by the Bishop of Alexandria, Cyril, in 415. Her works on the Geometry of Apollonius of Perga and on the Arithmetic of Diophantus of Alexandria, among others, were extremely important but they have been sadly lost. She was the inventor of the Astrolabe, an instrument in which theory and practice blend in a distinctive Alexandrian way. Hypatia has become a powerful reference for women's struggles in a male and intolerant world. In 2009, the Spanish director Alejandro Amenábar made a film of Hypatia's life entitled *Agora,* with Rachel Weisz as the protagonist. https://www.youtube.com/watch?v=zqzpHYfAdsE; https://www.britannica.com/print/article/279463.

2 **Alexandria**: Egyptian city founded in 332 BCE by the Macedonian King Alexander the Great who made it the Mediterranean capital of his empire. For many years, the new city kept Alexander's attitude of treating Greeks and non-Greeks as equals. After Alexander's death, his viceroy Ptolemy Soter took control of the city and founded a dynasty that presided over the golden years of the city. The early Ptolemies blended the religions of ancient Greece and Egypt in the cult of Serapis and made Alexandria the greatest Mediterranean environment for cultural exchange of knowledge, and a centre of Greek scholarship and science. The Museion, a research institute which included the famous Library, a repository for the all the scrolls and books known at the time and where they were translated into Greek, was founded and supported by the early Ptolemies. https://www.britannica.com/print/article/14376; https://www.youtube.com/watch?v=hcb8tmdC-sA

3 **Neo-platonic School**: Plotinus was the founder in the 3rd century of what was to become the last school of Greek philosophy. It achieved its best moments in the 3rd and 4th centuries. Plotinus followed Plato's philosophical thought and expanded it.

Hipatia era hija de Apolonio. Apolonio, el que cuidaba de guardar los rollos en los anaqueles de la Biblioteca. Apolonio, el responsable de que la Biblioteca mantuviera el ambiente de trabajo adecuado para cultivar las mejores mentes de la época. Época difícil la de Hipatia. Alejandría ya no era egipcia ni tampoco griega. Escribe la historia que los reyes griegos de Egipto, sucesores de Alejandro, heredaron y multiplicaron de este gran hombre su devoción al saber. Pero sucumbieron a la barbarie romana y cuando nació Hipatia, la ciudad mágica ya era un apéndice de Roma desde hacía tiempo. Ello significaba, para quienes no quieran recordarlo, que el poder cristiano calificaba la Biblioteca de burdel y de recinto pagano, y también su colección de manuscritos y a los sabios que en él se adentraban.

Apolonio fue el último de los contrabandistas de libros que enriquecieron sobremanera la Biblioteca. Los espías de culturas ajenas habían dejado de existir y sus nombres se conservaban como leyendas festivas. Apolonio contaba a sus hijos bellas historias sobre los antiguos espías y traficantes de libros. Hipatia lo escuchaba. Hipatia fue la tercera hija que diera a luz Dacia, esposa de Apolonio. Un año después de este nacimiento moría la madre dejando a la niña y a sus dos hermanos varones al cuidado de la vieja criada y el desolado padre. Apolonio no buscó mujer. Tenía la responsabilidad del conocimiento en su mano derecha y la crianza de sus hijos en la izquierda. Dedicó el resto de su vida (que fue breve) a educar a sus hijos para el saber, para custodiar lo que Apolonio, padre de Hipatia, consideraba que era el tesoro del mundo.

Heros y Aristarco, hijos de Apolonio, casaron jóvenes y eligieron para sí el camino del ganado y del cultivo del campo, respectivamente. Hipatia, en cambio, decidió comprometerse con el mar y con el tesoro de su Biblioteca. Durante esas horas en que Alejandría dormía la siesta, la niña se dedicaba a perseguir la sombra de su padre, bibliotecario ya medio ciego. Apolonio vio con placer larvado de sufrimiento que su hija tenía la mente despierta del padre y el atractivo iracundo de la madre. Y vio además que superaba con mucho a ambos. Pero era una mujer. Apolonio comprendió, entonces, que

Hypatia was the daughter of Apollonius.[4] Apollonius who cared for and guarded the rolls of manuscripts on the shelves of the Library. Apollonius, in charge of ensuring that the Library maintained the appropriate working environment for the cultivation of the best minds of the epoch. Hypatia's epoch was a difficult one. Alexandria was no longer Egyptian nor Greek. History records that the Greek kings of Egypt, the heirs of Alexander,[5] inherited and multiplied the devotion of that great man to knowledge. But they succumbed to Roman barbarity and when Hypatia was born, the magic city had already been an appendage of Rome for some time. That meant, for the benefit of those who may not wish to remember, that Christian power denominated the Library as a brothel and pagan precinct and likewise its collection of manuscripts and the wise men who used to penetrate its depths.

Apollonius was the last of the smugglers of books who greatly enriched the Library. The spies of other cultures had passed away and their names were preserved as celebrated legends. Apollonius used to tell his children beautiful stories about the ancient spies and book traffickers. Hypatia would listen to him. Hypatia was the third child whom Dacia, the wife of Apollonius, would bear. A year after her birth Hypatia's mother died leaving the girl and her two brothers in the care of the old maid and the disconsolate father. Apollonius did not seek another wife. He held responsibility for knowledge in his right hand and the upbringing of his children in his left. Apollonius dedicated the rest of his life (which was short) to instructing his children in knowledge, in order to safeguard what he, the father of Hypatia, considered to be the treasure of the world.

Heros and Aristarchus, the sons of Apollonius, married young and chose for themselves respectively the pathway of rearing cattle and the cultivation of the land. Hypatia, on the other hand, decided to commit herself to the sea and the treasure of her Library. During the hours of siesta time in Alexandria, the child dedicated herself to following the shadow of her father, the by now half-blind librarian. Apollonius saw with pleasure laced with pain that his daughter had the lively mind of her father and the attractive irascibility of her mother. And he saw moreover that she greatly surpassed both of her parents. But she was a woman. Apollonius understood then that he had to

---

4   **Apollonius**: It seems that the father of Hypatia was Theon of Alexandria. See Note 1.

5   **Alexander the Great**: (*c.* 356–323 BCE), Alexander was the King of Macedonia who conquered vast territories in the Mediterranean and founded the city of Alexandria. Under the dynasty of the Ptolemies, with its Museion and Library, the city that bears Alexander's name became the most important intellectual centre to follow the Greek tradition in the first centuries of our era.

debía ser duro con ella y más exigente de lo que fuera con sus hermanos y también mucho más tierno y dadivoso.

Hipatia crecía para llegar a ser sabia en una época en que la mujer pertenecía a uno o varios propietarios. La mujer, en la Alejandría de dominio romano, apenas si tenía otra opción vital que la esclavitud o la otra esclavitud, considerada como mal menor, llamada matrimonio. Apolonio, que amaba con serena locura a su hija, jamás se dijo: 'Educaré a Hipatia como a un hombre'. Su reto fue otro: 'Educaré a Hipatia para que sea una luz entre la ceguera de los grandes hombres'. Así le hablaba y le enseñaba: como enseña el perro a su amo a desafiar a la presa. Con humildad y firmeza le mostró el mundo en un libro y un libro capaz de deshacerse en mundos. Le mostró cómo descubrir la vida: observándola, a tientas, con cautela. Hipatia aprendió pronto que descubrir la vida consistía en sorprenderla. La niña era voluntariosa. 'Ahora, tiene que ser ahora', solía decirle como para abreviar ese largo tiempo que dura un aprendizaje. Aprendió a venerar de cada uno de esos libros que le enseñaba su padre las voces que encerraban la magia de sus signos. Amaba la palabra pero no la adoraba más que el mar, las costas y el puerto de Alejandría adonde iba a sentarse todos los atardeceres para llevar a cabo su juego favorito. Jugaba a saber. Provista de un retal de papiro y un buril jugaba a imaginarse sabia y reproductora de signos mágicos. Entraba, seguidamente, en el Serapeo a pedir a los dioses que su sueño fuera algo más real que la locura de creerlos.

Dionisia, la nodriza, era ya demasiado vieja para que Hipatia disfrutara de la imagen de una madre joven. A falta de otro espejo donde reflejarse, Hipatia se miraba en el silencio de los hombres más sabios y libres de Alejandría. Esta ausencia, lejos de masculinizarla, la hizo, si cabe, más mujer. Tan distinta de sus amigas como para que éstas la envidiaran y temieran a un tiempo. No fue una adolescente de facciones delicadas: sabía demasiado para tener para sí el rostro primoroso de las niñas bonitas y estaba destinada a ser una mujer de extraordinaria belleza. Hipatia adolescente trabajaba, sin prisas, sus atractivos de cortesana. De los griegos había aprendido que la belleza, al contrario del talento, se educa ocultándola a ojos innecesarios. Si hubo jóvenes temerosas de Hipatia era precisamente porque Hipatia jamás podría parecerse a ellas. A la edad de catorce años adivinó el placer tan intenso

be hard on her and more demanding than he was with her brothers, as well as being much more tender and generous.

Hypatia grew up to turn into a wise woman at a time when women belonged to one or several owners. Women in Roman-dominated Alexandria had hardly any other life choice but slavery or that other slavery, considered a lesser evil, called marriage. Apollonius, who loved his daughter madly and serenely, never said to himself: 'I'll bring up Hipatia like a man.' His aim was something else: 'I'll bring up Hypatia so that she may be a light among the blindness of great men.' Thus, he would speak to her and teach her: as the dog teaches its master to challenge the quarry. With firmness and humility, he showed her the world in a book and a book capable of unravelling into worlds. He showed her how to discover life: by observing it, cautiously feeling her way. Hypatia soon learned that discovering life consisted of surprising it. The child was strong-willed. 'Now, it has to be now', she used to say to him as if to cut short that long time that learning takes. From each one of those books that her father taught her she learned to venerate the words that encapsulated the magic of their signs. She loved words but did not adore them more than the sea, the coasts and the port of Alexandria where she used to go and sit at dusk every evening to play her favourite game. She played the game of knowledge. Armed with a strip of papyrus and a burin she played at imagining that she was a wise girl, a producer of magic signs. Right afterwards she would go into the Serapeum[6] to ask the gods to make her dream more real than the madness of believing in them.

Her wet nurse, Dyonisia, was now too old for Hypatia to enjoy the image of a young mother. Lacking another mirror in which to reflect her image, Hypatia saw herself in the silence of the wisest and freest men of Alexandria. This absence, far from masculinizing her, made her, were it possible, more feminine. So different from her female friends for them to envy and fear her at the same time. She was not an adolescent with delicate features: she knew too much to put on the exquisite face of pretty girls and she was destined to be a woman of extraordinary beauty. The adolescent Hypatia worked steadily at her courtesan attractiveness. She had learned from the Greeks that beauty, as distinct from talent, is cultivated by hiding it from prying eyes. If there were young women fearful of Hypatia it was precisely because Hypatia could never resemble them. At the age of fourteen she

---

6 **Serapeum**: Latin name given to temples or institutions dedicated to the Greek-Egyptian deity Serapis. See also Note 2. In Alexandria, the Serapeum was also part of the Library.

como efímero que se obtiene de los brazos de un amor y del sentimiento que este amor provoca. De esa fugacidad, de la que hablaban en sus libros Safo y Platón, aprendió las mil maneras de adiestrar y cultivar la ansiedad de Eros a fin de que Eros fuera eterno. El propio amor le hizo ver que la pasión de saber podía ser igualmente feliz y provechosa para aquella que el fuego convierte inmediatamente en brasas. Al contrario que el saber, el amor debía disfrutarse sin intentar poseerlo. Supo que jamás sería propiedad de un hombre. No les daría más que a los mismos dioses y recibiría de ellos un placer centuplicado. Hipatia había elegido el camino de ser ella misma, es decir: una lumbrera más de la primera y única Biblioteca.

Apolonio supo querer a su hija de modo que ella aprendiera todas las armas del amor que conceden placer y despiertan la generosidad de los hombres. Ella estaría, además, doblemente protegida por el escudo que en la mujer proporciona el conocimiento.

En el arte del aprendizaje tuvo Hipatia maestros ejemplares: el amor de un silencioso, humilde y excepcional hombre y el saber de la irrepetible Biblioteca. En el arte de la sabiduría sus maestros fueron: Eratóstenes, que rehízo el mundo al averiguar la curvatura de la Tierra y fijar sus dimensiones; Hiparco, que ordenó el mapa de las constelaciones y estimó el brillo de las

foresaw the intense and ephemeral pleasure that comes from the arms of a lover and the feeling that this love occasions. She learned from the fleeting nature of this love, about which Sappho[7] and Plato[8] spoke in their books, the one thousand ways to tame and cultivate erotic anxiety so that Eros[9] would become eternal. Love itself made her see that the passion for knowledge could be equally felicitous and advantageous for the woman whom fire immediately turns into hot embers. As opposed to knowledge, love ought to be enjoyed without trying to possess it. She understood that she would never belong to a man. She would never give men more than she gave to the gods themselves and she would receive from them a pleasure multiplied one hundred fold. Hypatia had chosen the way of being herself, that is, one more luminary in the leading and unique Library.

Apollonius knew how to love his daughter in such a way that she learned all the weapons of love that grant pleasure and awaken the generosity of men. Moreover, she would be doubly protected by the shield that learning gives to women.

During her early education, Hypatia had exemplary teachers: the love of a silent, humble and exceptional man and the knowledge contained in the irreplaceable Library. In her formative years, her teachers were: Eratosthenes,[10] who re-shaped the world by verifying the curvature of the of the Earth and establishing its dimensions; Hypparchus,[11]who arranged

---

7 **Sappho**: Female Greek poet born in the island of Lesbos (*c.* 630–*c.*570 BCE). Apart from her poems that stylised popular motifs, she is mostly celebrated for her love poems dedicated to the girls that lived with her. As a member of Lesbos high society, her main literary preoccupations were the cult of beauty and passionate amorous feelings.

8 **Plato**: Greek philosopher born *c.* 427 BCE who died in 347 BCE. One of the great and possibly the most influential names of classical Greek philosophy, he was a disciple of Socrates, and collector of his *Dialogues*, while Aristotle was one of his own disciples. Plato was the creator of the written dialectic form and his philosophical thought is seen as crucial to understand many posterior Westerns philosophers and writers. 'Many people associate Plato with a few central doctrines that are advocated in his writings: The world that appears to our senses is in some way defective and filled with error, but there is a more real and perfect realm, populated by entities (called "forms" or "ideas") that are eternal, changeless, and in some sense paradigmatic for the structure and character of the world presented to our senses.' https://plato.stanford.edu/entries/plato/#PlaCenDoc

9 **Eros**: the Greek god of love.

10 **Eratosthenes**: (*c.* 276, Libya–*c.* 194 BCE. Alexandria) he was an astronomer, geographer, mathematician and poet, the first to measure the size of the Earth by studying the differences in the sun's height during the winter and summer solstices. His estimations differ only by 90 km to the current beliefs. He was one of the directors of the Library of Alexandria. https://www.britannica.com/print/article/191064

11 **Hypparchus of Nicea**: a Greek astronomer from the 2nd century CE, he calculated

estrellas; Euclides, que sistematizó brillantemente la geometría y que en cierta ocasión dijo a su rey, mientras éste luchaba con un difícil problema matemático: 'No hay un camino real hacia la geometría'; Dionisio de Tracia, el hombre que definió las partes del discurso y que hizo en el estudio del lenguaje lo que Euclides ideó en la geometría; Herófilo, el fisiólogo que estableció de modo seguro que el cerebro y no el corazón es la sede de la inteligencia; Herón de Alejandría, inventor de cajas de engranajes y de aparatos de vapor, y autor de *Autómata*, la primera obra sobre robots; Apolonio de Pérgamo, el matemático que demostró las formas de las secciones cónicas, las curvas que como hoy se sabe siguen en sus órbitas los planetas, los cometas y las estrellas; Arquímedes, el mayor genio mecánico hasta

the map of the constellations and calculated the brilliance of the stars; Euclid,[12] who brilliantly systematized geometry and once said to his king while the latter was struggling with a mathematical problem: 'There is no royal road to geometry'; Dionysius Trax of Alexandria,[13] the man who defined the parts of discourse and who did in the world of language what Euclid devised in geometry; Herophilus,[14] the physiologist who established in a conclusive way that the brain, not the heart, is the seat of intelligence; Heron of Alexandria,[15] the inventor of gear boxes and steam apparatuses, and author of *Automatons*, the first work on robots; Apollonius of Perga,[16] the mathematician who demonstrated the shapes of conical sections, the curves that, as we now know, the planets, comets and stars follow in their orbits; Archimedes,[17] the greatest mechanical genius up until Leonardo da

---

the solar year in 365 days and 6 hours, and put together the first catalogue of stars. He is considered the founder of trigonometry.

12 **Euclid**: Greek mathematician who worked and taught in Alexandria *c*. 300 BCE. He was a mathematician of great influence over the centuries and was the creator of the Euclidean Algorithm, a technique used to obtain the greatest common divisor of two numbers.

13 **Dionysius Trax of Alexandria**: Greek grammarian (170–190 BCE) who was one of the initiators of the study of grammar as a scientific discipline.

14 **Herophilus**: (*c*. 335–*c*. 280 BCE) he was an Alexandrian physiologist considered the father of anatomy as he studied the human body at a time that the ban on human dissection was lifted. He investigated the brain, the organ he regarded as the centre of the nervous system. He also rendered accounts on the eye, salivary glands, and genital organs of both sexes, as well as the duodenum, the stomach and the prostate gland. His works, including a commentary on Hippocrates, of whom he had been a disciple, and treatises on anatomy were lost with the successive attacks that over the centuries destroyed the Library of Alexandria. https://www.britannica.com/print/article/263634

15 **Heron of Alexandria**: a Greek geometer and inventor who worked in Alexandria in the first century of our era. His works on geometry preserved for posterity a knowledge of the mathematics and engineering of Babylonia, ancient Egypt and the Greco-Roman world. https://www.britannica.com/print/article/263417

16 **Apollonius of Perga**: (*c*. 240–*c*. 190 BCE) he was a respected mathematician in Alexandria and his work as geometer in *Conics* is considered one of the greatest scientific works from the ancient world. Although his works are lost, we know of them through his disciples. He influenced the study of geometry in the Islamic world in medieval times, and in the Renaissance scientific revolution in Europe. https://www.britannica.com/print/article/30058

17 **Archimedes**: (*c*. 287–*c*. 212 BCE) from Syracuse. Archimedes was the best known mathematician and inventor of the ancient Greece. Archimedes studied with Euclid and worked with Eratosthenes. He is attributed with the discovery of the relation between the surface and volume of a sphere and its circumscribing cylinder. The Archimedes Principle is his formulation of a hydrostatic principle. His device for raising water is still valid today. https://www.britannica.com/print/article/32808

Leonardo da Vinci; el gastrónomo y geógrafo Ptolomeo, que compiló gran parte de lo que es hoy la astronomía y el poeta Calímaco, cuya pedantería lo llevó a decir: 'Un gran libro es un gran mal', y que mostraba más interés por la pulcritud de la expresión que por la profundidad de los sentimientos, aunque éstos aparezcan en sus famosos epigramas.

Belleza y sabiduría se conjugaban en la persona de Hipatia de un modo que hacía irritar a los jóvenes alejandrinos incapaces de conquistarla. Indiferente a las habladurías e inquinas de estos cristianos que despreciaban el Museion y sus estudiosos, Hipatia, última representante de la Grecia creadora de Alejandría, no escondía la clave del secreto para que uno pudiera tener todo el saber del mundo a su entera disposición. En sus primeros años de estudiante había robado a su antiguo maestro Eratóstenes el modo de aprovecharlo al máximo.

Además de astrónomo, historiador, geógrafo, filósofo, poeta, crítico teatral y matemático, Eratóstenes fue también director de la Biblioteca. En sus escritos –Hipatia se vanagloriaba de haberlo descubierto–, decía el maestro que en una ocasión hojeando un libro de papiro de la biblioteca leyó que en un puesto avanzado de la frontera meridional, en Siena, cerca de la primera catarata del Nilo, en el mediodía del 21 de junio, un palo vertical no proyectaba sombra. Esta observación, a primera vista tan sencilla y cotidiana, invitó a Eratóstenes a realizar un experimento. ¿Sucedería también en Alejandría, que los palos verticales no proyectaran sombras hacia el mediodía de un 21 de junio? Eratóstenes descubrió entonces que tampoco lo hacían y comprendió que la única respuesta posible a este fenómeno era la curvatura de la superficie terrestre. La diferencia observada en las longitudes de las sombras hacía necesario que la distancia entre Alejandría y Siena

Vinci;[18] the astronomer and geographer Ptolemy,[19] who compiled a large part of what is today Astronomy and the poet Callimachus,[20] whose pedantry led him to say: 'A great book is a great evil', and who showed more interest in the beauty of expressions than in the depth of feelings, although these appear in his famous epigrams.

Beauty and wisdom coalesced in the person of Hypatia in such a way as to irritate the young men of Alexandria incapable of seducing her. Indifferent to the idle gossip and spite of those Christians who despised the great Museion and its scholars, Hypatia, the last representative of creative Greece in Alexandria, did not hide the secret key for anyone to have all the knowledge in the world at his or her entire disposition. In her early years as a student she had stolen the way to get maximum profit out of it from her old teacher Eratosthenes.

Besides being an astronomer, historian, geographer, philosopher, poet, theatre critic and mathematician, Eratosthenes was also Head of the Library. In his writings —Hypatia took pride in having discovered it – the master said that once when leafing through a papyrus book in the library he read that in Siena, an outpost on the southern frontier, near the first waterfall on the Nile, at mid-day on the 21st of June, a vertical stake did not project a shadow. This observation, at first sight so mundane and simple, invited Eratosthenes to conduct an experiment. Would it also happen in Alexandria that at mid-day on the 21st of June vertical stakes would not project a shadow? Eratosthenes then discovered that they did not project a shadow there either and he understood that the only possible answer to this phenomenon was the curvature of the Earth. The difference observed in the longitudes of the shadows made it necessary that the distance between Siena and Alexandria was about seven degrees, approximately a fiftieth of the three hundred and

---

18 **Leonardo da Vinci**: possibly the best known painter, sculptor, engineer, musician, philosopher and inventor from 15th century Italy. Born in 1452 in Vinci, Toscana, he is the author of the famous *Giaconda*, one of the most emblematic paintings of the Italian Renaissance.

19 **Ptolemy**: an Egyptian astronomer, mathematician and geographer of Greek descent who worked in Alexandria in the 2nd century CE. His work as an astronomer, the *Almagest* (the name, meaning 'the greatest', indicates its Arabic and Greek hybrid nature) comes from all the achievements of the Greco-Roman science, in particular his geocentric model of the universe, the Ptolemaic system. https://www.britannica.print/article/482098

20 **Callimachus**: (*c.* 300–*c.* 249 BCE) Callimachus was a poet and a scholar of Libyan-Greek origin who wrote in Greek and worked in Alexandria under the patronage of the Ptolemies. He was responsible in his time for cataloguing the scrolls and books of the Library of Alexandria.

fuera de unos siete grados, aproximadamente una cincuentava parte de los trescientos sesenta grados que contiene la circunferencia de la Tierra. A fin de confirmar su hipótesis, contrató a un hombre para que midiera a pasos la distancia entre Alejandría y Siena: era de unos ochocientos kilómetros. Ochocientos kilómetros por cincuenta dan como resultado 40.000 kilómetros: ésta debía ser pues la circunferencia de la Tierra.

Fue así como Eratóstenes se convirtió en la primera persona que midió con precisión el tamaño del planeta. Y fue también de ese modo, con la aparente ingenuidad del sabio y sobre la base de la lectura de observaciones en un principio insustanciales de los libros de que disponía la Biblioteca, como Hipatia prosiguió con la investigación emprendida por los hombres que la precedieron. El cargo de director de la Biblioteca se daba al que era en su tiempo el mejor científico, lo que en el argot del medio se llamaba un *alfa* de la época, o mejor un *beta*, como lo pudo ser Eratóstenes pues, según decía uno de sus envidiosos contemporáneos, era en todo el segundo mejor del mundo. Y el secreto de tal poder intelectual, sabían los estudiosos, residía en la propia Biblioteca. Ella era la que confería a sus investigadores los instrumentos básicos para ser los primeros y mejores del mundo en todo. Hipatia, a la edad de veintinueve años, iba a alcanzar por sus propios méritos –no había persona que la igualara en sabiduría– el cargo de directora de esa institución sagrada.

Hipatia vivía sola. Dos criadas se ocupaban de cuidar la casa que había heredado de sus padres y un viejo jardinero había adquirido la costumbre de ocuparse tanto de las flores que cautivaban a Hipatia como de los sueños siempre atareados de su ama. Ella elegía sabiamente cuándo quería permanecer sola con sus pensamientos o bien estar acompañada en sus alegrías. Si su inteligencia era perfecta para alejar a aquellos hombres que difícilmente podían competir con ella en las ramas del conocimiento, su belleza conseguía siempre atraer a los más cultivados y justos. Dicen las fuentes que tuvo muchos pretendientes pero rechazó siempre todas las preposiciones matrimoniales. Se enamoró del gobernador romano de Alejandría, y también del estudiante Antonio, cuyas dotes para la ingeniería mecánica y la automación le auguraban un gran futuro. Y, sin embargo, recusó de plano la idea de casarse con uno u otro de sus enamorados. Ni entonces ni cuando la pasión fuera a transformarse en hábito. Y como los amaba, Hipatia prefirió conservarlos como amantes. Y con estos dos hombres, que dedicaron sus vidas a la esperanza de esposarla, Hipatia pensó, o sólo imaginó, que el matrimonio con cualquiera de ambos habría sido el

sixty degrees that the entire circumference of the Earth contained. In order to confirm his hypothesis, he contracted a man to measure in steps the distance between Alexandria and Siena: it was about eight hundred kilometres. Eight hundred kilometres by fifty gives a result of 40,000 kilometres, so this must therefore be the circumference of the earth.

Thus it was that Eratosthenes became the first to measure with precision the size of the planet. And it was also in this way, with the apparent ingenuity of the wise man and with her reading of seemingly inconsequential observations in books in the Library, that Hypatia continued the research undertaken by the men who preceded her. The post of Library Head was given to the man who was the best scientist of his time, what was called in the jargon of the milieu an *Alpha* of the epoch, or rather a *Beta,* as Erastothenes could have been, because, as one of his envious contemporaries used to say, he was second best in everything. And the scholars knew that the secret of such intellectual power lay in the Library itself. It was the Library that provided its researchers with the basic tools to be first and best at everything in the world. At the age of twenty-nine Hypatia was destined to achieve on her own merits – there was no one to equal her in knowledge – the post of Head of that sacred institution.

Hypatia lived alone. Two female servants worked at looking after the house she had inherited from her parents. And an old gardener had acquired the habit of looking after both the flowers that captivated Hypatia and the always buzzing dreams of his mistress. She chose wisely when she wanted to be alone with her thoughts or to have company in her joyful moments. If she had perfect intelligence to keep at a distance those men who could hardly compete with her in the branches of knowledge, her beauty always succeeded in attracting the most cultured and just. Sources say that she had many suitors but always rejected marriage proposals. She fell in love with the Roman governor of Alexandria, and also with Anthony the student, whose talents for mechanical engineering and automation augured a great future for him. Nevertheless, she flatly refused the idea of marrying either of her lovers. Neither then nor when her passion became transformed into a habit. And since she loved them, Hypatia preferred to keep them as lovers. And with these two men, who dedicated their lives to the hope of marrying her, Hypatia thought, or only imagined, that marriage to either of the two

castigo más dulce y placentero que los dioses habrían podido darle en la tierra. Sus argumentos femeninos, frente al orgullo continuamente agraviado de estos dos hombres que dejaron mujer e hijos para tratar de convencerla, se fundamentaban en que el gobernador era demasiado poderoso para tener como esposa a una mujer famosa y erudita, y en que el obsesivo Antonio –reía Hipatia– habría acabado convirtiendo la vivienda de ambos en un anexo de la Biblioteca. Amor y matrimonio eran cuerpos antitéticos para una mujer comprometida en vida con el ejercicio de la sabiduría.

En materia de hombres, otro mérito distinguía a la sabia Hipatia: de entre los diecisiete que en su vida amó, consiguió –siendo fértil– no traer al mundo hijo alguno de ellos.

Aun siendo Alejandría, en época de Hipatia, la mejor ciudad que Occidente hubiera visto jamás, no era, ni con mucho, la misma Alejandría de los Ptolomeos. Sus gentes ignoraban por completo los descubrimientos que tenían lugar dentro de la Biblioteca. Cultura, ciencia, saber, conocimiento eran para esas gentes, influidas por la barbarie cristiana, una suerte de ritos paganos y cuentos de hadas que ocupaban el pasatiempo de algunos privilegiados. La Alejandría romana de Hipatia estaba dividida. De un lado, la Iglesia cristiana que pretendía quedarse con todo el poder, y de otro, la inteligencia egipcia, griega, extranjera y cosmopolita tachada por los primeros de pagana. En esta realidad, Hipatia representaba para los cristianos el símbolo escandaloso y pecador de la ciencia y la cultura. Perseguían sus pasos, denigraban sus publicaciones, despreciaban su vida. Y, pese a los riesgos que implicaba su trabajo de investigadora y bibliotecaria, continuaba enseñando en la Biblioteca y publicando sus trabajos. Seguía viviendo como una mujer libre, sin privarse tampoco de la compañía de sus amigos, incluidos los políticos romanos.

Los cristianos, encabezados por Cirilo, arzobispo de Alejandría, declararon a Hipatia enemiga del pueblo. En primer lugar, por su cargo de directora de la Biblioteca y, sobre todo, porque en esta mujer se daban una serie de atributos que el cristianismo primitivo despreciaba. La fuerza de Hipatia correspondía a dos poderes: el de la seducción por ser mujer inteligente, bella y especialmente amada y el poder mágico que confería un saber que

would have been the sweetest and most pleasurable punishment that the gods could have meted out to her on earth. Her feminine arguments, in the face of the continuously offended pride of those men who left wife and children to try to convince her, were based on the fact that the governor was too powerful to have a famous and erudite woman as a wife, and that the obsessive Anthony – she used to laugh – would have ended up turning their dwelling into an annex of the Library. Love and marriage were antithetical bodies in the view of a woman whose life was committed to the exercise of knowledge.

When it came to men, another merit distinguished the wise Hypatia: out of the seventeen whom she loved during her life time she succeeded, during her fertile years, in not bringing a child from any of them into the world.

Although Alexandria was, in the time of Hypatia, the best city that the West had ever seen, it was not by a long chalk the same Alexandria of the Ptolemies.[21] Her inhabitants were completely unaware of the discoveries that took place within the Library. Culture, science, wisdom, knowledge, were in the opinion of those people influenced by Christian barbarity, a string of pagan rites and fairy tales that filled the leisure time of some privileged individuals. The Roman Alexandria of Hypatia was divided. On the one hand, the Christian Church which tried to retain all power, and on the other, Egyptian, Greek, foreign, cosmopolitan knowledge dismissed by the former as pagan. In this atmosphere Hypatia represented for the Christians the scandalous and sinful symbol of science and culture. They dogged her steps, they denigrated her publications, they despised her life. And in spite of the risks that her work as researcher and librarian implied, she continued teaching in the Library and publishing her works. She continued living as a free woman, without depriving herself of the company of her friends, including Roman politicians.

The Christians, headed by Cyril,[22] the Archbishop of Alexandria, declared Hypatia an enemy of the people. In the first place because of her post as Head of the Library and above all because a series of attributes that early Christianity despised could be observed together in that woman. The strength of Hypatia corresponded to two powers: that of seduction because she was an intelligent, beautiful and especially beloved woman, and the magical power

---

21 **Alexandria of the Ptolemies**: See Note 2.
22 **Cyril**: Saint Cyril of Alexandria (*c.* 376–444) was a power-obsessed Christian bishop of Alexandria who wanted to make the city a theocracy. He is alleged to have encouraged the killing of the 'pagan' Hypatia.

nadie podía igualar en su época. Había quienes la amaban y admiraban, y otros muchos también que la odiaban por lo mismo. Cirilo iba en cabeza de ese odio feroz hacia una mujer cuya forma de ser tenía la virtud de estimular toda la mezquindad del hombre envidioso y necio así como toda la pericia y honestidad del humanista y sabio. Cirilo, por ejemplo, no cesaba de condenarla públicamente por sus relaciones demasiado íntimas con el gobernador romano.

Antes de cumplir los treinta años conocía Hipatia el peligro que corría su vida dedicada a recuperar el saber y a ordenar el conocimiento. Cada uno de sus trabajos publicados tenía como escandalosa respuesta el escarnio de débiles y desaforados y el fervor de cuerdos y prudentes. Sus clases en el Museion eran alabadas por sus alumnos que asistían con el sigilo de quien tiene la posibilidad de adentrarse en el pozo del saber prohibido. Aquélla era precisamente la época en que un romano residente en Alejandría se encontraba entre la disyuntiva de elegir entre ser un cristiano tonto o un pagano cultivado.

Amenazas y ataques no desanimaban a Hipatia para que continuara publicando sus trabajos. Escribió innumerables libros que el fuego restituyó a la nada desde el primero al último. Por eso es que no ha habido modo de conocer el alcance seguramente extraordinario de sus descubrimientos y doctrinas. Apenas nos ha llegado noticia de algunas de sus teorías relacionadas, en este caso, con la institución que fue gloria y cerebro de la mayor ciudad del planeta. Fue la misma Hipatia quien se ocupó de profetizar el terrible final de la Biblioteca de Alejandría con estas palabras:

'Durante centenares de años la humanidad tendrá desperdigados todos los conocimientos del cosmos que hoy, sin lugar a dudas, ordena y unifica el Museion. Esta división de disciplinas producirá el caos del saber, que dejará de ser uno y múltiple hasta que una fuerza autómata igual o más poderosa que nosotros lo congregue a imagen y semejanza de la gran Biblioteca'.

Antonio, en sus escritos, atribuye estas palabras a su maestra Hipatia poniendo énfasis en el interés de aquélla por el estudio de los libros de Herón de Alejandría, en particular su obra *Autómata*.

Prosigue Antonio:

'Hipatia, maestra, pocos años antes de su muerte, exploró el saber de Dionisio de Tracia en el estudio del lenguaje. Tenía la convicción de que en el futuro un

conferred by a knowledge which no one in her time could equal. There were those who loved and admired her and many others too who hated her for the same reasons. Cyril was at the forefront of that ferocious hatred towards a woman whose way of being had the strength to stimulate all the meanness of envious and foolish men as well as all the acumen and honesty of wise humanists. As an example, Cyril did not stop condemning her in public for her too intimate relations with the Roman governor.

Before her thirtieth birthday Hypatia experienced the danger that threatened her life dedicated to recuperating and cataloguing knowledge. Every one of her published works brought as a scandalized response the scorn of the weak and hot-headed and the fervour of the wise and prudent. Her classes in the Museion were praised by her students, who attended class with the mark of those who had the opportunity to submerge themselves in the well of forbidden knowledge. That was precisely the time when a Roman resident of Alexandria was faced with the dilemma of choosing to be a foolish Christian or a cultured pagan.

Threats and attacks did not dishearten Hypatia from continuing to publish her works. She wrote countless books that fire reduced to nothing from the first to the last. It is for this reason that it has been impossible to find out the undoubtedly extraordinary extent of her discoveries and teachings. Hardly any news has reached us of her theories connected in this case with the institution that was the glory and brain of the greatest city of the planet. It was Hypatia herself who took the trouble to prophesy the terrible end of Alexandria in these words:

'For hundreds of years human kind will find scattered all the knowledge of the cosmos that today, without any doubt, the Museion catalogues and brings together. This separation of subjects will cause chaos in knowledge, which will cease to be one and multiple until an automatic force equal to or more powerful than us brings it together in the image of the great Library.'

In his writings Anthony[23] attributes these words to his teacher Hypatia emphasizing her interest in studying the books of Heron of Alexandria, in particular his work, *Automatons*.

Anthony continues:

'A few years before her death, Hypatia the teacher researched the knowledge of Dionysus of Thrace in the study of language. She was convinced that in the

---

23   This character seems to have been inspired by Hypatia's student Synesius of Cyrene. See Note 1.

autómata o aparato mecánico sería capaz de transportar a cualquier lugar del cosmos todo el saber contenido en los libros de la Biblioteca de Alejandría. Así lo explica la sabia Hipatia en sus obras, especialmente en la titulada *El saber automatizado*'.

Ningún texto nos ha quedado de la autora Hipatia. Apenas referencias. Frases desperdigadas sobre su saber y su vida, además de una inmerecida leyenda, es lo poco que conocemos de ella. Sus fanáticos enemigos cuidaron bien de destruir sus obras. Cuentan los biógrafos que las quemaron junto con su cuerpo en el umbral de la Biblioteca. Poco tiempo después, la Biblioteca de Alejandría, con el irrepetible saber de la humanidad que encerraba, ardió a manos de los mismos fanáticos que quemaron el cuerpo de la bibliotecaria.

Hipatia murió a la edad de treinta y cinco años. Una mañana, cuando se dirigía a su trabajo en el carruaje que la llevaba de su casa a la Biblioteca, los feligreses de Cirilo la asaltaron. La arrancaron del coche, la desnudaron, la arrastraron varios centenares de metros y armados con conchas marinas la desollaron viva. Pero el auténtico crimen contra Hipatia fue doble y más terrible: con la desaparición de sus obras sus asesinos castigaron al mundo con su olvido.

future an automaton or mechanical apparatus would be capable of carrying to any place in the cosmos all of the knowledge contained in the books in the Library of Alexandria. Thus, the wise Hypatia explains it in her works, especially in that titled *Automatic Knowledge*.'

No text has remained of Hypatia the author. Only a few references. The little that we know about her consists of scattered phrases about her knowledge and life as well as an undeserved legend. Her fanatical enemies took great care to destroy her works. Her biographers recount that they burned them with her body in the entrance to the Library. A short time afterwards the Library of Alexandria with the irreplaceable knowledge of humanity that it contained burned at the hands of the same fanatics who burned the body of the female librarian.

Hypatia died at the age of thirty-five. One morning, when she was going to work in the carriage that used to take her from her home to the Library, Cyril's parishioners attacked her. They pulled her from her carriage, stripped her naked, dragged her several hundred metres and armed with sea shells they skinned her alive. But the real crime against Hypatia was two-fold and more terrible: with the disappearance of her works her murderers punished the world by casting her into oblivion.

DESPARECIDA

THE WOMAN WHO DISAPPEARED

Original Spanish text from
El País Semanal, 4 April 1993, 4;
later collected in *Como una gota*
(Madrid: El País/ Aguilar, 1996, 101–105)
© Maruja Torres, 1993

MARUJA TORRES was born in Barcelona in 1943. For more than forty years she has been a widely respected journalist working for the Spanish press as a columnist and correspondent all over the world, particularly in Lebanon, Israel, and Latin America. Since the 1980s, she was one of the high profile names in the newspaper *El País.* However, in 2013, she ended her association with the newspaper when she had a disagreement with its director regarding her opinion columns. She has talked openly about this conflict in her latest autobiographical book *Diez veces siete. Una chica de barrio nunca se rinde* (2014), which is also a memoir of key moments of her life and of her work as a journalist. She is now retired and, as she puts it, enjoys seeing 'our old world' go by. At the beginning of her career, Maruja Torres was one of the key contributors to *Fotogramas*, a cinema magazine that defied Franco's censorship and where, together with her collaborations in satirical periodicals such as *Por favor* or *Papus,* amongst other weeklies, she developed her flair for humour, irony and political and social satire that is the hallmark of all her work. Her style is based on a clever reworking of colloquialisms that allows her to address serious issues with a deceptively detached approach. Some of her books draw on her life as a journalist, such as *Mujer en guerra* (1999), or *Amor América. Un viaje sentimental por América Latina* (1993), a moving account of a train journey through ten Latin-American countries where she combines the chronicle of what see sees with her memories of previous visits as a reporter. Particularly memorable are the chapters on the avalanche caused by the volcano Nevado del Ruiz that buried the city of Armero, in Colombia, in 1985, and the one on death of Juantxu Rodríguez, the young photographer who was murdered by US marines when they were both covering for *El País* the invasion of Panama that put an end to the Noriega era in 1989. As a journalist, she has

won several prizes such as the Francisco Cerecedo, the Víctor de la Serna, and the Premio Internacional de Periodismo Vázquez Montalbán in 2004 for her work for *El País*. An award-winning novelist too, her fiction is often inspired by her experiences as a young girl growing up in the Barcelona's district of *el Raval* (*Un calor tan cercano*, 1997), or her time living in Beirut (*La amante en guerra*, 2007). She has also written two thrillers and created the female detective Diana Dial: *Fácil de matar* (2011), and *Sin entrañas* (2012). In 2001 she received the recognition from her readers through the *Qué Leer* prize, and in the same year she was awarded the *Orden al mérito docente y cultural Gabriela Mistral* by the Chilean government. In 2006 Maruja Torres received the prestigious Medalla de Oro de las Bellas Artes for her contribution to culture.

Bibliography of Maruja Torres
Novels
¡*Oh, es él!* (Barcelona: Anagrama, 1986; Barcelona: Planeta, 2006).
Ceguera de amor (Culebrón del V Centenario) (Barcelona: Anagrama, 1991; Barcelona: Planeta, 2006).
Un calor tan cercano (Madrid: Alfaguara, 1997; Barcelona: Círculo de Lectores, 1997; Barcelona: Planeta, 2005; Barcelona: Planeta/ Booket, 2007).
Mientras vivimos (Barcelona: Planeta, 2000) *Premio Planeta 2000.*
Hombres de lluvia (Barcelona: Planeta, 2004; Barcelona: Círculo de Lectores, 2004; Barcelona: Planeta/ Booket, 2005).
La amante en guerra (Barcelona: Planeta, 2007; Barcelona: Planeta/ Booket, 2007).
Esperadme en el cielo (Barcelona: Destino, 2009) *Premio Nadal 2009.*
Fácil de matar (Barcelona: Planeta, 2011).
Sin entrañas (Barcelona: Planeta, 2012).

Journalism and autobiographical memoirs
Amor América. Un viaje sentimental por América Latina (Madrid: El País-Aguilar, 1993); published again in 2012 by El País Selección as *Las metáforas de América Latina.*
Como una gota: la vida alrededor, la vida desde dentro [a collection of her articles from *El País*] (Madrid: El País-Aguilar, 1996).
Mujer en guerra (Madrid: El País-Aguilar, 1999; Barcelona: Círculo de Lectores, 2000; Madrid: Suma de Letras, 2000; Barcelona: Planeta, 2005; Barcelona: Planeta / Booket: 2007).
Grandes pasiones de la historia [with Javier Reverte and Manuel Leguineche] (Madrid: El País Selección, 2012).
Diez veces siete. Una chica de barrio nunca se rinde (Barcelona: Planeta, 2014).
Manuela Carmena: en el diván de Maruja Torres (Barcelona: Paneta, 2015).

Short stories included in anthologies and journals (a selection)
'El cuarto hombre', in *El País Semanal* (28 July 1996).
'Cuestión de supervivencia', in J. de las Muelas (ed.), *29 Martinis (That's the Limit!)* (Barcelona: Edhasa, 1999).
'El velo y las lágrimas', in *Mujeres al alba* (Madrid: Alfaguara, 1999).

Further reading on Maruja Torres
Samuel Amell, 'El periodismo: su influencia e importancia en la novela del posfranquismo', *Castilla* 12 (1989), 7–14.
Antonio Chamorro Chicharro, 'Del periodismo a la novela', *Ínsula* 589–90 (1996), 14–17.

Gabriela Cordone, 'Las vías cerradas de América Latina: trayectos por *Amor América,* de Maruja Torres', in J. Peñate Rivero (ed.), *Relato de viaje y literaturas hispánicas* (Madrid: Visor, 257–71).

Salwa Mahmoud, 'El proceso nostálgico en *Esperadme en el cielo* de Maruja Torres: Surrealismo y metaficción', in H. Awaad and M. Insúa (eds), *Textos sin fronteras. Literatura y sociedad, II* (Pamplona: Universidad de Navarra [Ediciones Digitales del GRISO], 2010), 117–13. http://dadun.unav.edu/bitstream/10171/14250/1/09_Mahmoud_Salwa.pdf

Rosa Mora, 'Tres formas de recordar el presente', *El País,* 6 June 1993.

Rosa Mora, 'Vi América con tus ojos. El largo viaje de Maruja Torres', *El País* (Babelia), 19 June 1993.

Rosa Mora, 'Un duro viaje a la literatura', *El País* (Babelia), 25 January 1997.

María José Obiol, 'Artículos para oír y leer', *El País* (Babelia), 3 August 1996.

M. Cinta Ramblado Marinero, 'Conflictos generacionales: la relación madre-hija en *Un calor tan cercano* de Maruja Torres y *Beatriz y los cuerpos celestes* de Lucía Etxebarria', in M. C. Ramblado Marinero (ed.). *Construcciones culturales de la maternidad en España: la madre y la relación madre-hija en la literatura y el cine contemporáneos* (Alacant: Universitat d'Alacant, 2004), 63–78.

Blas Sánchez Dueñas, 'Búsquedas femeninas de la identidad: *Mientras vivimos,* de Maruja Torres', *Signa* 22 (2013), 621–45.

Care Santos, 'Soñar América', *El Ciervo,* January (1994), 35.

Further online information on Maruja Torres (a selection)

www.marujatorres.com
http://escritoras.com/escritoras/Maruja-Torres
www.eldiario.es/autores/maruja_torres/
http://elpais.com/autor/maruja_torres/a
http://www.cervantes.es/bibliotecas_documentacion_espanol/creadores/torres_maruja.htm
http://www.planetadelibros.com/autor/maruja-torres/000012705
http://www.abc.es/medios/20130516/abci-maruja-torres-pais-201305161954.html
http://www.marujatorres.com/bio/
http://www.elcultural.com/revista/letras/Hombres-de-lluvia/9456
http://elpais.com/diario/2007/03/31/babelia/1175298624_850215.html
http://www.elmundo.es/elmundo/encuentros/invitados/2014/06/13/maruja-torres/
http://www.juntadeandalucia.es/cultura/opencms/opencms/download/bibhuelva/Mientras-vivimos-Torres.pdf
https://www.youtube.com/watch?v=wwJ0aBdfSH4
https://www.youtube.com/watch?v=yuHRvp8S68E
https://www.youtube.com/watch?v=aGAl8bWBJ7g
https://www.youtube.com/watch?v=Y4rIYECsvHw

https://www.youtube.com/watch?v=ujYjZzHPbEg
https://www.youtube.com/watch?v=z1Rm5tN-ULE
https://www.youtube.com/watch?v=q9PzL05v8xg
https://www.youtube.com/watch?v=nWcd8ciiCFw
https://www.youtube.com/watch?v=ovYMwBA5l9o
https://www.youtube.com/watch?v=jV-IP5HpD2Q

DESAPARECIDA

La mujer hizo una pausa, miró a los otros y continuó su relato: 'Resultó increíblemente fácil. Salí del hotel y caminé por la calle Mallorca, hasta Bailén. En un portal vi un anuncio: "Se alquila piso". Anoté el teléfono indicado y llamé desde una cabina. Esa misma tarde formalicé el contrato. Lo que iba a ser un fin de semana en otra ciudad se convirtió en 15 años de vida'.

Ahora que lo pensaba, se daba cuenta de que la idea había madurado en ella progresivamente, de tal forma que no se sintió culpable cuando, por fin, cuajó, empujándola a realizar un acto tras otro con fría deliberación, como quien añade cuentas a un collar. Había jugado con ello desde que los niños, que ya no eran niños, empezaron a llegar tarde, una noche tras otra, y a encerrarse en sus habitaciones con el teléfono, relacionándose con un mundo propio que se encontraba al otro lado del portal y al que ella no conseguiría nunca pertenecer. Se dio cuenta de que eso no la dolía, sino de que más bien la aliviaba, igual que las frecuentes desapariciones de su marido, que al volver envuelto en perfume ajeno esgrimía reunions de negocios, sin que ella le preguntara, porque tampoco le importaba en absoluto. Se fue aislando en sí misma cada vez más, y finalmente conquistó un terreno que sólo estaba en su imaginación, pero que la reclamaba día tras día con mayor insistencia. Ociosa, daba vagas instrucciones a la asistenta y se metía en su dormitorio –que sólo era suyo cuando no estaba él y los chicos no interrumpían pidiendo cosas–, encendiendo al principio el pequeño televisor que tenía a los pies de la cama, y viendo de forma ausente cualquier cosa que pusieran, aunque poco a poco adquirió seguridad y comprendió que se sentía igualmente bien si la pantalla estaba apagada; tumbada primero encima de la colcha, y más adelante metida entre las sábanas, protegiendo sus sueños despiertos, como si estuviera enferma. Cuando ellos volvían y la encontraban en bata y pijama no les extrañaba, al fin y al cabo era ya tarde y nadie, durante el día, la podía fiscalizar. A la mujer de la limpieza todo le daba igual: atendía la casa con la misma indiferencia que ella la descuidaba.

THE WOMAN WHO DISAPPEARED

The woman stopped speaking for a moment, looked at the others and then went on with her story: 'It turned out to be incredibly easy. I went out of the hotel and walked along Calle Mallorca as far as Bailén.[1] In a doorway I saw a notice: "Flat to let". I made a note of the number it gave and called from a phone box. I signed the contract that same afternoon. What started off as a weekend away in another town turned into fifteen years of my life.'

When she thought about it now, she realized that she had only thought things out gradually, so she didn't feel guilty when it finally crystalized into shape, propelling her into taking one coldly deliberate step after another, like somebody threading beads in a necklace. She'd been toying with the idea ever since the children, who were no longer children, started to come in late night after night, and to lock themselves away in their rooms with the telephone, connecting with a world of their own, a world that was to be found on the other side of the street door, a world to which she would never belong. She realized that this wasn't a source of pain for her but was instead something of a relief, as were the frequent disappearances of her husband who, upon his return, enveloped in a cloud of someone else's perfume, would use the excuse of a business meeting, even though she never asked him about such things because she wasn't the slightest bit interested. She withdrew further and further into herself, finally conquering a land that only existed in her imagination and yet made more and more insistent claims on her as the days went by. With nothing to do, she would issue vague instructions to the cleaning lady and lock herself away in her bedroom – which was only hers when he wasn't there and when the children didn't come in asking for things – in the early days switching on the little television set that was kept at the foot of the bed and mindlessly watching anything that was on, although she gradually acquired a sense of security and realized she felt equally good if the screen was blank, at first lying on top of the bedspread, later slipping between the sheets, protecting her day dreaming, as if she were unwell. When they got home and found her still in her dressing gown and her pyjamas they weren't surprised, after all it was already late and nobody could keep an eye on her during the day. The cleaning woman couldn't care less, looking after the house with the same degree of indifference with which she neglected it.

---

1   **Mallorca** and **Bailén** are the names of two streets in Barcelona.

Todo esto ocurrió durante la primera etapa, que más tarde, mirando atrás, ella llamaría de calentamiento, porque en aquella época ni siquiera sabía lo que quería hacer.

La segunda etapa se inició cuando la mujer se vio a sí misma en el metro, como si estuviera contemplando a otra, sentada a prudente distancia, precisamente, de la asistenta, a quien había seguido cuando terminó su jornada. Bajó tras ella las escaleras del suburbano y se introdujo en el mismo vagón, que afortunadamente estaba lleno de gente sudorosa que miraba sin ver y en silencio. Cuando la otra se apeó en una lejana estación, la mujer no hizo ningún gesto, y siguió el trayecto hasta que el tren se detuvo durante largo rato y todos salieron excepto ella, que regresó al punto de partida sin moverse. Otro día salió al mismo tiempo que su asistenta, siguiéndola a distancia hasta la cola formada en una parada de autobús. Después de casi una hora, la otra descendió del vehículo, y ella también lo hizo, pero no se atrevió a continuar y la vio perderse en una calle bulliciosa en cuyos escaparates había prendas de vestir que no se parecían en nada a las que ella guardaba en sus armarios. Entró en una de las tiendas y compró, compró mucho, como si no tuviera nada que ponerse. Al volver a su casa, lo escondió todo en una maleta, debajo de la cama.

Y entonces comenzó la tercera etapa, que consistía en vestirse con las prendas ocultas y vivir en ellas mientras los demás no estaban en casa. Aquellos jerséis gruesos, tejidos con trenzas, y aquella faldas acrílicas, y los zapatos de medio tacón, e incluso los abalorios con que se adornaba, collares de colores agresivos y pendientes estrafalarios, determinaban en ella una nueva forma de caminar, de moverse, e incluso de hablar, porque iba de un lado a otro manteniendo imaginarias conversaciones con gente inventada. Siempre se cambiaba antes de que regresara su familia, salvo en una ocasión, en que olvidó quitarse el moño laqueado y su marido le dijo qué horror, vaya pinta que tienes esta noche.

Y un jueves, en que él le comunicó que tenía que pasar fuera de casa el fin de semana porque la empresa iba a impartir un cursillo en un hotel de Toledo, la mujer inventó sobre la marcha que una nueva amiga, una catalana a quien había conocido en la escuela de repostería, la había invitado a pasar con ella unos días en Barcelona. A su marido le pareció bien, y el viernes se marchó después de besarla en la mejilla. Los niños, que ya no eran tan

All this happened during the first stage, the one, looking back on it, she would call the 'warm up phase', because in those days she didn't know what she wanted to do.

The second stage began when the woman caught sight of herself on the Underground, as if she were looking at somebody else, sitting at a discreet distance, in fact, from the cleaning lady, whom she'd followed when she'd finished work. She followed her down the steps of the subway and got into the same carriage, which fortunately was full of sweaty people gazing with unseeing eyes and in silence. When the cleaning woman got off at one of the stations near the end of the line, she remained impassive and continued her journey until the train stopped for a long time and everybody got off except her. Without moving, she travelled back to the station she'd set off from. On another day she left at the same time as the cleaning lady, following her from a distance as far as the queue at the bus stop. After almost an hour, the cleaning woman got off the vehicle, and she did the same, but she didn't dare to go any further, and she saw the other woman melt into a bustling street whose shop windows displayed garments unlike anything hanging in her wardrobes. She went into one of the shops and bought some things, bought a great deal in fact, as if she had nothing to wear. When she got back to her house, she hid it all in a suitcase under the bed.

And then began the third stage, which consisted of dressing herself up in the hidden clothes and living in them when there was nobody in the house. Those thick cable-knitted jerseys, those acrylic skirts and the shoes with the medium heels, and even the glass beads, the necklaces in garish colours and the outlandish earrings with which she would adorn herself, would make her try a new way of walking, of moving around, even of speaking, because she would walk up and down holding imaginary conversations with people she'd made up. She always changed before her family came home, except once when she forgot to brush out the lacquered hair she'd swept into a bun on top of her head, and her husband said, for God's sake, you look a sight tonight.

And one Thursday, when he told her he was going to have to spend the weekend away from home because the company was holding a short course at a hotel in Toledo, the woman had there and then made up some story about how a new friend of hers, a Catalan she'd met at her baking class, had invited her to spend a few days with her in Barcelona. This suited the husband fine, and on the Friday he had set off after giving her a peck on the cheek. The children, who were no longer so little, were sleeping when

niños, estaban durmiendo cuando ella dejó sigilosamente el piso y diecisiete años de vida matrimonial detrás, con el desayuno para sus hijos preparado en la mesa y una nota para que no olvidaran apagar el gas por la noche.

Primero fue a un hotel, dio su nombre y colgó en el armario la ropa clandestina, que ahora ya no lo era y verdaderamente le gustaba. Paseó durante el fin de semana, y por último, el lunes, echó a andar con la maleta por la calle Mallorca hasta Bailén y poco después se instaló en un piso grande, con galería interior en la que colgaba la ropa, como el resto de las mujeres, antes de salir a fregar pisos y regresar de noche, agotada, para dormirse ante el televisor.

Y ahora estaba en un estudio, rodeada de focos y de gente, con unos desconocidos que la besuqueaban y decían que eran su familia y ella sentía una pereza absoluta, pero todos, incluido el simpático locutor, parecían tan felices.

she crept out of the flat leaving seventeen years of married life behind her, with the children's breakfast ready on the table and a note to remind them not to forget to turn off the gas at night.

She went first to a hotel, gave her name and used the wardrobe to hang up the clandestine clothing that was now no longer clandestine and which she really liked. She went out for walks over the weekend, and finally, on the Monday, she set off again on foot, suitcase in hand, along Calle Mallorca as far as Bailén, and shortly afterwards she settled in a large apartment which had an interior courtyard where she would hang up her clothes to dry, like the other women, before she went off to clean flats and return at night, worn out, to fall asleep in front of the television set.

And now here she was in a studio, surrounded by lights and people, with some people she didn't know covering her with kisses and saying they were her family, and she felt that she couldn't be bothered with it all, but everybody else, including the nice presenter, seemed so happy.

VIEJAS HISTORIAS

TALES FROM THE PAST

Original Spanish text from
La corriente del golfo
(Barcelona: Anagrama, 1993, 93–106)
©Soledad Puértolas, 1993

SOLEDAD PUÉRTOLAS was born in Zaragoza, in February of 1947, on a day 'con viento helador y rosquillas a la puerta de las iglesias' [of freezing wind and *rosquillas* being sold at the doors of the church], as she puts it in an autobiographical note. When she was fourteen, her family moved to Madrid, where she has lived ever since (she is now based in Pozuelo de Alarcón, not far from the capital). She graduated in Journalism, and studied Politics and Economics at the Universidad Complutense at a time, in Spain under Franco, when university life was more momentous outside the classroom than inside. In the early 1970s, and newly married, she spent a winter in Trondheim (Norway), and three years in Santa Barbara (California), where she taught Spanish and received a Master's Degree in Spanish and Portuguese Literature from the University of California, Santa Barbara (USA). Both stays abroad have left literary traces in her fiction. Apart from being a prolific novelist and a short-story writer, she is a regular contributor to newspapers and has written autobiographical texts, including the beautifully crafted *Con mi madre* (2001), an account of the period when, as a child, she was ill at the same time as her mother, a special time when a bond between mother and daughter was established for ever. She has also published literary criticism as well as reflections on her own work as a writer. With her carefully constructed plots, and her meticulous yet not dispassionate style, which has been described by her publisher Jorge Herralde as having a deceptive ease (*Turia,* 100 [2011], 202), she is widely acknowledged and respected as one of the best writers at the moment in Spain. Over the years, Soledad Puértolas has won a a number of literary accolades, such as the Premio Glauka for her career in 2001, the Premio de Cultura de la Comunidad de Madrid in 2012, and the José Antonio Labordeta de Literatura

in 2016 (for more prizes to individual books, see bibliography below). Her books have been translated into French, German, Turkish, Portuguese and English. Since 2010, Soledad Puértolas has held the seat labelled with the letter 'g' at the Real Academia Española, a remarkable achievement in such a traditionally male-dominated institution. Her inauguration speech dealt with *El Quijote*'s secondary characters.

Bibliography of Soledad Puértolas

Novels

El bandido doblemente armado. (Madrid: Legasa, 1979; Madrid: Trieste, 1982; Barcelona: Anagrama, 1988) – *Premio Sésamo 1979*.

Burdeos (Barcelona: Anagrama, 1986; Barcelona: RBA, 1992).

Todos mienten (Barcelona: Anagrama, 1988; Barcelona: RBA, 1992).

Queda la noche (Barcelona: Planeta, 1989; Barcelona: Anagrama, 1999) – *Premio Planeta 1989*.

Días del Arenal (Barcelona: Planeta, 1992; Barcelona: Anagrama 2000).

Si al atardecer llegara el mensajero (Barcelona: Anagrama, 1995; México: Seix Barral, 1995; Barcelona: Planeta/Booket, 2003).

Una vida inesperada (Barcelona: Anagrama, 1997; Barcelona: Círculo de Lectores, 1997).

La señora Berg (Barcelona: Anagrama, 1999; Barcelona: RBA 2001).

La rosa de plata (Madrid: Espasa, 1999; Barcelona: Círculo de Lectores, 1997).

Historia de un abrigo (Barcelona: Anagrama, 2005).

Cielo nocturno (Barcelona: Anagrama, 2008).

El clarinetista agradecido (Pamplona: Clínica – Universidad de Navarra, 2008).

Mi amor en vano (Barcelona: Anagrama, 2012).

Short story collections

Una enfermedad moral (Madrid: Trieste, 1982; Barcelona: Anagrama, 1987).

La corriente del golfo (Barcelona: Anagrama, 1993).

Gente que vino a mi boda (Barcelona: Anagrama, 1998).

A través de las ondas (Madrid: Ollero y Ramos, 1998).

Adiós a las novias (Barcelona: Anagrama, 2000) – *Premio Relatos NH 2001*.

Citas (Madrid: H. Kliczkowski, 2005).

Compañeras de viaje (Barcelona: Anagrama, 2010).

El fin (Barcelona: Anagrama, 2015).

Chicos y chicas (Barcelona: Anagrama, 2016).

Short stories included in anthologies (a selection)

'A través de las ondas', in Y. Navajo (ed.), *Doce relatos de mujeres* (Madrid: Alianza, 1982).

'Contra Fortinelli', in in B. Fernández Casasnovas and M. Iglesias Vicente (eds), *Relatos de mujeres. 2* (Madrid: Popular, 1988; 2011).

'El jardín de la señora Mussorgsky', in L. Freixas (ed.), *Los pecados capitales (Catorce cuentos inéditos)* (Barcelona: Grijalbo, 1990).

'La indiferencia de Eva', in F. Valls (ed.), *Son cuentos. Antología del relato breve español, 1975–1993* (Madrid: Espasa Calpe, 1993).

'The Origins of Desire' (trans. by Miriam Frank), in J. A. Masoliver Ródenas (ed.), *The Origins of Desire* (London: Serpent's Tail, 1993).

'Viejas historias', in Á. Encinar and A. Percival (eds), *Cuento español contemporáneo* (Madrid: Cátedra, 1993; 2001).

'El jardín de la señora Mussorgsky', in Á. Encinar (ed.), *Cuentos de este siglo: 30 narradoras españolas contemporáneas* (Barcelona: Lumen, 1995).

'La hija predilecta', in L. Feeixas (ed.), *Madres e hijas* (Barcelona: Anagrama, 1996).

'El inventor del tetrabrik', in M. Monmany (ed.), *Vidas de mujer* (Madrid: Alianza, 1998).

'El cuarto secreto', in J. Goñi and E. Butragueño (eds), *Relatos para un fin de milenio* (Barcelona: Plaza y Janés, 1998).

'A la hora que cierran los bares', in J. Andrews and M. Lunati (eds), *Contemporary Spanish Short Stories: Viajeros perdidos* (London: Bristol Classical Press, 1998).

'El hombre apoyado en un árbol', in Á. Encinar (ed.), *Historias de detectives* (Barcelona: Lumen, 1998).

'Un poeta en la piscina', in *Cuentos solidarios* (Madrid: ONCE, 1999).

'La carta desde el refugio', in *Mujeres al alba* (Madrid: Alfaguara, 1999).

'El origen del deseo', in J. M. Merino (ed.), *Cien años de cuentos (1898–1998). Antología del cuento español en castellano* (Madrid: Alfaguara, 1999).

'La corriente del golfo', in R. Hernández Viveros (ed.), *Relato español actual* (México, DF: Universidad Nacional Autónoma de México; Fondo de Cultura Económica, 2002).

'Pisando jardines', in *Orosia: Mujeres de sol a sol* (Jaca: Pirineum Multimedia, 2002).

'Ausencia', in *Mujeres en ruta* (Madrid: Línea Recta, 2005).

'Masajes', in L. Freixas (ed.), *Cuentos de amigas* (Barcelona: Anagrama, 2009).

Children's literature

La sombra de una noche (Madrid: Anaya, 1986; Barcelona: Ediciones del Bronce, 1996).

El recorrido de los animales (Madrid: Júcar, 1975; Madrid: Alfaguara, 1988; Valencia: Pre-textos, 1996).

El desván de la casa grande (Badalona: Parramón, 2007).

Autobiographical

Recuerdos de otra persona (Barcelona: Anagrama, 1996).

Con mi madre (Barcelona: Anagrama, 2001; Barcelona: Círculo de Lectores, 2001).

Imagen de Navarra (Madrid: El País-Aguilar, 1991).

Essays, reflections on her own work, and literary criticism

El Madrid de 'La lucha por la vida' (Madrid: Helios 1971).

'La gracia de la vida, la inmortalidad', *Lucanor* 6 (1991), 172.

La vida oculta (Barcelona: Anagrama, 1993) – *Premio Anagrama de Ensayo 1993.*

La vida se mueve (Madrid: El País-Aguilar, 1995).

'Rosa Chacel', in L. Freixas (ed.), *Retratos literarios. Escritores españoles del siglo XX evocados por sus contemporáneos* (Madrid: Espasa Calpe, 1997).

'Extremos de la creación', in A. Percival (ed.), *Escritores ante el espejo: estudio de la creatividad literaria* (Barcelona: Lumen, 1997), 267–74.

Como el sueño (Zaragoza: Gobierno de Aragón, 2003) – *Premio de las Letras Aragonesas.*

'Mujer del espejo', in E. L. Bergmann and R. Herr, *Mirrors and Echoes: Women's Writing in Twentieth Century Spain* (Berkeley, CA: Global Area, and International Archive; University of California Press, 2007), 17–21.

La Celestina, Edited by Soledad Puértolas (Madrid: Castalia, 2012).

Nostalgia de los demás (Valladolid: Secretariado de Publicaciones e Intercambio Editorial de la Universidad de Valladolid, 2014).

Further reading on Soledad Puértolas

Ramón Acín, 'Soledad Puértolas', in *Los dedos de la mano: Javier Tomeo, José María Latorre, Soledad Puértolas, Ignacio Martínez de Pisón* (Zaragoza: Mira Editores, 1992), 75–103.

Concha Alborg, 'Cuatro narradoras de la transición', in *Nuevos y novísimos. Algunas perspectivas críticas sobre la narrativa española desde la década de los 60* (Boulder, CO: Society of Spanish and Spanish-American Studies, 1987), 11–28.

Joaquín Arnáiz, 'Seis autores de medio siglo: entrevistas a Francisco Ayala, José Luis Sampedro, Miguel Delibes, Soledad Puértolas, Arturo Pérez Reverte, Almudena Grandes', *República de las Letras* 50 (1996), 1–29.

J. Ernesto Ayala-Dip, 'Conciencia y espíritu. Los ángeles y las batallas de los humanos', *El País*, 25 February 1995.

J. Ernesto Ayala-Dip, 'La vida reducida a cinco momentos. Una mujer piensa, habla y escribe sobre su situación en *Una vida inesperada*, la última novela de Soledad Puértolas', *El País*, 14 June 1997.

Nuria Azancot, 'Soledad Puértolas: "Hay una enorme confusión de criterios en la edición"', *El Cultural*, 12 May 2005. http://www.elcultural.com/revista/letras/Soledad-Puertolas/11971

Justo Barranco, 'Palabras para sobrevivir a una madre', *La Vanguardia* (Libros), 4 May 2001.

Eduardo Barraza, 'Escenas de la vida provisional: *Todos mienten* de Soledad Puértolas', in J. Arancibia, A. Mandel, and Y. Rosas (eds), *Literatura femenina*

contemporánea de España (Westminster, CA: Instituto Literario y Cultural Hispánico. 1991), 179–87.

Catherine G. Bellver, 'Two New Women Writers from Spain', *Letras Femeninas* 8.2 (1982), 3–7.

Emilie L. Bergmann, 'Mothers and Daughters in Transition and Beyond', in E. L. Bergmann and R. Herr, *Mirrors and Echoes: Women's Writing in Twentieth Century Spain* (Berkeley, CA: Global Area and International Archive; University of California Press, 2007), 108–17.

Frieda H. Blackwell, 'Conventions of Detective Fiction and Their Subversion in *A través de las ondas* and *Queda la noche* de Soledad Puértolas', *Letras Femeninas* 26.1–2 (2000), 171–83.

Frieda H. Blackwell, 'La mujer de la transición configurada en *Queda la noche* de Soledad Puértolas', in Á. Encinar y C. Valcárcel (eds), *Escritoras y compromiso. Literatura española e hispanoamericana de los siglos XX y XXI* (Madrid: Visor Libros, 2009), 369–77.

Francisco Calvo Serraller, ''Ausencia'. Así se titula uno de los cuentos del libro nuevo de Soledad Puértolas en el que un maestro pide una interpretación de un cuadro del Greco', E*l País* (Babelia), 31 January 2017. https://cultura.elpais.com/cultura/2017/01/30/actualidad/1485794627_158521.html

Tomás Camarero Arribas, 'Lógica de una narrativa en *Una enfermedad moral* de Soledad Puértolas', *Ventanal, Revista de Creación y Crítica* 14 (1988), 133–57.

Vicente Carmona, Jeffrey Lamb and Sherry Velasco, 'Conversando con Mercedes Abad, Cristina Fernández Cubas y Soledad Puértolas: "Feminismo y literatura no tienen nada que ver"', *Mester* 20. 2 (1991),157–65. http://escholarship.org/uc/item/9wx441f1#page-4

Nuria Carrillo, 'La expansión plural de un género: el cuento 1975–1993', *Ínsula* 568 (1994), 9–11.

Nora Catelli, 'Soledad Puértolas', *El Urogallo* 6 (1998), 43.

Nora Catelli, 'Los rasgos de un mestizaje. (La actual novela en castellano)', *Revista de Occidente* 122–3 (1991), 135–47.

María Dolores de Asís Garrote, *Última hora de la novela en España* (Madrid: Pirámide, 1996).

Christine Di Benedetto, 'Escritores y escritura en la obra novelística de Soledad Puértolas: las fronteras de la metaficción', in M. Álvarez, A. J. Gil González and M. Kunz (eds), *Metanarrativas hispánicas* (Zürich: Lit, 2012), 123–37.

Marguerite DiNonno Inteman, *El tema de la soledad en la narrativa de Soledad Puértolas* (Lewiston: Peter Lang, 1994).

Darcy Donahue, 'The Narrator in Soledad Puértolas' *Todos mienten*', *Letras Femeninas* 20.1–2 (1994), 101–108.

Ignacio Echevarría, 'La tristeza redimida. El talento narrativo de Soledad Puértolas, al servicio del relato', *El País*, 18 September 1993.

Ángeles Encinar, 'Escritoras españolas actuales: una perspectiva a través del cuento', *Hispanic Journal* 13.1 (1992), 181–91.

Carlos Galán Lorés, 'Los más jóvenes de los jóvenes', *Ínsula* 512–13 (1989), 14–15.

Francisca González Arias and Darío Villanueva, 'Soledad Puértolas: La ciudad de las almas', in D. Villanueva (ed.), *Los nuevos nombres: 1975–1990*, vol. IX, edited by F. Rico, *Historia y Crítica de la Literatura Española*, (Barcelona: Crítica, 1992), 371–75.

Alberto Gordo, 'Soledad Puértolas: "La novela peligra por culpa del mercado"', *El Cultural*, 13 May 2015. http://www.elcultural.com/noticias/letras/Soledad-Puertolas-La-novela-peligra-por-culpa-del-mercado/7769

Sonia Hernández, 'Arrieros somos. Un objeto, un abrigo, sirve de metáfora a Soledad Puértolas para adentrarse en las constantes humanas, como el amor o el miedo', *La Vanguardia* (Culturas), 3 August 2005.

Marisa Herrera Postlewate, '*Recuerdos de otra persona*: Redefining Autobiographical Writing', in *How and Why I Write: Redefining Hispanic Women's Writing and Experience* (New York: Peter Lang, 2003), 23–56.

Estelle Irizarry, 'Aventura y apertura en la nueva novela Española: *Queda la noche* de Soledad Puértolas', in D. Galván, A. K. Stoll, and P. Brown Yin (eds), *Studies in Honor of Donald W. Bleznick* (Newark, DE: Juan de la Cuesta, 1995), 59–74.

María del Mar López Cabrales, 'Soledad Puértolas. Al otro lado del espejo', in *Palabras de mujeres: escritoras españolas contemporáneas* (Madrid: Narcea, 2000), 117–34.

Rubén Loza Aguerrebere, 'Diálogo con Soledad Puértolas', in *Palabras abiertas: (entrevistas)* (Montevideo: Ediciones B Uruguay, 2011), 109–12.

Maricarmen R. Margenot, 'Creación de la identidad femenina y transgresión en dos relatos de Soledad Puértolas', in G. Cervantes Martín (ed.), *Selected Proceedings of the Pennsylvania Foreign Language Conference* (Pittsburg, PA: Duquesne University, Dept. of Modern Languages, 2003), 151–59.

Sonia Mattalia, 'Entre miradas: Las novelas de Soledad Puértolas', *Ventanal: Revista de Creación y Crítica* 14 (1988), 171–92.

Mercedes Mazquiarán de Rodríguez, 'Beyond Fiction: Voicing the Personal in Soledad Puértolas's *La vida oculta*', in M. Mazquiarán de Rodríguez (ed.), *Spanish Women Writers and the Essay: Gender Politics and the Self* (Columbia: University of Missouri Press, 1998), 231–49.

Charlene Merithew, 'Silencios poderosos: el tema de la quietud en los ensayos de Soledad Puértolas', *Monographic Review / Revista Monográfica* 16 (2000), 162–73.

Miguel Ángel Muñoz, 'Entrevista a Soledad Puértolas', in M. Á. Muñoz (ed.), *La familia del aire: entrevistas con cuentistas españoles* (Madrid: Páginas de Espuma, 2011), 41–45.

Gonzalo Navajas, 'Una estética para después del postmodernismo. La nostalgia

asertiva y la reciente novela española', *Revista de Estudios Hispánicos* 25.3 (1991), 129–51.

Gonzalo Navajas, 'Narrativa y género. La ficción actual desde la mujer', *Ínsula* 589–90 (1996), 37–39.

Gonzalo Navajas, *Más allá de la posmodernidad. Estética de la nueva novela y cine españoles* (Barcelona: Ediciones Universitarias de Barcelona, 1996).

Pilar Nieva de la Paz, 'De la realidad verificable a la ensoñación imaginativa: *El bandido doblemente armado*, de Soledad Puértolas; *Doce relatos de mujeres,* de Ymelda Navajo (ed.), y *La puerta de los sueños*, de Blanca Valdecasas', in *Narradoras españolas en la transición política (Textos y contextos)* (Madrid: Editorial Fundamentos, 2004), 301–12.

Dorothe Notte, 'Soledad Puértolas: El fugaz encanto de lo cotidiano', in Dieter Ingenschay and Hans-Jörg Neuschafer (eds), *Abriendo caminos. La literatura española desde 1975* (Barcelona: Lumen, 1994), 149–56.

María José Obiol, 'Fragmentos de memoria. El nexo de los relatos que recoge Soledad Puértolas en su *Gente que vino a mi boda* es lo efímero del tiempo', *El País*, 16 May 1998.

Carlos Ortega, 'La vida invertebrada', *El Urogallo* 94 (1994), 57–58.

Carlos Ortega, 'Soledad Puértolas desde dentro. La autora recupera desde el realismo interior las trazas de un nuevo hombre', *El País* (Babelia), 5 June 1999.

Janet Pérez, *Contemporary Women Writers of Spain* (Boston, MA: Twayne Publishers, 1988).

Randolph D. Pope, 'Misterios y epifanías en la narrativa de Soledad Puértolas', in A. Toro and D. Ingenschay (eds), *La novela española actual: autores y tendencias* (Kassel: Reichenberger, 1995), 271–301.

Ana Rodríguez Fischer, 'En la corriente de la vida', *El País* (Babelia), 25 May 2015. https://cultura.elpais.com/cultura/2015/05/20/babelia/1432114841_618565. html

Ana Rodríguez Fischer, 'Lo que no se ve', *El País* (Babelia), 4 October 2016. https://cultura.elpais.com/cultura/2016/09/28/babelia/1475078414_281562.html

Eugénie Romon, 'À la recherche de la mère perdue: *Historia de un abrigo* de Soledad Puértolas', *Pandora, Revue d'Études Hispaniques* 6 (2006), 213–21.

Eugénie Romon, 'Vers une mythologie arthurienne au féminin: *La rosa de plata* de Soledad Puértolas', in M. Ramond (ed.), *L'insistante/ La insistente* (Mexico/ Paris: Rilma 2 & ADHEL, 2008), 279–85.

Eugénie Romon, 'Les Shérézades dans *La rosa de plata* et dans les autres oeuvres de Soledad Puértolas', in C. François (ed.), *Le don de Sharazad: la mémoire des Mille et une nuits dans la littérature contemporaine* (Cergy: Université de Cergy-Pontoise, 2008), 97–113.

Eugénie Romon, 'De Soledad Puértolas a Diego Pita', in M. Ramond (ed.), *Les créations ont-elles un sexe? Les Travaux de Gradiva* (ADHEL, 2010), 131–34.

Eugénie Romon, '"A través de las ondas": entre relato policíaco y cuento de hadas', *Estudios Románicos* 19 (2010), 173–90.

Eugénie Romon, 'La singularité des territoires dans l'oeuvre de Soledad Puértolas', *Pandora, Revue d'Études Hispaniques* 10 (2010), 247–60.

Eugénie Romon, 'Le Madrid de Soledad Puértolas', in *Lire les villes: panoramas du monde urbain contemporain* (Tours: Presses Universitaires François Rabelais, 2012), 243–51.

Eugénie Romon, 'La femme dans l'oeuvre de Soledad Puértolas ou Gradiva en marche', in *Hommage à Michèle Ramond* (Paris: Indigo, 2013), 459–72.

Eugénie Romon, '*Si al atardecer llegara el mensajero* de Soledad Puértolas; l'odyssée corporale d'un messsager divin', in E. Tilly and A. Duprat (eds), *Corps et territoire* (Rennes: Publications de l'Université de Rennes, 2014), 175–88.

Eugénie Romon, 'Évolution de la figure du père dans l'oeuvre de Soledad Puértolas', in *Le père comme figure d'autorité* (Saint-Etienne: Publications de l'Université de Saint-Etienne -*Chaiers du GRIAS-CELEC*, 2014), 345–60.

Eugénie Romon, 'Jeux et joueurs dans l'oeuvre de Soledad Puértolas', in *Le jeu: ordre et liberté* (Le Mans: Éditions Cénomane, 2014), 272–82.

Eugénie Romon, 'Relations entre autobiographie et fiction dans l'oeuvre de Soledad Puértolas', in J.-P. Castellani (ed.), *Écriture de soi et autorité* (Tours: PUFR, 2016), 141–55.

Lorraine Ryan, 'Nada más que un espejismo: la inquieta realidad de la modernidad española a través de los relatos "La buena hija" de Almudena Grandes y "La hija predilecta" de Soledad Puértolas', in M. C. Ramblado Minero (ed.), *Construcciones culturales de la maternidad en España: la madre y la relación madre-hija en la literatura y el cine contemporáneos* (Alacant: Universitat d'Alacant, 2004), 45–61.

Santos Sanz Villanueva, 'Generación del 68', *El Urogallo* 26 (1988), 28–60.

Elizabeth A. Scarlett, 'Nomads and Schizos: Postmodern Trends in Body Writing', in *Under Construction: The Body in Spanish Novels* (Charlottesville: The University Press of Virginia, 1994), 166–85.

Lynn K. Talbot, 'Entrevista con Soledad Puértolas', *Hispania* 71.4 (1988), 882–83.

Mary Jane Treacy, 'Soledad Puértolas', in L. Gould Levine, E. Engleson Marson and G. Feiman Waldman (eds), *Spanish Women Writers: A Bio-Bibliographical Source Book* (Westport, CT and London: Greenwood Press, 1993), 397–403.

Tamara Townsend, *Memory and Identity in the Narratives of Soledad Puértolas: Constructing the Past and the Self* (Lanham, MD: Rowman & Littlefield, Lexington Books, 2014).

Akiko Tsuchiya, 'Language, Desire, and the Feminine Riddle in Soledad Puértolas's *La indiferencia de Eva*', *Revista de Estudios Hispánicos* 25.1 (1991), 69–79.

Turia, Revista Cultural dedicated its issue 100 to Soledad Puértolas in 2011.

http://www.ieturolenses.org/revista_turia/index.php/revista-cultural-turia-numero-100.html

Katica Urbanc, *Novela femenina, crítica feminista: cinco autoras españolas* (Toledo, Ohio: Textos Toledanos, 1996).

Katica Urbanc, 'Soledad Puértolas: "He vuelto a la realidad de otra manera"', *Espéculo, Revista Digital de Estudios Literarios* 8 (1998).

Fernando Valls, 'El renacimiento del cuento en España (1975-1990)', *Lucanor* 6 (1991), 27–42.

Anna M. Vilà, 'Algunos momentos efímeros', *La Vanguardia* (Libros), 9 June 2009.

Jun Wang, *El mundo novelístico de Soledad Puértolas* (Albalote, Granada: Editorial Comares, 2000).

Further online information on Soledad Puértolas (a selection)

htpp://www.escritores.org/puertolas.htm
http://escritoras.com/escritoras/escritora.php?i=47
www.rae.es/academicos/soledad-puertolas-villanueva
www.biografiasyvidas.com/biografia/p/puertolas.htm
http://elpais.com/autor/soledad_puertolas/a
https://aragonesesilustres.wikispaces.com/Soledad+Pu%C3%A9rtolas
https://www.youtube.com/watch?v=rEWQp-ZAsF8
https://www.youtube.com/watch?v=Uvbd3UvwDzg
https://www.cuartopoder.es/elblogdelverano/2014/08/02/nostalgia-de-los-demas/4362
https://www.youtube.com/watch?v=wCujDQcVUWM
https://www.youtube.com/watch?v=7eV3okbI0xo
http://cultura.elpais.com/cultura/2010/11/21/actualidad/1290294005_850215.html
http://www.heraldo.es/noticias/ocio-cultura/2016/10/10/soledad-puertolas-indaga-las-relaciones-humanas-chicos-chicas-1105576-1361024.html
http://juegodemanosmag.com/soledad-puertolas-y-lo-invisible-de-las-mujeres/
https://www.elimparcial.es/noticia/171844/los-lunes-de-el-imparcial/soledad-puertolas:-chicos-y-chicas.html
https://ttu-ir.tdl.org/ttu-ir/bitstream/handle/2346/21128/tesis.pdf?sequence=1
http://www.lecturalia.com/autor/189/soledad-puertolas
http://www.rtve.es/television/20160523/documental-soledad-puertolas-dime-estas-buscando/1352105.shtml
http://elpaissemanal.elpais.com/placeres/soledad-puertolas/
http://www.huffingtonpost.es/ovidio-parades/las-busquedas-de-soledad-_b_12260720.html
http://www.aragondigital.es/noticia.asp?notid=150650
http://www.cccb.org/en/participants/file/soledad-puertolas/35798
http://www.anagrama-ed.es/libro/narrativas-hispanicas/el-fin/9788433997944/NH_547

VIEJAS HISTORIAS

Ernesto, el ex marido de mi hermana pequeña, me llamaba frecuentemente por teléfono para ponerme al tanto de las crisis nerviosas de mi hermana, se desahogaba conmigo y me acababa pidiendo que tratara de calmarla a ella y de comprenderle a él, que hacía dos años que se había separado legalmente de Alicia y que no conseguía vivir sin su vigilancia. Su vida se estaba convirtiendo en un infierno.

Ernesto vivía con Rosana, una chica que por aquel entonces quería ser actriz y que años más tarde, también ella separada de Ernesto, lo consiguió. Vivían en Avilés desde hacía un par de meses porque, huyendo de mi hermana, Ernesto tenía un nuevo trabajo, dirigía el laboratorio de una de esas empresas que contaminan el ambiente. Realizaba estudios ecológicos, lo que para Ernesto era algo así como su caballo de batalla, y para la actriz, y para mi pobre hermana. En eso coincidían todos. Tenían razón, a pesar de su tono misionero. Pero si se ponían a hablar todos a la vez, tuvieran o no razón, yo era capaz de llevarles la contraria.

Eran escenas que habían tenido lugar antes de que se trasladaran a Avilés, y que cerraban las visitas de mi hermana, que se abrían con violencia y lamentaciones, pero que concluían siempre en una amigable conversación sobre la necesidad de preservar las zonas verdes del planeta. La menos amigable en aquel momento era yo, no porque estuviera en profundo desacuerdo con ellos, sino porque me irritaba aquella repentina transformación, esa súbita reconciliación basada en una idea general y humanitaria que los unía después de haber gritado y llorado (Alicia y Rosana lloraban las dos, muy espectacularmente, com si se tratara de una competición), haberse insultado y haberse maldecido, sin que aparentemente nada quedara en pie entre ellos. Pues bien, quedaba eso: su loable preocupación por la escalada de destrucción que estaba sufriendo la madre naturaleza. Y aunque todos sabemos que una cosa son las ideas y otra los sentimientos, no dejaba de desconcertarme, y de irritarme, que se produjera aquel desfase tan absoluto entre unas y otros y hasta llegaba a pensar que en algún momento mentían, porque no podía darse tanta radicalidad: o no se odiaban tanto, o las cuestiones ecológicas

TALES FROM THE PAST

Ernesto, the ex-husband of my younger sister, would often phone to bring me up to date on my sister's latest nervous crisis, pour his heart out and end up asking me to try to calm her down and to understand him, this man who had been legally separated from Alicia for two years now, and who was unable to live without her keeping an eye on him. His life was turning into hell on earth.

Ernesto lived with Rosana, a young girl who at about that time wanted to be an actress and who, years later, she too separated from Ernesto, achieved it. They'd been living in Avilés[1] for a couple of months or so because, in running away from my sister, Ernesto had landed a new job, in charge of the laboratories at one of those companies that pollute the environment. He was involved in ecological research, which was something of a hobby-horse for Ernesto, as well as for the actress, and my poor sister. On this at least they were all agreed. And they were right, in spite of their missionary tone. But when they all began to talk at once, irrespective of whether they were right or not, I was quite capable of taking the opposite point of view.

Before they moved to Avilés my sister's visits used to conclude with one of these scenes. The visits would begin in violence and wailings, yet would always end in a friendly conversation about the need to preserve the green zones of the planet. In those days, the least amicable one was myself, not because I felt I was in strong disagreement with them, but because that sharp transformation used to irritate me, that sudden reconciliation based on some general and humanitarian notion that brought them together again after they'd been shouting and weeping (Alicia and Rosana, the pair of them, crying in the most spectacular way, as if in competition with one another), after having insulted and cursed each other, without, apparently, there being any common ground left between them. Well, there was just one thing: their commendable preoccupation with the escalating destruction being suffered by Mother Nature. And even though we all know ideas are one thing and feelings another, I was continuously disconcerted and irritated that such an absolute imbalance should exist between one and the other, and I even came to believe that at times they were lying, because such a radical about-turn was not possible: either they didn't hate each other as much as they pretended,

---

1   **Avilés**: industrial and maritime town in Asturias, in northern Spain.

les importaban bastante poco. Algo tenía que fallar, algo había allí que no encajaba y que yo no conseguía ver. Era así, en aquel estado de perfecta connivencia e idílico acuerdo, como yo me los encontraba cuando, después de recibir la llamada desesperada de Ernesto, iba a recoger a Alicia, y nunca dejaba de pensar, inquieta y atemorizada, que en aquella ocasión me tocaría presenciar los gritos, las lágrimas, las violentas escenas que Ernesto me había contado por teléfono, pero nunca fue así, y aunque en sus caras se podían ver los signos de aquella explosión emocional –los ojos de Alicia y de Rosana estaban francamente rojos y sus maquillajes corridos; eran, inequívocamente, dos mujeres después de una batalla– los tres estaban tranquilamente sentados alrededor de la mesa baja del cuarto de estar, con una bebida entre las manos, preocupados, dadas las proporciones, alcance y dificultades del asunto que comentaban, pero plácidos.

El mismo Ernesto, con quien había hablado media hora antes y que me había pedido que fuera a ayudarlo a sacar a mi hermana de su casa, parecía no tener ya ningún deseo de poner punto final a aquella reunión. Me ofrecía una copa, se sentaba en el sofá, nos contemplaba con satisfacción y exponía sus teorías, encantado al parecer de encontrarse entre un público femenino tan incondicional. Tres mujeres que le miraban atentamente. Porque, hora es ya de confesarlo, Ernesto nos gustaba a las tres. Había sido yo quien se lo había presentado a mi hermana, como había sido ella quien había cometido tal vez aún mayor error al presentárselo a Rosana, y estábamos, las tres, a nuestro pesar, perfectamente convencidas de que Ernesto se merecía nuestra devoción. Sus ojos brillaban al mirarnos y se diría que existía en él un constante, puede que inconsciente, deseo de conquistarnos.

Cuando al fin bajábamos Alicia y yo en el ascensor, ella, ligeramente más achispada que yo, declaraba que nada de lo que había pasado le importaba mucho porque lo único que necesitaba para seguir viviendo era poder ver a Ernesto y atreverse a pensar que él todavía sentía algo por ella, y yo la entendía y la disculpaba, aunque no se lo decía, porque hasta yo podía sentir algo parecido, mucho más tibio y controlado, pero sabía, como ella, que Ernesto era irresistiblemente atractivo y, sabiéndolo también él, todavía jugaba con nosotras, sin querer descartar del todo la posibilidad de un reencuentro, una reconciliación, por muy fugaz que fuera, por mucho dolor que nos causara después. Bastante más sensata que Alicia, mayor y más

or the environment didn't matter that much to them. Something had to be wrong, there was something there that just didn't fit, that I wasn't able to see. Thus it was that I would find them, in that state of perfect collusion and idyllic accord, when I went to collect Alicia, after receiving Ernesto's desperate call, and I never stopped thinking, so worried and scared was I, that that would be the day it would be my turn to witness the screaming, the tears, the violent scenes that Ernesto had been telling me about over the phone, but it was never like that, and even though you could see the signs of that emotional outburst written all over their faces – Alicia and Rosana's eyes obviously red and their make-up all smeared; they were, unmistakably, two women after a battle – the three of them were sitting peacefully round the coffee table in the living room, a drink in their hands, worried, given the extent, the range and the difficulty of the subject they were discussing, but placid.

Ernesto himself, with whom I had been talking just half an hour before and who had asked me to go and help him get my sister out of his house, now appeared to have no desire whatsoever to bring the meeting to an end. He would offer me a drink, sit down on the sofa, look at us in a satisfied way and begin expounding his theories, apparently delighted to find himself before such a captive female audience. Three women all looking at him attentively. Because, and the time has come to confess the fact, Ernesto was a man that all three of us fancied. It had been I who introduced him to my sister, just as it had been she who had made perhaps the even greater mistake of introducing him to Rosana, and all three of us were perfectly convinced, in spite of ourselves, that Ernesto was worthy of our devotion. His eyes shone as he looked at us and it might be said that there was in him an ever present, perhaps unconscious, desire to seduce us.

When at last Alicia and I went down in the lift she, slightly more tipsy than I, would declare that none of what had happened mattered very much because the only thing she needed to carry on living was to be able to see Ernesto and dare to think that he still felt something for her, and I understood her and forgave her, although I didn't tell her so, because even I was capable of having similar feelings for him, albeit much more lukewarm and restrained even though I knew, as she did, that Ernesto was irresistibly attractive and, being aware of this fact himself, would still play with us without wanting to rule out forever the possibility of a further encounter, a reconciliation, however fleeting it might be, however much pain it might cause us later on. Somewhat more sensible, older and more experienced than Alicia, I managed

experimentada, yo conseguía ahogar aquel atisbo de esperanza sin excesivas dificultades, sin desmedidos esfuerzos, pero mi pobre y obstinada hermana se quedaba encasquillada, atrapada, y desde ese momento se iba preparando para la próxima escena. Se miraba en el espejo del ascensor y sin duda daba a su propia imagen una cita, todavía no determinada pero cierta, en aquel mismo lugar. Nos volveremos a ver.

Pero no estaba demasiado convencida del fundamento de sus ilusiones y no quería ir sola a su casa, de forma que me pedía que la dejara dormir en la mía, aunque fuera en el sofá, para evitar volver a pensar en Ernesto, para estar rodeada de gente, para no sacar las peores conclusions sobre su vida. Ajena al orden y a las costumbres de mi casa, repentinamente olvidada de todo, se daba un baño y se paseaba por la casa, canturreando envuelta en uno de mis albornoces, gastándoles bromas a mis hijos y a mi marido, y ya para entonces sus turbulencias emocionales parecían perfectamente superadas. Pero así era Alicia, y yo no podía asombrarme. Lo que no conseguía era convencer a mi marido de que su estado era crítico, porque él no acababa de creer que Alicia fuera capaz de violencias. Y yo misma terminaba concluyendo, cuando al día siguiente Alicia se despedía, bien arreglada, perfumada y maquillada, camino de su oficina, que todo aquello no tenía ninguna importancia y que debía dejar que mi hermana y su ex marido arreglaran sus problemas solos y, sobre todo, no sobresaltarme, porque cada vez que Ernesto me llamaba, en aquel tono marcadamente trágico, llegaba a pensar que Alicia había perdido la razón y mientras me dirigía hacia su casa en su búsqueda me decía que ya era hora de tomar una medida, de consultar a un médico.

Tantas veces se había dado esa situación y tantas veces la había arrojado de mi cabeza, que creo que ya estaba un poco inmunizada, aunque confieso que la decisión de Ernesto de trasladarse a vivir al norte me alivió. Al menos, ya no sería para Alicia tan tentador presentarse en su casa, y si lo hacía, a Ernesto no se le podía ocurrir llamarme en busca de ayuda, porque Avilés estaba lo bastante lejos como para que esa petición resultara excesiva.

Fue Alicia quien me lo comunicó, y percibí que, a pesar de sus quejas, en lo más profundo de su ser aprobaba la decisión de Ernesto, consciente de que la distancia entre dos personas que no han conseguido, para la desesperación de una de ellas, la armonía en el amor, es indiscutiblemente terapéutica.

to stifle those first stirrings of hope without too much difficulty, without disproportionate effort, but my poor, obstinate sister remained stuck in the groove, trapped, and from then on she would spend her time preparing for the next scene. She would look at herself in the mirror in the lift, doubtless planning a rendez-vous, not yet finalized but nonetheless certain, in that same place, with her own reflection. We'll see each other again.

But she wasn't too sure of how well-founded her dreams were and she didn't want to go home alone, so she would ask if I'd let her sleep at my house, even if it were on the sofa, to stop her thinking about Ernesto again, so that she could be surrounded by people, so that she wouldn't draw the worst conclusions about the way her life was going. Being a stranger to the arrangements and customs of my house, her mind suddenly oblivious to all that had happened, she would take a bath and wander through the house, humming, wrapped in one of my bathrobes, joking with my children and my husband, and by then her emotional storms appeared to have been perfectly overcome. But that was Alicia for you, and I couldn't claim to feel any surprise. What I failed to do was to convince my husband that her condition was critical, because he never showed any real signs of believing Alicia capable of violence. And when, on the following day Alicia took her leave of us, beautifully turned up, wearing perfume and make-up, on her way to her office, even I was left with the conclusion that none of it meant anything and that I should just leave my sister and her ex-husband to sort out their problems on their own and, above all, that I shouldn't be alarmed, because every time Ernesto called me in that oh-so-tragic tone of voice, I'd end up thinking Alicia had lost her mind and while I was on my way to his house to fetch her I'd tell myself the time had come to do something about it, to consult a doctor.

The situation had arisen so many times before and I had put it out of my mind so many times that I think by now I was a bit immune to it, although I must admit Ernesto's decision to move away and live in the north came as a relief. At least it wouldn't be so tempting for Alicia to just turn up at his house, and if she did, Ernesto couldn't possibly think he could call me up looking for help, because Avilés was far enough away to make such a request unreasonable.

It was Alicia who told me about it, and I could see that, in spite of her protests, deep down she agreed with Ernesto's decision, aware of the fact that putting a distance between two people who have, to the despair of one of them, failed to achieve harmony in love, is undoubtedly therapeutic.

Tal vez estaba ella cansada de sufrir, de llorar, gritar y reconciliarse al fin hablando de ecología, de venir a casa después de las peleas para bromear con mis hijos como si nada hubiera pasado y ella fuera la tía soltera y alegre de las novelas rosas. Esas escenas debían parecerle, al fin, unas iguales a otras, y debían dejarle la sensación de una repetición absurda, casi aburrida. Sin duda, ella también admitía la conveniencia de esa medida, que nunca se hubiera decidido a tomar, pero que la beneficiaba. Ahora empezaba su verdadera separación, ahora tenía que adaptarse a su nueva vida y tomar medidas para no dejarse hundir. Ernesto quedaba fuera de su alcance.

En todo caso, fue Alicia quien me dio la noticia. Ernesto no tuvo la delicadeza de llamarme para despedirse de mí. Sus llamadas respondían sólo a la urgencia, a la desesperación. Cuando se fue, en una huida que a todos nos pareció muy razonable, no consideró necesario hacérmelo saber.

No fui consciente de esa época de paz, porque es difícil valorar la calma cuando se tiene. Se añora en el mismo momento en que se pierde, y sólo entonces parece el mayor don que pueda obtenerse sobre la tierra. Entre tanto, no se piensa en ella porque ése es su regalo. En la verdadera calma no cabe el análisis. Pero me temo que estoy, ya, hablando de otra cosa: estoy hablando de mí.

No sé el tiempo que transcurrió hasta que volví a escuchar la voz de Ernesto. Lo primero que me asombró fue que aquel timbre tan conocido no sonara con ansiedad, no era un grito, una llamada de urgencia. Tenía una cadencia lenta, de cansancio, de contenido temor.

–¿Sabes dónde está Alicia?– me preguntó, después de interesarse brevemente por mi existencia.

–Supongo que estará en su casa– dije, comprendiendo de inmediato que él ya habría intentado localizarla allí.

–No está–confirmó–. Llevo tres días buscándola. No ha ido a trabajar desde hace cuatro días y su teléfono no contesta. Por eso te llamo.

–Puede que esté de viaje.

–En la oficina no saben nada. Pidió unos días de vacaciones, pero nadie sabe dónde está. Creí que teníais mucha confianza–. Ahora su voz cansada cobró un matiz de irritación, de reproche.

–Alicia es bastante mayor. No suele darme explicaciones de su vida– me defendí–. Y siempre ha hecho lo que le ha dado la gana, como seguramente sabes.

Una de las cosas que había hecho era quitarme el novio y casarse con

Perhaps she was tired of suffering, of crying, of screaming, of finally making up by talking about ecology, of coming home after the fights to joke with my children as if nothing has happened and as if she were the unmarried, merry aunt of sentimental novels. Those scenes must finally have all looked very much the same and must have left her with a feeling of absurd, almost boring, repetition. Doubtless she too could see the convenience of that move, which she herself would never have decided to undertake, although it was god for her. Now she started her real separation from him, now she had to adapt to her new life and to take steps to ensure she didn't let herself be overwhelmed. Ernesto was beyond her reach.

In any event, it was Alicia who told me the news. Ernesto didn't have the decency to call me to say goodbye. His calls came only in times of emergency and despair. When he left, making an escape that seemed highly reasonable to all of us, he didn't think it necessary to let me know.

I wasn't aware of that period of peace because it's difficult to put a price on calm when you have it. You long for peace of mind at the very moment that you're losing it, and only then does it seem like the greatest gift this earth has to offer. In the meantime you don't think about it, because peace of mind is its own gift. Analysis has no place in real peace of mind. But I'm afraid I'm talking about something else now: I'm talking about myself.

I don't know how long it was before I heard Ernesto's voice again. The first thing which surprised me was that his so familiar tone didn't sound anxious, it wasn't a shout, a cry for help. It had a slow, tired cadence to it, a note of controlled fear.

'Do you know where Alicia is?' he asked, having asked briefly after me.

'I assume she'll be at home', I said, realizing straight away that he'd already tried to track her down there.

'She's not there', he confirmed. 'I've been looking for her for days. She's not been in to work for four days and her phone isn't answering. That's why I'm calling you.'

'She could be away on a trip.'

'They don't know anything at her office. She asked for a few days holiday, but nobody knows where she is. I thought you two were very close.' His tired voice now held a trace of irritation, of reproach.

'Alicia is a big girl now. She doesn't usually tell me what's going on in her life', I countered. 'And she's always done whatever took her fancy, as you must surely know.'

One of the things she had done was to take away my boyfriend and

él sin mostrar jamás el menor remordimiento por ello. Supuse que Ernesto sabía a lo que yo me estaba refiriendo.

–¿La cees capaz de cometer una tontería?– me preguntó.

–¿Qué quieres decir?

–La última discusión que tuvimos fue bastante fuerte. En realidad, le dije cosas que no siento. Ya sabes cómo acaban esas peleas, uno acaba sacando lo peor, sólo por fastidiar, por hacer daño. De repente, todo se convierte en una cuestión de honor, de amor propio. Lo único importante en ese momento es vencer, humillar. Creo que me pasé de rosca.

–¿Cuándo fue eso?

–El viernes pasado.

–¿Fue Alicia a Avilés?

–Sí. Me quedé asombrado. Nunca pensé que vendría hasta aquí. Se presentó con una maleta y dijo que se quedaría en casa hasta estar perfectamente convencida de que no había nada entre ella y yo. Que necesitaba esa prueba antes de decidirse a olvidarme. Cielos, a veces pienso que está loca –suspiró–. Por eso me preocupa–. Al fín salía ese verbo: preocupar, que estaba en el fondo de la conversación.

–¿Cuánto tiempo se quedó?

–Muy poco. Yo estaba solo. Rosana estaba en Madrid, haciendo unas pruebas. Supongo que fue eso lo que me empujó a insultarla. Pensé que Alicia estaba enterada de la ausencia de Rosana, que, desde Madrid, nos seguía espiando. Me llené de ira. La insulté y la eché de casa. Le puse la maleta en la puerta, la cogí del brazo y la saqué al descansillo. Cerré la puerta y ya no la volví a abrir, aunque ella siguió tocando el timbre. Al fin, pidió el ascensor y se fue. Al poco tiempo, empezó a sonar el teléfono, pero no lo cogí. Y eso es todo lo que sé–. Volvió a suspirar–. Rosana vino el domingo y me hizo llamar a Alicia. En realidad, creo que Rosana siente simpatía por ella. No le pareció bien que la hubiera tratado así. Pero ya no pudimos encontrarla. La estamos buscando desde el lunes. ¿Dónde crees que puede estar? ¿No te parece extraño que no te haya dicho nada?

Me resistía a inquietarme, pero tampoco sentía ninguna necesidad de tranquilizar a Ernesto, cuyas llamadas nunca habían sido tranquilizadoras.

–Voy a intentar buscarla–dije.

Pero cuando colgué el teléfono comprendí que no sabía cómo hacerlo. No sabía mucho de la vida de mi hermana y no quería asustar a mis padres, que

marry him without ever showing the slightest remorse for having done so. I supposed that Ernesto knew what I was talking about.

'Do you think she's capable of doing something silly?' he asked me.

'What do you mean?'

'The last row we had was pretty bad. To tell you the truth, I said things to her I don't really feel. You know how these things end up, you show your worst side, just to upset or hurt the other person. It all suddenly becomes a question of honour, of pride. The only thing that's important at the time is to win, to humiliate. I think I went too far.'

'When was this?'

'Last Friday.'

'Did Alicia go to Avilés?'

'Yes. I was astonished. I never thought she'd come up here. She turned up with a suitcase and said she'd be staying at the house until she was thoroughly convinced there was nothing left between herself and me. That she needed proof of that before deciding whether to forget me. Honestly, sometimes I think she's crazy', he sighed. 'That's why I'm worried.' At last it had come out, that verb: to be worried. It was at the very root of the conversation.

'How long did she stay?'

'Not long. I was on my own. Rosana was in Madrid auditioning for a couple of parts. I suppose that was what drove me to insult her. I thought Alicia knew about Rosana's being away, that she'd been spying on us from Madrid. I got very angry. I called her names and threw her out of the house. I took her suitcase to the door, grabbed her by the arm and pushed her out onto the landing. I slammed the door and refused to open it again even though she kept ringing the bell. She finally called the lift and went. A little while later the phone began to ring, but I didn't answer it. And that's all I know." He sighed again. 'Rosana came back on the Sunday and made me call Alicia. To tell you the truth, I think Rosana rather likes her. She didn't think it was right that I should have treated her like that. But then we couldn't find her. We've been looking for her since Monday. Where do you think she could be? Don't you think it's odd that she hasn't said anything to you?'

I refused to start worrying, but neither did I feel any need to calm Ernesto down; his phone calls to me had never been reassuring.

'I'm going to try to find her', I said.

But when I hung up I realized I didn't know where to start. I didn't know very much about my sister's life and I didn't want to alarm my parents

eran los únicos que tal vez tenían algunos datos sobre sus actuales amistades. Me las arreglé para sacarles un par de nombres sin levantar demasiadas suspicacias, pero volví a encontrarme en un punto muerto. Nadie sabía nada.

Ernesto me volvió a llamar.

—¿Crees que debemos acudir a la policía?— me preguntó.

Yo tenía la mente paralizada y su sugerencia me sorprendió.

—Supongo que sí–dije–. Hazlo tú, por favor. Es algo que me impresiona demasiado.

Me telefoneó en cuanto la policía hizo sus investigaciones. Ni en las comisarías ni en los hospitales se sabía nada de mi hermana, y eso era todo lo que podía hacerse. Si tenían otras noticias, nos las comunicarían de inmediato.

Pero no nos llamaron.

Alicia apareció al lunes siguiente. Lo supimos porque telefoneamos a la oficina. Cuando hablé con ella, acababa de hablar con Ernesto.

—No entiendo por qué os habéis preocupado tanto— dijo—. Me he ido de viaje.

—Pero no se lo habías dicho a nadie.

—Soy bastante mayor, ¿no crees?

Algo parecido le había dicho yo a Ernesto hacía unos días.

—¿Fuiste sola?

Se rió.

—Ya que me lo preguntas, me fui con un chico.

Parecía bastante contenta, y me alegré. Tal vez había encontrado ya la forma de consolarse.

Sucedió otro período de calma, sin que yo dedicase mucho tiempo a las visicitudes amorosas de mi hermana. Y una tarde de invierno, sonó el timbre de mi puerta de una manera insistente. Era Ernesto. No quiso pasar, sólo pidió por favor que lo acompañara a un bar porque quería hablar conmigo a solas.

—Aquí no— dijo. No quiero molestar. Sois una familia.

Temblaba, no se había afeitado, me miraba fijamente bajo el mechón de pelo mojado que cubría su frente y parte de sus ojos. No di muchas explicaciones y me fui tras él. Anduvimos bajo la lluvia fría –yo sostenía el paraguas contra el viento y Ernesto no hacía nada por cubrirse– hasta encontrar un bar que le gustara. Éste no, decía, tiene demasiada luz, aquí hay demasiada gente, éste es horroroso… Al fin, se decidió, un poco resignado, y entramos y nos sentamos y pedimos algo de beber. Yo le observaba, esperando que empezara a hablar, ¿qué podía preguntarle?

who were the only ones who might have any information about her current circle of friends. I managed to get a couple of names out of them without raising too many suspicions, but I ran up against another dead end. Nobody knew anything.

Ernesto called me again.

'Do you think we should call the police?' he asked me.

My mind had gone blank and his suggestion took me by surprise.

'I suppose so', I said. 'Please, you do it. I find it too upsetting.'

He called me as soon as the police had carried out their enquiries. None of the police stations or hospitals knew anything about my sister, and that was all they could do. If they had anything further to report, they'd get in touch with us straight away.

But they didn't call.

Alicia turned up the following Monday. We found out about it because we phoned her office. When I spoke to her, she'd just been talking to Ernesto.

'I don't understand why you were so worried', she said. 'I've been away.'

'But you didn't say a word to anybody.'

'I'm a big girl now, aren't I?'

I'd said more or less the same thing to Ernesto a few days earlier.

'Did you go on your own?'

She laughed.

'Now you ask me, I went with a male friend.'

She sounded quite happy, and I was glad. Perhaps she'd already found a way of consoling herself.

There ensued another period of calm during which I paid little attention to the amorous vicissitudes of my sister. Then one winter's evening my front doorbell started to ring insistently. It was Ernesto. He didn't want to come in, he only wanted to ask me to go to some bar with him because he wanted to talk to me privately.

'Not here', he said. 'I don't want to bother you. You have a family.'

He was trembling, he hadn't shaved, he was staring at me from under a lock of damp hair that had fallen across his forehead and part of his eyes. I didn't say much by way of explanation and set off behind him. We walked along in the cold rain – I was holding my umbrella against the wind but Ernesto did nothing to cover himself up – until we found a bar he liked. Not this one, he'd say, it's too bright, there are too many people here, this one is awful... He finally made up his mind, somewhat resigned, and we went in, sat down and ordered something to drink. I kept my eyes on him, waiting for him to start speaking. What could I ask him?

Bebió, se pasó la mano por la cara, miró la superficie lisa de la mesa.

–Me ha dejado–dijo–. Se ha ido definitivamente.

–¿Quién?

Me devolvió una mirada de asombro, vacía, como si no me entendiera.

–Alicia–susurró.

–Creí que eras tú quien la había dejado.

Negó con la cabeza, volvió a restregarse la cara mojada.

–Cielos, no lo sabía, te lo aseguro, no me había dado cuenta. Es la única mujer a la que he querido. No soporto perderla. No quiere verme. Dice que nunca nos volveremos a ver.

Se puso a llorar. Sacó un pañuelo y se limpió la cara.

–Es tan raro todo esto, tan extraño.

–Has necesitado que Alicia te dejara para darte cuenta de que la querías– le dije, y supongo que era un reproche, por Alicia y tal vez por mí, que nunca le había dejado.

–Soy un estúpido, lo sé–dijo–. Pero estoy desesperado. Nunca volveré a tenerla.

–¿Para qué querías verme? No puedo hacer nada por ti.

Volvió a dedicarme una mirada de desconcierto.

–No lo sé– balbuceó –. De repente, me vi frente a tu casa. Supongo que eres la única persona a la que puedo decir esto.

–Siempre acudes a mí–dije, con mi viejo resentimiento–. Cuando Alicia te molestaba y querías que se fuera de tu casa, me llamabas para que me la llevara a la mía. Ahora que no quiere verte, me llamas para llorar sobre mi hombro. ¿No crees que eso es muy cómodo? Yo siempre estoy ahí, para ayudarte. Te saco de apuros y te consuelo. Deberías preguntarte por qué lo hago. Aunque ya es tarde. Me parece que me he cansado de ayudarte.

El vacío de sus ojos se convirtió en pánico y, a mi pesar, sentí compasión. No podía ayudarle, pero todavía me conmovía, y me acordé de Alicia cuando, después de una de sus violentas escenas y posterior reconciliación, se miraba al espejo del ascensor de la casa de Ernesto y se decía que él la amaba y que ella no podía renunciar. Al fin y al cabo, ahora se demostraba que tenía razón.

–Lo siento–murmuró–. Pero no te vayas. No puedes fallarme.

Decidió sobreponerse a su temor y se echó a reír. Fue entonces cuando comprendí que estaba verdaderamente borracho.

He took a drink, wiped his hand across his face and looked at the smooth surface of the table.

'She's left me', he said. 'She's gone for good.'

'Who?'

He answered me with an astonished, vacant look, as if he didn't understand my question.

'Alicia', he whispered.

'I thought it was you who'd left her.'

He shook his head and went back to mopping his wet face.

'Heavens, I didn't know, honestly, I didn't realize. She's the only woman I've ever loved. I can't bear to lose her. She doesn't want to see me. She says we'll never see each other again.'

He started to cry. He took out his handkerchief and wiped his face.

'This is all very odd, very peculiar.'

'You needed Alicia to leave you to make you realize you loved her', I told him, and I suppose it was a reproach, for Alicia and perhaps for me, who had never left him.

'I know I'm being really stupid', he said. 'But I'm desperate. I shall never have her again.'

'Why did you want to see me? I can't do anything for you.'

He gave me another disconcerted look.

'I don't know', he stammered. 'I suddenly found myself outside your house. I suppose you're the only person I can say this to.'

'You always turn to me', I said, feeling my old resentment. 'When Alicia used to bother you and you wanted her out of your house, you'd call me so I'd take her to mine. Now she doesn't want to see you, you call me to cry on my shoulder. Very handy, don't you think? I'm always there to help you. I get you out of tight posts and comfort you. You should ask yourself why I do it. Even though it's a bit late now. I think I've grown tired of helping you.'

The emptiness of his eyes turned to panic and in spite of myself I felt sorry for him. I couldn't help him, but he still moved me and I remembered how Alicia, after one of their violent scenes and subsequent reconciliations, would look at herself in the mirror in the lift at Ernesto's house and tell herself that he was in love with her and that she couldn't give him up. And when all was said and done, it turned out she was right.

'I'm sorry', he murmured. 'But don't go. You can't desert me.'

He made up his mind to overcome his fear and burst out laughing. It was then I understood he was completely drunk.

–Vámonos–le dije–. Prefiero andar bajo la lluvia.

Al ponerse de pie, empujó la mesa y su vaso cayó al suelo. Me excusé con el camarero, cogí a Ernesto del brazo y lo saqué a la calle. Al otro lado de la puerta de cristal del bar, el camarero se inclinó para recoger el vaso roto.

Anduvimos mucho rato, cobijados bajo mi paraguas, envueltos en el ruido de la lluvia, hablando cada uno sin escucharnos demasiado, contando retazos de vida y de ilusiones, sosteniéndonos mutuamente.

–¿Cómo va a terminar esto?– preguntó Ernesto.

De vez en cuando lo decía, como una frase de la que uno no se puede desprender, que termina por perder su verdadero significado y se convierte en algo desconocido, ajeno, salvador, una respuesta.

'Let's go', I said. 'I would rather walk in the rain.'

As he got to his feet he knocked against the table and his glass fell on the floor. I apologized to the waiter, took Ernesto by the arm, and led him out into the street. On the other side of the glass door to the bar the waiter had bent down to pick up the broken tumbler.

We walked for a long time, sheltering under my umbrella, enveloped in the noise of the rain, each of us talking without listening very much to what the other was saying, relating snippets of our lives and our hopes and dreams, giving each other mutual support.

'How's this all going to end?' asked Ernesto.

From time to time he'd say the same thing, like a phrase you can't get out of your mind, that ends up losing its real meaning and becomes something unknown, foreign, a life-saver, an answer.

CIRUGÍA PLÁSTICA

PLASTIC SURGERY

Original Spanish text from
Últimos narradores: Antología de la reciente narrativa breve española,
edited by Joseluís González and Pedro de Miguel
(Pamplona: Hierbaola, 1993, 179–90)
© María Eugenia Salaverri, 1993

MARÍA EUGENIA SALAVERRI was born in Bilbao in 1957. She is a
writer, a journalist, a songwriter, and above all a scriptwriter and film producer
who, together with cinema director Javier Rebollo, owns the film company
Karambola Producciones S. L. María Eugenia Salaverri is regularly involved
in the organization of the International Film Festival of San Sebastian. She
has also been a producer of debate programmes for Basque Television and
writes articles for *El País* and other publications such as *El Correo, ABC,
La Estafeta Literaria, Cuadernos Iberoamericanos, Pérgola, Tribuna Vasca*
and *La Gaceta del Norte*. In 1978, María Eugenia Salaverri published a
book of poems, *Retrato de un pájaro*, but she is best known for her work
as a short-story writer. *Un tango para tres hermanas* (1991) is a collection
in which she reveals her talent for charging an ordinary situation with a
hint of the nightmarish. Although very different from one another, all the
main characters in the book are women driven by their instinct to fight and
survive, and some of them travel from one story to another, thus giving the
book a purposeful sense of unity in spite of the diversity of literary strategies
deployed: diaries, letters, stories told by different narratorial voices, etc. In
2004, she published a second volume of stories, *¿Por qué te ríes?*, which
includes the one selected for this anthology, although under a different title:
'En Francia anochece antes'. It also features 'Noche en la autopista', which,
under the title 'Un taxi en la niebla', was awarded the Premio de Narración
Breve Julio Cortázar in 1999. María Eugenia Salaverri is a prominent figure
in the cultural life of the Basque Country: she teaches creative writing, is
responsible for the Club de Lectura 'Aurrez Aurre', based in the Azkuna
Zentroa (Centro Cultural de la Alhóndiga de Bilbao) and, since 2012, she has
been the President of the Asociación de Escritores de Euskadi/ Euskadiko

Idazleen Elkartea. She is also the organiser of the association's yearly conference which, in 2016, focussed on issues of literary authorship in the digital era. Maria Eugenia Salaverri has been awarded several prizes for her short stories, such as the Samaniego de Relatos in 1982, the 'Imagínate Euskadi' de Relatos in 1993, and the Narración Breve Julio Cortázar in 2005.

Bibliography of María Eugenia Salaverri

Poetry
Retrato de un pájaro (Bilbao: La Gran Enciclopedia Vasca, 1978).

Short story collections
Un tango para tres hermanas (Bilbao: Pérgola, 1991; 1997).
¿Por qué te ríes? (Bilbao: Bassarai, 2004).

Short stories in anthologies (a selection)
'Hazlo por mí', *Cuadernos Hipanoamericanos* 390 (1982), 615–23.
'La gardenia azul''', in J. L. Hernández and P. de Miguel (eds), *Narradores vascos. Antología de la narrativa breve vasca actual* (Pamplona: Hierbaola, 1992).
'Cirugía plástica', in J. L. Hernández and P. de Miguel (eds), *Últimos narradores. Antología de la reciente narrativa breve española* (Pamplona: Hierbaola, 1993).
'Plastiche Chirurgie', in G. Pichler (ed.), *Wespennest. Wespennest. Zeitschrift für brauchbare Texte und Bilder / Literatur aus Spanien* (Berlin: Verlag, 1995).
'Cirugía plástica', in R. Hernández Viveros (ed.), *Relato español actual* (México, DF: Universidad Nacional Autónoma de México; Fondo de Cultura Económica, 2002).
'El do de Anatoli', in *Bilbao, almacén de ficciones* (Bilbao: Alberdania, 2000).
'Un taxi en la niebla', in *Palimpsestos* (Murcia: Publicaciones de la Universidad de Murcia, 2005).
'Un perro en un bar', in *Lecturas entre paradas* (Bilbao: Diputación Foral de Bizkaia/ Trama Servicios Culturales, 2007).
'Supermercado', in *Historias del 8 de marzo* (Bilbao: Fundación Bilbao Bizkaia Kutxa, 2008).
'Julián y su padre', in *Literatura y placer* (Bilbao: Asociación de Escritores de Euskadi/ Euskadiko Idazleen Elkartea, 2010).
'Idolatría', in *Literatura y realidad* (Bilbao: Asociación de Escritores de Euskadi/ Euskadiko Idazleen Elkartea, 2013).
'Rosas en la noche', in *Bilbao de cine* (Bilbao: Bilbao Udala, 2008).
'Bilbao', in *Bizkaia vista por las mujeres* (Bilbao: Bizkaiko Foru Aldundia, 2013).

Cinema scripts
Calor… y celos (1996).
Marujas asesinas (2001).
Locos por el sexo (2006).
Anfitrioi berezia / El extraño anfitrión (2012).
Alaba zintzoa / La buena hija (2013).
Txarriboda / La matanza (2015).

El amigo imaginario (2015) [based on her short story 'Edificio España' from her collection *¿Por que te ríes?* (2004)].

Further reading on María Eugenia Salaverri

ABC guionistas, 'María Eugenia Salaverri: "En las noticias breves a veces hay una película"', *El Correo Español-El Pueblo Vasco*, 23 February 2006.

G. E. Bilbao, 'Un país de ensueño. María Eugenia Salaverri: "En un mundo donde hay castigos, también deber existir recompensas"', *El Correo Español-El Pueblo Vasco*, 26 November 1992.

Isabel Camacho, 'La crítica más imbécil te deja huella durante días', *El País*, 11 May 1999.

Cartelera, '*Marujas asesinas*, una comedia criminal', 14 July 2001.

Ciao, Revista Musical, 'Las chicas malas no saben perdonar', December 2001.

De Cine, 'Esto no es la biblioteca de Alejandría', February 2006.

María Luisa Idoate, 'Eugenia Salaverri: "Los personajes de mis cuentos son vulnerables, fuertes e incluso crueles al mismo tiempo"', *Deia*, 11 September 1991.

Ainhoa Iglesias, 'Entrevista a María Eugenia Salaverri', *Bilbao*, July 2004.

Gara, '*Alaba Zintzoa* presenta a una mujer desbordada por los problemas familiares y económicos', Kultura, 29 November 2013.

Lucía Martínez Odriozola, 'El guión se debe escribir para el personaje, no para el intérprete', *El Correo Español-El Pueblo Vasco*, 20 February 2006.

María José Mielgo, '"Todos mentimos sobre nosotros mismos, pero nuestros actos no mienten, dicen lo que somos en realidad". Entrevista con María Eugenia Salaverri', *Alborada, Revista Literaria*, January 2005.

Javier Pérez, 'Fallados los premios del certamen cultural "Imagínate Euskadi". María Eugenia Salaverri, primera en cuento', *El Correo Español-El Pueblo Vasco*, 19 November 1992.

Camila Pinzón Mendoza, 'Decálogo del escritor ideal en la era digital', *WMagazin*, 14 September 2017.

Ana Ramos, '"Lo que más me interesa es describir las emociones." María Eugenia Salaverri, escritora y guionista bilbaína, retrata con ironía y un toque de lirismo situaciones cotidianas en su libro de relatos *¿Por qué te ríes?*', *Deia*, 25 June 2004.

Txani Rodríguez, 'Obras escritas por mujeres copan las listas de los libros más vendidos', *Post Data*, 15 March 2016.

Beatriz Rucabado, 'Un thriller en euskera sobre muertes en serie', *El Mundo*, 10 April 2015.

Gorka Zabala, 'Días semilaborables', *Deia*, 14 October 1995.

Information online on María Eugenia Salaverri (a selection)
http://karambolaproducciones.com/es/karambola-producciones/
http://karambolaproducciones.com/es/documentales/bilbao-en-el-tiempo/
http://elpais.com/autor/maria_eugenia_salaverri/a
http://decine21.com/biografias/Maria-Eugenia-Salaverri-79424
http://www.escritoresdeeuskadi.com/es/asociados/36-asociados/autores/75-mo-
    eugenia-salaverri
https://www.youtube.com/watch?v=J0gQxLVQO7w
http://www.abcguionistas.com/noticias/guion/maria-eugenia-salaverri-en-las-
    noticias-breves-a-veces-hay-una-pelicula.html
http://www.bilbao.eus/bld/bitstream/handle/123456789/942/pergola16.
    pdf?sequence=1&rd=003123846035579633&rd=003123583151302417
http://www.elmundo.es/pais-vasco/2015/04/10/5527eba122601df8668b4570.html
http://txarribodafilm.com/en/
http://acescritores.com/primer-encuentro-estatal-asociaciones-escritores-se-aprueba-
    una-declaracion-treinta-demandas-del-sector/
http://elpais.com/diario/1999/05/11/paisvasco/926451626_850215.html

CIRUGÍA PLÁSTICA

En Francia anochece antes. Eso es así. A mí no me gusta hablar mal de este país porque a fin de cuentas si estoy aquí lo menos que puedo hacer es ser agradecida, pero las cosas como son: en Francia anochece antes y ésa es una de las tristezas de vivir aquí, que a eso de las nueve de la noche no hay un alma en la calle.

Nosotros tenemos un bar. Fran y yo. Abrimos hace ya tres años. Hacemos cocina vasca. Ponemos pinchos al mediodía y luego tenemos un menú con comidas normales, de las que hemos comido siempre, bacalao, pochas, arroz con leche. A los franceses les gustan mucho. También damos cenas, pero a la noche viene menos gente porque aquí todo el mundo se acuesta más temprano que allí. Así que a eso de las nueve, cuando comienza a flojear la clientela, yo suelo aprovechar para ponerme a limpiar. Limpio todo, la barra, los anaqueles, los vasos, pero sobre todo me aplico bien en las botellas, que se ven mucho. Soy muy limpia, pero la verdad es que no les saco brillo sólo por eso, sino sobre todo porque aquí piensan que los del otro lado del Pirineo somos todos unos guarros. Bueno, y también para dar ejemplo y que me vea Simone, que en cuanto nos quedamos sin clientes se va al extremo de la barra, donde se sienta Fran a leer el periódico, y comienza a darle palique sobre cualquier tontería. Generalmente Fran no le hace demasiado caso, es decir, no más que a cualquiera que entre y se ponga a charlar sobre fútbol o política o lo que sea, porque Fran es muy sociable y habla muy bien francés, pero a mí me molesta porque creo que no hace buen efecto entrar en un local y encontrarte al personal de cháchara, como si no tuviera nada mejor que hacer. Además hay otra cosa que me fastidia y es que si Fran no está, Simone no se dedica a buscar temas de conversación para hablar conmigo, pensara para qué, que yo hablo un francés pésimo, o sea que es de esa clase de chicas que resultan muy simpáticas y muy dicharacheras si hay hombres cerca y que si no, no abren la boca, y a mí esa gente me revienta.

–Mira, Simone– solía decirle antes– en un bar siempre hay trabajo para el que quiera trabajar, así que quien está mano sobre mano es porque le da la gana.

Y es cierto. Pero un día Fran me dijo que la dejara en paz, que ya cumple

PLASTIC SURGERY

It starts to get darker earlier in France. That's how it is. I don't like to run down this country because, when all's said and done, if I'm here the least I can do is be grateful, but that's the way things are: it gets dark earlier in France and that's one of the sad things about living here, the fact is that by around nine o'clock at night there's not a soul on the streets.

We've got a bar. Fran and I. We opened it three years ago. We serve Basque food. We do light bar snacks at midday and then we have a menu with the usual dishes – the sort of food we've always eaten – cod, pinto beans, rice pudding. The French like it a lot. We also provide evening meals, but not as many people turn out at night because round here everybody goes to bed earlier than they do there. So at around nine, when trade starts to slacken off, I usually seize the chance to get on with the cleaning. I clean everything, the bar, the shelves, the glasses, but what I pay particular attention to are the bottles, which are always on view. I'm very clean, although to tell you the truth that's not the only reason I leave them sparkling on, no, it's because round here they think that all of us who come from the other side of the Pyreness live like pigs. OK, it's also to set up an example and so Simone can see me – as soon as the last costumers leave she goes to the end of the bar, where Fran sits reading the paper, and she indulges in idle chitchat with him. Fran usually doesn't take much notice of her, I mean no more notice than he does of anybody else who comes in and starts nattering away to him about football or politics or whatever, because Fran is very sociable and he speaks very good French, but it bothers me because I don't think it creates the right impression for people to come into an establishment and find the staff chattering away as if they had nothing better to do. Besides, there's something else that annoys me, and that's the fact that if Fran isn't around, Simone doesn't spend her time searching for topics to make conversation with me, she obviously thinks what's the point, my French is very poor, in other words she's one of those girls who are very nice and chatty when there are men around, but if there aren't they don't open their mouth, and people like that really get on my nerves.

'Look, Simone', I used to say to her in the early days, 'in a bar there's always work for those who want to do it, so when somebody sits twiddling their thumbs it's because that's what they feel like doing.'

And it's true. But one day Fran told me to leave her alone, because when

cuando tiene que cumplir, que muchos clientes vienen a verla expresamente a ella, y que si seguía así terminaría por marcharse, así que ahora no le digo nada, simplemente quito el polvo de las botellas para que me vea y coja la indirecta y aunque es cierto que a veces alguien me ha dicho que cuando limpio parezco malhumorada y que aprieto los labios, yo suelo contestar que soy simplemente limpia y que si hago el trabajo a conciencia no voy a estar pendiente de qué cara pongo.

Así que esa noche, la noche de la que quiero hablar, cuando conocí a los Lucas, yo estoy limpiando botellas y Simone y Fran hablan en la esquina de la cafetería. Es Simone quien habla. Fran escucha y desde donde yo me encuentro puedo verle de perfil. Veo como se tira del labio inferior con los dedos una y otra vez, como si estuviera pensando en algo que requiriera mucha concentración, pero no logro ver la expresión de sus ojos. Posiblemente los tenga entornados, pienso, porque es así como suele mirar cuando hace ese gesto. Y entonces me acuerdo de que el día de nuestra boda también lo hizo. Fue precisamente en el momento en que le preguntaron eso de si promete honrarte y respetarte hasta que la muerte os separe. Bueno, pues sencillamente no contestó. Se quedó mirando al vacío, pellizcándose el labio de abajo como si la cosa no fuera con él, como si estuviera esperando a un autobús en la parada o algo así. Yo estaba atónita. El cura repitió tres veces la pregunta y entonces le di un codazo y le dije 'Fran', porque creí que no había oído. Pero no es que no oyera, lo que ocurría era que realmente se lo estaba pensando. Fue algo increíble. Allí estábamos los dos, de pie, delante de un montón de gente y él se lo estaba pensando. Ni siquiera se le ocurrió ponerse en mi lugar e imaginarse cómo podía sentirme allí plantada, esperando a ver qué decidía. Y en aquel momento me dije que no tendría nada de extraño si simplemente se diera la vuelta y se marchara. Con la cara que tenía hubiera resultado incluso normal. Pero de pronto giró la cabeza hacia mí, me miró a los ojos, parpadeó un par de veces y dijo: 'Sí'. De eso hace ya siete años, aún no habíamos venido a Francia, pero se me quedó grabado y siempre que le veo esa cara me pregunto qué estará pasando por su cabeza, porque creo que si algún día decidiera largarse sin más, sería después de haber puesto una expresión como ésa.

Pero esa noche, la noche en que después vinieron los Lucas, él parece de muy buen humor, y aunque escucha estirándose el labio, de pronto estalla en carcajadas.

–¿De qué habláis?–pregunto.

she's needed she does what she has to do, that a lot of customers come in expressly to see her, and that if I carried on like that she'd end up by walking out, so now I don't say a word to her, I simply wipe the dust off the bottles so she can see me and get the hint, and even though it's true that people sometimes tell me that when I'm cleaning I do look bad tempered and I purse my lips, I usually reply that I'm just a clean person and if I'm doing my job properly I don't have time to bother about the look on my face.

So that night, the night I want to tell you about, when I met the Lucases, I'm cleaning off the bottles and Simone and Fran are talking in the corner by the coffee machine. It's Simone who's doing the talking. Fran is listening and from where I'm standing I can see his face in profile. I watch how he pulls at his bottom lip with his fingers again and again, as if he was thinking about something that requires a lot of concentration, but I can't see the look in his eyes. Perhaps he's got them half closed, I think, because that's how he usually looks when he's doing that business with his lip. And then I remember that he did it on our wedding day too. It was at the precise moment he was asked if he promised to love and honour till death us did part. Well, he simply didn't reply. He just stood there staring into space, pinching his bottom lip as if it was nothing to do with him, as if he was queuing at a bus stop or something. I was amazed. The priest repeated the question three times and then I nudged him and said 'Fran' because I thought he hadn't heard. But it isn't that he hadn't heard him, the fact of the matter was he was thinking about it. It was unbelievable. There we were, the two of us, standing there in front of a crowd of people and he was thinking about it. It didn't even cross his mind to put himself in my place and imagine how I might feel, stuck there, waiting to see what he'd decide. And just at that moment I told myself I wouldn't be in the least bit surprised if he were simply to turn on his heel and walk away. Given that look on his face, it might even have been the normal thing for him to do. But he suddenly turned his head towards me, looked me in the eyes, blinked a couple of times and said 'yes'. That was seven years ago now, we hadn't yet come to France, but that moment was imprinted on my mind and whenever I see that look I wonder what's going through his head, because I think if he were to decide to just clear off some day without further ado, it would be after wearing an expression like that.

But that night, the night on which the Lucases later turned up, he seemed to be in a very good mood, and although he's listening and pulling at his lip, he suddenly bursts out laughing.

'What are you talking about?' I ask.

No me oyen, así que me quedo mirándoles e incluso sonrío mientras les miro. Luego pienso que sería lógico que fuera Simone quien limpiara y yo la que estuviera acompañando a Fran, pero hace ya demasiado tiempo que las cosas están así y aunque meses atrás he decidido que esa situación no me gusta nada, tampoco sé qué hacer para cambiarla.

Entonces llegan ellos, los Lucas. Primero entra él. Avanza balanceándose sobre unas piernas cortas y combadas, lanza una mirada general y de pronto, abriendo los brazos, dice en voz muy alta que no está mal el tugurio. Lo dice en español. 'Nada mal', repite.

Tiene unos treinta años y es de esa clase de tipos que son todo pecho, de esos que sentados parecen normales o incluso grandes y cuando se levantan tiene la misma estatura de un niño de doce años. Y ahí está, mirando el local con la misma satisfacción con la que lo miraría si fuera el propietario y sonriéndonos a todos con sus dientes mellados.

Fran se vuelve sorprendido, les mira, dice 'vaya, vaya', abandona con lentitud el taburete y se dirige hacia ellos.

—Mira quien está aquí— dice cuando llega junto al hombre, mientras le da en el brazo un puñetazo suave y luego un abrazo.

La chica se ha quedado un par de pasos atrás y permanece con la vista fija en la puntera de su zapato, haciendo círculos en el suelo hasta que el hombre la toma por el codo y la acerca a Fran.

—Ésta es Rosa—dice—. Fran, Rosa, Rosa, Fran.

Ella extiende la mano y Fran, que ha anvanzado un poco, como para besarla en la mejilla, cambia de idea y le estrecha la mano.

—Bueno, y ahora me presentarás a tu parienta, ¿no?— pegunta el hombre mirando fijamente a a Simone.

Entonces me seco las manos, salgo de la barra y me acerco. Nos damos la mano y nos quedamos mirándonos. Tienen un aspecto chocante. Los dos llevan vaqueros y camisetas de algodón, pero aun así tienen un aire endomingado, como si se hubieran arreglado para la ocasión. Tal vez no sea así, quizá él salga siempre a la calle con el pelo embadurnado en fijador y ella con esa diadema de perlas, pero la pinta que tienen es muy rara. Ella lleva unos zapatos blancos, con lazos de raso. Algunos de los lazos están deshilachados y me pregunto si se habrá comprado esos zapatos para su propia boda.

Fran hace las presentaciones. Dice que se llaman Lucas y Rosa. Yo digo 'Irma', y ellos me miran y luego se miran entre sí, como si nunca hubieran

They don't hear me, so I keep watching them and I even smile while I watch them. Then I think it would make more sense if it were Simone who was doing the cleaning and me who was sitting next to Fran, but things have been like this for a long while now, even though I made up my mind months ago that I didn't like the situation one little bit, nor do I know what I can do to change it.

Then they turned up, the Lucases. He comes in first. He comes in, swaying on short bandy legs, gives the place a general once over and then suddenly, throwing his arms open wide, he announces in a very loud voice that it's not a bad joint. He says this in Spanish. 'Not bad, not bad at all', he repeats.

He's about thirty years old and he's one of those people who are all chest, the sort of person that looks normal, even big, when they're sitting down, but when they stand up they've got the stature of a kid of twelve. And there he stands, looking round the place with the same air of satisfaction he would have if he were the owner, smiling at all of us with his chipped teeth.

Fran turns round, surprised, looks at them, says 'well, well', gets slowly up from his bar-stool and walks over to them.

'Look who's here', he says when he gets up to the man, giving him a light punch on the arm and then hugging him.

The girl has stopped a couple of paces behind and stays there, her eyes fixed on the tip of her shoe, tracing circles on the floor until the man takes her by the elbow and moves her closer to Fran.

'This is Rosa', he says. 'Fran, Rosa, Rosa, Fran.'

She stretches out her hand and Fran, who has moved forward a little as if to give her a kiss on the cheek, changes his mind and stretches out his hand.

'Right, and now you'll introduce me to the wife, won't you', asks the man staring at Simone.

Then I dry my hands, come out from behind the bar and go over to them. We shake hands and stand there looking at each other. There's something odd about them. They're both wearing jeans and cotton T-shirts, but they still have a Sunday-best look about them, as if they've got dressed up especially for the occasion. Perhaps it isn't like that at all, perhaps he always goes out plastered with hair oil and she with that pearl-studded Alice-band, but there is a very strange look about them. She's wearing white shoes with satin bows. Some of the bows are beginning to fray at the edges and I wonder if she has bought those shoes for her own weeding.

Fran makes the introductions. He says they're called Lucas and Rosa. I say 'Irma', and they look at me and then they look at each other, as if they'd

oído que nadie se llame de ese modo. Sonríen. Tods sonreímos. Fran explica que Lucas y él han hecho la mili juntos.

–Vi muchas fotos tuyas– comenta Lucas–. Tenías una foto de ella con un gato. Me acuerdo de aquel gato. Recuerdo que era un gato muy bonito, blanco. Aquella foto parecía un calendario.

No recuerdo haberme hecho nunca una foto con un gato, pero no digo nada. En realidad odio a los gatos. No me gustan los animales, pero supongo que podría haber salido en alguna foto con algún perro. Mi hermana tiene uno. Pero nadie que yo conozca tiene un gato y, aunque lo tuvieran, jamás me acercaría a él.

Fran endereza los hombros y suspira.

–Hace años de eso– dice.

Luego pregunta qué hacen ellos en Poitiers y como resulta que viven en Limoges, dice que tenemos que celebrarlo, que hay que sacar champán y festejar el encuentro. Nos sentamos en la mesa del fondo y Fran le pide a Simone que traiga una botella de brut. Hablamos del bar, de cómo se había enterado Lucas de la dirección por otro compañero de la mili y de las ganas que tenía de vernos.

Mientras, Simone ha traído la botella de champán y las copas. Nos sirve a Fran, a Lucas y a mí. Rosa tapa su copa con la mano y niega con la cabeza.

–Yo prefiero agua– dice, y su cara se vuelve roja como la grana.

–Está embarazada– comenta Lucas pasándole una mano por el pelo–. O al menos eso creemos, ¿verdad, Rosa? Aún no lo hemos confirmado porque sólo ha tenido una falta, pero estamos seguros porque nos hemos empleado a fondo, ¿eh, Rosa?

Rosa asiente varias veces. Al parecer tiene esa costumbre. Espera que Lucas hable y entonces ella cabecea tres o cuatro veces, como esos perros que adornan las ventanillas traseras de los coches.

Lucas explica que trabaja en un taller de reparaciones. Antes pasó unos años en Barcelona, pero se quedó sin empleo y alguien le buscó trabajo en Limoges y se vino.

–He hecho de todo, tío, de todo– dice, y sus ojos se vuelven graves y tristes, como si fuera a confesar algo inconfesable. Pero de pronto cambia

never heard of anybody with such a name. They smile. We all smile. Fran explains that he and Lucas did their military service[1] together.

'I saw a lot of photos of you', remarks Lucas. 'You used to have a photo of her with a cat. I remember that cat. I remember it was a very pretty white cat. That photo looked something off a calendar.'

I don't remember ever having my photo taken with a cat, but I don't say anything. To tell the truth, I hate cats. I don't like animals, although I suppose there could be a photo of me somewhere with some dog. My sister's got one. But nobody I know has a cat and even if they did, I'd never go anywhere near it.

Fran leans back and sighs.

'That was years ago', he says.

Then he asks what they're doing in Poitiers and how come they live in Limoges, he says we should have a celebration, that we must bring out the champagne and toast the reunion. We sit down at the table at the back and Fran asks Simone to bring a bottle of the best champagne. We talk about the bar, about how Lucas had tracked down the address through another friend who'd done military service with them and about how much he'd wanted to come and see us.

Simone, meanwhile, has brought the bottle of champagne and the glasses. She pours some for Fran, for Lucas and for me. Rosa puts her hand over the top of her glass and shakes her head.

'I would rather have water', she says, and her face turns as red as a beetroot.

'She's pregnant', remarks Lucas, stroking her hair with his hand. 'Or at least, we think she is. Isn't that right, Rosa? It's still not been confirmed because she's only missed once, but we're sure because we've been trying really hard, eh, Rosa?'

Rosa nods several times. It seems that this is a habit of hers. She waits for Lucas to speak and then she nods three or four times, like one of those dogs you see in the rear window of cars.

Lucas explains that he works in a garage. Before that he'd spent a few years in Barcelona, but he lost his job and somebody found work for him in Limoges and so he came.

'I've done everything, man, everything', he says, and his eyes turn serious and sad as if he was going to confess something that could not be confessed.

---

1 **Military service**: compulsory enlistment of young men for a period of approximately one year. It was legally suspended in Spain after 2001.

de expresión y pasando el índice por la mano de su mujer dice que ahora todo está bien. Después él y Fran comienzan a hablar de amigos comunes y a recordar anécdotas de cuando estaban en la mili.

–¿Tenéis hijos?– me pregunta Rosa de pronto.

Contesto que no. Luego miro a la barra. Han entrado clientes y Simone atiende a un hombre gigantesco que bebe cerveza mexicana con limón. Más allá una pareja formada por una rubia y un viejo están haciendo tonterías con la corbata del viejo. De vez en cuando se besuquean.

–No, todavía no– digo, pero Rosa no parece escucharme.

Hemos terminado de cenar y todos, excepto Rosa, estamos un poco achispados. Hemos comido como bestias. Tortillas, anchoas, tigres, champiñones, callos, queso, y todo regado con champán, lo que para mi gusto es un poco asqueroso y para el gusto de Fran, en estado normal, también. Pero hoy Fran no está muy normal que digamos. Ha bebido más de la cuenta y parece estar deseando hablar de cosas deprimentes. Ha contado con pelos y señales la muerte de su hermano. Su hermano se suicidó ahora hace un año tirándose al asfalto desde un puente. Fue algo terrible y Fran jamás lo menciona, ni siquiera conmigo, pero esta noche ha empezado a hablar de eso y luego se ha echado a llorar. Dice que muchas veces sueña que habla con su hermano y que al despertar le siente tan cerca como si pudiera tocarle.

–¿Es eso cierto?– pregunto–. ¿Por qué nunca me lo has contado?

Alza los hombros y se limita a jugar con una miga de pan. Entonces, no sé cómo, Lucas y él empiezan a hablar de coches. Lucas cuenta un chiste muy malo sobre Nicky Lauda y los dos se ríen. Se ríen alto y desde el otro lado de la mesa llega una vaharada de olor dulzón y picante de la loción fijadora de Lucas. Recuerdo que olí algo parecido hace mucho tiempo, pero aunque me esfuerzo no consigo recordar dónde fue.

–Pues yo no puedo dormir sola– dice Rosa de pronto.

Me está observando fijamente con sus grandes ojos negros mientras se retuerce un mechón de pelo con el índice. La miro extrañada porque nadie ha dicho nada sobre eso. Que yo sepa, estaban hablando sobre garajes. Estoy a punto de decírselo, pero en el último momento decido callar.

But his expression suddenly changes and drawing his index finger across his wife's hand he says that everything's fine now. Afterwards, he and Fran start talking about mutual friends and reminiscing about things that happened when they were doing their military service.

'Have you got any children?' Rosa suddenly asks me.

I answer no. Then I look at the bar. Some customers have come in and Simone is serving a huge man who's drinking Mexican beer with lemon. Further along a couple, a blonde and an older man, are doing silly things with the old chap's tie. Every now and again they start necking.

'No, not yet' I say, but Rosa doesn't appear to be listening to me.

We've finished dinner and everybody, except Rosa, is a bit tiddly. We've eaten enough to feed an army. Omelettes, anchovies, mussels cooked in spicy tomato sauce, mushrooms, tripe, cheese, and the whole lot washed down with champagne, which I find slightly revolting, as does Fran when he's in a normal mood. But today Fran is not, let us say, quite normal. He's had too much to drink and seems to want to talk about depressing things. He's given a blow-by-blow account of his brother's death. His brother committed suicide a year ago now by throwing himself off a bridge onto the road. It was terrible and Fran never mentions it, not even to me, but that night he started to talk about it and then he burst out crying. He says that he often dreams he's talking with his brother and that when he wakes up he feels he's so close he could touch him.

'Is that true?' I ask. 'Why have you never told me?'

He shrugs his shoulders and restricts himself to playing with a crumb of bread. Then, I don't know how they got into it, he and Lucas start talking about cars. Lucas tells a very bad joke about Nicky Lauda[2] and the two of them laugh. They laugh very loudly and from the other side of the table there comes a woft of Lucas's sickly sweet and racy hair lotion. I recall that I smelt something similar a long time ago, but try as I might I can't remember where it was.

'Well I can't sleep alone', says Rosa suddenly.

She's staring at me with her big dark eyes while she twirls a lock of hair round her index finger. I look at her in surprise because nobody's said a word about that. As far as I knew they were talking about garages. I'm on the point of telling her that, but at the last minute I decide to hold my tongue.

---

2   **Nicky Lauda**: racing driver born in Vienna in 1949. He was three times world champion (1975, 1977, 1984). He survived a horrific crash in 1976 but did not retire until 1985, after 25 career wins.

–Hasta que Lucas no llega, no me duermo– añade.

Parece esperar una respuesta.

–Caramba– digo. No se me ocurre nada mejor qué decir.

Ella asiente tres veces.

–Pueden ser las cuatro, o las cinco, la hora que sea. Me da igual, no me duermo. Y si empiezo a dormirme, me despierto. Pienso cosas. Pienso que tal vez haya tenido un accidente, o que alguien le ha atracado o que ha perdido la memoria y se encuentra en medio de una calle sin saber hacia dónde echar a andar. Y me lo paso fatal. De verdad.

Lo ha dicho de corrido, pero ahora se detiene y nos mira con ansiedad.

–Pobrecita chiquitina– dice Lucas mirándole tiernamente y acercando su cara a la de ella, que se aparta hacia un lado.

–Así que no me extraña que sueñes con tu hermano, Fran. No me extraña nada. Te entiendo muy bien– añade con voz rotunda.

Fran echa atrás el cuerpo y su silla se balancea únicamente sobre las patas traseras.

–Ah…– dice. No dice nada más. Cruza las manos tras la nuca mirando al aire y se queda pensativo y silencioso unos instantes.

Yo podría contar que una noche Fran no vino a casa. Fue hace un par de meses y cada vez que lo recuerdo me siento enferma. Podría contarlo ahora. Podría contarlo perfectamente y todos dejaríamos de mirar a Fran como si se tratara de alguien sensible que sufre pesadillas. Podría decirles que yo tampoco dormí. Que creí que no volvería nunca. Que paseé por toda la casa encendiendo y apagando luces. Pensaba 'vuelve, cariño, vuelve'. Y luego pensaba 'ojalá no me cruce nunca más contigo, cabrón de mierda, ojalá no vuelva a ponerte la vista encima porque te mato'. Y otra vez le rogaba que volviera. ¡Se lo rogaba! Hablaba con él como si estuviera allí delante. Quiero decir que hablaba en alto. Llegué a convencerme de que me había vuelto loca. Pero no. Simplemente sabía dónde estaba y con quién. Tiene gracia. Siempre se piensa que esas cosas no le van a pasar a una. Pero pasan.

Ahora los cuatro estamos en silencio. Simone retira los platos y se los lleva a la cocina desde donde nos llega un estruendo de cubertería y vajilla estrellándose en el suelo. Sin embargo, ni Fran ni yo nos movemos para ir a ver qué ha ocurrido. Estamos borrachos y nos da lo mismo. Al menos a mí me da igual. Estoy agotada y con gusto me iría a dormir ahora mismo. Me pesan los párpados y me siento envejecer por segundos. Es una sensación

'I don't get to sleep until Lucas comes to bed', she adds.

She seems to be waiting for a reply.

'Well I never', I venture. I can't think of anything better to say.

She nods three times.

'It could be four or five o'clock, any time at all. It's all the same to me, I can't get to sleep. And if I start to nod off, I wake up. I think about things. I think that may be he's had an accident, or that somebody has mugged him or that he's lost his memory and he's in the middle of a street and doesn't know which way to go. And I feel ghastly about it. I really do.'

She had gabbled all this out, but now she stops and looks at us anxiously.

'Poor little darling', says Lucas, looking at her tenderly and moving his face towards hers, which she turns away to one side.

'So it doesn't surprise me you have dreams about your brother, Fran. It doesn't surprise me at all. I understand you very well', she adds in a decisive voice.

Fran leans backwards and his chair is rocking on its rear legs only.

'Ah...', he says. He doesn't say anything else. He folds his hands behind his neck, looks into the air and remains silent, lost in his thoughts for a few seconds.

I could tell the story about how Fran didn't come home one night. It was a couple of months ago and every time I remember it I feel sick. I could tell the story now. I could very well do it and we would no longer be looking at Fran as if he were a sensitive person suffering from nightmares. I could tell them how I didn't sleep either. That I thought he'd never come back. That I went through the whole house switching lights on and off. I was thinking 'come back, darling, come back.' And then I thought 'I hope I never have to have anything more to do with you again, you bloody bastard, I hope I never set eyes on you again because I'll kill you.' And then I begged him to come home. I begged him! I spoke to him as if he was there in front of me. I mean I was talking out loud. I ended up convincing myself that I'd gone crazy. But no. I simply knew where he was and who he was with. It's funny. You always think that these things will never happen to you. But they do.

By now all four of us had fallen silent. Simone clears away the plates and takes them into the kitchen, from where there comes the sound of china and cutlery crashing to the floor. Neither Fran or I, however, make any move to go and see what's happened. We're quite drunk and we don't really care. At least I don't care. I'm absolutely exhausted and I'd happily go to bed this very minute. My eyelids are heavy and I can feel myself ageing by the

clarísima. Noto como me arrugo, como la piel se me vuelve fláccida y mate, como se descuelgan y derrumban los músculos, como si fueran los de una anciana decrépita. Apoyo la cabeza en la pared y cierro los ojos. Cuando los abro tengo la impresión de que ha pasado muchísimo tiempo. Creo que incluso he dormido. Pero ninguno parece haberlo advertido y supongo que si me hubiera dormido de verdad alguien diría algo. Necesito café. Pregunto a los demás y me levanto a poner tres cafés solos y un descafeinado para Rosa. Podría pedírselos a Simone, que sigue coqueteando con el gigante y agitando su melena rubia a diestro y siniestro, pero prefiero hacerlos yo para ver si así me espabilo.

Cuando vuelvo a la mesa, encuentro a Fran y a los Lucas muy animados. Les preguntó de qué hablaban y Fran dice que no estaban hablando, sino soñando.

—Soñamos con lo que pediríamos si se nos fuera a conceder el mayor deseo. Lucas se compraría una casa y un coche de carreras. Rosa quiere una habitación azul para el niño. Yo pediría un velero. ¿Y tú? ¿Qué pedirías tú, Irma?

Me quedo pensando. Es la primera vez que alguien me pregunta algo así y no sé qué responder ni por dónde empezar.

—Bueno— digo al fin—, una vez escuché una cosa muy curiosa que contó una mujer en la peluquería. Estaba bajo el secador, le hacían la manicura y ella hablaba alto mientras se miraba las manos. Dijo que había tenido un accidente. Su coche se incrustó en otro. Debió de ser un golpe tremendo, porque la mujer se estrelló contra el cristal delantero y salió disparada hacia la carretera. La ingresaron en la uvi y cuando salió de allí estaba totalmente desfigurada. Así que la operaron. Le hicieron cirugía facial en la nariz, en los ojos, en la boca. Y cuando le retiraron las vendas la mujer se miró en un espejo y se encontró con otra persona. Era algo así como diez años más joven que ella y también era más atractiva. Ella decía que lo que le habían hecho le hacía parecer diez veces más guapa. Así que todos sus amigos y su marido y sus hijos la felicitaban. Le decían que había tenido verdadera suerte con aquel accidente y que hay actrices que pagan millones para que les hagan algo parecido. Pero ella no se sentía a gusto con su nueva cara. Dijo que cada mañana, al despertarse, se preguntaba cuál de sus dos

second. It's a very clear sensation. I see how I'm getting wrinkled, how my skin is getting flabby and dull looking, how my muscles are dropping and collapsing as if they were the muscles of a decrepit old woman. I lean my head against the wall and close my eyes. When I open them again I have the impression that a great deal of time has passed. I think I might even have fallen asleep. But nobody seems to have noticed and I suppose that if I really had been asleep, somebody would say something. I need some coffee. I ask the others and get up to fetch three black coffees and one de-caff for Rosa. I could have asked Simone to get them – she's still flirting with the giant and tossing her blonde mane this way and that – but I prefer to get them myself to see if it will wake me up.

When I get back to the table I find Fran and the Lucases very excited about something. I ask them what they're talking about and Fran says that they weren't talking, they were dreaming.

'We're dreaming about what we'd ask for if we were granted the thing we wanted most in the world. Lucas would buy a house and a racing car. Rosa wants a blue bedroom for her baby. I'd ask for a saliling boat.'

'And what about you? What would you ask for, Irma?'

I get to thinking about it. This is the first time anybody has asked me anything like this and I don't know what to say or where to begin.

'Well', I say at last, 'I once heard something very strange, something a woman in the hairdresser's was talking about. She was under the dryer, they were doing her nails and she was talking loudly while was looking at her hands. She said she'd had an accident. Her car had smashed right into another one. It must have been a tremendous crash, because the woman was thrown against the front windscreen and hurled out onto the road. They admitted her to the intensive care unit and when she came out of there she was totally disfigured. So they operated on her. They gave her facial surgery on her nose, on her eyes, on her mouth. And when they took the bandages off the woman looked at herself in the mirror and found herself face to face with somebody else. It was somebody who looked about ten years younger than her and who was also more attractive. She was saying that what they had done to her made her look a thousand times prettier. So all her friends and her husband and her kids congratulated her. They told her that she'd had a really lucky accident and that there are actresses who pay millions to have something similar done to them. But she didn't feel happy with her new face. She said that every morning, when she woke up, she'd wonder which of her two faces would be looking back at her from

caras la miraría desde el espejo. Dijo que era una cosa muy extraña y muy desagradable tener dos caras diferentes.

Fran me mira con perplejidad. Parece molesto.

–¿Qué me quieres decir?– pregunta–. ¿Qué tiene que ver esa mujer contigo? La verdad es que no entiendo nada. Estamos hablando de lo que nos gustaría hacer y tú sales con una historia que no tiene ni pies ni cabeza. Esa mujer estaba loca. Tendría que estar agradecida. Tendría que dar gracias a Dios de que en este país exista una seguridad social que te haga todas esas cosas. En otros países la hubieran echado a la calle con sus cicatrices y todo. En África. O en Asia. Diles a los africanos que no te gusta tu cara. Diles que estabas llena de ojales y que te han puesto una piel nueva y que no te gusta. Díselo y verás. ¿O es que tú quieres que te hagan cirugía plástica? No entiendo nada. No sé si dices que quieres una nariz nueva o si estás diciendo que aquí hay alguien que tiene dos caras. ¿Es eso lo que pretendes decir? ¿Crees que yo tengo dos caras? Porque si es así, me gustaría saberlo.

–No es eso– contesto.

En realidad no tengo ganas de explicar nada. Lo que yo quiero, lo único que de verdad deseo es volver a mi casa. A veces cierro los ojos y me lo imagino. Imagino que he vuelto, que voy caminando y conozco los nombres de las calles, que cuando me hablan no tengo que esforzarme por entender qué dicen, que hay gente que me conoce y me saluda y con la que me paro a charlar un rato. Que no me encuentro tan sola. Hay mañanas que me despierto y siento que he vuelto a mi pueblo. Son sólo unos segundos, hasta que de verdad espabilo por completo y comprendo que no, que soy como la mujer del espejo, que tal vez nunca más volveré a ver mi verdadera, mi auténtica cara, la mía. Pero ¿cómo se explica algo así?

–No es eso– repito.

Fran se levanta de la mesa.

–¡Mierda!–dice.

Le oigo trajinar detrás de la barra, a mi espalda. Oigo que saca hielos de la máquina y que los echa en la cubitera, pero no me vuelvo para verle. En cambio, me empeño en convencer a Lucas y a Rosa de que se queden a dormir en nuestra casa y mientras insisto, miro fijamente una única burbuja de champán que asciende continuamente por mi copa. Las demás se han muerto hace rato, pero ella sigue subiendo, recta y solitaria, desde el mismo punto.

the mirror. She said that it was a very odd sensation and very unpleasant to have two different faces.

Fran is looking at me, perplexed. He looks annoyed.

'What are you trying to say?' he asks. 'What's that woman got to do with you? Honestly, I don't understand a word of it. We're talking about what we'd like to do and you come out with some story that doesn't make any sense. That woman was mad. She should be grateful. She should give thanks to God that there's National Health Service in this country that takes care of these things. In other countries she'd have been thrown out onto the street, scars and all. In Africa. Or in Asia. Tell people in Africa that you don't like your face. Tell them you were full of holes and they've given you a new skin and you don't like it. Tell them and you'll see. Or is that you'd like them to do some plastic surgery on you. I don't understand it at all. I don't know if you're saying that you want a new nose or if you're saying that there's somebody here who has two faces. Is that what you're trying to say? You think that I have two faces? Because if that's what you think, I'd like to know about it.'

'It's not that', I reply.

The fact of the matter is I don't want to explain anything. What I do want, the only thing I truly wish, is to go home. Sometimes I close my eyes and I imagine it. I imagine that I've gone back, that I'm walking along and I know the names of the streets, that when people talk to me I don't have to make an effort to understand what they're saying, that there are people who know me and who say hello and who I stop and chat to for a while. That I don't feel so alone. There are mornings when I wake up and I feel I've gone back to my home village. It only lasts a few seconds until I wake up completely and I understand that no, I'm like the woman in the mirror, that perhaps I'll never see my true, my real face, my own face again. But how do you explain something like that?

'It's not that', I repeat.

Fran gets up from the table.

'Shit!' he says.

I hear him bustling about behind the bar, behind me. I hear him getting ice cubes out of the machine and throwing them into the ice bucket but I don't turn round to look at him. Instead, I try to persuade Lucas and Rosa to sleep at our house and as I keep trying I stare at a single champagne bubble which is continually rising up through my glass. The rest died out some time ago, but this one keeps on rising, following its straight and solitary course, from the same point.

Ahora los Lucas se han ido a buscar su coche. Finalmente han desistido de viajar de noche y van a quedarse en la habitación de invitados. Mientras les aguardamos, Fran barre y yo recojo las sillas, las copas y el cenicero. Después me desmaquillo ante el espejo del baño. Pienso en lo que ha ocurrido esta noche, pienso en lo que ha dicho Fran, en lo que he contestado yo, pero ya no sé si a estas alturas eso importa. Me cepillo bien las uñas. Me peino. Me miro y veo que estoy igual de horrorosa que antes de peinarme. Luego abro la puerta.

–¡Lo prometiste, Fran, lo prometiste!– escucho decir a Simone.

Me quedo clavada en la puerta. Oigo que Fran contesta algo, pero no entiendo qué.

–¡Pero tú lo prometiste, Fran!– repite Simone.

Fran hace "Sshhh" y lanza una perorata en un francés rápido y nervioso.

Entonces vuelvo a entrar en el baño, cierro con el pasador y apoyo la espalda en la puerta. Intento pensar. Intento concentrarme y pensar, pero veo mi cara en el espejo y continuamente me viene a la cabeza la mujer de la peluquería así que apago la luz y me quedo quieta en la oscuridad sintiendo como me tiemblan las piernas.

Cuando Fran llama a la puerta no contesto. Le oigo mover el pestillo y llamarme, pero no contesto. Él comienza a aporrear la puerta y pienso 'vete. Vete, Fran. Márchate. Por favor, vete', pero tampoco digo nada.

Y entonces él pregunta:

–Irma, ¿estás bien? ¿Te encuentras bien, cariño? Dime, ¿estás bien?

The Lucases have gone to look for their car now. They've finally given up the idea of driving through the night and are going to stay in our guest room. While we wait for them, Fran sweeps up and I put the chairs on the tables, and collect the glasses and the ashtray. Afterwards, I clean off my make-up in front of the bathroom mirror. I think about what has happened tonight, I think about what Fran has said, about what I said in reply, but now I don't know if things happened the way I think they did or in some other way. Nor do I know whether that matters right now. I give my nails a good scrub. I comb my hair. I looked at myself in the mirror and see that I'm as much of a mess as I was before I combed my hair. Then I open de door.

'You promised, Fran, you promised!' I hear Simone saying.

I stand frozen in the doorway. I hear Fran say something in reply, but I can't make it out.

'But you promised, Fran!' Simone says again.

Fran goes 'Shhh' and launches into some long-winded spiel in rapid, nervous French.

Then I go back into the bathroom, I close the door and turn the lock and lean back against the door. I'm trying to think. I'm trying to concentrate and to think, but I see my face in the mirror and the woman in the hairdresser's keeps popping into my head, so I switch off the light and I stay there motionless in the dark, aware of how my legs are trembling.

When Fran knocks at the door I don't answer. I hear him trying the latch and calling out my name, but I don't answer. He starts pounding on the door and I think, 'go away, go away, Fran, clear off, please, just go way', but still I don't say anything.

And then he asks:

'Irma, are you OK? Are you feeling OK, darling? Tell me, are you OK?'

MI MADRE EN LA VENTANA

MY MOTHER AT THE WINDOW

Original Spanish text from *Madres e hijas*,
edited by Laura Freixas (Barcelona: Anagrama, 1996, 225–36);
slightly revised, it was later included in
Podría hacerte daño, by Luisa Castro
(La Coruña: Ediciones del Viento, 2005, 109–18)
© Luisa Castro, 1996.

LUISA CASTRO was born in the town of Foz, Galicia, in 1966. She studied Hispanic Philology in Santiago de Compostela, and did her postgraduate studies in Romance and Hispanic Philology at the Universidad Complutense, in Madrid, and at the Universitat de Barcelona. In 1994, having been awarded a Fulbright Scholarship, she studied cinema (script writing, direction, editing and production) at New York University. Luisa Castro writes both in Spanish and in Galician. As well as being a poet, novelist and short story writer, she has regularly contributed over the years to a number of Spanish and Galician newspapers such as *El País, El Mundo, ABC, El Periódico de Catalunya, Blanco y Negro, La Voz de Galicia, El Progreso de Lugo, Diario de Pontevedra* and the *Axencia Galega de Noticias*. She has been awarded several prizes for her journalistic work as a columnist, such as the Vieira de Plata de Periodismo in 2008, and the Puro Cora de Periodismo in 2009. She has lived in New York, Madrid, Barcelona, and Santiago de Compostela. She is now based in Bordeaux, where she is the Director of the Instituto Cervantes, having previously held the same post in Naples. She has taught creative writing at the University of Santiago de Compostela, Galician language and literature at the Centro Galego, in Barcelona, and adaptation of literature to cinema at the Institut d'Humanitats, also in Barcelona. As an academic, she has been invited all over the world to lecture on Galician and Spanish literature, as well as to read her own poetry and prose. Her poems have been translated into French, Italian, Hebrew, German, Korean, Turkish, and English. She has also worked in audiovisual media and, among other activities, she was the co-scriptwriter for the Spanish TV programme *Esta es mi tierra*, which in 2006 dedicated a special episode to her celebrated

novel *Viajes con mi padre* (2003). The programme also included a homage to Galician writer Álvaro Cunqueiro, who she considers a significant influence in her writing. In 2010, she was the director of *Cultura 10*, a programme for Galician Television which included thirty-five interviews with distinguished cultural figures. From a young age, she was considered one of the most promising poetry and prose writers of her generation and awarded important prizes such as a grant to Literary Creation in 1990, and, in 1992, another grant to write a cinema script based on her first novel, *El somier,* both awarded by the Spanish Ministry of Culture.

Bibliography of Luisa Castro

Poetry

Odisea definitiva (Madrid: Arnao, 1984; 2004).

Los versos del eunuco (Madrid: Hiperión, 1986; 2004) – *Premio Hiperión de Poesía.*

Baleas e baleas (Ferrol: Esquío, 1988, 2004) [Translation into German (20005)].

Ballenas (Madrid: Hiperión 1990; 2004) [Bilingual edition Spanish-Galician].

Los hábitos del artillero (Madrid: Visor, 1990; 2004) *–Premio Juan Carlos I de Poesía.*

De mí haré una estatua ecuestre (Madrid: Hiperión, 1997; 2004).

Señales con una sola bandera. Poesía reunida (1984-1997) (Madrid: Hiperión, 2004).

Amor mi señor (Barcelona: Tusquets, 2005) – *Libro del Año 2006 'Notodo.com'.*

Anthologies which include her poems

Las diosas blancas. Antología de la joven poesía española escrita por mujeres, R. Buenaventura (ed.) (Madrid: Hiperión, 1985).

20 poemas de amor y un par de canciones desesperadas, J. Munáriz (ed.) (Madrid: Hiperión, 1987).

Litoral, Revista de Poesía y Pensamiento, Issues 178, 179 and 180 (1988).

Queimar as meigas: Galicia y 50 años de poesía de mujer, E. Vázquez de Gey (ed.) (Madrid: Torremozas, 1988).

La emoción de la palabra, J. Uceda (ed.) (Ferrol: Sociedad de Cultura Valle-Inclán; Esquío, 1988).

Poesía gallega de hoy, B. Losada (ed.) (Madrid: Visor, 1990).

Fin de un milenio. Antología de la poesía gallega última, C. A. Molina (ed.) (Madrid: Libertarias, 1991).

Conversaciones y poemas. La nueva poesía femenina española en castellano, S. Keefe Ugalde (ed.) (Madrid: Siglo XXI, 1991).

Encuentro con José Hierro (Madrid: Ministerio de Cultura, 1992).

Propuestas poéticas para un fin de siglo, C. Rodríguez (ed.) (Madrid: Fundación Cultural Banesto, 1993).

Ellas tienen la palabra. Dos décadas de poesía española, N. Benegas (ed.) (Madrid: Hiperión, 1997).

Norte y sur de la poesía iberoamericana (Argentina, Brasil, Chile, Colombia, España, México, Venezuela), C. Triviño (ed.) (Madrid: Verbum, 1997).

Ángel González en la generación del 50. Diálogo con los poetas de la experiencia (Oviedo: Tribuna Ciudadana, 1998). http://www.cervantesvirtual.com/nd/ark:/59851/bmcmp526

Barcelona Poesía. 14 Festival Internacional de Poesía de Barcelona (Barcelona: Ajuntament de Barcelona, 1998).

Alén do azul, unha ducia de poetas galegos en Catalunya, X. L. García (ed) (A Coruña: Edicións do Castro, 1999).

Ni Ariadnas ni Penélopes. Quince escritoras españolas para el siglo XXI, C. Estévez (ed.) (Madrid: Castalia, 2002).

Poesía última (Actas 2003), B. Rodríguez Cañada and J. R. Trujillo (eds) (Puerto de Santa María: Fundación Rafael Alberti, 2004).

Lecturas para el cambio de siglo, P. de Miguel (ed.) (Madrid: Ediciones Internacionales Universitarias, 2004).

Di yo. Di tiempo. Poetas españolas contemporáneas, J. de Andrés and R. García Rayego (eds) (Madrid: Devenir, 2005).

Con voz propia. Estudio y antología comentada de la poesía escrita por mujeres (1970-2005), M. Rosal (ed.) (Sevilla: Renacimiento, 2006).

Seis siglos de poesía española escrita por mujeres, D. Romero, R. Catrina Imboden and I. López Guil (eds) (Berna: Peter Lang, 2007).

Mujeres que sueñan, J. Aguado Cedma (ed.) (Málaga: Puerta del Mar, 2007).

Metalingüísticos y sentimentales. Antología de la poesía española 1966-2000, M. Sanz (ed.) (Madrid: Nueva Biblioteca, 2007).

Novels

El somier (Barcelona: Anagrama, 1990) [Translations into Dutch (1993) and into Hebrew (2001)].

La fiebre amarilla (Barcelona: Anagrama, 1994, 2003) – *Premi Raimat 'Vi Jove' de Cultura.*

El secreto de la lejía (Barcelona: Planeta, 2001; 2004) – *Premio Azorín.*

Viajes con mi padre (Barcelona: Planeta, 2003).

La segunda mujer (Barcelona: Seix Barral, 2006; 2007; Barcelona: Círculo de Lectores, 2008) [Translation into Italian (2009)] – *Premio Biblioteca Breve.*

Short story collection

Podría hacerte daño (A Coruña: Ediciones del Viento, 2005) – *Premio Torrente Ballester.*

Short stories included in Spanish and Galician anthologies and magazines (a selection)

'Muertos', *Blanco y Negro*, 23 April 1989, 20–21.

'Un amor sobre ruedas', in *Cuentos sobre ruedas* (Madrid: Popular, 1990).

'A última xogada', in *Contos eróticos /elas* (Vigo: Xerais, 1990).

'Mi madre en la ventana', in L. Freixas (ed.), *Madres e hijas* (Barcelona: Anagrama, 1996).

'El amor inútil', in S. Martín (ed.), *Páginas amarillas* (Madrid: Lengua de Trapo, 1997).

'No es un regalo', in M. Monmany (ed.), *Vidas de mujer* (Madrid: Alianza, 1998).

'Story of my dog', and 'A woman and a chair', in J. Rutheford (ed.), *From the Beginning of the Sea. Anthology of Contemporary Galician Short Stories* (Brighton: Foreign Demand, 2008).

'Correspondencia', in L. Freixas (ed.), *Cuentos de amigas* (Barcelona: Anagrama, 2009).

'Chasco por Navidad' and 'La pequeña muerte', in F. Valls (ed.), *Mar de pirañas: nuevas voces del microrrelato español* (Palencia: Menoscuarto, 2012).

Collections of press articles

Diario de los años apresurados (Madrid: Hiperión, 1998) [Collection of articles published in *ABC* between 1987–1997].

Melancolía de sofá (Vigo: Xerais, 2009) [Collection of articles in Galician published in *La Voz de Galicia* between 2000–2006].

Essays and reflections on literature

'Los cuerpos presentes del vivir y del hablar', in *Las palabras de la tribu, escritura y habla* (Madrid: Cátedra & Ministerio de Cultura, 1993), 127–33.

'Falsos poetas', in P. de Miguel (ed.), *Articulismo español contemporáneo. Una antología* (Madrid: Clásicos Mare Nostrum, 2004), 280–82.

'Por amor al arte', in A. Orejudo (ed.), *En cuarentena. Nuevos narradores y críticos a principios del siglo XXI* (Murcia: Universidad de Murcia, 2004), 111–12.

'Carmen Martin Gaite', in L. Freixas (ed.), *Retratos literarios. Escritores españoles del siglo XX evocados por sus contemporáneos* (Madrid: Espasa, 1997), 306–307.

Further reading on Luisa Castro

Ernesto Ayala-Dip, 'Luisa Castro: *El secreto de la lejía*', *El País* (Babelia), 19 May 2001.

M. Barrado Timón, 'Luisa Castro reconoce que escribe "lo que me da la gana, absolutamente"', *Hoy Digital*, 22 May 2006.

Ángel Basanta, '*El somier'*, *ABC*, 15 December 1990.

Túa Blesa, 'Amor mi señor', *ABC* (El Cultural), 10 November 2005.

Fernando Castanedo, 'La intrusa: Luisa Castro', *El País*, 25 February 2006.

Pedro J. de la Peña, 'Artillería ligera', *El Mundo*, 10 June 1990.

Francisco Díaz de Castro, '*Señales sobre una bandera. Poesía reunida'*, *ABC* (El Cultural), 6 May 2004. http://www.elcultural.com/revista/letras/Senales-con-una-sola-bandera-Poesia-reunida/9453

Ángeles Encinar, 'En busca del secreto de la narrativa de Luisa Castro', in Á. Encinar and K. M. Glenn (eds), *La pluralidad narrativa. Escritores españoles (1984–2004)* (Madrid: Biblioteca Nueva, 2005), 149–61.

Belén Fortes, 'Luisa Castro: "'La falsedad, la conformidad y la complacencia son los mayores enemigos de la literatura"', *Barcelona Review*, July–August 2002. www.barcelonareview.com/31/s_lc_ent.htm

Juan-Manuel García-Precedo, *Intrahistory, Regeneration and National Identity, Past and Present: The Reflection of Nietzschean Unamuno on Arturo Pérez-Reverte and Luisa Castro* (PhD, University of Exeter, 2012).

Rosario G. Gómez, 'Luisa Castro cierra 25 años de historia en *Esta es mi tierra*', *El País,* 14 May 2006. http://elpais.com/diario/2006/05/14/radiotv/1147557603_850215.html

Kirsty Hooper, 'Alternative Genealogies? History and the Dilemma of "Origin" in Two Recent Novels by Galician Women', *Arizona Journal of Hispanic Cultural Studies* 10.1 (2006), 45–58.

Kirsty Hooper, 'Forum' in 'New Spaces, New Voices: Notes on Contemporary Galician Studies', *Journal of Spanish Cultural Studies* 7.2 (2006), 103–22.

Eduardo Larequi, 'Drama conyugal o alegoría política', *La Bitácora del Tigre*, 6 April 2006.

Alessandro Mistrorigo, 'Luisa Castro: Un eunuco me escribe versos', in D. Romero López, I. López Guil, R. C. Imboden and C. Albizu Yeregui (eds), *Seis siglos de poesía española escrita por mujeres. Pautas poéticas y revisiones críticas*, (Berna: Peter Lang, 2007), 527–38.

Ana María Moix, 'Golpes de luz', *El País* (Babelia), 5 April 2003. http://elpais.com/diario/2003/04/05/babelia/1049500218_850215.html

W. Michael Mudrovic, 'The Female Eunuch: Luisa Castro's *Los versos del eunuco*', in *Mirror, Mirror on the Page: Identity and Subjectivity in Spanish Women's Poetry* (Bethlehem: Leigh University Press, 2008), 140–96.

Antonio Ortega, 'Protagonista de sí misma', *El País* (Babelia), 25 April 2004. http://elpais.com/diario/2004/09/25/babelia/1096069833_850215.html

Antonio Ortega, 'La rebelión del corazón', *El País* (Babelia), 17 December 2005. http://elpais.com/diario/2005/12/17/babelia/1134780624_850215.html

Béatrice Rodríguez, 'Luisa Castro o la escritura doble', in A. Redondo Goicoechea (ed.), *Mujeres novelistas: jóvenes narradoras de los noventa* (Madrid: Narcea, 2003), 97–107.

Béatrice Rodríguez, 'Madrid ante la "década prodigiosa" o la ciudad y sus mitologías en *El secreto de la lejía* de Luisa Castro', in Javier Gómez-Montero (ed.), *Memoria literaria de la Transición española* (Madrid: Iberoamericana; Frankfurt am Main: Vervuert Verlag, 2007), 94–109.

Félix Romeo, 'Las nubes y las tormentas: *Viajes con mi padre*, Luisa Castro', *Revista de Libros*, 1 May 2003.

Jesús Ruiz Mantilla, 'Luisa Castro, poeta: "En poesía, la mujer es objeto; yo la he convertido en sujeto"', *El País* (La Cultura), 28 December 2005.

Jesús Ruiz Mantilla, 'Luisa Castro profundiza en el amor y el maltrato psicológico en *La segunda mujer*', *El País*, 21 February 2006. http://elpais.com/diario/2006/02/21/cultura/1140476404_850215.html

Gonzalo Santoja, 'La memoria sí está para cuentos', *El Mundo* (La Esfera), 19 January 1994.

Santos Sanz Villanueva, 'Luisa Castro: *Viajes con mi padre*', *El Cultural*, 13 February 2003.

Santos Sanz Villanueva, 'Luisa Castro: *Podría hacerte daño*', *ABC* (El Cultural), 14 July 2005.

Ricardo Senabre, *La segunda mujer*: Luisa Castro', *El Cultural*, 2 March 2006. www.elcultural.com.revista/letras/La_segunda_mujer/16670

Sharon Keefe Ugalde, *Conversaciones y poemas: La nueva poesía femenina española en castellano* (Madrid: Siglo Veintiuno, 1991).

Sharon Keefe Ugalde, 'The Feminization of Female Figures in Spanish Women's Poetry of the 1980s', *Studies in 20th Century Literature. Contemporary Spanish Poetry* 16 (1992), 165–84.

Juan Varela Portas de Orduna, 'Luisa Castro: Una virgen se debate pulsando con martillos el cuerpo inquebrantable', in P. Frohlicher *et al., Cien años de poesía: 72 poemas españoles del siglo XX: Estructuras poéticas y pautas críticas* (Bern, Switzerland: Peter Lang, 2001), 811–25.

John C. Wilcox, 'Visión y revisión en algunas poetas contemporáneas: Ámparo Amorós, Blanca Andreu, Luisa Castro y Almudena Guzmán', in B. Ciplijauskaite (ed.), *Novísimos, postnovísimos, clásicos: la poesía de los ochenta en España* (Madrid: Orígenes, 1990), 95–115.

Further online information on Luisa Castro (a selection)

http://amediavoz.com/castroLuisa.htm
http://escritoras.com/escritoras/Luisa-Castro
http://www.elcultural.com/revista/letras/Luisa-Castro/6378
http://elpais.com/autor/luisa_castro/a
http://www.planetadelibros.com/autor/luisa-castro/000012696
https://www.youtube.com/watch?v=gr_bN8W1uWI
http://www.elmundo.es/encuentros/invitados/2003/02/587/
http://www.rtve.es/alacarta/videos/esta-es-mi-tierra/esta-tierra-santiago-mondonedo-foz-viajes-luisa-castro/708876/
http://www.ojosdepapel.com/Index.aspx?article_id=2440
http://www.revistadelibros.com/articulos/viajes-con-mi-padre-de-luisa-castro
https://www.escritores.org/biografias/4589-castro-luisa
http://elprogreso.galiciae.com/noticia/153599/non-hai-nada-que-non-se-lle-perdoe-alguen-quen-amas-e-que-te-ama

MI MADRE EN LA VENTANA

Había una diferencia entre las madres y las mamás. Cuando en el colegio sor Águeda le preguntaba a Esther Alonso por su mamá, o cuando en el patio del colegio todas aquellas mujeres esperaban nuestra salida y sor Águeda le decía a Esther Alonso: 'Mira, tu mamá, te espera tu mamá', yo ya sabía que entre Esther Alonso y yo había un mundo de distancia y que entre aquellas mujeres no se encontraría nunca mi madre. Yo tenía madre, claro, pero no era una mamá. Cuando Esther Alonso decía 'mi mamá…' yo la sentía un poco ridícula y muy pequeña a mi lado. Sólo escucharla me obligaba a ponerme en un lugar incómodo, a sentirme más pequeña también. Era una cuestión de lenguaje pero me impedía ser amiga de Esther Alonso. Convivir con ella en el mismo pupitre era algo llevadero hasta que no se cruzaba por medio aquella palabra, o quizás otra como 'mi papá', o tal vez 'mi hermanito', todas pertenecientes a un vocabulario de una galaxia lejanísima de esas que gusta ver en los cómics pero que una nunca se arriesgaría a visitar.

A los hijos de papá y mamá los caracterizaba una bondad tierna y atontada y una inocencia peculiar, algo que siempre me daba un poco de pena. Y nunca dejaban de ser ellos mismos aunque esto supusiera mantenerse al margen de muchos juegos en los que tranquilamente no participaban. La conformidad tenía para mí un encanto arrollador y Esther Alonso era una niña quieta y conforme. No sé cómo nos veía Esther Alonso a las demás, aunque yo creo que no se enteraba. Esto de andarse poniendo en el lugar del otro es una debilidad de muy pocos, me parece.

Un día entré en la casa de Esther Alonso. Estaba en penumbra, pero se adivinaba una escenografía mínimamente suntuosa: lámparas, aparatos de música y tapices. Su madre estaba muy arreglada, como recién salida de la peluquería, le brillaba la cara y fumaba envuelta en una bata de casa con aves bordadas. No pareció muy perturbada por mi presencia y eso que no me conocía. Nos hizo la merienda y luego se retiró al salón a fumar. Esther y yo jugamos con sus juguetes alegremente hasta el anochecer.

Ese día volví a casa a la hora de cenar. Pensé que llegaba tarde pero mi madre todavía no había entrado en la cocina. Estaba apoyada en la ventana junto a mi hermana, viendo cómo mi padre construía detrás de la casa un

MY MOTHER AT THE WINDOW

There was a difference between the mothers and the mummies. When Sister Agatha asked after Esther Alonso's mummy in primary school, or when all those women were waiting in the school yard for us to come out and Sister Agatha used to say to Esther Alonso: 'Look, your mummy, your mummy's waiting for you', I already knew that between Esther Alonso and me there was a world of difference and that my mother would never be found among those women. Of course, I had a mother but she was not a mummy. When Esther Alonso would say 'my mummy', I felt she was a little ridiculous and very small beside me. Just listening to her used to force me into an uncomfortable space, and made me feel smaller too. It was a question of language but it prevented me from being friends with Esther Alonso. Being with her at the same desk was bearable provided that that word was not mentioned, or perhaps another like 'my daddy' or 'my little brother', all words belonging to a far away galaxy like those it is enjoyable to see in comics but which you would never risk visiting.

The children of mummies and daddies were characterized by a tender and other-worldly goodness and a strange naivety, something which always made me feel a little sorry for them. And they never stopped being themselves although this implied staying on the margin of many games which they were happy not to participate in. Conformity had an overwhelming charm in my view and Esther Alonso was a calm little conformist. I don't know how Esther Alonso would see the rest of us, although I don't think she was aware of all that. Going through life putting yourself in the place of others is a tendency of very few people, it seems to me.

One day I went into Esther Alonso's house. It was in semi-darkness, but you could make out a scene bordering on luxurious: lamps, music players and tapestries. Her mother was well turned out, as if she had just come from the hairdressing salon, her face was shining and she was smoking in a house coat embroidered with birds. She did not appear to be put out by my presence even though she did not know me. She made afternoon tea for us and then retired to the sitting room to smoke. Esther and I played happily with her toys until nightfall.

On that occasion I went back home at dinner time. I thought I was late but my mother had still not started to cook. She was leaning out of the window next to my sister, looking at my father building a garage for the

garaje para el coche. Era un garaje de madera como la cabaña del tío Tom. La parte de atrás de nuestro edificio estaba llena de construcciones de este tipo, más o menos artesanas y provisionales. Todos los vecinos se habían apresurado a construir su propio garaje en aquel lugar que el Ayuntamiento tenía reservado para zona verde y espacio comunitario. Quizás algún día llegaría una excavadora y retiraría todos aquellos tinglados y nadie se iba a oponer. Nosotros fuimos los últimos en montar nuestra choza y mi madre parecía muy satisfecha de ver a mi padre con maderas y serruchos finalmente decidido a dar aquel paso. Como estaba oscureciendo no pudimos ver la labor terminada, pero por la mañana el garaje me pareció una obra de arte. Era algo más grande que los otros, de madera nueva y pintada de blanco, y tenía una contundencia arquitectónica que casi nos pareció peligrosa.

—No debería quedar tan bien— fue la única objeción de mi madre —si fuera un poco peor no darían tantas ganas de tirarlo.

Mi padre estaba orgulloso y tranquilo.

—Nadie lo va a tirar. ¿No ves los demás? Tendrían que gastar mucho en destrozar los garitos. Y nadie se preocupa ya de eso, ¿por qué has de preocuparte tú?

—No sé.

Pasaron varios días sin que hubiera ningún contratiempo, y después de algunas semanas el garaje todavía seguía en pie. Hay pequeñas cosas, como ver cada mañana un garaje de madera en el mismo sitio, que parecen milagros. Por las tardes después de salir del colegio y antes de subir a casa, mi hermana y yo íbamos directas al garaje, dejábamos los libros encima del capó del 127 y jugábamos a perseguirnos y escondernos detrás de las ruedas del coche, o montábamos una cocina sobre los hatos de leña que mi padre amontonaba escrupulosamente en el escaso metro que sobraba frente al guardabarros. Aquello no tenía nada que ver con el espacioso desván de Esther Alonso, lleno de juguetes y rincones maravillosos, pero yo no era consciente de eso, a mí el garaje me parecía una conquista especial, un territorio ganado a los comanches, un submarino hallado en el fondo del mar.

Cuando hubo pasado el tiempo suficiente y ya nadie temía por el derrumbe del garaje, nuestros juegos se extendieron a los territorios vecinos. Cada bodega o caseta estaba separada de la siguiente por lindes que solo los usuarios conocíamos. Ningún extraño que se internara en aquel laberinto de chabolas podía imaginar el mapa de fronteras que lo atravesaban, pero nosotras conocíamos muy bien su trazado. La colonización particular de cada vecino impuso una repartición de hecho que nunca se discutió. Las leyes de

car behind the house. It was a wooden garage like Uncle Tom's cabin. The rear of our building was full of such more or less home-made and temporary constructions. All of the neighbors had rushed to build their own garage in that spot that the Town Hall had reserved as a green area and community space. Perhaps one day a digger would come and remove all those makeshift constructions and no one was going to object. We were the last to erect our shack and my mother seemed very pleased to see my father with planks and saws determined at last to take that step. As it was getting dark we were not able to see the job finished, but in the morning the garage looked to me like a work of art. It was rather bigger than the others, made of new wood and painted white, with an architectural solidity that almost seemed dangerous to us.

'It ought not to look so good' was the only objection of my mother. 'If it were a bit worse it wouldn't provoke the desire to tear it down.'

My father was proud and tranquil.

'Nobody is going to tear it down. Can't you see the others? They would have to spend a lot to destroy all of the shacks. And no one is bothered any longer about those; why do you have to bother yourself?'

'I don't know.'

Several days passed without any mishap, and the garage was still standing after some weeks. There are little things that seem like miracles such as seeing every morning a wooden garage in the same spot. After coming out of school in the afternoon and before going up to the flat, my sister and I would go straight to the garage, and leave our books on the bonnet of the 127 and we would chase each other and hide behind the wheels of the car, or we would set up a kitchen on the bundles of firewood that my father scrupulously piled up in the bare metre of space in front of the mud guard. That had nothing to do with Esther Alonso's spacious attic, full of marvellous toys and nooks, but I was not conscious of that, to me the garage appeared like an especial conquest, a territory won from the Comanches, a submarine found at the bottom of the sea.

When sufficient time had passed and no one was afraid any longer that the garage would be knocked down, our games expanded into neighbouring territory. Each cellar or hut was separated from the next by boundaries that only we residents knew. No stranger who entered that labyrinth of shanties could imagine the map of boundaries that crisscrossed it, but we knew the layout very well. The private construction of each resident imposed a de facto distribution that was never disputed. The laws of illegality are rather

la ilegalidad son bastante más estrictas que las oficiales, y nadie puso jamás en entredicho la distribución irregular de las parcelas. Algunas eran bastante más grandes que otras, para eso sus dueños habían corrido el riesgo de dar el primer paso. Los más temerarios abrieron camino, eligieron mejores localizaciones y se quedaron con más terreno. Los rezagados y temerosos como nosotros nos conformamos con el espacio que nos quedaba, y nunca sentimos envidia ni nada parecido por las ventajas de los primeros colonos.

Nuestro garaje sin embargo tenía una ganancia con respecto a los otros: por el lado derecho lindaba con un muro de cemento de un metro de altura, construido con todas las de la ley y que servía para segregar aquella floración de chabolas desordenadas de otro territorio donde empezaban los terrenos otorgados por el Ayuntamiento. Esta proximidad con el cemento armado daba a nuestro garaje una consistencia y una entidad que no tenían los otros, construidos con materiales de desecho o prefabricados. Precisamente, uno de los juegos que más me gustaba era pasearme haciendo equilibrios por encima de aquel muro firme, rodeando el lado derecho del garaje hasta alcanzar la parte de atrás no accesible de ninguna otra forma y que nos servía como lugar secreto.

A Esther Alonso no la invité el primer día a jugar sobre el muro. Esperé a que fuera tan mío como el garaje. Vino una tarde de otoño que aún hacía sol, la llevé directamente a las chabolas y le indiqué, subida al muro, el lugar recóndito. Pero Esther no se quiso subir.

—Quiero la merienda— me dijo.

Yo sabía que a mi madre no le iba a gustar que llevara a nadie a jugar al garaje. Ella pensaba que cuanto menos anduviéramos por allí, mejor. Pero quise satisfacer a Esther, pues en parte le debía aquella merienda. Mientras subía las escaleras de dos en dos ya me di cuenta que mis relaciones con Esther Alonso empezaban a enturbiarse con el fango del compromiso y que además no me interesaba mucho la amistad de un ser que prefería un trozo de pan con chocolate a mi oferta de lugares inaccesibles. Y además estaba mi madre, que no era una mamá de esas que te reciben con batas llenas de pavos reales y que te preparan la merienda ellas mismas.

—No, no, quédate—le dije a Esther—, yo traigo la merienda. Ahora vuelvo.

En un salto llegué a casa y ayudada de un taburete alcancé la alacena de la cocina y cogí las provisiones.

—¿Qué haces?

Mi madre enseguida detectó mi sigilo.

stricter than the laws of officialdom, and no one ever called into question the irregular distribution of the plots of land. Some were quite a bit bigger than others, to this end their owners had taken the risk of making the first move. The most daring opened the way, chose the best spots and gained the most territory. Those of us who were timid and in the rearguard accepted the space that was left, and we never felt envy or anything similar towards the advantages of the first settlers.

Nevertheless, our garage had an advantage over the others: on the right side it bordered on a concrete wall one metre high, built with planning permission, which served to demarcate that flowering of ramshackle shanties from another area where the plots granted by the Town Hall began. This proximity to the concrete wall gave our garage a solidity and presence that the others did not have, constructed with discarded or prefabricated materials. Actually, one of the games that I liked most was to walk without losing my balance along the top of that solid wall, running along the right side of the garage, until I reached the rear which was inaccessible in any other way and which served us as a secret spot.

On the first day I did not invite Esther Alonso to play on the wall. I waited until it was as mine as the garage. She came one autumn afternoon when it was still sunny, I took her straight to the shanties and from the top of the wall I pointed out the hidden place to her. But Esther had no wish to climb up.

'I want to have afternoon tea', she said to me.

I knew that my mother was not going to like me taking anyone to the garage to play. She thought that the less we went round there, the better. But I wanted to please Esther because for one thing I owed her that afternoon tea. While I was climbing the stairs two at a time, I already realized that my relationship with Esther Alonso was beginning to be sullied by the mud of compromise and that moreover the friendship of someone who preferred a bit of bread with chocolate to my offer of inaccessible places was of little interest to me. And in addition there was my mother, who was not the type of mummy who greets you in a housecoat covered in peacocks and makes afternoon tea for you.

'No, no, you stay there', I said to Esther. 'I'll bring you afternoon tea. I'll be back in a moment.'

In a bound I was home and with the help of a stool I reached the larder and took the food.

'What are you up to?'

My mother detected my secrecy right away.

–Tengo a una amiga abajo. Le llevo la merienda.

Mi madre reaccionó muy bien. No sé qué entendería por 'abajo'.

–No os hagáis daño–me dijo. Y eso se lo agradecí mucho.

Cuando volví a reunirme con Esther ya había sorpresas, y no buenas. Laura, la hija de mis vecinos, se había sumado a la expedición del lugar secreto. Me puso furiosa aquella intromisión. Sin siquiera mirar a Laura, que me sonreía como una idiota, me dirigí a Esther y le entregué la merienda requerida.

–Toma. Me lo ha dado mi 'mamá'–dije, – nos dice que no nos hagamos daño.

Y enseguida noté que Laura ponía una cara muy sorprendente, como de estar viendo un espectáculo inusual, y sin duda debía serlo al oírme a mí hablar de mi 'mamá' y del 'daño'. Yo misma me horroricé. El trozo de pan con chocolate dificultaba un poco mis planes de viajar a través del muro pero me subí tentada por el reto, y detrás, sin que nadie la invitara a jugar, se subió Laura, mi vecina, mientras Esther permaneció quieta y en tierra comiendo trocitos de chocolate con pan. Aunque no me hacía mucha gracia, yo estaba dispuesta a dejar entrar a Laura en el juego si veía que aquello animaba a Esther, pero cuando vi a mi vecina subida al muro mientras Esther se mantenía en el suelo, me sucedió algo muy raro.

–No. Tú no– le dije.

–¿Por qué yo no?–preguntó Laura, mientras mantenía el equilibrio con los brazos en cruz.

Con sólo tocarla la hubiera derribado pero me contuve.

–Porque no. Porque no quiero y ya está. Este muro es sólo mío y al lugar secreto viene Esther y no tú.

Esther comía trocitos de pan y parecía no oír nada. Yo la veía desde lo alto del muro sin inmutarse. Frente a mí, Laura intentaba avanzar.

–Te digo que no, vete a tu garaje–repetí–, éste es 'mi' garaje.

En las sienes de Laura crecían ríos, mientras se ponía pálida.

–Pero el muro no es tuyo, el muro no es tuyo– contestó–, y quiso dar un paso más.

–No sigas– la avisé.

Laura avanzó, y a mí la cabeza se me llenó de sangre, y luego hice lo que no tenía que haber hecho. Cuando recobré el equilibrio sobre el muro, ya no había vuelta atrás. Esther, impertérrita, con los pies clavados en el

'I've got a girlfriend downstairs. I'm taking her a snack.'

My mother reacted very well. I don't know what she understood by 'downstairs.'

'Don't hurt yourselves', she said. And I was grateful to her for saying that.

When I rejoined Esther, there were surprises, and not good ones. Laura, my neighbours' daughter, had joined the expedition to the secret place. That interference made me furious. Without even looking at Laura smiling at me like an idiot, I addressed Esther and handed her the requested snack.

'Here. My mummy gave it to me. She says we shouldn't hurt ourselves.'

And I noted at once that Laura was putting on a surprised expression, as if witnessing an unusual spectacle, which doubtless hearing me speaking of 'mummy' and 'hurt' was. I myself was horrified. The piece of bread and chocolate complicated my plan to go along the wall but I climbed up tempted by the challenge, and behind me up climbed Laura, my neighbour, without anyone having invited her to play, while Esther remained still on the ground eating bits of chocolate with bread. Although it did not appeal to me, I was ready to let Laura join in the game if I saw that that encouraged Esther, but when I saw Laura on top of the wall while Esther stayed on the ground, something strange happened to me.

'No, not you', I said to her.

'Why not me?' Laura asked, while she kept her balance with her arms in the shape of a cross.

By simply touching her I would have knocked her off but I controlled myself.

'Because not. Because I don't want it and that's it. This wall is mine alone and Esther is coming to the secret place and you're not.'

Esther was eating bits of bread and appeared not to hear anything. I saw that she was not reacting from the top of the wall. In front of me Laura was trying to go forwards.

'I'm telling you not to, go to your own garage', I repeated, "this garage is *mine.*'

Laura's temples were glistening with perspiration as she grew pale.

'But the wall isn't yours, the wall isn't yours', she answered, and tried to take another step.

'Don't go any further', I warned her.

Laura moved forward and the blood rushed to my head, and then I did what I shouldn't have done. When I recovered my balance on the wall, there was no turning back: Esther, unmoved, with her feet clamped to the

suelo, ahora comía trocitos de chocolate en vez de pan. Mi madre observaba la escena desde la ventana como un tercero. Y en la ventana de la casa de Laura vi a la madre de ésta moviendo los brazos y agitándose, muy excitada y sin peinar, como si algo horrendo la hubiera despertado y hubiera acudido desde el fondo de la cama donde según los vecinos se pasaba el día durmiendo sin que nada ni nadie la arrancara de allí. Ya me di cuenta de que algo irreparable había ocurrido, algo bastante grave para que aquella mujer que nunca se dejaba ver apareciera de pronto escandalizando por la ventana. Gritaba con todas sus fuerzas, me amenazaba.

–¡Te deshago, como te coja te deshago!– oí que se dirigía a mí– y tú, Laura, sube, no te acerques a ese animal.

Laura estaba tirada en el suelo. Yo misma la había derribado, pero me resultaba todo un poco exagerado. Sólo sangraba por una rodilla y lloraba desconsoladamente. Su madre desde la ventana se desgañitaba en amenazas y yo me moría de rabia y de vergüenza mientras Esther Alonso desaparecía como una gallina entre el laberinto de los garajes. Tres o cuatro cabezas se asomaron a las ventanas, llamadas por el escándalo. Por un momento me sentí en peligro, jamás había visto a nadie tan fuera de sí como lo estaba la madre de Laura, pero me tranquilizó pensar que no se atrevería a bajar y pegarme ante toda aquella gente, ella que no salía de su casa ni para comprar el pan. Mi madre se mantuvo todo el tiempo detrás de la ventana de nuestra casa, un poco retirada de medio cuerpo hacia dentro, sin intervenir. Laura, ensoberbecida por la sangre y la razón, se fue a su casa como un león herido, con el desprecio y la grandeza de los héroes derribados, repitiendo aquello que todavía resuena en mis oídos.

–No es tuyo, el muro no es tuyo.

Permanecí allí subida más tiempo del normal, creo, esperando no sé qué muestra de apoyo por parte de alguien, de mi 'mamá' quizás. Pero ella se retiró de la ventana, el refuerzo nunca llegó y allí me quedé sola.

Cuando subí a casa, llorando, se lo reproché.

–Y tú ahí, sin moverte. ¿Por qué no me defendiste?

Creo que me puse un poco dramática por aquel primer abandono, al que luego siguieron otros que fui encarando mejor, porque siempre tenían las mismas características: yo iba metiéndome sin querer en algún lío de esos que no te dejan dormir y cuando acudía a mi madre para encontrar justificación o consuelo hallaba a una mujer extraña que se lavaba las manos y que me dejaba perpleja con su imparcialidad.

ground, was now eating bits of chocolate instead of bread. My mother was watching the scene from the window like a third party. And at the window of Laura's house, I saw her mother waving her arms and flapping about, very agitated and disheveled, as if something horrible had woken her up and she had risen from the depths of her bed, which according to the neighbours was where she spent the day sleeping without anything or anybody being able to drag her from it. I realized that something irreparable had taken place, something serious enough for that woman who never showed herself to appear suddenly yelling and screaming out of the window. She was shouting with all her strength, threatening me.

'I'll tear you apart, when I get you, I'll tear you apart!' I heard her shouting at me. 'And Laura, you get upstairs, don't go near that brute.'

Laura was stretched out on the ground. I had knocked her down, but everything seemed a bit exaggerated to me. She was only bleeding from one knee and crying disconsolately. From her window her mother was showering me with threats and I was mortified with anger and shame while Esther Alonso was disappearing like a hen among the labyrinth of garages. Three or four people appeared at windows, summoned by the uproar. For a moment I thought I was in danger, I had never seen anyone so out of control as Laura's mother was, but the thought that she who never jumped out of bed even to buy bread would not dare to come down stairs and thump me calmed me down. All this time my mother stayed a bit back from our window, with half of her body inclined inwards, without intervening. Puffed up with a blood rush and reason on her side, Laura went off home like a wounded lion, showing the scorn and grandeur of fallen heroes, repeating what still sounds in my ear:

'It isn't yours, the wall isn't yours.'

I stayed up there for longer than usual, I think, waiting for some kind of backing from someone, my 'mummy' perhaps. But she drew back from the window, reinforcements never came and there I remained alone.

When I went home crying, I reproached my mother.

'And you stood there without moving. Why did you not defend me?'

I think I became a bit dramatic on account of that first abandonment, which was later followed by others that I faced better, because they always had the same features: despite myself I would get into some scrape or other that doesn't let you sleep and when I went to my mother in search of justification or consolation, I found a strange woman who washed her hands of it and left me perplexed with her impartiality.

–Ya ves– era como si me dijera ella–, apáñatelas.

No era indiferencia lo que me demostraba mi madre ni lo que apreciaba yo sino algo que fue teniendo para mí un significado muy hondo y un poco estremecedor, como si aquellos abandonos de mi madre fueran nuestro verdadero lazo, el único modo de recordarme la condición de nuestra mutua soledad.

Dejarse tentar por el demonio es un modo de llamar a Dios, el más desesperado quizás. Yo sé que en cada maldad o en cada situación de riesgo siempre ando buscando la clemencia de mi madre, su refrendo incondicional, ese apoyo que sé que nunca llegará, lo que me permite despreciar profundamente a las 'mamás' que justificarían la más grave abyección de sus hijos, con el desprecio hacia aquello que nunca le pertenecerá a uno, como el muro de cemento que rodeaba nuestro garaje. Yo puedo pasearme sobre esas cosas, usarlas de puente a lugares secretos, pero cualquier intento de poseerlas es el camino más recto hacia el desprecio y el ridículo. Lo mismo me ha pasado cuando he querido ver en mi madre a otra madre, por esa absurda tendencia que ya es vicio de ponerse en el pellejo de los otros, en el de Esther Alonso, en el de Laura Casín.

–Hasta esa mujer que se pasa el día borracha y en la cama sabe defender a su hija. ¿No lo ves?

Pero mi madre no veía nada, sólo me miraba con pena y estupefacción.

–No hay que empujar a nadie–me dijo sin alzar la voz.

–¡Tú no me vas a buscar al colegio!–repliqué.

La lista de reproches y de agravios fue larga. Recuerdo que terminé extenuada, prometiendo por mi parte que nunca más pegaría a nadie y haciéndole asegurar a mi madre que al día siguiente saldría un poco antes del trabajo y estaría esperándome a la salida del colegio. Pero la costumbre para un niño es toda su libertad, y a la mañana siguiente me pasé las cuatro horas de clase en un puro nervio esperando no encontrar a mi madre a la salida, deseando que los acontecimientos del día anterior no cambiaran nada entre nosotras. ¡Y al sonar la campana le agradecí tanto no verla entre aquellas cabezas de mamás olfativas! ¡Todo seguía igual entre nosotras! Y pude correr como cada día libre hacia mi casa, entremeterme a mi antojo en los escaparates, subir al trote las escaleras del portal, y sobre todo –lo que me hacía sentir tan bien– abrir la puerta de casa yo misma con mi propia llave, un derecho y una responsabilidad que aún no habían adquirido ninguna de mis amigas.

Al meter la llave en la cerradura enseguida noté que alguien abría por dentro. Mi madre había salido un poco antes del trabajo y sonreía frente a mí.

It was as if she were saying to me: 'There you are, sort it out for yourself.'

What my mother was demonstrating to me and what I felt was not indifference but something that began to take on a deeper and more frightening meaning, as if those abandonments on her part were our true bond, the only way of reminding me of our state of mutual loneliness.

Allowing oneself to be tempted by the devil is a way of calling upon God, maybe the most desperate way. I know that in every bad deed or in every risky situation I am always seeking my mother's forgiveness, her unconditional approval, that support that I know will never come, which allows me to despise deeply the 'mummies' who would justify the most seriously despicable action of their children, with scorn towards what will never belong to one, like the concrete wall surrounding our garage. I can walk over those things, use them as a bridge to secret places, but any attempt at taking possession of them is the straightest road to scorn and ridicule. The same has happened to me when I have tried to see another mother in my mother, owing to that absurd tendency which is by now a vice to put myself in other people's skin, in Esther Alonso's, in Laura Casín's.

'Even that woman who spends her day drunk in bed can defend her daughter. Don't you see that?'

But my mother did not see anything. She just looked at me with sorrow and astonishment.

'You shouldn't push anyone', she said without raising her voice.

'You don't come to collect me from school!' I replied.

The list of reproaches and regrets was long. I remember that I ended up worn out, promising on my part never to hit anyone again and making my mother promise that she would leave work a little earlier the following day and be waiting for me at the school exit. But habit for a child is its total freedom, and the following morning I spent the four hours in class a bunch of nerves hoping not to find my mother at the exit, wishing that the previous day's events wouldn't change anything between us. And when the bell went I thanked her so much for not seeing her among the heads of the tactile mummies! Everything remained the same between us! And the same as every day, I could run home freely, enjoying myself as I wished looking at the shop windows, running up the main stairs, and above all – something that made me feel so good – opening the door myself with my own key, a right and responsibility that none of my friends had yet acquired.

On inserting the key in the lock I noticed at once that someone inside was opening the door. My mother had left work a bit early and was smiling at me.

–No fui a buscarte. Así comemos antes.

Todavía puedo decir que estos descubrimientos que he ido haciendo de mi madre, este modo suyo de tomarme en serio y hasta de entregarme a la policía si hace falta, sin venderme por un regalo o un cariño, sigue resultándome estremecedor. En mi recuerdo es la máxima prueba del sentido de la verdad que ella tiene y del que yo carezco. Así como recuerdo varias escenas de tierno encubrimiento por parte de mi padre, de mi madre no recuerdo ni una sola concesión en lo que refiere a 'problemas reales o imaginarios con la justicia'. Al contrario, estoy segura de que su fría mirada sobre los hechos le impide ni siquiera sentir el más mínimo remordimiento por no acudir en mi ayuda cada vez que me precipito hacia algún pozo.

Pero, es curioso, nunca me expliqué cómo mi madre, que tenía tan arraigada la justicia y era tan ecuánime en sus juicios, se mostrara en cambio tan temerosa de la justicia de los otros sobre ella, esa justicia que podía derribarle el garaje ilegal, por ejemplo, por el que siguió temiendo hasta que se cayó de viejo. Aunque parecen dos cosas relacionadas, el amor y el miedo a la justicia, a mí me resultaban un poco incongruentes: no veía relación entre la impecabilidad moral de mi madre y su miedo congénito a las leyes. Y ambas actitudes me parecían el producto de una extrema desproporción. Observándola a ella y aun admirándola por este sentido exagerado de la justicia, he llegado a pensar que justo, realmente justo, sólo se puede ser si se es un poco gángster. Aquello que hizo la madre de Laura y que a mí me pareció un abuso de un adulto contra un niño era realmente un acto de justicia, algo que yo quisiera para mí: una madre borracha y despeinada defendiéndome desde la ventana, y no un juez con toga y peluca blanca. Porque un juez es un juez, pero un justo es otra cosa. Y, de algún modo, sólo se llega al delito por un ansia de justicia, como yo defendiendo como mío el muro que no era mío, reivindicando mi parcela privada ante los ojos atónitos y espantados de Esther Alonso. Aquel garaje de madera nunca nos trajo más problemas que el que he contado aquí, pero ya digo que mi madre siguió esperando cada día de la vida de aquella cabaña a que llegaran unos hombres uniformados y vinieran a meternos a todos en la cárcel, mientras que el incidente del muro se le olvidó al instante.

Se lo he recordado algún día, por oír una vez más lo que me sigue y me seguirá emocionando y escandalizando. Y ella sigue contestándome lo mismo que me contestó entonces, cuando subí a casa llorando en busca de un regazo consolador:

–Pero es que no era tuyo. Aquel muro no era tuyo.

'I didn't go to get you. So we can eat early.'

I can still say that those discoveries that I have been making about my mother, that way of hers of taking me seriously and even handing me over to the police if necessary, without selling me in exchange for a present or hug, still makes me tremble. In my memory it is the supreme proof of her sense of truth, something that I lack. Just as I recall some scenes of a tender cover up on my father's part, I cannot recall a single concession from my mother with regard to 'real or imaginary problems with the law.' On the contrary, I am certain that her cold overview of the facts prevents her from having the least bit of remorse for not coming to my aid every time I rush headlong towards some hole in the ground.

But, it's strange, I never understood how my mother, with her ingrained sense of justice and so balanced in her judgments, on the other hand should show herself to be so fearful of the judgement of others on her, that judgement, for example, that could knock down the illegal garage, for she suffered on that account until it fell down from old age. Although love and fear of the law seem two related things, they were a bit incongruous in my view: I could not see any connection between the moral rectitude of my mother and her innate fear of the law. And both attitudes seemed to me the result of an extreme disharmony. Observing her and still admiring her for this exaggerated sense of justice, I have come to think that one can only be upright, really upright, if one is a bit of a gangster. What Laura's mother did and what I thought was the bullying of a child by an adult, was really an act of justice, something I would want for myself: a disheveled, drunken mother defending me from the window, and not a judge wearing a gown and white wig. Because a judge is a judge but an upright person is something different. And in some way, one only arrives at the crime through a thirst for justice, like me defending the wall which wasn't mine, claiming my private plot of land in front of the astonished and fearful eyes of Esther Alonso. That wooden garage never brought us any more problems other than the one I have related here, but I can say that every day that that cabin was in existence my mother kept expecting men in uniforms to come and put us all in prison, while she forgot about the wall incident in an instant.

I've reminded her of it from time to time, to hear her once again say what continues and will continue to move and shock me. And she still answers me in the same way as she answered me then, when I went up to the flat crying and in search of a consoling lap.

'But the wall wasn't yours. That wall wasn't yours.'

Y entonces, pero siempre con sus ojos y nunca con su voz, yo la escucho muy claramente tratando de responderme a una pregunta que no sale de mi boca pero que está en mis ojos:

–Pues claro que soy tuya, claro que soy tu madre.

Y su cara mirándome con una mezcla de desconcierto e ingenuidad, como si no quisiera mentirme ni defraudarme, como si quisiera hacerme entender algo que desde muy pronto me inquietó, como si lo mejor que podía hacer por mí, más que ir a buscarme al colegio, fuera compartir conmigo la carga de saber que el ser yo su hija y ella mi madre era, en el fondo, un hecho tan innegable como perturbadoramente azaroso y casual.

And then, always with her eyes and never her mouth, I hear her very clearly trying to answer my question that remains in my eyes and is never spoken.

'But, of course, I'm yours, I'm your mother.'

And her face looking at me with a mixture of surprise and naivety, as if she didn't want to lie to me or deceive me, as if she wanted to make me understand something that disconcerted me from an early age, as if the best thing she could do for me instead of fetching me from school, was to share with me the burden of knowing that I was her daughter and she my mother, a fact both undeniable and perplexingly fateful and fortuitous.

SERÁS AIRE VOLADOR

YOU'LL BECOME A WHISPER OF AIR

Original Spanish text from *Aire nada más*
(Barcelona: Plaza y Janés, 1999, 191–98)
© Juana Salabert, 1999

JUANA SALABERT was born in Paris in 1962, the daughter of exiles from the Spanish Civil War. Her father was the writer and translator Miguel Salabert, author of the excellent novel *El exilio interior*, published in Spanish in 1988 but which was first out in French in 1961. Juana Salabert has a degree in Modern Languages from the Université Toulouse Le-Mirail and writes mostly in Spanish, although she considers herself very fortunate that she was brought up bilingual. Her first novel, *Arde lo que será*, was a finalist for the prestigious Premio Nadal in 1996 and, since then, she has published eight novels, some of which have been translated into French, as well as short stories and essays. The most significant of her essays is *Hijas de la ira: vidas rotas por la Guerra Civil* (2005), which brings together the testimony of ten women who experienced the Spanish Civil War as children: Ana María Matute, the writer and personal friend with whom she worked on many occasions; the actress Julia Gutiérrez Caba; the writer Josefina Aldecoa; the radio presenter and actress Juana Ginzo, among others. Her interest in Spanish and European history is the main focus of most of her novels, in which the dialogue between history and memory takes the form of a fictional story closely related to historical events. Exemplary of her fiction are *Velódromo de invierno* (2001), a novel about the Nazi persecution of Jews in France seen through the eyes of a young girl, in which the past has a profound effect on the present; *La noche ciega* (2005), about a family's troubles during the Civil War and a homage to the Republicans who lost it, and *El bulevar del miedo* (2007), where the past (the 1940s) once again defines the present in the life of its protagonist during the May 1968 events in Paris. Domestic violence is the subject of *La faz de la tierra* (2011), and her latest novel, an incursion into the *noir* genre, *La regla de oro* (2015), also touches on social preoccupations combined with the conventions of the detective novel. Juana Salabert publishes literary criticism and has extensively translated from French.

Bibliography of Juana Salabert

Novels
Arde lo que será (Barcelona: Destino, 1996) – *Finalist Premio Nadal.*
Varadero (Madrid: Alfaguara, 1996).
Mar de los espejos (Barcelona: Plaza & Janés, 1998).
Velódromo de invierno (Barcelona: Seix Barral, 2001; Madrid: Alianza, 2009) – *Premio Biblioteca Breve 2001*; *Le Vélodrome d'hiver* (Paris: Buchet/Chastel, 2007).
La noche ciega (Barcelona: Seix Barral, 2004) – *Finalist Premio Nacional de Narrativa 2005.*
El bulevar del miedo (Madrid: Alianza, 2007) – *VIII Premio Unicaja de Novela Fernando Quiñones; Finalist Premio Dashiel Hammett 2008.*
*La faz de la tierra (*Madrid: Alianza, 2011).
La regla de oro (Madrid: Alianza, 2015); *La régle d'or* (Paris: Métailié, 2017).

Short story collections
Aire nada más (Barcelona: Plaza & Janés, 1999).

Short stories (a selection)
'Salvo en la noche', *Premio Relatos Breves de la UNED 1998.*
'Adviento', *Finalist Premio NH de Relatos 2004.*
'Amigas de verano', in L.Freixas (ed.), *Cuentos de amigas* (Barcelona: Anagrama, 2009).

Essays on literature and history
'Texto sobre lectura y escritura para curso de verano "cuarentón" de la Universidad de Murcia dirigido por Antonio Orejudo', in A. Orejudo (ed.), *En cuarentena. Nuevos narradores y críticos a principios del siglo XXI* (Murcia: Universidad de Murcia, 2004), 167–69.
Hijas de la ira: vidas rotas por la Guerra Civil (Barcelona: Plaza y Janés, 2005; Madrid: Nocturna, 2009).
'Ana María Matute, a este lado del paraíso', *Campo de Agramante: Revista de Literatura* 22 (2015), 5–18.
http://www.cervantesvirtual.com/nd/ark:/59851/bmcxm099

Travel writing
Vive la vía: Estación Central (Barcelona: Plaza & Janés, 1999).

Children's literature
La bruja Marioneta (Madrid: Espasa Calpe, 2001).

Further reading on Juana Salabert

Fernando Castanedo, 'Verbo torrencial y muchas prisas', *Revista de Libros*, 1 December 2007. http://www.revistadelibros.com/articulos/el-bulevar-del-miedo-de-juana-salabert

Amelia Castilla, 'Juana Salabert profundiza en la memoria con *Mar de los espejos*', *El País* (Cultura), 24 March 1998. http://elpais.com/diario/1998/03/24/cultura/890694008_850215.html

M. José Díaz Cuesta, 'Salabert retrata en un libro la generación de los sesenta', *El País* (Cultura), 7 October 1999. http://elpais.com/diario/1999/10/07/cultura/939247205_850215.html

Pedro Espinosa, 'Salabert gana el Fernando Quiñones con una novela sobre los robos de arte', *El País*, 18 November 2006. http://elpais.com/diario/2006/11/18/andalucia/1163805738_850215.html

Luis García Jambrina, 'No olvidarás', *ABC* (Cultural), 28 April 2001.

Luis García Jambrina, 'La recuperación de la memoria histórica en tres novelas españolas', in A. Orejudo (ed.), *En cuarentena. Nuevos narradores y críticos a principios del siglo XXI* (Murcia: Universidad de Murcia, 2004), 79–95.

Jordi Gracia,'Interiores en guerra', *El País* (Babelia), 28 February 2004. http://elpais.com/diario/2004/02/28/babelia/1077929423_850215.html

Javier Goñi, 'Sólo creo en los escritores que son lectores fanáticos', *El País* (Cultura), 14 January 1996. http://elpais.com/diario/1996/01/14/cultura/821574001_850215.html

Tabea Alexa Linhard, 'The Maps of Nostalgia: Juana Salabert's *Velódromo de invierno*', *Revista Hispánica Moderna* 60.1 (2007), 61–77. http://www.jstor.org/stable/40647354

María del Mar López Cabrales, 'Juana Salabert. La confluencia de caminos', in *Palabras de mujeres. Escritoras españolas contemporáneas* (Madrid: Narcea, 2000), 63–72.

María del Mar Mañas Martínez, 'Juana Salabert o la persistencia de la memoria', in A. Redondo Goicoechea (ed.), *Mujeres novelistas: jóvenes narradoras de los noventa* (Madrid: Narcea, 2003), 59–77.

María José Obiol, 'Un antihéroe en dos tiempos', *El País*, 30 June 2007. http://elpais.com/diario/2007/06/30/babelia/1183161018_850215.html

Isabel Obiols, 'Juana Salabert gana el Premio Biblioteca Breve con una novela sobre el Holocausto', *El País* (Cultura), 29 March 20021. http://elpais.com/diario/2001/03/29/cultura/985816803_850215.html

J. Rodríguez Marcos, 'Cansadas de ser las hermanas pequeñas: Ana María Matute y Juana Salabert denuncian el machismo del mundo literario', *El País*, 6 August 2007.

Álvaro Romero Marco, 'Melodrama, laberinto y memoria en la novelística de Juana Salabert', in Á. Encinar and K. M. Glenn (eds), *La pluralidad narrativa.*

Escritores españoles contemporáneos (1984–2004) (Madrid: Biblioteca Nueva, 2003), 107–18.

H. Rosi Song, 'Anti-conformist Fiction: The Spanish Generation X', in M. E. Altisent (ed.), *A Companion to the Twentieth-Century Spanish Novel* (Woodbridge: Tamesis, 2008), 197–208.

Elisa Silió, 'Juana Salabert relata en *La noche ciega* las peripecias de una excéntrica familia durante la Guerra Civil', *El País* (Cultura), 19 January 2004. http://elpais.com/diario/2004/01/19/cultura/1074466804_850215.html

Isabelle Toulon, 'Juana Salabert', in N. Noyant (ed.), *La narrativa española de hoy (2000–2010). La imagen en el texto (2)* (Berna: Peter Lang, 2012), 315–37.

Further online information on Juana Salabert (a selection)

http://www.elcultural.com/noticias/letras/La-novela-negra-de-Juana-Salabert/7758
http://otrolunes.com/37/unos-escriben/juana-salabert-a-modo-de-biografia/
http://elpais.com/diario/1998/05/30/cultura/896479206_850215.html
http://www.mcnbiografias.com/app-bio/do/show?key=salabert-juana
http://www.eldiario.es/cultura/Juana-Salabert-novela-crisis-regla_0_384962007.html
http://www.agenciabalcells.com/autores/autor/juana-salabert/
http://www.nocturnaediciones.com/autor/4/salabert_juana
https://lecturassumergidas.com/2015/06/28/juana-salabert-de-nina-me-enamore-sin-remedio-de-poe/
https://www.youtube.com/watch?v=m3o5oQyrVhM
http://www.goodreads.com/book/show/5033875-vel-dromo-de-invierno
https://revistacalibre38.com/2016/12/19/resena-la-regla-del-oro-de-juana-salabert/
https://www.graphiclassic.es/juana-salabert-jv
http://www.march.es/conferencias/anteriores/voz.aspx?p1=22653
http://www.comentariosdelibros.com/comentario-velodromo-de-invierno-31idl31idc.htm
http://www.todostuslibros.com/autor/juana-salabert
http://amirvalle.com/a-titulo-personal/de-literatura/juana-salabert-libros-que-remueven-conciencias/
http://www.nuevatribuna.es/articulo/cultura---ocio/estoy-indignadisima-nos-hallamos-gran-estafa/20150429121739115286.html
http://www.publico.es/culturas/william-faulkner-espanola.html
http://elpais.com/diario/2007/08/06/ultima/1186351201_850215.html
http://elpais.com/diario/1998/05/13/madrid/895058679_850215.html
http://topcultural.es/2015/05/07/entrevista-a-juana-salabert-autora-de-la-novela-negra-la-regla-del-oro
https://editions-metailie.com/livre/la-regle-de-lor/

SERÁS AIRE VOLADOR

Para Ainhoa Carcavilla e Inés González

Soñé por un momento que serás aire,* le musité, su mano helada entre
las mías, mirando ese rostro desconocido que durante tanto tiempo fue el
mío. Pero él ya no podía oírme, porque el silencio lo había atrapado en
sus redes últimas, y los años más felices, aquella década de los ochenta
que compartimos jugando a intercambiarnos las identidades (nos divertía
confundir a la gente y ligarnos a las mismas chicas) se habían desvanecido
tras de nuestras huellas como humareda de teatro. No sé en qué instante
descubrimos que ya nunca habría paraísos, *Haway, Bombay,* retornan esos
estribillos ahora en mi memoria, o quizá los he tarareado sin darme cuenta en
voz alta en esta sala de espera de hospital donde nuestro hermano mayor y su
segunda mujer miran fijo ante sí, y yo fumo un pitillo tras otro, pese al cartel
que lo prohíbe, y a las reconvenciones de la enfermera menos simpática.
'Cállate, Miguel, no creo que sea el momento de cantar', dice mi padre, y
añade enseguida: 'buena vida perra me habéis dado … todos. Y tu madre
sin llegar, sólo faltaba un retraso del vuelo'. Mi madre es francesa y desde
que se divorciaron vive en París, la ciudad donde yo hubiese querido nacer,
con otro hombre, un arquitecto diez años menor. Una vez le mandé grabada
esa canción de Mecano *Cenando en París*, que Adrián y yo amábamos, y
poníamos una y otra vez en aquella vieja minicadena de nuestro cuarto
familiar, de ventanas tendidas sobre el paseo de Rosales, antes, mucho antes
de que él se adentrase por las sendas atroces de la heroína; desde entonces,
siempre que he ido a visitar a mi madre ésta me lleva a cenar a la mítica *La
Tour d'Argent*, sobre el Sena, y se maquilla y se viste a tope solo para mí, y

---

*   Like the title itself, many sentences in this story come from the lyrics of the Mecano
songs, a group whose music the protagonists used to like when they were younger. The
intertextual references are indicated in italics and the notes in the translation of the story
provide information in detail.

YOU'LL BECOME A WHISPER OF AIR

For Ainhoa Carcavilla and Inés González

For a moment I dreamt that you will be air,[1] I whispered to him, his icy
hand held in mine, looking at that unknown face which for so long was
mine. But he could no longer hear me, because silence had entrapped him
in her deathly nets, and the happiest years, the decade of the eighties that
we shared playing at exchanging identities (we enjoyed confusing people
and flirting with the same girls) had vanished behind our footprints like
theatrical smoke. I don't know at what precise point we discovered that there
never would be paradise, *Hawai, Mumbay,*[2] those refrains come back to my
memory now, or perhaps I have hummed them out loud without realizing it
in that hospital waiting room where our elder brother and his second wife
look straight ahead, and I am smoking one fag after another, in spite of the
poster prohibiting it and the admonitions of the least friendly nurse. 'Be
quiet, Miguel, I don't think it's the time to sing', says my father, adding
at once: 'Some shitty life you've given me, all of you. And your mother
still not here, a late flight is the last straw.' My mother is French and since
they got divorced, lives in Paris, the city where I would like to have been
born, with another man, an architect, ten years her junior. I once sent her
a recording of that song by Mecano, *Dining in Paris,*[3] that Adrian and I
loved, and used to play again and again on that old record player in our
family room, whose windows overlooked the Paseo of Rosales,[4] before, a
long time before, he ventured down the atrocious paths of heroin; since then,
every time I've gone to see my mother she takes me to dinner at the iconic
La Tour d'Argent,[5] on the Seine, and she makes herself up and dresses up

---

1   The narrator of this story remembers the years of his youth in the early 1980s shared
with his twin brother, Adrián, now dying of an AIDS related illness. They used to like
the electronic music of Mecano, a very popular band at the time. Juana Salabert's story
is cleverly peppered with lines from the lyrics of the Mecano songs, which captured the
mood of many urban kids in the early post-Franco era in Spain. The title of the story and
the opening sentence refer, in a slightly modified way, to the stanza of a song entitled *Aire*
[*Air*]: 'Aire, soñé que por un momento que era aire / aire, oxígeno, nitrógeno y argón / sin
forma definida ni color / fui aire volador'.
2   *Haway, Bombay*: the title of a Mecano song.
3   *Dining in Paris [Cenando en París]*: Another title of a Mecano song.
4   **Paseo de Rosales**: Popular avenue in central Madrid.
5   **La Tour d'Argent**: Historic restaurant in Paris, located in 15 Quai de la Tournelle.

ambos fingimos ante los ojos del maître y del resto de los comensales que no soy su hijo, sino un amante jovencito. A ella, tan divertida y tan insegura, siempre le horrorizó envejecer, 'habría que morir como Boris Vian, antes de cumplir los cuarenta', afirmaba… Bien, ahora sé –no lo intuyo, tengo la certeza más estricta y absoluta en ese sentido– que su avión no llegará a tiempo. Y que su hijo pequeño, mi gemelo nacido dos minutos después que yo, no cumplirá nunca cuarenta años, porque *la espuma de los días* se ha terminado para él, y navega ya a solas por unas aguas a las que no podré seguirlo, como le seguí en los años dorados por los bares de la noche y de las risas y la música entre amigos. 'Sois una generación perdida', decía Ernesto, mi hermano mayor, que entonces aún mostraba resabios de ex progre a punto de reconvertirse en yuppie sociata, Dios, qué discos coñazos escuchó durante años, esos cantautores, 'comprometidos', decía él, con su cara de fervor y gesto de santón hipócrita; luego le dio por las rancheras y la ópera, típico suyo, que siempre ha estado a la moda del instante… Supongo que ahora tratará de colarse en el PP, pero eso qué importa… Hace mucho que no mantenemos ninguna clase de relación. Para él y su nueva mujer (una tipa guapísima que apenas abre la boca la jode, porque su encefalograma es más plano que el de mi gemelo en coma desde esta mañana), yo soy un licenciado en letras que malgasta y desbarata su vida, trabaja de mensajero y vive en un cuchitril de alquiler en la plaza de Santa Ana –un lugar de pasillos entrecruzados habitado por putas muy amables, actores ancianos sin demasiadas ofertas ya para el cine o el teatro, y travestis que a veces me invitan a desayunar al bar DORIN, que tiene los camareros más estupendos del mundo–, un fracasado… Y Adrián es, *era*… En fin.

just for me, and we both pretend in the eyes of the head waiter and the rest of the diners that I'm not her son but a very young lover. Always so lively and insecure, she was always horrified by getting old, 'one ought to die like Boris Vian,[6] before one's fortieth birthday', she used to say ... Well, I now know – I don't know it instinctively, I know it with the most definite and absolute certainty – that her plane will not arrive on time. And I know that her youngest son, my twin brother who was born two minutes after me, will not make his fortieth birthday, because *the foam of his days*[7] has ebbed away, and he is now sailing alone through waters where I won't be able to follow him, as I followed him in the golden days through the all-night bars, and through the laughter and music in the company of friends. 'You are a lost generation', my eldest brother Ernesto used to say; at that time he still showed traces of being an ex-left wing engagé youngster about to turn into a champagne-socialist yuppie, God, what shitty records he used to listen to during those years, those 'politically committed' singer-songwriters, he used to say, with his earnest face and look of a priggish hypocrite; then the Mexican *rancheras* and opera, just typical of him, who has always been up-to-date with passing fashion... I suppose he'll now try and slip into the PP,[8] but what the heck... It's a long time since we had any sort of relationship. In the opinion of him and his new wife (a really pretty chick who every time she opens her mouth puts her foot in it, because her brain scan is flatter than my twin's who has been comatose since this morning), I'm a Humanities graduate who wastes and cheapens his life, works as a messenger and lives in a rented pig-sty in Santa Ana Square – a place with crisscrossing corridors, inhabited by loveable whores, ancient actors with few offers of work nowadays from theatre or cinema, and transvestites who sometimes invite me to breakfast in the DORIN bar, which has the most superb waiters in the world – a failure... And Adrián is, *was*... Well.

---

6   **Boris Vian (1920–1959)**: French polymath (he was a novelist, a poet, a musician, a singer, a translator and critic as well as an actor and an American jazz enthusiast) who indeed died at 39. Amongst other works, he was the author of the surrealist novel *L'Écume des jours* (1947) and is also remembered as the composer of a cult anti-war song from 1954, at the time of the colonial First Indochina War between France and the Viet Minh communist-nationalist revolutionaries. The song, entitled *Le Déserteur*, gives voice to a man who writes a letter to the French President declaring that he will not answer his call to arms and explains why. The song was forbidden by the French government until 1962.

7   Allusion to *L'Écume des jours* by Boris Vian. Literally meaning 'the foam of days', the best known translation into English of the novel bears the title *Froth on the Daydream*.

8   **PP**: the acronym for Partido Popular, a Spanish conservative party.

Me coloco las gafas negras, no quiero que me vean llorar, no *ellos*, al menos. Nada más anhelo regresar por espacio de un minuto o de unas horas o de toda una vida a la época de nuestros veinte años; aquellos ochenta en que todo parecía posible, hasta el sol de la felicidad, y Adrián, que era más vital, pero también el más frágil de nosotros dos, estaba obsesionado con la chica de Mecano (tenía fotos suyas chincheadas sobre la cabecera de su cama), y los dos salíamos de marcha al Rockola y a tantos sitios, y la ciudad nos pertenecía, y subidos a la moto que nuestra madre nos regaló al cumplir los veinte, cantábamos a voz en cuello aquello de *coca-cola para todos y algo de comer*, y *hoy no me puedo levantar*, y esa verdadera declaración de principios de la alegría de vivir que era *ya no puedo más y quiero salir pronto de aquí, quiero vivir con amigos, irme de copas y acostarme tarde, montar en moto, salir con las chicas, ir por la calle y sentirme libre*, y yo devoraba libros, porque ansiaba escribir ese libro que lo contendría todo, y estaba colgadísimo – me temo que siempre he tenido cierta vertiente *masoca* – de Lola, mi primera cuñada; y supongo que ella se daba cuenta, pero que no le importaba, porque nos quería a los dos, *Cástor y Pólux* nos llamaba en broma, y nos invitaba a los restaurantes más exóticos, nos regalaba discos, y escuchaba nuestras confidencias sin impacientarse nunca. Ni siquiera sé qué ha sido de Lola luego de que Ernesto la dejase tirada, quizá ni viva ya en Madrid, tal vez haya vuelto a su Ibiza natal... Adrián no se enamoraba por aquel entonces; después sí se enamoró, a lo bestia, y no sé qué sucedió, jamás

I put on my sunglasses, I don't want them to see me crying, at least, not *them*. My only yearning is to return for a minute or a few hours or a whole life to when we were twenty; those years in the eighties when everything seemed possible, even the sunshine of happiness, and Adrián, who was the livelier but also the more fragile of the two of us, was besotted with the female singer from the Mecano group[9] (he had photos of her pinned above his headboard), and we both went out on the town to the Rockola[10] and to so many places, and the city was ours, and astride the motorbike our mother presented us with on our twentieth birthday, we sang at the top of our voices that song about *Coca Cola for everyone and a bite to eat,*[11] and *today I can't get up,*[12] and that true declaration of the principles of the joy of living which was *I can't do any more and I want to get out of here quick, I want to live with my friends, go for some drinks and go to bed late, ride a motorbike, ride through the streets and feel free,*[13] and I devoured books, because I longed to write that book that would contain everything, and I was crazy about Lola, my first sister-in-law – I'm afraid I've always had a bit of a masochistic tendency; and I suppose she realized that, but didn't mind, Castor and Pollux[14] she used to call us in jest, and she invited us to the most exotic restaurants, she gave us records as a gift, and she listened to our secrets without ever getting exasperated. I don't even know what has become of Lola after Ernesto left her high and dry, perhaps she doesn't even live in Madrid any longer and has gone back to her native Ibiza... In those days Adrián did not fall in love; later he did really fall in love, head over heels, and I don't know what happened overnight, he never told me, and

---

9   Mecano had three members: two brothers, José and Nacho Cano, who both composed the group's songs, and the female singer Ana Torroja who, later on, once the group had dissolved, was to follow a solo career as a singer. With a very distinctive voice, she represented a different, fresher and more personal image of a group lead singer in those days.

10   **Rockola**: name of an extremely popular club in Madrid during the *movida* years in the early 1980s.

11   Lines from the Mecano song *Me colé en una fiesta* [*I sneaked into a party*]. The song is a good example of the male-oriented lyrics produced by the Cano brothers and sung by Ana Torroja as it gives voice to a boy that sneaks into a party and wants to attract the attention of a girl.

12   Another title of a popular Mecano song, *Hoy no me puedo levantar.*

13   Some lines from the Mecano song *Me voy de casa* [*I'm leaving home*].

14   **Castor and Polux**: Twin brothers in Greek and Roman mythology, known as Polydeuces to the Greeks. The twins were worshiped as gods who helped shipwrecked sailors and who brought favorable winds for those who made sacrifices to them. The Romans considered Castor and Pollux the patron gods of horses and of the Roman social order of mounted knights. http://www.mythencyclopedia.com/Ca-Cr/Castor-and-Pollux.html#ixzz4apYVIY4a

me lo contó, de la noche a la mañana, y al cabo de una fuerte depresión, se distanció de mí y desapareció por completo. Tras una larga búsqueda logré encontrarlo en una pensión barata de Atocha, cuya patrona había tirado sus cosas a la calle por escándalos e impago, y amenazaba con llamar a la policía. Se había enganchado muy deprisa a la heroína, se había entregado al caballo como quien se entrega a fondo a una causa perdida y al suicidio, y me miraba y pretendía no conocerme, y se negaba a dejar los picos, y yo me dejaba insultar y robar y agredir, a sabiendas de que no era culpa suya; y de nuevo volví a seguirlo, pero en esta ocasión hacia una infinita noche sin sol. Todo lo intenté, pero fue en vano, porque, lo vi de inmediato en la clara y nueva oscuridad de sus ojos, se estaba negando a la vida, y ansiaba el naufragio cual el capitán enloquecido de un buque fantasma de un cuento que alguna vez quizá Poe llegase a imaginar.

'Buena vida perra me habéis dado todos', vuelve a decir mi padre, 'tú, Ernesto, con tus tonterías políticas y tus detenciones en los setenta, aunque ahora, todo hay que reconocerlo, hayas sentado cabeza y mi ex mujer poniéndome los cuernos casi desde el primer año de matrimonio, y tú, Miguel, mucha carrera y muchos aires de artista, pero sin oficio ni beneficio, tú apareciéndome un día maldito con el cuento de que tu hermano la está palmando, y encima de SIDA, que tengo que andarle con mentiras a todos mis conocidos. Qué vergüenza, Dios Santo...'. Lo miro, a través de los cristales oscuros, y por primera vez siento en mi interior una oleada de compasión hacia el adusto general que en la infancia nos infundía un pavor y un respeto absolutos. Es un anciano con bolsas bajo los ojos y hombros encorvados, que de repente, al ver entrar a la enfermera, se echa a llorar sin pudor alguno, y grita '¡mi hijo, Dios mío, mi hijo!' Y entonces descubro que lo quiero, aunque lo siga odiando y anhelo abrazarlo, pero no lo hago, porque no corro, vuelo hacia esa UVI, empujando en mi carrera a los ATS. Y me lanzo a la cabecera de esa cama, chillo: '¡no toquen sus ojos, fuera de aquí!', y toco su cráneo pelado, pero en verdad estoy tocando su pelo rubio de otro tiempo, ése que amaban las chicas que lo telefoneaban y se citaban con él en las terrazas de Rosales, y reían sus ocurrencias porque nadie, nadie en este mundo jodido ha tenido nunca tanta gracia como él a sus dieciocho, diecinueve, veinte años. Antes de que empezase lo malo. En verdad estoy tocando al muchacho que se examinaba por mí de matemáticas –y yo por él de lengua y literatura– al que no *quería que le enseñasen la*

after a heavy depression, he grew away from me and disappeared completely. After a long search, I managed to find him in a cheap guest house in Atocha district,[15] whose landlady had thrown his effects into the street owing to bad behaviour and failure to pay, and was threatening to call the police. He had very quickly become hooked on heroin, he had surrendered himself to horse like someone who completely gives himself up to a lost cause and suicide, and he looked at me and claimed not to know me, and he refused to give up the heroin shots, and I let myself be insulted, robbed and attacked, in the knowledge that it wasn't his fault; and once again I began to follow him, but this time towards an unending night without sunlight. I tried everything, but it was in vain because, I saw it immediately in the clear, new darkness in his eyes, he was in denial of life, and longed for shipwreck like the mad captain of a ghost ship in a tale that Poe might have once thought up.

'Some shitty life you've all given me', my father says again, 'you, Ernesto, with your political nonsense and arrests in the seventies, but I've got to admit it, you've got your head together now, and my ex-wife cuckolding me almost from the first year of marriage, and you, Miguel, a load of studies and artistic airs and graces, but without work or gain, then appearing one cursed day telling the story about your brother kicking the bucket and with AIDS into the bargain, so that I have to go around telling lies to all the people I know. My God, what a shame...' I look at him through my dark lenses, and for the first time I feel a wave of compassion for the stern General who, when we were children, instilled in us absolute fear and respect. He's an old man with bags under his eyes and drooping shoulders, who on seeing the nurse come in suddenly bursts out crying without any restraint, and shouts out: 'my son, my God, my son!' And then I discover that I love him, although I still hate him and I long to hug him, but don't because I don't run but fly to the intensive care unit, pushing the nurses out of my way as I run. And I hurl myself at the headboard of his bed, screaming: 'don't touch his eyes, get out of here!', and I touch his shaved head, but I am really touching his former blond hair, that hair that was loved by the girls who used to phone him and arrange a date with him in the outside bars on Rosales, and laughed at his witty remarks because nobody, nobody in this fucked-up world has ever been as witty as he was when he was eighteen, nineteen, twenty. Before the bad things started. In truth I am touching the boy who took my mathematics exam for me – and I took his language and literature exam –

---

15 **Atocha**: District in central Madrid.

lección porque sabía que hay que dejarse siempre algo por aprender, al que amaba a la vida como la vida no iba, no sé por qué, más tarde a amarlo a él. Lo llamo, y rozo sus pómulos descarnados, y miro el verde estancado de sus ojos, y por mi mente desfilan a toda velocidad esas canciones de nuestras vidas, las que acuñaron las horas luminosas de nuestra primerísima juventud y de nuestra generación, Ernesto no sabe nada, es mentira que hayamos sido 'una generación perdida', buscábamos algo mejor, pero no sabíamos el qué, ni dónde se ocultaba siquiera el lugar de los sueños, aquél donde compartiríamos el vino no turbio de la amistad y la dicha de los cuerpos sin mácula y a la espera del porvenir donde llegar a ser adultos, pero no miserables. Lo abrazo, acuno ese esqueleto que fue mi hermano y la mitad de mi alma, le susurro las letras inolvidables que bailábamos encantados hasta la llegada de la siguiente luna, o del sol donde arder pletóricos, le recito los poemas que yo escribí para regalárselos y que él se los susurrase al oído de las chicas que le iban gustando (*impagable el detalle intelectual, muchas gracias*, me decía, *cómo descubriste lo mucho que se liga con las palabras, a ellas les enloquecen los sensibles, te lo dice un duro como yo*), le recuerdo las noches en vela de las temporadas de exámenes, cuando de repente dejábamos de estudiar y voceábamos, muertos de risa, *perdido en mi habitación/ sin saber qué hacer, no, no quites nunca esa canción/ no seas antiguo y déjate llevar*, hasta que mi padre aporreaba las paredes, y nos mandaba callar con '¡dejad dormir al mundo y poneos a las asignaturas, que si cargáis os juro que os mando a la fuerza a una academia de cadetes donde os hagan hombres a toque de corneta!'

Le recuerdo lo más hermoso, le digo 'mamá llegará enseguida', le ruego que no tenga miedo, pero ahora ya sólo podré tenerlo yo, que cierro sus párpados, y prometo escribir para él, solo para él, ese libro único que lo contiene todo y nunca se cierra, porque en sus páginas se extienden y acumulan el amor, y el placer y el tiempo de fortuna y el dolor y música de unas palabras que nos crean, nos salvaguardan y nos ayudan a vivir y a morir, a perder y a ganar, y a ganar, también, aquello que perdimos. Y le prometo, sí, *te lo prometo, Adrián, hermano, no despedirme nunca de*

the boy who *didn't want them to teach him the whole lesson*[16] because he knew that one should always leave something to learn, the boy who loved life as life, I don't know why, was later on not going to love him. I call him, and lightly stroke his emaciated cheeks, and I look at the stagnant greenness of his eyes, and through my mind goes a high speed parade of those songs in our lives, those that the luminous hours of our early youth and our generation coined, Ernesto knows nothing, it's a lie that we were 'a lost generation', we were in search of something better, but we didn't know what, not even where the place of dreams was hidden, that place where we would share the crystal wine of friendship and the happiness of unsullied bodies, waiting for the future in which we would become adults, but not bad people. I hug him, I cradle that skeleton that was my brother and half of my soul, I whisper to him the unforgettable words that we used to dance excitedly until the next moon came out, or the sun where we burned with unbridled happiness, I recite the poems that I wrote as a present for him and that I wished him to whisper into the ears of the girls that he liked at that moment in time (*I can't repay your gift, intellectual, many thanks*, he used to say to me, *how you've discovered how much one can pull with words, the sensitive men drive them mad, a hard man like me is telling you that*), I remind him of burning the midnight oil during exam time, when we would suddenly stop studying and, killing ourselves laughing, gave voice to: *lost in my bedroom / without knowing what to do, don't ever take that song off / don't be a square and let yourself go*[17] until my father banged on the wall with a stick and told us to be quiet: 'let people sleep and get studying, for if you fail your exams I swear I'll forcibly put you in a military academy where they will make men of you to the sound of the bugle!'

I remind him of what is more beautiful, I say to him 'mum will be here right now', I ask him not to be afraid, but now only I can be afraid any longer, I who close his eyelids, and promise to write for him, only him, that unique book that will contain everything and will never close, because love, pleasure, happy and painful times, and the music of words that fashion us, save us and help us to live and die, to win and lose, and to win also what we lost, stretch throughout and build up in those pages. And I promise him, yes, *I promise you, Adrián, my brother, never to take my leave of you,*

---

16 Another intertextual reference to a Mecano song: *No me enseñen la lección* [*Don't teach me a lesson*].

17 Some verses from the Mecano song entitled *Perdido en mi habitación* [*Lost in my bedroom*].

ti, que eres ya para siempre en mi memoria aire volador. *He decidido* ser consecuente con mi nueva dimensión, sin entrar en pormenores, *sabré, por ti*, hacer cosas mejores, *me convertiré en huracán, porque también para mí, ahora*, este cuarto es muy pequeño para las cosas que sueño. Las que voy a escribirte, a regalarte, a ti que fuiste y serás siempre el más hermoso *aire volador* que ha soplado en mi vida, esa vida que nos ha dado tanto, tanto, todo. En nuestras vidas, como en tu cinta favorita de entonces, Adrián, hermano, YA VIENE EL SOL.

for you will forever be in my memory a whisper of air.[18] *I have taken the decision* to act upon my new dimension without going into details, *thanks to you I'll be able to*, do better things, *I'll become a hurricane*,[19] *because for me* this room *is now* very small for the things that I am dreaming. The things that I am going to write to you, to present to you, to you who were and will always be the most *beautiful whisper of air*[20] that ever blew into my life, that life that has given us so much,[21] so much, everything. Into our lives, as into his favourite album of then, Adrián, my brother, THE SUN IS RISING.[22]

---

18   Another intertextual allusion to the Mecano song *Aire*.
19   *Aire* includes this line: 'me convertí en huracán' ['I became a hurricane']
20   See note 1.
21   This sentence has a striking resemblance to the folk Chilean singer-songwriter Violeta Parra's song *Gracias a la vida* [*Thanks to life*]. Amongst others, the Chilean singer-songwriter and politic activist Víctor Jara popularised the song in the late 1960s and early 1970s. He was assassinated by the Chilean dictator General Allende shortly after his coup d'etat in 1973.
22   Another title of a Mecano song: *Ya viene el sol*.

LOS MAYORALES EXHAUSTOS

THE EXHAUSTED FARMERS

Original Spanish text from *Cuentos de amigas*,
edited by Laura Freixas (Barcelona: Anagrama, 2009, 163–79)
©Paloma Díaz-Mas, 2009

PALOMA DÍAZ-MAS was born in Madrid in 1954. She graduated in Romance Philology and Journalism from the Universidad Complutense, in Madrid. After spending six years as a researcher on Sephardic Language and Literature at the Spanish National Research Council, the CSIC (Consejo Superior de Investigaciones Científicas), she then taught Spanish Golden Age and Sephardic Literature at the Universidad del País Vasco, in Vitoria, for eighteen years. She is currently back at the CSIC, in Madrid, where she is a Research Professor at the Council's Instituto de Lengua, Literatura y Antropología. Her two short periods as a visiting scholar at the University of Oregon, Eugene (USA) in 1998 and in 1990, form the basis of her ironic yet empathetic observations on American life in *Una ciudad llamada Eugenio* (1992). Paloma Díaz-Mas's academic training as a medievalist has influenced her literary output. Her historical novels are fine examples of her knowledge of history, particularly literary history and history of art, combined with a contemporary perspective seen through the lens of an ironic postmodern discourse. Questions of gender, class, race and religious intolerance are represented not as a thing of the past but as relevant to our times, something seen in *El rapto del Santo Grial* (1984), *El sueño de Venecia* (1992) and *La tierra fértil* (1999). She has also written books of an autobiographical nature, such as *Como un libro cerrado* (2005), her reflections on growing up in Franco's Spain that can be related to the short story chosen for this present collection, 'Los mayorales exhaustos' ['The exhausted farmers']. In it, she fictionalizes her experiences as a schoolgirl. Her latest novel, *Lo que olvidamos* (2016), a moving approach to Alzheimer's and old age, is a deep reflection on the ravaging effects of the passing of time, and on how inextricably linked private and collective memories are. Paloma Díaz-Mas has won many prizes throughout her literary career (see bibliography below), and is widely regarded as one of the best and most original writers in contemporary Spain.

Bibliography of Paloma Díaz-Mas

Novels

El rapto del Santo Grial, o el Caballero de la Verde Oliva (Barcelona: Anagrama, 1984; 2014) – *Finalist of Premio Herralde 1983.*
Tras las huellas de Artorius (Cáceres: Institución Cultural El Brocense, 1985) – *Premio Cáceres 1984.*
El sueño de Venecia (Barcelona: Anagrama, 1992) – *Premio Herralde 1992.*
La tierra fértil (Barcelona: Anagrama, 1999) – *Premio Euskadi 2000.*
Lo que olvidamos (Barcelona: Anagrama, 2016).

Short stories collections

Biografías de genios, traidores, sabios y suicidas, según antiguos documentos (Madrid: Editora Nacional, 1973) – Published in 2014 as an E-book with the title *Ilustres desconocidos.*
Nuestro milenio (Barcelona: Anagrama, 1987) – *Finalist of Premio Nacional de Narrativa 1987.*

Short stories included in anthologies and journals (a selection)

'En busca de un retrato', *Nuevas Letras,* 8 (1988) – later included in A. Encinar and A. Percival (eds), *Cuento español contemporáneo* (Madrid: Cátedra, 1993; 2001).
'Me sé todos los cuentos', *Lucanor*, 1 (1988).
'La discreta pecadora, o ejemplo de doncellas recogidas', in L. Freixas (ed.), *Cuentos eróticos* (Barcelona: Grijalbo, 1988) – later included in C. Estévez (ed.) *Relatos eróticos* (Madrid: Castalia/ Instituto de la Mujer, 1990).
'Las sergas de Hroswith', in F. Valls (ed.), *Son cuentos. Antología del relato breve español, 1975–1993* (Madrid: Espasa Calpe, 1993).
'The Ressurection of the Young Squire' (trans. by Dinny Thorold), in J. A. Masoliver Ródenas (ed.), *The Origins of Desire* (London: Serpent's Tail, 1993).
'La fiesta pasa', in Á. Encinar (ed.), *Cuentos de este siglo: 30 narradoras españolas contemporáneas* (Barcelona: Lumen, 1995).
'La niña sin alas', in L. Freixas (ed.), *Madres e hijas* (Barcelona: Anagrama, 1996).
'La obra maestra', in M. Lunati (ed.), *Rainy Days: Short Stories by Contemporary Spanish Women Writers* (Warminster: Aris & Pillips, 1997) [1st edn].
'La infanta Ofelia', in J. Andrews and M. Lunati (eds), *Contemporary Spanish Short Stories: Viajeros perdidos* (London: Bristol Classical Press, 1998).
'El señor Link visita a un autor', in M. Monmany (ed.), *Vidas de mujer* (Madrid: Alianza, 1998).
'El señor Link visita a un autor', in J. M. Merino (ed.), *Cien años de cuentos (1898-1998). Antología del cuento español en castellano* (Madrid: Alfaguara, 1999).
'El señor Link visita a un autor', in R. Hernández Viveros (ed.), *Relato español*

actual (México, DF: Universidad Nacional Autónoma de México; Fondo de Cultura Económica, 2002).

'Toda la culpa', in I. Diéz Ménguez (ed.), *Antología de cuentistas madrileñas* (Madrid: Ediciones La Librería, 2006).

'La visita del Comendador', in F. Marías (ed.), *Don Juan* (Zaragoza: 451 Editores, 2008).

'Los mayorales exhaustos', in L. Freixas (ed.), *Cuentos de amigas* (Barcelona: Anagrama, 2009).

Autobiographical
Una ciudad llamada Eugenio (Barcelona: Anagrama, 1992).
Como un libro cerrado (Barcelona: Anagrama, 2005).
Lo que aprendemos de los gatos (Barcelona: Anagrama, 2014).

Scholarly books
Los sefardíes: Historia, lengua, cultura (Zaragoza: Riopiedras, 1986; 1993; 1997) – *Finalist of Premio Nacional de Ensayo* – translated into English by George K. Zucker, *Shefardim. The Jews in Spain* (Chicago: The University of Chicago Press, 1992; 2004).

Poesía oral sefardí (Ferrol: Sociedad de Cultura Valle-Inclán; Esquío, 1994). https://www.academia.edu/31425678/Poes%C3%ADa_oral_sefard%C3%AD

Alberto Hemsi. Cancionero sefardí [annotated edition, with Edwin Seroussi and other scholars] (Jerusalem: The Jewish Music Research Centre, the Hebrew University of Jerusalem, 1995).

Romancero (ed.) (Barcelona, Crítica, 1994; 1997; abridged edn in 2001; updated edn in 2005).

Romancero Sefardí de Marruecos. Antología de tradición oral, with Susana Weich-Shahak (Madrid: Editorial Alpuerto, 1997).

Sem Tob de Carrión, *Proverbios morales* [ed. with Carlos Mota] (Madrid: Cátedra, 1998).

Fronteras e interculturalidad entre los sefardíes occidentales [ed. with Harm den Boer] (Amsterdam: Rodopi, 2006).

Judaísmo and Islam [with Cristina de la Puente] (Barcelona: Crítica, 2007).

Los sefardíes ante los retos del mundo contemporáneo. Identidad y mentalidades [with María Sánchez Pérez] (Madrid: CSIC, 2010).

Los sefardíes y la poesía tradicional hispánica del siglo XVIII. El Cancionero de Abraham Israel (Gibraltar, 1761–1770) [ed. with María Sánchez Pérez] (Madrid: CSIC, 2013).

Cartas sefardíes de Salónica. La Korespondensya (1906) [ed. with Teresa Madrid Álvarez-Piñer] (Barcelona: Tirocinio, 2014).

La Celestina [annotated edn, with other scholars] (Madrid: Real Academia Española de la Lengua, 2016).

Mujeres sefardíes lectoras y escritoras, with Elisa Martín Ortega (eds), (Madrid: Iberoamerican; –Frankfurt, Iberoamericana– Frankfurt: Vervuert, 2016).
A comprehensive list of her scholarly articles can be found at http://cchs.csic.es/es/personal/paloma.diazmas

Reflections on her own work
'Los nombres de mis personajes', in M. Mayoral and G. Gullón (eds), *El oficio de narrar* (Madrid: Cátedra / Ministerio de Cultura, 1990),pp.107–20.
'Memoria y olvido en mi narrativa', in P. Collard (ed.), *La memoria histórica en las letras españolas* (Genève: Librairie Droz, SA, 1997), 87–97.
'Mi vida en media página', in A. Percival (ed.), *Escritores ante el espejo. Estudio de la creatividad literaria* (Barcelona: Lumen, 1997), 313–21.
'Lugares y objetos en la génesis de la novela histórica', *Ínsula* 641 (2000), 23–24.
'La construcción de una escritora', in C. Henseler (ed.), *En sus propias palabras: escritoras españolas ante el mercado literario* (Madrid: Torremozas, 2003), 17–34.
'Del ensayo histórico a la novela histórica', *Boletín Hispánico Helvético* 6 (2005), 111–24.
'Cómo se escribe una novela histórica (o dos)', in J. Jurado Morales (ed.), *Reflexiones sobre la novela histórica* (Cádiz: Servicio de Publicaciones de la Universidad de Cádiz, 2006), 37–49.

Play
La informante (Toledo: Ébora, 1983) – *Premio Teatro Breve Rojas Zorrilla.*

Further reading on Paloma Díaz-Mas
Guillermo Altares, 'Premios literarios' *El Urogallo*, 90 (1993), 62–64.
J. Ernesto Ayala-Dip, 'El contemporáneo siglo XIII', *El País* (Babelia), 13 November 1999.
Catherine Bellver, 'Humour and the Resistance to Meaning in *El rapto del Santo Grial* by Paloma Díaz-Mas', *Romance Review* 87.1 (1996), 145–55.
Jeffrey Benham Brunner 'Figurative Fiction: Verbal and Visual Intertextuality in Paloma Díaz-Mas's *El sueño de Venecia*', *Anales de la Literatura Española Contemporánea* 27.2 (2002), 63–79.
Nuria María Carrillo Martín, 'El camino de la escritura. Entrevista con Paloma Díaz-Mas', *La Nueva Literatura Hispánica* 2 (1999), 91–101.
Reyes Coll-Tellechea, 'España a examen: *El sueño de Venecia* y la memoria histórica en un calidoscopio picaresco', *Confluencia* 13.2 (1998), 61–67.
Rosalía Cornejo-Parriego, 'Entrevista a Paloma Díaz-Mas', *Letras Peninsulares* 10.2–3 (1998), 479–89.
María Dolores de Asís Garrote, *Última hora de la novela en España* (Madrid: Pirámide, 1996).

María Luz Diéguez, 'Entrevista con Paloma Díaz-Mas', *Revista de Estudios Hispánicos* 22.1 (1988), 77–91.

Judith Drinkwater and John Macklin (1998) 'Keeping it in the Family: Secret Histories in Paloma Díaz-Mas's *El sueño de Venecia*', *Bulletin of Hispanic Studies* 75 (1998), 317–29.

Carmen Estévez, 'Introducción', in C. Estévez (ed.), *Relatos eróticos escritos por mujeres* (Madrid: Castalia, 1990), 7–26.

Iñaki Ezkerra, 'Paloma Díaz-Mas o las lecciones de delicadeza', *El Correo Español* (Territorios), 6 September 2014.

Ofelia Ferrán, 'La escritura y la historia: Entrevista con Paloma Díaz-Mas', *Anales de la Literatura Española Contemporánea* 22.1–2 (1997), 327–45. https://www.jstor.org/stable/27741363?seq=1#fndtn-page_scan_tab_contents

Jessica A. Folkart, 'El arte apropiado: Construcciones artísticas de la identidad española en *El sueño de Venecia* de Paloma Díaz-Mas', *Symposium* 58.2 (2004), 93–107.

Pablo Gil Casado, *La novela deshumanizada española (1958–1988)* (Barcelona: Anthropos, 1990).

Kathleen M. Glenn, 'Reading and Rewriting *El sueño de Venecia*', *Romance Languages Annual* 7 (1995), 483–90.

Kathleen M. Glenn, 'Reading Postmodernism in the Fiction of Cristina Fernández Cubas, Paloma Díaz-Mas and Marina Mayoral', *South Central Review, The Journal of the South Central Modern Language Association* 18.1/2 (2001), 78–93.

Miguel González San Martín, 'Ironías de la historia', *Margen Cultural* 8 (1993), 13–16.

Linda Gould Levine, 'The Female Body as Palimpsest in the Works of Carmen Gómez-Ojea, Paloma Díaz-Mas, Ana Rosetti', *Indiana Journal of Hispanic Literatures* 2.1 (1993), 181–206.

Germán Gullón, 'La novela histórica: ficción para convivir', *Ínsula* 641 (2000), 3–5.

Christine Henseler, 'The Sixth Chapter of *El sueño de Venecia*: Vision and Truth in Paloma Díaz-Mas', *Revista Hispánica Moderna* 52 (1999), 180–92.

Christine Henseler, 'Vision over Truth: *El sueño de Venecia* by Paloma Díaz-Mas', in *Contemporary Spanish Women's Narrative and the Publishing Industry* (Urbana and Chicago: University of Illinois, 2003), 21–41.

Juana Amelia Hernández, 'La postmodernidad en la ficción de Paloma Díaz-Mas', *Romance Languages Annual* 2 (1990), 450–54.

M. Eugenia Ibáñez, 'Paloma Díaz-Mas desmitifica la gènesi d'un escriptor', *El Periòdic*, 2 February 2005.

Heather Jerónimo, 'Angels or Monsters? Motherhood in the Dystopian World of Paloma Díaz-Mas's "La niña sin alas"', *Letras Femeninas* 41.2 (2015). http://firstmonday.org/ojs/index.php/lf/article/view/6717

Juan Ángel Juristo, 'La memoria es un relato', *La Vanguardia* (Culturas), 24 December 2016.

'María del Mar Mañas, 'Paloma Díaz-Mas: Tras las huellas de Petrocio Carpoaletti', *Dicenda. Cuadernos de Filología Hispánica* 16 (1998), 133–44.

Guadalupe Martí-Peña,'Los avatares de un cuadro: arte y literatura en *El sueño de Venecia* de Paloma Díaz-Mas y *El Velázquez de París* de Carmen Boullosa', *Extravío. Revista electrónica de literatura comparada* 3 (2008). <htttp://www.uv.es/extravio>

Salustiano Martín, '*El sueño de Venecia*. La verdad, el error y la memoria histórica', *Reseña* 237 (1993), 28.

Juan Antonio Masoliver Ródenas, 'Dueños del presente. Para los amantes de los gatos y para conversos', *La Vanguardia* (Culturas), 3 September 2014. https://www.pressreader.com/spain/la-vanguardia-culturas/20140903/281629598456458

Mercedes Mazquiarán de Rodríguez, 'Parody and the Truth of History in Paloma Díaz-Mas' *El sueño de Venecia*', *Letras Peninsulares* 8.1 (1995), 7–25.

Rafael M. Mérida-Jiménez, 'El medievalismo fértil de Paloma Díaz-Mas', *Lectora, Revista de dones i textualitat* 7 (2001), 127–34. https://www.researchgate.net/publication/277205802_El_medievalismo_fertil_de_Paloma_Diaz-Mas

Eunice Myers, 'The Quixerotic Quest: Paloma Díaz-Mas's "La discreta pecadora, o ejemplo de doncellas recogidas"', *Monographic Review / Revista Monográfica* 7 (1991), 146–55.

Gonzalo Navajas, 'Narrativa y género. La ficción actual desde la mujer', *Ínsula* 589–90 (1996), 37–39.

María José Obiol, 'El juego de la similitudes y las diferencias. Madurez en el oficio de contar', *El País* (Libros), 28 July 1985.

Elizabeth J. Ordóñez, 'Parody and Defiance. Subversive Challenges in the Texts of Díaz-Mas and Gómez Ojea', in *Voices of Their Own. Contemporary Spanish Narrative by Women* (Lewisburgh: Bucknell University Press, 1991), 150–73.

Janet Pérez, 'Characteristics of Erotic Brief Fiction by Women in Spain', *Monographic Review / Revista Monográfica* 7 (1991), 173–95.

Janet Pérez, 'Contemporary Spanish Women Writers and the Feminized Quest-Romance', *Monographic Review / Revista Monográfica* 8 (1992), 36–49.

Peregrina Pereiro, 'Maniobras discursivas y recreación histórica: *El sueño de Venecia* de Paloma Díaz-Mas', in *La novela española de los noventa: alternativas éticas a la postmodernidad* (Madrid: Pliegos, 2002), 23–47.

María A. Rey López, '*El sueño de Venecia* de Paloma Díaz-Mas: Reflexiones sobre la historiografía', *Letras Femeninas* 26.1–2 (2000), 185–92.

Domingo Ródenas de Moya, 'Somos lo que no recordamos', *El Periódico de Catalunya*, 2 November 2016. http://www.elperiodico.com/es/noticias/ocio-y-cultura/que-olvidamos-critica-paloma-diaz-mas-5601611

Neus Samblancat Miranda, '*El sueño de Venecia* o el guiño de los clásicos', *Lectora, Revista de dones i textualitat* 1 (1995), 105–10.

Santos Sanz Villanueva, 'Lo que olvidamos', *El Mundo* (El Cultural), 28 October 2016. http://www.elcultural.com/revista/letras/Lo-que-olvidamos/38718

María Elena Soliño, 'Revealing Beauty/ Revealing History in *El sueño de Venecia*', *Hispanic Review* 76.4 (2008), 335–59. http://www.jstor.org/stable/27668859

Adolfo Sotelo Vázquez, 'Fragmentos de memoria sin impostura', *La Vanguardia* (Culturas), 6 April 2005.

Robert C. Spires, '*El sueño de Venecia* and the Information Age: Deceiving Facts and Validating Fictions', *Revista Hispánica Moderna* 56.2 (2003), 387–97.

Nadal Suau, '*Lo que aprendemos de los gatos*. Paloma Díaz Mas', *El Cultural*, 5 September 2014. http://www.elcultural.com/revista/letras/Lo-que-aprendemos-de-los-gatos/35081

Ignacio Vidal-Folch, 'Introducción', in Paloma Díaz-Mas, *El rapto del Santo Grial. Nuestro milenio* (Barcelona: Anagrama, 1993), 7–13.

Carlos Zanón.'No olvides recordar', *El País* (Babelia), 17 October 2016. http://cultura.elpais.com/cultura/2016/10/13/babelia/1476359965_028768.html

Phyllis Zatlin, 'Women Novelists in Democratic Spain: Freedom to Express the Female Perspective', *Anales de la Literatura Española Contemporánea* 12 (1987), 29–44.

Fuencisla Zomeño, 'Feminism and Postmodernism in Paloma Díaz-Mas's "The World According to Valdés" and "In Search of a Portrait"', *Studies in 20th Century Literature* 26.2 (2002), Article 9. http://dx.doi.org/10.4148/2334-4415.1540

Further online information on Paloma Díaz-Mas (a selection)

http://escritoras.com/escritoras/Paloma-Diaz-Mas

http://cchs.csic.es/en/personal/paloma.diazmas

http://press.uchicago.edu/ucp/books/book/chicago/S/bo3641761.html

http://catalogo.artium.org/book/export/html/304

https://www.um.es/tonosdigital/znum18/secciones/perfiles-2-paloma.htm

http://www.elperiodico.com/es/noticias/ocio-y-cultura/paloma-diaz-mas-publica-que-aprendemos-los-gatos-3554773

http://www.subverso.es/?p=3545

http://sefardiweb.com/

http://www.march.es/conferencias/anteriores/voz.aspx?p1=242

http://www.lavanguardia.com/vida/20161017/411072477268/paloma-diaz-mas-explora-los-extremos-de-la-memoria-personal-y-colectiva-en-lo-que-olvidamos.html

http://revistas.ucm.es/index.php/DICE/article/viewFile/DICE9898110125A/12742

LOS MAYORALES EXHAUSTOS

Habíamos subido trabajosamente las escaleras empinadas –era un tercer piso sin ascensor– hasta detenernos en un descansillo tenebroso, ante una puerta pintada al aceite de marrón oscuro. Mamá tenía la respiración algo agitada por el esfuerzo y yo me había dado un golpe en la espinilla con el filo de uno de los escalones, demasiado altos para mí. Por la escalera, nos precedían y nos seguían niñas de distintas edades, algunas como yo y otras que me parecieron muy mayores; todas llevábamos el mismo uniforme, azul marino con falda tableada y cuello blanco, un cuello de plástico duro que parecía un collarín y se sujetaba con botoncitos al uniforme. Sólo que mi uniforme era nuevo y tenía aún la rigidez un punto áspera del apresto de las telas sin estrenar.

Se abrió la puerta y las niñas entraron deprisa, pero ordenadamente, como dicen que se debe hacer la evacuación de los incendios. Según entraban, iban dando los buenos días a una señora gordita, que esperaba junto a la puerta abierta. Eran como unas veinte niñas, pero tardaron muy poco en pasar. Luego mamá y la señora intercambiaron algunas palabras a las que no atendí, porque yo estaba demasiado ocupada siguiendo la trayectoria de las niñas desde el vestíbulo oscuro hacia una habitación cuyo interior no se veía, pero por cuya puerta entreabierta entraba a raudales la luz del sol.

Entonces mamá hizo algo que yo no había previsto: me besó en la frente, dio media vuelta y se perdió escaleras abajo, dejándome sola por primera vez. Tuve un momento de desconsuelo: ya sabía que venía al colegio, pero no se me había ocurrido pensar que eso significaba que mi madre me dejaría allí y se marcharía para volver dentro de mucho, mucho tiempo, quizás para no volver jamás.

La señora se inclinó hasta mi altura. Olía a una mezcla de ropa lavada con jabón Lagarto –un jabón de olor cáustico y picante, que mamá usaba para hacer la colada de las sábanas y las toallas– e interior de iglesia. En aquel tiempo las iglesias olían de una manera especial, a una mixtura de óleos perfumados, cera de velas y aroma de las flores que se marchitaban ante los altares de las Vírgenes, y bastaba pasar por delante de la puerta de una iglesia cualquiera para sentirse impregnado de aquel olor balsámico, relajante y un poco aceitoso, que salía en una bocanada del interior del templo

THE EXHAUSTED FARMERS

We had laboured up the steep steps – it was on the third floor with no lift access – until we came to a dark landing, facing a door painted in a heavy, dark chestnut gloss. Mum was rather short of breath owing to her exertions and I had struck one of my shinbones on the edge of the steps that were too high for me. Young girls of various ages went before and came after us the whole length of the stairway: some were like me and others seemed to me much older; we were all wearing the same marine blue uniform, with a pleated skirt and a hard plastic white collar which looked like a collar and was attached to the uniform with little buttons. The drawback was that my uniform was new and still had the rather rough stiffness from the starch in clothes worn for the first time.

The door opened and the girls came in quickly in orderly fashion, as they say one should carry out a fire evacuation. As they were entering, they each said good morning to a plumpish lady standing by the door. There were about twenty of them but they took no time at all to come in. Then Mum and the lady exchanged some words that I did not pay attention to, because I was too busy watching the passage of the girls from the dark entrance to a room whose interior you could not see but through whose half-open door you could see the bright sunshine rushing in.

Then Mum did something unexpected: she kissed me on the forehead, turned round and disappeared downstairs, leaving me alone for the first time. I was disconsolate for a moment: I already knew that I was going to school but it had not struck me that that meant that my mother would leave me there, and go away for a long, long time, perhaps never to return.

The lady bent down to my height. She smelled of a mixture of Lagarto soap[1] – a soap with a caustic and irritating smell, which Mum used to soak the sheets and towels in – and the inside of a church. In those days churches had a special smell, a mixture of scented oils, wax candles and the aroma of flowers wilting before the side altars of lady chapels, and it was enough to pass the door of any church to feel impregnated with that rather oily and soporific balsamic smell, that wafted out of the church into the street. The

---

1   **Lagarto soap**: Spanish soap from the 1914, currently marketed as an environmentally safe product. Effective and cheap, it remained very popular in Spanish households until powders and gels replaced it as the main washing product. www.lagarto.es

hacia la calle. Así olía la señora: como si se hubiera metido en una iglesia con la ropa recién lavada y tendida al sol. Luego supe que así era, en efecto.

Me saludó con una frase adornada de diminutivos como puntillas:

—Buenos días, Carmencita. Soy la señora Rosita.

Me cogió de la mano —la suya era carnosa y cálida, una mano maternal que me confortó en mi infortunio de haber sido abandonada— y me acercó suavemente a la pared del vestíbulo frontera a la puerta. Señaló la pared:

—¿Sabes quién es esa señora?

La señora aludida estaba pintada en un cuadro, colgado con una alcayata muy visible. Vestía de blanco desde la cabeza, cubierta con un velo, hasta los pies descalzos, y de sus manos salían haces de rayos de oro, que iban a dar directamente sobre la cabeza de unos hombres y mujeres arrodillados, que portaban en las manos cadenas rotas.

—La Virgen— contesté yo, porque ya había visto otras veces la misma señora más o menos representada igual, vestida de largo y sin zapatos ni calcetines, aunque no siempre hubiese a sus pies hombres y mujeres con cadenas.

—María, Nuestra Señora, Redentora de Cautivos. Por eso este colegio se llama María Redentora. Tienes que querer mucho a María, porque es nuestra madre. Y ¿sabes quién es este señor?

En la misma pared que María Redentora, separado de ella por un crucifijo, colgaba una foto enmarcada con cristal. Frontero a la pared había un perchero de estilo renacimiento español, de madera casi negra, lleno de medallones con cabezas de guerreros y animales fantásticos, y el perchero se reflejaba en el cristal de la fotografía. Pero aún así, parcialmente eclipsado por el reflejo de una percha de sombrero y de una cabeza de centurión romano, distinguí un rostro conocido.

—Es Franco— dije sin dudar.

—Su Excelencia el Generalísimo, Francisco Franco, Caudillo de España por la gracia de Dios. Tienes que querer mucho al Generalísimo, porque él es como un padre para todos los españoles.

Y así, de la mano y emparentadas por una súbita hermandad —las dos hijas de María, que era nuestra madre, y casi hijas del Generalísimo, que era como un padre para todos los españoles—, nos dirigimos a clase.

lady smelled like that, as if she had gone into a church wearing clothes that had recently been washed and hung out to dry in the sun. Later I learned that that was in effect the case.

She greeted me with words embroidered with diminutives like lace:

'Good morning, Carmencita. I am Miss Rosita.'

She took my hand – hers was fleshy and warm, a maternal hand that comforted me in my misfortune of having been abandoned – and led me gently to the entrance hall in front of the classroom door. She pointed to the door:

'Do you know who that lady is?'

The lady she referred to was in a painting hanging from a very visible hook. She was covered from top to toe in white, barefoot and wearing a veil, and from her hands shot shafts of golden light which went straight to the heads of kneeling men and women, carrying broken chains in their arms.

'The Virgin Mary', I answered, because I had already seen the same lady on other occasions in more or less the same pose, wearing long robes and without shoes or stockings, although there were not always men and women in chains at her feet.

'Our Lady, Mary, Redeemer of Captives. So, this school is called Mary the Redeemer. You must love Mary a lot because she is our mother. And do you know who that man is?'

Hanging on the same wall as Mary the Redeemer and separated from her by a crucifix, there was a photo in a glass frame. Facing the wall there was an almost-black wooden hat stand in Spanish renaissance style, covered in medallions of warrior heads and fantastic animals, and the hat stand was reflected in the glass of the photo. But despite being partially obscured by the reflection from a coat stand and the head of a Roman centurion, I made out a face I knew.

'It's Franco', I said without hesitation.

'His Excellency the *Generalísimo*, Francisco Franco, Leader of Spain by the grace of God. You must love the *Generalísimo* a lot, because he is like a father to all Spaniards.'[2]

And so, hand-in-hand and suddenly linked together in sisterhood, we two children of Mary, for she was our mother, and quasi daughters of Franco, for he was like a father to all Spaniards, went into class.

---

2 Doña Rosita's beliefs encapsulate the spirit of the so-called *Nacionalcatolicismo* (State and official Catholic Church brought together during Franco's dictatorship), which is represented by the symbols on her school's wall, common at the time in every classroom across the country. The story, however, presents the bright side of such a character: she is an inspiring teacher and awakes in her pupils a thirst for knowledge.

En el aula había cuatro mesas grandes, rectangulares, en torno a las cuales se sentaban en sillitas niñas de todas las edades, desde los cuatro o cinco años (la edad que yo tenía) hasta los nueve o diez, el curso de preparación para el ingreso en el bachillerato. Doña Rosita me colocó de pie junto a la mesa de las más pequeñas y me preguntó si sabía persignarme; le dije que sí, y eso pareció alegrarle mucho.

—A ver, haz la señal de la cruz.

Yo hice las dos señales de la cruz, la grande y la pequeña, es decir, la que iba desde la frente hasta el pecho y luego al hombro izquierdo y al derecho, para acabar cruzando el índice y el pulgar en una pequeña cruz que se ponía al final sobre la boca para besarla; y la otra, la que consistía en dibujar pequeñas cruces sobre el cuerpo: la primera, en la frente; la segunda, en la boca; la tercera, en el pecho. Mamá me lo había enseñado noche a noche, cuando, en la cama, rezaba antes de dormir. Se llamaba signarse y persignarse.

—Muy bien, ahora rezaremos juntas el padrenuestro.

Las niñas se pusieron en pie como movidas por un resorte, todas a la vez, y empezaron a trazar cruces sobre frente, boca y pecho. Algunas cruces me parecieron francamente chapuceras. Yo sabía que lo había hecho mucho mejor, y eso me llenó de orgullo; sin querer, había descubierto la competitividad profesional.

Tras la oración, las niñas se sentaron, y abrieron sus tareas. Como Doña Rosita era la única maestra de una veintena de niñas de diferentes edades y niveles, iba de una mesa a otra mandando tareas a una de las alumnas, corrigiendo las de otra, repasando la lectura de aquélla o haciendo leer en voz alta a otra más. A mí me dijo:

—Por ser el primer día de clase para ti, abre el cuaderno y dibuja lo que quieras. Cuando acabes, me lo enseñas.

Me dejó utilizar una caja de lápices de colores preciosos, que tenía lo menos cincuenta colores distintos, y en la que los azules y los verdes iban degradándose en una sinfonía de tonos y matices, y el rojo se decantaba desde un tono de sangre seca que parecía casi marrón hasta el rosa pálido, pasando por el color de la sangre, del tomate, de las fresas o de las rosas encarnadas; había amarillo limón y amarillo cadmio y amarillo pollito, y hasta un lápiz blanco que yo no supe para qué utilizar sobre el papel también blanco. Aunque yo no lo sabía entonces, el permiso para utilizar la caja 'grande' de lápices era un honor y un privilegio en aquella escuela, algo que se daba como premio muy especial, así que aquel gesto venía a equivaler a

There were four big rectangular tables in the classroom around which girls of all ages were sitting on little chairs; they went from four or five, the same age as me, up to nine or ten, the preparatory year for secondary school. Doña Rosita made me stand next to the table where the smallest were and asked me if I knew how to make the sign of the cross; I told her I did, and that seemed to cheer her up a lot.

'Let's see, make the sign of the cross.'

I performed the two signs of the cross, the big one and the little one, that is, the one that goes from the forehead to the breast and then the left and right shoulders, ending with making a cross from your index finger and thumb which you then kissed; and the shorter one, which consisted in making little signs of the cross on your forehead, your mouth, your breast. Mum had taught me that night after night, when I was praying in bed before going off to sleep. It was called making big and little signs of the cross.

'Very good, now we will all say together the Lord's Prayer.'

The girls all stood up together at the same time as though released by a spring, and began to make the sign of the cross on foreheads, lips and breasts. Some signs of the cross seemed to be downright botched. I knew that I had done it much better, which filled me with pride; without trying I had discovered professional competitiveness.

After the prayer, the girls sat down and opened their work tasks. As Doña Rosita was the only teacher for about twenty girls of varying ages and levels, she went from table to table telling one girl to do this, correcting the work of another, checking the reading of someone else or getting another to read out loud. To me she said:

'Since it's your first day in school, open your exercise book and draw anything you like. Show it to me when you've finished.'

She let me use a box of lovely colour pencils, which had about fifty different colours, in which the shades of blue and green became a symphony of shades and tones, and the reds went from a blood red tone which looked almost chestnut to a pale pink, taking in blood, tomato and strawberry red, or crimson red rose; there was lemon, cadmium and chicken yellow, and even a white pencil, which I was at a loss to know how to use on the paper which was white too. Although I did not know it then, permission to use the 'big' box of pencils was an honour and a privilege in that school, something which was allowed as a very special prize, so that gesture was equivalent

un regalo de bienvenida, como cuando los griegos antiguos, ante la llegada de un huésped, le obsequiaban con alguna de sus posesiones más preciadas.

Yo pinté una flor.

–Mira, Doña Rosita.

–Mire usted, Doña Rosita. Así lo tienes que decir– me corrigió con dulzura. Luego miró la flor–. Está muy bien, Carmencita, es una florecita muy bonita. Pero ¿no crees que le falta algo?

Examiné mi obra. Por más que miraba y remiraba, no acertaba a ver que faltase nada. Allí estaba la flor, con su corola (yo no sabía que se llamaba así) y su tallo (esa palabra sí la sabía), del cual salía una hoja. Incluso al pie de la flor crecían un par o tres de briznas de hierba.

Presidiendo la clase, sobre una peana adosada a la pared, había una imagen de bulto de la Virgen, Nuestra Señora, Redentora de Cautivos, y ante ella un búcaro con flores frescas. Doña Rosita tomó una flor (ahora sé que era una azucena) y me la mostró de forma que yo pudiese ver su interior.

Era la primera vez que yo miraba dentro de una flor y lo que vi me sorprendió. Hasta entonces me había quedado en la mera apariencia de las flores, en la tersura y la suavidad de sus pétalos. Pero nadie me había hecho notar que esa envoltura vistosa encerraba algo más: unos filamentos erectos y flexibles, en cuyo interior parecía latir la sangre, se elevaban en el interior de la flor; cada filamento sostenía en su extremo, delicadamente, algo que se asemejaba a un minúsculo grano de arroz. Doña Rosita me hizo pasar un dedo por uno de aquellos granos y en la yema quedó un polvo amarillento.

–Es el polen– me dijo doña Rosita. Y así aprendí yo una palabra nueva, y habría aprendido más si hubiera preguntado; pero de momento ya sabía lo que quería saber y tardé casi dos años en aprender los otros nombres importantes: corola, cáliz, estambres, pistilos.

–Ahora pinta otra flor.

Y yo pinté otra flor, ésta ya sí con su secreto interior al descubierto, exhibiendo impúdicamente unos órganos que yo entonces no sabía –no hubiera imaginado– que eran sexuales.

Desde entonces, todas las flores que dibujaba llevaban en su centro un pequeño surtidor de filamentos acabados en granos de arroz. Lo ponía incluso en las que llamábamos margaritas y que muchos años después supe que son en realidad una variedad de crisantemos *(Dendrathema grandiflora)*. Al principio los adultos se desconcertaban un poco al ver mis dibujos.

–¿Qué es esto? ¿Una araña?

to a welcoming gift as when the ancient Greeks welcomed a guest with one of their most valuable possessions.

I painted a flower.

'Look, Doña Rosita.'

'Please look, Doña Rosita. That's how you must address me', she corrected me kindly. Then she looked at the flower. 'It's very good, Carmencita, it's a very pretty little flower. But, don't you think there's something missing?'

I examined my work. However much I looked and looked again, I did not succeed in seeing anything that might be missing. There was the flower with its corolla (I didn't know that's what it was called) and its stalk (I did know that word) from which a leaf was growing. At the bottom of the flower one or two blades of grass were growing.

On a pedestal set into the wall there was an impressive statue of our Lady Redeemer of Captives presiding over the class, with a vase holding fresh flowers in front of it. Doña Rosita took a flower (now I know it was a lily) and showed it to me so that I could see the inside.

For the first time I was looking inside a flower and what I saw surprised me. Up until then I had stopped short at the appearance of flowers, in the smoothness and softness of their petals. But no one had drawn to my attention the fact that that showy exterior enveloped something more: erect and flexible filaments, inside which blood seemed to pulse, rose up in the interior of the flower; each filament delicately supported at its extremity something that looked like a minute grain of rice. Doña Rosita got me to pass my finger over one of those grains and a yellowish powder remained on my cuticle.

'That's the pollen', Doña Rosita said. And thus I learned a new word, and I would have learned more if I'd asked; but for the moment I already knew what I wanted to know and I took another two years to learn the other important names: corolla, calyx, stamens, pistils.

'Now paint another flower.'

And I painted another flower, this one definitely with its secret interior exposed, shamelessly exhibiting organs that I did not know then, nor could have imagined, were sexual.

Since then all the flowers that I drew had a little fountain of filaments topped with grains of rice in their center. I even put it in what we used to call daisies, which many years later I learned in fact were a type of chrysanthemum (*Dendrathema grandiflora*). At first the adults were a little disconcerted on seeing my drawings.

'What's that? A spider?'

–No, es el polen–contestaba yo, confundiendo el todo con la parte.

–Ah, qué bien, mira qué idea tiene, cómo se fija esta niña. Mira, mira, cómo ha pintado la flor, como una persona mayor– se decían unos a otros, y yo experimentaba por primera vez el orgullo de un hallazgo científico y la tentación de cualquier investigador: el llegar a creer que ha descubierto por sí mismo lo que en realidad ha aprendido de otros que sabían más.

Con el tiempo, los comentarios de los mayores –esos comentarios que los adultos hacen ante los niños, considerándolos, incomprensiblemente, sordos e incapaces de entender– me fueron enseñando que doña Rosita era lo que se llamaba una solterona. En una época en que el que una mujer se quedase soltera era algo peor que malo, algo ridículo y vergonzoso, doña Rosita se había quedado soltera, quizás por una elección inconsciente que ejerció de forma pasiva e indirecta, rechazando por pudor o por temor a varios pretendientes, como hicieron entonces tantas otras mujeres.

Era también una beata –eso decían los mayores, pensando que no les escuchábamos– que pasaba en la iglesia el tiempo que no estaba en la escuela. Besaba la mano de todos los curas, visitaba monjas y se comía los santos. No faltaba por la tarde al rosario ni a la novena y era camarera de la Virgen de la parroquia, un cargo que a mí me resultó siempre enigmático y que solo mucho más tarde supe que consistía en tener el privilegio de desnudar y revestir la imagen de la Virgen con la indumentaria y los ornamentos que le correspondiesen según el tiempo del año. Muy de mañana iba a la primera misa y llegaba a la escuela todavía con el velo puesto, impregnada de aquel aroma incensal de la parroquia que yo había detectado la primera vez.

Empezando el día con misa y comunión antes de su trabajo en la escuela, seguramente doña Rosita se sentía tocada por la Gracia divina. Pero no sé si se daba cuenta de que ella misma poseía, de forma permanente y sin posibilidad de perderla por ningún pequeño o gran pecado, otra gracia más divina todavía: la gracia de saber enseñar.

Empezó por enseñarme que 'Mi mamá me ama, mi mamá me mima, yo amo a mi mamá'. Primero a deletrearlo, luego a escribirlo trabajosamente a lápiz en el cuaderno de caligrafía. Pronto pasé de esa frase sencilla, llena de emes que parecían besos, a otras más complicadas. Y cuando un día pude escribir en la pizarra, sin faltas ni vacilaciones, una frase erizada de miedos ancestrales y de grupos consonánticos ('Los hombres primitivos, recluidos en las cavernas, temblaban de pavor ante el resplandor del relámpago y el

'No, it's the pollen', I would answer, confusing the whole with the part.

'Ah, right, look at her ideas, look how observant the little girl is. Look, look, how she has painted the flower, like an adult', they would say to one another, and I experienced for the first time the pride of making a scientific discovery and the temptation of any researcher: coming to believe that you have discovered something by yourself that you really learned from others who knew more.

As time passed, adult remarks – those remarks adults make in front of children, incomprehensibly considering them to be deaf and incapable of understanding – began to teach me that Doña Rosita was what was called a dyed-in-the-wool spinster. At a time when the fact that a woman might remain a spinster was something worse than bad, it was ridiculous and shameful, Doña Rosita had remained a spinster, perhaps by passively or indirectly exercising an unconscious choice, rejecting several suitors out of prudery or fear, as so many other women did then.

She was also an excessively pious woman – that is what the adults said, thinking that we were not listening to them – who spent her time in church when not in school. She kissed the hands of all priests, she visited nuns, and was devoted to the saints. She never failed to attend evening rosary or novenas, and she was a servant of the Virgin in the parish society, a post that always struck me as enigmatic and which I only learned much later earned one the privilege of taking off and putting on the appropriate clothes and jewels of the Virgin Mary according to the annual religious calendar. She went to the first Mass very early in the morning and arrived at school still wearing her mantilla, which was impregnated with that whiff of incense from the church that I had detected the first time.

By beginning the day by going to Mass and Communion before working in the school, Doña Rosita undoubtedly felt touched by the grace of God. But I don't know if she realized that, in a permanent way that no great or small sin could ever take away, she possessed an even more divine gift of grace: the ability to teach.

She began by teaching me that 'My mum loves me, my mum spoils me, I love my mum'; firstly, to spell it out, then to write it laboriously in pencil in my handwriting book. Soon I moved on from those simple sentences, full of the letter m that seemed like kisses, to other more complicated ones. And when one day I managed to write on the blackboard, without error or hesitation, a sentence bristling with consonants and ancestral fear: 'primitive men, cowering in caves, trembled with terror as the lightning flashed and the

retumbar del trueno'), doña Rosita me elogió ante toda la clase y yo sentí por primera vez el halago del aplauso público y también de la envidia secreta de mis compañeras.

¡Resultaba tan fácil aprender con ella! Era capaz de sacar enseñanzas, literalmente, de una mosca.

Una tarde calurosa de mayo, mientras nos afanábamos haciendo vainicas, dobladillos y puntos de cruz en el dechado de costura, entró un moscardón en la clase. El bicho, atontado, chocaba una y otra vez contra las paredes, contra la pizarra, planeaba en vuelo rasante sobre nuestras cabezas, asustando a las niñas más pequeñas. La clase empezó a alborotarse con una mezcla de asco y diversión.

–Apagad la luz– dijo doña Rosita.

La luz artificial fue apagada y el moscardón insistía en suicidarse contra los vidrios de las ventanas.

–Ahora abrid la ventana de par en par.

Y el moscardón, buscando la luz, salió por la ventana y, súbitamente libre, se perdió zumbando en la tarde calurosa. Tal vez muriera aquella misma noche, pero las pocas horas que le quedaban hasta el anochecer seguramente equivalían para él a largos años de vida.

Entonces doña Rosita escribió en la pizarra la frase que determinó mi vocación futura: 'La mosca busca la luz'.

La frase revoloteó sobre nuestras cabezas durante el resto de la tarde y yo, mientras con manos sudorosas ensuciaba el trapito de dechado de costura, tratando de hacer un dobladillo no demasiado torcido, no dejaba de pensar en por qué la mosca busca la luz, qué extraño atractivo tenía la luz para la mosca o para qué necesita uno luz cuando es un moscardón aturdido, por qué la necesita uno tanto que le vale lo mismo el sol que una bombilla, que parece que le va la vida en ello, en un poco de luz (todas habíamos visto cómo el moscardón estaba dispuesto a matarse a cabezazos contra las paredes blancas, contra los cristales, buscando precisamente la luz) y si todos los animales buscaban la luz tan desesperadamente o había otros que, por el contrario, la rehuían. Y allí creo que empezó a fraguarse mi tesis doctoral sobre fototactismo negativo de los invertebrados en el ecosistema marino o, lo que es lo mismo, por qué algunos organismos vivos que viven en el mar huyen de la luz, cuando la mayoría de los organismos la buscan como algo necesario para la vida.

Pero la gran revelación llegó tres cursos más tarde, durante mi cuarto otoño en la escuela de la Virgen redentora de cautivos. Doña Rosita nos había

thunder boomed', Doña Rosita praised me in front of the whole class and I felt for the first time the flattery of public applause as well as the secret envy of my fellow pupils.

It was so easy to learn with her! She was literally capable of getting learning out of a fly.

One very hot afternoon in May, while we were struggling to make hem stitches, drawnwork and cross stitches on our samplers, a big buzzing fly came into the classroom. The disorientated insect crashed time and again into the walls, the blackboard, it swooped just above our heads, frightening the smallest girls. The class became agitated in a mixture of enjoyment and disgust.

'Put out the light', Doña Rosita said.

The artificial light was put out and the big fly repeatedly tried to commit suicide against the window panes.

'Now open the window wide.'

And the fly, seeking the light, went out of the window and, suddenly free, buzzed away in the hot afternoon. Perhaps it would die that very night but the few hours that were left until nightfall surely meant long years of life for it.

Then Doña Rosita wrote on the blackboard the sentence that determined my future career: 'the fly seeks the light.'

The sentence swirled above our heads for the rest of the afternoon, and while my sweaty hands dirtied the little rag of my sewing sampler as I tried to do a hemstitch which was not too crooked, I could not help thinking about why the fly seeks the light, about what strange attraction the light held for the fly or for what reason one needs light when one is a stunned big fly, why one needs it so much that the sun is just as okay as a light bulb, that it seems that its life depends on that, on a little bit of light (we had all seen how the big fly was ready to kill itself by banging its head against the white walls, against the panes of glass, just looking for the light) and if all animals sought the light as desperately, or if there were others that on the contrary sought refuge from it. And I believe that it was there that my doctoral thesis on negative photosensitivity in invertebrates in the marine ecosystem was forged, or in other words, why some living organisms that inhabit the seas flee from light, while the majority of organisms seek the light as something essential for life.

But the great revelation came three years later, during my fourth autumn in the school of Our Lady, Redeemer of Captives. Doña Rosita had been

estado enseñando las distintas formas de las hojas. Había dibujado en la pizarra hojas simples y compuestas, enteras, onduladas, dentadas, aserradas, lobuladas, elípticas, lanceoladas, ovales, acorazonadas, sagitadas, lineales, aciculares. Y entonces nos pidió que, aprovechando el otoño, trajésemos la semana siguiente muestras de los distintos tipos de hojas caídas de los árboles que pudiéramos recoger.

El colegio estaba en un barrio urbano, un barrio viejo del centro de la ciudad en el que no había jardines, y todas las alumnas éramos vecinas del barrio. Así que la única manera de poder recoger una variedad de hojas caídas era conseguir que nuestros padres nos llevasen de paseo al Retiro, donde había muchos árboles distintos que estaban perdiendo las hojas en aquel mes de noviembre.

Durante la semana era imposible pensar en que mamá fuese conmigo al parque, así que le pedí insistentemente que me llevase el domingo, con la esperanza de recoger hojas.

El domingo siguiente amaneció lloviendo a mares y, por más que les rogué, mis padres no quisieron llevarme al parque. '¿No ves que no hace tiempo de ir al Retiro? ¡qué manía se te ha metido en la cabeza!' me decían, ciegos y sordos a mi necesidad científica.

A la salida de misa pasamos por la plazoleta de al lado de la iglesia. Con la fuerza de la lluvia, los cuatros plátanos escuálidos de la plazuela habían perdido casi todas sus hojas, que alfombraban la tierra. Había escampado ya un poco y, mientras mis padres charlaban en la plaza con unos conocidos del barrio, yo me dediqué a recoger del suelo las palmeadas hojas de color barquillo, todas mojadas y embarradas, pero hermosas y brillantes.

En casa, las sequé un poco con un trapo. Y durante toda la tarde, con la ayuda de unas tijeritas sin punta que utilizábamos en la escuela para los trabajos manuales, me dediqué a recortar las hojas de plátano, fabricando con ellas hojas de todas clases. Pronto me di cuenta de que me salían el lado derecho y el izquierdo distintos, lo cual las hacía poco creíbles como productos naturales, así que, para que me salieran simétricas, doblaba cada hoja en torno al eje de su nervio central y recortaba los dos lados al mismo tiempo, y de esa manera experimenté con mis propias manos la simetría bilateral de la mayoría de los organismos pluricelulares (aunque, desde luego, yo entonces no sabía lo que era bilateral, ni lo que eran organismos, ni había oído nunca la palabra pluricelular). Incluso llegué a pelar todo el nervio de una de ellas para elaborar así una larguísima hoja acicular, derecha y desnuda como una aguja.

teaching us the different shapes of leaves. She had drawn on the blackboard simple and complex leaves, whole, wavy, sharp, jagged leaves, leaves with lobes, elliptical, oval leaves, leaves shaped like a heart, arrow, or needle. And then she asked us, taking advantage of the autumn, to bring in samples the following week of the different types of fallen leaves that we could collect.

The school was in an urban area, an old quarter in the city center where there were no gardens and all of the girls lived locally. So the only way we could collect a variety of leaves was for us to get our parents to take us for a walk in the Retiro Park, where there were lots of different trees shedding their leaves that November.

During the week it was unthinkable for mum to take me to the park, so I incessantly asked her to take me on Sunday in the hope of collecting leaves.

The following Sunday dawned with the rain pouring down. And however much I beseeched them, my parents did not want to take me to the park. 'Can't you see it isn't the weather to go to the Retiro? What's got into your head?' they said to me, blind and deaf to my scientific needs.

On coming out of Mass we went through the little square at the side of the church. Due to the force of the rain, the four squalid plane trees in the dingy square had lost almost all of their leaves, which were carpeting the ground. It had by now cleared up a little, and while my parents chatted in the square to some people they knew from the neighbourhood, I set about collecting the palm-shaped leaves the colour of an ice cream cone, all soaked and muddy, but lovely and shiny.

I dried them a bit with a cloth at home. And throughout the afternoon, using a pair of blunt-nosed scissors which we used in school for manual tasks, I set about trimming the plane-tree leaves, making all types of leaves from them. I soon realized that the right and left sides were coming out differently, which gave them little credibility as products of nature, so in order to get them to come out symmetrically, I folded each leaf in two along the central nerve, and cut out both sides at the same time, and thus I experienced by my hands the bilateral symmetry of multicellular organisms (though, of course, at that time I did not know the meaning of bilateral, nor what organisms were, nor had I ever heard the word multicellular). I even managed to strip completely the whole nerve of one of them so as to make it into a very large pointed leaf, as erect and naked as a needle.

Al día siguiente, lunes, me presenté orgullosa ante doña Rosita. Llevaba catorce hojas con limbos y márgenes de las más diversas formas, todo un muestrario elaborado con la materia prima de los plátanos de la plaza de la iglesia. Ninguna niña había conseguido tantas hojas distintas; lo más, llevaban tres o cuatro hojas, de plátano, de castaño de indias, de acacia o del laurel que utilizaban sus madres en la cocina.

Al ver mi tesoro, doña Rosita sonrió enigmáticamente, pero en vez de desenmascarar mi impostura, empezó a preguntarme.

–Esta hoja, ¿qué es?

–Oval alveolada– decía yo.

–¿Y ésta?

–Sagitada lobulada.

–¿Y esta otra?

–Lanceolada entera.

Y así hasta catorce. Dije todos sus nombres. No había dos hojas iguales.

–Está muy bien– concluyó doña Rosita–. Has trabajado mucho y te lo has aprendido muy bien, que era lo importante. Pero estas hojas son todas de un mismo árbol: son hojas de plátano recortadas.

Me quedé estupefacta. ¿Cómo había podido saberlo? Doña Rosita me pareció de repente un pozo de ciencia, el colmo de la sabiduría, alguien capaz de distinguir el bien del mal, las hojas naturales de las recortadas. Pero ¿se debía su conocimiento a una rara intuición, o había en las hojas algo que revelaba su origen espurio, que las identificaba como hojas de plátano modificadas a filo de tijera, que las distinguía de las verdaderas hojas naturales? Miré mis hojas y las de mis compañeras y en las siguientes visitas al Retiro recogí más hojas para compararlas con las mías –las conservaba porque, pese a ser bastardas, mi maestra me había pedido que las dejase secar entre papel de periódico, las pegase en un cuaderno de páginas blancas sin rayar y escribiese debajo la descripción–, y así fui indagando, espoleada por una sola frase de doña Rosita, en todo el mundo de las hojas caducas y de las características que permitían distinguir las falsas de las verdaderas. Nunca le agradeceré bastante que, en lugar de castigarme por mi pequeña trampa, sembrase en mi corazón una sola frase que me obligó desde entonces a abrir los ojos ante el mundo vegetal: 'esas hojas son todas de un mismo árbol'.

El año siguiente era ya el examen de ingreso en el bachillerato, año de

On the following day, Monday, I stood full of pride before Doña Rosita. I was holding fourteen leaves whose limbs and borders were in the most diverse shapes, a complete showcase made from the prime matter from the plane trees in the church square. No girl had managed to produce so many different leaves; at the most they brought three or four leaves, from the plane tree, the horse chestnut, the acacia or laurel that their mothers used in the kitchen.

On seeing my treasure trove, Doña Rosita smiled enigmatically, but instead of unmasking my deception, she began to ask me questions.

'This leaf, what is it?'

'An oval alveolar leaf.'

'And this one?'

'A lobular sagittate leaf.'

'And this next one?'

'A complete lanceolate.'

And so on up to fourteen. I gave all of their names. No two leaves were the same.

'Very good', said Doña Rosita at the end. 'You have worked hard and have learned everything very well, which was the important thing. But these leaves are all from the same tree: they are plane tree leaves cut up.'

I was astounded. How had she been able to tell that? Suddenly Doña Rosita seemed to me like a fount of knowledge, the epitome of wisdom, someone able to distinguish good from evil, natural leaves from cut up ones. But did she owe her knowledge to rare intuition, or was there something in the leaves that revealed their false origin, that identified them as plane tree leaves modified by a scissor blade, that distinguished them from authentic natural leaves? I looked at my leaves and those of the other pupils and on my subsequent visits to the Retiro I collected more leaves to compare with mine – I kept them because, although they were illegitimate, my teacher had asked me to let them dry between sheets of newspaper, stick them in an exercise book with unlined white pages and write the description underneath – and so, spurred on by a single sentence from Doña Rosita, I proceeded to investigate the world of withered leaves and the characteristics that would allow one to distinguish the true from the false. I will never be able to thank her enough for, instead of punishing me for my little trick, sowing in my heart a single sentence that obliged me from then on to open my eyes to the plant world: 'those leaves are all from the same tree.'

The following year was already the year of the examination for entry to

las divisiones de dos cifras en el divisor y de dictados inverosímiles, ya que la división y el dictado (en el que no se podían cometer más de dos faltas de ortografía) eran las pruebas clave del examen. Teníamos un cuaderno de rayas en el que íbamos escribiendo frases llenas de dificultades ortográficas y de *nonsense*: 'El velero valeroso navega por el mar embravecido', 'Los mayorales, exhaustos, se sentaron en un poyo para cebar a la gallina y a los pollitos', 'La abadesa, leyendo el breviario, veía abrevar a los caballos'.

Levanté la mano con el dedo índice muy derecho, como me habían enseñado a hacer cuando quería preguntar algo:

–¿Qué quieres, Carmencita? ¿Hay algo que no entiendas bien?

– ¿No sería mejor que los mayorales exhaustos viesen abrevar a los caballos?–pregunté con una lógica aplastante.

–Bueno, a lo mejor tienes razón: si quieres puedes probar. Coge las partes de estas dos frases y prueba a escribir en el cuaderno lo que te parezca más lógico.

Me puse a ello, pero no era tan fácil como parecía, porque, aunque a mí me parecía claro que los mayorales tenían más que ver con los caballos que las abadesas, algunos de los elementos de cada frase podían combinarse de varias maneras: 'los mayorales exhaustos, leyendo el breviario, veían abrevar a los caballos' y 'la abadesa se sentó en un poyo para cebar a las gallinas y a los pollitos'. ¿O quizás 'los mayorales exhaustos se sentaron en un poyo con la abadesa para ver abrevar a los caballos' y 'la abadesa, leyendo el breviario, sentada en un poyo, cebaba a las gallinas y a los pollitos?' ¿O 'los mayorales se sentaron en un poyo para cebar a los caballos' y 'la abadesa, exhausta, leyendo el breviario, veía abrevar a las gallinas y los pollitos?' Hecha un auténtico lío, llené más de dos planas con las distintas posibilidades; acabé desechando la mayoría, guiada por un instinto que me indicaba alguna incongruencia, y al final me quedé con dos oraciones que me parecieron las mejores: 'la abadesa, leyendo el breviario, cebaba a las gallinas y a los pollitos' y 'los mayorales exhaustos se sentaron en un poyo para ver abrevar a los caballos'. No era un prodigio de lógica, pero al menos estaba mejor que al principio.

Lo que yo no sabía entonces es que con su pequeña indicación ('prueba a escribir en el cuaderno lo que te parezca más lógico') doña Rosita no sólo me estaba produciendo un estado de confusión, sino introduciéndome en el

secondary school, the year of double figure division and unlikely dictations, because division and dictation (in which no more than two spelling mistakes were allowed) were the key tests in the exam. We had an exercise book with two margins in which we used to write nonsensical sentences full of spelling difficulties: 'The valiant sailing ship sails through the raging sea', 'The exhausted farmers sat on a stone bench to feed the hen and the little chickens', 'While reading her breviary, the abbess saw the horses being watered.'

I raised my hand with my index finger in the air, as I had been taught to do when I wanted to ask a question.

'What do you want, Carmencita? Is there something that you do not completely understand?'

'Would it not be better for the exhausted farmers to see the horses being watered?' I asked with overwhelming logic.

'Well, you're probably right; you can try it if you like. Take the parts of these two sentences and try to write in your exercise book what you think is more logical.'

I set about it, but it was not as easy as it seemed because, although it seemed clear to me that the farmers had more to do with horses than the abbess, some elements of each sentence could be combined in several ways: 'the exhausted farmers, reading their breviary, saw the horses being watered' and 'the abbess sat on a stone bench to feed the hens and the little chicks.' Or perhaps 'the exhausted farmers sat on a wooden bench with the abbess to watch the horses being watered' and 'the abbess, sitting on a stone bench reading the breviary, fed the hens and the little chicks?' Or 'the farmers sat on a wooden bench to feed the horses' and 'while sitting on a stone bench reading the breviary, the exhausted abbess watched the hens and little chicks being watered?' In a complete muddle, I filled more than two sides with different possibilities; I ended up by discarding the majority, guided by an instinct that indicated some incongruity to me, and finally I was left with two sentences that seemed the best to me: 'while reading her breviary, the abbess fed the hens and little chicks' and 'the exhausted farmers sat on a stone bench to watch the horses being watered.' It wasn't prodigious logic, but it was at least better than at the beginning.

What I did not know then is that with her simple instruction ('try to write in your exercise book what seems more logical to you'), Doña Rosita was not just sowing doubt in my mind but introducing me to the basic principle of scientific method: trial and error. Moreover, though I did not know it then

principio fundamental del método científico: ensayo y error. Y que, aunque tampoco lo supiera entonces –lo aprendí casi quince años después–, lo que estaba haciendo era un cálculo matemático de probabilidades (combinaciones de N elementos tomados de n en n), donde los elementos eran los mayorales, el hecho de estar exhausto, el poyo, el breviario, la abadesa, las gallinas y los pollitos, y los caballos, y n el número de elementos que introducía en cada frase.

Cuando le enseñé a doña Rosita las dos frases que había elegido, empezó– como casi siempre hacía: ése era el secreto de su gracia para enseñar–con un elogio, para continuar con una pregunta que sembraba la inquietud de la confusión:

–Las dos frases están muy bien. Pero ¿por qué has escogido éstas y no otras?

No supe qué contestar. Intuía vagamente que otras frases eran erróneas o incongruentes, que algunas de las posibilidades que había barajado no eran aceptables o tenían en su interior algo que rechinaba, que no acababa de cuadrar; pero no sabía explicar la causa. Y ahí, en mi pequeña humillación escolar, aprendí otro principio básico de la ciencia: que no solo hay que llegar al resultado correcto, sino que es imprescindible demostrar cómo y por qué.

Aprobé el ingreso de bachillerato, empecé a estudiar en el instituto y ya no volví al colegio de María Redentora, aunque a veces veía a doña Rosita por las calles del barrio; casi siempre ella venía de la iglesia o iba a la parroquia y me daba dos besos apresurados, me preguntaba brevemente por mis estudios y se marchaba enseguida, reclamada por sus devociones o sus obligaciones. Dos años después mi familia se cambió de casa, fuimos a vivir a otro barrio y dejé de ver a mi antigua maestra.

No sé qué fue de ella, ni cuándo cerró el colegio, ni qué hizo después, ni siquiera sé si vive. Por no saber, ahora caigo en la cuenta de que nunca supe su apellido. Los niños pequeños no solíamos conocer el apellido de nuestros maestros de la escuela y ahora ya no puedo preguntar a nadie, porque las personas que la conocieron han muerto o yo he perdido el contacto con ellas, o ni siquiera se acuerdan ya de doña Rosita, que es sólo un confuso recuerdo en su memoria.

Aquella mujer sin apellido determinó, sin embargo, toda mi vida posterior. Con los maestros establecemos la primera relación laboral de nuestras vidas. Visto en perspectiva, doña Rosita fue mi primera jefa, y luego he tenido muchas más.

either – it was something that I learned almost fifteen years later – what I was doing was a mathematical calculation of probabilities (combinations of N elements going from n to n), where the elements were the farmers, the fact of being exhausted, the stone bench, the prayer book, the abbess, the hens and the little chicks, and the horses, and n was the number of elements that I put into each sentence.

When I showed Doña Rosita the two sentences that I had chosen, she began – as she almost always did: that was the secret of her gift for teaching – with praise, and then followed with a question that sowed the concern with doubt:

'The two sentences are okay. But, why have you chosen those and not others?'

I did not know what to answer. I had a vague intuition that the other sentences were erroneous or incongruous, that some of the possibilities that I had mooted were not acceptable or had something that grated internally, which did not fit together; but I did not know how to explain why. And right there, in my little academic humiliation, I learned another basic principle of science: that it is not only necessary to achieve the right result but it is essential to demonstrate how and why.

I passed the entrance exam for secondary school, began to go to that school and never returned to Mary the Redeemer primary school, although I sometimes saw Doña Rosita walking through the neighbourhood streets; she was almost always going to or coming from the parish church and she would greet me with two hurried kisses, enquire briefly about my studies and walk away at once, summoned by her duties or devotions. Two years later my family moved house, we went to live in another neighbourhood and I stopped seeing my former teacher. I don't know what became of her, nor when the school closed and what she did after that, nor even if she is still alive. In my ignorance of that, I now realize that I never knew her surname. Little children like me did not usually know the surnames of our primary school teachers and now I cannot ask anyone, because those who knew her are dead or I have lost contact with them, or they no longer remember Doña Rosita, who is only a hazy memory in their mind.

Nevertheless, that woman without a surname determined my subsequent life. We establish the first working relationship in our lives with our primary school teachers. Seen in retrospect, Doña Rosita was my first boss, and I have had many more since.

I am now in charge of a research laboratory in which there are more

Ahora dirijo un laboratorio de investigación en el que trabajan más de treinta personas, la mayoría mujeres. La jefa, por tanto, soy yo; sé que mis colaboradores me llaman a mis espaldas *está-muy-bien-pero*…, aunque no saben que ese mote que me han puesto se debe a que procuro aplicar con ellos el mismo método que utilizaba mi primera maestra: que nunca falte el elogio por el esfuerzo realizado, pero que a continuación surja la pregunta que siembra la duda, que hace reflexionar y abre un mundo de nuevas perspectivas. Ése fue el mejor legado que me dejó mi maestra sin apellidos.

Otra cosa que tampoco saben mis compañeros es que todavía a veces, cuando en una tarde de otoño salgo del laboratorio después de muchas horas de trabajo (exhausta, como aquellos mayorales que cebaban a los pollitos), voy recogiendo del suelo las hojas caídas de los árboles y luego, en casa, me entretengo en recortar sus bordes con un pequeño bisturí, creando hojas inventadas de especies vegetales que no existen, producto de una mutación que no sucedió jamás pero que yo, pequeña divinidad, soy capaz de crear con mis propias manos.

than thirty people working, the majority of them women. Therefore I am the boss; I know that my fellow workers call me *it's-okay-but* behind my back, although they don't know that that nickname they've given me is due to the fact that I apply to them the same method that my first teacher used with me: let there always be praise for the effort made, but let the question immediately follow that sows doubt, makes them think and opens a world of new perspectives. That was the best legacy that my teacher without a surname left me.

Another thing that my co-workers do not know is that sometimes, when I leave the laboratory – exhausted like those farmers who fed the little chicks – after many hours of work on an autumn evening, I walk along picking up off the ground the leaves that have fallen from the trees, and then at home I amuse myself by trimming the edges with a little scalpel, creating invented leaves of non-existent plant species, the result of a mutation that never happened but that I, as a little goddess, am capable of creating with my own hands.

COCINITAS

PLAYING HOUSES

Original Spanish text from *Fantasías animadas*
(Barcelona: Anagrama, 2010, 111–27)
© Berta Marsé, 2010

BERTA MARSÉ was born in Barcelona in 1969. She defines herself as the daughter of an 'escritor y [una] extremeña' – her father being Juan Marsé, one of the most significant literary figures of the second half of the twentieth century in Spain, and her mother being from the Extremadura region. Berta Marsé is, to some extent, a self-taught intellectual who worked first for publishers and cinema producers as reader of manuscripts and script editor before starting her career as a writer. She has published two collections of short stories so far: *En jaque* (2006), which includes 'La tortuga', a story that was awarded the Premio Gabriel Aresti. In 2013 *En jaque* was translated into French. In 2010 she published a second book of stories, *Fantasías animadas*, which was very well received by critics. In both volumes, she displays a perceptive use of everyday language in which the dialogue cleverly constructs the peculiarities of her diverse and fascinating characters. Rather than being 'fantasies', her stories expose how ordinary lives are shaped by social constraints, although sentimentality is never an option. As early as 2008, she was included in an anthology of young Spanish writers published in Germany (see bibliography below). She has written for the newspaper *El País*, and has contributed to literary journals such as *Eñe* and *Turia, Revista Cultural*. In 2015, along with other writers and photographers, she was part of the team behind *Barcelona*, a book which tells the history of the city since 1870 through a number of literary and visual contributions. Berta Marsé is currently working on her first novel which will be entitled *Las leyes del azar*.

Bibliography of Berta Marsé

Short story collections

En jaque (Barcelona: Anagrama, 2006) – includes 'La tortuga', which was awarded the *Premio Gabriel Aresti – En écheq* (Paris: Christian Bourgois Éditeur, 2013).
Fantasías animadas (Barcelona: Anagrama, 2010).

Short stories included in anthologies and journals (a selection)

'Nacha', in M. Thomas Bosshard (ed.), *Pasodoble/ Junge Spanische Literatur* (Berlin: Wagenbach Verlag, 2008).

'Gran Noche de Gala', in G. Pellicer and F. Valls (eds), *Siglo XXI. Los nuevos nombres del cuento español actual* (Palencia: Menoscuarto, 2010).

'Piragüismo ("Placeres adultos")', in A. Neuman (ed.), *Pequeñas resistencias 5. Antología del nuevo cuento español (2001–2010)* (Madrid: Páginas de Espuma, 2010).

'Cocinitas', in C. Velasco Rengel (ed.), *Watchwomen: narradoras del siglo 21* (Zaragoza: Institución Fernando el Católico, 2011).

'La visita', *Turia, Revista Cultural* 99 (2011), 64–71.

'Gran Noche de Gala', in Á. Encinar and C. Valcárcel (eds), *En breve. Cuentos de escritoras españolas (1975–2010)* (Madrid: Biblioteca Nueva, 2012).

'Lo de Don Vito', in Á. Encinar (ed.), *Cuento español actual (1992–2012)* (Madrid: Cátedra, 2013).

'La visita: un recuerdo terrorífico', *Sibila, Revista de Arte, Música y Literatura* 42 (2014), 22–24.

Reflections on her own writing

[On the contemporary Spanish short story and the influences on her own writing – no title], in Á. Encinar (ed.), *Cuento español actual (1992–2012)* (Madrid: Cátedra, 2013), 321–22.

Other publications

Barcelona [with Ricardo Feriche, Javier Velasco, and photographers Català-Roca, Colita, Pomés, Masats, Cartier-Bresson, Erwitt, Avedon, Kouidelka, Newton and Parr] (Barcelona: La Fábrica, 2015).

Further reading on Berta Marsé

Pedro Donoso, 'Impulsos adolescentes', *Revista de Libros* 163–64 (2010), 44.

Álex Gutiérrez, 'Mat en set' [interview with Berta Marsé], *Benzina: Revista d'Excepcions Culturals* 1 (2006), 58–59.

David Morán, 'Berta Marsé debuta en la literatura con el libro de cuentos *En jaque*', *ABC*, 23 February 2006. http://www.abc.es/hemeroteca/historico-23-02-2006/

abc/Catalunya/berta-marse-debuta-en-la-literatura-con-el-libro-de-cuentos-en-jaque_142479889374.html

Josep A. Muñoz, '*Fantasías animadas*, de Berta Marsé', *Revista de Letras*, 25 April 2010. http://www.revistadeletras.net/fantasias-animadas-de-berta-marse

María Jesús Orozco Vera, '*En breve. Cuentos de escritoras españolas (1975–2010). Estudio y antología de Ángeles Encinar y Carmen Valcárcel*', Pasavento: Revista de Estudios Hispánicos 1.2 (2013), 395–400.

Annette Paatz, '¿Retiradas o Noches de Gala? Carmen Martín Gaite y Berta Marsé o el cuento de mujeres del siglo XX al XXI', in Á. Encinar and C. Valcárcel (eds), *En breve. Cuentos de escritoras españolas (1975–2010). Estudios y antología* (Madrid: Biblioteca Nueva, 2012), 191–208.

Juan Carlos Peinado, '¿Y ahora que lo sabemos, qué?, *Revista de Libros* 114 (2006), 46–47.

Further information online on Berta Marsé (a selection)

http://www.elperiodico.com/es/noticias/ocio-y-cultura/berta-marse-publica-fantasias-animadas-defiende-las-opiniones-padre-243636

http://conversesformentor.com/speaker/berta-marse/

http://elpais.com/autor/berta_marse/a

http://www.agenciabalcells.com/autores/autor/berta-marse/

http://revistadeletras.net/fantasias-animadas-de-berta-marse/

https://www.youtube.com/watch?v=0HHp7V6lnnA

http://acabodeleerymegusta.blogspot.co.uk/2015/10/berta-marse.html

http://www.elcultural.com/revista/letras/Fantasias-animadas/26540

https://depunoyletra.com/2010/06/23/entrevista-berta-marse/

http://www.diariodesevilla.es/entrevistas/falta-publicar-escribir-sentirte-escritor_0_344365563.html#!

http://www.abc.es/hemeroteca/historico-23-02-2006/abc/Catalunya/berta-marse-debuta-en-la-literatura-con-el-libro-de-cuentos-en-jaque_142479889374.html

http://www.blogseitb.com/pompasdepapel/2010/01/25/la-fantasia-realista-de-berta-marse/

http://www.revistadelibros.com/articulos/en-jaque-relatos-de-berta-marse

https://acabodeleerymegusta.blogspot.co.uk/2017/04/berta-marse.html

COCINITAS

Para ver el mundo en un grano de arena,
y el firmamento en una flor silvestre,
sostén el universo en la palma de tu mano
y la eternidad en una hora.

Augurios de inocencia, William Blake

A punto de empezar a jugar a cocinitas –como siempre, Lorena se ha pedido la Señora de la Casa para trajinar con los cacharros y dar órdenes, y a Susi le toca de Vecina con Lumbago que viene a tomar café y a charlar por los codos–, cuando de pronto ha sonado el timbre de la puerta y ha aparecido la madre de la vecinita de arriba para invitarlas a jugar con su colmado nuevo.

Ambas, Susi y Lorena, de siete años, vecinas puerta con puerta, han superado ya el impacto, el asombro, la fascinación y la rabia profunda que les causó el colmado con caja registradora que los Reyes Magos trajeron a la repipi de Natalie. Entraron a verlo cogiditas de la mano y se quedaron mudas de envidia, con los ojos como platos. Un despampanante colmado, con su toldo a rayas rojas y blancas, con sus latas de conserva, sus hueveras, sus tomates y sus ristras de ajos colgando. La Navidad pasó, pero desde entonces ambas sueñan con poner, más tarde o más temprano, sus delicadas zarpas sobre el colmado de Natalie. De hecho ya lo tienen todo planeado y calculado para no perder ni un segundo en repartir papeles y entrar en materia, para aprovechar el tiempo al máximo y a fondo, cuando llegue tan anhelado momento.

Pues bien, a punto de empezar a jugar a cocinitas, como siempre, cuando la madre de Natalie ha venido a pedirlas para una hora de juego porque, ha dicho con su acento extranjero, la suya lleva días *rrr*esfriada y se abu*rrr*e mucho. Y las madres de Lorena y Susi, que por las tardes toman café y charlan por los codos en casa de una o de la otra, han preparado bocadillos de mortadela y las han peinado: a Lorena con una cola de caballo, a Susi con dos moñitos altos que sostienen y esconden la goma de las gafas. En el ascensor las niñas se han pellizcado los brazos la una a la otra, presas de la agitación: ¡A por el colmado!

Las bases del juego están claritas desde el día en que lo admiraron por primera vez: Lorena va a hacer de Señora Dependienta y Susi de Señora Compradora, que no mola tanto –no hace paquetes ni manipula la caja

PLAYING HOUSES

To see the world in a grain of sand
And heaven in a wild flower
Hold infinity in the palm of your hand
And eternity in an hour.

Auguries of Innocence, William Blake

Just as they were about to play houses as usual, Lorena has asked to be the lady of the house to get busy with the pots and pans and give orders, and it falls to Susi to play the neighbour with lumbago who drops in for a coffee and talks ten to the dozen, when suddenly the doorbell rings and the mother of the little girl upstairs has turned up to invite them to play with her daughter's new grocery store.

Both the seven-year-olds, Susi and Lorena, who are next door neighbours, have already got over the impact, the astonishment, fascination and deep anger which the grocery store complete with a cash register that the Three Kings brought to that know-it-all Natalie. Hand in hand they went in to see it and were struck dumb with envy, their eyes agog. A stunning grocery store with its red and white striped awning, with its tins of food, its egg trays, its tomatoes and its strings of hanging garlic. Christmas has passed, but since then both dream of sooner or later getting their delicate claws on Natalie's grocery store. In fact they have already planned and plotted how to divide up roles and get straight down to it in order not to lose even one second when the anxiously awaited moment comes.

Well, just when they were about to play houses as usual, along comes Natalie's mother to ask them to come and play for an hour because, as she said in her foreign accent, her daughter has spent days with a *heavy* cold and is so *bor-ed*. And Susi and Lorena's mothers, who take afternoon tea and speak nonstop in one or the other's house, have prepared mortadella sandwiches and have combed their hair: Lorena with a pony tail, and Susi with two little buns on the top which hold up and hide the elastic attached to her glasses. In the lift the little girls pinched each other's arms, caught up in the excitement. Let's go get the grocery store!

The rules of the game have been quite clear since the day on which they admired it for the first time: Lorena will play the role of the lady shop assistant and Susi that of the lady shopper, which is a less exciting deal –

registradora, sin ninguna duda lo mejor del juego–, pero para compensar se lleva el cochecito de las gemelas de Lorena, equipado con todo lo que cree necesario, que no es precisamente poco.

En sus planes, claro, no han contado con Natalie, que es cursi pero no tonta y se da cuenta enseguida de que no hay papel para ella en esta obra; porque nada más cerrarse la puerta de su habitación y empezar la cuenta atrás, sus espabiladas vecinitas lanzan los bocatas a lo alto del armario y entran sin más en faena: Lorena poniéndose un mandil sobre el chándal de la escuela y precipitándose sobre la caja registradora, que empieza a abrir y cerrar compulsivamente. Susi cubriendo a las gemelas con una mantita y luego echándose ella, con arte femenino, el chal de su madre por los hombros.

–Y yo, ¿de qué hago?– pregunta Natalie, dueña y señora del colmado.

Está de pie, con sus dos trenzas muy rubias, herencia de su madre alemana. O su pijama ha encogido mucho o los días de fiebre la han estirado sádicamente por las muñecas y los tobillos. También inspiran un poco de lástima las aletas rojas y escamadas de su nariz. Pero Susi y Lorena tiemblan de apremiantes deseos de trajinar el colmado, no pueden apiadarse de nada. Y prosigue el tumulto de los preparativos del juego. Es la misma Natalie quien, viéndolas mirar de reojo la medalla que lleva colgada al pecho –es de su madre, que fue campeona de natación–, propone:

–¿Vale que yo era una nadadora que se preparaba para las olimpiadas y venía a por verdurita fresca?

Susi detiene su actividad para mirarla a la cara. Ahora es más bajita que Natalie, pero más compacta y resistente. Con sus ojos aumentados tras los cristales de las gafas, y sus dos moños como dos antenas, parece un robot programado para jugar duro. En su expresión corporal se ve claramente que no piensa compartir con nadie su papel de Señora Compradora:

–¿Vale que yo no tenía gemelas sino trillizas pero una me había salido mal y eras tú, que siempre estabas enferma?

–¡Sí, hombre!– protesta Natalie.

–O de gemela rarita o haces cola– amenaza Susi, aferrada en tensión al cochecito–. Pero va a ser una hora mínimo, porque a mí no me sacan de aquí ni los Reyes Magos de Oriente.

Natalie teme que si se muestra débil sus vecinas la atropellarán y abusarán de su colmado, por eso clava sus uñas donde sabe que Susi, que es más bruta pero más inocente que Lorena, tiene una herida secreta.

she will not wrap things up nor work the cash register – but in return she takes the pram of Lorena's twin dolls, equipped with everything necessary, which is not exactly a little.

Of course, they have not taken Natalie into their plans; she is a bit twee, but not a fool, and immediately realizes that there is no place for her in this role play because the door of her bedroom is no sooner closed and the countdown started than her cunning little neighbours throw their sandwiches on top of the cupboard and get straight down to business: Lorena putting an apron over her school track suit and rushing to the cash register, which she starts to open and close compulsively, and Susi covering the twin dolls with a little blanket and then, with feminine wiles, throwing her mother's shawl over her shoulders.

'And me, what do I do?' asks Natalie, the lady and owner of the store.

She's standing with her two blond tresses, inherited from her German mother. Either her pajamas have shrunk a lot or the days of high temperatures have sadistically made her wrists and ankles stretch. Her red nostrils and the flaking skin on her nose also induce some pity. But Susi and Lorena tremble with the overwhelming desire to mess around with the grocery store, and they can't take pity on anything. And the noise of the game being set up continues. It is Natalie herself who, seeing them glance sideways at the medal she wears hanging from her neck – it belongs to her mother who was a champion swimmer – proposes:

'Is it okay if I play a swimmer preparing for the Olympic Games who comes to buy some fresh vegetables?'

Susi stops what she is doing to look her in the face. She is now a little smaller than Natalie but stronger and more solid. With her eyes enlarged behind her lenses, and her two buns like antennae, she looks like a robot programmed to play hard ball. In her body language it can be seen that she is not intending to share the role of housewife shopper with anyone.

'How about I don't have twin dolls but triplets, one of whom has turned out sick and that's you, who are always sick?'

'No way!' Natalie protests.

'Either you play the strange twin or you join the queue', Susi threatens her, clinging on tensely to the pram. 'But it's going to be at least an hour, because not even the Three Kings from the East will budge me from here.'

Natalie fears that if she shows her weak side, her neighbours will walk all over her and take over her grocery store, and so digs her nails into where she knows that Susi, who is rougher but more naïve than Lorena, has a secret wound.

—Ya, seguro— se burla—. Te haces la chula porque no te han traído lo que te has pedido.

—¡Tú qué sabes lo que me he pedido! Sólo Lorena y los Reyes lo saben, y tú no.

Defendiendo su secreto ante Natalie, Susi la excluye de su mundo y de su juego. Natalie es hija de madre soltera, alemana, nadadora, todo muy moderno y muy exótico para Susi, y encima es rubia, saca buenas notas, a menudo no va al cole porque se resfría, y tiene un colmado que te cagas. ¿Qué no tiene Natalie? Natalie no tiene una amiga como Lorena. Susi y Lorena, uña y carne, relámpago y trueno; aunque ahora mismo Lorena continúe abriendo y cerrando la caja registradora con placer y concentración máximos, como si no existiera nada más en este mundo y en esta hora. Natalie mide sus propias fuerzas y las de Susi, que espera su decisión en actitud inflexible, sacando barriga, cejas en alto y brazos cruzados.

—Vaaale— cede. A Natalie le da un poco de miedo Susi cuando se pone tan seria que ni parpadea y parece que esos ojos intensos, oscuros como agujeros, se la van a tragar—. De gemela rara, pero que ya sepa hablar.

—Mamá, agua, caca, y ya— enumera Susi, estirando los tres dedos del medio, el pulgar apretando el meñique.

—Qué morro… – murmura Natalie, derrotada al fin por la determinación de sus vecinas y por su propia debilidad—: Ellas se piden lo mejor y yo tengo que hacer de bebé tonto, cuando el colmado es mío...

El colmado es suyo, es doloroso pero es la verdad. Susi y Lorena, que han crecido juntas y apenas tienen que hablar para entenderse, se miran con cómplice preocupación. Van a tener que aflojar un poco la presión sobre Natalie, aunque esté apagada y griposa, y por lo tanto sea fácil de avasallar. Van a tener que aflojar porque, desgraciadamente, injustamente, en medio de la habitación ordenada que comparte con su hermana, que también es rubia y ya tiene novio, los Reyes Magos de Oriente dejaron un exuberante colmado con caja registradora. Fueron así de generosos con ella mientras que a Lorena, cuya lista abarcaba las dos caras de un folio con letra menuda, sólo le dejaron el cochecito de las gemelas, y Susi, que lo había apostado todo a un único y ambicioso regalo, tuvo que conformarse con un libro sobre caballos y unos leotardos. Fue una desilusión muy amarga que Susi tragó como pudo, y que de vez en cuando vuelve para golpear los cristales

'Right, okay', she says mockingly. 'You're showing off because they didn't bring you what you asked for yourself.'

'How do you know what I asked for? Only Lorena and the Kings know that, and you don't.'

Keeping her secret from Natalie, Susi shuts her out from her world and the game. Natalie is the daughter of a single mother, a German, a swimmer, all very modern and exotic for Susi, and into the bargain, she's blond, gets good marks, frequently misses school because she gets colds, and has one helluva grocery store. What doesn't Natalie have? She doesn't have a friend like Lorena. Susi and Lorena are as thick as thieves, two peas in a pod, although Lorena keeps opening and closing the cash register with maximum enjoyment and concentration, as if there were nothing else in the world at this moment in time. Natalie sizes up her own and Susi's strength, the latter waiting for her decision with a stern look, sticking out her tummy, arching her eyebrows and arms folded.

'O-kay', she concedes. When Susi becomes so serious that she doesn't even blink and it seems that those deep eyes, as dark as holes, are going to swallow her up, she makes Natalie a little afraid. 'I'll be the strange twin, but one who can already talk.'

'Mummy, water, pooh, and that's it', Susi counts out, stretching out her three middle fingers, her thumb squeezing her little finger.

'What a cheek...' murmurs Natalie, finally overcome by the determination of her neighbours and her own weakness: 'they ask for what's best and I have to play the dumb baby, when it's my grocery store...'

It's painful but true: the store is hers. Susi and Lorena, who have grown up together and hardly need to speak to understand each other, exchange worried, complicit looks. They are going to have to ease the pressure on Natalie, even though she is out of sorts and full of the flu, and so easy to subjugate. They are going to have to ease up because, unfortunately and unjustly, in the middle of the tidy room that she shares with her sister, who is also blond and already has a boy friend, the Three Wise Men from the East left a splendid grocery store with a cash register. So they were generous to her, whereas they only left the pram with twin dolls for Lorena, whose list, written in small handwriting, covered both sides of a sheet of paper, and Susi who had gambled everything on one single ambitious present, had to make do with a book on horses and a pair of leotards. It was a very bitter disappointment which Susi swallowed as best she could, and which from time to time comes back to smack the graduated lenses of her glasses; but

graduados de sus lentes; pero no va a permitir que la rabia estropee su hora de juego, así que aprieta los dientes y mete a Natalie en el cochecito de las muñecas, mientras Lorena coloca la caja registradora en su lugar, mirándola con devoción. Luego se dan la espalda y cada una se concentra en su personaje unos segundos, los últimos segundos de silencio en esta miniatura microscópica.

–¡Hasta luego, cariño! ¡Nos vamos al súper!–grita Susi.

Y es que, sin más, ha empezado el juego.

–Buenas tardes, señora… Domínguez– dice Lorena con un lápiz en la oreja, en jarras frente al colmado del que ha tomado feliz posesión.

–¿Domínguez?– cuestiona Susi.

–No se me ha ocurrido otro.

–Ya. Pero eso no vale. Cualquiera menos el nuestro. ¡Volvemos a empezar!

Susi da media vuelta. Se quita el chal y se lo vuelve a poner en el mismo gesto envolvente y enérgico. Lorena aprovecha para abrir y cerrar una vez más, con espasmos de éxtasis, la bendita caja registradora. Desde su pasivo rol de bebé con el pulgar en la boca, Natalie vigila de reojo la invasión de su espacio y de sus cosas.

–¡Hasta luego, cariño! ¡Nos vamos al súper!– repite Susi, añadiendo de pronto–: Nena, dile adiós a papá.

Desprevenida, Natalie agita el puño en una improvisación que convence a sus exigentes, mandonas y preparadas vecinas que asienten a la par: ¡Ahora sí!

–Buenas tardes, guapa–le dice la Señora Vendedora a la Señora Compradora.

Natalie no sabe muy bien por qué les ha dado la risa floja pero, por si acaso, les sigue la corriente; emoción de haber puesto los motores en marcha y empezado por fin el viaje…

–Oye–dice Lorena–, ¿tu marido no debería estar trabajando?

–¿Qué quiere decir, Señora Vendedora?

–No, que te estoy hablando en serio, Susi. Cuando las señoras van al súper los maridos trabajan.

–Pues el mío no.

–¿Por qué? ¿Está enfermo?

–Sí.

–¿Y qué tiene? ¿O aún no lo saben?

–Aún no lo saben, pero es algo gordo.

–¿Se muere?

she is not going to allow her anger to spoil her hour of play, so she grits her teeth and forces Natalie into the twins' pram, while Lorena puts the cash register in its place, looking at it lovingly. Then they turn their backs on one another, and each concentrates on her role for a few seconds, the last seconds of silence in that miniature mise-en-scène.

'So long, darling. We're off to the supermarket', shouts Susi.

And with that, the game has got under way.

'Good afternoon, Mrs ... Domínguez', says Lorena with a pencil behind her ear, arms on her hips in front of the store which she is happy to have taken possession of.

'Domínguez?' Susi challenges.

'I couldn't think of another name.'

'Okay, but that one's no good. Any one except ours. Let's start again!'

Susi half turns round. She takes off her shawl and puts it on again with the same all embracing and energetic move. Lorena takes the chance to open and close once again the holy grail of the cash register trembling with excitement. In her passive role as the baby sucking her thumb, Natalie surveys out of the corner of her eye the invasion of her space and things.

'Bye, bye, darling. We're off to the supermarket', Susi says again, suddenly adding: 'say goodbye to daddy, dear.'

Caught off guard, Natalie shakes her fist in a gesture that convinces her demanding, bossy and street-wise neighbours, who approve in unison: 'now, that's more like it.'

'Good afternoon, love', the lady shopkeeper says to the lady shopper.

Natalie does not know exactly why she has given them a thin smile, but just in case she goes with the flow; the excitement of finally having got the engine started and the journey underway...

'Hold on', says Lorena. 'Shouldn't your husband be working?'

'What do you mean, Mrs Shopkeeper?'

'No, I mean it, Susi. When housewives go to the supermarket, their husbands are working.'

'Well, mine isn't.'

'Why? Is he sick?'

'Yes.'

'And what's the matter with him? Or do they not know yet?'

'They don't know yet, but it is something serious.'

'Is he dying?'

–Sí, sí. Yo diría que sí. Oye, Señora Vendedora, ¿tiene limones?

–A ver, a veeer–. Aparte de los tomates y de un puñado de plátanos pegados, sólo hay limones a la vista–. Ah, pues sí, los últimos. ¡Mire qué bonitos, mire qué bien huelen!

Lorena aprieta el limón de plástico contra la nariz de Susi, que aspira con fuerza.

–Mmm, sí. A mi marido le encantan.

–Pobre.

–No, pobre yo. Es pesadísimo.

Risas de nuevo, pero esta vez son alegres y electrizantes. Risas que escapan silbando entre huecos de dientes que han caído, entre dientes de leche colgando o de sierra a medio salir. Natalie protesta porque, como era de esperar, no le hacen ni caso.

–¡Tú, calla!–grita Susi, con una agresividad inesperada–. ¡Cochina, que eres una cochina!

–Ha hecho llorar a la nena, Señora Compradora–advierte Lorena.

Compradora y Vendedora, ceñudas y peligrosas, miran a la nena con expectación. Natalie se repone del susto y reacciona obedeciendo:

–¡Buaaaa…!

–¿No quiere usted doscientos gramos de mortadela cortada muy finita?– pregunta la Señora Vendedora.

Así se lo ha oído Lorena a su madre en el mercado, y se muere por fingir que corta unas lonchas y las empaqueta. Sin esperar confirmación de la Señora Compradora, muy ocupada en intentar levantar a la trilliza llorona, coge el rulo de mortadela de plástico y finge que la corta finita, canturreando exultante, mientras Susi está logrando encajarse a Natalie en la cadera.

–Ea, no llores más– la consuela; hasta que de pronto huele algo, quizá el aliento a jarabe de Natalie, quizá su miedo a quedarse atrás, y la mira sin parpadear con sus severos ojos–. Aquí huele a caca… ¿No huele usted a caca, Señora Vendedora? Me parece que esta niña lleva plasta.

Pero Lorena está concentradísima envolviendo la mortadela imaginaria en un paquetito, como una auténtica profesional.

–Tenga–dice, triunfal.

–Eh, un momento, un momento…-se alarma Natalie, haciéndose con el paquete–. ¿De dónde has cogido esos papeles, Lorena? ¡Son los apuntes de mi hermana!

'Yes, yes. I'd say so. Now listen, Mrs Shopkeeper, are there any lemons?'

'Let me seeee...' Apart from the tomatoes and a bunch of bananas stuck together, there are only lemons on display. 'Ah, yes, the last ones. Look at how nice they are, how nice they smell.'

Lorena presses the plastic lemon against Susi's nose, and she takes a deep breath.

'Mmm, yes. My husband loves them.'

'Poor thing.'

'No, I'm the poor thing. He's boring.'

More laughter, but this time it's jolly and electrifying. Laughter that whistles out through the gaps in lost teeth, between milk teeth still hanging on or incisor teeth half-way out. Natalie protests because, as was to be expected, they take not a jot of notice of her.

'You shut up!' shouts Susi, with unexpected aggression. 'Dirty pig, you're a dirty pig!'

'You've made the baby cry, Mrs Customer', Lorena warns.

Client and shopkeeper, frowning and threatening, look at the baby with expectation. Natalie recovers from her fright and reacts obediently:

'Boo-hoo!...'

'Do you not want two hundred grams of finely cut mortadella?' asks the lady shopkeeper.

She has heard her mother speaking like this in the market, and she is dying to pretend that she is cutting some slices and wrapping them up. Without waiting for assent from the lady customer, who is very occupied in trying to lift the sniveling triplet, she picks up the roll of plastic mortadella, and pretends that she is slicing it very thinly, humming exultantly, while Susi is managing to settle Natalie on her hip.

'There, there, don't cry any more', she consoles her, until she suddenly smells something, perhaps Natalie's breath smelling of syrup, perhaps her fear at being left behind, and her severe eyes look at her without blinking. 'There's a smell of pooh here... Can't you smell pooh, Mrs Shopkeeper? I think this baby's done a big pooh.'

But Lorena is concentrating on wrapping up the imaginary mortadella in a little packet like a true professional.

'Here you are', she says triumphantly.

'Wait a minute, wait a minute', Natalie becomes alarmed, snatching the packet.

'Where did you get that paper, Lorena? They're my sister's school notes.'

–¡Hija mía, te he dicho mil veces que con la comida no se juega!– interviene Susi, devolviendo a Natalie al cochecito y arrebatándole la mortadela.

–Son treinta y cinco con cuarenta– dice Lorena, tecleando de nuevo sin venir a cuento, mientras Susi le arranca el chupete a una muñeca y se lo pone a Natalie bruscamente.

–Hay que ver lo que pesa la niña esta…–se queja, muy teatrera–, y yo con el lumbago a tope.

–Pues, ¿sabe qué, Señora Compradora?, que a mí también me duele el lumbago de tanto trabajar, y que cuando sea mayor me voy a ir a Marina D'Or, que allí hay vacaciones todo el año.

–Es una idea genial, Señora Vendedora.

–Pues si quiere se puede venir conmigo en cuanto se le muera el marido y, bueno, ¿qué más le pongo? Tengo latas de melocotón en almíbar, huevos de gallina…

–Póngame, póngame… ¡Ay, déjeme que lo piense!

Mientras la Señora Compradora se lo piensa, la Señora Vendedora abre y cierra la caja registradora cuatro veces.

–Bueno, vale ya, ¿no?–protesta Natalie–. ¡Que me la vas a estropear!

–¿No tiene chuletas de ternera?– exclama Susi, excitada por el golpe de inspiración.

Lorena repasa nerviosamente toda su mercancía, la que vende en el colmado de Natalie y la que aguarda en la despensa de su imaginación, lista también para la venta.

–Pues no me quedan, no– se lamenta, hasta que de pronto repara en algo–. ¡Pero tengo de cerdo!

–De cerdo no quiero.

–¿Cómo que no? Chuletas de cerdo buenas, bonitas y baratas.

Susi asiente sin mucho entusiasmo; no sabe por qué, pero a veces la inventiva y el talento improvisador de Lorena la irritan profundamente. Natalie observa como Lorena, agitando su alegre cola de caballo, se hace con el ramo de rosas que su hermana tiene en su mesa de estudio:

'Child, I've told you a thousand times that you don't play with food!' interjects Susi, putting Natalie back in the pram and grabbing the mortadella off her.

'That'll be thirty-five euros and 40 cents', says Lorena, once again touching the keys for no reason whatsoever, while Susi grabs a dummy from a doll and roughly sticks it into Natalie's mouth.

'You'll never believe how heavy that baby is', she complains, very theatrically, 'and me with my full-on lumbago...'

'Well, do you know what, Mrs Shopper? My lumbago is causing me pain from so much work, and when I'm older I'm going to go to Marina d'Or,[1] for you can go on holiday there all year round.'

'Brilliant idea, Mrs Shopkeeper.'

'Well, if you want, you can come with me as soon as your husband dies and, now, can I get you anything else? I have tins of peaches in syrup, hen's eggs...'

'Yes, give me some... Well, let me think about it!'

While the lady shopper is thinking about it, the lady shopkeeper opens and closes the cash register four times in a row.

'Right, that's it, okay?' protests Natalie. 'You're going to break it.'

'Don't you have beef chops?' Susi exclaims, excited by a stroke of inspiration.

Lorena goes over all of her stock nervously, what she is selling in Natalie's grocery store and what she is keeping in the pantry of her imagination, also ready to be sold.

'I've got none left, none at all', she says with regret, until she suddenly spots something. 'But I've got pork chops!'

'I don't want pork chops.'

'Why not? Good, nice, cheap pork chops.'

Susi agrees unenthusiastically; she doesn't know why but sometimes Lorena's inventiveness and talent for improvisation deeply irritate her. Natalie looks on as Lorena, shaking her jolly pony tail, picks up the bunch of roses that her sister has on her desk.

---

1   **Marina d'Or**, the so-called *ciudad de vacaciones* [the holiday city], is a mostly family-orientated holiday resort with hotels, spas, and appartments located in Oropesa del Mar, on the Valencian coast. Given the mild climate of the area, it has been advertised by a popular female TV presenter as the place to go on holiday all year round. A product of the building fever and land speculation of the pre-financial crisis era, it is marketed to attract middle-class holiday makers.

–Ni se te ocurra… ¡Que se las ha regalado su novio por San Valentín!

Pero Lorena ignora a Natalie y deshoja las rosas sin compasión.

–Su vecina pasó antes por aquí y se llevó todas las chuletas de ternera– va diciendo–. Se ve que tenía prisa y se fue corriendo como una *insolación*.*

–¿Quién, la hija de la nadadora? No me diga más, si es que ésa es una cochina que va detrás del pobre Jordi, el pesao del ático que se pasa el día ensayando al piano.

–Fue novio mío– presume la Señora Vendedora.

Lorena desempeña su tarea con alto grado de perfección técnica: las hojas arrancadas a la rosa, rojas y aterciopeladas, son ahora chuletas de cerdo que ordena primorosamente en una hoja llena de apuntes de matemáticas. Integrada e inspirada, Lorena vive el juego en su plenitud, mientras Susi está demasiado pendiente de Natalie, y Natalie pendiente de las flores y los apuntes de su hermana.

–¿Le pongo un poquito de perejil?

–Póngame de todo–dice Susi–, que hoy es San Valentín y tengo invitados famosos a cenar.

–¿Ah, sííí?–se interesa Lorena, pestañeando con picardía, cortando los tallos con un cúter que ha encontrado, y envolviéndolo todo como si fuera un regalo de cumpleaños.

–Mi hermana me va a matar…– murmura Natalie.

–Tenga, son veintisiete justitos–. Aunque la compra no ha terminado, Lorena teclea la caja registradora con afición. Luego suspira–: Me encanta ese peinado, Señora Compradora, ¿quién se lo ha hecho?

–Mi madre. Me pone la goma de las gafas debajo de los moños y así no se me caen.

–Se os ha olvidado una cosa muy importante– interrumpe Natalie.

–¿El qué?–preguntan las dos a la vez.

–Tu dinero, Susi, ¿con qué vas a pagar?

–Pagaré con tarjeta.

–¡De eso nada!–salta Lorena–, que entonces no puedo usar la caja registradora.

---

* See footnote 2 in the translation.

'Don't even think about it... They're a Valentine present from her boyfriend.'

But Lorena ignores Natalie and mercilessly takes the petals off the roses:

'Your neighbour called in before and bought all the beef chops', she goes on. She was obviously in a hurry and she took off quickly like *sunstroke*.'[2]

'Who? The swimmer's daughter? Don't tell me any more, for that one's a pig who is chasing poor Jordi, that nuisance on the top floor who spends all day doing piano practice.'

'He was my boyfriend', says the lady shopkeeper presumptuously.

Lorena carries out her task with a high degree of technical skill: the red, velvety petals plucked from the roses are now the pork chops which she arranges beautifully on a sheet of paper full of mathematics notes. Fully engrossed and inspired Lorena is living out the game in its entirety, while Susi is too caught up with Natalie and Natalie with her sister's flowers and school notes.

'Do you want a little parsley?'

'Give me a bit of everything', says Susi, 'because today is Valentine's day and I've invited famous guests to dinner.'

'Ah, is that right?' Lorena gets interested, flashing her eyelashes in a coquettish way, and cutting the stalks with a sharp knife that she has found, and wrapping everything up as though it were a birthday gift.

'My sister is going to kill me...' murmurs Natalie.

'Here you are, that will be twenty seven euros exactly.' Although the shopping is not over, Lorena enthusiastically presses the keys of the cash register. Then she sighs: 'I love that hair style, Mrs Shopper, who did your hair?'

'My mother. She puts the elastic band of my glasses under my buns so my glasses don't fall off.'

'But you've both forgotten something very important', Natalie interrupts her.

'What?', both of them ask at the same time.

'Your money, Susi. What are you going to pay with?'

'I'll pay with my card.'

'You'll do no such thing!' Lorena interjects, 'because then I can't use the cash register.'

---

2   Lorena's enthusiasm when playing the role of Mrs Shopkeepper leads her to get confused with two words of similar phonetics: *como una exhalación*, which means doing something very quickly, in the blink of an eye, what she actually meant to say, and *insolación*, which means sunstroke.

Susi está de su parte, puesto que compartirá su momento estelar, la operación del recuento total y devolución del cambio, apoteosis de toda Señora Vendedora que se precie.

–Ya has abierto y cerrado bastantes veces, ¿no te parece?– opina Natalie.

–¡Pues mira, una más!–replica Lorena, hundiendo la tecla del siete hasta que hace *clic*, y sacando un puñado de monedas de plástico–: Toma, Susi, para que me pagues cuando me hayas comprado todo, pero todo todo, dentro de una hora.

–Media–corrige Natalie–. O menos, os quedan unos minutos. ¿Se puede saber qué haces ahora?

–Fumo–dice Lorena, con el lápiz en la boca–. Cuando sea mayor, fumaré Fortuna.

–Y yo– se apunta Susi.

–Pues yo no. Fumar es malo.

–¿Sabe que le digo, Señora Compradora? Que su trilliza es insoportable y repelente, y que si al final viene conmigo a Marina d'Or se me trae sólo a las gemelas, ¿vale?

–Vale, pero venga, venga…– Susi se impacienta. Natalie les ha echado el tiempo encima y hay que seguir adelante–. Póngame leche para esta niña que no me come nada… Pero le decía que esta noche me viene a cenar el padrino de las trillizas, un cantante que es muy famoso…

–Ah, sí, sí– dice Lorena. Fue novio mío.

–… así que póngame algo un poco de lujo, no sé, ¿no tiene pechinas de esas negras?

–¿Mejillones?

–No, esas pechinas negras que tienen una perla dentro.

–Ostras–dice Natalie–. En alemán se dicen *austern*.

–¡Huy, qué sabionda la nena!–exclama Lorena–. Sabe matemáticas, alemán, ¡todo!

–Venga, venga…– se apresura Susi, sacando del cochecito un enorme biberón de juguete–. Mientras me pone las *austern* yo le doy el bibe para que se calle.

Lorena localiza rápidamente el joyero de las hermanas en un ángulo de la estantería, saca un collar de cuentas y empieza a cortarlo con unas tijeras. Natalie protesta, pero Susi le mete el chupete en la boca, aferrando su nuca

Susi is on her side, since she will share her moment in the limelight, the operation of adding everything up and returning change, the highlight of every lady shopkeeper with a sense of esteem.

'You've already opened and closed it more than enough, don't you think?' says Natalie.

'Well, just look, there's one more go', replies Lorena, pressing down the number seven key until it clicks, and taking out a handful of plastic coins. 'Here, take it, Susi, so you can pay me when you've bought everything, really everything, in an hour's time.'

'Half an hour', Natalie corrects her. 'Or less, you two have a few minutes left. May I ask what you're doing now?'

'I'm smoking', says Lorena, with the pencil in her mouth. 'When I grow up, I'll smoke Fortuna.'[3]

'And me too', Susi joins in.

'Well, I shan't. Smoking is bad.'

'Do you know what, Mrs Shopper? Your triplet is unbearable and disgusting, and if you decide to come to Marina d'Or with me just bring along the twins, alright?'

'Alright, but come on, come on', says Susi impatiently. Natalie has drawn their attention to the time and they must get on. 'Give me milk for this child who won't eat anything for me... Well, as I was telling you, tonight the triplet's godfather, a very famous singer, is coming to dinner...'

'Ah, yes, yes', says Lorena, 'he was my boyfriend.'

'So give me something on the expensive side; I don't know, don't you have any of those big black clams?'

'Mussels?'

'No, those big black clams that have a pearl inside them.'

'Oysters', says Natalie. 'In German they're called *austern*.'

'Wow, what a know all this child is!' exclaims Lorena. 'She knows Maths, German, everything!'

'Come on, come on', Susi bustles about, taking out of the pram a big toy baby's bottle. 'While you're serving me with the *austern*, I'll give this baby her bottle to keep her quiet.'

Lorena finds the sisters' jewellery box on a corner of the shelves, takes out a necklace and begins to cut the beads with scissors. Natalie protests, but Susi sticks the bottle in her mouth, holding her neck tightly with her

---

3 **Fortuna**, a Spanish brand of tobacco, popular at one time amongst women smokers and cheaper than the American ones, such as Marlboro or Winston.

con la otra mano. Cuando Lorena coge el cúter para abrir los mejillones a la fuerza, Natalie aumenta los gruñidos y Susi propone a voces:

–¿Vale que yo llevaba un móvil en el bolso y me llamaban que por fin se había muerto el marido y así podía casarme con el cantante famoso en la cena de San Valentín?

La idea de Susi, como muchas de sus ideas, es confusa y poco resolutiva.

–Bueno, vale, venga– consiente Lorena, por no discutir en la recta final.

–Sí. Vaya. Ah. Bueno– va diciendo Susi al teléfono imaginario que sujeta entre el hombro y la mejilla–. Ya está. Era el médico del hospital.

–Fue novio mío–dice Lorena, que ha abierto con el cúter los mejillones del colmado de Natalie y les está metiendo cuentas del collar una a una.

De pronto ven que Natalie, en medio del fragor imparable del juego, se ha quedado adormecida con el biberón en la boca, y les da un ataque de risa histérica, agachándose sobre el talón del pie para no mearse encima; ni un segundo el tiempo que les queda van a perder en ir al baño.

–¿Mami? – murmura Natalie, con un hilo de voz.

Han golpeado a la puerta, eso significa que el tiempo se acaba y hay que resolver ya.

–*Es geth mir nicht gut* (No me encuentro bien)–murmura Natalie.

–¿Qué dice?–pregunta Susi.

–Yo qué sé–contesta Lorena.

–*Mir ist kalt* (Tengo frío).

–Está tiritando y no se le entiende nada– dice Susi, tapándola instintivamente.

–¡Deprisa, deprisa, Susi!

Se sitúan una frente a otra. Dos Señoras responsables, una al mando del negocio y de la caja registradora, la otra al volante de un cochecito en el que duermen tres niñas. Vendedora y Compradora carraspean, se ponen serias y, con una calma sorprendente, encaran la recta de salida de forma sencilla, sobria, perfecta.

–Dígame, Señora Vendedora, ¿cuánto es?

Lorena teclea con aplomo, con experiencia, y luego pronuncia una cifra complicada con una sonrisa tan serena que asusta:

–Ochenta y nueve euros con cuarenta y siete céntimos, cuarenta y cinco para usted.

other hand. When Lorena picks up the sharp knife to force open the mussels, Natalie increases her grunting and Susi shouts out:

'Is it okay if I had a mobile phone in my handbag and someone called to tell me that at last my husband had died and so I could get married to the famous singer during the Valentine's day dinner?'

Like many of Susi's ideas, this one is confusing and inconclusive.

'Well, okay, okay', Lorena agrees to avoid quarrelling on the home straight.

'Yes. Imagine that. Ah, good!' Susi is saying into the imaginary phone held between her cheek and shoulder. 'That's that. It was the doctor from the hospital.'

'He was my boyfriend once', says Lorena, who has opened the mussels from Natalie's grocery store with the sharp knife and is putting the necklace beads into them one by one.

Suddenly they see that, amid the non-stop hubbub of the game, Natalie has gone to sleep with the teat in her mouth, and they are seized with an attack of hysterical laughter, bending over on their heels to stop wetting themselves; they aren't going to waste a second of the time left to them by going to the toilet.

'Mummy?' Natalie whispers in a small voice.

They have banged on the door, which means that time is up and a decision has to be made.

'*Es geht mir nicht gut* (I don't feel well)', Natalie whispers.

'What's she saying?' asks Susi.

'How do I know?' answers Lorena.

'*Mir ist kalt* (I'm cold).'

'She's shivering and you can't make out anything she's saying', says Suzi, instinctively wrapping her up.

'Quick, quick, Suzi!'

One stands in front of the other. Two responsible ladies, one in charge of the business and the cash register, the other steering a pram in which three little girls are asleep. Buyer and seller clear their throats, become serious, and with surprising calm, face the home straight in a simple, sober and perfect way,

'Tell me, Mrs Shopkeeper, how much is it?'

Lorena presses the keys with aplomb, with experience, and then states a complicated figure with such a serene smile that it is frightening:

'Eighty-nine euros plus forty-seven cents, forty-five for you.'

–Tenga.

–Deme.

Se produce el intercambio sin ningún incidente.

–Gracias y adiós, Señora Compradora. ¡Nos vemos en Marina d'Or!

Ya está, el juego ha terminado. Lorena está sofocada y satisfecha, pero Susi parece ensimismada; dentro de poco estará otra vez en su habitación, y tendrá que vérselas de nuevo con su infancia frustrada, con el vacío que han dejado todas la muñecas y los peluches que ya no están, todos los juguetes de los que se deshizo para hacer espacio al regalo soñado, la bolsa llena de paja y el barreño para el agua aún bajo la cama...

–No estés triste–le dice Lorena–. El año que viene te lo traerán, ya lo verás.

–Sí, vale– se esfuerza Susi, resistiendo los envites de la tristeza.

El año que viene; pero mientras volverán a sus cocinitas, a compartir el cuidado de las gemelas de Lorena, y a hojear juntas ese libro de caballos.

–Qué bonito es, ¿verdad?– suspira Lorena por el colmado. Luego mira a Natalie, que parece dormida con las piernas colgándole a cada lado del cochecito–. No hay derecho. ¿Tú crees que se lo han traído porque no tiene padre?

–Qué va, si son alemanas... Se lo han traído– sostiene Susi –porque ha sacado buenas notas y no pega a su hermana. Mira, Lorena, si a mí no me han traído lo que me he pedido ha sido por lo del comedor del cole, que los Reyes Magos lo ven todo, ¿no has pensado?

–¿Tú crees? ¿Crees que te han visto meterte el escalope en los bolsillos?

–Estoy segura. Lo que no entiendo es por qué me traen leotardos, si los odio. Son unos cabrones...

Alguien, la madre de Natalie, vuelve a golpear discretamente la puerta. Se ha acabado el tiempo de juego. Mientras Lorena recoge el estropicio, Susi espabila a Natalie.

–Natalie... Natalie, despierta que ya nos vamos.

Susi la acompaña hasta su cama entre los restos de la batalla: los mejillones rajados, el collar de la hermana y las flores del enamorado, añicos todo, los apuntes inservibles, el joyero saqueado, la caja registradora encasquillada, el colmado arrasado.

–No me importa–dice Natalie, sin pena ni rabia–. Me comprarán otro.

'Here you are.'

'I'll take it.'

The exchange takes place without further ado.

'Thanks and good bye, Mrs Buyer. We'll see each other in Marina d'Or.'

That's it, the game is over. Lorena is breathless and happy, but Susi seems lost in thought; she will shortly be in her room again, and she will have to contend once again with her frustrated fantasy, with the vacuum left by all the dolls and soft toys that are no longer there, all the toys that she got rid of to make way for the longed for gift, the bag filled with straw and the bowl for water still under her bed...

'Don't be sad', Lorena says to her. 'They'll bring it to you next year, you'll see.'

'Yes, okay', Susi tries to be resilient, fighting off the bouts of sadness.

Next year; but in the meantime they'll go back to their playing at houses, sharing, caring for Lorena's twin dolls, and turning the pages together of that book about horses.

'How pretty it is, isn't it?' Lorena sighs at the grocery shop. Then she looks at Natalie, who appears to be asleep with a leg hanging out of each side of the buggy. 'It's not right. Do you think they brought it to her because she hasn't got a father?'

'Get away, they're Germans...' 'They brought it to her', Susi maintains, 'because she got good marks and doesn't hit her sister. Look, Lorena, if they didn't bring me what I asked for it's because of what happened in the refectory at school, because the Three Kings see everything, haven't you thought about that?'

'You think so? Do you think they saw you putting the escalope in your pocket?'

'I'm sure. What I don't understand is why they brought me a pair of leotards, if I hate them. They are bastards...'

Someone, Natalie's mother, discretely knocks on the door again. Playtime has finished. While Lorena tidies up the mess, Susi wakens up Natalie:

'Natalie... Natalie, wake up, we're going now.'

Susi takes her to her bed amid the remnants of battle: the shredded mussels, her sister's necklace and her boyfriend's flowers, all smashed to pieces, the school notes unusable, the jewelry box ransacked, the cash register jammed, the grocery store in ruins.

'I don't care', says Natalie, neither aggrieved nor angry. 'They'll buy me another one.'

–Tan chulo como éste, fijo que no les queda ni uno– asegura Susi en su oído.

Una vez acostada y tapada por Susi hasta la barbilla, Natalie saca su medalla por encima de la colcha.

–Los Reyes Magos no existen, Susi. Ni Papá Noel tampoco. Son los padres los que eligen y compran los regalos. Mi madre me lo comprará…

–¿Qué dice?–pregunta Lorena, asomando de pronto tras el colmado.

Por la mirada que Susi le devuelve, Lorena comprende que se trata de algo serio y se acerca a su amiga. En la cabecera de la cama de Natalie, volcadas ambas sobre su rostro encendido por la fiebre, parecen desenchufadas de repente.

–A ver– dice Natalie, mirando a una y a otra–. ¿Adónde llevasteis vuestra carta?

–Al Caprabo – dice Susi–. Se la dimos las dos a la vez.

–¿A qué Rey se la disteis? ¿Os acordáis?

–Pues claro– dice Susi–. Yo al Baltasar y ésta al Gaspar, al pelirrojo…

–Y… ¿no se parecía a Manolo, nuestro portero, el Rey Gaspar? Y el paje, ¿no os recordó a mi hermana?

Susi y Lorena se dan la mano sobre la colcha y comparten un escalofrío. Ambas se habían fijado, pero no se lo habían dicho la una a la otra, no se lo habían dicho ni a sí mismas. Natalie sigue hablando, la dulzura de su voz contrasta con la crueldad de sus palabras:

–Nos estuvimos riendo de vosotras toooda la noche.

–Mientes…– dice Susi, resistiéndose aún a la dramática revelación, pero herida en lo más profundo de su desconfiado ser.

–Lorena, busca ahí–. Natalie levanta un bracito con esfuerzo y señala el escritorio de su hermana–. Debajo de esa carpeta rosa está la carta de Susi.

–¡Mientes para vengarte porque te hemos destrozado el colmado, y la caja registradora, y las cosas de tu hermana!–Pero Natalie niega con la cabeza, sus trenzas rubias se retuercen sobre la almohada–. ¡Y porque te hemos robado, mira!

Susi muestra a la enferma todo lo que extrae de sus bolsillos: unas cuantas monedas de plástico, un limón, un minicartón de leche, un par de clips para el pelo que Natalie ha debido de perder en el cochecito y un trozo reseco de escalope.

'As good as this one, sure there's not another one', Susi says into her ear.

Once put to bed and covered up to her chin by Susi, Natalie sticks her medal out of the top of the quilt:

'The Three Kings don't exist, Susi. Neither does Father Christmas. It's our parents who choose and pay for the presents. My mother will buy it for me...'

'What are you saying?' asks Lorena, suddenly appearing from behind the grocery store.

From the look that Susi directs at her, Lorena understands that it is something important and she goes towards her friend. Standing beside Natalie's headboard, both bend over her face flushed with fever, and they suddenly seem switched off.

'Let's see', says Natalie looking from one to the other. 'Where did you take your letter to?'

'To the Caprabo supermarket', says Susi. 'We both gave ours to them at the same time.'

'To which King did you give it? Do you remember?'

'Of course', says Susi. 'I gave mine to Balthazar, and she gave hers to Gaspar, the red-haired one.'

'And did King Gaspar not look like our caretaker Manolo? And the page, did he not remind you of my sister?'

Susi and Lorena hold hands above the quilt and each shivers. Both had noticed that, but neither had said anything to the other, they hadn't even said it to themselves. Natalie goes on talking, the sweetness of her tone contrasting with her cruel words:

'We were laughing at you all night long.'

'You're lying', says Susi, still fighting against the dramatic revelation, but wounded in the deepest part of her distrusting being.

'Lorena, look over there.' Natalie raises her little arm with an effort and points to her sister's writing desk. 'Susi's letter is under that pink file.'

'You're lying to get your own back because we destroyed your grocery store, the cash register and your sister's things.' But Natalie shakes her head no, her blond tresses twisting on the pillow. 'And because we stole from you, look!'

Susi shows the patient everything she takes out of her pockets: some plastic coins, a lemon, a small carton of milk, a pair of hair grips that Natalie must have lost in the buggy and a dried up bit of escalope.

–¡¡Mira!!– grita, con los ojos llenos de lágrimas de rabia, pero Natalie aprieta la medalla de su madre y sonríe.

–Susi...– dice Lorena, ya con la carta en la mano.

Falseando la voz, y sin dejar de sonreír en ningún momento, Natalie recita de memoria:

–Queridos Reyes Magos: lo que más me gusta del mundo mundial son los caballos. Por eso este año me pido un poni, y nada más. Sólo quiero un poni. Muchas gracias. Soy la Susi.

'Look!' she shouts, with her eyes full of angry tears, but Natalie squeezes her mother's medal and smiles.

'Susi...' says Lorena, with the letter now in her hand.

Putting on a false voice, and without breaking her smile, Natalie recites from memory:

'Dear Wise Kings, what I like best in the whole world are horses. So, I am asking for a pony and nothing else. I only want a pony. Thank you very much. My name is Susi.'

A SELECTION OF CRITICAL WORKS
ON SPANISH WOMEN'S WRITING SINCE 1997

(DEALING WITH MORE THAN ONE SINGLE AUTHOR)

Martha Ackelsberg, *Free Women of Spain: Anarchism and Struggle for the Emancipation of Women* (Edinburgh: AK Press, 2005).

Jean Andrews, 'Poetry and Silence in Post-War Spain: Carmen Conde, Lucía Sánchez Saornil and Pilar de Valderrama', in M. Bragança and P. Tame (eds), *The Long Aftermath: Cultural Legacies of Europe at War, 1936–2016* (New York and Oxford: Berghahn, 2016), 40–59.

Josefa Álvarez (ed.), *Laberintos de género: muerte, sacrificio y dolor en la literatura femenina en España* (Sevilla: Renacimiento, 2016).

María Angulo Egea and Teodoro León Gross (eds), *Artículo femenino singular. Diez mujeres fundamentales en la historia del articulismo español* (Cádiz: Ediciones APN; Fundación Alcántara; Asociación de la Prensa de Cádiz; Fundación Manuel Alcántara, 2011).

Milagros Arizmendi and Guadalupe Arbona Abascal (eds), *Letra de mujer (La escritura femenina y sus protagonistas analizados desde otra perspectiva)* (Madrid: Ediciones del Laberinto, 2008).

Christine Arkinstall, 'Towards a Female Symbolic: Re-Presenting Mothers and Daughters in Contemporary Spanish Narrative by Women', in A. Giorgio (ed.), *Writing Mothers and Daughters: Renegotiating the Mother in Western European Narratives by Women* (New York: Berghahn Books, 2002), 47–84.

Encarnación Barranquero Texeira (ed.), *Mujeres en la Guerra Civil y el franquismo: violencia, silencio y memoria de los tiempos difíciles* (Málaga: Centro de Ediciones de la Diputación Provincial de Málaga, 2010).

Emilie L. Bergmann and Richard Herr (eds), *Mirrors and Echoes: Women's Writing in Twentieth-Century Spain* (Berkeley: Global Area, and International Archive; University of California Press, 2007).

Marguerita Bernard and Ivana Rota (eds), *Mujer, prensa y libertad: (España 1883–1939)* (Sevilla: Renacimiento, 2015).

María José Blanco and Claire Williams (eds), *Feminine Singular: Women Growing Up through Life-Writing in the Luso-Hispanic World* (Oxford: Peter Lang, 2017).

Anny Brooksbank Jones, *Women in Contemporary Spain* (Manchester: Manchester University Press, 1997).

L. Buonomo, *Maschere. Le scritture delle donne nelle culture iberiche* (Roma: Bulzoni, 1994).

Anna Caballé (ed.), *La vida escrita por las mujeres* (4 vols.) (Barcelona: Círculo de Lectores, 2003).

Nuria Capdevila-Argüelles, *Autoras inciertas. Voces olvidadas de nuestro feminismo* (Madrid: horas y HORAS, 2008).

Nuria Capdevila-Argüelles, *Artistas y precursoras. Un siglo de autoras Roësset* (Madrid: horas y HORAS, 2013).

Isabel Carrero Suárez and María Socorro Suárez Lafuente (eds), *Como mujeres: releyendo a escritoras del XIX y XX* (Oviedo: Principado de Asturias, Dirección Regional de la Mujer, 1994).

Susana Cavalho (ed.), *Estudios en honor de Janet Pérez. El sujeto femenino en escritoras hispánicas* (Potomac, MA: Scripta Humanitistica, 1998).

María Cibreiro and Francisca López (eds), *Global Issues in Contemporary Hispanic Women's Writing: Shaping Gender, the Environment, and Politics* (Ney York: Routledge, 2013).

Biruté Ciplijauskaité, *La construcción del* yo *femenino en la literatura* (Cádiz: Servicio de Publicaciones de la Universidad de Cádiz, 2004).

Raquel Conde Peñalosa, *Mujeres novelistas y novelas de mujeres en la postguerra española (1940–1965). Catálogo bio-bibliográfico* (Madrid: Fundación Universitaria Española, 2004).

Rosalía Cornejo-Parriego, *Entre mujeres: política de la amistad y el deseo en la narrativa española contemporánea* (Madrid: Biblioteca Nueva, 2002).

Cristobal Cuevas García and Enrique Baena (eds), *Escribir mujer. Narradoras españolas hoy* (Publicaciones del Congreso de Literatura Española Contemporánea, 2000).

Catherine Davies and Jane Whetnall (eds), *Hers Ancient and Modern: Women's Writing in Spain and Brazil* (Manchester: Spanish and Portuguese Studies, University of Manchester, 1997).

Catherine Davies, *Spanish Women's Writing 1849–1996* (London and Atlantic Highlands, NJ: The Athlone Press, 1998).

Josefina de Andrés Argente and Rosa García Rayego (eds), *Las damas negras: novela policíaca escrita por mujeres* (Madrid: Fundamentos, 2011).

Ángeles de la Concha and Raquel Osborne (eds), *Las mujeres y los niños primero: discursos de la maternidad* (Barcelona: Icaria, 2004).

Inmaculada de la Fuente, *Mujeres de la posguerra,* (Barcelona: Planeta, 2002).

Xon de Ros, and Geraldine Hazburn (eds), *A Companion to Spanish Women's Studies* (Woodbridge: Tamesis, 2011).

Marta Duch, *Dones públiques. Política i gènere a l'Espanya del segle XX* (Tarragona: Arola, 2004).

Ángela Ena Bordonada (ed.), *La otra Edad de Plata: temas, géneros y creadores (1898–1936)* (Madrid: Editorial Complutense, 2013).

Ángeles Encinar and Carmen Valcárcel (eds), *Escritoras y compromiso. Literatura española e hispanoamericana de los siglos XX y XXI* (Madrid: Visor, 2009).

Victoria Lorée Enders and Pamela Beth Radcliff (eds), *Constructing Spanish Womanhood: Female Identity in Modern Spain* (Albany, NY: State University of New York Press, 1999).

Pura Fernández and Marie-Linda Ortega (eds), *La mujer de letras o letraherida: discurso y representaciones de la mujer escritora en el siglo XXI* (Madrid: CSIC, 2008).

Ofelia Ferrán and Kathleen M. Glenn (eds), *Women's Narrative and Film in Twentieth-Century Spain: A World of Difference* (New York: Routledge, 2002).

Laura Freixas, (ed.), *Ser mujer* (Madrid: Temas de Hoy, 2000).

Laura Freixas, *Literatura y mujeres: escritoras, público y crítica en la España actual* (Barcelona: Destino, 2000).

Laura Freixas, *La novela femenil y sus lectrices: La desvalorización de las mujeres y lo femenino en la crítica literaria española actual* (Córdoba: Servicio de Publicaciones de la Universidad de Córdoba, 2008).

Laura Freixas, *El silencio de la madres (y otras reflexiones sobre las mujeres en la cultura)* (Barcelona: Aresta, 2015).

Bernard Fouques and Antonio Martínez González (eds), *Imágenes de mujeres/ Images de femmes* (Caen: Université de Caen, 1998).

Yvonne Fuentes and Margaret R. Parker (eds), *Leading Ladies: Mujeres en la literatura hispana y las artes* (Baton Rouge: Louisiana State University Press, 2006).

Fuera de orden: Mujeres de la Vanguardia Española [María Blanchard; Norah Borges; Maruja Mallo; Olga Sacharoff; Ángeles Santos; Remedios Varo] (Madrid: Fundación Cultural Mapfre Vida, 1999).

Jairo García Jaramillo, *La mitad ignorada: (en torno a las mujeres intelectuales de la Segunda República)* (Madrid: Devenir/Juan Pastor, 2013).

Elisa Garrido, *Historia de las mujeres en España*(Madrid: Síntesis, 1997).

Kathleen M. Glenn and Kathleen McNerney (eds), *Visions and Revisions: Women's Narrative in 20th-Century Spain* (Amsterdam: Rodopi, 2008).

Shelley Godsland, *Killing Carmens: Women's Crime Fiction from Spain* (Cardiff: University of Wales Press, 2007).

María Gómez Martín, *No son batallas lo que quiero contar: la mujer medieval en la novela histórica de autora* (Oviedo: KRK, 2012).

Helena González Fernández, *Género y nación: la construcción de un espacio literario* (Madrid: Icaria, 2009).

Christina Henseler, *En sus propias palabras: escritoras españolas ante el mercado literario* (Madrid: Torremozas, 2003).

Marisa Herrera Postlewate, *How and Why I Write: Redefining Hispanic Women's Writing and Experience* (New York: Peter Lang, 2003).

Joan M. Hoffman, *Voces femeninas de España: una antología* (San Juan, Puerto Rico: Penélope Academic Press, 2015).

Elizabeth Teresa Howe, *Autobiographical Writing by Early Modern Hispanic Women* (Farnham, Surrey: Ashgate, 2015).

Alastair Hurst (ed.), *Writing Women: Essays on the Representation of Women in Contemporary Western Literature* (Victoria: Antípodas Monographs, 2002).

Catherine Jagoe, Ada Blanco and Cristina Enríquez de Salamanca (eds), *La mujer en los discursos de género: textos y contextos en el siglo XIX* (Barcelona: Icaria, 1998).

Roberta Johnson and Maite Zubiaurre (eds.), *Antología del pensamiento feminista español (1726-2011)* (Madrid: Ediciones Cátedra, Universitat de València, 2012).

Ursula Jung, *Autorinnen des Spanischen Barok: weibliche Autorschaft in weltichen und religiösen kontextexten* (Aufl.- Heidenberg: Winter, 2010).

Nino Kebade, *Romance and Exemplarity in Post-War Spanish Women's Narratives* (Woodbridge: Tamesis, 2009).

Susan Kirkpatrick, *Mujer, modernismo y vanguardia en España: 1898–1931* (Madrid: Cátedra, 2003).

Sarah Leggott, *History and Autobiography in Contemporary Spanish Women's Testimonial Writings* (Lewisburgh: Bucknell University Press, 2001).

Sarah Leggott, *The Writings of Memory: Life-writing by Women in Early Twentieth-Century Spain* (Lewisburgh: Bucknell University Press, 2008).

Sarah Leggot, *Memory, War, and Dictatorship in Recent Spanish Fiction by Women* (Lewisburgh: Bucknell University Press, 2015).

Elizabeth Franklin Lewis, *Women Writers in the Spanish Enlightenment: the Pursuit of Happiness* (Aldershot: Ashgate Publishing, 2004).

María del Mar López Cabrales, *Palabras de mujeres. Escritoras españolas contemporáneas* (Madrid: Narcea, 2003).

María del Mar López Cabrales, 'Tras el rostro/ rastro oculto de las mujeres en la Generación del 27', *Letras Femeninas*, Spring (1999), 173–87.

Shirley Mangini González, *Recuerdos de la resistencia: la voz de las mujeres de la guerra civil española,* trans. by T. Kennedy (Barcelona: Península, 1997).

Susan Martin-Márquez, *Feminist Discourse and Spanish Cinema: Sight Unseen* (Oxford: Oxford University Press, 1999).

Rafael M. Mérida Jiménez (ed.), *Mujer y género en las letras hispánicas* (Lleida: Universitat de Lleida, 2008).

Rafael M. Mérida Jiménez, *Mujer y cultura literaria en las letras ibéricas medievales y del renacimiento trempano* (Kassel: Edition Reichenberger, 2011).

Pepa Merlo (ed.), *Peces en la tierra: antología de mujeres poetas en torno a la Generación del 1927* (Sevilla: Fundación José Manuel Lara, 2010).

Nina Molinaro, 'Narrating Women in the Post-War Spanish Novel', in M. Altisent (ed.), *A Companion to the Twentieth-Century Spanish Novel* (Woodbridge: Tamesis, 2008), 161–73.

Lucía Montejo Gurruchaga and Nieves Baranda Leturio (eds), *Las mujeres escritoras en la historia de la literatura española* (Madrid: UNED, 2002).

Ana María Muñoz, Carmen Gregorio Gil and Adelina Sánchez Espinosa (eds),

Cuerpos de mujeres: miradas, representaciones e identitades (Granada: Universidad de Granada, 2007).

Mary Nash, *Rojas: las mujeres republicanas en la Guerra Civil*, trans. by I. Cifuentes (Madrid: Taurus, 2006).

Pilar Nieva de la Paz, *Narradoras españolas en la transición política (Textos y contextos)* (Madrid: Editorial Fundamentos, 2004).

Pilar Nieva-de la Paz (ed.), *Roles de género y cambio social en la literatura española del siglo XX* (Amsterdam: Rodopi, 2009).

Patricia O'Byrne, *Post-War Spanish Women Novelists and the Recuperation of Historical Memory* (Woodbridge: Tamesis, 2014).

Julián Olivares (ed.), *Studies on Women's Poetry of the Golden Age: tras el espejo la musa escribe* (Woodbridge: Tamesis, 2009).

Janet Pérez and Maureen Ihrie (eds), *The Feminist Encyclopaedia of Spanish Literature* (Westport: Greenwood Press, 2002).

Janet Pérez, Monica Jato and Sharon Keefe Ugalde (eds), *Mujer, creación, exilio (España 1939–1975)* (Barcelona: Icaria, 2009).

María José Porro Herrera and Blas Sánchez Dueñas (eds), *Mujer y memoria: representaciones, identidades y códigos* (Córdoba: Servicio de Publicaciones de la Universidad de Córdoba, 2009).

Cinta Ramblado-Minero (ed.), *Construcciones culturales de la maternidad en España: la madre y la relación madre-hija en la literatura y el cine contemporáneos* (Alacant: Centre d'Estudis sobre la Dona, Universitat d'Alacant, 2006).

Alicia Redondo Goicoechea (ed.), *Mujeres novelistas: jóvenes narradoras de los noventa* (Madrid: Narcea, 2003).

Manuel Francisco Reina (ed.), *Mujeres de carne y verso: antología poética femenina en lengua española del siglo XX* (Madrid: La Esfera de los Libros, 2001).

María Pilar Rodríguez, *Vidas impropias: Transformaciones del sujeto femenino en la narrativa española contemporánea* (West Lafayette, IND: Purdue University Press, 2000).

Lissette Rolón-Collazo, *Figuraciones: mujeres en Carmen Martín Gaite, revistas feministas y 'Hola'* (Madrid: Iberoamericana, 2002).

Assumpta Roura (ed.), *Un inmenso prostíbulo: mujer y moralidad durante el franquismo* (Barcelona: Editorial Base, 2005).

Juana Sabadell Nieto, *Desbordamientos: transformaciones culturales y políticas de las mujeres* (Barcelona: Icaria, 2011).

Iñigo Sánchez Llama *(ed.), Antología de la prensa periódica isabelina escrita por mujeres, 1843–1894* (Cádiz: Servicio de Publicaciones de la Universidad de Cádiz, 2001).

María Isabel Sancho Rodríguez, Lourdes Ruiz Solves and Francisco Gutiérrez García (eds), *Estudios sobre lengua, literatura y mujer* (Jaén: Universidad de Jaén, 2006).

Cristina Segura Graíño (ed.), *Feminismo y misoginia en la literatura española: fuentes literarias para la historia de las mujeres* (Madrid: Narcea, 2001).

Theresa Ann Smith, *Emerging Female Citizen: Gender and Enlightment in Spain* (Berkeley, CA: University of California Press, 2008).

Maureen Tobin Stanley and Gesa Zin, *Female exiles in Twentieth and Twenty-First Century Europe* (New York; Basingstoke, England: Palgrave Macmillan, 2007).

Meri Torras Francès, *Tomando cartas ern el asunto. Las amistades peligrosas de las mujeres con el género epistolar* (Zaragoza: Prensas Universitarias de Zaragoza, 2015).

Meri Torras, *Soy como consiga que me imaginéis: la construcción de la subjetividad en las autobiografías epistolares de Gertrudis Gómez de Avellaneda y Sor Juana Inés de la Cruz* (Cádiz: Servicio de Publicaciones de la Universidad de Cádiz, 2003).

Tiffany Trotman (ed.) *The Changing Spanish Family: Essays on New Views in Litearture, cinema and Theatre* (Jefferson, N.C. and London: McFarland, 2011).

Julia Varela, *Mujeres con voz propia: Carmen Baroja y Nessi, Zenobia Camprubí Aymar y María Teresa León Goyri: análisis sociológico de las autobiografías de tres mujeres de la bueguesía liberal española* (Madrid: Ediciones Morata, 2011).

María Francisca Vilches Frutos and Pilar Nieva de la Paz (eds), *Imágenes femeninas en la literatura española y las artes escénicas* (Philadelphia, PA: Society of Spanish and Spanish-American Studies, 2012).

Marina Villaba Álvarez (ed.) *Mujeres novelistas en el panorama literario del siglo XX* (Cuenca: Ediciones de la Universidad de Castilla-La Mancha, 2000).

Lisa Vollendorf (ed.), *Recovering Spanish Feminist Tradition* (New York: The Modern Language Association of America, 2001). [Spanish translation as *Literatura y feminismo en España (s. XV–XXI)* (Barcelona: Icaria, 2005)].

Nancy Vosburg and Jacky Collins (eds), *Lesbian Realities/ Lesbian Fictions in Contemporary Spain* (Lewisburg: Bucknell University Press, 2011).

Mercedes Yusta Rodrigo, *Madres Coraje contra Franco: la Unión de Mujeres Españolas en Francia: del anarquismo a la Guerra Fría* (Madrid: Cátedra, 2009).

Iris M. Zavala, *Breve historia feminista de la literatura española (en lengua castellana)* (Barcelona: Anthropos, 1998).

A SELECTION OF ANTHOLOGIES
OF SPANISH *CUENTOS* AND STUDIES
ON THE SHORT-STORY GENRE SINCE 1997

Anthologies (entry by title; chronologically ordered)

Páginas amarillas, edited by Antonio Álamo. Prologue by Sabas Martín (Madrid: Lengua de Trapo, 1997).

Proceder a sabiendas: antología de la narrativa de vanguardia española (1923–1936), edited by Domingo Ródenas de Moya (Barcelona: Alba, 1997).

Relatos para un fin de milenio, edited by Elena Butragueño and Javier Goñi (Barcelona: Plaza y Janés, 1998).

Gentes del 98, edited by Elena Butragueño and Javier Goñi (Barcelona: Plaza y Janés, 1998).

Contemporary Spanish Short Stories: Viajeros perdidos, edited by Jean Andrews and Montserrat Lunati (London: Bristol Classical Press, 1998).

Historias de detectives, edited by Ángeles Encinar (Barcelona: Lumen, 1998).

Los mejores relatos españoles del siglo XX: una antología, edited by José María Merino (Madrid: Alfaguara, 1998).

Los cuentos que cuentan, edited by J. A. Masoliver y Fernando Valls (Barcelona: Anagrama, 1998).

Narradores españoles de hoy, edited by Alberto Hernández Vásquez (Veracruz: Cultura de Veracruz, 1998).

Vidas de mujer, edited by Mercedes Monmany (Madrid: Alianza, 1998).

Antología del cuento español, 1. Siglos XIII–XVIII, edited by Arturo Ramoneda (Madrid: Alianza, 1999).

Antología del cuento español, 2. Siglos XIX–XX, edited by Arturo Ramoneda (Madrid: Alianza, 1999).

Cien años de cuentos (1898–1998). Antología del cuento español en castellano, edited by José María Merino (Madrid: Alfaguara, 1999).

Lo del amor es un cuento (2 vols), (Madrid: Ópera Prima, 1999).

Mujeres al alba, Prologue by Victoria Camps (Madrid: Alfaguara, 1999).

Relatos de mujeres I, II, y III (Madrid: Editorial Popular, 1990–1999).

Mudances/Mudanzas, (Barcelona: Columna; Bronce, 1999).

29 Dry Martinis (That's the limit!), edited by Javier de las Muelas (Barcelona: Edhasa, 1999).

Cuentos apátridas, edited by Enrique de Hériz (Madrid: Ediciones B, 1999).

Cuentos solidarios, (Madrid: ONCE, 1999).

Antología de cuentos del siglo XX, edited by J. L. Suárez Granada (Madrid: Bruño, 1999).

Spanish Short Stories, edited by John King (London and New York: Penguin, 1999).

Relatos a la carta. Historias y recetas de cocina, edited by Viviana Paletta and Javier Sáez de Ibarra, prologue by Tununa Mercado (Madrid: Páginas de Espuma, 2000).

Rumores de mar. Relatos sobre el mar, edited by Viviana Paletta and Javier Sáez de Ibarra, prologue by José María Merino (Madrid: Páginas de Espuma, 2000).

Vidas sobre raíles. Cuentos de trenes, (Madrid: Páginas de Espuma, 2000).

Pequeñas resistencias. Antología del nuevo cuento español, edited by Andrés Neuman, prologue by José María Merino (Madrid: Páginas de Espuma, 2002).

Galería de hiperbreves, edited by Círculo Cultural Faroni (Barcelona: Tusquets, 2001).

Por favor, sea breve. Antología de relatos hiperbreves, edited by Clara Obligado (Madrid: Páginas de Espuma, 2001).

Nosotros los solitarios, (Valencia: Pre-Textos, 2001).

El cuento español en el siglo XIX: autores raros y olvidados, edited by Jaume Pont (Lleida: Edicions Universitat de Lleida, 2001).

Cuento español contemporáneo, edited by Ángeles Encinar and Anthony Percival (Madrid: Cátedra, 2001).

Relato español actual, edited by Raúl Hernández Viveros (México, DF: Universidad Nacional Autónoma de México; Fondo de Cultura Económica, 2002).

Ni Ariadnas ni Penélopes (quince escritoras españolas para el siglo veintinuno), edited by Carmen Estévez (Madrid: Castalia, 2002).

Molto vivace. Cuentos de música, edited by Viviana Paletta and Javier Sáez de Ibarra, prologue by Hipólito G. Navarro (Madrid: Páginas de Espuma, 2002).

Antología de cuentos e historias mínimas (siglos XIX y XX), edited by Miguel Díez Rodríguez (Madrid: Espasa Calpe, 2002).

Orosia: Mujeres de sol a sol (Jaca: Pirineum Multimedia, 2002).

La vida alrededor (Cuentos de cine), edited by Miguel Ángel Oreste (Málaga: Zut Ediciones, 2002).

I love NY. Diez autores en busca de una ciudad (Barcelona: Planeta, 2002).

Amores de película. Grandes pasiones que han hecho historia (Madrid: El País, 2002).

Antología de la ciencia ficción española (1982–2002), edited by Julián Díez (Barcelona: Minotauro, 2003).

Spain: A Traveller's Literary Companion, edited and translated by Peter Bush and Lisa Dillman (Berkeley, CA: Whereabouts Press, 2003).

Jóvenes protagonistas: cuentos del siglo XX, edited by Tomás Rodríguez (Madrid: Castalia Prima, 2004).

Lecturas para el cambio de siglo, edited by Pedro de Miguel (Madrid: Ediciones Internacionales Universitarias, 2004).

Golpes. Ficciones de la crueldad social, edited by Eloy Fernández Porta and Vicente Muñoz Alvárez (Barcelona: DVD Ediciones, 2004).

Mujeres en ruta, (Madrid: Línea Recta, 2005).

Todo un placer. Antología de relatos eróticos femeninos, edited by Elena Medel (Córdoba: Berenice, 2005).

Antología de cuentistas madrileñas, edited by Isabel Díez Ménguez (Madrid: Ediciones La Librería, 2006).

Contar las olas. Trece cuentos para bañistas, edited by Ronaldo Menéndez (Madrid: Lengua de Trapo, 2006).

Qué me cuentas, edited by Amalia Vilches (Madrid: Páginas de Espuma, 2006).

Las vidas de Eva, prologue by Santiago Dexeus *(*Barcelona: Destino, 2007).

Mujeres que sueñan, edited by Jesús Aguado (Centro de Ediciones de la Diputación de Málaga, Col. Puerta del Mar, 2007).

Relatos de viajes, miradas de mujeres, edited by María del Mar Gallego Durán y Eloy Navarro Domínguez (Sevilla: Ediciones Alfar, 2007).

Mutantes. Narrativa española de última generación, edited by Julio Ortega and Juan Francisco Ferré (Córdoba: Berenice, 2007).

Partes de guerra, edited by Ignacio Martínez de Pisón (Barcelona: RBA, 2008).

Ficción Sur. Antología de cuentistas andaluces, edited by Juan Jacinto Muñoz Rengel (Granada: Traspiés, 2008).

Drácula, edited by Fernando Marías (Madrid: Editorial 451, 2008).

Frankenstein, edited by Fernando Marías (Madrid: Editorial 451, 2008).

La realidad oculta. Cuentos fantásticos españoles del siglo XX, edited by David Roas and Ana Casas (Palencia: Menoscuarto, 2008).

Jeckill and Hyde, edited by Fernando Marías (Madrid: Editorial 451, 2009).

Cuentos de amigas, edited by Laura Freixas (Barcelona: Anagrama, 2009).

Un deseo propio. Antología de escritoras españolas contemporáneas, edited by Inma Pertusa and Nancy Vosburg (Barcelona: Bruguera, 2009).

Perturbaciones. Antología del relato fantástico español actual, edited by Juan Jacinto Muñoz Rengel (Madrid: Salto de Página, 2009).

22 escarabajos. Antología hispánica del cuento Beatle, edited by Mario Cuenca Sandoval (Madrid: Paginas de Espuma, 2009).

Pequeñas resistencias, 5. Antología del nuevo cuento español (2001–2010), edited by Andrés Neuman, prologue by Eloy Tizón (Madrid: Páginas de Espuma, 2010).

Aquelarre: antología del cuento español actual, edited by Antonio Rómar and Pablo Mazo Agüero (Madrid: Salto de Página, 2010).

Three Centuries of Spanish Short Stories. Literary Selection and Activities for the Student of Spanish, edited by Astrid A. Billat (Newburyport, MA: Focus Publishing, 2010).

Siglo XXI. Los nuevos nombres del cuento español actual, edited by Gemma Pellicer and Fernando Valls (Palencia: Menoscuarto, 2010).

Cincuenta cuentos breves: una antología comentada, edited by Miguel Díez and María Paz Díez Taboada (Madrid: Catedra, 2011).

Watchwomen: narradoras del siglo 21, edited by Carmen Velasco Rengel (Zaragoza: Institución Fernando el Católico, 2011).

Rusia imaginada, edited by Care Santos (Madrid: Nevsky Prospects, 2011).

En breve. Cuentos de escritoras españolas (1975–2010). Estudios y antología, edited by Ángeles Encinar y Carmen Varcárcel (Madrid: Biblioteca Nueva, 2012).

Steampunk: antología retrofuturista, edited by J. Félix Palma (Madrid: Fábulas de Albión, 2012).

Mar de pirañas. Nuevas voces del microrrelato actual, edited by Fernando Valls (Palencia: Menoscuarto, 2012).

Bleak House Inn. Diez huéspedes en casa de Dickens, edited by Care Santos (Madrid: Fábulas de Albión, 2012).

Ls mil caras del monstruo, edited by Ana Casas (Barcelona: Bracket Cultura, 2012).

Madrid, con perdón, edited by Mercedes Cebrián (Madrid: Caballo de Troya, 2012).

Prospectivas. Antología de ciencia ficción española actual, edited by Fernando Ángel Moreno (Madrid: Salto de Página, 2012).

Bajo treinta. Antología de nueva narrativa española, edited by Juan Gómez Becerra (Madrid: Salto de Página, 2013).

Última temporada. Antología de nuevos narradores españoles, edited by Alberto Olmos (Madrid: Lengua de Trapo, 2013).

Cuento español actual (1992–2012), edited by Ángeles Encinar (Madrid: Cátedra, 2014).

La vida después (Cuentos de cine), edited by Miguel Ángel Oreste (Málaga: Zut Ediciones, 2014).

MicroBerlin. De minificciones y microrrelatos, edited by Ottmar Ette, Dieter Ingenschay, Frieldhelm Schmidt-Welle and Fernando Valls (Madrid: Iberoamericana; Frankfurt am Main: Vervuert, 2015).

Studies on the short story

Irene Andres-Suárez and Antonio Rivas (eds), *La era de la brevedad. El microrrelato hispánico* (Palencia: Menoscuarto, 2008).

Irene Andres-Suárez and Antonio Rivas (eds), *El microrrelato español. Una estética de la elipsis* (Palencia: Menoscuarto, 2010).

María Luisa Antonaya Núñez-Castelo, 'El ciclo de cuentos como género narrativo en la literatura española', *Rilce* 16.3 (2000), 433–78.

Montserrat Amores and Rebeca Martín (eds), *Estudios sobre el cuento español del siglo XIX* (Vigo: Editorial Academia del Hispanismo, 2008).

Ana L. Baquero Escudero, *El cuento en la historia literaria: la difícil autonomía de un género* (Vigo: Editorial Academia del Hispanismo, 2011).

Eduardo Becerra and Ricardo Piglia (eds), *El arquero inmóvil: nuevas poéticas sobre el cuento* (Madrid: Páginas de Espuma, 2006).

Ana Calvo Revilla and Javier Navascués (eds), *Las fronteras del microrrelato: Teoría y crítica del microrrelato español e hispanoamericano* (Madrid: Iberoamericana; Frankfurt am Main: Vervuert, 2012).

Ana Casas, *El cuento español en la posguerra* (Madrid: Marenostrum, 2007).

Geneviève Champeau, Jean-François Carcelén, Georges Tyras and Fernando Valls (eds), *Nuevos derroteros de la narrativa española actual* (Zaragoza: Prensas Universitarias de Zaragoza, 2011).

Epicteto Díaz Navarro and José Ramón González (eds), *El cuento español en el siglo XX* (Madrid: Alianza, 2002).

Ángeles Encinar, *Siguiendo el hilo: Estudios sobre el cuento español actual* (Villeurbane, Lyon: Orbis Tertius, 2015).

Edward H. Friedman (ed.), *El cuento: arte y análisis* (Upper Saddle River, NJ: Prentice Hall, 2003).

Teresa Gómez Trueba (ed.), *Mundos mínimos: el microrrelato en la literatura española contemporánea* (Gijón: Libros del Pexe, 2007).

Barbara Lounsberry *et al.* (eds), *The Tales We Tell: Perspectives on the Short Story* (Westport, CO and London: Greenwood Press, 1998).

Paul March-Russell, *The Short Story: An Introduction* (Edinburgh: Edinburgh University Press, 2009).

Azucena Mollejo, *El cuento español de 1970 a 2000: cuatro escritores de Madrid: Francisco Umbral, Rosa Montero, Almudena Grandes y Javier Marías* (Madrid: Pliegos de Bibliofilia, 2002).

Salvador Montesa (ed.), *Narrativas de la posmodernidad del cuento al microrrelato*, (Málaga: Publicaciones del Congreso de Literatura Española Contemporánea, 2009).

Miguel Ángel Muñoz, *La familia del aire: entrevistas con cuentistas madrileñas* (Madrid: Páginas de Espuma, 2011).

Antonio Orejudo (ed.), *En cuarentena: nuevos narradores y críticos del siglo XXI* (Murcia: Universidad de Murcia, 2004).

Ricardo Paglia, *Formas breves* (Barcelona: Anagrama, 2000).

Juan Paredes, *Para una teoría del relato. Las formas narrativas breves* (Madrid: Biblioteca Nueva, 2004).

José Romera Castillo and Francisco Gutiérrez Carbajo (eds), *El cuento en la década de los noventa: actas del X Seminario Internacional del Instituto de Semiótica Literaria, Teatral y Nuevas Tecnologías de la UNED (Madrid, 31 de mayo–2 de junio de 2000)* (Madrid: Visor Libros; UNED, 2001).

Alfred Sargatal, *Introducción al cuento literario* (Barcelona: Laertes, 2004).

Fernando Valls (ed.), *Soplando vidrio y otros estudios sobre el microrrelato español* (Madrid: Páginas de Espuma, 2008).

Sombras del mundo. Estudios sobre el cuento español contemporáneo (1944–2015), edited by Fernando Valls (Madrid: Iberoamericana; Frankfurt am Main: Vervuert, 2016).